THE HISTORICAL
AND
MYSTICAL CHRIST

THE THEOLOGY LIBRARY

The translation of the entire library
is under the direction of the Rev.
Louis J. Putz, C.S.C., University
of Notre Dame

THE HISTORICAL
AND
MYSTICAL CHRIST

75285

By a group of theologians
under the editorship of
A. M. Henry, O.P.

Translated by Angeline Bouchard

Fides Publishers Inc.
Notre Dame, Indiana

Library of Congress Catalog Card Number: 54-10891

NIHIL OBSTAT:
Albert L. Schlitzer, C.S.C., S.T.D.
University of Notre Dame

IMPRIMATUR:
✠ Leo A. Pursley, D.D.
Bishop of Fort Wayne

NIHIL OBSTAT:
Th. Camelot, O.P.
Stud. reg. in Fac. "Le Saulchoir"

IMPRIMI POTEST:
V. Ducattillon, O.P.
Prior prov.

IMPRIMATUR:
Parisiis, die 15a *martii,* 1954
M. Potevin
Vic. gen.

1st Printing   1958
2nd Printing   1963

Published originally by Les Editions du Cerf, 29,
Boulevard Latour-Maubourg, Paris 7, France

Manufactured by American Book–Stratford Press, Inc., New York
 55

Faithfully Dedicated

to

Our Lady Immaculate

PLAN OF THE THEOLOGY LIBRARY

VOLUME FIVE
The Historical and Mystical Christ

CONTENTS

INTRODUCTION

Theology is the science of God. It is concerned not with things in themselves but with things in their relationship to God. That is to say, theology deals with the way things depend upon God, their Author and Exemplar, or the way they return to Him, their End. This twofold point of view has determined the plan of Parts I and II of our study. In Part I, we considered how creatures proceed from God and how He governs them. In Part II, we saw how man, a spiritual creature and the image of God, returns toward his end and his beatitude.

And yet this circular approach does not exhaust the consideration of all the divine truths that have been revealed to us. In actual fact man has strayed from the path that leads him back to his Author; and it has pleased God in His mercy to send His Son and to redeem man. To complete the circle of our theological undertaking, therefore, we have yet to study the life, death, and Resurrection of our Savior, as well as the whole Economy of facts, "mysteries," gifts, and means that make up the work of our salvation.

Many of our readers may be surprised that we have waited until the third and last part of our study to deal with the mystery of our Redemption. We shall answer this question—or objection—at once, according to the five following points:

1. FIDELITY TO ST. THOMAS

It is not our intention to present a new theology, a new organization of known truths, interesting as this might be. Our purpose is to introduce beginners or more advanced students to traditional theology. That is why we have chosen to transmit in the most compelling way possible the common theology of the Church, looking for guidance to her Common Doctor who—in the apt words of Father Liégé—"has introduced the smallest amount of purely systematic thought into his theology" (*Theology Library,* Vol. I, p. 280). That is why we have adopted St. Thomas' own plan.

The fact remains that this first reason would be no more than an excuse—the excuse of fidelity—if the Angelic Doctor's plan had not kept its value and its reasons despite the objections that certain minds have raised against it for the past seven centuries.

We have already presented these reasons in our Volume I (p. 270-275). We again stress our adherence to St. Thomas simply to bring out a few important points.

2. THEOLOGY—NOT SPIRITUALITY OR PEDAGOGY

The primary and fundamental role of theology is to inform us as to what we may or may not say concerning God and His mysteries. Theology is also a grammar in its own way. For example, is it permissible to say that "God suffered," "God died," that "Christ assumed human nature in its entirety," that "the Immaculate Conception is a privilege of the divine maternity," that "the priest's absolution constitutes in itself alone the whole form of the sacrament of penance"? And so on. Theology may not let any of these questions go unanswered. This grammatical concern is not a matter of purism. It grows out of the exigencies of organization and development to which the plan of St. Thomas' *Summa Theologiae* seems to correspond perfectly. If theology were to begin with a study of Christ, for instance, there would be danger of confusing the attributes of His divinity with those of His humanity and the result would be very poor theology.

If devotion is an obstacle to basic theological distinctions, it deserves to be severely criticized. For it is an abuse of devotion—or of spirituality—to depend upon it totally for the construction of a theology. Theology has its own objective norms that the theologian must honor, regardless of the devotional movement of which he is a part. This is all the more true since in his fervor he may tend to ignore the possible vagaries of certain forms of piety.

On the other hand, it goes without saying that we never abuse theology when we depend upon it to nourish our spiritual life. But the fruits of theology ripen slowly. They demand continual contact, assiduous study, a stripping of our thought, the use of abstract ideas, and even technical apparatus, that may seem too burdensome for minds overly eager for immediate results. Those who want to reap at once a harvest of helps and consolations for their spiritual life will do best not to follow this ascetic method. They would too soon be disappointed, and without good reason. The theology that we are presenting to them is not a "spirituality" whose delicious savor they can taste without any effort on their part.

Neither is theology a pedagogy for adolescents—a fortiori for children. We have already pointed this out with regard to morality

(Vol. IV, p. 204); but we must not fear to repeat it often, for there seems to be a general lack of understanding as to what is to be expected of theology. Indeed, there are catechisms based on the plan of St. Thomas' *Summa,* and this plan seems better than that of certain other catechisms built upon Kantian rationalism. But it is very difficult to instill such concepts in the minds of children who know nothing of sacred history, who have never prayed the Psalms, and who have never even learned by heart the Gospel's Beatitudes —the fundamental charter of our religion—or the hymn to charity of I Corinthians 13.

Clearly, the division of subject matter and the organization of knowledge in theology call for a certain relativity and flexibility. Such flexibility is even more indispensable in view of the varying needs of different minds. The cultivation of faith in children demands that they be taught fundamental concepts, beginning with the Gospel of Christ taken literally. It also requires a certain concomitant education of their minds and hearts, of their whole beings, just as this fundamental training is presumably given to those who are studying theology.

Let us draw three conclusions from what has been said:

Theology does not seek to "nourish" the soul of the Christian directly, but to give him a clear and vital understanding of the basic truths of his faith. If he is studious and persevering, his interior life will inevitably profit, and the fruits that he will obtain— while they will ripen more slowly—will be stronger and more savory, and also more abundant than those he could gather in a hurry from a book of spirituality.

Theology by itself does not fulfill all the expectations of minds and souls. Many other types of works are needed in conjunction with it: catechisms, manuals, books of spirituality, etc., which correspond to different ages or stages in the cultivation of the faith— or to the diverse needs of men's souls.

Even on the "scientific" level where theology aspires to establish itself, there are many useful books for students. There is no single "plan" that exhausts all possible ways of considering the deposit of faith and of understanding it. Relatively speaking, the architecture of Thomism is a masterpiece. And yet it is useful, even for Thomists, to be acquainted with other methods of organizing knowledge that stress certain points that have been passed over by Thomism. Such works will suggest to the mind new comparisons that would inevitably be unthought of by those who read only one book: *Timeo hominem unius libri*—"I fear the man of one book." This fear is just as valid in the case of certain Thomists as it is of certain Scotists, Suarezians, or Liguorists, who lock themselves up in their own "school" and refuse to hear of any other.

3. THEOLOGY EMBRACES MORE THAN CHRISTOLOGY

The theologian considers God and the things of God from God's point of view. While this is a very lofty ambition, it is one to which faith spontaneously invites the believer.

Now, seen from this aspect, the concrete economy of salvation, sublime as it may be, cannot be given first consideration. It is secondary, and in a certain respect accidental. It shares in its own way the contingent state of all things freely decided upon and created by God. It is precisely the theologian's task to determine in what measure and for what reasons the Incarnation was or was not necessary, once God had created man. The complete answer to this question already calls for some grasp of the deposit of faith.

Therefore, we do not minimize the importance of Christ in the economy of our salvation when we study Him only after the creation and the return of created beings to God. On the contrary, by doing this we bring out Christ's role as the "Way" that leads us to God. True, Christ is also our "Truth" and our "Life," but only inasmuch as He is God. The life He gives us is none other than the life that the Father has given to just, God-fearing men since the beginning of time. This truth is made clearer to us when we study the treatise on grace, for example, or the treatise on God and on the divine missions, before we study the treatise on Christ. Theology is more than a simple Christology.

While it is true—as we shall soon point out—that theology attains to God only through Christ, nevertheless theology orders its science (or its "wisdom") only after it has reached the goal to which Christ has led it. Our Savior wants to be considered by theology in the light of faith, that is with the eyes of God. It is from this point of view that the ordering and the relative importance of the parts of our treatment must be judged.

It would be naïve and gravely erroneous to judge the importance of each part of our theological study solely by its position in the total plan or by its number of pages. Just because the treatise on Christ comes after the treatise on the habits and virtues does not mean it is less important. Nor does the fact that the treatise on justice is about as long as the treatise on God indicate that the two are of comparable theological value. We have many things to say about justice or about sins like lying or disobedience, whereas we can only stammer a few words on the simplicity of God. It would be foolish to try to determine the relative importance and quality of these matters on the basis of their quantity and position.

4. THEOLOGY, THE KNOWLEDGE OF GOD THROUGH CHRIST AND IN CHRIST

Finally, we come to the most important thing we have to say in this connection. Even though the person of Christ and His economy of salvation are studied in the last part of our theology, let no one imagine that His testimony has for a moment been absent from the theologian's mind in any of the other parts. Union with God—to which the believer dedicates himself and in which the theologian seeks an understanding of his faith—is granted to us only through the testimony of the Savior. Whatever we believe and know of our faith is what Christ sees and tells us. It is the law of all types of faiths to depend totally upon the vision and testimony of another. Theological faith is not exempt from this law: it is founded in its entirety upon the testimony of Christ, who is not only the Great Witness, but the Witness of God who authenticated by His coming the testimony of the prophets. Without this divine Witness, there is no supernatural faith, no divine knowledge, and no theology.

We must go further still. True, our faith rests upon the vision of Christ, who alone can tell us what He sees and knows. But Christ's vision is not only a safeguard for our faith, Christ is not merely an exterior witness, someone whom we could forget after having heard what He had to say; our faith has no other goal than to assimilate itself to the knowledge that Christ possesses of God and of the things of God.

God did not send us an ordinary witness. He sent us His Son. And we who have received the adoption of sons must do more than listen to Christ. We must also assimilate ourselves totally to Him, imitate Him in His own way of seeing things, and above all in His love. We must substitute Him for ourselves, within ourselves. It is the Holy Spirit who accomplishes this by making us understand all that Christ has told us, by making us see and hear all things in His Spirit just as He sees and hears them.

It was not through lack of logic, therefore, that we constantly relied on New Testament doctrine in our preceding volumes, and cited from it continually. Neither faith nor theology are conceivable outside the vision that Christ possesses and outside His teachings. Even our moral theology in its entirety rests upon the assurance we now have that Christ, seated at the right hand of God, has already inaugurated our eternal life with the Father. Even when we are not studying Christ in Himself, He never ceases being present in our theology as the Witness upon whom we base all that we assert, and as the Model and Exemplar whose mind and life we are striving to penetrate.

5. THEOLOGY IS A WHOLE

It must be clear by now that theology is not to be read like a "science" book which would continue indefinitely to develop conclusions implicitly contained in the initial premises. Nor must we read theology like a story or a novel that follows a straight line from the first episode to the last. Theology develops not so much by multiplying its conclusions, or by indefinitely going over the history of each dogma, as by multiplying its angles of vision on its one and only object.

The theologian is like a fisherman who has discovered a precious pearl or a diamond and cannot stop admiring its beauty. He is like a scribe who draws forth from his treasure things ever old and ever new. He does not so much want to see new truths as to multiply the number of angles from which he views his one and only object.

In theology everything is related. There are no "specialists" who can dispense with knowing things in which they are less interested, for then they would risk being ignorant of what is best in their "specialty." The treatise on Christ is presented in this volume, after several others, solely because everything cannot be said at once in a single sentence or word, the way God expresses Himself in His Word. But the theologian who reads the first two parts of our theological study grasps them perfectly only if he has the third part present in his mind (and the treatise on Christ in particular). Theology is a whole, like the perfect figure of the circle, and none of its parts can be detached at will.

And now we must explain the plan of this fifth volume, *The Historical and Mystical Christ*. The work is centered on two mysteries, that of Christ and of Mary and the Church. The mystery of

Christ will be the subject of the first four chapters and will be considered under various aspects. First will be the mystery of the Incarnation, through which God became man for our salvation. Here we shall not study the life and history of our Savior, but rather the mystery of the hypostatic union, its fitness, the perfections that result from it for the assumed human nature, and the prerogatives of the God-man. This will be the subject matter of the first chapter. In a second chapter we shall consider our Savior's life—His action and conduct, His teaching, His miracles. We shall reserve the entire third chapter for a study of His great work: the Redemption through His Passion, Death, and Resurrection, by which our salvation was consummated. Finally, in Chapter IV we shall consider the epic of His glory.

It can be said that our first subject for consideration (Chapter I) will be the mystery of the Incarnation in the mind of God and in His plan for our salvation. Our second consideration (Chapters II, III, and IV) will be "the mysteries" (words, acts, sufferings) concretely lived by the Word Incarnate, Jesus Christ. In a sense, these later chapters deal with the execution of the divine plan.

As the reader will see, we have inserted a number of illustrations into this volume. Perhaps it would be wise to repeat what we said earlier (Vol. I. p. 219), namely, that they are not meant primarily to adorn our theology.

In this very concrete presentation of the economy of salvation just as God has willed it by His free choice and just as the Church is living it, the theologian's first task, which is to become acquainted with the facts, cannot be limited to the reading of propositions. He must live with the Church, listen, look, be receptive and attentive to all these "documents" which also include the graffiti of the catacombs, the frescoes of the Roman basilicas, the mosaics of the Byzantine churches, the symbols in baptisteries, the ornaments for liturgical ceremonies, and even the chanting of the office at the present time.

A liturgy cannot be reconstructed solely from the rubrics we may possess. We must also enter into the community as it prayed, and participate in its movement. And likewise, *mutatis mutandis,* in order to penetrate to the inward faith of the Church we must enter as completely as possible into the movement of her Tradition and into the authentic manifestations of her life. The theologian rediscovers God's Word not only in the parchments of doctors, but also in all the cultural, liturgical, artistic, and social expressions of the faith of Christians through the ages. The Holy Spirit, who modulates the one melody of the Gospel upon the lyre of the Church, makes new chords vibrate each day, in each generation, in each people, in each mind and heart. Hence God's words, to which the theologian listens, are rich with a thousand resonances, none of which must be neglected.

Finally, as to the theologian's second task, which is to construct, organize, and set the facts in order, as well as to answer the questions which they evoke—this work cannot be reduced to a mere superimposing of new terms upon ancient propositions. In his supreme concern to "preserve the deposit," the theologian is called to orientate at his humble level the march of the Church through the succeeding crises which she continually encounters. It is up to the theologian to confront each fact, each event, with the norms of Scripture, and to give the reasons which lead the magisterium to approve or censure a new style of architecture, a particular picture, a type of confessional, or a new devotion.

Thus, it was not for the pleasure of the eyes that we inserted so many illustrations into this volume. We have simply tried to fulfill all these tasks of theology, especially in the sacramental domain in which "practice" reigns supreme because it is a "fact."

Chapter I

THE MYSTERY OF THE INCARNATION
OR THE MYSTERY OF THE UNION
OF THE TWO NATURES

by H.-M. Manteau-Bonamy, O.P.
and A.-M. Henry, O.P.

An Outline of the Development of Christology, by
H.-M. Manteau-Bonamy

I. SCRIPTURAL TESTIMONY ON THE INCARNATION OF THE WORD

The Historical Context
  1. The testimony of the Gospels
  2. The testimony of St. Paul

II. FROM THE ORIGINS OF THE CHURCH TO THE FIRST CONCILIAR DECISIONS (1ST TO 4TH CENTURIES)

1st Phase: Gnosticism and Anti-Gnosticism
  1. The two forms of Gnosticism
  2. The first Catholic reactions (after the Apostles)
     St. Ignatius of Antioch
     St. Irenaeus
  3. The first positions of the schools
     (a) The beginnings of the Alexandrian school
     (b) Tertullian and the first tendencies of Latin Christology
Conclusions
2nd Phase: The Trinitarian Aspect of Christology
  1. Adoptionism
  2. The beginnings of the School of Antioch and Arianism
  3. The radical dualism of Photinus

1

TABLES

THEOLOGICAL REFLECTIONS
by A.-M. Henry, O.P.

Chapter I

THE MYSTERY OF THE INCARNATION

OUTLINE OF THE DEVELOPMENT OF CHRISTOLOGY

I. Scriptural Testimony on the Incarnation of the Word

To the Christian eager to discover the Son of God made man, all the New Testament writings offer a privileged source of information. But three parts of the New Testament in particular will command attention: St. Paul, the Synoptics, and St. John.

If their value is to be rightly understood, these writings must be placed in their historical context and considered from the point of view of each of their respective authors.

The Historical Context

Two Elements:

1. *Historical Proof.* At the time these works were written, there were still many persons who had witnessed or heard of the life and works of the Galilean named Jesus. It was generally known that this man had claimed to be the long-awaited Messias; that He had clearly affirmed He was the Son of God; that He had proved the truth of His words, and died to uphold His claim. No one denied that He had told the truth, for His formidable affirmations had been supported by extraordinary facts, by miracles—the last being His Resurrection—which had astounded everyone. These are undeniable facts.

2. *The Testimony of the Faith.* Even at this early period there were faithful followers of this Man all over the world, who worshipped Him as God, accepted His declarations to the letter, and looked upon Him as identical to the Father and the Spirit. Every day the promises He had made before reascending to His Father were being realized before their eyes. They were living by Him, they were living His life all over again. Christian thought, to the extent that it existed at all, was certainly not speculative. It was above all practical, born of experience. The behavior of Christians

4

was guided by Jesus' life, words, counsels, and way of reacting to evil. But speculation about His person and His psychology had scarcely begun. We find only a few traces of it in the writings of St. John. One thing alone mattered and sufficed: God had come to earth; He had dwelt among men and gone back to prepare a place for them in His kingdom.

1. THE TESTIMONY OF THE GOSPELS

There is no need to distinguish St. John from the others, or to treat him apart from them. He, too, was a witness—and a reliable one. He presented the same Christ as the Synoptics, and thus completed their testimony. The Synoptics reflected the catechesis or ordinary teaching of primitive Christianity, and were concerned only with the concrete facts of Jesus' life. John, on the other hand, added personal reflections to his testimony, which were the fruit of his long and ardent contemplation. All of the Evangelists, for that matter, took care to maintain the strictest objectivity. Their tone was serene, almost impassive. God had become man: such was their unanimous affirmation.

1. The *humanity* of Jesus presented no difficulty. They had all known this man and seen Him live. And St. John merely summed up their common testimony: "What was from the beginning, what we have heard, what we have seen with our eyes, what we have looked upon and our hands handled: of the Word of Life . . . we announce to you, in order that you also may have fellowship with us, and that our fellowship may be with the Father, and with his Son Jesus Christ" (I Jn. 1:1-3).

2. Was the same true of His *divinity?* To grasp the import of the New Testament writings and to remember their historical context, we must see how Jesus got men to acknowledge Him as God. In a word, we must understand the divine pedagogy of Christ.

(a) *Steppingstones or preparations*

The Jews, to whom Christ addressed Himself, read the Bible incessantly. Beyond that, they were familiar with the sacred texts to an amazing degree. Their minds were imbued with Messianism and monotheism, and with everything that pertained strictly to the things of God. Even the message of the Incarnation was given to the Blessed Virgin in the most authentically biblical style.

(b) *Obstacles and controversies*

Unfortunately, in our Lord's time very few Jews had preserved the ancient revelation of the Messias in its true tradition. In consequence, Jesus was constantly confronted with a distorted Messianic conception, and He had to correct patiently warped ideas. He gradually led His audiences from the notion of a temporal and unduly nationalistic Messias who was to restore the kingdom of Israel to the idea of a universal Messias who would found a kingdom "not of this world." He was the true Messias: the ruler of a kingdom wholly within men's souls, a kingdom that would be manifested only on the last day. He told them: "Hereafter you shall see the Son of Man sitting at the right hand of the Power and coming upon the clouds of heaven" (Mt. 26:64).

And when He spoke like this, He meant He was the Messias announced by the prophets: "All things that have been written by the prophets concerning the Son of Man will be accomplished. For he will be delivered to the Gentiles, and will be mocked and scourged and spit upon; and after they have scourged him, they will put him to death; and on the third day he will rise again" (Lk. 18:31-33).

A more serious obstacle to the acceptance of Jesus' doctrine was the intransigent monotheism of the Jews. Surely it was to Israel's credit that it had so jealously guarded the doctrine of the "one God." This chosen people had faced untold difficulties, overcome many hardships, and even committed crimes in defending this doctrine so universally rejected by others. Is it not human to stiffen one's position in the face of a contrary position with which one is forced to have frequent contacts?

At any rate, Jesus had to deal with people who were scandalized that a man should declare Himself to be the Son of God in the sense of unequivocally identifying Himself with God.

Evidently St. John—who composed his Gospel many years after the Holy Ghost had made clear all that Jesus had said and done—flatly affirmed the divinity of Christ: He *was* before Abraham existed (Jn. 8:58); He had been glorified before the world existed (Jn. 17:5); He was to reascend to heaven whence He had come (Jn. 6:38,63); and furthermore He had claimed the power of almighty God for Himself—He acts in union with the Father and with the same authority (Jn. 14:11,20).

In the discourse after the Last Supper, Jesus formally taught His divinity. Nevertheless, St. John's testimony was no different from that of the Synoptics. It is St. Matthew who reported St. Peter's famous declaration: "Thou art the Christ, the Son of the living God" (Matt. 16:16). St. Mark took up St. Peter's catechesis in the parable of the murderous vine-dressers, contrasting the servants with the son of the master of the vineyard. The audience could not fail to understand that Christ was speaking of Himself and thus indicating His unique position as the Messias, the Son of God, as compared with the prophets.

All through His teaching, Jesus corrected the Jews' doctrine on the Messias and strove to orientate them toward the fullest acceptance of Himself: "But I tell you that one greater than the temple is here. But if you knew what this means, 'I desire mercy, and not sacrifice,' you would never have condemned the innocent; for the Son of Man is Lord even of the Sabbath" (Mt. 12:6-8; cf. Lk. 6:5; Mk. 2:27).

Although Jesus is the Son of David, He is none the less David's "Lord" (Mt. 22:41 ff.; Mk. 12:35 ff.; Lk. 20:41 ff.). He declared to His listeners: "But blessed are your eyes . . . and your ears . . . For amen I say to you, many prophets and just men have longed to see what you see . . . and to hear what you hear . . ." (Mt. 13:16-17). For here was One greater than the Temple, greater than Jonas, and greater than Solomon (cf. Mt. 12:41-42).

After His declarations with regard to His power in a realm until then reserved to God alone, we must take up His affirmations about His person. We know that Jesus liked to call Himself the Son of Man. In the Book of Daniel (7:13) this expression signified man coming on the clouds of heaven and exercising universal power. Doubtless, the listeners did not grasp the full significance of these words, for this interpretation of Daniel was not very well known in our Lord's day. They tended rather to understand them in the prophetic sense of Isaias announcing the "son of man," the Servant of Yahweh who would expiate the sins of his people by his death.

And yet at the same time that He called Himself "the Son of Man," Jesus declared He was superior to the angels: "So will it be at the end of the world. The Son of Man will send forth his angels, and they will gather out of his kingdom all scandals . . ." (Mt. 13:40-41).

Thus, little by little Jesus unveiled His personal relationship with the Father: His dependence, His equality, and finally His oneness with Him. It is this threefold revelation that St. John brings out so clearly throughout his Gospel.

(c) Demands and promises

Jesus was not content to argue, to prove to men's minds who He was. He made positive demands that bore witness to His power, to the certitude of His claims. Total faith in Him is necessary: if He calls, we must leave everything and follow Him; He demands to be loved more than we love our fathers and mothers (Mt. 10:37). To attain to His heavenly Father, we must acknowledge Him publicly (Mt. 10:32). Divine life is given by Him, but in the way He Himself has determined. The Eucharistic promise which He fulfilled on the eve of His death was made with authority and without any compromise. It is so because He said it (Jn. 6). He promised to send the Paraclete; and the Holy Spirit did in fact descend upon Mary and the Apostles with a great demonstration of power.

(d) The exterior proofs of His divinity

These proofs are of two kinds: miracles and the fulfilment of the prophecies concerning Him.

Jesus often worked His miracles in connection with an affirmation of His divinity. This is evident in St. John, who likes to introduce each of Jesus' major teachings by a typical miracle; but this is also the case in the Synoptics. "Which is easier, to say, 'Thy sins are forgiven thee,' or to say, 'Arise and walk'? But that you may know that the Son of Man has power on earth to forgive sins"— He said to the paralytic—"I say to thee, arise, take up thy pallet and go to thy house" (Lk. 5:23-24; cf. also Mk. 2:9-10; Mt. 9:5-6).

Jesus accomplished all the prophecies in His person. From the moment shortly after man's fall in the Garden of Eden, when Yahweh announced that the seed of a woman would crush the head of the serpent (Gen. 3:14-15), all of sacred history has been the gradual unfolding of this promise. Abraham's faith was the definitive inspiration for seeking the true, promised Savior, who was to be a descendant of Abraham. But it was God Himself who mercifully answered the Jews' prayers. In his prophetic 109th Psalm, David recognized the Savior as His Lord and as the eternal Priest according to the order of Melchisedech. Jesus took up Melchisedech's offering and gave His body and His blood under the species of bread and wine. Isaias announced that a Virgin would conceive; and in his eyes, as well as in those of a number of the prophets, the Servant of Yahweh was the man of sorrows. We need only reread the Gospel of St. Matthew to realize how perfectly Jesus fulfilled the prophecies of the Old Testament. Actually Matthew was addressing himself to the Jews, for whom the fulfilment of the prophecies was the best argument for the authenticity of the Messias.

Were the hearers and enemies of Jesus mistaken about His affirmations concerning His Person? No, they recognized the divine character of His claims; but they did not always accept them. It depended on the dispositions of their hearts, as Jesus Himself pointed out so often.

However, it was the great testimony of His Resurrection and Ascension that manifested His divinity most brilliantly. Everyone knew that He had died a genuine death, His enemies and Apostles alike. Thus the Resurrection was an irrefutable proof of His divine Sonship.

St. John gave the synthesis of this twofold testimony of the humanity and divinity of Jesus in his prologues to his first Epistle and to his Gospel. He took up once again the view expressed in the Synoptics and by other Apostles, unifying it by pointing out the precise purpose of the Incarnation: The Son of God became man so that man might become the son of God. And this goal had been attained by the Passion, Death, Resurrection, and Ascension of Jesus. St. Paul clearly demonstrated, just as St. John did, that through the Spirit of Christ we become the sons of the Father. On the other hand, since St. Paul was addressing himself directly to pagans, he insisted above all on the means by which men can become sons of God: incorporation into the Redemption of Christ.

2. THE TESTIMONY OF ST. PAUL

Was this a testimony? Yes, it was the testimony of the first generation of Christians. Is there anything more to it? Yes. Although St. Paul had not known Christ in the flesh, he had met Him on the road to Damascus and been enlightened by Him. Besides, he compared his Gospel with those of the other Apostles. Finally, there were still many witnesses of Christ's life at that time, and Paul knew them.

The significance of his testimony

We could very well reconstruct the principal events in the life of Christ from what St. Paul tells us. But the testimony of St. Paul's letters is not limited to that. They make us understand the scope and meaning of the coming of God among men. We must not forget that the pagan milieu in which Paul found himself had its own particular needs and demands. Morals were in need of reform. Paganism could not be Christianized unless it died to its idols. It was not simply a matter of redressing erring minds, as in the case of the Jews: the minds of the pagans had to be totally revolutionized. That is why the Christ of St. Paul was the Savior; the One who from His Cross enabled man to regain his true dignity, and even to become a child of light, a son of the Father.

Then the Cross, which had been a stumbling-block for the Jews, became foolishness for the Gentiles (I Cor. 1:23). "But the foolish things of the world has God chosen to put to shame the 'wise' " (I Cor. 1:27). Thus the Jesus of St. Paul is God presenting Himself in a state of abasement.

"Have this mind in you which was also in Christ Jesus, who though he was by nature God, did not consider being equal to God a thing to be clung to, but emptied himself, taking the nature of a slave and being made like unto men. And appearing in the form of man, he humbled himself, becoming obedient to death, even to death on a cross" (Phil. 2:5-8).

To make the pagans break off entirely with the past, St. Paul asked them to be imitators of Jesus in all things (Eph. 5:1; I Cor. 4:16; 11:1). And they were to do more than imitate. They were to live Christ's own life through mortification (II Cor. 4:10). They were to forgive one another, as Jesus had forgiven (Col. 3:13).

As in the Synoptics, Jesus is presented in St. Paul's writings with divine qualities and prerogatives. Paul commanded absolute faith in Jesus (Epistle to the Romans); he laid great stress on God's plan for the world, which had been realized in Jesus. Finally, he looked upon the Resurrection as the major argument for the divinity of Jesus: "And if Christ has not risen, vain then is our preaching, vain too is your faith" (I Cor. 15:14).

To sum up, all of the witnesses of Jesus demonstrate one thing: their faith in Christ the son of Mary, who is equally the Son of the Father. The unity of the person was not yet denied or even discussed by those around them. However, in the last testimony, which is St. John's, we catch a glimpse of the coming attacks against the mystery of God made man.

II. From the Origins of the Church to the First Conciliar Decisions

(First Century to the middle of the Fourth Century)

The Gospels and the other revealed writings make it clear that Jesus came to save what was lost. This soteriological view penetrated the belief of the first Christians. However we must not imagine that they approached their belief with any abstract considerations. They affirmed their allegiance to the Savior in the very fabric of their lives. But was this not an implicit recognition that the Savior was at once the Son of the Father, who existed from all eternity and became man out of love, and also true man, born of a woman, the Virgin Mary? As man, Christ experienced all our weaknesses except sin; as God, He raises up the body from death and the soul from sin. The faith of the first Christians, therefore, was a faith lived all of a piece, in which love had its place. As yet there were few abstract reflections concerning this Being in whom the divine and the human were so closely united.

But during this Apostolic period, a vast flood of ideas poured over the whole Roman Empire, taking the name of *Gnosis* in the second century. The multitude of Gnostic sects were imbued with more or less watered-down Platonistic ideas, and were likewise influenced by contemporary mythology. Although they contradicted one another, they had one idea in common: only spiritual and mystical knowledge can deliver man from evil, for spirit is good and matter is bad.

Whether in Rome or in the Orient, Christianity was judged almost everywhere in the Empire in the light of the Gnostic theses. Obviously, Jesus, the head of the new religion, was the favorite target of all critics. It is of the greatest importance to grasp this fact at the outset of any theological study of the Incarnation.

It was only in the second half of the fourth century that the Church officially defined her belief in Christ the God-man; she did this to refute Apollinarianism, the first formal heresy relating to the mystery of the Incarnation. And yet that is no reason for neglecting earlier Catholic thought, which firmly opposed the Gnostic aberrations right from the beginning. It would seem that if we understand the orientation of the doctrinal movement from its origins we shall be better able to grasp both the scope of the Patristic affirmations, the authority of the Conciliar decisions, and the riches of theological doctrine properly so-called. Besides, is this not an excellent way of being initiated into the problem of the Incarnation? Such will be our line of approach in the present theological introduction to the mystery of Christ Jesus.

The First Phase
Gnosticism and Anti-Gnosticism

1. THE TWO FORMS OF GNOSTICISM

The fundamental dogma of Gnosticism, if it can be called dogma, is that whatever has a material origin is without value. It follows that for the "Gnostic Christians" the coming of the Son of God in human flesh was scarcely comprehensible.

From the start, they were shocked by the sensible, physical realism of the Redemption. In Syria there were some (Simon, Menander, Saturninus) who affirmed that the heavenly Christ, sent into the earthly world to save men, *appeared* to suffer and die like a real man, but in reality neither suffered nor died. Others, especially in Alexandria, admitted the Incarnation in a certain respect, but did not admit the Redemption. Basilides, for example, declared that on Calvary Joseph of Arimathea was substituted for Jesus. Valentinus claimed that Christ arrived on earth with a pneumatic or psychic body, and that Mary was simply a transitory dwelling for this body. Marcion was more radical in his views. He went back to the source of Gnostic philosoɔ͵y, which is a divine dualism: there is the evil God, the Creator, the God of the Jews; and the good God, the Savior, the God of the New Testament. He affirmed that Christ, an emanation of the good God, could not have had a human origin; and that Jesus appeared suddenly in the fifteenth year of the reign of Tiberius.

Side by side with this so-called *Docetist* (δοχεῖν = to appear: Christ only appears to be a man) interpretation of the Incarnation of God, Christian Gnosticism presented Christ as a lesser god. In fact, the Gnostic theory of the emanation of eons was applied to Jesus. The Redeemer, emanated from the good God, is a demiurge who, though transcendent, is not God Himself. This is an important point, for while the Gnostic Christians more or less denatured the human side of the Savior, we should not mistake them for champions of the divinity of this same Savior. To quote Father Lebreton:

Christ was stripped by Docetism of His real humanity; by the theory of eons, of His divinity. As a diminished god, an apparent man, he was now no more than an indefinite figure whose role was reduced to a manifestation of the superior world. His Redemption through the Cross was wiped out. Salvation was simply a participation in the divine life through incorporation into Christ. It was the communication to a few initiates of the secrets concerning the divine emanations, the creation of the world . . .[1]

In the face of such a conception of the mystery of Jesus, authentic Christians could not fail to react vigorously.

2. THE FIRST CATHOLIC REACTIONS (AFTER THE APOSTLES)

St. Ignatius of Antioch († c. 110)

In the letters he wrote during his famous journey from Antioch to Rome, where he was to suffer martyrdom, Ignatius forcefully attacked the Docetist error, which was so popular around him. To this end, he presented the Incarnation as intimately related to the Redemption. Writing to the Ephesians, he said:

Beware of the heretics. They are difficult to cure. There is only one physician . . . who came in the flesh, the true God . . . Jesus Christ, our Lord (*Ad Ephes.* 7:2).
If Christ suffered only in appearance, why am I in chains? . . . By His Cross, in His Passion, He calls you to Himself, you who are His members (*Ad Smyrn.* 10-11).

St. Ignatius is, so to speak, midway between St. John and St. Paul. From the former he took his doctrine of the Word, his insistence on relating the unity of Christians to the unity of Christ with His Father, on binding the Eucharistic dogma to the Christological dogma, and on speaking of Christ, "the Life." To the latter he owed his predilection for the crucified Christ, his very concrete view of the reality of the Incarnation, the Redemption, and of the "economy" of our salvation.

His contribution consists in his distinguishing within the concrete unity of Christ the human and divine elements, which he named respectively "flesh" and "spirit." While these terms are imperfect, their meaning was very exact coming from his pen.

[1] Jules Lebreton, S. J., *History of the Dogma of the Trinity* (London, Burns, Oates and Washbourne, 1939).

St. Irenaeus († end of the 2nd century)

St. Irenaeus fought the fundamental error of those Gnostics who opposed and separated God the Father and God the Creator; the Word (Logos) and Christ Jesus; the flesh that is damned and the spirit that is life. He vigorously affirmed the oneness of God, the oneness of Christ, and the oneness of the work of salvation.

His affirmation of the unity of Christ was called for precisely by his faith in the God who saves us:

"The Word of God, Jesus Christ our Lord, became what we are so as to make us what He Himself is" (*Adversus haereses,* V, prol., Rouët de Journel, No. 248).

This affirmation postulates that the human and the divine are permanently united in the person of the Savior. At the same time it demands belief in the reality of His human nature: He was made flesh to save the flesh. It is St. John's "The Word was made flesh," henceforth to be expressed by the technical term "Incarnation" (σάρχωσις) which St. Irenaeus seems to have been the first to use.

In addition, the great Bishop of Lyons stressed heavily the cosmic aspect of the Incarnation. By His descent into the depths of the flesh, the Word contracted a mysterious union not only with one individual human nature, but in a very real—although as yet un-specified—way with the human race as a whole. He gathers up humanity, "recapitulates" it in Himself, to reconcile it with His Father and to deify it. "God became man so that man might become God." This thesis was to be well loved by St. Athanasius, St. Gregory Nazianzen, and St. Cyril of Alexandria.

Here is a manifestation of the human mind in search not of a "superior knowledge," of an exclusive "Gnosis," but of all the values included in the object of faith, so as to grasp its inward coherence and to present it under the form of a rational construction, with humble adherence to the deposit of faith.

3. THE FIRST POSITIONS OF THE SCHOOLS

(a) *The beginnings of the Alexandrian School* [2]

The doctrine of St. Irenaeus, which stresses the unity of the God-man above all else, is encountered among the founders of the

---

[2] Neither Alexandria nor Antioch possessed a school in the strict sense of the word, but only a *tradition.*

Alexandrian school. Captivated by Platonic philosophy and at the same time ardent Christians firmly attached to the Catholic Faith, Clement and Origen wrote commentaries on Scripture according to the *allegorical,* or mystical method.

Clement of Alexandria († c. 215)

In studying Christ by this method, Clement left the human element somewhat in the background, and stressed Christ's divine transcendence. Inevitably, he was accused of Docetism. Indeed, quite a number of his expressions laid him open to such criticism. On the other hand, we must not exaggerate. While Clement's theology is vigorously theocentric, it affirms no less boldly the humanity of Jesus and His very real sufferings on Calvary.

Origen († 255)

When the Word became incarnate, He remained the divine Word in His essence (οὐσία); the human nature that He assumed had all the reality and the properties of a substance like our own. On this point Origen simply followed common tradition. But the problem to be solved was precisely that of the union of the human and the divine in Christ. And to this problem Origen applied himself.

The soul of Jesus served as his point of departure. In accordance with his philosophical doctrine, he held that Christ's soul was created at the beginning of the world, as were all other souls; and that this human soul was united in its entirety to the Word through love. It became a single spirit with the Word (application of I Cor. 6:17). It was a curious attempt, and one whose inadequacy should be noted. In addition to resting on the gratuitous and false notion of the pre-existence of souls, it ran the danger of terminating in the concept of a purely moral union external to the being of Jesus.

On the other hand, the substance of the soul thus united to the Word serves as an intermediary and it is through this substance that the Word united Himself to human flesh so as to be born a man. To make this union more palpable, Origen used the comparison of iron plunged into fire and becoming "all fire." Thus is human nature changed and "transformed into God."

The tendency of Alexandrian Christology is easily discernible. Jesus was considered above all as the Word in whom the human element seems to be absorbed by the divine, just as they insisted that in Scripture the "letter" must give way to the "spirit."

The first Christian artists, trained in classical education and in pagan studios, made no innovations but simply adapted ancient themes to the new iconography.

Thus their pictures of Christ were inspired now by Hermes the ram-bearer, to represent the Good Shepherd pursuing the lost sheep; or again by the pagan Aristaeus, and sometimes too, as in this illustration in the cemetery of Domitilla, by the theme of Orpheus, the divine shepherd surrounded by his flock.

We need not be surprised at the introduction of mythological or legendary themes in Christian iconography. Christians are human, and they do not change their imagination or their feelings when they change their faith.

They no longer believed that Orpheus or Ulysses or Aeneas or some other hero had descended into hell, but their imagination remained imbued with these legends. And Christ spontaneously became for them the divine Orpheus, or the divine Hermes, or the divine Aristaeus. The old heroes or even the gods of mythology served as imaginative props to the thought of the faithful.

Christians no longer believed in the sun-god or the gods of the stars, but Christ was spontaneously acclaimed by them as the unconquered sun, *sol invictus,* who enlightens minds and hearts; and the sun and the moon were always represented as gigantic chariots, guided by some "intelligence," that daily traversed the vast ambit of heaven and hell. Christians no longer believed in the river gods, but they used the same human figures that formerly personified them.

In this picture the artist represents the divine Shepherd in the likeness of the pagan Orpheus. This is one of the most ancient representations of Christ that we have (second century).

We shall see that the School of Antioch, on the contrary, was more concerned with respecting the realities of biblical history and with safeguarding the values proper to the humanity of Christ. More rationalistic and less mystical in its approach than the Alexandrian school, it ended by separating Jesus from the Word. It no longer saw in Him anything but a man united to God by a purely moral union. Here is the starting point of the great controversies of the fifth century.

(b) *Tertullian († c. 220) and the first tendencies of Latin Christology*

While Tertullian was less original as a thinker than Irenaeus or Origen, he none the less deserves special attention. He was the first Christian writer of the West, and can be considered as the creator of the Latin theological vocabulary.

The mystical vision of the problem of Christ, so dear to the Alexandrians, was foreign to this positive, juristic, and above all, moralistic mind. In combating Docetism, he insisted with pleasure and with a very crude realism upon the humiliations and abasements of Jesus in His human state. He even went so far as to deny Him physical beauty. His noble concern was to keep very close to the Scriptural texts.

Far more interesting still was his theological interpretation. Tertullian distinguished with precision two "substances" in Christ:

the divine substance, which he called "spirit,"
the human substance, which he called "flesh,"

and in the human substance, he again distinguished two substances:

the body,
the soul.

This was decided progress in the analysis of the dogma, and the advances made at that time were never afterward lost. To sum up, there is:

one Christ
- God
- man
  - soul
  - body

This progress was to be clarified in two ways: These two sub-stances retain their respective properties: *salva est proprietas utri-usque substantiae* (*Adversus Praxeam, 27, De carne Christi, 5*). It was not until the fifth century that the term "natures" was used instead of "substances." Later on, Pope St. Leo (449) and the Council of Chalcedon (451) took up the same formulas. Finally, it was decided that since these properties belong to the same con-crete subject, they can be used interchangeably. We can therefore say: "God was born, was crucified, and died," we can speak of "the sufferings of God." This was to be called the *communication of idioms* (ἰδίωμα = property).

Tertullian's very positive turn of mind and the fact that he was called on to defend Christ's humanity more than His divinity (against the Docetists) led him to put less emphasis on the unity of Christ than upon His duality. Without going so far as to state, as is sometimes done, that his influence was preponderant upon Latin Catholicism, we must admit that his theology, within its lim-itations, opened the way to Christian thought and offered it precise and reliable means of expression.

CONCLUSIONS

In the face of Christian Gnosticism—considered primarily as a negation of the fleshly reality of the Savior—the mystery which is Christ gradually became clearer to the minds of the faithful until the middle of the 3rd century.

To correct as serious a deviation as Gnosticism, a twofold trend began to take form among Catholics. First, a mystical trend (today we would call it "ontological"), according to which the Word, while remaining fully Himself in His divine Being, truly assumed our flesh and allowed it to be crucified on Calvary for our salvation. The Incarnation and the Redemption were conceived as a descent and invasion by the divine that was so penetrating it extended to the entire human race in an intimate even if mysterious way. Irenaeus and the Alexandrians were the principal representatives of this movement.

Starting from the opposite direction, Tertullian was the principal initiator of a more tangible and positive trend, according to which—as Scripture literally attests—Jesus is at once the man of sorrows (soul and body) and the Son of God glorified even in His flesh. The first of these two representations of the mystery of the Incarnation stresses the *unity* of the Word made flesh; the second stops at the distinctions that are necessary to our conception of the God-man.

Beginning with the second half of the third century until the end of the fourth century, the problem of Christ became the problem of His *divinity*. Is He truly God? If so, how can the absolute transcendence of the Godhead be safeguarded? Is the Word who became incarnate distinguishable from God?

We can see at once that the answers to these questions touch the heart of the mystery of Jesus, a being whom we know to be perfectly one and yet extremely complex as well. Without making a detailed study of the Trinitarian aspect of this problem, it is fitting to emphasize its Christological consequences.

The Second Phase
The Trinitarian Aspect of Christology

1. ADOPTIONISM

To the extent that their Docetism was not absolute, that is did not flatly deny all reality to Christ's humanity, the Gnostic Christians already looked upon Jesus as a man in whom the Logos, the divine eon, had descended in order to accomplish spiritually the Redemption. To their minds, therefore, Jesus was truly born of Mary and Joseph just as other men are born.

More explicitly, Paul of Samosata, Bishop of Antioch between 260 and 268, affirmed that Christ was not God but a human person adopted by God. In his effort to safeguard the oneness of God, Paul of Samosata refused to see in the man Jesus of the Gospels the eternal Son equal to the Father and personally distinct from Him. This position, which was condemned by the Council of Antioch in 268, later received the name of *Adoptionism*.

2. BEGINNINGS OF THE SCHOOL OF ANTIOCH AND ARIANISM

In about 260 there arose in Antioch under the direction of the priest, Lucian, a school of thought which insisted on a literal reading of the Gospel. Without being a disciple of Paul of Samosata, St. Lucian considered Christ to be a man concretely constituted just like other men. From this position arose the tendency to make a human person of the God-man and thus to divide Christ, just as Paul of Samosata had done for other reasons.

In 318, an Alexandrian priest by the name of Arius, who had been won over by the ideas of Lucian and his disciples, pushed the distinction of persons between the Father and Christ to its utmost limit. The Word, according to Arius, was unlike men in that He was eternal in the image of God, but with regard to the one Father He was only a creature, the instrument of Creation and of the Redemption. Such a theory was not only a Christological error, but a denial of the dogma of the Trinity, since it denied the equality of the Word with the One from whom He proceeds.

On the other hand, Arius also fell into error, for psychological reasons, on the human constitution of the Word Incarnate. Since he looked upon the Word as fallible by nature, he held that the Word had the same relation to the body that is usually attributed to the soul. That was his way of explaining the ignorance and other mental shortcomings that he alleged Christ manifested in His earthly life.

The first Ecumenical Council—the Council of Nicea—condemned Arius and defined the consubstantiality of the Word with His Father (ὁμοούσιος τῷ πατεί). The dogma of the divinity of the Word was clearly stated, but on the other hand the mystery of Christ the God-man had not yet been correctly presented.

3. THE RADICAL DUALISM OF PHOTINUS

Lucian's disciples and the friends of Arius (such as Eusebius of Nicomedia, Asterius of Cappadocia, Enomius, etc.) refused to accept the formula of consubstantiality (ὁμοούσιος). The upshot of this refusal was a very intricate conflict in which the Arians, the semi-Arians and the defenders of Nicea fought a battle royal. But since this was strictly a Trinitarian question, it is not pertinent to discuss it here.

Meanwhile Photinus, the Bishop of Sirmium, following an ardent Nicean, Marcellus of Ancyrus, took to task the friends of Arius who denied the equality of the Divine Persons. But then Photinus fell into the opposite error: God is One, and Jesus, born miraculously of Mary and of the Holy Spirit, was simply a man who through his holiness deserved to become the adopted son of the One God. This was his thesis.

Like Paul of Samosata, Photinus radically separated Christ from God. It may seem easier to maintain the unity of the God-man when, like the Arians, one reduces the person of the Word to the level of created things. On the other hand nothing is gained if the unity of Christ has been safeguarded by sacrificing His divinity. Thus, while the Arians and the Photinians were in violent opposition to one another, they were fundamentally very close in their views. In their eyes, Jesus, the man of the Gospels, was not the Person eternally consubstantial with the Father. Christ was no longer God, but simply one of God's creatures.

With Photinus, the Christological problem—together with the difficulties proper to it—found its place among the Trinitarian controversies. Apollinarius of Laodicea was to seek a solution to the problem and with him the dogma of the Incarnation entered its decisive phase.

III. The Period of the Conciliar Definitions

(From the Middle of the Fourth Century to the End of the Seventh Century)

1. APOLLINARIANISM AND ANTI-APOLLINARIANISM (EAST)

(a) *Apollinarius of Laodicea († c. 390)*

Any effort to confine Jesus within the realm of created beings revealed by Scriptural history results either in the lowering of the Word to their level (and this was the Arian error) or else, if the personal oneness of God is upheld, in dividing Christ personally (and this was the most common position of the School of Antioch).

The principal concern of Apollinarius of Laodicea was to defend the *unity* of Christ, the God-man, against Lucian of Antioch and his disciples. A stout defender of Nicea, Apollinarius safeguarded the unity of Christ by the following reasoning: It is evident that two complete realities cannot constitute a single being; since Christ constitutes but a single being and since His divinity cannot be anything but complete, Christ must be incomplete from the point of view of His humanity. It was impossible to doubt the reality of His body (the revival of Docetism in the third century had no influence in the Church); Christ's soul must therefore be denied. Under the pressure of his opponents, Apollinarius finally admitted the existence of a *sensible* soul in Christ, but denied that He had an *intellectual* soul. He held that the Word took the place of the latter.

This position obviously brought him close to the Alexandrian school. He could make his own the great thesis of this school: it is the same Christ, the eternal Son, who died on the Cross. To quote Apollinarius' words: "The incarnate nature of the divine Word is one." However, he sacrificed the humanity of the Word, and his adversaries, the disciples of Lucian, were quick to be scandalized by his position.

(b) *The zenith of the school of Antioch (360-430)*

Lucian's disciples were not all Arians. Diodorus of Tarsus († c. 391) and Theodore of Mopsuestia († 428), the most outstanding of this period, were outspokenly anti-Arian. But faithful to the tradition of Antioch, they could not bear to see the humanity of Christ destroyed, as Apollinarius was trying to do. They held that the Word in Jesus Christ had assumed an *authentically human being,* declaring that He had not modified "the son of man." But does not this amount to stating that there are two "Christs"—the Son of the Father *and* the son of Mary, held together by a purely moral union? We can now see why Theodorus finally repudiated the tradition of Antioch and denied the *communication of idioms.* To his mind, it was the man and not the Word who died, and thus he fell into the opposite error.

(c) *St. Athanasius (295-373)*

While St. Athanasius was above all the undisputed champion of the consubstantiality of the Word with God His Father, he also played an important role in the conflict between Apollinarius and the school of Antioch.

True, he did not grasp the full scope of the error and danger in the Apollinarian position. In 362, when a synod was called together in Alexandria through his efforts, he tried to reconcile all Catholics on the problem of Christ. In fact, he did bring about agreement between both parties on the essential point: the Incarnation is not simply the moral presence of the Word within Jesus, as in the case of the prophets or the saints (against Antioch); the Word Himself was made flesh, just as Scripture declares. However, Christ's body is not deprived of a soul: neither of a sensible or a spiritual soul (against Apollinarius), for "it is not only by the body but also through the soul that the Word accomplished salvation." Christ does not consist of two distinct beings; there is a single subject for both His human and divine operations.

The fact remains that the agreement reached at the synod was superficial. The two parties continued to evolve in their separate directions. The Apollinarians went so far as to claim they were followers of Athanasius and put certain writings into circulation to support this claim which they dishonestly attributed to Athanasius. But they were quickly attacked by St. Basil of Caesarea and condemned by the Council of Rome under Pope St. Damasus (380), as well as by the Council of Constantinople of 381. It should be noted that Pope Damasus likewise condemned the Antiochan theory of the "two sons" in Christ.

St. Athanasius' doctrine is that of Irenaeus and of Alexandrian theology: the Word made Himself visible to us so as to enable us to know the invisible Father. The saint looks at everything from the point of view of Christ's divinity. And in order to explain the deifying power exercised by Jesus, St. Athanasius compared Christ's humanity to an instrument (ὄργανον) in the service of the Word. This analogy was to have great significance afterwards.

Moreover, St. Athanasius followed St. Ignatius and St. Irenaeus in stressing the soteriological argument as the proof of Christ's perfect humanity. The Cappadocians likewise did not hesitate to declare that the Word Incarnate had to have a human soul by reason of His essentially Redemptive mission, as we see from St. Gregory Nazianzen's terse formula: "Only that which is assumed by the Word is healed; and only that which is united to God is saved."

Before entering upon a discussion of the great Nestorian and Monophysite controversies, which were solved by the Council of Chalcedon through the authority of Pope St. Leo the Great, it will help us to understand their full significance if we follow the evolution of Latin theology after Tertullian.

2. CHRISTOLOGY IN THE WEST BEFORE EPHESUS (431)

Tertullian had given the Christology of the West its first decisive expression. After him Christology continued to perfect itself, but it did not deviate in the essentials.

Tertullian, as we may remember, had distinguished two substances in the one and only Christ: perfect divinity and perfect humanity, soul and body. The Latin tradition repeated his formulas, especially during the fourth and fifth centuries.

Certain of the Fathers such as St. Hilary, St. Jerome, St. Augustine, and St. Vincent of Lérins, often sought help from him, without of course turning to him exclusively. The bishops of Africa, with St. Augustine at their head, had occasion to show they were heirs of Tertullian's thought in a very special way. The monk Leporius (circa 415) feared the divine Majesty would be diminished by the affirmation: "The Word was born a man," and claimed the correct expression was: "The Word was born *with* a man" or else "a man was born who had God with him." To Leporius' mind, this was the only way to avoid confusing the divine and the human properties in Christ. He felt that this would also make it easier for him to explain the ignorance and weaknesses Jesus manifested during His earthly life.

But the bishops of Africa succeeded in making the loyal Leporius retract. They showed him that the duality he had introduced in Christ was too radical and that the reasons which had led him to take this erroneous position could easily be explained even if the divine origin were held to be the *only personal origin* of the Word Incarnate. To quote the formula of retraction:

"The faith that we must profess unfalteringly is faith in the one and only Son of God who is ever inseparable. A giant composed of two substances, as He is called, He truly performed the works of a man during His entire earthly life, and He has always possessed whatever belongs to God."

In the eyes of St. Augustine, the Incarnation is the work of the entire Trinity; while Scripture attributes it to the Holy Ghost, Jesus is not for that reason the Son of the Holy Ghost, but the only Son of the Father, and all human elements come to Him from Mary ever Virgin, who is perfectly His Mother.

In the matter of the primacy of divine action in the Incarnation, St. Augustine affirmed the presence of Jesus' rational soul, as against Apollinarius, but he considered the soul as an intermediary between the Word and the flesh He assumed. On the other hand there was no question of any temporal priority of soul over body, for the union of the two elements took place at the very instant of the Incarnation (against Origen). Moreover, St. Augustine admitted a perfect *communication of idioms,* which Leporius had denied.

Thus St. Augustine transmitted Tertullian's formulas to the West, after giving them greater doctrinal precision. Leo the Great was to adopt them almost to the letter, and to use them as the cornerstone of the Council of Chalcedon. St. Augustine was even more careful than Tertullian to attribute the fulfilment of the Incarnation, even in its human details, to the almighty power of God alone, so as to safeguard the unity of Christ's person. He was equally meticulous in referring this same Christ's fleshly origin to the Blessed Virgin alone, so as to bring out the specific perfection of His humanity.

Finally, in the psychological order St. Augustine took a position concerning Christ's knowledge which should be noted, because it has become accepted doctrine. Arius, as we remember, had eliminated the rational soul of the Word Incarnate because to his mind the Word, eternal but created, was as fallible as the human soul. A soul would therefore have been useless to Jesus. In consequence, Arius attributed to the Word the ignorance of Judgment Day referred to by St. Mark (13:32). While this attribution was intolerable to the Fathers, the admission of such ignorance gave these same Fathers a basis for insisting, as against Apollinarius, upon the presence of a rational soul in Christ.

In actual fact, does ignorance of any kind exist in the Word Incarnate?

To quote Father Lebreton:

"The influence of St. Augustine upon this question was particularly felt through his theological doctrine of ignorance and sin. St. Athanasius, and St. Cyril of Alexandria even more than he, saw the ignorance of our Savior as born of a merciful intention: as they saw it, it was an application of the general plan of the Incarnation by which the Son of God took our weaknesses upon Himself in order to heal them all.

"St. Augustine, on the other hand, distinguishes ignorance from all our other infirmities: hunger, thirst, and even death. He says that the Son of God took on all these things, but not ignorance, because ignorance is not only the consequence but also the principle of sin . . . If Christ saves us from this abyss, it is not by plunging into it Himself: 'He is our knowledge, He is our wisdom, it is He who makes us believe in temporal things; it is He who reveals eternal things to us as well' (*De Trinitate*, XIII, 19:24; P.L. 42, 1034)." [3]

This point presents no difficulty to St. Augustine, who affirms as vigorously as the Eastern Fathers the redemptive motive of the Incarnation. His formula: "Si homo non periisset, Filius hominis non venisset" ("if man had not fallen, the Son of man would not have come") (*Sermo* 174:2) will always remain famous. It was

[3] Lebreton, *op. cit.*

also the indirect object of certain discussions which we shall have to mention.

While Leporius in the West obliged St. Augustine and the whole Latin episcopate to bestir themselves, in the East, Nestorius, the Patriarch of Constantinople, ushered in a grave crisis for the same reasons, and the Eastern Church has suffered its consequences even until our own day.

3. THE NESTORIAN AND MONOPHYSITE CRISES

(a) *The state of men's minds at the time of the Nestorian crisis*

The conflict took place between Constantinople and Alexandria. This fact must be stressed if we want to understand the bitterness of the struggle which was perhaps as much an expression of rivalry between episcopal sees as of theological differences. It is easy to state the doctrinal disagreement, inasmuch as Nestorius, the Patriarch of Constantinople, followed the line of thought of the School of Antioch in every respect, whereas his antagonist St. Cyril, the Patriarch of Alexandria, was one of the most brilliant lights of the Alexandrian School. The East produced no Tertullian to settle their differences. Although the vocabulary dealing with the Blessed Trinity was already well developed in the East, such was not the case for Christological dogma.

While the West already distinguished *substance* or *nature* from *person*—two substances united in Christ in a single person—the terms *nature, hypostasis,* and *person* all had about the same meaning in Antioch as well as in Egypt. This is why the partisans of Antioch, whose primary concern was to safeguard the perfection of Christ the Man, spoke equivalently of two natures (οὐσία) as if they were two hypostases. As these writers presented them, the two natures had such distinct individualities that the union between the divine and the human was no more than a "connecting link" or "conjunction," a "relation" or "inhabitation" of the Word in His "human temple."

The Alexandrians, on the other hand, who had a penetrating insight into the personal unity of Christ, fully accepted Apollinarius' formula, which they then thought to be the work of Athanasius: "An incarnate nature of the Word of God" (σεσαρχωμένη). As they saw it, the union was accomplished in the hypostasis or divine nature of the Word.

The positions of St. Cyril of Alexandria and of Nestorius were characterized respectively by personal Monophysism and equally personal Dyophysism.

(b) *The Nestorian crisis and the Council of Ephesus (431)*

The conflict broke out with regard to the title "Mother of God" which had been given to the Blessed Virgin Mary. Now, if Mary were called the "Mother of God" (θεοτόκος = *Theotokos*), would not this be reducing the person of the Word of God to a pure creature as Arius had done, or else, if the divinity of Christ were maintained, would not the Blessed Virgin become a goddess? Inasmuch as Christ is first of all a man, although not a pure man but "a man united to God," Mary was neither the "Mother of the man alone" ('Ανθρωποτόκος), nor the "Mother of God" (θεοτόκος), but on the contrary the "Mother of Christ," that is, the Mother of the man in whom God dwells (Χριστοτόκος). Such was the thesis of Nestorius.

In the name of the traditional doctrine of Alexandria as well as in the name of the entire Eastern Church, St. Cyril protested vigorously: if Mary is not the Mother of God, then Christ is not God and in Him the human and the divine are two hypostases or distinct natures. Moreover, the term "Theotokos" was traditional and therefore most venerable.

While the first argument was accepted by almost no one except the Alexandrians, the second argument aroused even the followers of Nestorius, such as John of Antioch who accused his friend from Constantinople of contravening the whole of tradition. We should note that St. Cyril wanted to champion both tradition and his own doctrine. If Christ were not to be divided in two, it was necessary to say that the unity within Him derives solely from the Word; and that while His human nature and His divine nature are distinct, there exists a "physical union" between them, and that the divine nature or Person realizes this union within itself.

Tixeront aptly says that, for St. Cyril, "Christ is one, not through, but in spite of, the union." [4] The bishop of Alexandria succeeded in having the Ecumenical Council of Ephesus (431) accept his reasons against Nestorius. We should remark, however, that the Fathers of this Council were far more concerned with rejecting the

[4] Joseph A. Tixeront, *History of Dogmas* (St. Louis, B. Herder, 1916), Vol. III, p. 64.

radical dualism of Nestorius than with confirming St. Cyril's own position. They unhesitatingly approved the letter in which St. Cyril affirmed the unity of Christ. However, they were more reticent with regard to another letter accompanied with anathemas in which St. Cyril fulminated against the detractors of the "Theotokos" and imposed formulas that had Monophysite tendencies.

Unfortunately, the Council did not permit the opponents to present their views, and in consequence its decisions were violently contested. Calm was not restored until St. Cyril and St. John of Antioch agreed on the so-called "formula of union" (433). The Alexandrian recanted his expressions "one nature" and "physical union," and they were replaced by the terms "one person" and "union of two natures." The Antiochan for his part admitted the term "union," and abandoned the very contestable expression "simple conjunction."

(c) *The Monophysite crisis and the Council of Chalcedon (451)*

Peace was far from reigning in men's minds after the act of union of 433. St. Cyril's partisans, in particular, were concerned to see him affirm the union of two natures as if he were renouncing his formula of the "μία φύσις." They also attacked the works of Diodorus of Tarsus and Theodore of Mopsuestia. But the protagonists in the Nestorian quarrel died one after the other (John of Antioch in 442 and St. Cyril in 444). Nestorius was no longer in the lists. Only Theodoret of Cyrus—the most reliable theologian of the Antioch school—remained on the scene. He finally signed the formula of 433. St. Cyril was replaced in the see of Alexandria by Dioscurus, who did not measure up to his predecessor either in wisdom or in holiness.

It was precisely at this moment that a monk from Constantinople, Eutyches, became the ardent defender of all Cyrillian ideas. All-powerful at the court, he badgered the Nestorians, but fell into the opposite excess. He maintained the thesis of "μία φύσις," and would not hear of two natures in Christ. After the union, he declared, there was only one nature and not two; the divine nature remained what it had been and absorbed the human nature, just as the water of the sea dissolves and absorbs a drop of honey that has fallen into it. These ideas began to spread, and Eutyches grouped around himself all the opponents of the union of 433.

Attacked by Theodoret in 447, and condemned by a council of Constantinople in 448, Eutyches appealed to Pope St. Leo.

St. Leo the Great was already acquainted with the Nestorian question. In 430, when he was an influential deacon, he had called upon Cassian to refute Nestorius. This monk from Marseilles, who had been involved in the Leporius affair, soon recognized in Nestorius' ideas those of Leporius, which St. Augustine and the Latin Bishops had refuted with the help of Tertullian's formulas.

These circumstances easily explain St. Leo's answer to Flavian, the Patriarch of Constantinople, with regard to Eutyches: While the personal dualism of Nestorius divided Christ, the strict Monophysism of Eutyches did not respect the perfection proper to the humanity and the divinity of the God-man. Eutyches' view was therefore at least as intolerable as that of Nestorius. In this *Tome to Flavian,* the Pope vigorously affirmed the unity of the person while safeguarding the distinct properties of each nature:

> The Son of God, descending from His heavenly dwelling without being separated from the glory of the Father, was born in a new order and according to a new nativity . . . The God who cannot suffer did not disdain to become a suffering man . . . One and the same (being) is truly the Son of God and the Son of man . . . (Denz. No. 144).

This letter gave credit to the theology of Antioch for whatever correct views it held, but it displeased the Monophysites as well as the intransigent Cyrillians who did not find in it their "μία φύσις" formula. It was under these conditions that Dioscurus of Alexandria called a council in Ephesus (449) at which Eutyches was rehabilitated, Theodoret condemned, and the anathemas of Cyril noisily acclaimed. This is a sad episode which has gone down in history under the name of "The Robber Council of Ephesus" by which St. Leo stigmatized it.

Against this robbery, the Pope asked the Emperor Theodosius to call a general council. Being partial to Eutyches, Theodosius turned a deaf ear to the Pope's plea. Soon afterward the Emperor died, and his successor Marcian convoked a new council in 451. First held in Nicea with a representation of almost 600 bishops, it was later transferred to Chalcedon. After passionate debates, dogmatic pronouncements were made. The decree was directed expressly at Nestorius and Eutyches, against whom it held up the faith of Nicea, the letters of St. Cyril to Nestorius and to John of Antioch, and above all St. Leo's *Tome to Flavian:*

We must confess one and the same Son, our Lord Jesus Christ, complete in His divinity and complete in His humanity, true God and true man . . . one and the same Christ . . . in two natures, without admixture, without transformation, without division, without separation; for the union has not suppressed the difference of natures, each has preserved its proper mode of being, and has come together with the other in a single person or hypostasis (Denz. 148).

Thus the doctrine of the Church concerning the Incarnation and the vocabulary appropriate to this doctrine were definitively set forth: "In Christ there is unity of person and duality of natures."

Inasmuch as the decision of Chalcedon seemed to be a return to the "Antiochan" positions, the Nestorians triumphed and the Monophysites resisted openly in Palestine and in Egypt. This was the beginning of a long period of discussions and turmoil that would continue until the end of the seventh century. The Alexandrian influence was particularly felt at the Second Council of Constantinople (the Fifth Ecumenical Council) in 553, where all the partisans of Antioch were condemned, including Theodoret. On the other hand, the Third Council of Constantinople (681) condemned certain Monophysites who no longer insisted upon a single nature but claimed a unity of wills in Christ: "a single will" ("μόνη θέλησις," whence the name "Monothelism" for this heresy). This condemnation marked the rupture of religious unity in the East, the ruin of the Persian Church, and schisms in the Churches of Syria and Egypt.

4. GREEK THEOLOGY AFTER THE COUNCIL OF CHALCEDON: LEO OF BYZANTIUM— MAXIMUS THE CONFESSOR.

The conciliar decisions that canonized the Christological formula, "one person, two natures in Christ," were not the fruit of an extensive process of reasoning. The Church did not *explain* the Mystery of Christ in a philosophical formula; she merely *presented* it to the mind in a formula that was particularly suited to this Mystery. And it was not in the light of a reasoned notion of nature and person that this Mystery was defined in Ephesus or Chalcedon, but in the light of Scripture and of uncontested Tradition. There had not been any doctrinal evolution, but simply the conceptual clarification that was necessary to put an end to ambiguities and to guide every Christian who wanted to have a deeper understanding of his faith in the Word Incarnate, his Savior.

After the Church had established the Christological dogma through her infallible Magisterium, certain men—including Leo of Byzantium († 542) and St. Maximus the Confessor († 662)—tried to explain in a rational manner the significance hidden beneath the terms defined. Wishing to prove that Chalcedon and Ephesus were in harmony, Leo of Byzantium had recourse to Aristotle's categories:

> Nature implies the idea of being (simply); the hypostasis implies in addition the idea of *being apart:* the former indicates the species, the latter reveals the individual; the former bears the mark of the universal, the latter separates the particular from the general. . . .[5]

Since a nature without a hypostasis does not exist in real life but only in the mind, it seems that the human nature of the Christ *who exists* must also be a hypostasis. But this is precisely what the two councils had denied. Therefore, Leo continued, if the human nature does not exist by itself then it must find its subject in the Word. Christ's humanity is *enhypostasised* (ἐνυπόστατον). Thus, the union in Christ is not a "physical union," but a *hypostatic union*. This term was to have great success.

Leo of Byzantium vigorously rejected Nestorian dualism as well as strict Monophysism; in the end he came to look upon the Mystery of Christ from the same point of view as St. Cyril. We know that the latter abandoned the "μία φύσις" when he realized that this expression did not represent the *personal oneness* of the God-man. Like St. Cyril, Leo of Byzantium had an ontological conception—if we may say so—of this Mystery: there is only one being, one existence in Christ, for the Person of the Word is, by itself alone, the complete guarantee of unity. Therefore the unity is not the result of the unification of two natures into a third. As was said against the Monophysites, "Christ is one in spite of the union, not because of it." In the eyes of Leo of Byzantium, the basis upon which a rational theology of the Incarnation can be established is this: there is a single Person who maintains the unity between the two natures.

The theology of St. Maximus the Confessor, on the other hand, is entirely directed against Monothelism. It clarifies what has been called the "theandric operation" of Christ. In the works of Pseudo-Dionysius the term "theandric" was used to explain the perfect

---

[5] Cited in Tixeront, *op. cit.,* Vol. III, p. 154.

harmony in the activities of the God-man (θεὸς ἀνηρ). But a Mono-physitic interpretation of this term had denied Christ's human nature the power to be the principle of its own operations. As St. Maximus saw it, if we must grant the Person of the Word all-inclusive authority over His human as well as His divine activities, it is none the less necessary to carefully distinguish the specificity of each of these activities. That is why the formula "theandric operation" tends to express the fundamental harmony that results from the single intention and practical direction given by the Word Incarnate to His human and divine activities.

5. CONCLUSION: THE BALANCE-SHEET OF THEOLOGY IN THE EAST: ST. JOHN DAMASCENE.

To clarify the attainments of theology in the East at the close of the Patristic Age, we could not do better than to present briefly the position of St. John Damascene († c. 749).

Faithful to the method of Leo of Byzantium, St. John in his doctrine on the Incarnation "rigorously deduces the theological and dogmatic conclusions of the hypostatic union." On this point he was the forerunner of the thirteenth century theologians, in the exposition of the corollaries to the dogma of the hypostatic union.[6] He has actually been called the St. Thomas of the East.

Let us summarize his conclusions on the problem of Christ:

Granted that the Person of the Word is the sole guarantor of the oneness of His being even though it has a double function of subsistence (divine subsistence in the divine nature, and human subsistence in the humanity of Christ), the Word Incarnate can be said to be "composite according to His two natures." It follows that:

(a) There is a mutual compenetration of natures: the humanity participates intimately in the divine energy, just as in man the body participates in the spiritual energy of the soul.

(b) The humanity of Jesus must be adored, inasmuch as it cannot be separated from the Word who is its subject.

(c) As man, Christ is God's Son and not His servant; for the servant relationship is one that affects the person, just as does the relationship of a son. And the Person of Christ is the Son and not the servant of the Father.

[6] A. Michel, "Hypostatique (Union)" in *Dictionnaire de Théologie Catholique* (henceforth to be designated as D. T. C.), cols. 504, 505.

(d) There is a perfect *communication of idioms,* and St. John Damascene states its laws.

(e) In the psychological order:

absence of all ignorance in Christ;

absence of any passions which would be incompatible with His absolute perfection;

duality of operations coinciding with the duality of natures.

After St. John Damascene, the East ceased to be in the forefront of the great theological problems. The West had already prepared itself with Boethius († 525) for a reasoned conception of the notions used in Catholic dogma. However it was not until the eleventh century—two centuries after the renaissance of learning due to Charlemagne—that the so-called *Age of Scholasticism* opened in the West.

In closing our summary of the long and laborious formation of dogma and of its theological elaboration in the East, it is important to repeat once again that the soteriological argument was the major one for all the defenders of faith in Christ.

Father Rivière declares: "To prove that the Savior was true man, it was pointed out that our nature needed to be redeemed and rehabilitated. Consequently if Jesus Christ had not been a man like us and of our substance, He would not have been able to give us the examples of virtue which we needed, nor would He have been able to suffer and die to wrest us from death and from sin. Such was the reasoning of St. Irenaeus and Tertullian against Docetism. Later, the Cappadocians opposed Apollinarius with very similar considerations. Likewise, to maintain the effective divinity of Christ, St. Athanasius argued against Arius, and St. Cyril argued against Nestorius that this principle of the Redemption could not be efficacious if it were fulfilled by an ordinary man or by any mere creature. Only He who made man in the beginning was capable of redeeming him. Only the eternal Son of God could return to us the rights we had lost to adoptive sonship. Only He who was without sin would obtain forgiveness for sinners." [7]

There was practically explicit unanimity in looking upon the Redemption as the determining motive of the Incarnation of the Word. On the other hand, the Mystery of Christ—"one in two natures"—was constantly being explained from very different points of view even within the bosom of the Catholic Church.

[7] Jean Rivière, *The Doctrine of the Atonement* (London, Kegan Paul, 1909).

Barring the extremes incompatible with the Faith, this mystery can in fact be legitimately approached either from the angle of oneness or from the angle of duality. This twofold choice resulted in the founding of a twofold theology: one stressing the divine penetration of the Word within the human; the other manifesting the integrity and the glorification of the human in its union with the Word.

This is the explanation of the diverse but in no sense contradictory positions of Clement of Alexandria *and* Tertullian, of the Council of Ephesus *and* the Council of Chalcedon, of the School of Alexandria (St. Cyril) *and* the School of Antioch (Theodoret), and in more general terms of the positions of the Greeks *and* the Latins. Theirs were complementary positions in which man's intelligence found adequate justification for this Mystery which is unfathomable here below and necessarily very complex. This twofold option was to cause perpetual theological conflicts in the West from the eleventh century up to and including our own time.

IV. The Theological Doctrine of the Incarnation
(In The West)

1. FROM ST. ANSELM TO ST. THOMAS AQUINAS (11TH–13TH CENTURIES)

(a) *The Christological problem in the eleventh century*

When St. Anselm, the first great Christian thinker, ushered in the age of theological speculation, there was complete agreement in the West on the formulas of Ephesus and Chalcedon.

In the immediate deductions from these formulas, we find the same unanimity: a single Person in Christ, the divine Person (against Nestorius); two natures, the divine nature and the human nature, body and soul (against Eutyches). Likewise, it was recognized against the Manichaeans that the Word had "assumed" both a body and a soul, and that neither the body nor the soul pre-existed before the union (against Origen).

It was over the *mode of union* in the Person and over the role played by human nature that the debate arose. In fact, this union still remained to be explained, and in some measure clarified: Are the body and the soul united in such a way as to form an individual being, a supposit, a man? Did the Word assume a particular, determinate man? These passionate debates gave rise, especially in the twelfth century, to several very divergent conceptions. In order to grasp these views it is important to understand, and to describe the context in which the theology of the Incarnation was being worked out.

St. Anselm followed the Latin trend and reasoned about the mystery from the point of view of the duality of natures. For him, the Incarnation was the problem of the union of the human and the divine in the Son of God. And he attached capital importance to the fact that this union is realized precisely within the *Son* of God:

> If any other Person (besides the Son) had become incarnate, there would have been two sons in the Trinity, namely, the Son of God who is the Son even before the Incarnation, and the one who, through the Incarnation, would have become the son of the Virgin. Then in the (divine) Persons, who must always be equal, there would have been an inequality by reason of the (unequal) dignity of the nativities.[8]

The Incarnation also demands that the Person who assumes the humanity be begotten, because man normally comes into existence by way of generation. Thus, St. Anselm continues:

> If the Father had become incarnate, there would be two grandsons in the Trinity: the Father would in fact be the grandson of the Virgin's parents according to humanity; and the Word, without being a man, would none the less be the grandson of the Virgin (inasmuch as He is eternally begotten by the Father).[9]

Nowadays, such argumentation makes us smile. But it should not go unnoticed by anyone who wants to understand the orientation of the Christological problem in the Middle Ages and to grasp the speculative effort of theology from that period until our own time.

To give a rational explanation of the Incarnation as it actually took place, it was thought necessary to declare that divine power—attributed to the Holy Spirit as in the witness of the Gospel—miraculously fecundated the Blessed Virgin Mary. That is how the man *begotten* in her was immediately *assumed* by the eternal Son in whom alone the *union* of the divine and the human was perfectly consummated.

[8] *Cur Deus Homo*, Book II, Chapter 9.
[9] *Ibid.*

Thus, there was a *generation* in Mary, an assumption [10] of that which was begotten in her, and the *union* of that which was temporally begotten to the eternally begotten divine Person. These are the various movements that theologians affirmed to be essential to the Incarnation. They did not see these movements as temporal stages, but as logically distinct steps: the reason there was no succession between the generation, the assumption, and the union, is that divine power realized it all in a single instant.

The problem that remained unsolved was the following: was that which was begotten strictly a man constituted like other men? If so, was He not a human person? If not, how could Christ be truly a man like ourselves? Three answers were given, which have gone down in the history of doctrine as the "Three Opinions."

(b) *The "Three Opinions" (See Table, pp. 60-61 below)*

1. The so-called opinion of the "supposit assumed" by the Word (first opinion).

The first opinion was the heir to a long tradition which found expression in the very terms used by the councils and often repeated by the Fathers before and after Ephesus. It had many authorities in its favor (in 1184 over 150 such authorities were alleged to exist), and was synthesized in the formula: *Filius Dei assumpsit hominem* (the Son of God assumed a man). In the mystery of the Word Incarnate, they saw a given man constituted at the term of his generation in Mary, with a rational soul and a human body. This man was assumed by the Word and personally united to the Word, and he became the Word. There was no transformation of natures, each of which kept all that was proper to it. Thus, according to this opinion, we can say: just as God became man, so a man became God. There would therefore be a single person in Christ, but two supposits.

We cannot give a clear explanation of how this could be or actually was understood. The defenders of this opinion made an affirmation and did not try too much to understand it. They were conscious of echoing a tradition of long standing, and nothing more. But for those who sought to penetrate the inward significance of these pronouncements and to develop their consequences, difficulties

[10] The term "assumption" is a technical one and signifies in the theology of the Incarnation the act by which the Word took humanity to Himself (*ad-sumere*).

arose. Did not the insistence on speaking of "this man assumed" by the "Word" impair the unity of Christ by introducing a second person into His being? Did it not become impossible to explain the proposition that was affirmed: "The Son of God is this man"? Criticism is always easy, and it was not lacking in this instance.

2. The so-called opinion of "the Word clothed with humanity" (Abelard: third opinion).

The interpretation of Abelard, "that subtle dialectician of Mount St. Genevieve," appeared as a reaction against the first opinion. The inclusion of human nature in Christ, he held, must be to the exclusion of any new reality that might constitute a second person in Him. Now, in the eyes of Abelard, every rational substance, according to the definition of Boethius, constitutes a person. And a human nature, resulting from the union of soul and body, is indeed a reality of this sort. How, then, could one avoid introducing a fourth person into the bosom of the Trinity? His answer was by dissociating the elements of the nature assumed.

Indeed, Abelard held that the soul and the body of Christ were very real, like those that constitute every other human nature. But, as he saw it, it sufficed for the Word to have assumed them separately to safeguard the fact of the Incarnation. Since body and soul would not be united substantially to one another, they could not then constitute the new person that must at all costs be excluded. And the Word clothed Himself with this soul and this body, disunited from one another, as if they were garments; meanwhile He remained unchanged in His divinity. In this way, He could appear as one of us, *habitu inventus ut homo.*

To Abelard, only in this sense was it permissible to say: "God became man." The current formulas of his day on the mysteries were to be understood in this figurative, improper sense. The term "man" could signify only the parts of a human nature, not a substantial reality, *non est aliquid.* Indeed, this opinion of Abelard's has been called "Christological nihilism."

To avoid the embryonic Nestorianism of the first opinion, a position had been taken that could no longer maintain the reality of the human nature assumed. Pope Alexander III, who had upheld this thesis when he was still a cardinal, condemned it in 1177. Between these extreme opinions, a third position found its place: the so-called opinion of the "composite Person," the intermediate or second opinion.

3. The so-called opinion of the "composite Person" (second opinion).

The second opinion refuses to admit, with the first opinion, that the reality presupposed to have been assumed was a man, or more precisely *this* man. The reality in question could only be "humanity." The expression "this man" implies a subject subsisting in a human nature; whereas the term "humanity" simply evokes the essential, constitutive marks that belong to all men. Therefore "this man" must refer to the human reality *united* to the Word. In consequence, the term *supposit* must be used only to designate the Person of the Word who is the sole supposit of both natures. Inasmuch as He is the Word, Christ is an absolutely simple Person; and yet this Person can be said to be *composite* in that it subsists in two natures. Therein lies the difference between the second and the first opinions.

As against the third opinion (Abelard's), this view supports the substantial union between the body and the soul of the human nature assumed. This nature is *something* (the neuter *aliquid*) that is taken on by the Word, without however being *someone* (the masculine *aliquis*).

(c) *The* Sentences *of Peter Lombard* (*completed about 1150*)

We have a clear knowledge of the "three opinions" thanks to the study made of them in his *Sentences* by Peter Lombard, the famous Parisian teacher of the twelfth century. As we know, this work was practically the "manual of studies" for the entire Middle Ages until the sixteenth century, when the *Summa Theologiae* of St. Thomas Aquinas began to dethrone it.

In Book III, Distinction Six of the *Sentences,* the author showed that while all three opinions can be attributed to St. Augustine, the second relies above all on the authority of St. John Damascene. It was indeed the Damascene who declared that the hypostasis of Christ is *composite* by reason of the two natures.

Thus Peter Lombard introduced into Latin theology this heir to Greek theology. Until that time, only the Western Fathers were known (St. Augustine, St. Ambrose, and St. Hilary). On the other hand, we would be wrong to think that St. John Damascene changed the orientation of Latin Christology in the twelfth century. Rather it was the prevailing thought of the time that assimilated him, for while his writings were predominantly unitary in their approach they were interpreted from the dualistic point of view.

Actually, Peter Lombard in his study of the Word Incarnate crystallized the tradition begun by St. Anselm, as we can see from the organization of the *Sentences*. Here is the outline of this work, which St. Thomas has passed on to us:

I. The Incarnation of God (III *Sent.*, dist. 1-5).
    1. The Person who assumes (dist. 1).
    2. The nature assumed (dist. 2-4).
    3. The union of the One who assumes and of the reality assumed (dist. 5).

II. The Particular Condition of the Word Incarnate (dist. 6-22).
    1. What it is fitting that Christ should have by reason of the union (dist. 6-12).
        A. The way of union is explained (the three opinions, dist. 6).
        The manner of speaking of this union (the laws of the communication of idioms, dist. 7).
        B. The consequences of the union.
            a. What is fitting to the divine nature by reason of its union to the human nature (one or two sons in Christ, dist. 8).
            b. What is fitting to the human nature by reason of its union to the divine nature (worship due to Christ, dist. 9).
            c. What is fitting to the person of Christ by reason of the human nature assumed (problems of His predestination and adoption, dist. 10; is He a creature? dist. 11; how is He impeccable? dist. 12).
    2. What is fitting to Christ by reason of His human nature, exalted by the Incarnation (dist. 13-22).
        A. What was assumed with the human nature (dist. 13—grace).
        The psychology of Christ (knowledge, passions of the soul, etc.)
        Capacity for corporeal suffering.
        B. The activities that belong to the human nature (dist. 17-20).
        the will in Christ;

Christ's merit for Himself;
Christ's merit to redeem the world of sin (that is
why He is a Mediator);
Christ's satisfaction and His Priesthood.
C. The death of Christ and its consequences (dist.
21-22).

It was within this framework that the masters were to study and teach the theology of Christ until the sixteenth century. Peter Lombard had a number of commentators, including St. Bonaventure and St. Albert the Great. However his most famous commentator was St. Thomas Aquinas, who succeeded in bringing the theology of the Incarnation to a high level of perfection, as we shall soon show.

2. ST. THOMAS AQUINAS AND THE THIRTEENTH CENTURY

(a) *The* Commentary on the Sentences (*1256*)

With regard to the problem of the Incarnation, St. Thomas, as a young commentator on the *Sentences,* had his attention fixed continually upon the "three opinions." True, only the second opinion (the so-called opinion of the "composite person") had been generally accepted since the end of the twelfth century. But the Angelic Doctor went to greater pains than anyone else to stress the importance of this position, by comparing it often with the two others, particularly with the first opinion. He accepted the Augustinian tradition which St. Anselm had taken up again.

The theologians of the thirteenth century never ceased repeating that in the Incarnation it was extremely *fitting* that the eternally begotten Son should assume a nature produced by generation. And St. Thomas brought out this same point in his *Commentary on the Sentences.* We should note, however, that St. Anselm's doctrine had been weakened. They no longer said it was *necessary* that the Son of God become incarnate, but only that it was supremely *fitting.*

The theological problem of the Incarnation was now seen as follows: on the one hand was the divine aspect, and on the other was the human aspect; how was the *union* of the divine and the human accomplished solely in the divine Person of the Word, in conformity with the Catholic Faith? Here was St. Thomas' answer:

In the Incarnation there are two things to consider, namely the person who assumes and the nature assumed. On the side of the person who assumes, the Incarnation is designated by the name of *mission:* and this originates in the Father alone . . . On the side of the nature assumed, the Incarnation takes the name of *temporal conception* or *nativity*. Now, it is a totally gratuitous gift for this nature to be assumed into the personally divine unity, and the author of this conception is . . . the Holy Spirit (to whom gratuitous works are attributed).[11]

Inasmuch as the divine Person is *immutable,* the Incarnation could be accomplished only by the ascent of the begotten human nature toward this Person. The mission of the Word is strictly a Trinitarian problem; the conception and assumption of the human nature constitute the Christological problem. This is what we must keep in mind. If we want to catch a rational "glimpse" of the mode in which this mystery is realized, here is the plan according to which the humanity was instantaneously united to the Word:

Without any doubt it was within one and the same instant that the following took place: the physical *change* of the blood of Mary into the flesh of Christ—and the *formation* of the organs—and the *animation* of the organized body—and finally the *assumption* of the animated body into the *unity* of the divine Person.

Against the first opinion, St. Thomas specified: *that which* was assumed was not a reality that existed by itself, even though it was a reality, namely a perfectly constituted human nature. On the other hand, the second opinion appeared to present some difficulties. After all, was not the fundamental problem that of unifying everything in the divine Word and thus safeguarding His absolute simplicity? Hence the term "composite Person" seemed an equivocal expression to all the theologians of that time. This second opinion was adopted strictly as an opinion.[12] And yet it was better than the other two because it was the only one that explained the affirmations of our faith: "This man is God"—"God is this man"—"the man did not become God; but it is a fact that this man is God," etc., according to the law of the communication of idioms.

And what of the psychological and corporeal conditions of Christ? Since the Incarnation must be explained in terms of an (instantaneous) *ascent* of the human toward the Person of the Word, it is supremely fitting to consider the humanity as being already endowed with all sorts of perfections both natural and

[11] III *sent.,* dist. 4, q. 1, a. 1, solut. 2 ad 2.
[12] *Ibid.,* q. 5, a. 2, c.

supernatural (the natural perfections of unclouded knowledge, the spontaneity that belongs to man in willing and acting, the absence of corporeal defects, etc.; the supernatural perfections of habitual grace, the virtues, and the gifts) and that this endowment be prior (logically) to the *union* which perfects all things in Christ. In short, we must acknowledge that in Christ all the qualities were present that were requisite for a nature destined from the first instant of its formation to the supreme dignity of *existing only in dependence upon the Word.*

This is a very brief summary of the doctrine of the young St. Thomas Aquinas, which was the faithful echo of his contemporaries' views.

(b) *From the* Commentary on the Sentences *to the* Summa Theologiae

As the commentator on the *Sentences,* St. Thomas paid close attention to everything Scripture, the Fathers, and the Councils had to say. Alas! when the young professor first taught in Paris (1254–1259), his only sources of reference were a few Patristic texts, and then they were texts that had passed through several hands before reaching Peter Lombard and his commentators. But at the end of 1259 St. Thomas returned to Italy, and continued to teach there until 1267–1268. It was his good fortune, as early as 1259–1260, to discover a number of conciliar and Patristic collections recently brought from the East, which were rightly or wrongly attributed to various Fathers of Greece, Asia Minor, or Egypt. From then on, the Angelic Doctor made it his first task to study the thought of these authors as revealed in the newly found texts.

In his *Summa contra Gentiles* (Book IV, Chapters 28 ff.), he set up—with the help of these writings and those of St. Augustine's which were already known—a critical catalogue of the various heresies, at the end of which he set forth the true position of the Catholic Faith (Chapter 39). One of these heresies seemed to hold greater interest for him than the others, and he gave special attention to it. This was the heresy of Photinus (cf. above, p. 21), which was given first place because it perhaps seemed to him to be one of the farthest removed from the Catholic religion. Perhaps, too, it gave him an opportunity to reflect more deeply upon the Christology of St. John, St. Paul, and the Cappadocian and Alexandrian Fathers:

There were men like Ebion and Cerinthus, and later Paul of Samosata and Photinus, who confessed that Christ was wholly human. They imagined that The Godhead was in Him not by nature but according to a certain excellent participation of the divine glory, a participation that He was thought to have merited by His works . . . But this position destroys the mystery of the Incarnation. In fact, under such conditions, it is not God who assumed flesh to become man, but rather man who made himself God. And this is contrary to the affirmation of St. John: "The Word was made flesh" (Jn. 1:14). They affirm instead that the flesh was made the (divine) Word. Moreover, by taking such a (position), instead of saying that the Son of God came down, they insist above all on the glorification or the ascent of man (toward God); but then there is no longer any truth in the words of the Apostle (St. Paul): ". . . Jesus, who though he was by nature God, . . . emptied himself, taking the nature of a slave . . ." (Phil. 2:6-7). Likewise, the Lord's affirmation: "I have come down from heaven" (Jn. 6:38) is no longer true, but on the contrary only this one is true: "I ascend to my Father" (Jn. 20:17). And yet Scripture joins the two (movements). The Lord Himself has said: "And no one has ascended into heaven except him who has descended from heaven: the Son of Man who is in heaven" (Jn. 3:13). . . . It is in these two movements (of descent and of ascent) that we can affirm at once the humanity and the divinity (in the unity of Christ).[13]

Thenceforth, in St. Thomas' mind, the name of Photinus was connected with all errors which placed primary emphasis on the perfecting of man or his elevation toward God in the person of Christ. This position seemed to him diametrically opposed to that of the Manichaeans and of Valentinus (cf. p. 12), who saw only the downward movement of the divine into the human.

But as between the pure becoming of man that Photinus preached and pure "kenosis" (the annihilation of the divine in the human) of the Manichaeans, the Angelic Doctor found a golden mean: *the Word descended into the human by taking the human to Himself.* This conclusion seemed so rich and fruitful to him that it became the focal point of his *Summa Theologiae,* the point to which he referred all questions concerning the mystery of Christ in order to solve them. St. Thomas consciously revived the most authentic Tradition of the Church that had been inaugurated by the sacred writers, and that made up the heart of the thinking of St. Ignatius of Antioch, St. Athanasius, St. Cyril, St. Hilary of Poitiers, St. Augustine, St. Leo of Byzantium, and St. John Damascene.

(c) The Summa Theologiae (*IIIa Pars, 1272–1273*)

In his *Summa Theologiae,* St. Thomas no longer viewed the Incarnation, as he did in the *Sentences,* from the viewpoint of an

[13] *Summa contra Gentiles,* Book IV, Chapter 28.

ascent of the human toward the Person of the Word, from which ascent union would result. He affirmed the *mystery as already accomplished,* that is, he affirmed the hypostatic union. The Incarnation as he saw it was primarily a mystery of unity; and it is in this unity, guaranteed by the divine Person, that the theologian must take rational cognizance of the duality of natures: divine and human. In other words, he approached the mystery from the point of view of the Word in His function of subsisting in humanity.

It became clear that if there was no human person in Christ this was due not to a deficiency but to a superabundance. For when it is affirmed at the outset that the divine Person subsists in the human nature, the conclusion necessarily follows: there is no human person properly so-called.[14] This was a far cry from the argumentation of the *Sentences* in which the absence of the human person had been explained as follows: the nature was assumed by the Word before having attained to its own proper subsistence at the end of the process of human generation.[15]

After studying the three "opinions" one after the other, St. Thomas declared that far from being opinions—that is, positions that men were more or less free to take or leave—the first and the third "opinions" were formal heresies which revived those of Nestorius and Photinus, [16] whereas the second was the true teaching of the Catholic Faith. St. Thomas' assurance on this point can readily be understood if we remember that the second opinion comes from the Greek Fathers through St. John Damascene. When the expression "composite Word" is thus reinstated in its unitary context it regains all the primitive power and truth which it could not have with Peter Lombard and his commentators, who were of a dualistic turn of mind.

Hence, the human nature of Christ was compared to an instrument that the Word came to take up; but at the same time it was firmly maintained that the Word subsists in the human nature and communicates to it His personal existence. While the notion of instrument is inadmissible in the view of Nestorius, it became— when thus understood—the best help for our limited minds, dazzled by the unfathomable mystery of the hypostatic union.[17] Nestorius,

[14] Cf. IIIa, q. 2, a. 2, ad 2 and 3.
[15] Cf. IIIa, q. 2, a. 6, c.
[16] Cf. *ibid.*
[17] Cf. *ibid.,* ad 4.

and Photinus even more than he, considered the Incarnation as the ultimate perfection of man existing by himself within the Word; whereas we must follow the Councils in considering the Incarnation as the mystery of a "God who truly became man."

The great originality of the *Summa* also consists in giving a theological explanation of the hypostatic union without allowing *generation* to intervene. From the point of view of the divine Person the union is not restricted to the Son alone, since each of the divine Persons has equal power to subsist in the human; from the point of view of the nature assumed, the fact of generation is not essential, inasmuch as the Word could just as well have assumed an angelic as a human nature.

The task of the author of the *Summa,* therefore, was to distinguish the multiple problems posed by this great mystery of our faith. After having considered the profound fitness of the Incarnation—which is the fitness of divine mercy in the face of the disorder to which Adam's sin had reduced the human race—he went right to the heart of the matter: what the hypostatic union is and what is explained through it (IIIa, q. 2-26). Then, by means of this study of what cannot not be, he set out to explain the conditions in which the Incarnation was in fact realized. That is the theological problem of the life of Jesus from His conception in the womb of the Virgin Mary until His death, His Resurrection, and His glorious Ascension which includes the study of the Mother of God and the study of the Redemption (IIIa, q. 27-59).

When the Angelic Doctor's plan for his treatise on the Incarnation is compared with that of Peter Lombard, we can see the wisdom of the former's choice: the whole work is centered on the hypostatic union as the light that allows us to penetrate a mystery that must necessarily remain obscure to us here below. And is not careful reflection on the plan of a work the best initiation to the thought that governed its development? Here is St. Thomas' plan:

I. The Fitness and Harmonies of the Incarnation (q. 1).

II. The Way to Understand the Hypostatic Union.

    1. The Union itself (q. 2—the essential question);

    2. the Union considered in the person assuming (q. 3);

    3. the Union considered in the nature assumed:

        a. in the human nature iself (q. 4-6);

        b. in the parts that accompany the nature assumed:

    1) the spiritual perfections (grace, knowledge, power) (q. 7-13),

    2) the infirmities of body and soul (q. 14-15).

III. What is Explained by the Hypostatic Union.

    1. What is fitting to Christ in Himself:

        a. according to the exchanges in Him between the human and the divine (communication of idioms) (q. 16);

        b. according to unity or duality: unity of being (q. 17); duality of wills and operations (q. 18-19).

    2. What is fitting to Christ by comparison with His Father:

        a. the relationship of Christ to His Father: subjection (q. 20); prayer (q. 21); priesthood (q. 22);

        b. the relationship of the Father to Christ: adoption? (q. 23); predestination (q. 24).

    3. What is fitting to Christ by comparison of Him with us:

        a. adoration on our part (q. 25);

        b. Christ is our Mediator who leads us to God (q. 26).

The entire treatise gravitates around the hypostatic union, which is its indisputable foundation. The theologian gives the reasons for the union after it has been realized and not during the process of realization. Thus St. Thomas perfected the Anselmian tradition by correcting it, as his forceful words show:

> The mystery of the Incarnation is not to be looked upon as an ascent, as it were, of a man already existing and mounting up to the dignity of the union, as the heretic Photinus maintained. Rather is it to be considered as a descent, by reason of the perfect Word of God taking unto Himself the imperfection of our nature, according to Jn. 6:38: *I have come down from heaven.*[18]

To show that everything that must be attributed to Christ in accordance with His condition as man (grace, virtues, gifts, knowledge, etc.) is an *effective consequence* of the hypostatic union, St. Thomas continues:

> But the mystery of the Incarnation is considered as a condescension of the fullness of the Godhead into human nature rather than as the promotion of human nature, already existing, as it were, to the Godhead. Therefore in the man Christ there was perfection of spiritual life from the very beginning.[19]

This gives us a vivid picture of St. Thomas' profound thought toward the end of his life. Not only must we deny all *real* becoming

[18] IIIa, q. 33, a. 3, ad 3.
[19] IIIa, q. 34, a. 1, ad 1.

of man into God, but if we want to explain this ineffable mystery without danger of error we must even stop thinking of it as a simple ascent of the human toward the Word. We must always keep the following point of view: through the Incarnation, the divine Word descended deep within human nature by taking it to Himself. It is impossible to lay too much stress on this fundamental point of the Christology of St. Thomas Aquinas.

Thus the fitness of the Incarnation and its fundamental motive, discussed in the first question of the *Tertia Pars* really constitute the marrow of the entire *Summa:* the intimate diffusion of the absolute Goodness which is God, a diffusion accomplished in the most superlative way since it culminates in making a created nature subsist in a divine Person, for the purpose of the Redemption.

But because for us and for our salvation, uniting the human nature to His Person, He (the Son of God) became the child of a woman, for this reason do we say that He was born in the flesh.[20]

St. Thomas took this affirmation of St. Cyril's and made it his own, because, after the example of the Greek Fathers, he understood very well that "in (Christ) dwells all the fullness of the Godhead bodily" (Col. 2:9); and that in consequence of this not only did the Savior Himself as man but also all the members of His "body which is the Church" benefit from divine graces and favors. By a unique right, the God-man, the first among His brothers, possesses the perfection of holiness, of knowledge, and of power that can bring all men back to God.

The Holiness of Christ. Christ possesses grace at once in a measure and beyond measure. His sanctifying grace, like that of every other man, is measured by His personal nature, but this grace is far from being the foundation of His union with God. For the sanctifying grace of Christ results from the hypostatic union, and it is in this sense that St. Augustine writes that "grace is in a certain respect natural in Christ-the-man."

On the other hand, Christ possesses grace without measure if we consider His power as sanctifier. As God, Christ can give grace in His own right; He can even give the Holy Spirit. As man, it belongs to Him to do this instrumentally, for His humanity was from the beginning the instrument of the Godhead, conjoined to it forever. As the liturgy of the Mass exclaims: *Tu solus Sanctus*—"Thou only art Holy!"

[20] IIIa, q. 35, a. 2, ad 2.

The knowledge of Christ. It is because He is the Word made man that it is fitting to claim for Christ the knowledge proper to man: the knowledge that is acquired through the senses; [21] and the knowledge that belongs only to the blessed in heaven, which He had even before the glorification of His body.[22] To sum up St. Thomas' views: The soul of Christ personally united to the Word is closer to the Word than any creature. It therefore receives more perfectly than any other creature the communication of the light in which God is seen by the Word. It follows that the soul of Christ sees more perfectly than other creatures the primordial truth that is the essence of God.

Thus, since Christ before His Passion was not only a "wayfarer" but also a "blessed," His soul could know the angels in the same way as men's souls do after death. This is what is called infused knowledge or the knowledge of pure spirits.

The marks of the state of the God-man. It is easy for us to realize that when the Son of God assumed a body and came into the world to make full satisfaction for the sins of the human race He had to take on "bodily defects, to wit, death, hunger, thirst, etc." [23] He was also obliged to experience such states of soul as sensible pain, sadness, fear, astonishment, etc., with the exception of ignorance.[24]

This is the doctrine of St. Augustine, as we mentioned earlier (cf. p. 25 ff. above). In addition, the Angelic Doctor carried the thought of the Bishop of Hippo further by showing that the human will of Christ could have been in opposition to the divine will, since it possessed the natural and spontaneous tendency to avoid all pain and suffering. And yet the consciously and freely expressed will of Jesus could never contravene the will of His Father, that is the will of the Blessed Trinity as a whole.[25] From this came the possibility of our Savior's meriting for Himself something that He did not yet have, namely the glory of His body and the worship that is due to His body; and of meriting for us, His members, all the graces that we need.[26]

[21] Cf. IIIa, q. 12.
[22] Cf. IIIa, q. 10 and 11.
[23] Cf. IIIa, q. 14, a. 1.
[24] Cf. IIIa, q. 15.
[25] Cf. IIIa, q. 18, a. 5.
[26] Cf. IIIa, q. 19.

Christ the Pantocrator (All-Ruler) of the Cathedral of Cefalù in Sicily (an Arabo-Norman monument decorated with mosaics of the twelfth century deutero-Byzantine type).

As soon as the Church emerged from the catacombs and became established in her temples, a new so-called "triumphal" art appeared. The Savior was no longer represented as the beardless youth of the catacombs, but as a Syrian in the prime of life, with a black beard and a virile aspect. This new representation can no doubt be explained by the influence of miniatures. "Jesus laid down the law to the Christian world in the attitude of command used by emperors, standing, or seated upon a throne studded with precious stones. He was clothed in a toga and a pallium; a halo surrounded His head with a luminous circle upon which a cross was soon to be delineated, resplendent with the "A" and the "Ω": this was the Christ the Pantocrator." (A. Michel, *Histoire generale de l'art, des debuts de l'art chrétien à la fin de la période romane* [Paris, A. Colin, 1905], p. 43.)

This majestic figure, inspired by the Apocalypse, was perfectly suited to a Church in which the emperor himself was "the bishop from the outside" and the one who convoked the Councils. It was to preside over the prayers of Christians for centuries, and the Sicilian artists of the twelfth century were again to reproduce it. The "A" and the "Ω" are replaced in this picture by other letters which are also the seal of Christ.

Christ, the sole Mediator between God and men.

1. The Priesthood of Christ. The Epistle to the Hebrews tells us that we have "a great high priest who has passed into the heavens, Jesus the Son of God" (Heb. 4:14). The proper function of the priest is to be a mediator between God and the people. On the one hand he transmits divine things to the people, whence the name *sacerdos*—"he who gives sacred things." To quote the words of Malachias regarding priests: "For the lips of the priest shall keep knowledge, and they shall seek the law at his mouth" (Mal. 2:7). On the other hand, the priest offers to God the prayers of the people and makes satisfaction to God in a certain respect for the sins of the people. Whence St. Paul's words: "For every high priest taken from among men is appointed for men in the things pertaining to God, that he may offer gifts and sacrifices for sins" (Heb. 5:1).

Now these words apply perfectly to Christ. Through Him the gifts of God are transmitted to men, as St. Peter declares: "(Christ) has granted us the very great and precious promises, so that through them you may become partakers of the divine nature" (II Pet. 1:4). Likewise, Christ has reconciled the human race with God, as it is written in the Epistle to the Colossians: "For it has pleased God the Father that in (Christ) all his fullness should dwell, and that through him he should reconcile to himself all things" (Col. 1:20). It was therefore eminently fitting that Christ should be a priest.[27]

Christ was not only a priest, He was also a perfect offering; for He was at once an offering for sin, a peace offering, and a holocaust.

That is why His priesthood was established first of all to expiate the sins of the world. It is the mark of His priesthood that it is the source of all other priesthoods: the priesthood of the Old Law which was the figure of His own, and the priesthood of the New Law, which He keeps alive and efficacious in His own Person.[28]

2. The worship that is due to Christ. St. John Damascene writes: "Inasmuch as God the Word has become incarnate, the flesh of Christ is adored not for itself but because it is united according to the hypostasis to the Word of God." Worship of the humanity of

[27] Cf. IIIa, q. 22.
[28] Cf. IIIa, q. 26.

Christ can be a true adoration of latria, provided the worship rendered to this humanity hypostatically united to the Word is addressed to the Person of the Word Himself. That is why the worship of the Sacred Heart is so legitimate. Crucifixes and even pictures can be the object of the worship of latria if the intention of the worshipper is directed to Christ Himself.[29]

If we are to hold fast to the essentials of the mystery of the Incarnation, we cannot unfold the riches of the *Summa Theologiae* all at once. It suffices to say that the reader who understands that the Incarnation is above all the mystery of the divine Person of the Son descending deep within human nature and taking it to Himself has penetrated the thought of the Angelic Doctor on our Savior and has grasped what matters most.

3. FROM DUNS SCOTUS TO OUR OWN TIME

A. The Scholastic controversies

(a) *The question of the person in Christ*

The position of St. Thomas in the *Summa Theologiae* was not accepted as soon as it was known. Until the sixteenth century all theologians continued to read Peter Lombard's *Sentences,* and his doctrine either inspired or guided their own. That is why even after Cajetan—one of the greatest commentators of the *Summa*—had definitively brought about the adoption of St. Thomas' *Summa* (at the beginning of the sixteenth century), many theologians were still under the influence of Peter Lombard's Christology.

Soon after St. Thomas' time, the Franciscan Duns Scotus († 1308) set out to show that the mystery of the Incarnation can be perfectly explained by considering it as the assumption of a man by the Word. He stressed the historical aspect of the Word Incarnate. When the human nature of Jesus is considered by itself, there is apparently nothing to distinguish it from any other human nature. Only faith tells us that this man depends in all that He is upon the Word. And, yet, this man has His own existence, as well as a real relation of human sonship to Mary, His Mother.

To explain such a singular case, Scotus declared it was necessary to deepen the metaphysical notion of the *person*. Since it is a dogma of Faith that the human nature of Christ does not constitute an

[29] Cf. IIIa, q. 25.

independent person, said Scotus, Jesus was never an "isolated man." He was a man "assumed by the Word" from the first instant of His conception. Therefore the definition of a person would be: a rational nature not assumed by a superior person. Thus, to give a theological explanation of the fundamental problem of Christology, to wit, the absence of a human person in Christ, Scotus concluded to a *negative* notion of the person. By such reasoning, we can say in effect that Christ is a "man assumed," that is, that in Him is a true man who possesses in His own right not only what depends upon His nature (physical and psychical operations), but likewise the existence that every human person possesses. The human *to be* of Christ was the focal point of the difficulties regarding the Incarnation for St. Thomas' disciples in the following centuries.

Capreolus († 1444) affirmed that if Christ had the human existence that was attributed to Him, He would necessarily be a "supposit" or "human person." This assertion cut all the arguments short by identifying *person* and *existence*. Thereafter, the Incarnation was looked upon as the mystery of the unity of the person and of the *esse* of the God-man. And so the problem of the unity of being, which had been only a secondary object of study for St. Thomas, took first place in treatises on the Incarnation. Actually, St. Thomas had attacked this problem only in Question 17 of the *Tertia Pars*. The new orientation led to the theological explanation of the Mystery of Christ by the philosophical distinction between nature (or essence) and existence in created being; a distinction which Scotus implicitly denied but which Capreolus explicitly affirmed.

However, according to Cajetan (1534) and to the majority of Thomist theologians, Capreolus' answer was not pertinent. For while nature is really distinct from existence, existence is no less really distinct from the person. The person adds to the nature "a subsistential mode" that makes the nature incommunicable, that is, incapable of belonging to any other individual; the person gives the nature its singularity and permits it to receive its own existence.

Since in the human generation of Christ in Mary, His human nature was assumed by the Word at the very instant the generative process terminated, it follows that this human nature never had the human subsistential mode capable of giving it a human *esse*. Such was Cajetan's view. It denied the affirmation of Capreolus, and was not in agreement with the eclecticism of Suarez († 1617), who came later. Suarez rejected the distinction between essence and existence with the Scotists, but agreed with the Thomists in keeping the real distinction between person and existence. Actually, the position of Cajetan is more solid metaphysically and theologically than that of either Capreolus or Suarez.

We should, however, keep in mind the underlying thought that guided these various systematizations. While we may not agree with Duns Scotus in his metaphysical arguments—and it is scarcely possible to agree with them—we should not neglect his fundamental option. Scotus wanted to give a full explanation of the historical Christ just as the Gospels present Him—born of Mary, suffering and dying on the Cross, and thus manifesting a very real human *life*. Was it not in order to forcefully affirm this human life in Christ that Scotus distinguished two existences in Him: the human and the divine?

The Thomists, with Cajetan at their head, had another and no less meritorious concern: to show that a theology with unreliable philosophical foundations is in danger of falling into doctrinal error.

But was the only answer to this question to be found in the rational order? Is it not equally important to show how Scotus was related to such great and authentically Catholic thinkers on this point as Theodoret in the East and Tertullian in the West, for both of whom Christ was first of all the *man* of the Gospels? And with regard to the Incarnation, we always come back to this two-fold option whose terms are apparently incompatible: the option of a Christ who is the Word becoming man, and the option of a Christ who is a man assumed by the Word. St. Thomas Aquinas and Duns Scotus are the orthodox heirs of the School of Alexandria and the School of Antioch respectively.

(b) *The motive of the Incarnation*

We now understand why Duns Scotus centered his whole doctrine of the Incarnation on the predestination of Christ-the-man, who was first of all to be exalted and recognized as the King of all creation. But this point of view led him to a conclusion with weighty consequences: the Incarnation could not have been formally decreed with a view to making reparation for original sin (the soteriological view); it must have been decreed with a view to giving all creation the sublime completion that it possesses in the Person of the God-man. With this in mind, Scotus vigorously fought the Augustinian dictum: "If man had not sinned, the Word would not have become incarnate." As Scotus saw it, the Incarnation would have been realized whether man had fallen or whether he had remained in the state of original justice. And now the question of the "motive" came to the fore in Christology.

Since the twelfth century, the motive of the Incarnation had certainly been considered a problem, but one of secondary importance. St. Thomas had qualified his answer by saying that a motive could be assigned for such a mystery only if it were considered as an actual fact made known and manifested to us by Scripture. It could not be considered in the abstract, in its pure essence. For outside of the actual fact we have only "mental pictures," and all our theories on the presupposed will of God are without foundation. Now an attentive study of Holy Scripture compels us to interpret the motive for the Incarnation of God in the soteriological sense.

Since the time of Scotus, the problem of the motive for the Incarnation has become the leitmotiv of passionate debates between the Scotists and the Thomists. In recent years the Scotists have even tried to place the conflict within the domain of Scripture itself, by appealing to all the texts that might be used to corroborate the rational position of Scotus. While the Church has never made any pronouncement on the matter, she has constantly affirmed the redemptive character of the Incarnation; and she has renewed this affirmation in recent times in a way that deserves particular attention, by instituting the Feast of Christ the King.

B. The Errors Condemned

(a) *The Protestant doctrine*

Luther's doctrine on the Incarnation was elaborated within the same framework as his theology of justification by faith in Christ. Here are Luther's own words on the subject:

We must not picture Christ as a private, innocent person—as did the Scholastics, Jerome and others—a person who would be holy and just in himself. It is true that Jesus Christ is a very pure person; but we must not stop there: you have not yet understood Christ, even if you know that He is God and man. But you will truly understand Him if you believe that this very pure and very innocent person has been given to you by the Father to be a pontiff and savior, or rather to be your slave, and who by stripping himself of his innocence and his holiness puts on your sinful person, bears your sin, your death, and your curse, becomes for you a victim and accursed, so as to deliver you from the malediction of the law.[30]

We know the Protestant thesis of forensic justification: the Christian would be justified not by a real gift and a real change in himself but by a pure "declaration" of God which, by virtue of Christ's merits, would not impute his sins to him. This excessive abasement of the Word within the human, this kenosis that goes so far as to put on "the sinful person" of the sinner, together with his sin and his malediction, is as it were the echo in Christology of the Lutheran doctrine of justification.

This excessive abasement of the Word within the human (strict kenosis) was minimized by the Protestant theologians of the following centuries. For the liberal Protestants of our own time, Christ is a man who became God, and no longer God who became man, and a man of sin. The Protestant theory of the Incarnation of the Word, which is a consequence of their doctrine on the Redemption and on justification, is incompatible with the Catholic Faith, as defined by the Council of Trent in its Sixth Session. (See especially Chapter 3, and Canons 10 ff., Denz., 820 ff.)

(b) Günther and Rosmini

To understand these errors we must remember that since the Renaissance the philosophic notion of the *person* had become psychological. Less and less consideration was given to the substantial, metaphysical nature of personality, which is the philosophic foundation of Christology as well as of the theology of the Trinity.

In the nineteenth century, Günther echoed the current philosophy by defining personality as "the possession of oneself by the consciousness of oneself and of one's acts." From then on, the psychological point of view took precedence over the purely metaphysical approach of the ancients. We can see how undue emphasis came to be placed on the dualism of natures in Christ by the development of the thesis of the two consciousnesses of self within Him: the one as God and the other as man. Günther was condemned in 1857.

To Rosmini's way of thinking, "it seems we must believe that in Christ's humanity the human will was so completely taken over by the Holy Ghost in its adherence to the objective being, that is,

[30] Luther, *Comment. in Gal. 3:13, Werke,* Weimar Edition, Vol. 40, p. 448.

to the Word, that Christ's human will totally surrendered to the Word the government of the man. Thus, the Word personally took over this government, and thereby became incarnate. The human will, together with the other powers, remained subject to this will, to the power of the Word; and the Word, the first principle of this theandric being, accomplished all things or had them accomplished by the other powers, with the consent of His divine will. Thus the human will ceased to be personal in the man, and what in other men constituted the person remained simply the nature in Christ" (Prop. 27). This view, which was really the reiteration of the Nestorian position, was condemned by the Holy Office on December 14, 1887.

PRESENT-DAY PERSPECTIVES OF CHRISTOLOGY

The study of the mystery of the Incarnation has its place in our own day in the great current of thought that is guiding the revival of biblical and historical studies. This awareness of the deposit of faith contained in Scripture and authentic Tradition has had the advantage of emerging from the abstract quarrels that have been waged since the fourteenth century. And yet if we stop at this positive stage of our Faith, we are in danger of forgetting the rational value that dogmas must take on in order to be presented theologically.

Let us conclude this outline of the doctrinal problem of the Incarnation by affirming once more, with qualified authority, that the mystery of the Incarnation (as well as all the other mysteries of our Faith) must be grasped from two complementary points of view if they are to be rightly understood by our intellect. As Cardinal Suhard writes:

We once more find that the truth lies in uniting and harmonizing these two symmetrical statements. The God of Israel has the right to be called "the true God" because, combining all perfections, He is both pure spirit and creator, the One of whom it can be said "True praise of Thee is silence," and "All ye works of the Lord, bless the Lord."

The problem is not solved by an abstract formula; the solution itself is alive and is found in a person, the Word of God. He is revealed to us by the Incarnation, "taking the nature of a slave" (Phil. 2:7) come among men, at the same time the equal of the Father by His nature as God. The God of the philosophers is thus outstripped in grandeur, and that of the philanthropists in nearness to man. The Lord we adore is not a compromise between two extremes, but the fullness of both in the mystery of His Person . . .[31]

[31] Suhard, *The Church Today* (Chicago, Fides, 1953), pp. 196-197.

The perspectives that the idea of an incarnate God opens up both for faith and for humanism are admissible only within the *hypothesis* of the economy of salvation that Revelation presents to us as a fact. If we forgot that God created the world freely and out of love, and that He saved it freely by becoming incarnate out of "charity," we would be losing the meaning of God and the meaning of man.

But in theology we must not conclude as if the problem raised by our faith could be solved here below. It is not up to the mystery to restrict itself within the limits of our intellect, which is still under the dominion of the senses. On the contrary, it is up to our intellect to reach out toward the mystery that it can approach but never fathom.

In the light of the mystery of the Incarnation, man, starting from his faith and from all its potentialities, rectifies his attitude and even his life. Knowing that Christ is the God made flesh in whom alone he will find salvation and supreme happiness, he will allow himself to be seized in the depths of his being. He will look to this divine Person, so admirably humanized, as his exemplary personality. A burning faith in Christ will be his sole rule of conduct, his "prudence" of every moment. He will repeat with St. Paul, the most perfect model of the Christian: "It is now no longer I that live, but Christ lives in me" (Gal. 2:20).

II

TABLES

A. THE THREE OPINIONS OF PETER LOMBARD [1]

An attempt to explain if, and in what sense, the dogmatic formulas:

> Deus factus est homo
> Jesus Christus est verus Deus
> Jesus Christus est verus homo

imply the following:

> Deus est homo
> Homo est Deus
> Homo factus est Deus

and if "homo" in these statements signifies "aliquid." (See p. 37 ff. above.)

[1] This table was drawn up by A.-M. H. from typewritten notes for the course given by P.-H. Dondaine, O.P.

The "Three Opinions" recorded

Theses Common to All Three:
$\begin{cases} \text{1. One Person in Christ: the divine} \\ \text{2. Two natures: the Godhead, the} \\ \text{3. Body and soul are assumed by} \\ \text{4. Body and soul do not temporally} \end{cases}$

PARTICULAR THESES	FIRST OPINION
Concerning the way in which the body and the soul are united to the Word.	Body and soul are united and constitute one substance: *this man*, whom the Word unites to Himself substantially, without introducing him into His Personality (that is, the Word does not subsist in this substance; but the Word is this man and "this man is the Word"). Christ is the Word of God who takes on and who is this man.
Regarding *what* is assumed.	It is a man, *this man*.
Regarding what the word *Man* designates in Christ.	The composite of soul and body, which is a substance in its own right, and constitutes a supposit or hypostasis.
Regarding the mode of union.	A substantial union in the sense that it unites a substance to the Word, without, however, integrating this substance to His Personality.
Concerning the supposit(s) or hypostasis (hypostases)	Two supposits (or hypostases): $\left\{\begin{array}{l} \text{— One created, this man, a composite subsisting} \\ \text{in a body and a soul.} \\ \text{— The other uncreated, the Word who subsists} \\ \text{only in His divine nature.} \end{array}\right.$
Corollaries. How is "Deus factus est homo" to be understood?	God (the Son) became this man, that is, He began to be this rational substance.
How is "Deus est homo" to be understood?	God (the Son) is this man.
How is *homo* attributed to *Deus?*	Substantially. Homo indicates *the one* that the Word is, by reason of the union. The one who assumes, the Word, is the assumed, this man.
"Homo est Deus" signifies:	This man is God (the Son).
Christ is:	Someone (who assumes) and something (a supposit assumed). Two realities (duo neutraliter), two supposits, but one Person.
In Christ the Person of the Word is:	Simple, after the union as well as before, for the man does not affect the Personality of the Word.

by Peter Lombard

Person of the Word (against Nestorius).
humanity (against Eutyches).
the Word (against the Manichaeans, the Docetists, and the Gnostics).
pre-exist before the union (against Origen?).

SECOND OPINION (Outline of the Future Thomistic synthesis)	THIRD OPINION (The school of Abelard)
Body and soul are united to constitute *this humanity* in which the Word subsists so as to make it to be this man.	Body and soul are *separately* united to the Word of God, after the mode of extrinsic accidents (like garments).
Christ is the Word of God who takes on this humanity.	Christ is the Word of God who takes on this body on the one hand, and this separated soul on the other (body and soul are separated for fear of introducing a new Person into the Trinity).
It is a humanity; *this humanity.*	It is *this body* and *this soul,* separately.
The *real* whole which includes the humanity and the divine Person who renders it subsistent.	The body and soul, separately, which do not constitute a substance.
A substantial union in the sense that it joins to the Word a nature of the substantial order, in which the Word subsists by constituting it a substance.	An accidental union, extrinsically uniting the body and the soul to the Word.
A single uncreated supposit (or hypostasis), the Word, who subsists substantially in two natures: His Godhead and His humanity.	A single uncreated supposit (or hypostasis), the Word, who subsists substantially in His Godhead, accidentally in His soul and in His body.
God (the Son) became man, that is, He began to subsist also in a human nature.	God (the Son) took on the body and soul of a man.
God (the Son) is man.	The proposition *Deus est homo* is improper: God (the Son) possesses a body and a soul; He is humanized (just as one would say: he is clothed).
Substantially. Homo indicates *what* the Word is by reason of the union. The one who assumes, the Word, is not the assumed, the humanity.	Accidentally. Homo indicates *how* the Word exists by reason of the union: provided with a body and a soul, Homo is not a substantial predicate but an accidental one.
This man (the Person who subsists in this humanity) is God.	The one who possesses this soul and this body is God (the Son).
One, possessing a unity "per se": a supposit, a Person.	One, possessing an accidental unity, like that between Peter and his whiteness.
Composite, in this sense that after the union it subsists in two natures.	Simple, after the union as well as before, for the body and the soul add only accidental being to the Word.

B. AN OUTLINE OF THE CHRISTOLOGICAL HERESIES

by DOM G. GHYSENS

1. The revealed deposit concerning the being of Christ can be approached and has in fact been developed historically from two different angles: the *Trinitarian* point of view, which is that of the relationship between Jesus Christ with God His Father and with the Holy Ghost, as well as with the divine nature; and the specifically *Christological* point of view, which is that of the interior constitution of Christ, that is, of the relationships between His two natures.

All the Trinitarian heresies have a bearing on Christology because they falsify more or less seriously the divine nature or the distinct personality of the Son. We shall not discuss this point any further, except with respect to Arianism. On the other hand, every Christological error does not necessarily imply an error on the Trinitarian level, since the Son is generally spoken of only in His incarnated state.

2. To enable the reader to find his way in the complicated labyrinth of Christological heresies, we shall present these heresies chronologically on the vertical axis of our table, and show their logical relationships on the horizontal axis.

The double lines in the center mark off the *position of equilibrium* maintained by the Catholic Faith and by Thomistic theology. This equilibrium results from an exact evaluation and a judicious apportionment of the two poles of Christology: on the one hand the perfect duality, integrity, and distinction of the elements constituting Christ, namely, the divine and the human; on the other hand the ontological unity of His divine Personality.

This position of equilibrium can be found on three different levels: the primitive or Scriptural revealed deposit; the dogmatic formulas defined by the Magisterium, especially by the Council of Chalcedon (451); and finally the Christology of St. Thomas, which succeeded in constituting a rational synthesis in which both poles are accepted and made to buttress one another. This is not to say that this theology is complete or even without defect. A modern mind will no doubt find that Thomistic theology pays too little attention to the central problem of the human consciousness of Jesus.

Starting from the center, and within the scope of orthodox theology (that is, of the theology authorized by the Church) we see two divergent and often unduly partisan tendencies. Each of these trends is opposed to the other, and tends to become identified with the heresies beyond its extreme limits. Actually, the two theologies are in no sense mutually exclusive, rather they are incomplete and complementary. We must therefore consider them together, and integrate them into a superior synthesis, thus correcting the one by the other and causing them to exert reciprocal influence.

When the limits of orthodoxy are exceeded at either extreme, these two opposite tendencies elicit the various Christological heresies whose deviations from the truth are all the more pronounced in the measure that they stray from the center (cf. Diagram below, pp. 64-65). To the *right* of the center we have placed the tendency that starts out from the divine unity of the Word and explains less and less adequately the integral humanity of Christ, if it even admits its existence at all. The extreme expression of this trend was Docetism, which volatilized Christ's humanity into a mere semblance of reality.

To the *left* of the center, we have set down the tendency that starts from the human fact of Jesus of Nazareth and then has great difficulty explaining, even admitting, the true, ontological unity of Christ, and finally His very divinity. The extreme expression of this position was the Adoptionism of the second and third centuries, and in more recent times the liberal Protestantism and modernism of the nineteenth and twentieth centuries which volatilize the divinity of Jesus.

Need we add that the positions to the right and to the left on our diagram could just as well have been reversed? They have nothing to do with the conservatism or progressivism with which the words "right" and "left" are currently associated.

3. The diagram gives us an idea of the chronological succession and interaction of the heresies. Obviously, we cannot classify or even mention the vast throng of theologians who have studied Christology (most of whom merely repeat what the leaders of their school say). However it seems useful and instructive to point out a contemporary controversy in which the two opposite tendencies of the fourth and fifth centuries once again confronted each other. This controversy arose particularly around the Christology of the *Assumptus Homo* developed by a great Franciscan

theologian, Father Déodat de Basly († 1937). The "Antiochan" or leftist tendency was reaffirmed by this theologian and his disciples, especially L. Seiller and E. Longpré; by the Strasbourg theologians, notably A. Gaudel and E. Amann; by an eminent Jesuit, Father Galtier, in a very remarkable work, *L'Unité du Christ* (Paris, 1939); by Father Glorieux of Lille; and finally by scholars who had succeeded in bringing to light the greater part of the theological and exegetical work of Theodore of Mopsuestia, and who tend to favor his Christology (E. Amann, R. Devreesse).

The rightist or "Alexandrian" tendency is richly orchestrated by Dom H. Diepen, O.S.B., whose copious and vehement articles denounce a latent adoptionism in Father Déodat de Basly (*Revue thomiste,* 1949, 1950, 1951).

These two theologies have a rightful place in the Church on condition that they do not yield to the partisan spirit or exclude the underlying intuition of the opposite theology.

There is a judicious presentation of this controversy by Father Dondaine, O.P., in the *Revue des Sciences philosophiques et théologiques* (1951), pp. 609-613. From a more general point of view, one can read with profit the penetrating pages of Father Congar, O.P., in *Chrétiens désunis* (Paris, 1939), pp. 48-56, and in *Christ, Our Lady and the Church* (Westminster, Md., Newman, 1957). It should be noted that one of the "Antiochan" theologians has recently been warned by the Holy Office. An article by Father Seiller, O.F.M., entitled "La psychologie humaine du Christ et l'unité de personne" has been placed on the Index (Decree of the Holy Office, July 12, 1952, A.A.S., 1951, p. 561).

4. *Arianism* must be left out of consideration here, for it unites the two heretical tendencies, adding Apollinarianism and Adoptionism to its own Trinitarian error. The most serious error of Arius was obviously his denial of the strict, consubstantial divinity of the Word. As he saw it, the Word was only the first creature of the unbegotten Father, and the instrument in the Father's hands for the creation of all other beings. Moreover, like Apollinarius, and long before him, Arius claimed that the humanity of Jesus possessed no rational soul, for, to his mind, the Word took the place of a human soul in Christ. He held that Jesus was subject to ignorance, imperfection, and moral progress, just like other men.

Arianism was condemned above all by the Council of Nicea in 325, which introduced the following text concerning our Lord

Jesus Christ in its baptismal creed: "the only-begotten Son of the Father, that is, of the substance of the Father, God (issuing from) God, Light (issuing from) Light, true God (issuing from) true God, begotten not made; being of one substance with the Father; by whom (through whose intermediary) all things were made" (Denz. 54).

It should be no surprise that the columns to the extreme left and right are empty from the twelfth century on. As controversies and disagreements faded away and as the faith of the Church was better defined, extreme positions became untenable and problems were brought back closer to the center of orthodoxy.

III

THEOLOGICAL REFLECTIONS

The brief historical synthesis that we have just given presents successively all the principles of a theory of the Incarnation. Without taking up this synthesis again, we shall now approach a number of questions and reflections with the purpose of bringing out more forcefully the principles already given and developing the more important points.

As the preceding Table shows, "the Christological doctrine of the Church follows as it were a royal road between Nestorianism, condemned by the Council of Ephesus (431), and Monophysitism, condemned by the Council of Chalcedon (October, 451)." These words are taken from Father Congar's excellent little work, *Christ. Our Lady, and the Church* (Newman, 1957), which deserves to be read in its entirety.

I. GEOGRAPHY AND HISTORY IN CHRISTOLOGY

And yet, as our Table likewise shows, we would be wrong to condemn those theologians who do not follow exactly the middle of the royal road on which the Councils take their stand—so long as the Church herself has not warned them that they are in danger of being separated from her Body.

While it is the role of the Church to guard the deposit of faith, she does not impose a single explanation of these truths. Hence the wide margin that is allowed to the theology accepted within the Church, either to the left or to the right, in order to bring out as far as it is humanly possible the complementary and apparently opposed elements of the same mystery. The theology that succeeds in being inscribed in the dead center is a rarity. It is therefore wise to consider all the elements stressed either to the left or to the right, so as to realize how difficult it is to keep them together on the royal road toward the summit.

Thus, while there are two heresies that theologians must guard against at the two extreme limits of Christological doctrine, nevertheless there are two "tendencies" that theologians may legitimately follow, so long as they do not exceed certain norms (that is, so long as they can explain the deposit of faith) and so long as they do not become so inflexible that they systematically exclude the opposite tendency. On the contrary, when rightly understood, these "tendencies" are part of the patrimony of the Church. They both have their traditions which have not ceased to enrich the Church.

The first opponents of the faith of the Church were the Docetists, sprung from the Gnostic sects. It was against them for the most part that St. John wrote his Gospel and his Epistles, and that the first creeds formulated the deposit of faith. The Word was made flesh, and His flesh is real. He was born of the Virgin Mary, suffered, died, and rose from the dead.

On the one hand there was general agreement on the reality of Christ's flesh (i.e., humanity—the word *flesh* is often synonymous with *man* in Biblical terminology). On the other hand, divergence of thought soon began to appear here and there. In the East, from the days of Apostolic preaching in those regions, the emphasis was on the *transfiguration* of the human nature. The fundamental thought of the Christian East was that the Resurrection of Christ had a decisive transforming action that glorified His nature, and that every man is now deified by his incorporation in Christ.

This doctrine was traditional long before Ephesus and Chalcedon, and Monophysitism emerged from the obstinate inflexibility of those who preferred ill-starred formulas to the spirit of the ante- and post-cyrillian tradition. The Monophysite "tendency" that finds expression in this doctrine is generally speaking that of the entire Eastern tradition.

As Dom O. Rousseau writes: "Palamitism, which is the most characteristic doctrine of Orthodoxy is only its extreme development: the light of Tabor going as far as to reveal the hidden virtualities of our nature, subjugated through ascesis. And the whole ascesis of the Eastern Fathers is at bottom directed to making our nature translucid by the practice of *apatheia* until God can see His own reflection in man" (*Vers l'unité Chrétienne*, No. 51, March 1953, p. 4).

The tendency of the West is altogether different. As we have seen, the Eastern tendency was Monophysitic from the start. And this was a very orthodox tendency, in harmony with the preaching of the Apostles who had gone everywhere preaching the Resurrection of Christ, the glorification of human nature, and our deification. In the Eastern conception, Godhead and humanity were not opposed to one another. On the contrary: the more one saw God the more exalted was the human nature that God assumed and transfigured.

The West did not know the preaching of the Apostles in the same way, and it almost completely ignored the Christological quarrels of the first centuries. When the Council of Chalcedon defined, one person, two natures, this did not solve any vital question for the West. Acceptance of this doctrine for the West was no problem. The West had its attention fixed elsewhere. For all Augustine's polemics against Pelagius, Pelagianism—and what would later be called Semi-Pelagianism—was not dead. There were quarrels about the goodness of human nature, or its weakness, or its malice. Viewed in this light, grace appeared less as a deification than as a cure, and the sacraments were looked upon primarily as remedies.

In the wake of St. Augustine, the West was drawn into a usually pessimistic view of human nature. In truth, "the theology of extrinsic grace of the Protestant Reformation is only the tendency of Western theology pushed to its extreme limit, to the point of making it disagree with the truths of traditional theology" (O. Rousseau, *op. cit.*). For Protestant theology, the intrinsic transformation must be situated in the realm of eschatology. This is the extreme limit of the Western tendency, just as Palamitism is the extreme limit of the Eastern tendency. There is this difference between them, however, that the Eastern extreme, for very good reasons, has not received the same anathemas.

We must keep this history and geography of theology in mind, so that we may not shut ourselves up and harden ourselves in our own Latin "tendency." We would have much to gain by more careful study of Eastern theology, in which the idea of resurrection is the dominant, organizing, and unifying force of all theological knowledge. An event such as the rehabilitation of the Easter Vigil in the Latin-rite churches gives added power to the liturgical tradition that theology puts to use.

As Father Dondaine writes:

> The uneasiness that a particular theology causes its adversary—its Catholic adversary, of course—should warn us of the limits of this theology.
>
> On both sides it may happen that a system is defended and its consequences are developed, and from that point on exclusive and impossible pronouncements are made in an infinitely mysterious domain in which the decisive light can come only from Revelation. Instead of listening to *all* the voices of Revelation, instead of catching its *echo* in the whole of tradition, there is an unconscious tendency to choose, to push aside or undervalue the voices that do not harmonize too well with the system adopted. That is clearly the case with Father Déodat: his ears are attuned only to the "Damasian" formulary, and he takes exception to St. Cyril and the Three Chapters. But does not Dom Diepen also sometimes identify "Tradition" with St. Maximus and St. Damascene? He constructs his Christology on the principles of St. Cyril, and he seems quite unmoved by the "2,000" Patristic texts with which his opponents threaten to confront him.
>
> That is the ordinary compensating factor of theological systems. It is difficult to judge the value of the implications of a thesis, and to determine just how well they encompass the mysterious domain of the deposit of faith. It is difficult, too, to resist the temptation to reconstruct this deposit a priori and to assign limits to it. The Theologian's safeguard is the inspiring attention to the whole deposit of faith that is to be found in a St. Augustine and almost as much in a St. Thomas Aquinas. Indeed, we must be grateful to the theologians who push the principles of a system to their utmost consequences, for they make it possible for us to judge such a system not so much in terms of its internal coherence as of its harmony with the *totality* of the deposit.
>
> In the present case we are not sure that either of the two systems—the system of the *Assumptus homo* or that of the "personal appropriation"—will succeed in completely ousting the other. There are still two temptations in Christology: the temptation of Apollinarius who sacrifices the human integrity of Christ to the union, and that of Nestorius, who sacrifices the union to the integrity. And to drive away this twofold temptation, two theologies are perhaps necessary. At any rate, the better qualified of the two will be the one whose principles prove themselves to be more completely receptive to the demands of the other. (Bulletin de Théologie dogmatique, in *Revue des sciences philosophiques et Théologiques*, 1951, No. 4, pp. 610-611.)

II. GEMINAE GIGAS SUBSTANTIAE

History has the advantage of teaching us the extreme implications of various theses. Today we perceive what the authors of these theses did not always see themselves. Fascinating as one or another system may be, we become too well aware of its limits to imprison ourselves within it. We are better acquainted with the risks of each one, and we also know what must not be allowed to be lost if we are to maintain an integral faith in the *"Geminae gigas substantiae"* —in the Hero of twofold substance (Cf. Hymn by St. Ambrose, sung at Vespers for Christmas in the Dominican rite).

To speak accurately of this mystery, the great principle of St. Thomas is that we must conceive the Incarnation not as an ascending movement, going from man toward God, but as a descending movement going from God toward humanity. To quote St. Thomas: "The mystery of the Incarnation is considered as a condescension of the fullness of the Godhead into human nature rather than as the promotion of human nature, already existing, as it were, to the Godhead" (*Summa,* IIIa, q. 34, ad 1).

We can indeed see where the consideration of an "ascent" leads. It is at once a temptation to Dyophysitism, and even to Nestorianism or Photinism. Moreover, St. Thomas bases his view upon Scripture. According to the ascending conception, "God would not have assumed flesh to become man, but rather a man of flesh would have become God. And thus St. John's words (1:14) would not be true: The Word was made flesh. The contrary would be true: Flesh became the Word" (*Contra Gent.* 4:28).

Let us go further. To speak accurately of this mystery, we must conceive it *in facto esse* and not *in fieri.* In other words, we must think in terms of the accomplished fact and not in terms of the becoming of generation. To start out, as do St. Anselm and the Sententiaries, from what Mary conceived in her womb and end with the consideration of the God-man is to return to this ascending conception and to face the risks it entails. A proper understanding of the mystery demands that we consider it in itself, independently of the paths of access that God has chosen for Himself. Whatever the manner in which He came into the world, a man is God. This is the fact which our intellects must strive to understand. The primary problem is not that of the generation, but the problem of subsistence, or, if we prefer, the problem of the *"I"* of Christ.

To speak accurately of this mystery, must we always maintain that it is not a man but a human nature that has been assumed? The theology of the *Assumptus Homo* (a man assumed) is indeed difficult to defend. It is an open and tempting door to Nestorianism.

On the other hand, we must acknowledge with Father Dondaine

(*op. cit.,* p. 613—cf. p. 68 above) that the theory of the "two subjects" is not necessarily "implied, far from it, in any use of this venerable formula." St. Thomas sensed the difference when he labeled as heretical the theory of the two supposits (IIIa, q. 2, a. 6), whereas he simply brushed aside as improper the formula *assumpsit hominem* (IIIa, q. 4, a. 3). Therefore, while we must deny this formula a place in sound theology, we must be willing to see whatever worth it may have. Father H. Dondaine invites us to recognize in it "a millenary witness to the protest of the faith against the mutilation that Apollinarius inflicted upon Christ" (*op. cit.,* p. 613).

If we deny the formula *Assumptus Homo,* we must beware lest we fall into the error—to our way of thinking—of the "third opinion," or even into Origen's error. The Alexandrian doctor thought that Christ's soul had pre-existed before His body. This thesis no longer holds much appeal for our present-day anthropological trend of mind, but we might find echoes of it in certain spiritualities that are unaware of what it implies. The "third opinion," out of fear of Nestorianism, held that the Word had assumed body and soul separately.

We must also avoid any theory that would deny Christ a human will, free and capable of meriting, or deny Him a human intelligence; any theory that would "replace" the interplay of these superior faculties by the action of the divine Word. It was against these errors that St. Thomas Aquinas wrote his Question 6 (IIIa) on the order of the parts assumed. The flesh, the soul, the mind, were not assumed separately, but in a certain order (a logical and not a temporal order): first, the mind, then the soul, and finally the flesh.

Christ is a perfect man. Any theology which, under the pretext of maintaining the rights of the divine hypostasis, takes something away from His humanity—whether it be its freedom, its capacity to merit, or even, as some have said, its autonomy, its independence, its self-determination—may be suspected of mutilating Catholic truth. But inversely, any theology that, under the pretext of exalting the man, would no longer consider in this humanity even the effects of its immediate dependence upon the Word through the hypostatic union would be guilty of a serious omission. We can judge from this point of view certain artistic representations of Christ since the Renaissance, or certain modern writings in which

Jesus is called "big brother" or "pal" with a wholly human warmth.

While these considerations are sketchy, we deem them essential and sufficient to place the reader on his guard against grave errors. They will help him to judge exaggerations in devotional preaching. They can also be useful for testing the value of the religious education given to children and adolescents.

To take only two examples, borrowed from Father Congar, we shall cite first H.-Ed. Hengstenberg: "In nature, Christ is God and man, but He is solely God in His Person." [1] And on the other hand, here is the spontaneous answer of certain Catholic young ladies when the chaplain of their high school asked them if Jesus Christ had a human soul: "Oh no, since He is God." This answer, regardless of the excuses we may have for it, should make us weigh the influence of our Catholic teaching. As for Hengstenberg's proposition, it is ambiguous and dangerous. Strictly speaking, we might just as well say: Christ, in His Person, is man and God, since His Person is realized and activated in a twofold nature (whereas we would not say, for example: Christ is man and God with respect to His body). But most of all, the fact that the human nature of Christ is individuated, hypostasised, and receives its existence only through and in the Word who "terminates" it does not signify that Christ does not have the moral personality that every other man has and that consists in possessing His own human intellect and free will. We get a better understanding of the dangers of this proposition through the various consequences which its author draws from it.

III. THE "I" OF CHRIST

Christian thought relating to Christ, at once man and God and yet truly one, has come to conceive of the principle of union as solely the hypostasis. Thus the mystery of the Incarnation lies in this divine hypostasis, capable of "terminating" a created, human nature and of making it participate in its own existence. The task of theology with respect to this mystery consists in showing on the one hand how the faith of the Church has come to this final conclusion, and how on the other hand the function of the hypostasis of the Word in relation to the human nature of Christ is to be understood: to terminate this nature, to be its principle of existence,

[1] Congar, *op. cit.,* p. 61.

individuality, and personality. In other words, theology must tell us how it is that the Word is the "I" of Christ's humanity.

This is how St. Thomas, at the end of twelve chapters in which he has applied himself to refuting the historical errors of Christology, shows how the faith of the Church must be defined and how in fact it has been defined: one person, two natures.

It is therefore manifest that, in accordance with the Catholic Faith as it has been transmitted to us, we must say that there are in Christ the perfect divine nature and a perfect human nature, that is, a nature constituted of a human body and a soul endowed with reason. We must also say that these two natures are united in Christ not simply by inhabitation (God *dwelling* in the soul of Jesus); nor in an accidental manner, as a man might be united to a garment; nor by a possession or a simple personal ownership (the error of those who posit two hypostases in one person in Christ; since the hypostasis is what is most complete in the genus of substance, the union according to the person and not according to the hypostasis would be a union according to accidental ownership). These two natures are united according to a single hypostasis and supposit. In this way alone can we preserve what has been transmitted in Scripture concerning the Incarnation. Since, as we have shown, Holy Scripture applies without distinction the attributes of God to this man and the attributes of this man to God, it follows that it must be one and the same being of whom these things are said.

But since contraries cannot be said of the same subject from the same point of view, and since the divine and the human that are attributed to Christ— such things, for example, as being *impassible* and having *suffered,* being *dead* and being *immortal*—are opposites then the human and the divine must be attributed to Christ from two different points of view.

Thus, if we consider the one to whom the divine and the human are attributed, there is no distinction to make, and we find perfect unity. But if we consider in themselves the divine and human properties which are attributed, then we must distinguish. Natural properties are attributed to each thing according to its nature. For example, we attribute to that which is naturally heavy the property of tending by its nature toward the center of the earth. And since what is human and what is divine are attributed to Christ according to one nature or to the other, we must say that in Christ there are two natures without confusion or mixture.

However, the one to whom the natural properties are attributed, according to the nature of the genus of substance, is the hypostasis and supposit of that nature. Therefore, since it is impossible to divide the one to whom are attributed both what is human and what is divine, we must say that Christ is a hypostasis, a supposit, having a human and a divine nature. Thus everything that is divine can be attributed to this man from the fact that this man evokes a supposit of divine as well as of human nature; and inversely the human properties can be attributed to the Word of God inasmuch as He is the supposit of a human nature.

It is clear from all this that while the Son came in the flesh, it does not follow that either the Father or the Holy Ghost became incarnate, since the

Incarnation is not a union according to the nature—in which the three divine Persons are united—but a union according to the hypostasis of the Person, according to which the Persons are distinct. And hence, just as in the Trinity there are several Persons in a single nature, so in the mystery of the Incarnation there is one Person subsisting in several natures (*Contra Gentiles,* Book IV, Ch. 39).

Since we must understand the union of the divine and the human in the Incarnation in terms of the Person, and not in some other way, our chief concern in this mystery must be what the Person is and what its function is. Let us begin by defining all the terms we are using:

We speak of *supposit, hypostasis,* of an *individual subject,* and of a *subsisting individual.* We must realize that all these words are synonyms. If it is a question of an individual of the rational species (or of the metaphysical genus of intellects: see Lexicon), then this individual is called a *person.* Thus, the human individual is a person; and similarly we call the supposit of the divine nature a Person.

Modern philosophy would prefer to speak of the "I." It is our opinion that, philosophically speaking, this is still another synonym for supposit or hypostasis.

Let us look more closely at this supposit, at this real entity, that exists, that is the subject of operations. Then we shall be able to arrive at the various metaphysical principles which constitute it.

Paul is a hypostasis. The hypostasis is the ultimate subject, the one to whom we attribute existence, acts, and operations. I say: Paul walks, Paul thinks. Obviously it is his mind that thinks and his legs that walk. But the fact remains that Paul is the ultimate subject to whom all his parts belong. It is Paul who walks, reasons, is blond and fair, and who exists. The hypostasis sets before us the real being in its concrete totality, the whole that exists in its own right. Paul, this pebble, this planet, this flower that I shall call "Joie de vivre"—these are all hypostases. (A little humor is necessary to anyone who wants to enter the mysterious realm of being which is metaphysics, for otherwise he is in danger of being trapped by his own words—hence the name "Joie de vivre"!) And so this flower, "Joie de vivre," is a supposit, a hypostasis. If this flower spoke, it would say "I" in such a way that no other being could say it in the same way of itself.

The hypostasis is the ultimate subject to which everything is attributed, because it really sustains all its parts in existence and relates them to itself. In particular, it sustains its accidents (see Lexicon), that is, it dominates them and thereby distinguishes itself from them. Thus, Paul is blond and fair, "Joie de vivre" is red. And yet Paul is not the same thing as the fairness attributed to him; "Joie de vivre" is not identical to the redness of its petals or to the perfume it breathes out, or to its size or its age. What, then, is "Joie de vivre"?

What is Paul if he is neither his blondness, his fairness, his size, his age, his weight, his location, nor his friendly relations? Paul is the ultimate support of all that can be attributed to him. Paul is that which cannot be subjected in anything else since it is the ultimate subject. Paul is that which stands by itself, apart from other things, that which *subsists,* high enough in the genuses or categories of essences (see Lexicon for *category*) "to draw these accidents in its wake and order them to itself, while at the same time remaining fundamentally the same with or without them: and, to this end, it must be *complete* enough in itself, sufficiently integrated in all its essential parts to be *self-sufficient,* to exist autonomously. That is the meaning of substance, hypostasis."

Let us go further. The hypostasis possesses not only *these accidents* that we have mentioned: quantity, quality, etc. It also possesses elements that are more intrinsic to itself: its own nature, its existence. "Joie de vivre" is a plant, it possesses *its plant nature* with all the elements proper to it. Paul is a man, and he possesses *his human nature,* with all its elements. Likewise, "Joie de vivre" and Paul both possess *existence.* Thus, the hypostasis or supposit is the *habens naturam* and the *habens esse*: it is that which possesses nature, that which possesses being. Or if we prefer, the hypostasis is that which *subsists* in a given nature, or that which *subsists* in its being.

To subsist, that is, to exercise being in one's own right, so as to be absolutely incommunicable: this is what characterizes the hypostasis. The hypostasis is that which is, that which exercises by itself, for itself, in itself, the act of existing. The end of the creative act of God is to put into existence a hypostasis which appropriates the existence received. We must, however, carefully distinguish that which exists (the term *quod*) from the act of existence (the term *quo*) by which the hypostasis exists: God alone is His own act of existence.

Here, then, are the two metaphysical principles that we find in the definition of every created being: the hypostasis and the act of existing or existence. Some will say that existence is a constituent of the supposit; others, including the majority of Thomists, will not admit this. But whatever the thesis, the act of existing cannot be identified metaphysically with the hypostasis. The created supposit is not its own existence. Outside of God, existence is not the subject that subsists by itself, it is the act of a nature.

We have just written the word: nature. This is the third term of our philosophical trinity (hypostasis, existence, nature). What is the relationship between nature and hypostasis?

Let us remember that we have defined hypostasis as that which possesses a nature, that which possesses being. We must therefore distinguish the hypostasis from nature, just as we have distinguished the hypostasis from the act of being.

1. The first way of distinguishing nature from supposit or hypostasis is from the point of view of the individuation of material beings.

On the one hand we have *humanity,* the essence common to all men—what the Scholastics called *second substance;* and on the other hand we have Paul: Paul is a *first substance,* "the true substance, that which is truly a being, something that exists purely and simply."

The multiplicity of subjects in one and the same nature has imposed this distinction. Nature or essence is common to all the individuals of the human race. But the subjects who possess this nature are many and diverse.

Thus, seen under this aspect, essence is characterized by its logical *communicability* to created subjects, whereas the subject is characterized by its *incommunicability* to other subjects. Humanity (in the sense of nature) can be attributed to Peter, Paul, etc. But Paul cannot be attributed to any other subject but himself. He is the ultimate and logically incommunicable subject. It follows that there is more in *Paul* than in his *human essence*: the latter includes only those elements which go to make up every man. Paul possesses in addition elements that are individual and belong to him alone, thus making him a unique case distinct from every other human case.

2. There is also a second way of distinguishing essence from supposit, which starts out from a more metaphysical point of view. It touches being in what is most inward, most real, and most de-

finitive about it. This is the distinction that we must consider here.

The point of view of material individuation is limited. It applies only to material substances. But what about instances in which matter plays no part? And hence what about instances in which there is no common essence or "species"? While humanity exists quite as much in Peter, as in Paul, Jean, and Lucy, "Gabrielity" exists only in the Angel Gabriel. Are we to say that the Angel Gabriel *is* his Gabrielity purely and simply, and that Gabrielity is no different from Gabriel? Certainly not, for only God's nature possesses existence by itself and in itself. God's is the only necessary nature. Every other created being, on the contrary, is contingent: it would not exist unless God had created it. Created being is an essence to which existence has been granted, it is an essence that is "terminated" individually, that is unique and incommunicable, and that is the immediate subject of its act of being.

The created supposit is a metaphysically "composite" whole. It *has* a nature, it is not its own nature. Its nature limits its being,— defines, measures, and determines it. Nature is a formal principle of being that causes the supposit to be this and not that; that causes it to be very precisely this and not one of the infinite number of possible beings. Only in God, whose essence is rich with all possible virtualities without any limit whatever, are essence and existence one and the same.

We see how this approach brings us closer to the depths of being than the first point of view. We are no longer considering whether nature receives or does not receive individuating determinations (the case of material species). We see that whatever the case, created nature cannot be the whole of the creature.

Here, then, are three metaphysical principles: supposit, essence (or nature), and existence. Can we go further and set forth what constitutes the supposit or ultimate subject, now that we have seen that it is a metaphysically "composite" whole? And can we specify what the relationship of this supposit is to existence?

Where does the supposit get its privilege to *subsist,* that is, to be inherently cohesive, to exercise its own act of being, to order to itself all the elements or principles that integrate the subsisting reality? Its existence (i.e., its act of existing) does not contribute all this, for existence is a pure "act," and this principle cannot explain the ordering unity of the supposit, of that which subsists by itself and draws everything into its own unity, including existence.

Nor can the privilege of subsisting come to the supposit from its essence, for the essence possesses only a formal or numerical unity and it existence is contingent. Essence and existence "are ordered to a term that embraces and establishes them in its unity: the subsisting being itself, the hypostasis, in which is properly verified the ontological unity of the substance, the existence in itself."

With Cajetan, we shall say that the supposit adds to the nature that which connotes the existence which actuates it. Cajetan (and the Dominican school after him) does not make existence a constituent of the supposit. The supposit is simply the immediate subject of the act of being: it is *this thing* which is.

Since the sixteenth century, the word *subsistence* has been used to designate the substantial mode that terminates the essence and renders it strictly incommunicable. In other words, subsistence designates what makes an essence to be a supposit, an immediate subject of the act of being. (The term *subsistencia* for St. Thomas was synonymous with hypostasis.) Here, then, are the three metaphysical principles—simple, indivisible, and really distinct—that are to be found in every created being: essence, subsistence, and existence.

If the supposit is a person, the subsistence is called personality. That is what metaphysically constitutes the person, what confers incommunicability upon him, and makes him to be a unique case, an "I" who exists, who is a son or a father, who has a given nature, etc.

Among the ten categories (see Lexicon) of being, subsistence and personality are reducible to the first genus of substance. But subsistence is not a specific difference, it is *"the ultimate and pure term of a substantial nature."* And the supposit (or the person) is "this terminated nature, perfectly completed so that it can exist in its own right."

Existence, or the act of being, which "actuates" both the nature and the supposit, is metaphysically distinguishable from the one and the other. The supposit is the immediate subject of being; nature enters into the supposit, as its formal principle, and is the subject of being only through the supposit. With John of St. Thomas, we note that the essence (or nature) possesses an "intransigent" unity that admits of no additions or subtractions. It corresponds exactly to its definition. The supposit, on the contrary, is indefinable and receptive. It receives within its unity all the individuating marks, all the accidents of its unique case.

All these metaphysical explanations will help us if we want the definitions of our Faith to be more than words for us—*flatus vocis,* gusts of wind. Regardless of the philosophy they may prefer, those who have the responsibility of preserving the deposit of faith must constantly make use of philosophical terms. It is only by laboriously considering the concept of the person that theology can, insofar as it is humanly possible, clarify the mystery of the Trinity (a single nature in three Persons), and the mystery of the Incarnation (a single Person in two natures).

In the theology of the Holy Trinity, the important thing is to grasp the *distinct,* incommunicable character, the unique case of the Person. Theology is thus brought to see that each divine Person is a "pure relation" whereby it is distinguished from the other Persons even while it constitutes a single nature and a single being in union with them.

In the mystery of the Incarnation, the fact to be grasped is the proper *function* of the hypostasis (or Person) which consists in "terminating" the individual nature. Inasmuch as there is only one Person in Christ, we must say that the human nature of the Savior does not constitute a separate subsistent being, a distinct supposit; His human nature is "hypostasized": it is the Word who "terminates" it, that is, who constitutes it as *first substance,* as an individual, a hypostasis, a Person. It is the Word who communicates to it subsistence and existence. The human nature is entirely assumed within the hypostasis—the Person—of the Word. The human "I" of Christ is the "I" of the Word. This type of substantial and yet non-essential union would be unthinkable if we had not perceived in every created substance the necessary distinction between nature (even individual nature) and hypostasis. This distinction enables our minds to understand the unique case of Christ and to say: it is not contradictory. All progress in theology proceeds by way of philosophical attention to the conditions of created substance.

IV. VARIOUS INTERPRETATIONS OF THE WORD "PERSON"

We have defined the person as the *individual* of a rational nature, and we have said that personality is that which *metaphysically constitutes the person.*

Now, modern language brings confusion to these terms because it does not mean the same things when it speaks of person and of personality. The interest of ancient philosophy lay on the ontological level, on the level of being, whereas modern philosophy is concerned with act, or with the psychological condition rather than with being itself. Thus, for Leibnitz, the person is the consciousness or remembrance of self. For Kant, liberty constitutes the personality. Renouvier defines the person as thought and will; Ravaisson, as intelligent will; for Lachelier, the person is thought and love, and so on. The person is no longer considered as a substance, but as a "value," and on the ethical level instead of the ontological or metaphysical level. It goes without saying that when the unity of the "person" in Christ is thus understood, we immediately fall into the Monophysite (or at least the Monothelite) heresy.

We must therefore distinguish the different levels at which the notion of personality can be considered.

1. The psychological level. From this point of view, personality is defined by the totality of the specific qualities of the human *nature*: intelligence and will, consciousness and liberty, and so on. On this level personality is part of the nature; and therefore Christ has two personalities, and we can say that He has an autonomous human personality. Actually, there is no communication or exchange or confusion of natures. His two natures are distinct, unconfused, unmixed, and entire.

2. The moral level. Personality is here defined in terms of value. It is the virtue of the person who has "character," a penetrating mind, a firm will, and greatness of soul; it is susceptible to growth. On this level, personality also belongs to the nature. It is a quality of the nature—of the individual nature and not of the common nature or of the species, but still a quality of the nature. It would therefore be true, from this point of view, that Christ has a human personality: that is, a quality or power which is identified with His human will.

3. And finally, the metaphysical level. Seen from this aspect, personality is the principle that terminates the human nature of Christ, constituting it a unique and incommunicable substance, the substance that makes it possible for this man, Jesus, to say: "I" in such a way that no other being can say it with reference to the being of whom He says it. On this level, Christ has no human personality; the Word takes the place of His human personality.

In this union, nothing is taken away from the human nature of Christ. Jesus is really and wholly a man, but that which "terminates" His nature and constitutes Him to be this man, Jesus, is the Word. In a sense we could say: that which constitutes the "human person" of Christ, which personifies Him as a man, is the Word; for the Word, in Christ, plays the role of the term that completes the nature, hypostasizing and personifying it. But this is an ambivalent expression. Taken in another sense, it is false and absurd, for if the function of the Word is to "personify" the human nature of Christ, then there is no human person in Him, nor human personality. The one Word of God exists and acts in two natures. The "I" through which the human nature of Jesus finds expression is the "I" of the Word of God.

Enough has now been said to show that it is only on this metaphysical or ontological level that the person is the ultimate subject to which everything else is attributed, including the psychological and moral personalities. These two last-named personalities belong to the "I" of Christ and are attributable to Him. The "I" of Christ belongs to Him alone, and has no other subject but Him.

And now, two closing remarks:

A. Human nature, as we have said, *is united* to the divine nature in the one hypostasis of the Word. And on the other hand, the divine nature *unites itself* to the human nature in the one subsistence of the Word-Man. These two unions are not metaphysically alike. The former is a real relation; the latter can only be a relation of reason (see Lexicon), since there can be no real change in God. The Word of God is not modified by this union.

B. The "principle" and the "term" of the Incarnation are not to be confused. The Incarnation, or the sending, or the mission, concerns the Word alone. At the *term* of this mission, the human nature is hypostatically united to the Word alone. In its *principle,* on the contrary, inasmuch as God acts through His Nature, which the three divine Persons possess in common, we must say that *the Father, the Son, and the Holy Spirit* have brought about the union of the human nature to the one Person of the Word.

V. THE UNITY OF CHRIST

One Person, two natures: which of the two takes precedence? Which is more fundamental? Are we to say that Christ is one or that He is twofold? We have said that the ultimate *subject* of the created being is the supposit, *that* which exists, which possesses a nature. The supposit evokes the whole of the created being. And whatever is true of a subject in its entirety belongs to it more completely than what belongs to it according to one of its parts (for example, its nature). Since the duality of natures does not entail a duality of supposits, Christ is one purely and simply in His entirety, whereas He is "several" from the point of view of the relationship of His natures to His Person.

We should also note that we would have failed in our theological explanations if we had been led to the conclusion that Christ is "two." It is precisely to clarify the revealed truth of faith that there is only *one* Christ, at once God and man, that the theological thought of the Church concluded in her Conciliar definitions: one Person, two natures. From this point of view, the "first opinion" which posits two hypostases is a blow at theological thought because it necessarily "divides" Christ.

But if Christ is fundamentally one, what of His *esse,* of His act of being? Are there two *esse's* in Christ, or only one?

This is a delicate question. Is the *esse* (the act of being) attributable to the supposit or to the nature? If the *esse* is attributed to the supposit, then there is only one *esse*. If, on the other hand, the *esse* must be attributed to the natures, then there are two *esse's*. Strictly speaking, we do not say that "human nature" exists, but that Peter, Paul, and John exist. Being is attributed to the nature inasmuch as the nature is the formal principle (or the *quo*: see Lexicon). And being is attributed to the supposit inasmuch as it is the subject (or the *quod*: see Lexicon). Thus, neither the nature nor the parts receive the attribution of the *esse* properly so-called. It is only the complete supposit that *is*.

That is why, according to the "first opinion"—which claims that Christ has two supposits—there are two *to be*'s. The "third opinion" —according to which the divine Person is united accidentally to the disjoined elements of the human nature—holds that there is a substantial *to be* (the Word) and an accidental *to be* (the elements assumed). According to the "second opinion"—the only one which seems to us in complete harmony with orthodox Faith—there is only one *to be*: there is only one supposit and the human nature does not supervene as an accident. Moreover, if Christ is one, it is inevitable that there is only one *to be*. How otherwise could we interpret Jesus' affirmation: "Before Abraham came to be, I am"

(Jn. 8:58)? Since oneness is based on being, where there are two beings there is no longer unity. However, there is no reason why a single being should not be fundamentally consistent with several principles *quo* (cf. Lexicon).

Theologians must therefore consider these "principles *quo*," to clarify what they mean. Actually, we can conceive of a being as having: a) essential parts; and b) accidental parts. These are two different principles *quo*. For example:

a) Socrates is a man, *by reason of his humanity* (essential part).

b) Socrates is white, *by reason of his whiteness* (accidental part).

The accident of whiteness remains extrinsic to the personal being, and the existence that whiteness brings to the subject is accidental. Accidents can be multiplied (size, virtues, relations, etc.) without compromising the unity of the subject. That is how the third opinion tried to save the unity of being in Christ, to the detriment of the unity of His human nature. According to this view, Christ is a man in the same way that Socrates is white.

The "second opinion," on the other hand, sees the one being of Christ related to two principles *quo* which are both *substantial* parts. Thus, a man's head, body, and soul are substantial parts of him. If one of these parts is taken away, he is no longer a man. In like manner, Christ's human nature is united to the pre-existing being of the Word as a principle *quo*, after the manner of *an additional substantial part*.

What images could we use to translate this truth? The use of images in this case is difficult, not to say impossible, because Christ is absolutely unique and also because we are dealing with being itself, at a depth where all images must be left behind or even rejected. As a guide to the mind, however, we shall use the example of a man born blind who later gains his sight. Thus the Word exists in the first place only in His divine nature, and afterwards He is "humanified."

From the start we must note two essential differences between this example and the case of Christ. On the one hand, the sight of the man born blind and later miraculously cured is not a *substantial* attribute of the man. Important as sight is, it is possible to be a man (an animal endowed with intelligence) and still be blind; whereas the humanity that belongs to the Word Incarnate is one of His substantial parts. On the other hand, sight brings to the man born blind a new accidental *being*. He can now see, whereas before he was blind. In the case of Christ, humanity adds nothing to the Word of God (there is only a relation of reason between the Word and His humanity). It is the humanity (a real relation to the Word) that reaps all the benefit from its assumption by the Son of God.

We must not say that the humanity of the Word Incarnate is as it were a power (see Lexicon) with relation to its *act,* for God cannot be the act of any created power (that would mean that a created being can *become* God). And yet God cannot be one of the terms of a *becoming*: that is, He cannot become what He was not before. (God *is,* and that is the sum of it.) It follows that the Word is not the *informing* act of the humanity of Christ, He is its *terminal* act. The Word completes the created nature without being compounded with it.

The relationship of Christ's humanity to the Word is not one of a power to its act, but of individual nature to its hypostasis. The mystery of Christ consists in the fact that this hypostasis which gives the individual human nature its incommunicability, its individuality, is uncreated. In other words, the human nature of Christ is "personified" by the divine Person of the Word, and that is why it is actuated (terminal act) by the divine existence of the Word.

If we were pressed to give another example—and one that is not simply an image!—we would call to mind the beatific vision, in which God is the *terminating act* of our intellect and yet He does not *inform* our intellect. On the threshold of such a great mystery, theology can explain the revealed truths of faith only by affirming these distinctions. All the power of theology, and its joy as well, lies in finding the real basis of this mystery in the structure of created being. Thus, theology—in its efforts to grasp its object—holds a knife in the back of philosophy, if we may say so, and forces it to carry on to the utmost limit certain analyses that would remain superficial if it were not for faith's burning insistence.

VI. QUESTIONS OF LANGUAGE

In the knowledge of faith, it is through the propositions of the Creed which have been transmitted to us that we attain to the Truth which we cleave to. Thus, questions of language and grammar are not matters of purism in theology. They are essential to it. An error in mode of expression, if it is a grave one, implies heresy or the danger of being swept into it.

Questions of language are particularly thorny in all that concerns Christ. Inasmuch as He is man and God, it seems as if we can speak of Him indifferently either as man or as God. And yet there is only one Person in Christ. It follows that we cannot say anything we please concerning Him, and the discernment between heterodox and orthodox propositions is most enlightening on the authenticity of our faith.

It would be easy to point out in the New Testament the propositions which express the "exchange of properties" in Christ, that is, propositions in which human properties are attributed to God, and divine properties attributed to this man, Jesus. St. John says, for instance: "The Word was made flesh" (that is, was made man). Here "flesh" is attributed to the Word. Or again St. Paul says: "Christ Jesus, who though he was by nature God . . . emptied himself, taking the nature of a slave" (Phil. 2:6-7). That is to say, He took the nature of man. And we could give many more examples. We have even seen that St. Thomas argued from this manner of speaking among the inspired writers to establish the dogma of the hypostatic union.

Inasmuch as we have received the orthodox Faith of the Church from the whole of Tradition, we can understand the rules of this exchange of attributes, we can state them and also justify them.

The general rule is that we can attribute the properties of human nature to God, and reciprocally we can attribute the properties of the divine nature to this Man. And we can do this because there is a single supposit in two natures. However, we cannot attribute human properties to the divine nature, nor reciprocally divine properties to the human nature, because the natures remain distinct and attribution is based on identity. This is what is known as the "law of the communication of idioms. (The word idiom comes from the Greek "ἰδίωμα," which signifies property.)

The theologian Billuart has translated this law by declaring: *Concreta de concretis, et non abstracta de abstractis.* This signifies that we can always attribute concrete realities to other concrete realities, but that we cannot attribute an abstract word designating a nature to an abstract word designating another nature. Thus we can say: God is this man (two concrete words), or, this man is God. But we cannot say: this humanity is the Godhead.

Here is another, and simpler rule that St. Thomas gives us in his *Summa* (IIIa, q. 16, a. 5):

Now concrete words stand for the hypostasis of the nature; and hence of concrete words we may predicate indifferently what belongs to either nature —whether the word of which they are predicated refers to one nature, as the word *Christ*, by which is signified *both the Godhead anointing and the manhood anointed;* or to the divine nature alone, as this word *God* or *the Son of God;* or to the manhood alone, as this word *Man* or *Jesus.* Hence Pope Leo says: "It is of no consequence from what substance we name Christ; because since the unity of person remains inseparably, one and the same is altogether Son of Man by His flesh, and altogether Son of God by the Godhead which He has with the Father."

Thus, we can say: Christ suffered, God suffered and died, this man is God.

Special cases. Can we say: "God *became* man"? This is a dangerous proposition that must be rightly understood. In actual fact, there is no change in God. When we say "God became man" we mean that a human nature was united to the pre-existing divine nature. We are not positing any newness in God, but pointing to newness solely on the side of the nature assumed, which began to be united to God. To take any other view of the matter in this case amounts to heresy.

Can we say: "Man was made God"? This proposition is erroneous because a human *supposit* cannot become God. The truth of the matter is that "it happened that a man was God." But it is difficult to understand the proposition in this way.

Can we say: "Christ is a creature"? Following the rule we have stated, it is just as true to say that Christ is the Creator as to say that Christ was created. However, the Arian affirmation: "Christ is a creature"—which signifies that the Word is not God—is heretical. That is why this proposition is offensive to our way of thinking. We must clarify the rule we have given, following St. Thomas (IIIa, q. 16, a. 8, ad 2):

. . . things of which we may doubt to what nature they belong, are not to be predicated without a qualification. Hence (St. John Damascene) . . . adds that *the one hypostasis,* i.e. of Christ, *is uncreated in its Godhead and created in its manhood:* even so conversely, we may not say without qualification, *Christ is incorporeal* or *impassible;* in order to avoid the error of Manes, who held that Christ had not a true body, nor truly suffered, but we must say, with a qualification, that Christ was incorporeal and impassible *in His Godhead.*

Can we say: "This man began to exist"? Obviously, this is a false formula, since "this man" designates the hypostasis, and the hypostasis is eternal. Thus Jesus said: "Before Abraham came to be, I am" (Jn. 8:58). And the author of the Epistle to the Hebrews said: "Jesus Christ is the same, yesterday and today, yes, and forever" (Heb. 13:8).

Can we say: "Christ, as man, is a creature"? The expression "Christ, as man" can designate either the supposit or the nature. If it designates the supposit it amounts to saying: "Christ inasmuch as He is the Word" or "Christ inasmuch as He is man" since there is but one supposit. It is tantamount to affirming: "Christ, inasmuch as He is *that man,* is a creature." And that is false, for the supposit is eternal.

On the other hand, if the expression "Christ as man" designates the nature, then the proposition is true. Let us note, however, that grammatically the word "man" in this proposition refers more to the nature than to the supposit. It is as if we said: "Christ, inasmuch as He is man," with the clear implication that the word man is an attribute that designates an attributed nature. Thus, in its obvious sense, the proposition is perfectly true. This would not be the case, as we have pointed out, if we said: "Christ, inasmuch as He is that man, is a creature."

We must make the same judgment concerning the proposition: "Christ, as man, is God." The same reasons that led us to accept the preceding proposition oblige us to deny this one in the final analysis.

Can we say: "Christ, as man, is a Person, or a hypostasis, or a reality with a human nature"? We must apply the same rule here as in previous cases. If the phrase "as man" designates the supposit, there is no difficulty. The proposition is true. If the phrase designates the human nature, then one of two things applies: either the proposition signifies that it is fitting to this human nature, as to every other, to be in a person, and in this sense the proposition is true. For the only reality that subsists in Christ's human nature is a Person. Or else the proposition signifies that the human nature of Christ is an independent (metaphysical) personality, caused by the very principles of this nature. And in that sense, the proposition is false: the human nature of Christ does not subsist, nor does it exist by itself apart from the Word. While the human nature of Christ is real, we cannot say that it is a subsisting reality.

Can we say: "Christ, as man, is the adopted son of God"? Sonship and adoption properly belong only to the Person. And since there is only one Person in Christ, in no sense is it true that Christ, the Son of God by nature, can be His adopted son. There is this difference between the habitual grace of Christ and our own that this grace does make us truly adopted sons of God, whereas in Christ this grace is simply an effect of the grace of union by which the Word is personally united to human nature in Jesus.

Can we say: "Christ is subject to the Father"? This proposition is true, but it is dangerous in view of the error of Arius, who professed that the Word was inferior to the Father. Therefore we must specify: "Christ, with regard to His human nature, is subject to the Father."

Can we say: "Christ is subject to Himself"? This proposition can be understood in several ways. First, it could be understood to mean that in Christ there are two hypostases, the one exercising dominion over the other, which would be subject to it. That is the heresy of Nestorius. Thus understood, the proposition is false. Secondly, it can be interpreted to mean that Christ possesses two natures, the one subject to the other. This would amount to saying that Christ, in the nature that He has in common with us, is subject to Himself, in the nature that He has in common with the Father. And this is true. It should however be noted that "Christ" is a personal name, and that "Himself" also designates His Person. Therefore, what is proper to Christ by reason of one of His natures must not be attributed to Him without being precisely qualified. We must say: Christ, inasmuch as He is man, is subject to Himself, or else, Christ is master of Himself inasmuch as He Himself is man.

Can we say: "Christ was predestined to be the Son of God"? Yes, this can certainly be said, since St. Paul says so himself (Rom. 1:4). The important thing is to understand it correctly. We must not interpret it to mean that the human nature was predestined to be the son of God, for predestination, like sonship or adoption, belongs properly to the person and not to the nature. The predestination St. Paul speaks of is attributed to the Person of Christ, but to this Person inasmuch as He subsists in the human nature and not inasmuch as He subsists in Himself or in the divine nature. In this sense—and this is what St. Paul means—it is true that Christ, inasmuch as He subsists in a human nature, was predestined to be the Son of God. It is not natural to Him to be so predestined; it is the effect of the grace of union in Him.

Can we say: "The whole divine nature became incarnate"? We

have it from St. John Damascene, who declares: "The whole divine nature in one of its hypostases became incarnate." We can indeed say that the whole divine nature (in one of its hypostases) became incarnate, since each divine Person possesses the totality of the divine nature just as much as does the Blessed Trinity as a whole. This does not signify, of course, that the whole Trinity became incarnate.

We could cite many more examples of this sort. Those already given suffice to show the scope and complexity of the theology of the "communication of idioms." The grandeur of our faith lies in our being able to say as we look upon this man Jesus, without in any sense renouncing the absolute monotheism of Abraham and Moses: "My Lord and my God!" (Jn. 20:28). And yet we have seen that all the complexity of human language also comes into play.

We must avoid as much as possible formulas which may be exact but too subtle, or formulas that are ambiguous and can lead simple souls astray. There may even be reason at times to rectify correct formulas that simple souls use too simply. For such formulas can lead them into error or at least make them forget a part of the total truth.

To cite only one such instance, we believe it is sometimes harmful to the devotion of simple souls always to speak of the Eucharist as "le Bon Dieu," and to announce: "I shall bring you le Bon Dieu," or "I shall receive le Bon Dieu." Certainly, such expressions are true. But they are dangerous from two points of view. On the one hand, they entail the risk of making us forget that "le Bon Dieu" is everywhere, at every moment, in every circumstance, and that we can pray to Him anywhere and not only before the Blessed Sacrament. On the other hand, these words, when they are said in a certain way that seems to have done away with the mystery of faith, lead our enemies to understand that we truly adore appearances, or at least the "accidents" of bread, and they are quick to accuse us of idolatry. Of course, Christians are not idolaters, and yet the temptation to Monophysitism still seems very real among certain ones. These risks are not insignificant. It is therefore better to follow the mode of expression of the liturgy. For the liturgy possesses true mastery of language and grammar, because it is the teacher of the art of praying and of professing the orthodox Faith. Now, when the liturgy speaks of the Eucharist, it ordinarily says:

"the Body of Christ." And likewise, it designates the feast of the Eucharist by the precise term of "Corpus Christi"—the Feast of the Body of Christ—or the Feast of the Blessed Sacrament. For the sake of our faith and our devotion, let us strive to imitate the language of the liturgy.

In the following pages (pp. 94-96), we shall give another example of these problems of language with regard to our adopted sonship and to the "Our Father."

VII. VOLITION, OPERATION, MERIT

Since there are two natures in Christ, there must also be two natural operations and two wills in Him, as defined by the Third Council of Constantinople (680–681).

However, we should notice that those who spoke of a *single* operation in Christ did not always have the same point of view. It seems that Sergius, Patriarch of Constantinople, at first spoke of a single "energy" to signify a single active principle. His error, as we shall show, was to conceive of the operations of Christ's human nature in a purely passive way, as if the human faculties of Christ were no more than purely passive instruments in the hands of the Word.

But since Christ's human nature is complete, we must realize that He possesses, in addition to His divine will, a human faculty of volition, and that this faculty is not inert even though it is wholly subject to God. And like every human will, this human will of Christ produces two acts of volition: the first, the simple, spontaneous, and direct volition that adheres to what is presented to it as an end; the second, reasoned volition involving choice, that decides upon the means and circumstances and adheres to them. Christ possessed free will, capable of merit, inasmuch as He was a *viator* (wayfarer) as well as a *comprehensor* (the possessor of the good promised, at the end of the pilgrimage).

Finally, Christ, like every other man, possessed not only a rational appetite (will), but also a sensible appetite whose spontaneous movement could tend toward things that were not in accord with God's will. But on the level of rational will, this movement represented only velleity as long as the deliberate will did not assume it.

The divine and human operations of Christ must be understood without confusion, just like the natures which are at their source.

But these operations must also be considered in a certain order and in a certain manner.

The Mono-energism of Severus of Antioch and his disciples acknowledged two categories of works performed by Christ, but since there could only be one operator it held that there could only be one operation. It pointed out that several categories of human works can be distinguished, such as touching, which is the operation of the hand, or walking, which is an operation of the feet, and yet there is only one operation, since the soul operates through the hands or through the feet. And so it held that Jesus Christ had a human nature moved and governed by the divine nature, thus making one operator and one operation. This comparison is an oversimplification. The activity of Christ's human nature—endowed with reason and deliberate volition—cannot be compared to the activity of a foot or of a hand in man.

We must distinguish a twofold action in the agent (see Lexicon) moved:

a) an action that derives from its own nature;

b) an action that is impressed upon it by the agent on which it depends (principal agent).

Thus, the action of a knife is to cut. This is its proper action that derives from its "form" (from its nature), and this action belongs to the human agent only insofar as he makes use of it. We cannot do anything we please with a knife. Likewise, the action of a pliers is to grasp a nail and pull it out. We do not cut bread with a pliers, but with a knife. Once again, the action of fire is to heat, and the blacksmith uses fire for this purpose. It is the form of a tool that determines its action. But the operation impressed on the tool by the motion of the human agent is the operation of the human agent himself. Thus, the figure that emerges from stone when a statue is completed derives from the artist who held the chisel (and this is the only correct assertion of Mono-energism), as well as (secondarily) from the chisel held by the artist.

Therefore, whenever the mover and the thing moved have different forms, there must be two operations: the operation of the moving agent and the operation proper to the thing moved. This is true, even though the thing moved participates in the operation of the moving agent and even though the mover makes use of the operation proper to the thing moved. Consequently there is a communion from the one to the other.

Let us apply this truth to the case of Christ. Christ possesses two distinct natures, and therefore two operations proper to these natures. However, His human nature is subject to the divine nature, as the instrument to its agent. Since God makes use of the sacred humanity of our Savior to save us, the human nature of Jesus is the instrumental, efficacious cause of our salvation. The intimate life of our Lord, all that He did and said, all that He suffered, all the sentiments of His heart, all that He is now doing, are productive of salvation for men. And this brings us to consider the merit that belongs to Christ in His sacred humanity.

Let us call to mind what merit is (cf. *Theology Library* Vol. III, p. 399 ff.). Eternal life belongs only to God by nature, and no man can win it by his own efforts. But God is free to give eternal life to His friends, as a reward for their good works. If a man makes the fullest use of all his resources, God sees it and recognizes it, and it is fitting that He should reward this man according to His magnificence as God (merit of fitness, *ex congruo*). If a man is taken up and vivified by the Holy Spirit, that is, if a seed of eternal life, grace, is sown into his heart, and if this seed bears fruit, it is fitting that this man should attain the eternal life to which God has ordered him (merit of justice, or at least condign merit, *ex condigno*). This "justice" and this "merit" do not lessen the gratuity of salvation, because it belongs to God to order the soul to eternal life, just as it belongs to the Creator to make a given seed that He has created bear a particular kind of fruit.

Now, Christ had the use of His free will from the first instant of life. He therefore merited through each of His acts, through each of His free choices. He merited His own glory for Himself. Moreover, He had been constituted by God as the principle of salvation for all men, just as Adam had been constituted the principle of the whole human race. And therefore He merited not only His own personal glory, but salvation and grace for all men. (Corroboration of this doctrine of Christ's universal merit can be found in many texts of the Council of Trent. Cf. Denz. Nos. 790, 795, 799, 836, and 842.)

This doctrine has induced theologians to compare Adam and Christ from the point of view of their relationship to the human race, and to point out in what manner humanity is contained in Christ. Certain modern theologians speak of the *inclusion* of the whole of human nature or of the whole human race in Christ. It is better to say that Christ *virtually contains* all the grace of which the human race is capable. It is a "virtual" containment. In other words, it is containment by a universal (exemplary and efficient) *cause* which pre-contains its effects. Since grace in creatures is not of the substantial order, it cannot be on the level of substance or of nature that Christ "contains" humanity in order to heal it and raise it up to Himself.

There is also another difference between Adam and Christ: When Adam sinned, he "wounded" our nature; and thenceforth every human nature has been a bearer of this wound.[2] We receive original sin through our nature when we are born, and this sin infects our personal soul. Christ, on the other hand, by His personal action upon us, touches our personal soul, and through the salvation of our soul He heals our whole nature.

VIII. THE GRACE OF CHRIST AND OUR GRACE

In Christ there are three kinds of grace to be distinguished: 1. The grace of union; 2. habitual grace; 3. capital grace, which is not really distinct from habitual grace but evokes the latter by reason of its function as the source of all grace.

1. *The grace of union.* It is a unique grace for a man to possess the personal being of the Son of God. This grace transcends all other graces.

Let us note that there are two correlative ways of understanding the word "grace" (Cf. *Theology Library,* Vol. III, pp. 359-409). The word "grace" can signify, on the one hand, the will of God that forgives or that communicates its gracious gifts. And on the other hand, it signifies the gift of God that corresponds to this favor, or if we prefer, the divine favor that takes body in a given subject. Since God cannot change, if God "grants his favor" to someone who did not have it previously, this means that there is something new not in God but in the recipient of the favor. And this "something new" is what we call grace.

When we consider grace in the first sense, it is easy to see that the union of the Incarnation is a grace. For by the Incarnation a man was raised not only to know and love God as He is in Himself

---

[2] Obviously neither Christ nor His august Mother were touched with original sin itself. However by God's decree and Christ's free choice they both suffered some of the consequences of original sin, i.e. suffering and death. (Translator's note.)

—the way habitual grace does for us—but raised to the personal being of God.

Considering grace in the second sense, it is more difficult to explain what the grace of union in Christ corresponds to. Habitual grace is a "quality," a *habitus*. In short, it is a help, an assistance in some external manner by which the soul is capable of divine knowledge and love.

But in the case of the Incarnation the question is not merely one of *operations* of knowledge and love, it is a question of *existence*: that is, being the Son of God. There can be no intermediary between the nature and the hypostasis. Habitual grace is the intermediary (in the sense that the quality of a subject can be called an intermediary) by which we know and love God. The grace of union, on the other hand, is the union itself. If we consider the divine hypostasis given to the human nature, then the grace of union is an uncreated gift. If we consider human nature as united to the hypostasis of the Word, then the grace of union is a created gift, it is a real relation of union.

It goes without saying that this grace of union is not the consequence of any merit whatsoever. Christ could not merit before He could act (humanly), and He could not act before the hypostatic union. And if no merit of Christ's can precede such a union, then that is all the more reason, so it seems, why no merit of man can precede it. True, the liturgy sings that the Blessed Virgin "deserved" to bear our Redeemer. But this must not be understood to mean that she merited the Incarnation by a condign merit, but that she was faithful to the grace that made her to be the Mother of God, and that she thus attained to a degree of purity and holiness that befitted the divine Maternity.

A final question will make us see at what a profound level of being the grace of union lies. Can we say that the grace of union is natural to Christ the man? Admittedly, this association of words—nature-grace—shocks our sense of fitness. However we must remember that "natural" has two meanings. It can signify "essential," "proceeding from the very principles of a being." It is in this sense that it is "natural" for fire to burn. And in this sense the grace of union is not natural to Christ, if we understand that it is caused by the principles of His human nature; but it is natural to Him if we understand the grace of union as caused by the principles of His divine nature. Natural can also signify "native," "possessed from birth." It is in this sense that the nature of one man can be different from that of another. In this sense the grace of union is natural to Christ.

2. *Habitual grace.* Habitual grace in Christ is a kind of natural property of the union. Habitual grace flows from the grace of union the way bright light comes from the sun, the way the glory of a soul follows from the presence of God. The grace of union made the human nature subsist divinely, but left it intact; habitual grace, flowing naturally from the grace of union, disposes the nature to *operate divinely.*

The grace of Christ (i.e., His habitual grace) is a grace of supreme intensity and total efficacy. It is the grace of the One who was chosen by God to be the principle of diffusion of all grace. This grace is without measure—although it is "finite" since it is a quality of the soul—and it cannot increase since it flows from the hypostatic union. Christ's habitual grace is the grace existing in the humanity of the One who is the Son of God by nature.

This last proposition indicates the vast difference between our condition as sons and that of the God-man. We receive a grace that constitutes us the adopted sons of God. Christ, on the contrary, is not the Son of God through grace. He possesses grace in His own right from the fact that He is the Son of God by nature. Since our grace as adopted sons is created, the entire Trinity shares in it; whereas the Father alone is the origin of the sonship of Jesus. The sanctifying grace of Christ, therefore, derives in His soul from His quality as Son of God, and does not in any sense make Him an adopted son.

Certain theologians—such as Father Émile Mersch, S.J.—have thought that the grace of the Christian, because it is a participation in the grace of Christ, assimilates us in a special and wholly new way to the Son of God; and that from this point of view the grace of the Christian is specifically different from the grace of Adam. We do not think this is the correct approach. Grace remains a participation of the divine nature (II Peter 1:4). It is not specifically different in Adam and in ourselves; and it would not have been any more different if the Father or the Holy Ghost had become incarnate. The grace of the Christian is created, and it derives—as do all of God's external works—from the Trinity as a whole.

The advantage of the plan adopted by this theological study is that it makes the above distinction very clear by approaching the study of grace as distinct and separate from the treatise on Christ. The Three Persons cause grace in us by adopting us, the Three Persons give themselves to us as the object of our happiness and dwell in us simultaneously.

Are we then to say that "the Trinity is our Father"? In truth, as we have seen, our grace derives from the Trinity as a whole, and in this sense we are the sons of the Father, of the Son, and of the Holy Ghost. However, we still shall not say that "the Trinity is our Father." Why? Not because it isn't true, but because that is not the way the sacred writers from whom we get our divine knowledge usually express themselves. Let us try to understand that— we would not be truly theologizing if we were content merely to answer that we must not speak in that way because Scripture does not do so habitually; we must on the contrary seek to disclose the specific reason why Holy Scripture speaks the way it does.

The reason is that the divine Persons produce our grace and adoption, as they produce every other created thing, according to their mutual order and according to the mode that is *appropriate* to their personal character. St. Thomas says luminously: "Therefore adoption, though common to the whole Trinity, is appropriated to the Father as its author; to the Son, as its exemplar; to the Holy Ghost, as imprinting on us the likeness of this exemplar" (IIIa, q. 23, a. 2, ad 3). There would be no purpose in Scripture's "appropriating" the fatherhood of God so often and so expressively to the Father if we could not have some devotion in calling Him "our Father" in a special way.

Similarly, St. Paul's exhortation to us to be conformable to the image of the Son would be almost valueless if we could not consider Jesus as our model of sonship (cf. Rom. 8:29) before we considered Him as our Father.

Finally, Scripture's presentation of the affinities between the Holy Ghost and the life of the soul that loves the Father with filial love would be useless if we could not learn here and now to recognize the role and the Person of the Holy Spirit in all that is proper to Him and distinct from the other Persons. True, our understanding of this role is bound to be mysterious, hidden, and still very imperfect, but it will put us on the path of the perfect knowledge that will be given to us in the vision of the Three in heaven. This vision will certainly not be a "novelty" for those whom the

Three Divine Persons have thus initiated into their intimate life.

Therefore it is very useful and the highest wisdom, when we say the *Our Father*, to address ourselves to the Father of our Lord Jesus Christ, and always to pray the *Our Father* the way Christ does and in union with Him, in the Holy Spirit. When we pray in this way, we follow the practice of the Church, which is our teacher through her liturgy. It is certainly not forbidden to pray *also* to the Son alone, and to the Holy Ghost separately, but we must not seek to put any originality into such prayers. We must follow the discretion of the liturgy and not forget the distinctions in the origins and the missions of the Divine Persons as Scripture presents them to us.

Thus the grace that constitutes us the adopted sons of God is produced in us by the Father, the Son, and the Holy Ghost, according to the order of their origins and of their missions, and it makes us return to the Father according to the inverse order.

We should judge severely any theology that would stop before the fact that grace is equally produced by the Three Persons, and would induce its disciples to set aside the formulas or the ways of praying and of returning to God common to the sacred writers who were inspired by the Holy Ghost. Formulas such as "the Trinity, our Father," which are not traditional—and which are not in the style of the Apostolic letters—should *ordinarily* be avoided. On the other hand, formulas in which "God" unquestionably designates "the Father" are completely in harmony with similar formulas of St. Paul.

3. *Capital grace.* Actually, the individual grace of Christ and His capital grace are one and the same reality. But His individual grace designates the adornment of His soul, and His capital grace designates His power of universal influence, inasmuch as "of His fullness we have all received" (John 1:16).

On this point, we cannot compare the influence of Adam with that of Christ. Or at least, if we do compare them as St. Paul does in Romans 5:15, we must take into account the differences between them. Adam committed an actual, personal sin, whose sequel and consequence was original sin. Now, original sin passed into human nature through Adam's actual sin and is transmitted to us, together with our human nature, by way of generation.

The grace of Christ, on the other hand, does not come to us by way of nature. It comes to us solely through the personal action of

Christ. In Christ there are not two perfections, in the way that there were two imperfections in Adam. When the economy of the head of the race proved to be disastrous, God replaced it by an Economy of the Head in grace, the universal principle of the life of the sons of God, and this Head is not the head of the race. Grace is due to the soul of Christ as a connatural principle and as a natural property (in the sense defined above). Thus, all grace necessarily has its origin, its principle, and its eminent locus in the soul of Christ.

We have just said that Christ is our Head in grace. Let us pay careful attention to what the word "head" means. The Latin word for head is *caput,* which implies an organic relationship between the head and the members, and a like influence exerted by the head on the members. This meaning of the word "head" must be applied to Christ, when we speak of Him as our "Head."

The word "head," John of St. Thomas tells us, presupposes a conformity of nature, a connaturality, and it signifies a dignity of principle, of perfection, a function of active cause either through interior influence or through exterior direction. As for St. Thomas, he simply retained the three properties of the head in the human body, thus setting up three priorities: a priority of order (in the sense of being first in line); a priority of perfection (in the sense of a masterpiece—*chef-d'oeuvre*);[3] and a priority of activity as the source of influence (in the sense of the head of a nation or of an army, etc.).

Thus, Christ is our Head, and His grace is a "capital" grace (from the Latin *caput*): 1) because this grace comes first; 2) because this grace is perfect; and 3) because it is the cause from which supernatural life flows into all the members of the Church: the Blessed Virgin, angels, and men. The Church is not a body after the manner of a social or political body. As Cajetan tells us (*Tract. de fide et operibus,* cap. 9), the Church is a body whose organic unity is much closer to the unity of a natural body, for the Head of the Church quickens the members by His Spirit and unites them by His life-giving influence that makes the whole body grow.

But how can Christ in His humanity be the cause of grace? Is

---

[3] In English, the word "masterpiece" does not have its etymological origin in the word "head," whereas the French word "chef-d'oeuvre" is a derivative of the French word "chef" which in turn is derived from the Latin *caput.* (Translator's note.)

not God alone the cause of grace (see *Theology Library,* Vol. III, p. 387)? Before St. Thomas, the theologians of the twelfth and thirteenth centuries (and St. Thomas himself in his *Commentary on the Sentences*) held that the sacred humanity of our Savior *prepared* and *disposed* souls to receive grace. But the study of Greek sources, particularly St. Athanasius and St. Cyril, convinced St. Thomas that there is a much deeper and more mysterious communion between the divine and the human operations of Christ. And by means of his notion of instrumentality, St. Thomas was able (in the *Summa Theologiae*) to attribute the efficient causality of salvation to the Savior's humanity.

To sum up St. Thomas' view once again: The Godhead made use of the humanity as its *conjoined instrument* in the one Person of the Word, for the work of salvation. And Christ likewise makes use of the sacraments as *separated instruments,* or as prolongations of His humanity, to apply to men the effects of His redemptive work.

We have already noted briefly (see p. 90 above) how we could distinguish two "operations" in instances in which the principal agent and the instrument have diverse forms. When we apply this law to the present case, we ask what is the *operation that belongs properly* to the humanity of Christ in His different mysteries and what is the operation that belongs properly to the seven sacraments. In other words, what is the work that belongs properly to the principal salvific acts of Christ—His passion, death, descent into hell, His resurrection and ascension—in the divine operation that brought us salvation? And likewise, what is the proper and specific work of Baptism, Confirmation, the Eucharist, Penance, Extreme Unction, Holy Orders, and Matrimony?

A theology that sought to exalt the divine power at work through these instruments by minimizing the differences between the effects of these mysteries or of these sacraments would be detrimental to the reality of the *human* nature and *human* operations of Christ. It would be tempted—and already tainted—by Docetism.

On the other hand, a theology that tended to give greater attention to the particular form of each sacrament, to the point of seeing the efficacy of these sacraments only in the human gestures and the act of faith to which they give rise, would be detrimental to the primacy of the divine Power in whom "we live and move and have our being" (Acts 17:28) and whose efficacy infinitely surpasses that of our own acts. That is the temptation of Nestorianism and of certain theologies that unduly separate the two natures of Christ in their efforts to distinguish them.

We must therefore say at one and the same time (not separating these two affirmations): "Christ quickens us by His influence" *and*: "He is the object to which we cleave through this same influence."

Likewise, the sacraments are at one and the same time:

a) *Intentional* intermediaries, that is, signs that present salutary *objects* to us so that our hearts may cleave to them (the theological virtues) and so that we may externally accept them (the religious gestures of our profession of faith, repentance, charity, etc., in the sacrament)—and this aspect applies to the sacraments of the Old Law as well as to those of the New Law;

b) *Efficacious* intermediaries, that is, instruments of the sanctifying and life-giving activity of Christ—and this second aspect of the sacraments is a privilege applicable only to the sacraments of the New Law.

In other words, Christ makes contact with our hearts by the natural presentation—at once sensible, social, and human—of our objects of faith and our motives for believing; [4] and He makes contact with us by a divine mark that penetrates the very depths of our beings, the very root of our freedom and of our act of faith. The power of Christ does not suppress our personal acceptance through faith under the pretext that it is taking our faith into custody; on the contrary, His power enters into symbiosis with our acceptance through faith so as to bring it to fullest fruition.

We can judge the success of a theology by the way it discovers the *organic unity* of these two aspects: the objective presentation to our faith of the mystery or of the sacrament, and the instrumental efficacy of this mystery or of this sacrament—meanwhile recognizing the importance of each of them without detriment to the other.

Three Remarks

1. The function of Headship that belongs properly to Christ the man is exercised over our entire beings. The influence of Christ

[4] For example, in Baptism the object of faith presented to us consists in the death and the resurrection of Christ who saves us; and the motive for believing presented to us is God who speaks and reveals Himself to us through Christ.

is not exerted soul to soul, but man to man. The whole humanity of Christ is an instrument that derives its influence from its union with the Word of God—and this includes His body which is also united to the Word through the soul. And on the other hand, the grace of Christ makes contact with our souls in a very human way, through sensible sacraments, and, very humanly again, through the salvation of our whole beings. The grace of the Holy Ghost deposits in us the seed of the resurrection of our bodies.

2. Christ is the Head of all men, but by different rights and in varying degrees. This point will be developed in the chapter on the Church, but we can briefly cite St. Thomas Aquinas here:

> Christ is the Head of all men, but diversely. For, first and principally, He is the Head of such as are united to Him by glory (the blessed in heaven); secondly, of those who are actually united to Him by charity (whether they are living here on earth or are now in purgatory); thirdly, of those who are actually united to Him by faith (all believers who are in the state of mortal sin); fourthly, of those who are united to Him merely in potentiality which is not yet reduced to act, yet will be reduced to act according to divine predestination (the predestined); fifthly, of those who are united to Him in potentiality which will never be reduced to act. Such are those men . . . who . . . on their departure from this world, wholly cease to be members of Christ, as being no longer in potentiality to be united to Christ (IIIa, q. 8, a. 3, c.).

This method of presenting the hierarchy of the members of Christ made it possible for St. Thomas to include in the "Body of the Church" the just of the Old Covenant (same article, answer to the third objection).

We can easily see the difference in the meaning of the expression "Body of the Church" as used by St. Thomas and by many modern theologians. St. Thomas took the point of view of salvation and of the efficacy of Christ's work. In this sense, all who are united to Christ by faith benefit from His action and are in the Body of His Church. Modern theology, on the contrary, usually takes the point of view of the ecclesiastical institution founded on the objective faith (Revelation) received from Christ and from the Apostles, and on the sacraments of this faith. According to this second approach, only those belong to the Body of the Church who outwardly profess this faith, submitting to the same Creed and participating in the same sacraments. From this point of view, there will be among the saved some who do not belong to the Body of the Church, and some of those who belong to this Body may not be saved.

3. The comprehensiveness that we have seen in the word "head" —in Latin, *caput* (at once *head* and *governor*)—is totally justified when this word is applied to Christ. Christ is truly our *Head*, and He *governs* us universally, on His own authority. The title of head can be applied in the Church to others than Christ, but the word then ceases to have the same comprehensiveness. Neither the Pope nor the Bishops are our *Head*. They are only our governors, and in a doubly restricted sense: a) even the Pope does not govern by his own authority, for he is only the Vicar of Christ; b) his government is not universal, since it lasts only for the time of his pontificate, since he has real power only over baptized Christians, and since he is subject to the institutional norms established by Christ.

As for the devil or Anti-Christ, it would be improper to call him the "head" of the wicked from either point of view. Evil divides, and the wicked, far from forming a single body, are a multitude. It is closer to the truth to say that the devil is a tempter, a seducer, a deceiver, an instigator.

IX. THE STRENGTH AND THE WEAKNESSES OF CHRIST

The divine nature personally united to the human nature of the Savior gives to the latter a unique dignity and nobility. Are this dignity and nobility beyond measure, or do they remain within human bounds? Did Christ lack certain qualities and activities proper to man, by reason of the fact that His human nature subsists only in the Word of God? For example, even though Christ possessed infused knowledge, was He able to acquire certain information, just like any child or man, as He grew up and progressed in years? Could Christ be taught by His parents, by teachers? Can we say that Christ had faith? Hope? The virtue of repentance? Is it permissible to think that Christ could laugh? Why did He weep? How can we understand the fact that He prayed, since He was God? Was it fitting that Christ's life should be spent without sickness? Did Christ have, in addition to His rational will, a sensible will (or appetite)? How can we explain the free will of Christ, since it was not possible for Him to do wrong? How can we understand that Christ could have wanted anything different from what God willed ("Yet not as I will, but as Thou willest"

Mt. 26:39)? Was it possible for a conflict of wills to exist in Christ? Was the soul of Christ capable of doing all that it willed? In particular, was it able to work all the miracles it willed? And so on.

The reasons man can offer are trifling in the face of such a great mystery. The answers to these questions are likely to be futile unless they are founded first of all upon a careful reading of the Gospels. It is from the Gospels that we must learn how Christ actually acted while on earth. The theologian's role is not to invent these things, but simply to "understand" them rightly, that is to try to show the agreement of Christ's actions with what faith teaches about the twofold nature and about the personality of Jesus.

Without going into all of Jesus' actions, we shall simply note two different types of activity which He carried on:

On the one hand, Jesus looked, observed, questioned, investigated, and made decisions on the basis of the information He gained. He lived with others, apparently like all other men, sharing their condition, speaking their language. He was indebted to the fabric of relationships constituted by His environment and His epoch. Examples: Mk. 5:31-33—the miracle of the woman suffering with a hemorrhage. In this case Jesus looked around Him to see who had touched Him. Mk. 6:33-34—Jesus invited His Apostles to withdraw with Him to a desert place in order to rest, but many people guessed where He was going and came after Him. Then Jesus *had compassion upon them, and began to teach them.* Thus, He seemed to change His plans in view of unexpected circumstances. Mk. 10:21—the rich young man. Jesus listened to him, and then St. Mark tells us, looking upon him, loved him." Surely this was very human behavior.

But on the other hand, from the point of view of knowledge alone, Jesus gave evidence of mysterious powers. Examples: Jn. 1:50—Jesus had "seen" Nathanael before His eyes could rest upon him. Jn. 2:24—"But Jesus did not trust himself to them, in that he *knew* all men." Jn. 4:17-18—Jesus revealed the Samaritan woman's private life to her. Jn. 4:50—Jesus said to the centurion, "Go thy way, thy son lives." Jn. 7:15—"How does this man come by learning, since he has not studied?" And Jesus answered: "My teaching is not my own, but his who sent me." Jn. 6:46—". . . not that anyone has seen the Father except him who is from God, he has seen the Father."

Thus the psychology of Christ, seems to transcend history. Jesus was the one who saw God, who knew, who was aware, who revealed what He knew. But from another point of view the human soul of Christ would have been imperfect if it had not been endowed with a knowledge of its own which was connatural to it, and Christ would have possessed His human intellect to no purpose if He had not made use of His reason.

In its efforts to discern all the resources of knowledge which the soul of Christ possesses, theology must distinguish, first, the knowledge of vision. Without the beatific vision, Christ would simply have had *faith* in His divine Personality. He spoke otherwise. We must therefore recognize that He had the beatific vision. Besides it was fitting that He "who had brought many sons into glory" (Heb. 2:10) should know in advance the goal toward which He was leading us.

Secondly, infused knowledge. Actually beatific knowledge does not take the place of all natural knowledge of the intellect. On the contrary, the beatific vision presupposes and strengthens nature. It was fitting that the soul of Christ, hypostatically united to the Word should receive certain intellectual communications directly from the Word. Thus we see that He knew Scripture without having learned it.

Thirdly, innate knowledge. This is the knowledge we do not receive from the outside, but which we possess from the very fact that we have an intellect. It is something we possess at birth, but it can increase. Such for example is the knowledge of all first principles, e.g. "A thing cannot be and not be at the same time in the same way." Of course, in addition to this knowledge, Christ also had the knowledge of vision which was likewise innate.

Finally, acquired or experimental knowledge. This explains the words of St. Paul to the Hebrews: "He . . . learned obedience from the things that He suffered" (Heb. 5:8). From this last point of view, the knowledge of Christ could progress, and it did progress effectively through the images or contacts of His sensible experience. But Christ, the universal Doctor of the human race, had nothing to learn either from His parents (the Blessed Virgin, on the contrary, had much to learn from Him) or from any man.

With regard to the power of Christ, theology shows the agreement between faith and evangelical *fact* through the help of a twofold principle:

1. Christ is a man and "it was right that he should in all things be made like unto his brethren" (Heb. 2:17).

2. The human soul of Christ can be considered in two ways: either in itself, or as the instrument of the Godhead that makes use of it. But if the operation that emanates from Christ's soul exceeds its natural powers, then the effect of this operation must be attributed strictly to God and not to Christ's soul. In virtue of these principles we can say that the soul of Christ was not all-powerful, since this privilege belongs only to God. We can also say that Christ's soul did not have all power over creatures or even over His own body, because that is not natural to the human soul. And yet we can say that Christ's soul could do all that it wanted, for it never wanted anything that did not befit it. (Mk. 7:24 and Mt. 9:30-31 are to be explained in this sense.)

It should be noted that the efficacy of Christ's will did not prevent Him from praying. Christ obtained what He wanted because His will was "reasonable" and He never wanted anything that was not wise. Christ also prayed because His will was well-ordered, that is, always obedient to God. He prayed visibly, as an example to us.

Finally, with regard to the weaknesses of our Savior, we must distinguish between the corporeal, emotional, and spiritual weaknesses.

1. Bodily weaknesses. It was fitting that the body assumed by the One who had come to take charge of us and to save us should be subject to corporeal infirmities. But in Him these infirmities were not the consequence of original sin. He assumed them voluntarily. Besides, He assumed only the infirmities that are common to all (and sickness is not among them), and those that entail no spiritual infirmity. Thus Christ experienced hunger, thirst, fatigue, the extremes of heat and cold, inclement weather, blows, bruises, and death. None of these things were punishments in His case, because He willed them.

2. Spiritual and emotional weaknesses.

A. Christ never committed the slightest sin. This would have been impossible for the One who was the God-man and whose function was to be the Savior. We must understand the words "He made Him to be sin" (II Cor. 5:21) in the sense of a personal and relative appropriation, that is of an attribution to the Head of what belongs only to the members, the Head taking the place of the others out of affection and sympathy.

B. Nor was there in Christ, as there is in all other men born of Adam, a source of immoderate desires. For in Him everything was harmoniously and hierarchically subject to superior power.

C. There was no ignorance in Christ.

D. But the soul of Christ experienced those passions natural to man that are good: Christ knew sensible pain, fear, anguish, sadness, joy, surprise, and anger.

While we may not find an explanation for all of Christ's strengths and weaknesses, their simultaneous and harmonious coexistence accords with our faith in a Savior who was at once a wayfarer and a possessor of the beatific vision (*viator* and *comprehensor*). Christ was a *comprehensor,* that is the possessor of the eternal happiness for which we are striving and hoping, inasmuch as He was one Person with the Word. That is why He possessed neither faith nor hope. But Christ was also a *viator,* that is, in progress toward this beatitude; although He possessed the beatific vision, His passible, corruptible, human nature, subject to painful impressions from the outside, still lacked many things.

Indeed, metaphysics and psychology always fall short of fathoming Christ. Since theology came of age in the twelfth and thirteenth centuries, it has used Aristotelian philosophy almost exclusively. It may be that certain modern philosophies of existence or of the "I" may, without losing anything that has been acquired through Aristotelian philosophy, bring new and as yet unexploited resources to theology. The fact remains that these new philosophies represent a new departure for the theologian, and consequently one that is not without risk.

X. OUR ADORATION OF CHRIST AND OUR DEVOTIONS TO HIM

Theology must not be content with giving us a sound understanding of the mystery of Christ in terms of our faith. Granted what we know about Christ, theology must also dictate to us the proper attitudes we must take in our relationships with Him, and it must pass judgment on the "devotions" prevalent among the faithful.

The principle that must govern our attitude is the following: Since we recognize a single Person in Christ, we must render one and the same identical worship to the humanity and to the divinity of our Savior. But inasmuch as there are two natures in this one Person, our "motives of homage" may be distinct.

Theology attempts to clarify what this single worship must be by making the distinction between the worship of adoration, the worship of *latria,* and the worship of *dulia.* The Latin word *adoratio* (adoration) has a rather flexible meaning in the usage of the Church. Originally, it seems to have designated simply a certain bodily gesture: a total prostration, the most total exterior humiliation possible. Thus Nathan came before King David and "worshipped" him (III Kings 1:23). That is to say, he prostrated himself before the king, with his face against the earth as a mark of homage.

And it is precisely because there is no more perfect way to express reverence and exterior submission, that this gesture is most appropriate in the presence of God, and that it began to be reserved for God alone. It is in this sense that Mardochai refused to "worship" Aman (Esther 3:2). The gesture of adoration or worship could have been appropriate either for God or for creatures; and yet as soon as it became the expression of a *total* interior homage (spiritual adoration), it could fittingly be applied only to God.

The words *latria* and *dulia* have the same meaning etymologically, and signify a kind of servitude. But the usage of the Church has given them different meanings. The worship of *latria* is that which is addressed to God alone; the worship of *dulia* is addressed to creatures. Highest among creatures, we honor and venerate the Blessed Virgin Mary, Mother of God, with a worship of *hyperdulia.*

Thus, the worship we must render to the sacred humanity of the Savior is the worship of *latria,* since worship is addressed to the Person and we honor only one Person in Christ. We must therefore adore the human nature of Christ with the worship of *latria* because it is the human nature of the Word. And in like manner, we must adore His flesh and His wounds.

However, we may ask ourselves what our reason is for adoring the one Person of Christ. This is called the motive of homage. Inasmuch as Christ has two natures, we can have two motives of homage in worshipping Him. Thus, we can honor a king because of his supreme authority over the whole kingdom, and also respect him for his excellent qualities as a fencer or a horseman. Likewise.

we can honor the one Person of Christ in His divinity or in His human nature. The second motive of homage would be the basis for worship of *dulia*—or more precisely, in view of the fact that His human perfections are the highest conceivable, worship of *hyperdulia*.

It is important to note that the second form of worship of Christ is legitimate only if it does not exclude the first. The worship of *hyperdulia* must presuppose the worship of *latria* (for the perfections of Christ's human nature derive from its union to the Godhead); and such worship must not be separated from the worship of *latria*. For in very truth there is only one reality, one Person in Christ. It would be heresy (Nestorianism) to have two kinds of worship for Christ. And yet when we adore Christ, we can *add* a second motive of homage in consideration of His human perfections.

In order to avoid possible errors, the Church has not authorized the official worship of *hyperdulia* as applied to Christ. As Father Héris writes: "The danger would lie in going no further than this inferior veneration, in seeing only the man in Christ and forgetting that He is God. The believer must therefore consider the humanity of Christ first and above all in its union to the Word . . . Once this is granted, all sentiments of admiration, veneration, and praise for the created perfections of Jesus are permissible: but these sentiments are simply added to the essential worship, completing and perfecting it in a more or less explicit manner" (*Le Verbe incarné,* Vol. III, pp. 323-324).

The worship we render to the images of the Savior or to His Cross also calls for explanation. It is true that we worship them with the worship of *latria*. The reason for this is that through images our intellect turns with a single movement to the original which they represent. The function of an image is always to refer us to something other than itself.

The Cross of Christ is a case in point. It represents Christ crucified. When we honor His Cross we are addressing our homage to Christ Himself. When we adore relics of the true Cross, we have additional motives of homage.

As we know, the worship of images gave rise to violent and bloody quarrels in the East, particularly at the time of Emperor Leo III, the Iconoclast (717–740). It seems that the religious influence of the Moslems played some part in instigating these iconoclastic quarrels. It is significant that the Church reacted, as was her privilege, on behalf of the law of the Incarnation, according to which God became one of us and allowed Himself to be seen, heard, approached, and touched. In view of this, the Church does not fear to nurture the nearness of Christ among the faithful through the greatest possible use of images. Moreover, images instruct the uneducated and rekindle religious fervor.

Among the various devotions to Christ, the Church encourages Christians to honor in particular the *Precious Blood,* the *Five Wounds,* and the *Sacred Heart.* Certain other devotions, such as devotion to the Sacred Head (Decree of the Holy Office, June 18, 1938), have been set aside.

The history of devotion to the Sacred Heart is a long one, and it is still being written. In the early days, the Fathers, following St. John, liked to consider the wound in Christ's Side from which came forth "the sacraments that fashion the Church" (the water and the blood). Their motive of homage was more specifically the constitution of this Church in which we have found life through Christ's sacrifice. Certain medieval mystics, like St. Mechthild and St. Gertrude, contemplated, within the wound, the heart wounded and broken through its excessive love. In the seventeenth century, St. Margaret Mary stressed Jesus' love for us. The Sacred Heart, the sign of this twofold love, divine and human, may be said to embody all devotions, all mysteries, and all feasts. Monsieur Olier and St. John Eudes were attracted to the interior life of Jesus. A discussion of all these matters will be found in "Le mystère du Sacré-Coeur," in *La Vie Spirituelle* for June, 1952 (by A. Viard, Ch.-V. Héris, J. Jacques, P. Démann, J.-A. Robilliard, etc.)

XI. THE MOTIVE AND FITNESS OF THE INCARNATION

This is undoubtedly the first question that theology must grapple with. Before an artisan undertakes a given work, he asks himself if it is fitting to perform this work, and the motive for it. Likewise, in seeking to enter into the views that determine God's initiatives, the theologian should begin his study of the Incarnation by inquiring into its motive.

But this question is the boldest of them all. It compels us to open the impenetrable sanctuary of God's own thoughts and affections, and we cannot gain even the slightest access to it except through the preliminary consideration of the divine works. It is therefore legitimate for us, who are on the level of believers, to approach the theology of the motive of the Incarnation only at the end of our study. That is what we are doing.

Is it fitting that God should become incarnate? Supreme audacity of the theologian who would scrutinize what is or is not fitting to God Himself! Actually, this is not exactly the question before us. The Incarnation is fitting to God, inasmuch as God did become incarnate. Fortunately, the theologian's purpose is an humbler one. His faith, eager for vision, wants to perceive reasons, or at least coherences, harmonies, and it asks itself how it can find in the nature of God something that makes the Incarnation supremely fitting.

A preliminary question might be asked, namely whether the Incarnation is possible? And this was the question that certain theologians of the twelfth and thirteenth centuries, before St. Thomas, actually asked themselves. But when we ask, with St. Thomas, whether it is fitting that God should become incarnate, the possibility of the Incarnation is thereby taken for granted.

The coherence that theology is seeking here finds magnificent support in the theme of goodness: since it is of the nature of goodness to communicate itself, it is fitting that God, who is good, should communicate Himself supremely to His creatures. And since on the other hand the Incarnation represents the supreme communication of God to His creatures, it is supremely "fitting."

We see the scope of the argument: the theologian is not searching for a necessity, but for a fitness. God is free. He is under no necessity whatever to become incarnate, but it *befits* His infinite goodness that He should do so. Since "goodness tends to diffuse itself" there is no better way God can show forth His goodness than by giving Himself to His creatures as totally as possible, that is, by becoming incarnate.

Let us go one step further. So far, we have considered only the nature of God. Let us now look at the human creature to whom God wants to unite Himself.

It so happens that man has sinned and that the calamity of sin cries out for the goodness and mercy of God. It was fitting that God should raise up fallen man. It was particularly fitting to God, for He thus showed forth His mercy and His wisdom. But it was also fitting to man, who is capable of being raised up again. It would have been less fitting—if it had been fitting at all—that God should assume an angelic nature, incapable of improvement or of half-measures. An angel either sets himself against God instantaneously by a mortal sin, or he keeps his state of grace perfectly. An angel commits no venial sins; he makes his ultimate choice once and for all. Finally, the Incarnation of God was fitting to the perfection of the universe, of which man is in a sense the supreme achievement.

Certainly, there were several possible ways of raising up fallen man and of saving him. The Incarnation was one of them. It was not necessary. There would have been no injustice if God had forgiven without demanding any satisfaction. But if He wanted justice that would satisfy Him *ex condigno,* condignly, then God had to become man. Through the Incarnation, the salvation that God brought to man showed forth not only His mercy but also His supereminent justice. He likewise signified the dignity which He wanted man to have, by giving him the power to *redeem himself.* Thus, the Incarnation was necessary for the perfect Redemption upon which God had decided and that can be formulated as follows: no forgiveness without satisfaction on the part of man.

Does this mean that if man had not sinned God would perhaps have become incarnate anyway? This is a burning question, that has been considerably embittered by the quarrels of theologians since Duns Scotus. Ruppert of Deutz, in the twelfth century, answered this question affirmatively. Albert the Great, in the thirteenth century, also answered in the affirmative. St. Bonaventure expounded the reasons for and against, and finally answered in the negative. St. Thomas Aquinas hesitated. In his commentary on St. Paul, he said that it was a useless question, "because God ordained that things should be done in accordance with what they had become. We do not know what He would have ordained if He had not foreseen sin; and yet authorized Scripture seems to say that He would not have become incarnate if man had not sinned. And I am inclined to agree with this view" (*In I Tim. 1:15*).

Until the thirteenth century the thought of the sacred writers, of the Fathers, and of the theologians seems to have been unanimous: Scripture presents Jesus to us as the One who came *to save us.* (Cf. Lk. 5:32; 19:10; Mt. 18:11; Jn. 3:17; Gal. 4:5; I Tim 1:15.) The *motive* for which God actually came into the world is our salvation.

That is precisely what St. Thomas Aquinas said: God alone can reveal to us the *motive* of His supreme gift, and He has told us and shown us by His very works that this motive is our redemption. But the fact that the Word became incarnate to save us does not make Him any less the end for which all things exist. Whatever the particular *motive* for which He came, inasmuch as He did actually come He is evidently the *end* of all created things. He could have come without any motive, or with a different motive, and He would still have been the end of creation. And yet we have never been told that He would have come whether we had sinned or not. That depends entirely upon His free choice.

Duns Scotus, on the contrary, and all Scotists after him, think that God's decision is unconditioned. Practically all Franciscans hold this view, in opposition to their own St. Bonaventure. The Scotist view is that Christ is willed absolutely, because God loves Himself and wants to be loved by someone outside Himself who can love Him as much as He deserves to be loved. In taking this approach the Scotists end by untying the knot of the Incarnation-Redemption, which is so strong in the New Testament and in traditional theology, in favor of another relationship: *Creation-Incarnation*. As they see it, even prior to its redemptive aspect, the Incarnation constitutes the created order in which God is most loved.

Moreover, this thesis is open to a number of objections: 1) It lacks the support of Tradition. 2) It tends to reverse the order of values between sanctifying grace and the grace of union (as we have shown, the greatest thing about Christ's soul is not His love for God; the habitual grace from which this love flows is itself an emanation of the grace of union). 3) It tends to place the Redemption and the Cross in the rank of secondary functions. 4) It presents a Man-God who is distinct from the human race, whereas in fact God communicates Himself totally and Christ is the *Head* of all men. 5) This is an a priori thesis concerning only what we can know through God's words and works.

On the other hand, we must agree with the Scotists and the Thomists (as against any false and narrow interpretation of Thomism) that: 1) Christ is the one who receives the greatest gift from God, who is most loved by Him, and who offers Him supreme worship and love. 2) Christ is the source of all graces for the elect, whose holiness brings glory to Him. 3) Christ is the cause (exemplary, efficient, and final) of our predestination. 4) Christ is the end of the order of grace.

On these questions, read the authoritative presentation by Father Ch.-V. Héris, *Le motif de l'Incarnation* (Auxerre, 1939).

XII. THE DELAY OF THE INCARNATION

If God came for our salvation, how is it that He came so late? And now that He has come, why must we wait centuries until salvation is universally manifested in its glory? These are questions concerning the *time* of salvation.

As for the time before Christ, theology finds an answer in Scripture, especially in Gal. 4:4: "When the fullness of time came . . ." and explains the delay by the principle of the necessary *preparation* of the human race and the correlative preparation of divine teaching.

As for the time after Christ, New Testament writings often present it as a time of repentance ("Repent, for the kingdom of God is at hand"). It is the role of theology to apply this theme of repentance to the delayed manifestation. The time left to the Church is a respite given to men so that they may repent and come back to God with Christ.

But what is the significance of the universe after Christ? St. Paul says: "Creation was made subject to vanity . . . in hope, because creation itself also will be delivered from its slavery to corruption into the freedom of the glory of the sons of God" (Rom. 8:20-21). What, then, is the meaning of the material world which we are using? Must everything pass through the fire? Does not the labor of Christians engaged in temporal tasks simply increase or improve the volume of what must pass through the flood of fire? On this subject, read P.-A. Liégé, "Incarnation et transcendance" (Supplément, *Équipes enseignantes,* Third Quarter, 1952–1953, pp. 3-7). Here are to be found a few simple principles concerning a subject that is less than simple.

BIBLIOGRAPHY *

The bibliography for the life and historicity of Christ is given at the end of Chapter II. Only those works are listed here that concern the mystery of the Incarnation—the mystery of the union of two natures in one Person.

The history of the dogma of the Incarnation:

Grandmaison, Leonce de, S.J. *Jesus Christ, His Person, His Message, His Credentials.* 3 vols. New York: Sheed and Ward, 1930–1934.

Lebreton, Jules, S.J. *History of the Dogma of the Trinity,* vol. I, "The Origins." London: Burns, Oates and Washbourne, 1939.

The encyclopedia *Le Christ* (Paris: Bloud and Gay, 1946) should be consulted, as well as works on patrology and the history of the Church.

* The bibliographies in this volume have been translated from the French, with the substitution of English titles wherever possible. Additional entries in English have also been made.

Important exegetical works:

Allo, B. *Le scandale de Jésus.* Paris: Grasset, 1927.
Braun, F. *Où en est le problème de Jésus.* Paris: Gabalda, 1932.
————. *Jésus* (history and criticism). Tournai: Casterman.
Guitton, Jean. *The Problem of Jesus* (Divinity and Resurrection). New York: Kenedy, 1955.
Lemonnyer, A. *Notre Christ.* Paris: Desclée, 1914.
Lepin, M. M. *Le Christ Jésus* (His historical existence and Divinity). Paris: Bloud and Gay, 1929.

The theology of the Incarnation:

Bouessé, H. *Le Sauveur du monde* and *Le Mystère de l'Incarnation,* in vol. IV, Coll. *Doctrina Sacra.* Chambery: Collège théol. dominicain, 1953.
Dewailly, L. M. *Jésus-Christ, Parole de Dieu.* Paris: Cerf, 1945.
Galtier, P. *L'unité du Christ.* Paris: Beauchesne, 1939.
Gaudel, A. *Le Mystère de l'Homme-Dieu.* 2 vols. Paris: Bloud and Gay, 1939.
Heris, C. V., O.P. *The Mystery of Christ.* Westminster, Md.: Newman, 1950.
Joret, D. *Par Jésus-Christ Notre-Seigneur.* Paris: Desclée, 1925.
Montcheuil, Yves de, S.J. *Le Christ.* Paris: Centre univ. Cath., 1944.
————. *Leçons sur le Christ.* Paris: Éd. de l'épi.
Mugnier, F. *Roi, prophète, prêtre avec le Christ.* Paris: Lethielleux.
Schwalm, P. *Le Christ d'après saint Thomas d'Aquin.* Paris: Lethielleux, 1910.
Thomas Aquinas, St. "The Mystery of the Incarnation," in *Summa Theol.,* III, 1-26.
Vonier, Dom A., O.S.B. "The Personality of Christ," in vol. I, *Collected Works.* Westminster, Md.: Newman, 1952.

Christological heresies in general:

Gaudel, A. *Le Mystère de l'Homme Dieu,* vol. I, pp. 162-173; vol. II, pp. 6-50.
Riedmatten, H. de, O.P. *Les Actes de Paul de Samosate. Étude sur la christologie du IIe au IVe siècle.* Fribourg, 1952.
Tixeront, Joseph A. *History of Dogmas.* 3 vols. St. Louis: Herder, 1921.
Le Christ, Encyclopédie populaire des connaissances religieuses. Paris: 1935. Contains an excellent summary, "Le dogme christologique du IIe au IVe siècle," by G. Bardy, pp. 393-415; and "Les grandes controverses christologiques," by E. Amann, pp. 416-440.

Particular heresies:

Bardy, G. *Paul de Samosate. Étude historique.* Louvain-Paris: 1929 (see Riedmatten's critique).
Jugie, M. *Nestorius et la controverse nestorienne.* Paris: 1912.
Lebon, J. *Le monophysisme sévérien.* Louvain: 1909.
Nestorius. *Le livre d'Héraclide de Damas.* Paris: 1910.
Voisin, G. *L'apollinarisme.* Louvain-Paris: 1901.
For the controversy over *baslisme,* see the extensive bibliography given by D. Diepen in *Revue Thomiste,* 1949, p. 431, n. 1.
For a sympathetic treatment of the Christology of P. Deodat de Basly, see A. Gaudel's "La Théologie de l'Assumptus Homo" in *Revue des Sciences Religieuses,* 1937 and 1938.
See the list of the works by D. Diepen in *Revue Thomiste,* 1949, pp. 433-434.

The Christ of the royal portal of the Cathedral of Chartres (twelfth century).

The triumphal theme of *Christ the Pantocrator* that we first saw in the East in the fifth and sixth centuries was carried on into the Middle Ages, inspiring the Romanesque sculpture and painting of the twelfth century in France. It culminated in this royal portal of Chartres in one of the most powerful creations of the French Middle Ages.

This is the Christ of the Apocalypse. He is holding the sealed book which is the book of life, and he is surrounded by the four winged animals that represent the Evangelists.

The oval in which Christ is placed is called the mandorla. In medieval symbolism it is the sign of glory, just as the cruciform halo is the sign of divinity, and the simple halo the sign of holiness. The mandorla is to be found in all artistic representations of Christ from the tenth to the twelfth century, since their themes are always glorious. There is the theme of the Apocalyptic vision (Moissac, Saint-Sernin, Carennac, Saint-Trophime d'Arles, Charlieu, Chartres, etc.); the theme of the Ascension (Cahors, Angoulême, Montceaux, l'Étoile, Anzy-le-duc); the theme of the Last Judgment Conques, Autun); the theme of the Transfiguration (La Charité-sur-Loire); and the theme of the Apostles' Mission on Pentecost (Vézelay).

Neither the mandorla nor the nimbus are medieval creations. The Greeks already surrounded the heads of their gods with halos to distinguish them from other men. We also find the nimbus in the earliest representations of the Greek Buddha in India.

The mandorla appeared in the Syrian and Byzantine manuscripts that inspired the Romanesque artists. It also surrounded the Christ in majesty of the fresco of Baouit (Egypt, circa fifth century), and the Christ of the Ascension on the phials of Monza (circa 600), which reproduce the mosaics of the Palestinian basilicas.

Chapter II

THE LIFE OF JESUS

by A. M. Henry, O.P.

117

Chapter II

THE LIFE OF JESUS

In our first chapter we considered the mystery of the God-man, that is, the mystery of one Person—the Person of Christ—who is both man and God. In a certain sense, a study such as that, made outside of time and history, does not suffice. The Word was made flesh, and dwelt among us. He has a history. We must now follow Jesus in the course of His earthly life from His conception to His resurrection, and up until the moment when He consummated the work of our salvation at the right hand of His Father.

I. THE CONCEPTION

Mary conceived in her womb, not by man but by the Holy Spirit. St. Luke assures us of this in his record of the dialogue between the Angel Gabriel and Mary. After the angel had announced to Mary that she would conceive and bring forth a son, she answered: "How shall this happen, since I do not know man?" (Lk. 1:34). Mary had already made up her mind to remain a virgin consecrated to the Lord God. And the angel said to her: "The Holy Spirit shall come upon thee and the power of the Most High shall overshadow thee" (Lk. 1:35). Thus, it was the Holy Spirit who took the initiative. It is of Him that the work of the Incarnation is predicated by appropriation.

However, let us not say that the Holy Spirit is the Father of Jesus, or that He was the Spouse of the Blessed Virgin Mary. Scripture, which is our only guide to the understanding of this mystery, does not say anything of the sort. The Father of our Lord Jesus Christ is God the Father.

Since the Incarnation is an exterior work of God, the Three Persons necesarily had an equal part in it, each according to His order. We must even affirm that their operation is indivisible. The Three Persons brought about the union of the human nature with the Word of God in Mary's womb. And yet in revealing the Incarnation to us, Scripture has *appropriated* it to the Holy Spirit, inasmuch as it usually attributes to Him the works of life, power,

118

and miracles. By appropriation, the Holy Spirit is the source of life. That does not mean that the Father and the Son are not equally the source of life. It simply means that the Holy Spirit is the source of life in a special, incommunicable way which still escapes our comprehension, but that already helps us to know Him in the familiar and intimate way we shall know Him in Eternity.

II. THE BIRTH

This is the same mystery under another aspect. The Word was born a second time. His first birth is eternal, divine, spiritual. It has neither a before nor an after, neither beginning nor end. His second birth was temporal and according to the flesh. St. Cyril of Alexandria says: "He was born according to the flesh" (Ep. 4), in a text canonized by the Council of Ephesus (Part I, Chapter 8), "because for us and for our salvation He united to Himself according to His Person that which was human and proceeded from woman." Although there is only one Person in Christ, we must say that He was born twice, because He has two natures.

Theologians have asked themselves whether it can be said that there are "two sonships" in Christ. This expression actually seems to have a Nestorian flavor, and we must put it to the test. This we shall do by distinguishing the *subject* of the sonship from its *cause*. If we consider the subject—or the term—of the filiation, that is, of the twofold relationship of Jesus to the Father and to Mary, we must say that it is absolutely unique. In this sense, there is only one sonship, since there is only one Person, eternally begotten by the Father and temporally brought forth by Mary. If on the other hand we consider the cause of the filiation, then we must say that there are two sonships just as there are two natures. It is the same as if the father of a family added adopted children to his own children, and thus acquired two "paternities."

Moreover, we must make it clear that the filial relation of Jesus to His Father is a "relation of reason" (see Lexicon), and not a real relation; for any relationship that is applied to God for a temporal reason does not posit anything real in God. And yet we can say that Jesus is really the son of Mary, inasmuch as Mary is really His mother (Mary's motherhood implies a real relation proceeding from herself to Jesus). Thus we say that God is really the Lord, by reason of the fact that creatures are really subject to Him.

We must never question the physical and biological reality of

Jesus' mysterious birth. The Blessed Virgin can truly be called the Mother of God because she brought forth, if we may say so, God Himself. The fact that she gave God only His human nature, and obviously not His Godhead, does not exempt us from calling her the Mother of God. For motherhood, no less than sonship, can be attributed only to the person (and not to the nature), and in Christ there is a single Person in two natures.

The same grace of union that made the Word of God man in the Incarnation also made Mary His divine Mother. We have already seen what flows from this grace of union in Christ (Chapter I, above). We shall also see the effects upon Mary of her divine maternity (Chapter IV, below).

III. THE EPIPHANY

The salvation Christ has brought us concerns all men, whatever their condition. And so it was fitting that the birth of Jesus, humble as it was, should be immediately made manifest to the representatives of all peoples and all conditions: Jews and pagans, shepherds and kings. St. Augustine tells us: "The shepherds were Israelites, the Magi were Gentiles (that is, members of the pagan nations). The former were neighbors, the latter lived far away. Both Israelites and Gentiles came together at the cornerstone" (*Sermon 202* on the Epiphany).

IV. THE CIRCUMCISION

St. Thomas Aquinas finds no less than seven reasons why Christ chose to be circumcised: 1. To prove the reality of His human flesh, against the heresiarchs: the Manichaeans, the Apollinarians, and the Valentinians. 2. To ratify the circumcision instituted earlier by God Himself. 3. To show that He was of the race of Abraham, who had received the command to be circumcised as a sign of his faith in Christ. 4. To prevent the Jews from not receiving Him under the pretext that He had not been circumcised. 5. To enjoin us to practice the virtue of obedience after His example: He was circumcised on the eighth day, as the law prescribed. 6. So as not to reject the remedy by which the body of sin was usually purified, once He had assumed this body of sin, or at least its exact likeness. 7. To liberate others from the burden of the law, by taking this burden upon Himself, in accordance with St. Paul's words: "God sent his Son, . . . born under the Law, that he might redeem those who were under the Law" (Gal. 4:4-5).

In a more general way, Christ willed to be born under the law so as to redeem those who were under the law and so that the justification of the law might be "accomplished" in His members. That is why He also wanted to be presented in the Temple and why He willed that His Mother should fulfill the observances of the law forty days after His birth, even though she had no need of purification. Jesus came not to triumph over the enemies of Israel by working wonders of all kinds, but to redeem sinners by His patience and by His death. It was fitting, therefore, that He should conform until death to the devout practices of the Israelites.

V. BAPTISM

Each of Christ's mysteries teaches its own lesson and brings its own grace. His baptism was no exception.

The liturgy (Paschal Vigil) points out that when Christ went into the Jordan He sanctified all the waters by which we would be baptized. In a more general way, Christ, through His own baptism, wanted to raise baptism to the stature of a sacrament.

In primitive symbolism, the waters are the seat of the Dragon, that is, of the Evil One, the Emperor of death and of the Powers of darkness. When Christ went into the waters, He symbolically crushed the Dragon and prophetically conquered death (and together with it the sins for which death is the punishment).

John's baptism also teaches other lessons: From the moment of His baptism, Christ manifested Himself as the Son of God, filled with the Holy Spirit; He gave us an example to accustom us to baptism, and at the same time officially accredited the prophetic and preparatory mission of John the Baptist. In a homily on John 3:34, Scotus Eriugena says very cogently: "We can compare the benefit that the catechumens derive from the teachings of the faith before their baptism to the good that John's baptism wrought in men before the baptism of Christ. John preached penance, announced the baptism of Christ, and drew men to the knowledge of the truth that has been manifested to the world. Likewise, the ministers of Christ begin by teaching, and then point out sins and promise their remission in the baptism of Christ."

John's baptism was only preparatory. It was not the baptism in the Spirit that Christ came to being. Therefore, those whom

John had baptized had to be baptized anew after the Resurrection (Cf. Acts 19:1 ff.).

To sum up, the reason Christ willed to be baptized when He obviously had no need of it was to induce men to receive the baptism of which they were in dire need.

St. Ambroise has said: "Let no one exempt himself from the bath of grace, since Christ did not exempt Himself from the bath of penance" (*In Luc.*, 3:21).

VI. THE DAILY LIFE AND BEHAVIOR OF JESUS

The Word was made flesh and dwelt among us. How did He react to society, law, and custom? Did He prefer the solitary life to the public life, or vice versa? Did He practice austerities, or live a simple life without austerities? Did He prefer poverty or comfort? Obviously, it is in the Gospel that we must seek answers to these questions. But even when he possesses the answers, the believer will still have the deep-seated need of understanding and of inquiring into the "reasons" behind the answers.

Now, we see that except for a few rare manifestations, at His birth and in the Temple, Christ led a hidden life until His baptism by John, which inaugurated His public life. We see, too, that this public life began by a forty-day retreat in the desert, and that afterwards He interrupted His public life from time to time by periods of solitude. Isidore tells us that our Lord had three kinds of refuge: "Boats, mountains, and the desert, and it was to one of these that He went each time He was pressed by the crowd" (*De vet. et nov. test.*, q. 36, No. 50).

Likewise, we see that Jesus led a life of perfect chastity, preserving continence and counseling others to do the same (Mt. 19:12). And yet He does not seem to have led a particularly austere life. John the Baptist "had a garment of camel's hair and a leathern girdle about his loins, and his food was locusts and wild honey" (Mt. 3:4); he came "neither eating nor drinking" (Mt. 11:18), whereas "the Son of Man came eating and drinking, and they say, 'Behold a glutton and a wine-drinker, a friend of publicans and sinners!'" (Mt. 11:19). Jesus sat at table not only with the "perfect" but also with sinners: "And it came to pass as he was at table in the house, that, behold, many publicans and sinners came to the table with Jesus and his disciples" (Mt. 9:10), and He accepted the invitation of Simon the Pharisee "to dine with him"

(Lk. 7:36) quite as well as the invitation to the marriage feast of Cana.

There was surprise among the Jews that the disciples of John the Baptist and the Pharisees fasted, whereas neither Jesus nor His disciples did (Mt. 9:14; Mk. 2:18; Lk. 5:33). And yet, after His baptism, He fasted "forty days and forty nights" (Mt. 4:2) in the desert. Nor did He have a "comfortable life, though He seems to have held to a certain moderation even in this. In the apostolic band, a fund of money had been set up, and Judas was in charge of it (Jn. 13:29). There were also a few women who provided for them "out of their means" (Lk. 8:3). Finally, Jesus liked to withdraw from time to time among his friends in Bethany (Lk. 10:38; Mk. 11:11; Mt. 21:17).

We see that Jesus conformed in all things with the requirements of the Mosaic Law, and even taught that He had "not come to destroy, but to fulfill" (Mt. 5:17). And yet on certain occasions He acted as if He were above the law. Thus, He worked cures on the Sabbath (Mk. 3:4-5; Lk. 14:3-4; Jn. 5:9); He allowed His disciples to pluck ears of grain on the Sabbath (Mt. 12:1; Mk. 2:23; Lk. 6:1); He corrected the disciples' legalistic conception of pure and impure foods (Mt. 15:11); He publicly justified His attitude concerning the Sabbath (Jn. 7:23) in spite of the fact that the Pharisees considered Him a man who did not keep the Sabbath (Jn. 9:16).

The explanation of these various attitudes is to be found in the goal our Savior had set for Himself, that is in His mission. For it was His mission that determined His goal.

He Himself has told us that He came "to bear witness to the truth" (Jn. 18:37), or to preach (Lk. 4:18, 43). Obviously, neither preaching, nor teaching, nor bearing witness are compatible with a solitary life. People had to hear Him, to learn from His gestures and attitudes, to see the kind of a life He led and to follow its example. They had to be stirred by His miracles that confirmed His doctrine and His testimony. And yet Christ did not always appear in public. Sometimes He would slip away alone or with His Apostles either to get some rest and renew His energies (Mk. 6:31), to pray (Lk. 6:12), or again, apparently, to flee from the adulation of men (Jn. 6:15). All this was for our instruction.

Christ also came to save sinners (cf. I Tim. 1:15). In this, too, the public life fitted His purpose better than a retired and hidden life. Like a good shepherd who goes out to seek his lost sheep, like a good doctor who visits his patient, He gave us the example of real solicitude.

But healing us was not everything. Jesus also wanted to bring us back to the Father (see Rom. 5:2). This purpose demanded that He should live among men, and attract them by giving them confidence.

The reason our Savior did not live the ascetic life that John the Baptist led was that He might conform in all things with the Jews' way of life. He who wants to conquer souls must, in accordance with St. Paul's words, become "all things to all men" (I Cor. 9:22); otherwise, he will remain a stranger among those whom he wants to win over by his example. Food and drink are not so essential but that they can be sacrificed to this pastoral principle. As St. Paul says, "the kingdom of God does not consist in food and drink" (Rom. 14:17), but "in justice and peace and joy in the Holy Spirit" (*ibid.*). It was better to give the example of this perfect meekness than an example of fasting and abstinence that might have been misunderstood. And yet Jesus did not scorn austerity. He wanted His disciple John the Baptist to stand out through his fasting, his abstinence, and his austerities of all kinds, and He, too, gave us the example of it at the beginning of His public life.

With regard to poverty, however, there was no danger of being misunderstood, whereas wealth might have deluded many concerning our Savior's intentions. He chose, therefore, to live in the most total poverty possible. The Son of Man had "nowhere to lay His head" (Mt. 8:20). He did not even have the money to pay the Temple tax for Himself and His Apostle, and He had to work a miracle to obtain the indispensable stater (Mt. 17:26). Finally, He wanted His Apostles to be free from all attachment to this world's goods, and He commanded them: "Do not keep gold, or silver, or money in your girdles, nor wallet for your journey, nor two tunics, nor sandals, nor staff" (Mt. 10:9-10).

Thus did He show that it was not the power of money but the power of the Spirit alone that gave authority and efficacy to His own and His Apostles' mission. He would not have anyone believe that His Apostles preached out of greed, and He gave them full freedom of mind by commanding them to be detached from earthly possessions. Judas' purse must have had very little in it, and he had turned away from the spirit of the Lord by his covetousness even before his treason (cf. Jn. 12:6). As for the gifts of the holy women, they were providential means of livelihood for the Apostles. Such help was customary among the Jews, and it did not detract from the Apostles' poverty. If these gifts could have aroused any suspicions, the Apostles would have refused them, as St. Paul—who had the Spirit of Christ and obeyed His lessons—wanted to do (II Cor. 11:7-9).

As to Christ's attitude with respect to the Law, we have His own words: "Do not think that I have come to destroy the Law or the Prophets. I have not come to destroy, but to fulfill" (Mt. 5:17). Thus did He eliminate one of the pretexts the Jews had for calumniating Him. At the same time, the Law found in Him its completion, its fulfillment, its ultimate reason for being. To quote St. Paul: "God sent his Son, . . . born under the Law, that he might redeem those who were under the Law" (Gal. 4:4-5).

The apparent derogation of the law that the Jews condemned (healing on the Sabbath, the plucking of grain on the Sabbath) was justified in the name of the Law itself, since the precepts did not forbid what was necessary to maintain life: "Does not each one of you on the Sabbath loose his ox or ass from the manger, and lead it forth to water?" (Lk. 13:15). And again: "Which of you shall have an ass or an ox fall into a pit, and will not immediately draw him up on the Sabbath?" (Lk. 14:5). As for food, of its nature it is neither pure nor impure, or rather all food is pure. If any food is impure it is by virtue of the significance attached to it in a given circumstance. We must give up observances that have lost all meaning (cf. Gal. 4:9).

VII. THE TEMPTATION

Christ inaugurated His public life by His baptism, during which He was shown to be the Son of God. Then He went to the desert, "led by the Spirit" (Lk. 4:1) "to be tempted by the devil" (Mt. 4:1). Why this temptation, at the start of His mission, and in the desert?

The purpose, as presented by the Evangelists, seems perfectly clear. There is an obvious parallelism between the scene of the temptation of Christ, inaugurating the Messias' career, and the scene of Adam's temptation inaugurating human history. By the defeat of the first Adam, "the whole world (fell into) the power of the evil one" (I Jn. 5:19). Christ came as a second Adam to begin human history all over again, or at least to reconstitute it upon new foundations. He came to break the ancient bond between the world and Satan and to dethrone the latter. That is why His entrance into battle was heralded by a single combat against Satan, the beginning of a struggle that would end only with Christ's death.

Father Lagrange explains it to us as follows:

"Satan is the 'the god of this world' (II Cor. 4:4); he rules those kingdoms of the world over which he can hold sway. He sees an enemy rise up who is declared to be the son of God and who will therefore work for the advancement of His kingdom. Without delay, he tries to parry the blow by making Him contradict Himself—at first without His knowing it perhaps, but later on more overtly. But Satan is defeated, not in that his empire is already destroyed but in that he has been unable to prevent Jesus from undertaking His work according to God's intentions and in the dispositions that God wills." [1]

Jesus went to the desert because that is the classical site for combats with evil spirits; His action was therefore significant—inhabited areas are the seat of other types of temptation. How are we to visualize His temptation? The Evangelists suggest a very concrete situation: Jesus had fasted; He was hungry. The devil came and spoke to Him. Perhaps we should not condemn the notion of an "interior vision," but such a view minimizes the temptation. Besides, the Gospel seems to indicate something else. It was a temptation presented to the eyes, the understanding, the imagination. It seems more consistent with the text to think that the devil appeared to Christ in a human form and spoke to Him as one man to another. In fact, the devil's suggestion was wholly exterior. An evil suggestion could not arise within Jesus' soul, for the temptation of the flesh always implies a certain connivance of the soul with sin (inasmuch as this temptation does not express itself in a natural desire or pleasure that Christ could well have had, but in a desire or pleasure contrary to reason). And so we see that Jesus was tried outwardly. The devil strove to win Him over by words, images, and suggestions.

The first temptation was that of hunger. It was typical. "Satan asked the Son of God to provide for His needs by His supernatural power. This was only a first step. Why, then, should He be subject to harder needs than those of seeking His food, why accept the hard-

[1] M. J. Lagrange, O.P., *The Gospel of Jesus Christ* (Westminster, Md., Newman, 1943), 2 vols. in one.

ships of the road, the machinations of the scribes, and all the things that make ordinary men suffer? If Jesus had listened, He would not have drunk the chalice in the end. He cut His tempter short: food and drink are not all of man and are not worth such a deviation from human ways. For food as well as for clothing, men must trust to God's help (Mt. 6:25 ff.)." [2]

The second temptation was cruder. The devil took Jesus up to the pinnacle of the Temple. We must not interpret this temptation as if Jesus had climbed up on the devil's back or had held on to his neck. "If Jesus had followed the devil into the air, what significance would there have been in the invitation to throw Himself down from a height of a few hundred yards? Jesus would already have yielded to Satan's wishes." [3]

The devil simply led Jesus to Jerusalem and to the pinnacle of the Temple. He even made use of the words of Scripture, tempting Him to seduce the people by working wonders. That is the perpetual temptation of those who "ask for signs" (I Cor. 1:22), or who, inversely, want to seduce the imagination by working wonders. The kingdom of God does not come in this way, and the Lord is not to be tempted.

Then the devil staked all that he had. He led Jesus upon a high mountain and offered to make a bargain with Him, promising Him all the kingdoms of the world. But Jesus is not to reign in Satan's manner and with Satan's pomp. His mission is "to proceed always and everywhere through the adoration of God alone." [4]

Thus, just as Christ was to conquer our death by His own death, He chose to conquer our temptations by His temptations. He proved Himself a compassionate shepherd by taking upon Himself our temptations, with the exception of sin. And by overcoming temptation He gave us the power to overcome it in our turn, since it is through His strength within us that we master temptation. Besides, He gave us the example of His humility and His patience. He did not choose to conquer the devil by arms and exterior power, but by proving Himself the stronger in the realm of justice, truth, love, and humility; or at least by showing Himself to be strong in those areas where the devil could only display weakness or nothing-

[2] *Op. cit.*
[3] *Op. cit.*
[4] *Op. cit.*

ness. It was fitting that He who was to teach the ways of God should first have manifested such virtues.

Finally, it is remarkable that the order of the suggestions or temptations conceived by the devil should so cleverly correspond to our own weaknesses, and be such obvious replicas of the temptations of the first Adam. To quote St. Thomas: "A suggestion cannot be made to everybody in the same way; it must arise from those things towards which each one has an inclination" (IIIa, q. 41, a. 4). After Christ had fasted for forty days and was hungry, Satan began by tempting Him with food, hoping thereby to open the door to other temptations concerning His Messianic role and His Person. Likewise, the serpent had tempted Adam by presenting him a fruit from the forbidden tree, beautiful to look at and good to eat, and then suggesting that if he consented to eat of it he would be like God, knowing good and evil. But there is a difference between Adam's temptation and Christ's. Adam succumbed to the temptation. Satan had the initiative and was the victor. Christ, on the other hand, went out to meet Satan in the desert; He had come to dethrone Satan. It was Christ who took the initiative in this gigantic duel in which the Prince of darkness and death was finally overthrown.

VIII. THE PREACHING OF JESUS

With regard to the preaching of Christ, the first question that presents itself is this: How is it that Christ chose to preach only to the Jews, and not to the pagans? He Himself declared that He had not been "sent except to the lost sheep of the house of Israel" (Mt. 15:24).

We have the first reason from St. Paul: "For I say that Christ Jesus has been a minister of the circumcision in order to show God's fidelity in confirming the promises made to our fathers" (Rom. 15:8). It was indeed necessary that Christ should present Himself as the One who came to fulfill the promises. By His fidelity to these promises, Jesus obviated all possibility of calumny and excuses on the part of the Jews.

And yet these promises had a meaning of their own. God, who does all things "in weight, and . . . in measure" (Is. 28:17), had prepared His people of Israel for centuries, teaching them to believe in the one true God, so that they might be ready to receive the good news of salvation at the proper time, and then communicate these tidings to the pagan nations.

Moreover, the Jews had to merit the right to rule over the pagan peoples. This power was actually the stake for which Christ was fighting and which He would win by the Cross (Apoc. 2:27-28 and Phil. 2:8 ff.). That is why Christ did not preach to the pagans before His Passion. But after His Resurrection He said to His Apostles: "Go, therefore, and make disciples of all nations" (Mt. 28:19).

At the same time, we know that Christ did not refuse His teaching and His salvation to the pagans or the Samaritans that He met without having sought them out—and this fitted in perfectly with His plan of salvation. The following examples can be cited: the centurion (Mt. 8:10); the Syrophoenician woman (Mk. 7:26); the Canaanite woman (Mt. 15:22); and the Samaritan woman (Jn. 4:7 ff.).

But why did Christ want to be "a stone of stumbling and . . . a rock of offense" (Is. 8:14) even to His own people? Why did He choose to be severe with the Pharisees, the Scribes, and the leaders of the people, when He came to teach meekness and to proclaim mercy and salvation?

When put in this way, the question does not seem to hit home. The choice is not between mercy and severity. And if this were the choice, it would have to be in favor of mercy. Actually, that is the choice Christ made in such cases as those of the adulterous woman (Jn. 8:11) and the good thief (Lk. 23:43). But on the other hand an apostle must never betray the truth. Where truth is in danger, it is not merciful to respect established disorder or lies. It is better to cause scandal to many than to betray the truth upon which salvation rests and to deceive men by seemingly approving lies and vices. Thus our Savior could not humor the vices of the Pharisees as they would have liked Him to. Nor did He allow Himself to be influenced by His disciples' remark: "Dost Thou know that the Pharisees have taken offense at hearing this saying?" (Mt. 15:12).

Theology has much to say about the extent of Christ's doctrine, and His way of presenting it. Christ spoke "openly to the world" (Jn. 18:20), but His disciples could not bear the whole truth (cf. Jn. 16:12); and so He did not tell them everything, but left it up to the Spirit of truth to teach what He Himself had not said (Cf.

Jn. 16:13). Christ also spoke in parables, so that the truth might not be despised. In this way, those who had ears to hear could hear, and those whose hearts were hardened did not scorn what they had understood in their own way. To quote St. Hilary: "His teaching was darkness for carnal men, His words were night for unbelievers" (*In Mat.,* cap. 20). And yet our Lord did not leave His disciples without the necessary explanations when these seemed opportune (Mt. 13:36 ff.).

Finally, it is most remarkable that Christ did not write His doctrine. Our Scripture is not a Koran. The Truth that Christ has to impart to us exceeds anything that can be written, for He Himself is the Truth. Beyond all the texts and words, everything we believe leads us to the Word Himself and in Himself. The difference between the Old Law and the New is here manifest: whereas the Old Law had been written "on tablets of stone" (II Cor. 3:3), the law of the Spirit of life is "written not with ink but by the Spirit of the living God on fleshly tablets of the heart" (*ibid.*).

IX. THE MIRACLES

The theologian's first task here again is to take an inventory of the facts and to inquire very simply into what they set forth. The inventory itself already calls for certain distinctions. For example, are we to include the apparitions of the risen Christ among the miracles? The baptism of Jesus, the fast in the desert, the triumphal entry into Jerusalem, the unexpected cure of the woman suffering from the hemorrhage, the foretelling of the Passion, the water and the blood that flowed from Christ's side on the Cross, the wonders in the skies and upon the earth after His death—all these supernatural facts are of rather diverse types.

This brief enumeration makes us realize that the category of "miracles" in the Gospels derives from the more comprehensive genus of "signs." While all the *signs* presented by Jesus were not miracles, it seems that all of His miracles signified something. What did they signify? This is the second question which theology must answer. As a prelude to this answer, we can point out that the most advantageous classification of Christ's miracles would *not* be according to the type of objects or persons, such as, for example: miracles in the skies (the star of the Magi, the darkening of the sun at the death of Christ), miracles affecting the elements (Jesus walking on the waters, the calming of the storm, the water changed into wine, the coin found in the fish's mouth, the multiplication of the loaves), miracles concerning animals and living beings (the miraculous catches of fish, the dried-up fig-tree), miracles over the human body (cures, and wonders like Zachary's dumbness), miracles in which the angels intervene (the Annunciation, the apparition of the angels to the shepherds, and later on after the Temptation, after the Resurrection, after the Ascension), miracles attendant upon apparitions of the risen Christ, etc.

The most advantageous way to classify Christ's miracles is according to their signification, or at least according to the various intentions of the Evangelists who record them. It is certain that from this point of view the miracles recorded by St. John are very important. St. John did not report all the miracles but only a few of them that presented a prophetic teaching of considerable scope: the miracle of the man born blind, the symbol of baptism; the cure of the lame man at the pool of Bethsaida, another sign of spiritual resurrection; the multiplication of the loaves, a miracle ordered to the Eucharist; the marriage feast of Cana, a prophetic miracle announcing the hour of the Passion and baptism; the blood and the water from Christ's side, the symbols of the sacraments; the miraculous catch of fish after the Resurrection, in which St. John himself notes that 153 fish were caught, a symbolic number full of significance.

Besides, St. John indicated the meaning of Christ's miracles to us: they were the manifestation of the works of God (Jn. 9:3). The miraculous works of Jesus bore witness that the Father had sent Him (Jn. 5:36). They were the divine seal of His mission, for by His miracles God Himself set His seal upon Him (Jn. 6:27). And Jesus declared: "The works that I do in the name of my Father, these bear witness concerning me" (Jn. 10:25). "The Father dwelling in me, it is he who does the works. Do you believe that I am in the Father and the Father in me? Otherwise believe because of the works themselves" (Jn. 14:10-12). "If I had not done among them works such as no one else has done, they would have no sin. But now they have seen, and have hated both me and my Father" (Jn. 15:24). Words of this sort occur frequently in St. John's Gospel.

We can sum up this teaching by saying that Jesus worked His miracles to confirm His doctrine and to attest to His divine power. They are the divine seal set upon His words and upon His prophetic acts. Our Savior did not work miracles simply to strike men's imaginations and to satisfy a certain natural desire in man for the marvelous. He even went so far as to chide those who asked Him to work miracles on that account (Mt. 16:4). He worked miracles for the salvation of souls, so as to confirm to believers the doctrine that they heard and the testimony that they were expected to acknowledge.

This explains why our Lord worked miracles in the presence of those whose hearts were disposed to hear Him, and why He refused to work wonders for the Jews who asked Him for a sign but whose hearts were closed. This is how we must interpret the fact that in Nazareth Jesus "could not work any miracle" (Mk. 6:5). It was not that Jesus had lost the capacity to work miracles—He was still God—but because these miracles would have been useless, and spiritually barren. His miracles were never the kind that the Jews sought (cf. I Cor. 1:22)—wonders that are such a shock to the imagination and the psyche that they in some way inhibit freedom. On the contrary, Christ's miracles respected the freedom of faith, and addressed themselves to this freedom. There is always one divine *Truth* which we seek, in which we believe and put our trust. Miracles simply attest to the fact that we are indeed in the presence of this Truth.

In the matter of miracles, there is an important difference between the first coming of Christ, in which the authority of God was always accompanied by the weakness of the flesh, and His second coming "with great power and majesty" (Mt. 24:30).

Now that we have clarified the purpose of Christ's miracles, it would be wise to consider their time and place, the conditions under which they were worked, and the way Jesus approached them.

Jesus' first miracle took place in Cana. For the first thirty years of His life before His baptism, Jesus did not work any miracles. This fact corroborates what we have just said as to the purpose of His miracles: He began to work miracles at the time He began to preach and to bear witness to His mission. His miracles attested to the truth of His words and of His testimony. Besides, it was fitting that He should live a reasonable length of time without working miracles, in order to prove the reality of His human nature. We are in no way obliged to believe the wonders and legends surrounding the childhood of Christ, which have come down to us only through the Apocrypha.

Christ did not will to use His thaumaturgical power during His Passion, so that all justice and redemption might be effectively accomplished in Him for our sakes.

As to the manner in which Christ worked miracles, we notice that sometimes He commanded and worked them on His own authority—as when He said to the dead Lazarus: "Lazarus, come forth!" (Jn. 11:43). At other times He prayed and asked God that what He desired might be done, as in the case of the multiplication of the loaves (cf. Mt. 14:19). That was because Christ had to demonstrate that He was God and also the Son of God, the envoy of the Father, who did only what the Father commanded Him to do.

We also see that at times Jesus worked directly, as when He said to the royal official: "Go thy way, thy son lives" (Jn. 4:50). At other times, He began by making certain signs, as when "he put his fingers into the man's ears, and spitting, he touched his tongue" (Mk. 7:33) before curing the deaf and dumb man. Evidently, it was for our instruction that Jesus did these things, and we should pay attention to them and seek their meaning in each of His miracles.

When Jesus told the man born blind: "Go, wash in the pool of Siloe" (Jn. 9:7), He was intimating that all blessings would henceforth come through Him. Siloe was the symbol of life under God's protection. It was from the pool of Siloe "that water was drawn, the symbol of divine blessings, during the Feast of the Tabernacles." [5] St. John was very careful to note that the word "Siloe" meant "sent" (Jn. 9:7). And he seemed particularly fond of speaking of Jesus as the One who had been sent (Jn. 3:17, 34; 5:36, etc.).

X. THE TRANSFIGURATION

We shall deal with the Resurrection of Jesus later on. As a prelude to it, the miracle of the Transfiguration deserves special attention, not because it is the greatest of His miracles but because it is the most significant of them all. As far as miracles go, the restoration of Lazarus to life may have been greater. As a sign, however, the Transfiguration contains many diverse and mysterious aspects that are not to be found in the other miraculous accounts.

[5] D. Mollat, S. J., *L'Évangile selon Saint Jean* (Paris, Éditions du Cerf, 1953), p. 123.

It is the role of theology to discover the meaning of all these aspects of the Transfiguration and bring them into a synthesis.

Let us simply reread the account of the Transfiguration, setting the Synoptics side by side (Lk. 9:28-36; Mk. 9:1-7; Mt. 17:1-8), and study the different elements of the scene as we go along.

Luke 9:28 notes: "Now it came to pass about eight days after these words . . ." There is no need to labor the number eight, as the word "about" ("ὡσεί") indicates. For one thing, numerical precision of this sort was not customary for Luke, and besides Matthew and Mark, whose writings Luke knew well, say: "After six days." But we should keep in mind the relationship that the Gospel of Luke establishes between Jesus' discourse on His Passion and Resurrection on the one hand and the Transfiguration on the other.

Jesus had just shown His disciples that "the Son of Man must suffer many things" (Lk. 9:22) "and be rejected by the elders and chief priests and Scribes, and be put to death" (Lk. 9:22; Mk. 8:31; Mt. 16:21), "and on the third day rise again" (ibid.). This prediction had so disturbed the disciples that Peter in his naïveté wanted to help Him (Mt. 16:22), or rather to encourage Him in what seemed to be a moment of weakness. We know that Peter had a very high idea of Jesus' mission because this episode occurred immediately after he had confessed Jesus to be "the Christ, the Son of the living God" (Mt. 16:16) in Caesarea Philippi.

Peter said to Jesus: "Far be it from thee, O Lord: this will never happen to thee" (Mt. 16:22). But Jesus turned and said to Peter: "Get behind me, satan, thou art a scandal to me: for thou dost not mind the things of God, but those of men" (Mk. 8:33; Mt. 16:23). Then He began to tell His disciples that each one of them must carry his cross and follow Him. The minds of the disciples were still filled with these predictions and these words of advice when Jesus led them up a mountain so that He might be transfigured before their eyes. Such is the impression the Gospels leave with us, by stressing the relationship between these talks and the miracle that occurred soon afterward.

We are therefore justified in thinking that after Jesus had confirmed Peter in his faith (Mt. 16:17) and had prophetically announced the Passion, He wanted to give His Apostles confidence by showing them in advance the glory of His Resurrection and of the resurrection to which He was leading those who believed in Him. Before we entered the narrow path of tribulations and the

Cross, it was fitting that Christ should show us in advance where this path led, and that He should encourage us in our expectation that "the body of our lowliness" would be refashioned, "conforming it to the body of his glory" (Phil. 3:21). Thus did He anticipate Thomas's question: "Lord, we do not know where thou art going, and how can we know the way?" (Jn. 14:5).

Jesus took with Him Peter, James, and John (Lk. 9:28; Mk. 9:1; Mt. 17:1). He had refused to give the Scribes and the Pharisees the signs that their arrogance demanded of Him. But now He gave a sign to His Apostles to strengthen them in their faith for the moment when the Father would "forsake" His Son on the Cross (see Mk. 15:34). And yet Jesus did not take all His Apostles and disciples with Him. Perhaps after such a divine manifestation, some of them would have tried to prevent Him from following His sorrowful path, or else would have refused to believe in Him any more. He did not even take all His Apostles, but only three, His closest friends whom He chose to be His witnesses, as in the case of the resurrection of Jairus' daughter (Mk. 5:37), and during His agony at Gethsemani (Mk. 14:33). It was Peter who had recognized Jesus as the Messias, the Son of God, in Caesarea. John was the disciple Jesus loved; James, his brother, was to be the first Apostle to bear witness to Jesus with his blood (Acts 12:2).

"And his face shone as the sun, and his garments became white as snow" (Mt. 17:2). We may wonder how it happened that Christ's body had not been luminous from His conception. Following the argumentation of St. Paul (I Cor. 15:44-49), it seems that it is the Spirit within us who will give brightness and glory to our bodies. Inasmuch as Jesus was personally united to the Word of God and also filled with grace from the moment of His conception, it would have been natural for His glory to shine forth through His own body from the time of His birth. But Jesus willed to save us by taking on our body of sin, except for the sin. In other words, He took on our corruptible flesh, "our body of lowliness" (Phil. 3:21). The Transfiguration was to be provisional. That is another reason why it was a miracle. It was the miraculous radiance of a body which, according to God's plan, would be glorious only after the Passion.

The miracle was further confirmed by the fact that His clothing also became luminous. "His garments became white as snow"

(Mt. 17:2), "as no fuller on earth can whiten" (Mk. 9:3), "a radiant white" (Lk. 9:29). They already suggested the "dazzling raiment" of the angels after the Resurrection (Lk. 24:4). According to the Fathers, these garments are the symbols of the glory of the saints, resplendent with the glory of Christ. This exegesis, which seems subtle, may take its inspiration from Isaias 49:18: "thou shalt be clothed with all these as with an ornament"; and from the Apocalypse, 19:8.

"And behold, two men were talking with him. And these were Moses and Elias, who, appearing in glory, spoke of his death, which he was to fulfill in Jerusalem" (Lk. 9:30-31). This mention of Christ's death stresses once again the close tie that Luke saw between the discourse on the Passion and the Transfiguration. To strengthen the souls of His Apostles, Jesus brought forward those who had risked death for God's sake. Moses had risked his life when, upon God's command, he had presented himself before the Pharaoh (Ex. 3:10 and 5:1); Elias had done the same when he too obeyed God and presented himself to Achab (III Kgs. 18:1). Elias and Moses rendered homage to the Cross, to teach a lesson to the Jews for whom the Cross was a stumbling-block (I Cor. 1:23). And first of all, they wanted to teach Peter a lesson, who had himself been a stumbling-block on this matter (cf. Mt. 16:23) for Christ.

There are many other reasons why Elias and Moses were present. Moses represented the Law, and Elias, the Prophets. Jesus, who had come not to abolish but to fulfill the Law and the Prophets, willed that these two personages should bear witness to Him before His Apostles. Jesus also showed that He was greater than they, even though they were models of meekness and zeal for everyone, because He sent for them and had power over them. Their apparition does not signify that their bodies were unreal. Very probably they had bodies like those the angels assume in their apparitions.

The mysterious manifestation of God that crowned the Transfiguration at once calls to mind the Baptism of Jesus. In both instances, the Father presented His Son. This similarity is suggestive. Baptism is the sacrament of the first generation and of divine adoption, the sacrament that gives us *grace,* the seed of eternal life. The Transfiguration is the sign of the second generation, in which we shall be consummated in *glory.* On the Jordan, the Holy Spirit appeared under the form of a dove, and on Mount Sion He appeared under the form of a luminous cloud that enveloped them all, a vision that corresponds to Daniel 7:13, and that announced Matthew 26:64 as well as the Apocalypse 1:7 (cf. also Ex. 19:9,16; 24:15,16; Deut. 4:11; III Kings 8:10,12; Ps. 17:12; 96:2). The cloud calls to mind the cloud that miraculously led the Hebrews away from the Pharaoh and out of Egypt (Ex. 13:21). In every context it designates the protective power of God. The dove is the symbol of baptismal innocence, and the cloud is the symbol of glorious brightness and eternal refreshment, safe from all harm.

When they heard the Father's voice, "the disciples fell on their faces and were exceedingly afraid" (Mt. 17:6). Such terror is quite normal in the presence of the glory of God (cf. Dan. 8:17; 10:9). To lie prostrate against the earth is to take an attitude of adoration (cf. I Mac. 4:40,55; Dan. 8:17-18; 10:9,15). In this case, it was not a supernatural apparition that stooped down to touch and raise up the terrorized ones (Dan. 8:18; 10:10,18). It was Jesus Himself (Mt. 17:7), as befitted His mission.

To sum up, the Transfiguration was an admirable confirmation of the doctrine and the mission of Jesus, through the testimony of the Old Covenant. It was also a prophetic annunciation of His glory after His Passion, and of our glory after we die. The Transfiguration is the sacrament of the glory that will be given us when Christ returns. As a central scene of the Bible, at the juncture of the two Testaments, it introduces us to the hour for which our Savior came into the world, and it opens our minds to its mystery.

REFLECTIONS AND PERSPECTIVES

The first question we ask ourselves is this: What place does the life of Jesus hold in our religion?

There is no doubt whatever but that knowledge of Jesus is at the heart of Christianity. It even marks the originality of our religion by comparison with Islam, for example, and even with Judaism and all the other religions. Christianity is not the religion of a book, in the sense that Islam is, nor is it first of all a doctrine. Christianity is the knowledge, the imitation, the love, of a Person who is Christ. Necessary as the Sacred Books are for faithfully preserving the revealed message and for transmitting it to us, nevertheless they are not fundamental. It is not absolutely necessary to know how to read to be a Christian. But it is necessary to have "heard of" Christ, the Savior, the Son of God, who was crucified, died, and rose again;

and it is necessary to believe in Him. Whereas Islam is first of all the acceptance of the Koran, and afterward and secondarily the imitation of the Prophet, Christianity is just the reverse. It is first of all and essentially a cleaving to Christ, an "imitation of Jesus."

Before Christianity became a doctrine, it was an Event, and this event is at the heart of all Christian doctrine: God intervened in human history by raising Jesus His Son from the dead. And this was not the only event. God intervened many times in the history of Israel, and likewise before the Resurrection of Jesus. Abraham's call, the freeing of his son, the passage of the Red Sea, the promulgation of the Law on Sinai, the march through the desert, the entrance into the promised land, the reign of David, the construction of the Temple and its first destruction, the exile, the return, all the words of Yahweh's prophets, the birth of Christ, His teaching, His miracles and His whole life—all these things are events that matter in our religious history. And yet they have meaning and value only in relation to the central Event that explains and shows the scope of each of them: the Resurrection of Christ. In fact, the preceding events are no longer exactly what they are for us when considered by those who do not believe in the Resurrection of Jesus: the Jews and the Moslems.

With the Resurrection, God showed that He saved and assumed control of the whole human race, all of human history, and universal history as well. Like a magnet amid iron filings, God brings all events and all men in historical contact with Himself. No one can change the fact that Abraham was called, that Moses gave the Law, that Christ rose from the dead, and that the Church preserves His Word and the sacraments of His Word. "No nation ever had gods so close to it as our God is to us."

The whole of Christian life is impregnated with this mystery of proximity. Since God came into our world to meet us and save us, the Christian does not have to flee from the world in order to find God. He knows that human history is imbued with the Incarnation and with the divine. He needs only to flee from sin.

We shall better understand the originality of our religion if we compare it once again with Islam. The Moslem recognizes only a transcendent God, a remote God that no one can approach. The Moslem is a servant, a worthy servant of a very lofty monarch no doubt, but not really a friend of Allah. This conception influences all the forms of Mohammedan religious life. There is a striking contrast between the mosque and the center of Christian worship, the church, "even when (the mosque's) builders have borrowed the carvings and decorative motives of the church. At first the mosque had no roof, and it generally contains a large central court. But the exterior walls of its enclosure are opaque, without any openings that filter light, such as cathedral windows do. And no one can enter a mosque until he has passed by way of the basin of ritual ablutions . . . Even though the wooden doors are often ornamented and the arch-stones of the vaults are alternately dark and bright, the nave is bare and stripped, without any of the statues that make earthly beauties the intermediaries that raise up the adorer's soul to his one God; for the representation of human figures is prohibited. There are only Arabic inscriptions on the walls, commemorating the Law in a rigid and solemn manner" (L. Massignon, *Situation de l'Islam,* Paris, Geuthner, 1939, p. 6).

The same thing that is true of Islamic architecture also applies to decoration, furniture, writing, customs, salutations and greetings, clothing, etc., whose form M. Massignon scrupulously analyzes: "Moslem decorative art does not seek to imitate the Creator in His works by means of relief and volume in artistic forms, but evokes Him by His very absence in a fragile, unfinished presentation, as perishable as a veil, that simply underlines with serene resignation the fugitive passage of things that perish, and everything is perishable 'except His face.' The artist's medium is malleable, humble, without depth: plaster, stucco. And ornamentation consists of incrustations instead of reliefs. The artist's subjects are geometric forms, but forms that are geometrically open. It is a calling to mind, a visible figuration of a thesis of fundamental dogmatic theology, namely that figures and forms do not exist in themselves and are incessantly recreated by God. And so we find intersecting polygons, arcs of circles with variable radii, the *arabesque,* which is essentially a sort of indefinite negation of closed geometric forms that prevents us from contemplating the beauty of a circle in itself or the beauty of a closed polygon (as Greek thought did) as if it were a magic and planetary pentacle" (*Ibid.,* p. 6-7).

This beautiful page on the expressions of Moslem life makes us understand by contrast how much of the human and sensible our religion of the Word "Incarnate" has kept. Christianity has not been afraid to assume the expressions of "Greek thought," as well as those of Slavic culture and of many others as well. In principle, everything that is human can be baptized and can serve as a means of getting close to God. The immanence of Christianity must be so great that all peoples can approach Christ in their own homes, without leaving their country, or having to give up their language, their culture, or their civilization. Everything that is human can become Christian.

But this is not merely a question of immanence. Not only is God close to us by reason of the humanity He assumed, He is also transcendent to everything we can touch, see, or even know. From this point of view, the Christian acknowledges—as does the Moslem —that God is humanly unknowable, that "no one has ever seen Him." The Church has always recognized certain vocations or certain forms of life that seem to bear witness to God's transcendence much more than to the proximity of the God who became man. The Moslems are not alone in proclaiming the formula "God is one," or in their sense of the terrifying precariousness of all that passes in this world, or in the building of high cloistered walls behind which men retire "for God alone." Christian deserts and the walls of monasteries isolate men even more than do mosques. Thus Christianity can likewise assume, at least in part, the stripped and austere religious expressions of Moslem architecture and furnishings.

And yet Christianity cannot go as far as the Moslems in this respect. The monk who withdraws from the world "for God alone" knows very well that God walked upon our earth, and that by approaching Him in His sacred Humanity he will have a chance to approach His Godhead as well. The mosque transformed into a Christian temple may fail to acquire frescoes and statues and stained glass windows. After all, these things are secondary. But it is absolutely necessary that such a Christianized mosque receive the sacramental Body of Christ. Thus, a visible and sensible element is introduced into religion which calls for all the other elements by a sort of logical necessity. The Christian is not above possessing through images those things that he cannot possess in reality at every moment, such as, for instance, the Body of Christ in His sacrament.

How could a Christian separate himself from his brothers and their action in this world or from the important events of history, now that God has in a way united Himself to man's history by coming into the world? For the Christian, the "sense of God" cannot be simply the sense of His metaphysical transcendence. It is also the sense of the Love that has brought God so close to us and made Him so human. The believer is not only a servant who prostrates himself in adoration before God. He also eats at God's table. Human life is not merely a nothingness before God. Now that God also has a human life, all that is human cannot fail to hold the attention of the believer.

The Jesus we must know

We can know Jesus in many ways, but all of them do not reveal Him to us as He really is. Certain ways may be very erudite, and yet give us only a superficial understanding of Him. Others may leave many facts out of consideration and yet be more real. The little child who believes that Jesus is God knows more, in the sense that he possesses a loftier truth about Him, than the modern scholar, the ethnological and philological historian, who "explains" all His words and actions but reduces His life to that of "an eminent human personality." The history of Jesus possesses another dimension for the believer than that which "history" is capable of revealing.

While Jesus is certainly an historical personage, He is that and more besides. He is the Word made flesh. The believer cannot abstract from his faith in order to know Jesus, and his faith gives him a knowledge of all the words and acts of Christ that is far superior to the knowledge of which the historian, as such, is capable, even though this knowledge of faith takes advantage of all that the historian can give. Not only is the knowledge of faith deeper, but it is also more extensive. For example, it discovers relationships between events or between words that purely historical analysis cannot bring out. Theological knowledge of Christ is nourished by these "relationships," particularly the relationships of "typology," or those that are implied by the "titles" given to Christ. Let us open up a few paths for research in the field of this knowledge.

1. *The typology of Christ.* The five classical themes of the Old Testament as seen by the Fathers are as follows: Adam and paradise, Noah and the flood, Abraham and the sacrifice of Isaac, Moses and the exodus, Josue and the crossing of the Jordan into Jericho. All of these themes have a traditional significance with relation to Christ, the Church, Baptism, and the Eucharist. The typology of these various events should be studied in their relationship to these four realities.

Track down in the New Testament and in the Fathers the texts that designate Christ as the new Adam, the new Abel, the priest according to the order of Melchisedech, the new Abraham, the new Isaac, the new Israel, the new Joseph, the heir of David, the new Solomon. What does each of them designate when applied to Christ?

2. *The titles of Christ*. Study in the Old Testament and in Tradition the significance of the titles Christ applied to Himself or that others gave Him: Son of man, Servant of God, King, Doctor, Prophet, Preacher, Priest, Messias, Shepherd, Pastor, Door of the sheepfold, Altar, Victim.

3. *The life of Christ compared with Israelite life in general*. Study the actions and words of Christ in terms of Jewish usage. In particular, the Circumcision, the Purification of Mary and the Presentation of Jesus in the Temple, His words concerning rest on the Sabbath, concerning the Pasch, His citations from the Psalms or from other portions of Scripture, His sermons to the Jews and to the pagans, His teaching on food and fasting. Study the meaning of the miracles reported by St. John, in their relation to the teaching of Christ and to the mystery of His death and resurrection. Consider from this point of view the role of worship in Christ's life. What is the place of (exterior) worship of God in His life? How did He inaugurate the Christian religion? What are the fundamental rites He instituted, what "spirit of the liturgy" can we draw from the Gospel? What must also be the respective place of preaching and worship in the life of the apostle (of the bishop or priest)?

4. *The temptation of Christ*. Also study the temptation of Christ in relation to the temptation of the first man, and in relation to the temptations of every sinful man. The problem of Christ's temptation is one of the touchstones that reveal the psychology of Christ. The only temptation that Adam could know and to which he could yield was the temptation of pride. He could not know the temptation of the flesh as long as all his powers remained in the order in which they had been created by God, the flesh subject to the intellect. The flesh could only become a temptation for Adam after a previous disorder in the intellect had allowed the flesh to emancipate itself. But such a temptation—whether it be in the mind "tempted" by pride, or in the flesh (that is, in the mind tempted by the seduction of the flesh)—is the sign of sin: of a sin that has already been consummated or of a sin that has begun to take root in the soul because it has found secret complicity there.

Temptations of that sort are unthinkable in the soul of Christ. It is absolutely impossible that Christ should ever have been the accomplice to a temptation. The temptation of Christ must be conceived as an action exterior to Christ, and in relation to which the soul of Christ was purely passive, offering no active complicity. The temptation of the world or of the flesh could not exist in the soul of Christ. Only the temptation of Satan, that is, the ordeal of the externally seductive actions of Satan, was possible.

5. *The virtues of Christ.* An attentive reading of the Gospels should bring out a certain number of virtues that are particularly characteristic of the soul of Christ. Modern theologians have but little concern for this because they have established a general catalogue of virtues, perfectly arranged and organized, that corresponds exactly, according to their way of thinking, with the perfect structure of the soul. And since the soul of Christ is perfect, it possesses all these qualities.

We have already made the twofold criticism that this systematization of the virtues calls for (Vol. III, pp. 204-208). Judicious as this systematization may be, it still remains relative, and dependent upon a philosophical system that is excellent perhaps, but subject to improvement. Besides, this list of virtues indicates essential perfections, but not the existential intensity of this or that virtue in the soul of this or that just man. Nor does it bring out the particular luster that one virue or another takes on in the life of various saints. It is precisely the "intensity," the luster of this or that virtue in the soul of Christ that must be of particular interest to he theologian.

The theologian cannot consider the life of Christ simply as the life of a just man, even if he qualifies it as "particularly eminent." The existence of a saint is always particular. No saint is or can be perfectly imitable by everyone. The country where he lived, the circumstances of his life, his temperament, his personal grace, his epoch—all these things "particularize" his existence so that the luster that finally accrues to this or that virtue will be personal and will not necessarily be of interest to every Christian life. Such is not entirely the case of Christ, for His life is a norm for all men. It is therefore important for us to know the particular intensity in Christ's life of those virtues known as the "evangelical" virtues: patience, meekness and humility of heart, "humility," etc., and to explain them as far as possible in terms of His mission and of His love.

BIBLIOGRAPHY

There are countless works on the life of Jesus. Those cited here are the more valuable ones from our own century.

Adam, Karl. *The Christ of Faith*. New York: Sheed and Ward, 1957.

Bardy, G., Tricot, A., and a group of specialists, *The encyclopedia Le Christ*. Paris: Bloud and Gay, 1946.

Daniel-Rops, Henry J. *Jesus and His Times,* Catholic ed. New York: Dutton, 1954.

Felder, Hilarin. *Jesus of Nazareth*. Milwaukee: 1953.

Grandmaison, L. de, S.J. *Jesus Christ, His Person, His Message, His Credentials*. 3 vols. New York: Sheed and Ward, 1930–1934.

Guardini, Romano. *The Lord*. Chicago: Regnery, 1955.

Imschoot, O. Van. *Jésus-Christ*. Paris: Desclée.

Lagrange, M. J., O.P. *The Gospel of Jesus Christ*. 2 vols. in 1. Westminster, Md.: Newman, 1943.

Lebreton, J., S.J. *The Life and Teaching of Jesus Christ Our Lord*. 2 vols. in 1. New York: Macmillan, 1957.

Lelong, M. H. *Jésus et son pays*. Paris: Cerf.

Papini, Giovanni. *Life of Christ*. New York: Harcourt, Brace, 1923.

Prat, Ferdinand, S.J. *Jesus Christ, His Life, His Teachings, and His Work*. 2 vols. Milwaukee: Bruce, 1950.

Ricciotti, Giuseppe. *The Life of Christ*. Milwaukee: Bruce, 1947.

William, Franz M. *The Life of Jesus Christ*. St. Louis: Herder, 1936.

The Theology of Christ in the New Testament:

Amiot, F. *L'enseignement de saint Paul*. 2 vols. Paris: Gabalda.

Cerfaux, L. *La Voix vivante de l'Évangile au début de l'Église*.

————. *Le Christ dans la théologie de saint Paul*. Paris: Cerf, 1952.

Prat, F. *Theology of St. Paul*. 2 vols. Westminster, Md.: Newman, 1946.

Additional works on the theology of the life of Christ:

Brillet, G. *La vie intérieure de Jésus; Jésus parmi les hommes*. Paris: Desclée.

Chollet, Msgr. *La psychologie du Christ*. Paris: Lethielleux, 1903.

Marmion, Dom Columba, O.S.B. *Christ in His Mysteries*. St. Louis: Herder, 1924.

Thomas Aquinas, St. "The Life of Jesus," in *Summa Theol.,* III, 27-59.

Before we begin the chapter on "The Redemption" we have an important point to make.

Theologians are accustomed to dividing Christological doctrine into two parts which would seem to exclude one another: they call the first part *The Incarnation,* and the other, *The Redemption.* The one studies the mystery of the Word Incarnate, and the other, the mystery of the Redeemer. But who can fail to see that the Incarnation itself is redemptive and that our Redemption was wrought by every act of the God-man? God became incarnate to save us, and His sufferings save us only because they are the sufferings of a man who is God. We have already seen and we shall note again that He could have saved us, if He had so willed, by the least of His acts, even though the "satisfaction" would then not have been perfect in "justice." We must therefore consider the Redemption as an aspect of the mystery of the Incarnation, as God has conceived it, and we must not forget to apply to the Passion of Christ all that we have said concerning the acts of the God-man.

Now that we have made this point, we must add that while the Redemption is an aspect of the mystery of the Incarnation, it has its privileged moment. Jesus had His "hour," His "day," and it was for that hour or that day that He became incarnate. His whole life and work were in some way concentrated in that hour and are summed up in it. It is at this privileged moment that we must study the redemptive mystery in which the Incarnation has its purpose and its consummation. That is our reason for introducing this study in the third and not in the second chapter.

The perspective of this chapter will therefore be at once outside of time and in time. It will be considered outside of time in the same sense as our first chapter, for the Redemption is an *aspect* of the mystery of the Incarnation, and we must consider it theologically as such. This does not imply that the Incarnation was realized outside of time, but only that we have studied it from a non-temporal point of view in which it is "the union of two natures in one divine Person," and that we are studying the Redemption here from the point of view in which it is "the operation of a God-man." From this vantage point we shall be able to make a useful comparison between Catholic doctrine and certain ancient and modern theories

145

on the "redemption" or the "salvation" of man. We shall also approach the Redemption as it unfolded in time, because the Redemption was the work of the God-man "Jesus," and was realized at a precise moment of time upon Calvary.

To conclude, let us add that in our first perspective we are evoking the whole mystery of the redemptive work, without excluding the Resurrection and the Ascension, which are the other side of the mystery of the Cross. We are considering the theandric operation of the death and the Resurrection of Christ. In our second perspective we shall not include the glorious moments in the epic of Christ, but shall reserve an analysis of these for Chapter IV on "The Glorious Epic of Jesus Christ."

Chapter III

THE REDEMPTION

by M. Mellet, O.P.

I. THE HISTORY OF THE DOGMA OF THE REDEMPTION

1. The Experience of the Redemption in Antiquity
2. The Redemption in Holy Scripture
   (a) The Redemption in the Old Testament
   (b) The Redemption in the New Testament
3. The Redemption in the Tradition of the Fathers
   (a) The Redemption according to the Apostolic and Ante-Nicene Fathers
   (b) The Redemption according to the Post-Nicene Fathers
       A. The Rights of the Devil
       B. Salvation through Deification
4. The Redemption in Theological Tradition
5. The Redemption in the Liturgy and Devotion
6. The Redemption in Art
7. The Heresies and the Magisterium

THE THEOLOGY OF THE MYSTERY OF THE REDEMPTION

1. The Harmonies of the Mystery of the Redemption
2. The Necessity or Fitness of the Redemption
3. The Historical Fact of the Redemption
   (a) Our Savior's Sufferings
   (b) The Actors in the Passion
4. The Redemptive Power of the Passion
   (a) The Sinner's Deification through the Incarnation
   (b) The Moral Efficacy of the Passion
   (c) The Merit of the Passion
   (d) Satisfaction through the Passion
   (e) The Sacrifice of the Cross

Chapter III

THE REDEMPTION

"The Christian religion," says Pascal, "consists in the mystery of the Redeemer who, by uniting the human and divine natures in Himself, raised men out of the corruption of sin in order to reconcile them to God in His divine Person" (*Pensees,* Brunschvicg Edition, No. 556). This reflection of Pascal's expresses with exactitude the significance of the dogma of the Redemption in Catholic doctrine and experience. This doctrine and this experience have, throughout their history and in their present state of development, constantly tended to concentrate Christian faith and life around Christ crucified. St. Paul attests to this fact in one of his letters to the Corinthians: "For I determined not to know anything among you, except Jesus Christ and him crucified" (I Cor. 2:2).

We know the Pascalian proof of a religion's truth: "It must have known our nature. It must have known greatness and insignificance, and the reason for each of them. What religion except the Christian religion has known these things?" (*Pensees* Brunsch. No. 433). In the Christian religion we have Jesus Christ, the Mediator of God and men by His Cross. Now, it is by Jesus Christ crucified that we know God, and "not only do we know God through Jesus Christ alone, but we also know ourselves through Jesus Christ alone" (Brunsch. No. 548).

Jesus Christ crucified reveals God to us, "who is rich in mercy, by reason of his very great love wherewith he has loved us even when we were dead by reason of our sins, brought us to life together with Christ" (Eph. 2:4-5). But Jesus Christ reveals to us the exacting justice of God, as well as His merciful love. "In him we have redemption through his blood" (Eph. 1:7), for "without the shedding of blood there is no forgiveness" (Heb. 9:22).

In consequence of men's sins, the mystery of the Incarnation of the Word *is consummated* in the mystery of the Cross. Thus, the Incarnation is not the supreme limit of God's tenderness for man. Sin has made of man a wretched creature whose fate depends on the totally gratuitous initiative of divine mercy. And this in turn has led God to outdo Himself by joining His justice and His love on the Cross.

149

Not only do we know God through Jesus Christ, but we know ourselves through Him, "for this God is none other than the Repairer of our wretchedness" (Pascal's *Pensees,* Brunsch. No. 547), of our lost grandeur. It is in the service of human ends that God pours out His love and exercises His justice. Man, the son of God, aspires to be united to his principle, to become Godlike. The Incarnation reminds him of his secret yearning, and makes a superabundant response to it; but the Cross reminds him that he is a prodigal son, and that henceforth he cannot reach the object of his aspirations until he has first been raised up from the depths to which he has fallen. And so the Redemption weds and completes the immense and painful effort that lifts sinful man above himself. It is through the Redemption that guilty man is liberated from his chains and united to God.

Historically, the mystery of the Redemption has been conceived and represented in various ways. We shall merely mention the two that correspond to the two aspects of sin. Sin is a fall of man, an offense against God. The Redemption shows us the misery of man as the slave of evil, and the greatness of God wronged by sin. The Redemption rescues man and makes satisfaction to God. It has an anthropocentric, subjective value on the one hand, and an objective, theocentric value on the other. There is no question of making a choice between them, for they are inseparable.

The mystery of the Redemption remains "to the Jews indeed a stumbling-block and to the Gentiles foolishness" (I Cor. 1:23). To quote the Catechism of the Council of Trent:

> Indeed, if one thing more than another presents difficulty to the mind and understanding of man, assuredly it is the mystery of the cross, which, beyond all doubt, must be considered the most difficult of all; so much so that only with great difficulty can we grasp the fact that our salvation depends on the cross, and on Him who for us was nailed thereon . . . Since, therefore, nothing is so far above the reach of human reason as the mystery of the cross, the Lord immediately after the fall ceased not, both by figures and prophecies, to signify the death by which His Son was to die" (Translation by John A. McHugh, O.P. and Charles J. Callan, O.P., Joseph F. Wagner, Inc., 1934, p. 52).

Even before these figures and oracles, whose purpose was to remove the stumbling-block for the Jews, God had long been preparing the pagan soul to understand "the folly of the Cross" by showing that He willed a bloody redemption and that all men were one in the obedience as well as in the disobedience of a single man (cf. Rom. 5:19).

I. The History of the Dogma of the Redemption

1. THE EXPERIENCE OF THE REDEMPTION IN ANTIQUITY

There is no doubt that Christianity is summed up in the mysteries of the Redemption. And yet it must be said that even outside Christianity we can discover an unconscious preparation for this dogma, a latent presence of this mystery in the human soul. If it is true that "it suffices to have the slightest notion of God and of the human soul to arrive at a certain concept of the Redemption," [1] how could this idea fail to arise outside the Christian faith and Christian life?

Why should a religion of divine origin show no similarity to religions of human origin? "Quite the contrary . . . It is essential that the true religion should satisfy all genuine human needs, that a supernatural religion should answer all natural aspirations, that it should adapt itself when it appears to all the wholesome trends of the time, and that it should make itself known only at the moment when souls are to some extent disposed to accept it." [2]

Nicolas Berdyaev remarks:

"In the end every man will come to realize that it is impossible to be content with the law . . . The thirst for the Redemption . . . was already inherent in the pre-Christian world. We find it in the ancient mysteries that recall the sufferings of the gods. This thirst corresponds to the vast hope of seeing God and the gods come to man's help in solving the excruciating problem of good and evil, of seeing them share human sufferings . . . It is a need for finding a suffering and expiating God, that is a God who shares in the tragic destiny of the world." [3]

This thirst has found powerful expression in the Greco-Roman and Egyptian cults that were in vogue at the time Christianity was born.[4] Osiris in Egypt, Dionysus in Greece, Attis in Phrygia, and Adonis in Phoenicia were all honored as gods who suffered, died, rose again, and offered their incarnations to the imitation of their

[1] J. Rivière, art. "Rédemption," DTC, 13, col. 1913.
[2] Pinard de La Boulaye, S.J., *Etude comparée des religions* (Paris, Beauchesne, 1922), Vol. I, p. 477.
[3] *Destiny of Man* (Naperville, Ill., Allenson, 1954).
[4] Cf. A. J. Festugière, O.P., *L'Idéal religieux des Grecs et l'Évangile* (Paris, Gabalda, 1932), p. 107 ff.

faithful.[5] The same idea of salvation can be discovered in all religions. They all have some notion of sin, a notion that is often uncouth, in which moral and physical evil tend to be confused, and in which the resultant notion of salvation is grossly materialistic. But for all its shortcomings, this idea brings into the picture an avenging god who must be appeased by rites of purification and expiation.

The most eloquent of these rites consists in shedding the blood of an expiatory victim. This seems to represent man's inherent conviction that God possesses supreme dominion over life, and that man is under the necessity of rendering homage to God by offering Him what is most precious in man's life. But this rite also represents the solidarity among the members of a human group. The origin of the idea of community lies in identity of blood. Later, with the Stoics, the idea of spiritual solidarity among men and even among all beings made its appearance. The sinner surrenders himself to death—the radical form of purification and expiation—through an intermediary person.

It is easy to make comparisons between paganism and Christian beliefs and practices. Neither the apologists of Christianity nor its opponents have failed to make use of these comparisons.[6] Actually, the points of contact between paganism and Christianity are really superficial, interesting as they may be because of the common preoccupations that they reveal. "The idea that the god dies and rises again to lead his faithful to eternal life does not exist in any of the mystery religions." [7] "The death of the god is not an expiatory sacrifice," but the culmination of erotic adventures. This remark is of utmost importance. It points to the total absence in paganism of one of the essential elements of Christian dogma: the element of love. For it is through love that the Father sent His Son to save sinful man, and it is through love that this Son died for sinners. Therein lies the transcendent originality of the Christian faith. That is the basic "mystery" of Christian salvation.[8] This originality and this

---

[5] Cf. B. Allo, O.P., "Les dieux sauveurs du paganisme gréco-romain" in *Revue des sciences philosophiques et théologiques*, Vol. XV, 1926, p. 534. Cf. also L. de Grandmaison, S.J., "Gods who died and rose again" in *Jesus Christ, His Person, His Message, His Credentials* (New York, Sheed & Ward), 1935–1937.

[6] Cf. A. Loisy, *Les mystères paiens et le mystère chrétien* (Paris, 1919).

[7] A. Boulanger, *Orphée* (Paris, 1925), p. 102.

[8] A. J. Festugière, O.P., *op. cit.*, p. 133 ff.

mystery are perfectly brought out by the opposition of the ancient philosophers to the mystery cults. Plotinus declares: "Divine law does not permit us, if we have become evil, to ask others through prayers to forget themselves in order to save us. The gods are not to neglect their own lives in order to attend to our private affairs." [9]

Attempts have also been made to compare Christ with certain personages of antiquity, such as Socrates. When we recognize the sublimity that belongs to Jesus alone, we do not minimize the greatness of that lofty Greek, whom the Fathers of the Church greatly admired but who has been set up in opposition to us by the Church's enemies. The death of Jesus was not simply a heroic act, it was essentially an act of religion and an act of love. Socrates did not die for anyone else. He died neither for God nor for men. Jesus freely chose to die to honor God His Father, and to save sinners, His brothers. Lastly, Jesus' death was not the end of an earthly life and the completion of a limited mission as was Socrates'. The death of Jesus was the full exercise of a divine vocation, and the beginning of a life and of an activity that assumed the totality of human nature through the medium of time and space. [10]

2. THE REDEMPTION IN HOLY SCRIPTURE

The redemptive love that the devotees to the savior-gods did not know and that the philosophers deliberately repudiated is the burden of the growing revelation of the Bible, until it reaches its fullest expression on the Cross.

(a) *The Redemption in the Old Testament*

The Old Testament is the figure of the New (Heb. 10:1). What strikes us from the outset in the history of God's people is the universal and lavish use of bloody sacrifice, a practice that betrays a lively sense of guilt, and faith in salvation through peace with Yahweh. As St. Paul remarks: "with blood almost everything is cleansed according to the Law, and without the shedding of blood there is no forgiveness" (Heb. 9:22). All the important acts of the life of Israel were sealed by a bloody sacrifice. The sacrifice of the paschal lamb was the focal point of Jewish worship.

The ritual of the sacrifice was regulated by Yahweh Himself, with a view to spiritual instruction. He sought to awaken the soul of

[9] *Enneads*, 3, 2, c. 9, no. 10-13.
[10] Cf. Th. Deman, O.P., *Socrate et Jésus* (Paris, 1944), p. 172.

Israel to the meaning of sin and the need of forgiveness by imposing expiatory practices. But Israel paid little attention to its God's teachings, and soon sank into a debauchery of blood which God found abhorrent. Then came the prophets: Isaias, Amos, and Osee. They tried to replace a meaningless ritualism by a religion of expiation and love, such as St. Paul would later preach (Heb. 9:9-10). This is what Isaias had in mind when he gave us his remarkable description of the Servant of Yahweh (42:1-4; 52:13; 53:12). This is an "historical enigma" (to quote Duhm) that critics declare they cannot solve, but to which faith finds the key in Jesus Christ. Later on, when the Savior came, He could be recognized at once. His presence added nothing to the picture the prophets had given of Him, even though the men for whom He was to suffer succeeded in covering over this portrait. Israel obstinately refused to recognize Jesus as the Messias, and it has continued to await the triumphal coming of its Messias even though this has meant imagining a second Messias whose humiliating mission would be to suffer and die.[11]

(b) *The Redemption in the New Testament*

With the New Testament we pass from the prophetic descriptions to the presence of the reality. This is the era of the "good news of great joy which shall be to all the people; for today . . . a Savior has been born to you" (Lk. 2:10-11).

In the Synoptic Gospels, the Savior's role is to inaugurate "the kingdom of God" among men. But men are sinners. Their interior conversion is the indispensable prerequisite for their entrance into the kingdom. To deliver them from their sins, Jesus preached the mercy of God to them, and called them to faith. He came to teach men that He was the Son of God and that He would redeem them through His death and resurrection. And He died for them, of His own free will, through love for His Father and for sinners.

The kingdom of God is spiritual, interior, and only the *blessed* of the Sermon on the Mount will have access to it. Thus, one of the most important doubts was laid to rest: the Savior was a spiritual Messias, who gave Himself "as a ransom" for men enslaved to their sins (Mt. 20:28; Mk. 10:45); and who had to pass through suffering and death (Mt. 16:21-22; 17:22; 20:17-19).

The Last Supper was the culminating moment of the revelation:

[11] Cf. Joseph Bonsirven, S.J., *Le Judaïsme palestinien au temps de Jésus Christ* (Paris, Beauchesne, 1935), Vol. I, p. 580 ff.

Until the end of time Jesus would be the sacrifice which sinful men would need to renew and preserve as their covenant with God. After this sacrifice had been accomplished once and for all in a bloody manner upon the Cross, it would continue to be perpetuated sacramentally. But the redemptive work of Jesus did not end with His death. His death, the supreme act of His love, merited for Him the resurrection of His mortal body and His all-powerful glory. His death inaugurated the life of His Mystical Body. A jubilant thought sustained the newborn Church: "Jesus . . . was delivered up for our sins, and rose again for our justification" (Rom. 4:25).

St. Paul was the herald of this conviction, the preacher par excellence of the mystery of the Redemption. So great has his role been in the formation of the doctrine of the Redemption that independent critics do not fear to denounce him as the creator of Christian soteriology.

". . . all have sinned and have need of the glory of God. They are justified freely by his grace through the redemption which is in Christ Jesus" (Rom. 3:23-24). This is the starting point of St. Paul's thought. Sin, grace—between these two poles unfolds the Pauline drama of the Redemption. The Redemption confronts sin as the manifestation of the "very great love" of God the Father (Eph. 2:4) in "the fullness of time" (Gal. 4:4).

It is through Jesus that God saves sinners. Jesus can assume this role because He is God with His Father and equally man with us. "For our sakes (God) made him to be sin who knew nothing of sin, so that in him we might become the justice of God" (II Cor. 5:21). Being a man like us, Jesus is the second Adam who has made reparation for the sin of the first Adam. Whereas Adam brought us to ruin by his disobedience, Jesus saved us by His obedience. In this famous parallel, St. Paul sums up his entire theology of the universe and of salvation.

Jesus saves us by offering Himself up to God as a ransom for us (I Tim. 2:6), as a propitiatory sacrifice (Rom. 3:25), as a mediator of reconciliation (Rom. 5:9-10; Eph. 2:14-18; I Tim. 2:5-6). Jesus is the instrument of propitiation who abolishes the powerless victims of the Law (Rom. 3:25). St. Paul stresses the role of blood in our deliverance (Eph. 1:5-10; 2:1-18; Col. 1:22). But he places even greater emphasis on the essential role of love. Jesus saves us because His sacrifice is pleasing to God, but God accepts this sacrifice only by virtue of the charity that inspires it (Eph. 5:2, 25; Gal.

2:20). The love of the Savior is twofold: it is love for us sinners (Rom. 5:8-9), and love for God (Phil. 2:6-11).

Strictly speaking, Jesus did not take our place with respect to the blood He shed for us, nor with respect to the sentiments that filled His Redeemer's soul. He was one with us, as the head is one with its members. To express this unprecedented unity, St. Paul had to forge a whole new vocabulary: *commortui, consepulti, conressuscitati in Christo*. We are associated with Christ in His death, His burial, and His Resurrection.

In the Epistle to the Hebrews, the Redemption appears in the light of worship rather than in a mystical light. It is a more deeply Jewish approach. The Law is as powerless to provide true worship of God as to provide interior holiness to souls. The Law must surrender before the one perfect sacrifice, the sacrifice of Christ (Heb. 9:9-14). The decisive value of this sacrifice derives from the sentiments and the love that inspire it (Heb. 2:9-10, 14-18; 5:7-9; 10:5-9), and still more from the person of the Savior (Heb. 7:26-28). Moreover, this sacrifice is infinitely more our own than the ancient sacrifices, because Jesus is one of us, like to us in all things except sin (Heb. 2:14, 17; 4:15). In short, the human personality of the Savior is inseparable from His role as priest and victim, and this role sums up His life (Heb. 10:5-6). The Resurrection is the full development and exercise of this personality and of this life as priest and victim (Heb. 5:6; 6:20; 7:21-25).

St. Paul, it is true, merely stresses the interior value of the sacrifice of Jesus Christ here and there in his Epistles, giving more emphasis to the efficacy of His sacrifice. With St. John, however, these interior values are given first place. "God . . . has first loved us, and sent his Son a propitiation for our sins" (I Jn. 4:10). "God is love. In this has the love of God been shown in our case, that God has sent his only-begotten Son into the world that we may live through him" (I Jn. 4:8-9). "For God so loved the world that he gave his only-begotten Son, that those who believe in him may not perish, but may have life everlasting" (Jn. 3:16).

And while the total initiative for salvation flows from the Father's love, the love of the Son answers that of His Father. Jesus loves His Father, and He loves us. "Greater love than this no one has, that one lay down his life for his friends" (Jn. 15:13). Jesus is the Good Shepherd who died for His flock through love (Jn. 10:11, 15, 16); He is the loving Son who died for the honor of His Father

(Jn. 10:18). The decisive proof that He died through love lies in His absolute freedom. No one took His life from Him, but He laid it down of Himself (Jn. 10:18), and He did so only when "His hour" had come: "Jesus, knowing that the hour had come for him to pass out of this world to the Father, having loved his own who were in the world, loved them to the end" (Jn. 13:1).

3. THE REDEMPTION IN THE TRADITION OF THE FATHERS

(a) *The Redemption according to the Apostolic and Ante-Nicene Fathers*

This first age of the Church possessed all the themes of present-day soteriology. Being primarily concerned with the reality of salvation, the Fathers were resolutely opposed to the Docetists. They thought with a simple and powerful realism about our Savior's humanity, even about His flesh, and about the history of His Passion. As a mark of their conviction, they often repeated the axiom: "Only that which has been assumed is saved." To quote St. Ambrose: "He borrowed from us what He was to offer as His own for us, so as to procure the price of our redemption from us . . . For what is the motive of the Incarnation if not that the flesh that sinned should redeem itself?" [12] Thus Jesus Christ had to be totally a man so that the whole of man might be saved in Him.

With regard to the modalities of salvation, the first Fathers drew their interpretations from Scripture: images of redemption, expiation, sacrifice, and reconciliation. But beyond these images, they recognized the secret source of the drama of Redemption to be love. In the second century, Clement of Rome wrote: "It is because of His love for us that Jesus Christ gave His blood for us, according to the will of God, His flesh for our flesh, His soul for our souls" (I Cor. 49:6). On the other hand, this love did not make the Redemption any less necessary, since God had decided to work the Redemption by way of justice. "Indeed, what could cover our sins, except His justice?" asks the author of the *Epistle to Diognetus* (9:4).

With St. Irenaeus in the second century, ideas already familiar to his predecessors were organized into the imposing doctrine of the "recapitulation" of all things in Christ. Sin, from which Jesus saves us, is a ferment of disunion, decomposition. It breaks the bonds

[12] *De Incarn. Dom. Sacram.*, 54, 56, P.L., 16, 832.

that unite us to God and sets us against one another—*Ubi peccata, ibi multitudo,* to quote Origen. It disorganizes the world, which is made subject to sin against its will (Rom. 8:10). The Word became incarnate; and by that very fact humanity was deified, order and peace were restored in the universe. For the Word Incarnate is the keystone of the universe. He virtually bears within Himself the whole of humanity, and even the universe itself. He recapitulates humanity within Himself and thus saves it "in principle," leaving to each individual the task of ratifying this salvation by his personal acceptance.

The remarkable thing about this soteriology is that it inscribes salvation in the Incarnation, even prior to the meritorious acts and Passion of the Savior. This is the "physical theory" of salvation. It is far from being exclusive. St. Irenaeus expressed in magnificent terms the mustering at the Cross: "Through the wood of the Cross, the work of the Word of God became manifest to all: His hands were stretched upon it to gather together all men. Two hands extended, for there are two peoples dispersed over the whole earth. A single head at the center, for there is one God above all, in the midst of all, and in all." [13]

(b) *The Redemption according to the Post-Nicene Fathers*

A. The rights of the devil

Certain historians, notably J. Turmel, claim to follow what they tendentiously call "the theory of the rights of the devil" in their analysis of the Fathers of the great era. According to them, St. Irenaeus would have been the first known defender of this theory. The point of departure of this "theory" consists in the scriptural terms "redemption," "ransom," "price." If we "have been bought at a great price" (I Cor. 6:20), it is because we were the slaves, the captives of someone to whom a ransom had to be paid in exchange for our liberation. But who could this someone be? Certain Fathers answered: it is God, offended by sin. Others said: it is the devil. Scripture often denounces the power of the devil in the sinful world (Jn. 12:31; 14:30; Col. 1:13; I Jn. 3:8). It follows that delivering us from evil means delivering us from the Evil One. In fact, "everyone who commits sin is a slave of sin" (Jn. 8:34).

[13] *Adv. Haer.*, 5, 17, P.G. 1171-2. Cf. also H. de Lubac, *Catholicism* (New York, Longmans, 1950).

"He who commits sin is of the devil" (I Jn. 3:8), for "to whom you offer yourselves as slaves for obedience, to him whom you obey you are the slaves" (Rom. 6:16).

With this picture as a basis, a dramatic literature began to develop, branching out in various directions. At times God the Father or the Son would negotiate our deliverance with the devil. The blood of Christ was the currency of exchange. Again, the devil, who as the executor of God's justice had rights over sinners, would exceed his rights and attack the innocent Christ. Then he would be justly stripped of his rights over us (the theory of the abuse of power).[14] Or else the devil who had conquered man was in turn conquered by a man, Jesus Christ, who thus avenged humanity (the theory of revenge).[15]

The authors and preachers of the Middle Ages and the audiences of the "mysteries" were very fond of this imagery, which they developed with questionable taste. While the imagery is perfectly legitimate, it is not without danger. Certain of the Fathers have judged it severely.[16]

B. Salvation through deification

Jesus died for us. Clearly, His death was not the price of our lives paid to the enemy of God, the instigator of evil. But then, how shall we interpret the words "for us"? By way of substitution? Of identification? The general trend of Patristic thought seems to have been more in the direction of identification than of substitution, although the expressions used encouraged interpretations favoring substitution more than once. While we should beware of oversimplified classifications, we can say that the idea of identification conforms to the genius of the Greeks, while the idea of substitution is more attuned to the Latin genius.

The most fruitful and the deepest idea that Greek Patrology of the fourth and fifth centuries has left us is the idea of the deification of Christians through the Incarnation. This idea has already become part of the riches of Tradition, since St. Irenaeus had

[14] Cf. J. Rivière, *Le dogme de la Rédemption chez saint Augustin,* pp. 77, 100; also his work *Le dogme de la Rédemption après saint Augustin,* pp. 22-32, 82-90.

[15] Cf. St. Augustine, *De Trinit.,* 13, 17, 22, P.L. 42 (1032–1033).

[16] Cf. St. Gregory Nazianzen, *Oratio* 45, 22, P.G. 361, 653. St. John Damascene, *De fide orthod.,* 3, 27, P. G. 94, 1096; cf. J. Rivière, *Le dogme de la Rédemption, Études critiques et documents,* pp. 146-240.

held it at the end of the second century. But it was not until the fourth and fifth centuries that it received its fullest expression and attained its most far-reaching influence on the whole of Christology. God became man so that man might become God. Through the hypostatic presence of the Word in human nature, this nature, gathered up in Christ, was deified and consequently saved.[17]

True, this sublime view of the so-called "physical" theory of salvation is joined in the thought of the Greek Fathers to certain Platonistic conceptions. But it can be extricated from these notions. While it has never been defined, it must be considered as one of the major elements of the traditional "deposit" in Christology.

It must be admitted, however, that this doctrine tends to relegate the life and the Passion of the Savior to the background. The Latin Fathers, on the contrary, lay great emphasis on these two elements in their so-called "mystical" theory: First and above all, Jesus saves us by His merits and consequently by His Passion. As St. Ambrose expresses it: "While the mysteries of the assumption of the flesh (the Incarnation) and of the Passion are equally admirable, nevertheless the plenitude of faith (in the economy of salvation) resides in the mystery of the Passion" (De Spir. Sto, 3, 17).

Seen in this perspective, the acts of our Savior take first place. By contrast, they appear to be exterior to sinners and give Christ the juridical aspect of a substitute: He suffered and died in our place. The Latin Fathers avoid this juridical extrinsicism, thanks to the doctrine of the Mystical Body which is indebted to them, and above all to St. Augustine, for so many admirable terms. The Savior and we are one, just as the head and the members of the body are one. Thus, we cannot say that Christ takes our place, for we suffer, die, and merit in union with Him. There is no substitution where there is identity. In speaking of us, our Savior says: "They are Myself." [18]

Unfortunately, the classical theology of the Redemption, constructed upon the juridical notions of merit and satisfaction, ignored for all practical purposes the Greek doctrine of deification through the Incarnation. Moreover, it impoverished its own Latin

---

[17] Cf. J. Gross, La divinisation du chrétien d'après les Pères Grecs (Paris, 1938).
[18] St. Augustine, In Johan., tract. 108, P. L. 35, 1916. Cf. E. Mersch, S.J., The Mystical Body of Christ (St. Louis, B. Herder, 1951).

sources by neglecting to plunge these notions into the life-giving waters of the Latin doctrine of the Mystical Body.

4. THE REDEMPTION IN THEOLOGICAL TRADITION

The Patristic age possessed from the beginning all the themes of present-day soteriology. But these themes had not yet been synthesized into a true "theology." That was to be the work of the Middle Ages.

Saint Anselm

St. Anselm (1033–1109) exerted a decisive influence upon soteriology. In his *Cur Deus homo,* this "first philosopher-theologian" [19] got rid of the fantasy about the rights of the devil, and organized doctrine around the notion of "satisfaction." He set out to demonstrate *"per rationes necessarias"* how the redemptive Incarnation was a necessity, given the sinful condition of the human race.

His reasoning was simple. Human sin is infinite, inasmuch as it is essentially the violation of honor due to God. Of its very nature, therefore, sin demands an infinite compensation or "satisfaction." Now, sinful man is fundamentally incapable of providing such satisfaction. Two solutions are possible: either God will abandon man to his deserved misfortune and renounce His original plan, or else God will simply forgive man. But on the one hand God has no intention of giving up His initial purpose. He must therefore save man. And on the other hand, it is not "fitting" that God should forgive man without demanding adequate reparation. When the problem is presented in these terms, the only solution is the intervention of a savior who is both man and God. Since the death of this God-man is voluntary and free, an act of perfect supererogation by an innocent being, it makes infinite reparation for man's sin and wins infinite merit for Christ in our behalf.

This soteriology is original because it introduces the concept of "satisfaction." This does not keep it from being thoroughly traditional, for the concept of satisfaction is merely the scientific transcription of the simple Scriptural notions of sacrifice, expiation, and reconciliation. But this concept, borrowed from the field of law, orientated the Catholic theology of the Redemption toward a legalism in which it lost the interior significance of salvation.

[19] According to Bainvel.

The Redemption took on the aspect of a contract, of a bargain between God the Father, who had been offended, and His Son as the victim: the Son suffered and died to make reparation for the offense committed against the Father. Thus the corporeal Passion and death of the Savior were given first place in the economy of the Redemption, to the detriment of His interior dispositions of obedience and love. At the same time, this Passion and death owed their power of satisfaction to their supererogatory character, which gave them a power to save which belonged to them alone, but which set them apart from the rest of Christ's life. It was only later that even His smallest acts were recognized to have saving power.

This legalism is based on an ill-founded trust in rational logic and upon the desire to prove dogma. St. Anselm allowed himself to make use of a certain imagery which, while not as puerile as the image of the rights of the devil, did not sufficiently respect the mystery. Withal, *Cur Deus homo,* is a powerful work which exerted a decisive influence on the ulterior development of the dogma of the Redemption.

From St. Anselm to St. Thomas Aquinas

St. Anselm's trust in reason was echoed by Abelard, but unfortunately without the counterpoise of an equally religious sentiment. And yet curiously enough, Abelard's rationalism sought to emphasize the subjective realities of the Passion. Christ saved us not by performing an efficacious act, but by giving us a lesson in loving. Our salvation depends upon our docility to this lesson. The mystery of the Redemption, for Abelard, is a mystery of *pedagogy.* This conception, which radically eliminates the theory of the rights of the devil, was to reappear on many occasions. But Abelard went further, he went too far: Not only does the devil have no rights over us, but he has not received any power from God to punish us. Consequently, our Savior did not have to "deliver us from the devil's yoke." The devil would thus be incapable of preventing us from understanding the lesson of love that the Cross teaches and from making answer to it by our love.

Abelard's theories were condemned in 1140 by the Council of Sens (Denz. No. 371). Orthodox thought strengthened its reliance on Tradition: Jesus Christ saved us not only by His example but also by a mysterious and real bond between His Passion and ourselves. And on the whole, there was a rallying to the Anselmian theory of satisfaction. William of Auvergne, and then Alexander of Hales and St. Bonaventure among the representatives of the first Franciscan school, took over this theology. However, they substituted the idea of "fitness" for St. Anselm's notion of "necessary reasons." In their concern for safeguarding the transcendence of God's reasons and the freedom of His initiative in the modalities of salvation, they renounced the imperatives of an overly human logic.

St. Thomas Aquinas (1225–1274)

The thought of the Angelic Doctor appears to have been consistent throughout his life, starting with his *Commentary on the Sentences* which he wrote at the start of his doctrinal career. It offers nothing distinctly new by comparison with St. Anselm. The subject-matter of *Cur Deus homo* was simply transposed, using the theme of "fitness" in place of the theme of "necessary reasons."

In the absence of any new innovation on his part, the particular contribution of St. Thomas on this as well as on so many other questions was a powerful synthesis in which he gathered up and organized the scattered elements of the earlier theology. This synthesis was constructed with the help of the clarified notions of *merit, satisfaction,* and *sacrifice,* and completed by the strictly Thomistic notion of *efficiency* (Summa, IIIa, q. 46).

Christ saves us in two ways: "Morally"—by His Passion and death He merits our salvation for us, He makes satisfaction and He offers Himself as a sacrifice for us and in our place. He also saves us "physically"—through His suffering, dying, and triumphant humanity He effectively transmits to us the grace of God. The idea of "re-purchase" is secondary and emptied of any reference to the alleged rights of the devil (IIIa, q. 49, a. 2).

In this fourfold modality the Passion and death of Christ play the preponderant part in our salvation, but they are not exclusive for St. Thomas, as they are for St. Anselm. It is through His whole life that Jesus merits, satisfies, offers Himself for us, and transmits grace to us. The least of His activities possesses a truly infinite value by reason of the infinite Person who inspires it. To understand the power attached to all the elements of the epic of Redemption, it is indispensable to go back to this double interior principle, at once human and divine.

After St. Thomas

After St. Thomas, the only name to remember is that of Duns Scotus. And even then the originality of the "subtle Doctor" often consists in misconstruing the theses of St. Thomas. For St. Thomas, sin assumes a sort of infinitude by reason of the infinite character of God who has been offended. That is why in the plan of Redemption as God actually conceives it, the Savior "must" be able to present infinite merits. Such is the case with Christ. His merits are infinite by reason of His divine Person and because of His charity.

Duns Scotus, on the other hand, considers Christ's Person and His charity as "extrinsic denominations." Sin is not really infinite, because it proceeds from a finite being; and Christ's merits are not infinite either, because merit is the property of a human and therefore of a finite act. As he sees it, there can be question only of a free decision by God, who accepts these merits. So free is this decision that if God should so decide, any man at all could offer Him acceptable satisfaction for the whole human race.

We have come a long way from St. Anselm's views. But the supreme liberty of God, which St. Thomas so deeply respected, has not benefited by this interpretation and truth has suffered. If we have been saved, we no longer owe it to Christ but to God's free decision. Dogma was considerably impoverished by this "extrinsicism" which is so foreign to Tradition.

The thought of Duns Scotus cropped up here and there among the theologians of the next few centuries. We find it for example in Malebranche's Occasionalism: Jesus is only the occasional or distributive cause of the true "goods." [20] Thenceforth theologians were divided into two schools, and disputes were almost entirely over questions of secondary interest: the malice of sin, the necessity of adequate satisfaction, the value of the satisfaction of Christ.[21] Looking beyond the schools, the Church turned to the theology of St. Thomas to discover once again the scientific expression that corresponds to her understanding of the dogma.

[20] *Méditations chrétiennes,* Méditation 14, No. 10. (Paris, H. Gouhier, 1938), p. 81.
[21] Cf. Suarez, *De Incar.,* disp. 4, sect. 3-12 (Paris, Vives) Vol. 17, pp. 55, 186.

5. THE REDEMPTION IN THE LITURGY AND DEVOTION

Even though the canonical and Patristic expressions of the Redemption are rather limited, the expression of the Redemption as lived in the Church and in the souls of Christians amply compensates for this lack. We would have made a liturgical approach to the Redemption sooner if we had not planned to discuss it here as a synthesis of the formulas considered above.

During the first centuries, the testimony of Christian life spoke in a singularly stirring way through the blood of the martyrs. Martyrdom, the perfect imitation of Christ crucified, is the Christian's peremptory profession of faith in the Redemption that saves him. In the words of St. Ignatius of Antioch: "It is in order to associate myself to His Passion that I suffer everything, and it is He who became completely a man who gives me the strength to do it" (*Ad Smyrn.*, 4).

Beginning in the eighth century, a devotion concerned specifically with the Passion appeared in the liturgy. Until then, Easter had been the Church's only feast. The Passion and the Resurrection had been associated in one and the same indivisible mystery: the Paschal mystery and the mystery of baptism. There had been no thought of solemnizing the days that preceded Easter by a special evocation of the Passion. But in the eighth century, this unity was broken. "Holy Week" was gradually organized and dramatized, until it achieved a splendor which our own epoch has lost. This liturgy reached its height in the fifteenth century. That was the era when Arnould Gréban brought the "mystery" of the Passion to the theater, under the porches of the churches, and when the faithful began to make "the way of the Cross" and to say their prayers at "tombs," some of which have become famous.[22]

The feasts of the Passion began to multiply: the Finding and the Exaltation of the Holy Cross, the feasts of the Precious Blood, of the Crown of Thorns, of the Lance and the Nails, etc. Beginning with the tenth century, the cross and the crucifix became objects of adoration, and their worship spread irresistibly. By the sixteenth century, the sorrowful crucifix, which had replaced the hieratic image of antiquity and of the East, was everywhere present in the public and private religious life of Christians.

[22] Cf. E. Male, *Religious Art from the 12th to the 18th Century* (New York, Pantheon, 1949).

In the Patristic age, with a few rare exceptions, Christian devotion addressed itself spontaneously to the divine Word through the sacred humanity of the Savior. Later, especially after St. Anselm in the eleventh century, a new sentiment began to develop which found expression in the devotion to the Five Wounds. St. Bernard, in the twelfth century, gave great impetus to this movement through the devotion to the Wounded Heart of Christ. St. Gertrude, St. Mechthild, and St. Bridget inherited his legacy.

In the thirteenth century, the mendicant Orders of St. Dominic and St. Francis brought a decisive impulse to this devotion through their stigmatics. In the Franciscan soul, as exemplified by St. Francis of Assisi, St. Bonaventure, St. Bernardine of Siena, and St. Angela of Foligno, devotion to the Passion took on the colors of human tenderness. In the Dominican school, with Blessed Henry Suso, Tauler, and St. Catherine of Siena, this devotion took a slightly different form.

Then came the author of the *Imitation of Jesus Christ* (see Book II, Chapters 1 and 12), who "made a synthesis of the entire Christological spirituality of the Middle Ages" (P. Pourrat). And St. Teresa of Avila's ardent piety took it up (*Autobiography, Chapters 9 and 12*), as did Louis Chardon during the seventeenth century with his theological contemplation (*La Croix de Jésus*). Pascal, sorrowful in soul, wrote about "the mystery of Jesus" in letters of fire. Bérulle, with his serene and metaphysical piety, cultivated "the interior" of the Savior and His "states," thus opening the way to the great devotion to the Sacred Heart, whose heroes were to be St. John Eudes and St. Margaret Mary.

Devotion to the Sacred Heart is really a form of devotion to the Passion, since this Heart is the Wounded Heart of the Crucified. Even though such famous orators as Bossuet and Bourdaloue thundered in their pulpits about Christ condemned and chastised by God, devotion to the Sacred Heart drew Christians to the mystery of mysteries: redemptive love. From that time on, the Christian soul instinctively went out to "this Heart that has so loved men."

6. THE REDEMPTION IN ART

Art is a particularly eloquent witness to faith, through the devotion that is its inexhaustible and ever varied source of inspiration. Now, it is a remarkable fact that the first Christians rarely represented Christ on the Cross, but preferred to depict Him in His triumph. They may have wanted to spare their crucified Master the pagan insults of which we find examples in the graffiti of the Palatine, where a Christian is shown worshiping a crucified man with a donkey's head, and in the mockery of a Celsus.[23] Or it may be that a certain Docetist tendency inspired this early Christian art.

At any rate, the most popular image of Christ among Christians was for a long time the solemn representation which we know as the "Byzantine Christ." It was not until the Latin Middle Ages that we find the human and suffering Christ, so familiar to us now, hanging upon the Cross. This trend was due primarily to the influence of St. Francis of Assisi. Grünewald of Colmar's splendid portrayal of the horrors of the Passion was the most pathetic representation of the suffering Christ, but artistic efforts afterward deteriorated into intolerable affectations. Sometimes dramatic scenes were added to the image of Christ, some of them imposing but others of questionable taste.

The fifteenth century was fond of the Crucified as the fountain of life or of the Crucified under the mystical wine press, themes inspired by the theologians and the mystics. During this period we also frequently find compositions whose theological intention is evident: Christ crucified carried in the arms of the eternal Father, surmounted by the dove of the Holy Ghost; or the dead Christ resting on His Father's knees. It was during this era that the worship of the Holy Face began to gain favor.[24]

7. THE HERESIES AND THE MAGISTERIUM

The dogma of the Redemption developed peacefully on the whole. Formal soteriological heresies did not arise until quite late, and they helped to develop the dogma. The earliest errors the historian encounters are generally Christological: Docetist errors of Manichaean origin. They denied the reality of the Savior's flesh, and consequently the reality of His Passion and death. Then there were the Gnostic errors that denied the objective reality of the Passion,

[23] Cf. P. de Labriolle, La réaction payenne (Paris, L'Artisan du Livre, 1934), p. 174.
[24] Cf. Germaine Maillet and Broussole, in Le Christ, encyclopédie populaire (Paris, Bloud & Gay, 1946), pp. 879-976; G. de Jerphanion, "L'image de Jésus-Christ dans l'art chrétien" in La voix des Monuments (Rome, Pontificio instituto orientale, 1938), p. 11.

claiming that Christ saves us not by His acts but by His teaching and His example.

At the beginning of the fifth century, *Pelagianism* called the whole dogma of the Redemption into question. Claiming that man could assure his justification by his own efforts, it would have made the Redemption by Christ's death useless. *Nestorianism* in the fifth century "divided" Christ into two persons and attributed the Passion to His human person, thus stripping His Passion of its redemptive power, which derives from the Godhead of the Word. Gottschalk's *Predestinationism* in the ninth century denied the universality of the redemptive efficacy of the Passion: Jesus Christ died only for the predestined (Denz., No. 318). This error was taken up again by Jansenius in the seventeenth century (Denz., No. 1096 and 1294), and by Quesnel in the eighteenth century (Denz., No. 1382).

In the twelfth century, Abelard refused to see anything but an example of love in the mystery of the Cross, and denied it any objective efficacy. This conception was again taken up in the sixteenth century by the *Socinians,* a dissident Protestant sect. According to them, God saves us by a simple forgiveness independently of the Passion, which is a testimony of love but without any objective efficacy over our sins. To the extent that there are sins to expiate, each one must expiate in his own name. It is impossible for Christ to expiate for us, for adequate expiation would have to be eternal and to be renewed as many times as sins are committed.

Socinianism was essentially a reaction against the extreme theses of primitive *Orthodox Protestantism,* which held that the Redemption by the bloody Passion was necessary and exclusive of all collaboration on our part. If we did collaborate, it would imply that the Savior's merits and satisfaction were insufficient. Moreover, such collaboration is impossible. Since we are sinners to the core, incapable of any virtuous act whatever, what personal merit could we bring to the foot of the Cross? By virtue of this absolute pessimism, which destroys all hope of a genuine interior conversion, the Passion saves us only by a juridical, exterior imputation of the merits of Jesus Christ. We remain what we are, radically and totally corrupted, but God throws the cloak of Christ's blood over our sins.

The juridical imputation of Christ's satisfaction to us is the corollary of the theory of substitution. Christ on the Cross is simply substituted for sinners. Thus, St. Anselm's dictum, "He made satisfaction in our place" must be changed to: "He was really punished." As Luther saw it, Jesus Christ must be considered not as "an innocent, private person, but as a sinner who is guilty of and who bears the sins of Paul, Peter, and David." It follows that Christ must die. Here is the language that Luther attributed to the Father when He sent His Son into the world and put our sins upon Him: "Be Peter the renegade, Paul the persecutor, David the adulterer, be the sinner who ate the apple of Paradise, in short be the person who committed the sins of all men. Consequently, you must pay and make satisfaction for them. The Law comes and says: 'I find Him to be a sinner to such an extent that He took upon Himself the sins of all men and that I see sin in Him alone. He must therefore die upon the Cross.' And so the Law fell upon Him and put Him to death. By this means the world was delivered and purified of its sins." [25]

This gloomy soteriology is based on the idea of an inexorable expiation that leaves no place for love. The Catholic theory of "vicarious satisfaction" presupposes that it is love beyond all other motives that moves God and His Christ. The Protestant conception of expiation, on the contrary, sees only implacable justice in God.

In the face of such doctrines, we can understand the reaction of *Liberal Protestantism* which originated with Kant and Hegel. These German philosophers interpreted the Christian dogma philosophically, and presented Christ-the-Redeemer as the symbol and the supreme success of the human race in its effort to be delivered from evil. The Protestant subjectivism that was the historical successor to Kantian and Hegelian rationalism also saw the Savior in this light, with many variations in points of view. Schleiermacher, an important representative of this form of Protestantism, interpreted the dogma as a function of religious experience. This experience may be summed up as the conflict within us between our attraction to God and our attraction to things of sense. Christ delivers us from this struggle in the sense that within Him are accomplished full consciousness of God and freedom from sin, as well as the power to communicate this perfect experience to His faithful.

There was no longer any question of expiation or substitution here. The cold and truly revolting rationalism of the early dialecti-

[25] Cited by L. Richard, *Le dogme de la Rédemption,* p. 130.

cians gave place to a pietistic sentimentality that easily followed from Luther's "doctrine" of *faith alone*. This anti-intellectual and anti-dogmatic Protestantism was animated by a profound moral and religious sentiment in the case of such men as A. Sabatier and A. Réville. As they saw it, the work of Jesus consisted in realizing within the individual and within society, the attitude of dependence that is the condition for the efficacy of divine forgiveness. The death of Jesus was a pathetic appeal to us, to make us enter into this disposition. Jesus is only a man, but in him the Love of God was manifested in an eloquent manner. His Passion and death were the consequences of our sins, by virtue of the solidarity of the human race. The case of Jesus is akin to that of the martyrs, who are the inevitable victims of the wicked, as with Socrates; but Jesus is infinitely more and better than they.

Obviously, the effort of Liberal Protestantism has been toward freeing the dogma of the Redemption from all "mythicism" and legalism, and toward retaining only its moral significance: it is an appeal to God's mercy, the source of our salvation. Unfortunately, the subjectivism of this liberal critique of the old concept of expiation vitiates whatever it might have of truth and common sense.

The excesses of this subjectivism have provoked a vigorous return to dogma. The most famous representative of this movement is the great contemporary theologian, Karl Barth. He accuses Protestant theology of having "fallen back fatally and in many different ways into the pagan conception that the Fathers of the Church had legitimately and successfully combated in the first centuries . . . This 'great theological and ecclesiastical disaster' would not have occurred if faith in the only-begotten Son of God had not disappeared beneath the confusion of mitigating interpretations." [26]

Catholics can rejoice over the number of essential points of agreement between themselves and Karl Barth. However one difficulty remains. Dr. Barth clings to his uncompromising anti-intellectualism, inspired by the rigid Calvinistic pessimism behind which he has entrenched himself. As far as the dogma of the Redemption is concerned, this difficulty consists in the stultifying determinism that the Calvinistic doctrine of predestination imposes upon the unfolding of our salvation in Christ. Nowhere in this interpretation does love, the essential reality of this drama, appear. Everything is governed by God's impassible sovereignty.

[26] *Credo,* French translation (Paris, 1936), p. 67.

It is certainly not in *Modernism,* whether Catholic or Protestant, that Karl Barth—the determined opponent of Modernism—can discover the true notion of love. Modernism, for which religious certitude is based solely on religious experience, literally dissolves the dogma of the Redemption. First of all, it claims that Christ is not God in historical reality, but only in the faith of His disciples. He is actually only a man, and it is therefore illusory to speak of the redemptive value of His Passion. Moreover, modernists (such as Loisy) declare that Jesus Christ had no intention of dying to expiate our sins; and that the doctrine of Christ's expiatory death is a creation of St. Paul's. They hold that the progress of the sciences demands that the Christian doctrine of the Redemption be reformed, and certain other points of doctrine as well.[27]

It has fallen to Catholic exegetes, texts in hand, to show the Evangelical origin of the traditional doctrine. And they have done it victoriously. With regard to the progress of science that would oblige us to recognize only a "symbol" and not an "absolute and indestructible truth" in the necessity of expiating sin by the death of a just man, theology agrees that symbolism has its rightful place. However, it upholds the fundamental reality of Christ's expiatory death and the essential truth of His satisfaction, because this death was in the service of Love and this satisfaction was the effect of Love. In its attempt to understand the mystery of the Redemption, Modernism has not considered Love as its inspiration and in its acts, any more than has the dogmatism of Karl Barth.

This grave omission is no doubt the sanction as well as the principle of all the errors concerning the dogma of the Redemption, including the errors that consisted in insisting exclusively on the value of love as against the overly legalistic conceptions of salvation. To fathom this mystery, dogmatic truth is mindful both of the sentiments of our Savior's soul and of the objective values of His sufferings and death. Catholic theology, heedful of the Church's salutary reactions against heresy, has applied itself to the harmonious synthesis of the elements that the heresies dissociated.

Before going any further, let us consider a few of the canons in which the Church has steadfastly affirmed her faith.

Jesus "came down from heaven" to "restore" our nature, lost

---

[27] Cf. Encyclical *Pascendi,* issued by Pope St. Pius X, Denz. No. 2076, 2094; and the Decree of the Holy Office dated July 4, 1857, Props. 38 and 64, Denz. No. 2038, 2064.

through Adam, said the Second Council of Orange in 530 (Denz., No. 194). He came "to deliver the human race," added the Second Council of Toledo in 675 (Denz., No. 282). In 1441, the Decree to the Jacobites of the Council of Florence specified that He is the one mediator who wrests us from the devil (Denz., 711).

In combatting one or another of the heresies, the Magisterium clarified the role of the Redeemer. Against the Pelagians, the Council of Carthage, in 418, pointed to our Savior as the center of the religious life of the individual (Denz., 103-104): It is through Him that we receive the graces we need, not only for knowledge but for action as well. On several occasions, the Church has taught the universality of the Redemption: at the Council of Quierzy in 853 (Denz., No. 318-319); against the Jansenists in 1690 (Denz., 1294–1295); and against Quesnel in 1713 (Denz., 1380, 1382). In these instances she stressed that the Savior dominates the religion of the whole human family, inasmuch as He died for all men.

Jesus saves us at the price of His blood, according to the Third Council of Valencia in 855 (Denz., No. 323). But this must not make us neglect the principle of our salvation, namely the love of the Savior who died "spontaneously" (Second Council of Constantinople in 553, Denz., No. 215; First Lateran Council in 649, Denz., No. 255). Finally, it is His Godhead that confers infinite efficacy upon His Passion, and even on the smallest drop of His blood, as Clement VI wrote in 1343 (Denz., No. 550). For He is "one of the Trinity" according to the Eastern expression (John II in 534, Denz., No. 201, par. 1; Second Council of Constantinople, Denz., No. 223).

At the Council of Trent, held from 1545 to 1563, the Church has summed up her doctrine on the Redemption in the solid and ample chapters and accompanying canons of Sessions 5, 6, and 22 (Denz., No. 787, 793, 938). We are sinners, powerless to justify ourselves either through nature or through the Law. We have only the justice of Christ (Denz., 793-794). The Father of mercy (Denz., 799) is the "efficient cause" of our salvation. The Council teaches (against Socinianism) that the Savior's role is not simply an exemplary one: Jesus is the *meritorious cause* of our salvation in His Passion. In addition to His meritorious activity, He also offers *satisfaction* for us to His Father on the Cross (Denz., 799, and Session 14, Denz., 904, 905, concerning the sacrament of Penance);

and He likewise offers *sacrifice,* to which the sacrifice of the Mass is identical (Denz., 938, 940, 951). In addition, there is the special influence of the Head on His members, an influence that precedes, accompanies, and follows their virtuous acts and renders them meritorious (Denz., 809).

This doctrine implies the rejection of the Protestant conception of justification through mere imputation. The justice of Christ wins for us true satisfaction and interior renewal (Denz., 792 and 820). It is also an affirmation of our power to merit and satisfy personally, without impinging upon the infinite merits or upon the unique satisfaction of the Savior (Denz., 809 and 906). Pope Pius V reaffirmed this doctrine against Baïus (Denz., 1059). One of the distinctive marks of the soteriology of the Council of Trent, which was so deeply inspired by Tradition, is the use of the scholarly notions of merit and, especially, of satisfaction.

In our own time, the teaching of the Magisterium gives less consideration to dogmatic matters than to spiritual aspects of the mystery in which the age-old thought and devotion of the Church toward her Savior are condensed: the priesthood and the kingship of Christ, the charity of Christ, devotion to the Sacred Heart. The controversial trend of thought provoked among theologians by the heresies has given way to loving meditation, and the analysis of the mystery has yielded to the discovery of its sources: "the very great love" of the Father and the tenderness of the Son who has loved sinners "to the end." [28]

II. The Theology of the Mystery of the Redemption

We have turned for inspiration to the theology of St. Thomas, as presented in the "Tertia Pars" of his *Summa Theologiae.* For this theology, as we see it, is the most rigorous, the most faithful to Tradition and to Scripture, and the one that best expresses the teaching of the Magisterium.

Four fundamental themes present themselves to the theologian's mind: The Word Incarnate saved us by way of *merit, satisfaction, sacrifice,* and *efficiency.* Now charity is the soul of these four functions; and it is within the Mystical Body that the quadruple effect of the Redemption is communicated by the Savior to His sinful members.

[28] Cf. *Le Sacré-Coeur,* Pontifical texts with commentary by Paul Galtier, S. J. (Paris, Desclée de Brouwer), 1936.

1. THE HARMONIES OF THE MYSTERY OF THE REDEMPTION

Before going any further, it will be helpful if we grasp the "harmonies" of the mystery of the Redemption, that is, those of its related aspects that are either necessary or optional.

Man was created in the image of his God, in order to glorify God by an homage of love. But instead, man aspired to equal God and refused to give Him his heart's submission. Now, some see in this rebellion the first stage in man's conquest of his own personality. But in reality it was the supreme insult to God, the downfall of man. This offense called for reparation, this downfall cried out for rehabilitation: an onerous reparation, a painful rehabilitation. But what a cynical joke these would be if they were not the work of love! Yet the sinner was henceforth powerless to make this love spring up from his guilty heart in a way that would be acceptable to God. That is the root of the pathetic distress that inspired the ancient Tragedies. We can emerge from this abyss only with the help of a Savior.

Jesus Christ can be the Savior of sinful men because He is man and God, and because there is no sin in Him. He took these two natures, which are hostile in this world because of our souls' rebelliousness, and united them hypostatically without confusing or changing them, in order to reconcile them in Himself. Our redemption was assured by the very fact of His presence among us. For in His very constitution, in His psychology and His life, He was "the Redeemer" even before He actually redeemed us by certain privileged acts.

We were saved from the moment there was someone among us to render to God efficaciously the worship that is His due (Lk. 2:49), to obey Him even to death (Phil. 2:8), and "to give his life as a ransom for many" (Mt. 20:28). He is the one to whom God has made us belong, for He "has become for us God-given wisdom, and justice, and sanctification, and redemption" (I Cor. 1:30). "Neither is there salvation in any other. For there is no other name under heaven given to men by which we must be saved" (Acts 4:12).

2. THE NECESSITY OR FITNESS OF THE REDEMPTION

If Jesus is the only way out of our misfortune, is the Redemption necessary? The dialectic of certain Fathers seems to conclude in the affirmative. For example, St. Athanasius writes: "It was unfitting that creatures endowed with reason and admitted to a participation in the Word should perish, and should fall into nothingness through corruption. For it was not worthy of God that His works should be destroyed by the devil's deceit . . . If God had not created man, no one would think of accusing God of weakness. But now that in fact God did create man, so that he might live, it would be absurd that man should perish, and worse still that he should perish under the eyes of his author . . . It would be improper and unworthy of God's excellence." [1]

We find the same argumentation in St. Gregory the Great,[2] and in many others. We know how St. Anselm intended to demonstrate the fact of the Redemption by starting from the demands of God's justice and the insolvency of man. But this demonstration is fallacious, for nothing obliges God to conform to the imperatives of a justice that we necessarily conceive in human terms. As for the sense of guilt in the sinner's heart and the sense of recovered liberty in the Christian's soul, they do not serve as principles from which to deduce the historic fact of the Redemption or the timeless fact of God's will to save man. The universality of the practice of bloody sacrifice and the need of forgiveness can only prove the permanence of certain sentiments in the heart of man.

Reason cannot prove the existence of a divine Redemption in the face of dialecticians who distrust the resources of human logic, or of traditionalists who are the eager interpreters of religious facts. On the other hand, reason is aware of the divine and human *fitness* of such a Redemption.

Some insist that reason protests against the picture of God that the dogma of the Cross gives us: a bloody tyrant who might perfectly well forgive without more ado but prefers to set in motion the apparatus of a savage justice and takes pleasure in the suffering of an innocent victim. Natural reason also protests against the idea of a change or a relenting in the will of the One who is changeless in His plans as well as in His nature, whose works are without re-

[1] *De Incarnatione Verbi*, 6, P.G. 25, 108.
[2] *Moralia*, 17, 20, P.L. 76, 32-33.

pentance and who cannot forgive what must be punished. "Who is this God," asks J. Turmel, "who puts God to death to appease God?" [3]

The reason of the believer invites the defenders of "reason" to some attempt at modesty: "For my thoughts are not your thoughts: nor your ways my ways, saith the Lord" (Is. 55:8). The most rigorous justice that divine forgiveness demands can be the most eloquent revelation of love, inasmuch as in God mercy always precedes justice. No merit or right of God's creatures can ever shake God's supreme changelessness, since "in rewarding our merits, He crowns His own gifts" (Second Council of Orange). The reason God died in the human nature He assumed was so that we sinners, the members of the Savior, might die in Him. Finally, when we speak of "appeasing" God, we do not mean that there is a "passion" in God. All we mean to suggest is that God is watching over our interests and wills their successful realization.

When the Christian's reason thinks about the economy of the Redemption, it can see in God only absolute liberty and total initiative, and the absence of any "necessity" anterior to His will. God can save or not save the sinner without injury to any of His attributes: He is the sole judge of the ultimate reason for His acts, and this reason is His glory. There is a certain necessity in this economy, but it follows upon a "hypothetical" divine decision. Granted the hypothesis that God has decided to save the world, and to save it not only by way of pardon but also by way of adequate satisfaction, it is necessary that a Savior should intervene, raised up by God Himself, a Savior who is innocent and also God, a Savior who is loving and obedient even unto death.

Why did God choose this plan of salvation, among others that were equally possible? In what way does this plan assure Him greater glory? God alone knows. We can merely say with St. Irenaeus: "The glory of God is living man." God glorifies Himself in His creatures by making them happy in Him. Their happiness is His glory. Inasmuch as God cannot benefit in any way from His works, it is man's advantage alone that has inspired His choice.

And lastly, the economy of the Redemption, as God has conceived it, can be explained by God's desire to teach man by means he would best understand. This economy reveals to us something that we would not have understood as well if things had been differ-

[3] *Hist. des dogmes*, Vol. I, pp. 450-455.

ent, namely the disproportion between sin and God's infinite justice. In the same light, man is made to see the infinite mercy, "the very great love" of God for man. By the reparation that God demands for our sins, and the cooperation that He expects of us on the Savior's Cross, He makes known to us the importance He attaches to our moral activity, the sublime idea He has of our worth, and the great respect He still has for us in spite of the insults He has received from us. To quote St. Leo the Great: "O Christian, recognize your dignity!"

In this economy, the incomparable and all-powerful wisdom of God shines forth. For God's wisdom makes use even of the evil that He has foreseen, permitted, and integrated into His plan, for the honor of His name and to the advantage of man. Thus the Redemption is not simply the patching up of a work that has been spoiled, it is much more than that. God has taken what He had so marvelously created in the beginning, and He has even more marvelously re-created it in the Savior.

In the twofold perspective, divine and human, from which the drama of our salvation must be viewed, meditation opens up many avenues that lead to the heart of the mystery. But all of them start from the will of God, a will that is absolutely gratuitous and that transcends all our reasons. Whatever the reason we may choose, it will never lead us to the justification of the views and actions of God. The "fitness" and harmonies of the Redemption may captivate those who are already following the divine "choragus," as Clement of Alexandria calls Christ. But they cannot prove that He has come to those who are still seeking Him.

3. THE HISTORICAL FACT OF THE REDEMPTION

God's eternal will to save man was realized in a dramatic episode of human history. We must look upon the hero and the various actors in this drama not with indiscreet curiosity, but with reverent attention.

(a) Our Savior's Sufferings

The immensity of Christ's sufferings stirs up our emotions, which are further stimulated by spiritual writers, the efforts of preachers, and the pathetic portrayals of artists. Although theology examines this suffering with apparent serenity, its sober analyses, which are more moving than oratorical or literary effects, actually penetrate deeper into the mystery (cf. for example, St. Thomas Aquinas, *Summa,* IIIa, q. 46, a. 4).

Theology does not claim that our Savior had to or actually did experience all possible human sufferings during His Passion. Excruciating as were the torments of the Cross, man's cruelty now possesses resources to cause far worse sufferings, as we know too well! Moreover, it is erroneous to place an emphasis on physical suffering that should belong first of all, in a drama of moral redemption, to spiritual suffering.

The fact remains that Jesus willed to undergo one of the most terrible tortures, in order to redeem us. Crucifixion was conceived in such a way as not to leave any point of the organism without suffering. Besides, to get some idea of the intensity and depth of our Lord's suffering, we must remember the exquisite sensibility of His pure body, born of the Virgin Mary and untouched by any of the sicknesses that dull our sensations. On the contrary, His body was offered up to the maximum of pain by a will that held absolute sway over His whole being and kept Him at the peak of consciousness; whereas in us one pain inhibits another, and the will strives to anaesthetize all discomfort.

During those three days of unmitigated tragedy, the universe of human suffering was really concentrated in the heart and soul of Jesus. He experienced all the pain that men can inflict: from foreigners and from fellow-countrymen, from strangers and from His closest friends, from the lowly and the great. He experienced all the grief that can ravage a man's heart: the infidelity of His friends, denial by one of them and the treason by another; the vilest affronts to His reputation and to His manly honor. He was treated as a liar, He was stripped naked before His compatriots, He faced the universal disgust which dissolves courage; and at the end, He was apparently abandoned even by His Father.

Amid this ocean of horrors which Grünewald has painted for us with an extremism that is far preferable to the mawkishness of so many paintings, the Savior's soul was plunged in the infinite, inamissible joy of the beatific vision. Moralists distinguish between man's spontaneous volition and his deliberate volition. The former cannot help instinctively resisting suffering in all its forms, for it is incapable of grasping the ends of suffering. Deliberate volition, on the other hand, can accept and even will this suffering and find its joy in it. Such is the joy that delights in giving the supreme proof of love. It is the joy of the martyrs. And yet no martyr experienced this joy the way Christ did, because no one ever loved as He did.

But the Savior's joy was incomparably more powerful and radiant, and its source was more certain; for it was rooted in the vision of God. So great is the joy of the elect that neither tears nor sorrow are possible for them (Apoc. 21:4), and even their flesh is glorified. Our divine Lord had to exert His will in a special way to stop the flood of joy from invading His soul, for this joy would have made it impossible for Him to suffer. This is the profound truth underlying St. Paul's words: "Jesus, who for the joy set before him, endured a cross, despising shame" (Heb. 12:2).

Even during His deepest humiliation, our Savior retained the unity of His being and of His consciousness. It was the divine Person of the Word Incarnate who endured these humiliations and sufferings, even while He experienced in the highest portions of His soul the supreme human joy of the beatific vision.

(b) *The Actors in the Passion*

The Redemption is a drama which unfolds on several stages simultaneously, in accordance with a manifold chronology. There is a visible stage, but also an invisible stage where the eternal secrets of this drama find expression. On the visible stage, men move about, on the invisible stage the Godhead acts. Between the two, the Hero of the drama plays His role. While He appears to be swept along by the plot, in reality it is He who calls the turns and brings about a permanent union between these two worlds, which have been at war until then but now are reconciled by Him.

The striking thing about the unfolding of the Passion is the supreme freedom with which the Savior moves through it, *sponte passum* in the words of the Lateran Council (Denz., 225; cf. Second Council of Constantinople, Denz., 215). He suffers freely, and He repeatedly affirms this freedom: "No one takes (my life) from me, but I lay it down of myself. I have the power to lay it down, and I have the power to take it up again. Such is the command I have received from my Father" (Jn. 10:18). He is free with regard to the men who are His torturers; they are merely His unknowing instruments. He is free likewise with regard to God His Father. True, Jesus dies out of obedience—as is fitting to make reparation for man's original disobedience—but far from contradicting His freedom, this obedience is its supreme expression. It is by reason of what is most spontaneous and free in Him that Jesus conforms to the will of His Father. And this freedom-giving quality is His love for the Father. His obedience is not merely passive. Jesus is not content to let others act; He efficaciously directs the agents of the execution and takes the initiative when "His hour" has come. "Arise, let us go from here!" (Jn. 14:31).

In the last analysis, the Father is the ultimate author of the economy of salvation, through and because of His Son's obedience. When we say "the Father" we mean the Holy Trinity, since the Trinity is indivisible in all of its external works (Fourteenth Council of Toledo, Denz., 284). It is the Blessed Trinity that redeems us, and the Word who redeems us within the Trinity. To understand the full depth of St. Paul's words: "He . . . has not spared even his own Son but has delivered him for us all" (Rom. 8:32), we must look up to God Himself. If we are to understand the secret of our Savior "obedient even unto death on a Cross," we must turn to the mystery of the eternal relations between the Three Persons, in whom the Son receives everything from His Father without being inferior to the Father in any respect. And though the human "extras" of the drama of the Passion are actually serving to carry out the Son's obedience and the Father's will, this does not lessen their guilt in the least. Of course, we can make hierarchical distinctions in the scale of responsibility, as did the theologians of the Middle Ages, between the *majores* or leaders, the *minores,* or members of the sheeplike and lustful crowd, and intermediaries like Judas.

We must look beyond the bloody scene in which base human passions play a parody of justice around Christ, and discern the will of God to save us and the loving obedience of Christ. If we do this, it will be impossible to give any but a spiritual and religious significance to this drama: The Passion is a mystery of redemptive love.

4. THE REDEMPTIVE POWER OF THE PASSION

Now that we have entered into the Savior's soul through the Gospel account of the Passion, we must strive to find there the mysterious modalities of our salvation through the Passion.

Several theological systems have tried with varying degrees of success to give us a satisfactory explanation of the redemptive efficacy of the Passion. The least attractive of these explanations is the one based on *punishment:* Jesus saved us by His Passion because He suffered in our place the punishment we deserved. This theme was formerly favored by orthodox Protestants and also by many Catholic preachers, for example Bossuet and Bourdaloue. It has been abandoned in our own day with good reason, because of the odious character it attributes to divine justice and because of the impropriety of a substitution that disregards the inalienability of sin.

Another explanation, and a better one, is based on the principle of *expiation.* Christ is not the object of God's awful vengeance, but it is a general law that sin must be expiated by suffering. Our Savior endured in our place sufferings that are equivalent to those we should have endured, thus paying off our debts. The weakness of this system rests in the excessive importance it gives to penal suffering, to the detriment of the moral values that are inseparable from sin and its reparation.

The theology of *reparation* places primary emphasis on moral values, without disregarding the physical and penal aspect of expiation. If the life and death of Christ have the power to save, it is above all by reason of His love for His Father and for us, and by reason of the hypostatic union of His suffering humanity with the Person of the Word. When the Passion is thus endowed with infinite value, it superabundantly re-establishes the moral equilibrium of the world destroyed by sin. While penal suffering, both physical and spiritual, has a significant place in the Passion, we must look upon it first of all as a drama of love. It is by virtue of this love that the Passion makes reparation for sin—if it is indeed true that sin is essentially a refusal to love.

It is in this direction that the Latin Fathers influenced the development of the theology of the Redemption. According to this view the Passion has a preponderant role. The Greek Fathers, on the contrary, preferred the notion of a Redemption accomplished by the very fact of the Incarnation of the Word. This is the sublime theme, Platonistic in savor, of the sinner's deification through the Incarnation.[4]

[4] Cf. J. Gross, *op. cit.*

Romanesque portals present the triumphant Christ to us, and the piers of the Gothic cathedrals represent the Beautiful God teaching. The later Middle Ages, on the other hand, preferred sorrowful representations of the Passion of Christ. With the invasion of religious sentiment into the realm of art, there were increasing numbers of portrayals of the Carrying of the Cross, the Crucifixion, the Pietà, and the Burial of Christ. This change in Christian iconography has been explained by the influence of Scotism, the tender devotion of St. Francis, the mysticism of Tauler, Henry Suso, etc.

We should not minimize the importance of isolated statues and paintings during this period. What art lost in monumental dimensions, it gained in sensitivity. In centering their efforts on a single subject, artists became more interested in facial expressions. From there, it was only a step to affectation, pathos, and a taste for the macabre; and certain artists made the step. French art, however, never ceased producing works which, though expressing the varying temperaments of their authors, maintained the plastic qualities of French genius, with its scholarly discretion and simplicity, its sobriety in means of expression, and its concern for professional skill.

Need we stress the interior emotion that is written on the face of the Virgin Mary, the fervent and sorrowful faith that joins her Mother's hands in a gesture of adoration and offering before the Body of the Savior, fixed by the redemptive death in a permanent attitude of sacrifice and abandonment? The quality of the design is at the service of an extraordinary power of expression, and this with a sobriety of means and a reserve that make of it an eminently religious work.

Unfortunately, the centuries that followed have given us religious works of unequal caliber. Academicism imprisoned expression within "canons of beauty" that often won out over the search for interior religion.

And have we not yielded to this tendency ourselves? Do we not prove it by our astonishment and scandal before certain modern religious works that upset our academic prejudices?

What can we expect of an artist if not the expression of the religious universe he bears within him and with which he communes at length before bringing it forth in forms proper to his inspiration, his genius, and his character, themselves the products of his race and his time? Thus, his work will be truly religious only in the measure that it is faithful to his interior vision of the Christian mystery. That is what Rouault means when he says that the artist must obey his interior order.

We must contemplate this "Christ of the outrages" long and silently, and look upon the face of this derided Christ, heavy with all of human suffering, in order to enter into its mystery and understand all that the artist has wanted to tell us about it. Above all, we must look upon it with infinite respect, and with a completely open mind and heart that will make us receptive to the divine and will draw us into the soul of this Savior who communes with human tragedy without ceasing to commune with immutable Peace. What we perceive beyond this is as unutterable as the silence of mental prayer.

When an artist has caught the image of his contemplation with such power, should we be surprised that he dares to take a few liberties with forms? Let us rather try to understand that there would be a kind of impropriety in speaking of anatomy to one who is trying to grasp the soul of his God.

The Christ of the Outrages, by G. Rouault (1935).

(a) *The sinner's deification through the Incarnation.*

Pagan antiquity was tormented by the human yearning for union with God, for man can be happy only by being like God and being united to Him. Jesus Christ answers this age-old yearning. Through the Incarnation, man, who had been separated from God by his sinfulness, was once again united to his God. Thus the Incarnation is essentially redemptive. In the words of St. Athanasius: "Because the Word of God, the eternal Son of the Father, clothed Himself with flesh and became man, we have been delivered." [5] Even our flesh has been made "like to the Word." [6] How does this assimilation to the Word touch individual men? By reason of the real unity of all men in the subsistent humanity in which they participate. When the Word assumed human nature, He assumed and deified all men within Himself.

In this view, the acts of the Passion of Jesus receive much less attention. There is no need of using the concept of substitution to explain how the Redemption is applied to sinners. Whereas the Latins seek to explain how the Redeemer's acts during His Passion are truly His own and can be attributed to us, the Greeks start from the premise that the acts of the Passion are our own, that each one of us merits, makes satisfaction, and offers sacrifice in the person of Christ. And yet Latin and Eastern theology must find a common meeting ground. On the one hand, the acts of the Passion of the Word are really the Incarnation in its second phase, its decisive expression and the plenary exercise of its efficacy: on the Cross, Jesus is the perfect mediator. On the other hand, within the Mystical Body there reigns a vital identity which makes the legalism of substitution meaningless.

Far from being opposed, the two theologies of the Redemption mutually complement one another. The alleged opposition that certain historians such as Harnack have discovered between the juridical realism of the West and the speculative mysticism of the East is purely artificial. There is no truth in the view which contrasts the two, showing the West as obsessed by an oppressive picture of an avenging God weighing the Redemption on the scales of quantitative justice, and the East as inclined to confuse the Redemption with the Incarnation and to forget the capital role of the Passion.

[5] *Contra Arian.*, orat. 2, 60, P.G. 26, 290; *ibid., Epist. ad Epict.* 7, P.G. 20, 1062.

[6] *Oratio*, 3, 33, P.G. 26, 395.

The East and the West are in reality so little opposed that it is easy to glean "realistic" texts among the Greeks that exalt the Passion and adopt the legalism of substitution, and to find "mystical" texts among the Latins in favor of the Redemptive Incarnation.

(b) *The moral efficacy of the Passion*

Merit, satisfaction, sacrifice, instrumental efficiency—these are the multiple modalities of one and the same causality, the causality of the Passion. One and the same agent can produce a single effect by different but simultaneous ways, when this agent acts intelligently and freely.

The first and most obvious way anything is a cause is by producing the effect of itself. This is physical causality. An architect is the cause of a house and God is the cause of the world in the sense that they are, properly speaking, the authors of the house and of the world, which have come directly from them. Likewise, when we say that the Passion is the cause of our salvation, this is what we mean: The architect is the principal cause of the house, whereas the carpenter who executes his plan is its instrumental cause; God is the principal cause, that is, the principle of our salvation, whereas the Passion is its instrumental cause.

The second way of producing an effect is to make it proceed not from oneself but from another agent that one induces to act. This is moral causality, that sets into motion intelligent and free agents. After his day's work, the laborer has the right to receive the wages his employer has agreed to pay him. It is in return for his work that the "boss" pays the sum due. Now, merit, satisfaction, and sacrifice come within the category of moral causality. Through His sufferings and death, Jesus acquired rights to our salvation. He presents these rights to His Father, and by reason of these rights the Father saves us.

The Passion of our Lord is the *physical* cause of our salvation: this assertion signifies that the grace which is restored to the sinful human race really passes through the sacred Humanity of the suffering and dying Christ, and through His Humanity into our own individual beings.

The Passion of our Lord is the *moral* cause of our salvation: this assertion signifies that God grants His salvation to sinful humanity in consideration of the merits, the satisfaction, and the sacrifice of Christ in His Passion.

Physical causality demands the direct intervention of the sacred, suffering Humanity, whereas in moral causality this sacred Humanity intervenes only in an exterior manner. In its physical causality, the Passion produces our salvation; in its moral causality, it assures the conditions demanded for salvation. On the other hand, in terms of physical causality the sacred Humanity cooperates only instrumentally in the work of our salvation, whereas moral causality demands the total initiative and activity of the suffering Savior. It goes without saying that these two causalities are intimately interrelated. The Passion is the infinite, meritorious cause of our salvation. Whence this infinite value? From the hypostatic presence of the Word in the sacred Humanity. The human actions and sufferings of our Savior are the human actions and sufferings of an infinite Person. When these actions are clothed by this Person with a power that surpasses them, they become as it were instruments of the Person. The merits, satisfaction, and sacrifice of Christ in His Passion are the instruments of the Word for our salvation. Conversely, in Christ the "animate instrument" of God, the efficiency of the Passion necessarily brings into play His human consciousness and liberty, that is, the very principles of His moral, meritorious, satisfactory, and sacrificial activity.

Thus the two causalities of the Passion are simultaneous and indissociable. The instant the Savior freely surrenders Himself to His Father through love and obedience, as the instrument of our salvation, He posits an act that has value for us in terms of merit, satisfaction, and sacrifice. And the instant He merits, satisfies, and sacrifices Himself for us, He is the instrument of the Word, the divine Person responsible for His merits, His satisfaction, and His sacrifice, and who confers upon them an infinite value for salvation.

A careful analysis of the human act will reveal that the principle of merit, satisfaction, and sacrifice is charity. And if we look deep into the human heart of our Savior, we shall see that He made Himself the instrument of God, "obedient even to death on a Cross," because of His love; and that it is through His love for us that the grace of our salvation finds its way to us. From whichever way we look at it, the mystery of the Cross is a mystery of love. Does this amount to forgetting the drama of tears and blood that is the price of our Redemption? Certainly not! But it is the realization that suffering, whether corporeal or spiritual, is capable of religious merit and satisfaction, and has instrumental power to save only inasmuch as this suffering is a function of love. "It was not Christ's death but the love of the dying Christ that was pleasing to God— *Non mors sed voluntas placuit ipsius morientis.*" This thought of St. Bernard's (Letter 190, to Innocent, 2, P.L. 182, 1053) is the necessary foundation of any sound theology of the Redemption.

(c) *The merit of the Passion*

According to the Council of Trent, only those are saved "to whom the merit of the Passion is communicated"; for "there is bestowed upon them, through the merit of His Passion, the grace by which they are made just" (Session VI, Chapter 3, Denz., 795). In analyzing the various causes of our salvation, the same Council came to the conclusion that Jesus Christ, the meritorious cause "when we were enemies" (Rom. 5:10), merited our justification for us on the Cross by His most holy Passion, "by reason of his very great love wherewith he has loved us" (Eph. 2:4). (Cf. Denz., 799).

The notion of merit used by the Council had been traditional in theology since St. Anselm. It appeared in the texts of the Magisterium in 1343 with the Bull of Clement VI on indulgences (Denz., 552), and in the Decree to the Jacobites of the Council of Florence (Denz., 711). It was also used in the canons prepared by the Vatican Council.

We shall not discuss again the general notion of merit which was analyzed in the volume on morals. Let us simply call to mind that merit is a property of the virtuous act. It apparently belongs to the field of law. But in reality it belongs to the "biological" realm. The plant that has been properly watered "merits" its flower and its fruit, because it has been faithful to the law of its being. The conscious and free being who acts in conformity with his nature, merits that his being should grow and achieve fulfillment. It is love that enables the free being to be faithful to his inner law. Love is the source and the measure of merit.

When the internal principles of merit are considered in themselves, we find that no one can merit for another. Merit is a property of the human act. It belongs to the person responsible for this act, and is applicable only to this person. But if we trace back to the initial source of merit—which is the free choice of the Creator— the answer depends on what God has done. If God confers upon an individual a principle that truly constitutes him a "public being," and extends the scope of his activity beyond his own particular interests, then this individual can merit strictly for others by the same right that he can merit for himself, for then other persons are simply the totality of this "public being."

Now, by a divine dispensation, Jesus Christ is one of us but He towers above and embraces all of us. "He is the head of his body, the Church; he, who is the beginning, the firstborn from the dead, that in all things he may have the first place. For it has pleased God the Father that in him all his fullness should dwell, and that through him he should reconcile to himself all things, whether on the earth or in the heavens, making peace through the blood of his cross" (Col. 1:18-20). In the thought of God and in reality, Jesus and we are one. "We are Himself," as St. Augustine says (*In Jn. Tract.*, 111, P.L. 35, 1929). In fact, Jesus Himself has declared: "And for them I sanctify myself" (Jn. 17:19). St. Augustine comments on these words by adding "because they, too, are myself" (*In Jn., Tract.*, 108, P.L. 35, 1916). Thus Jesus, our Head, merits strictly for us His members, for the head and the members form the total Christ.

Jesus merited by suffering for the sake of justice. When an individual man in the state of grace suffers for justice' sake, he merits his own personal salvation. Therefore Jesus merited ours. To "suffer for justice' sake" signifies fighting against the powers of evil so that the kingdom of God may supplant them. No virtuous activity could conform more closely to the Law of man, and therefore be more meritorious before God.

"For why did Christ, at the set time, die for the wicked when as yet we were weak? For scarcely in behalf of a just man does one die; yet perhaps one might bring himself to die for a good man. But God commends his charity towards us, because when as yet we were sinners, Christ died for us" (Rom. 5:6-9). While Christ died out of a spirit of religion and obedience, He died also and above all through love. It is in the love of Jesus that we must discover the principle of the merit of His Passion and death.

And yet, precisely in view of this love, we can wonder wherein lay the need of suffering so much for justice' sake simply to merit our salvation. The wails of the newborn babe in Bethlehem would have sufficed, according to St. Ambrose (*In Luc,* 2, 41, P.L. 15, 1568), for they already expressed this love loudly enough. But Jesus impatiently awaited the supreme hour (Jn. 12:27; Lk. 12:49-

50). His "hour" would be the moment when He would express in a decisive manner the immensity of His love for His Father and for us, and His burning thirst for justice; the moment when the excessive gravity of sin would be revealed to the frivolity of sinful men. "For the wages of sin is death" (Rom. 6:23). We would not have understood what sin is if God had not conformed to the established relationship between crime and punishment in the matter of reparation for sin. Jesus merited by His invisible love, but this love "had" to be manifested to us.

(d) *Satisfaction through the Passion*

The Passion of Christ is meritorious in a general way, but it is also meritorious in three specific ways: because Christ makes satisfaction through His Passion; because He offers Himself up as a sacrifice in His Passion; and because He willingly becomes the instrument of a divine activity in His Passion.

The notion of merit that specifically involves the idea of satisfaction has direct soteriological significance. The Church was planning to define this concept at the Vatican Council, which was interrupted by the War of 1870. Today, she makes frequent use of this idea. In its analysis of the causes of justification, the Council of Trent declared: "Jesus Christ made satisfaction for us to God the Father, by His most holy Passion on the wood of the Cross" (Session VI, chap. 7, Denz., 799). Against the Protestants, the Council also called for our collaboration with the Savior's satisfaction. For, far from impinging upon the infinite sufficiency of the Passion, our satisfactions have value only through Christ's (Session XIV, Chap. 8, Denz., 904-905).

It is true that the concept of satisfaction is unknown to Patristic tradition outside the doctrine of penance (since Tertullian). However this concept is traditional and Scriptural in its application to the Passion, in the sense that it follows from the closely-related notion of expiation by substitution and from the idea of ransom, both common in Scripture and among the Fathers.

Certain liberal historians (Ritschl) have claimed the antecedents of the concept of satisfaction are to be found in the Germanic custom of the "wergild." [7] The Church did not wait until she

[7] Germanic law admits of a pecuniary compensation (wergild) for all offenses, whatever their nature, which dispenses the guilty person from suffering the punishment he deserves. Thus satisfaction and punishment are different and distinct.

learned Germanic law to make the sinner choose between reparation for his sin and eternal damnation. St. Paul declared that "one
died for all" (II Cor. 5:14-15). St. John saw Christ as "a propitiation for our sins, not for ours only but also for those of the whole
world" (I Jn. 2:2; 4:10). In the vocabulary of the New Testament,
Jesus is presented as dying "for us," and again as dying "for our
sins" (Mt. 20:28; I Jn. 2:2; Rom. 5:8; I Cor. 15:3; I Pet. 3:18,
etc.).

Let us inquire into the theological meaning of satisfaction. Satisfaction is made when the person offended is offered something that
he loves as much or more than he detests the offense he has suffered. This is a complex notion, involving two elements: a moral
element and a penal element. Now, each of these elements tends
to become inflexible either in the direction of exclusive moral
reparation for the offense sin has caused to the honor of God, or in
the direction of exclusive and total acquittal of the punishment due
to sin. According to the definition borrowed from St. Thomas, satisfaction is essentially a moral work deriving from the virtue of
justice and even more from the virtue of charity.

Restitution of what one has stolen is a work of justice. In the
case before us, what we have refused to give and what must be
restored is not a thing but an interior act of submission, of reverence, and love. It is necessary to compensate, to "do enough"
(*satis-facere*), to render equal value not according to our own
standards but according to the objective measure of the offense committed. But how can we make restitution to God, whose love is
infinite? How can we span the abyss of a betrayed love that we
owe in a supreme degree? Agreement can be reached only by
means of a compromise. Obviously, the principle and measure of
this compromise is the good will of the One offended: He demands
of His offender only what he is capable of offering in restitution.
For lack of any "equivalence" between the restitution and the debt
owed, He accepts a "sufficiency."

Such a satisfaction implies the meeting of two wills, of two
loves: Out of His love for sinful man, God demands reparation;
for to be exacting toward man is to honor him. And yet He does
not demand more of man than he can do. The sinner in turn wants
to make reparation and strives to do it to the best of his ability,
out of his love for his offended God.

From this communion of love is born the need of a penalty in satisfaction. It does not suffice to love today, in order to make reparation for one's refusal to love yesterday. The love of which I am capable today is due in its entirety today, and the fact remains that yesterday I refused my love to God, and I gave it to another. This adulterous use of my heart should cause my conscience pain, the pain of repentance whose source is love. And this repentance calls for punishment.

Satisfaction is a work of justice, but it is less a matter of re-establishing an equality of justice than of reconciling two friends.

We must also discard the odious anthropomorphism of an avenging God who, because He is powerless to get restitution from men who are insolvent debtors, vents His wrath against the Innocent One, constituted their representative through love. Instead of this intolerable caricature, theology presents the Savior to us at the center of two formerly hostile loves, which are reconciled in Him and which accomplish in Him the justice for which they both hungered.

Because God loves the sinner, He demands reparation for his sin, but because the sinner is insolvent God asks of him only what he can do. God could well have asked no more than that of the sinner. But He loves the sinner too much not to rehabilitate him totally, adequately, in His sight. God's love for the sinner leads Him to demand a reparation that adequately covers all the sins of the world, and He gives the sinner the means of providing this reparation: Jesus Christ. Inasmuch as Jesus is innocent, transcending the human community and yet a member of it, inasmuch as He is the God-man, His Passion is a satisfaction that is more than objectively sufficient, a satisfaction that is really superabundant, infinite, for the sins of the whole world. Now, contrary to the opinion of St. Anselm (*Cur Deus Homo,* I, 20-21, P.L. 151, 392-394), it is not absolutely necessary that Jesus should take on the responsibility for this satisfaction, because it is not necessary that God demand it. And yet, if it were necessary Jesus alone would have the power to pay this debt. Jesus' satisfaction goes far beyond the compromise with which God's love for us could have been content.[8] The most rigorous justice in the service of the most merciful love reveals "the riches of his grace" (Eph. 1:7).

Conscious as we may be of this sublime economy of our Re-

[8] However, let us not forget that Christ's satisfaction precedes and obtains our love, even while it prepares the reparation it desires.

demption, we cannot help having the impression that it rests on the fragile foundation of a fiction. Because of His love, God demands adequate satisfaction of the sinner, but He also provides the sinner with the means of making this satisfaction in the Person of Christ. But this plan presupposes that the Savior's work of satisfaction be considered identical with the sinner's. There is a substitution here. But is such a substitution possible? Can Christ make satisfaction in such a way that it is we who make satisfaction and we who are delivered from sin in truth and not by imputation? This question touches the nerve center of the dogma of the Redemption.

Now as we have said, merit is radically inalienable because it is a property of a moral act, which is personal by its very nature. Satisfaction, on the other hand, can in one of its aspects be transferred. Here we must distinguish between the strictly satisfactory element of satisfaction which is transmissible, and the medicinal element which is not transmissible. Clearly, even though another can make restitution in my name for what I have stolen, I myself must take the remedy for my illness. However, satisfaction, in its formally reparative aspect, can be exercised by a third party and its results placed to the credit of the insolvent debtor. "Vicarious satisfaction" is possible on two counts, by reason of the bonds that unite Christ to men in the Mystical Body.

In the name of friendship, it is possible to make satisfaction for others before God. It goes without saying that it is indispensable to be on terms of friendship with God in order to plead before Him the cause of our friend the sinner. But that is perfectly feasible in that such a substitution presupposes a greater supernatural love through which God receives greater honor. Friendship's effectiveness in this instance rests upon the objective nature of satisfaction. The homage that our friend the sinner has refused to give God is in a certain respect exterior to his person and it can therefore be rendered by another person, providing this satisfaction is really imputable to the sinner. And besides, we can be our friend's instruments in terms of exterior activity.

Friendship, more than any other bond between men, creates an instrumental state, whose effect is attributable to the principal cause. Friendship implies such an identity of thought and will that what is thought, willed, and done by one of two friends appears spontaneously to be thought, willed, and done by the other. Peter makes satisfaction for Paul by doing in Paul's name what Paul, the sinner, would do if he saw the light. True, if Paul is to be effectively saved by this transfer, he must sooner or later—when he has recovered his good judgment—ratify Peter's action of which he can avail himself before God.

That is how Jesus saves us. Through His friendship for us, Jesus is our instrument, His will is our own will, our most genuine will. What He does, we in our powerlessness to make satisfaction, do in Him. All we have to do is to ratify this "representation" in order that the satisfaction of Christ may not only make restitution to God of what we have stolen from Him but also restore to us the life of God that we have lost.

Moreover, the bonds that unite us to Jesus Christ are closer than the bonds of friendship. Jesus is our Head, our Leader, we are His members. In the Mystical Body our bonds to Him are not only moral but in a certain respect "biological." These bonds are also the opposite of the bonds that friendship creates: As members of Christ our Head, we are His instruments. This is not a case of substitution, of representation, but of identity. There are no longer two persons, but "a single mystical person." "It is now no longer I that live, but Christ lives in me" (Gal. 2:20) and makes satisfaction in me, providing I am at least truly a member of this body.

(e) *The sacrifice of the Cross*

The Passion of Christ has value not only in terms of merit and satisfaction, which are more recent theological notions, it has value also as a sacrifice.

The sacrifice of Christ, according to the Epistle to the Hebrews, abrogates the empty sacrifices of the Law. It is the only definitive sacrifice that brings into play not a purely legal holiness but a new, interior holiness. This sacrifice is made up essentially of the love and obedience of the One who offers Himself. These spiritual values are a compelling proof of its transcendent originality as compared with ancient sacrifices, regardless of the claims of certain religious historians.

Let us call to mind what sacrifice is. Sacrifice is the act of the virtue of religion, which in turn derives from the virtue of justice. Its object is to render to God the worship that is due to Him as Creator by His creatures. Therein lies the formal difference between sacrifice and satisfaction. Satisfaction presupposes that a right of God has been violated and must be restored; sacrifice implies a duty that all men must perform. The former is called for by a failure which increases man's dependence, the latter flows from an inferiority that existed prior to any guilt. One is a reparation, the other is a homage.

An analysis of sacrifice shows that it has two composite elements, as does satisfaction: an interior element and a sensible, exterior element. But satisfaction must give God something that is primarily of an interior order, just as sin is; whereas sacrifice is formally of the sensible order, even though it is the sign of an interior homage that is really its most important element. In sacrifice the external act is an offering that transfers the thing offered to God from the realm of the profane to the sacred, that "consecrates" it, makes it sacred (*sacrum-facere*). A radical and definitive way of consecrating a thing to God is to "immolate" it to Him. This is the most eloquent expression of interior worship, of offering. In fact, this immolation corresponds to spiritual sacrifice, to an interior attitude of renunciation whose external, sensible immolation is only its symbol and completion.

The homage due to God by His creatures is inevitably affected by the historical state of those creatures. The sacrifice of sinful man, whose sin has consisted precisely in refusing this homage to God, necessarily takes on an aspect of "reparation," in order to be acceptable to God, to "appease" Him, and to make Him "propitious" to the sinner. The sacrifice of men in our historical situation is necessarily "offered in the form of satisfaction." We can therefore understand that consciousness of guilt has led the religious man spontaneously and universally to offer sacrifice in the extreme form of bloody immolation.

The religious condition of the sinner is tragic. He is obligated to render to God the worship that is His due, and yet it is impossible for him to offer God anything whatever that might be acceptable to Him. For, through his sin, he is the enemy of God. And if God is willing to be reconciled with him, the sinner does not know under what conditions and by what rites. It is necessary that God Himself designate the victim of sacrifice that He will accept, and that He compose the ritual for the sinner. That is why "in this has the love of God been shown in our case, that God has sent his only-begotten Son into the world that we may live through him. In this is the love . . . that he has . . . sent his Son a propitiation for our sins" (I Jn. 4:9-10). "God has sent forth (Christ Jesus) as a propitiation by his blood through faith" (Rom. 3:25). The initiative belongs to God alone, "for it has pleased God the Father that in (Christ) all his fullness should dwell, and that through him he should reconcile to himself all things, whether on the earth or in the heavens, making peace through the blood of his cross" (Col. 1:20).

Sacrifice is a work of justice, whose purpose is to render to God the worship that is His due. But what worship does God expect, if not the worship "in spirit and in truth" (Jn. 4:24) of love? Charity is the matter of the virtue of religion as well as its inspiration and its most perfect exercise. Charity is necessarily "religious": to love is also to adore. It is by reason of this love that sacrifice can fulfill its function of pacifying an offended God and of uniting the sinner to Him. The external offering is only the symbol of the perfect interior offering which underlies all love. To love is to give what is most intimately oneself. It is we ourselves and not our exterior goods that God wants. Consumed with love of God and also stimulated by repentance, the saint yearns to be delivered up, "dedicated," "consecrated," wholly and irrevocably to God. He aspires to the immolation of the heart, of which external immolation is only a meager proof.

We can now form some idea of the prodigious value of the sacrifice of Jesus Christ. "Upon the altar of the Cross" He visibly offered His sufferings as homage and reparation to His offended Father and He immolated His life. His love was the imperious mover of His offering: He offered Himself. No victim has ever offered itself more truthfully, because none ever offered itself more freely. No one has ever possessed himself so perfectly, or been so free from the obligation to expiate personal sins and exempt from the forces of interior dispersion that would have hindered the total recollection of his being in love.

It is in this quasi-infinite love, rather than in the shedding of the blood, that the Father who loves us received the expected sacrifice. How could He still take pleasure in blood after having so long rejected it? (See Heb. 10:5.) And yet it was in blood that the expiatory sacrifice proportionate to the sin that condemned us to death was formally accomplished. For sacrifice is formally an external act. It is in this blood that the love of our Savior found definitive expression, since "greater love than this no one has, that one lay down his life for his friends" (John 15:13).

It is because of the shedding of blood that the Passion has a specific value in the Redeemer's life. True, Jesus was constantly in a state of sacrifice throughout His life, as the French School loved to point out. And yet it was only when He died that Jesus was really in the act of sacrifice.

Jesus immolated Himself "for us," "for our sins": There could be no more magnificent proof of His immense love, of His ardent passion for the honor of God. Jesus could substitute Himself for us in the expiatory sacrifice that as sinners we owed to God, just as He could substitute Himself for us in making satisfaction, because God His Father had constituted Him the victim for powerless sinners, and because He was one with them before God.

The religious function that this Leader exercised in His sacrifice suggests an important complementary aspect: In His sacrifice Jesus was at once victim and priest, since He offered and immolated Himself. Now, He is a priest through the essential consecration of His humanity by the hypostatic union. Jesus Christ is not only the principle of the divine life of the members of His Mystical Body; He is also their priest, their Leader in the worship they must render to God His Father. The sacrifice of the Cross, the central act of His priesthood, is at the very heart of the mystery of the Incarnation of God and of the Redemption of men.

(f) The Passion, the "Instrument" of our Salvation

"Christ's Passion, according as it is compared with His Godhead, operates in an *efficient* manner; but in so far as it is compared with the will of Christ's soul it acts in a *meritorious* manner. Considered as being within Christ's very flesh, it acts by way of *satisfaction*, inasmuch as we are liberated by it from the debt of punishment; while inasmuch as we are freed from the servitude of guilt, it acts by way of *redemption*. But in so far as we are reconciled with God it acts by way of *sacrifice*" (St. Thomas Aquinas, *Summa,* IIIa, q. 48, a. 6, ad 3).

In meriting, making satisfaction, and sacrificing Himself for us on the Cross, Jesus exercised an essentially human activity the effect of which was human: a right to our salvation. But these same actions and His same Passion, human, meritorious, satisfactory, and sacrificial, were also the instruments of God. An essentially divine activity was exercised through these human acts and the effect obtained was divine in nature: the grace of our salvation.

As the instrumental cause of our salvation, the sacred humanity of our Savior acted during the Passion after the manner of the sacraments. His humanity is the supreme sacrament.

St. Cyril presented to the Council of Ephesus the mystery of the saving power of the Word Incarnate in words that have been approved by later Councils: "If anyone refuses to acknowledge that the flesh of Christ is life-giving . . . because it is the flesh of the Word Himself, who has the power of giving life to all things, let him be anathema." The Greek Fathers preferred to consider the saving power of the Passion under this "physical" aspect, rather than under the moral aspect of merit and satisfaction favored by Latin theology. According to St. John Damascene's classical dictum, which echoes the whole of Eastern tradition, the humanity of Christ is the instrument of His Godhead.

The Greek Fathers drew this realism directly from Scripture. For example, the parable of the vine (Jn. 15) clearly suggests it. Moreover, the redemptive efficacy attributed to the Passion is only the logical development of the theology of the union of the two natures in Christ.

To understand these fundamentals, we must first of all call to mind a few principles concerning instrumental causality. There are two types of efficient causes: the principal cause and the instrumental cause. The principal cause gives the initial impulse to the causal influx and to the effect produced; it can also associate to itself an agent upon which it may impress its own movement and which it may apply to the production of the effect desired. This agent thus becomes the instrument of the principal cause.

The mark of the instrument is to be a caused cause that acts and produces its effect only in the measure that it is under the influence of the principal cause. Thus, the instrument is really an instrument only at the moment it is in the hands of the initial agent. Outside of this privileged instant when it communes with an activity that surpasses its own powers, it is only a "thing," limited to the form and activity that are proper to it.

The instrument is thus intimately bound up with the action that the principal agent exercises together with it. Is it possible to discern the instrument's particular contribution? Let us consider the tool in the hand of the workman: the totality of the effect produced belongs simultaneously to the tool and to the workman. Together they constitute an inseparable tandem in the unity of their action.

But we see that this "thing," which has become a tool in the workman's hand, modifies and adapts the influx it receives, in accordance with its own form, with a view to the effect desired. And this tool applies the influx it receives from the workman to the matter to be worked upon. The paintbrush and the chisel are both vehicles in their own particular way, according to their own form, carrying the artist's effort and applying it to a canvas or to marble.

These philosophical notions should help us to form an idea of the saving efficacy of Christ's humanity. By virtue of the hypostatic union, two natures are present in the one Person of the Word, not confused in their essence and their activity and yet intimately united in their action. The sacred Humanity is the instrument of the Godhead, *organon Divinitatis,* according to the Greek Fathers' expression. The humanity is at the service of the Godhead, to obtain effects sought by the Godhead which exceed the powers of the humanity.

Now, this instrument is more than a tool in the hand of an artisan. It is a "conjoined" instrument, like a member of the body in its relation to the soul, and even much more than a member in its relation to the body. For the sacred humanity is capable of taking its own initiatives. It is an "animate instrument" conscious of its role as an instrument and communing by its intelligence, its will, and its love, with the activity of the Divine Artisan.

Thanks to the closeness of the hypostatic union of the two natures and of the perfect penetration of the human will by the divine will, this admirable instrument is exempt from the inevitable inadequacies of human instruments in the hands of artistic geniuses. It is truer than ever in the case of Christ that the effect obtained belongs in common, in its totality, to the instrument and to the principal cause. It is God and it is the Man Jesus who saves us.

And yet we can discern in our salvation the mark of the sacred humanity, of the intelligence and the heart of Jesus, of His consciousness and His liberty, and even of His flesh. Through His human intelligence, Jesus communes with the thought of God concerning the salvation of the world; and by His infused knowledge He knows each and every sinner. Through His human will He communes with the will of the Father for saving each sinner. And freely, out of love, He delivers up His soul and His body to suffering and death, in God's service. He is an animate instrument in the hands of God, and on the other hand He is in contact with us so as to apply to us the grace of salvation that God causes to pass through His intelligence, His will, and His flesh. Thus, our divine life depends essentially upon Christ the Man, since, as a sacrament, it is He who assures its transmission to us, and since, as the unique sacrament, it is He whose human will governs the diffusion of this divine life.

As the instrumental cause of our salvation, Jesus is incomparably more precious to sinners than He would be if His Passion were merely its "occasional" cause, as Duns Scotus and Malebranche thought; or if, according to certain ancient and modern theologians, He were only the "moral" cause of salvation. If He were the "occasional" cause, then God alone would save us, and the sacred humanity would not intervene even in the production of the grace of salvation. God would simply decide to grant salvation on condition that Christ suffered and died. If our Savior were solely the "moral" cause of salvation, He would acquire rights to our salvation that He would transmit to us but He would not accomplish this salvation Himself. Neither occasional causality nor moral causality take into account the efficacy of the saving Passion.

"Intentional" causality, which Cardinal Billot, S.J., elaborated, is not acceptable either. According to the Cardinal, the role of the instrument in the intention of the principal cause would be only to designate this cause or to provide it with the matter on which it would operate, and consequently to dispose this matter to receive the action of the principal cause: this would be intentional and dispositive activity. Thus, by virtue of a divine intention, the Passion of Christ designates and presents to God the creatures to be saved, and likewise disposes and prepares them effectively to receive the grace of their salvation from God. This theory, in which the exigencies of a genuine instrumentality are not met, brings us back to the errors of occasionalism, and encourages us to rally to the ingenuously realistic interpretation inherited from the Fathers.

As the Fathers saw it, the spiritual strength of the grace of salvation flows from the bosom of God through the sacred humanity to each one of us. Indeed, such realism raises difficulties and remains mysterious. How are we to conceive of the movement of this spiritual force through the body of Christ, and the contact that the Passion must have with each of us, even though it is historically so far removed?

The bodies of men are animate, filled with spirit. While it is philosophically inconceivable that a body should be the subject in which a spiritual energy dwells, it is however philosophically thinkable that a body should be a canal through which this spiritual energy passes: the body is the instrument of the soul. Thus, the flesh of the suffering Christ can be the instrument of grace, just as the sacraments are. At any rate, His body is the instrument of grace through His soul, for His flesh is the instrument of His Godhead only because it is first of all the instrument of His soul, of His intelligence, and of His love. These spiritual realities do not constitute an obstacle to perfect instrumentality in God's service; and by virtue of the hypostatic union they can permanently bear the grace that it is their mission to distribute to us.

The same is true of the contact established between the act of the Passion and the sinners that successively come under its spiritual action, even though with the passage of time they are further and further removed from the sensible reality of the Passion. The Redemption transcends history and geography. It is above all the work of the Eternal and the Immense, of the principal Cause. And the Instrument whom the Redemption uses, subject to time and place, retains within Himself the same will that He had during His Passion. He can reach all men, whom He has not ceased to know and to love, by the contact of His mind and of His love. This contact is normally realized through preaching and through the sacraments of faith.

We must bear in mind that the Passion is less a bloody episode of history than an invisible drama of the soul. Through His infinite charity toward God, Jesus communes with the infinite presence of God. Through His infused knowledge, and through His immense love for us, Jesus, the man of His own time and country, is the man of all times and all countries. He knows and loves each and every man, His members, and wants to be the saving instrument of God for each one of them. This loving will, which places Him at the service of God, commands the actions and passions of His body. And these are at the service of God for our salvation. While the act of the Passion is completed, His divine and human wills that command this act still remain unchanged. Moreover, this act is etched in the glorious scars of His glorified flesh. Thus, a "virtual" contact is possible between us and the Passion. There can also be a spiritual contact between us and the spiritual aspects of the Passion.

The Redeemer accomplishes our salvation by His blood and by His love, and more by His love than by His blood. For He comes to us through His blood only because He has first come through love. Likewise, we must go to the Redeemer both through faith and through the sacraments, and more by faith than by the sacraments. For we must go to Him through the sacraments only because we have first gone to Him through faith. It is through faith, by virtue of the Passion, that the sinner opens his soul to the grace of his Deliverer; and it is through the sacraments of the Passion that he receives this grace effectively. Through faith we are united to the mind and heart of the suffering Christ, which are the sources of His merit, of His satisfaction, and of His sacrifice. But His mind and heart are also the essential centers of His instrumentality in the hands of His Father, and consequently of our return to God.

At the same time, living faith does not suffice without the sacraments that Jesus instituted. Faith aspires to participate through the sacraments in the reality of Jesus, "whom God has set forth as a propitiation by His blood through faith" (Rom. 3:25). It aspires to participate in His sacred Humanity, once subject to suffering but now glorious, to participate in His bruised flesh and in His burning charity, because of which "we . . . have believed the love that God has in our behalf" (I Jn. 4:16).

(g) *The effects of the Passion*

Gleaning in Patristic tradition, we can reduce the effects of the Passion to three: 1) It delivers us from sin, the devil, and punishment; 2) it reconciles us with God; 3) it makes the fullness of joy available to us.

Although we are subject to the inward incitements of evil, we know that we can overcome them in Christ, and that in spite of our sins we have received through Him the spirit of adoption to love God as our Father (Rom. 8:15). Although we are condemned to suffering and death, which are the ransom for sin, we at least know their significance and satisfactory value in Christ. Through Christ, suffering and death cease to belong to the realm of blind Fate; for He came to "deliver them, who throughout their life were kept in servitude by the fear of death" (Heb. 2:15). Henceforth, suffering and death are transfigured by love and repentance. The exultant accents of the first Christian writers give us some idea of the value of this liberation. The Savior also wrests us from the devil, our tempter, by withdrawing us from the mortal attraction that he has had for us ever since we freely joined his ranks through sin.

To be happy, we must resemble God and be united to Him. Jesus is the answer to this yearning which tormented the souls of antiquity. In His sacrifice, He is the Mediator through whom "we . . . have access . . . to the Father" (Eph. 2:18). For the Father sees His likeness in Him and is well pleased with Him.

Finally, not only does Jesus reconcile us with God even in this life, but He opens heaven to us. That is, He reassures us as to our eternal destiny, for where He is He also wants us to be with Him (Jn. 17:24).

(h) *The universality of the Redemption*

Christ died for all men. Against the heresies that seek to limit the effects of the Redemption to a privileged few, the teaching of the Church has been clear and constant. In 475, the Council of Arles anathematized those who claimed that Christ did not die for all and does not will the salvation of all men. In 849, this anathematization was repeated against Gottschalk by the Council of Quierzy-sur-Oise (Denz., 318-319). The Council of Trent taught, against the Protestants, that all men are the beneficiaries of the Cross of Christ and that they are saved if they do not put obstacles in the way of their redemption (Session VII, Chap. 3, Denz., 795). In the seventeenth century, Popes Innocent X and Alexander VII condemned the theses of Jansenius and then of Quesnel, and declared that Christ did not die only for the predestinate, nor only for the faithful, nor only for the elect (Denz., 1096, 1294, 1382).

This doctrine was formulated in precise terms by St. Paul: "God our Savior . . . wishes all men to be saved and to come to the knowledge of the truth. For there is one God, and one Mediator between God and men, himself man, Christ Jesus, who gave himself a ransom for all" (I Tim. 2:4-6).

Leo XIII, in the Encyclical *Annum sacrum,* teaches that all men, including pagans, are the subjects of Christ because He died for all. And Pius XII, in his Encyclical *Mystici Corporis,* deduces our obligations of brotherly love from this doctrine:

"The love of the divine Spouse is so vast that it embraces in His Spouse the whole human race without exception. Men may be separated by nationality and race, but our Savior poured out His Blood to reconcile all men to God through the Cross, and to bid them all unite in one Body. Genuine love of the Church therefore is not satisfied with our being within this Body members one of another, . . . we must also recognize as brothers of Christ according to the flesh, destined together with us to eternal salvation those others who have not yet joined us in the body of the Church.

"There are some unfortunately, today especially, who proudly boast of enmity, of hate and spite as something that elevates and honors the dignity of man and his power. Let us, however, follow on after our King of peace, the while we gaze with sorrow on the pernicious consequences of that teaching. He has taught us not only to have love for those of a different nation and a different race (Lk. 10:33-37), but to love even our enemies (Lk. 6:27-35; Mt. 5:44-48). While Our heart overflows with the sweetness of the Apostle's teaching We chant with him the length, the breadth, the height, the depth of the charity of Christ (Eph. 3:18), which neither diversity of race or culture, neither the wasteless tracts of ocean, nor wars, be their cause just or unjust, can ever weaken or destroy." [9]

REFLECTIONS AND PERSPECTIVES

Questions of vocabulary. Even when the words we use are thoroughly valid, they always fail to encompass the mystery they are trying to express. That is why the theologian must constantly scrutinize his words, to discern what they intend to say, what they do say effectively, and what they do not say. Words often have a history of their own. The theologian should discover when and how they were introduced into theology, how permanent their use has been, and whether their significance has undergone very noticeable change in current terminology. Only in this way will he be able to point out the relative inequality between what they really signify and the mysterious reality that they designate in the language of Christianity.

We have already pointed out in passing the evolution of certain words like *Apostle, charity, will,* and *prudence.* We shall point out the evolution of others, such as *penance.* Here we purpose to call attention to the words *economy, salvation, redemption, repurchase, satisfaction,* and *liberation.*

The present volume, together with the next, traditionally falls under the heading of *The Economy of Salvation.* What does the word *economy* mean? Obviously, it has nothing in common with the somewhat miserly virtue of thrift, unless it be pointed out that this so-called quality is an abuse and a deformation of the virtue of the good governor, the good administrator, the good manager, or the good architect. But in the language of Christianity, the word

[9] Encyclical, *Mystici Corporis Christi,* June 29, 1943. English translation by the Paulist Press, Par. 108-109, pp. 32-33.

economy designates something else again. "The economy of salvation" is God's plan to save all men, the Dispensation God has established for salvation. It is a secret hidden in God for many centuries and revealed in His Son Jesus Christ. Objectively, it is revealed and contained in its entirety in Christ. Subjectively, it consists in believing in Jesus Christ. It is an "economy of faith" (I Tim. 1:4) that supersedes the old "economy of the Law." The apostle's task is to reveal the Economy (cf. I Cor. 9:17). It becomes his responsibility, his function. But ordinarily the word *economy* designates God's Plan, His Dispensation, His Mystery (cf. Eph. 2:10; 3:2). St. Paul even links the two words and speaks of "the Dispensation of the Mystery" (Eph. 3:9). On this subject, see L. Bouyer, "Mysterion," in *Mystery and Mysticism* (London, Blackfriars, 1956).

The words that theologically express the reality of salvation: *redemption, repurchase, satisfaction,* must also be considered in their relation to the reality they are meant to designate, and in relation to their origins.

The word *redemption* was spontaneously discovered and used at a time when slaves were being repurchased. It has been said, doubtless with truth, that the word *liberation,* which evokes so many other things to the modern mind, originally corresponded quite closely to what it means today. Actually, a living religion creates its own vocabulary, and certain words of our Christian language point out, in their origins, epochs when Christianity was very much alive. There are countless modern words and expressions (such as *Catholic Action, militant, labor priest, area of want, ecclesial, lay apostolate,* etc.). And these new words are a good sign, even if the philologist is legitimately dissatisfied with certain ones (e.g. the atrocious tautology: "missionary apostolate").

The word *salvation* deserves close attention. What precisely does it signify? Or rather, to what salvation does it refer? Does it apply to the salvation of the soul alone, to the salvation of the soul and then of the body, to the salvation of the whole man, to the salvation of the world, or to cosmic salvation?

We know that original sin has infected our very nature. It is through the nature each of us receives at birth that original sin invades the soul. But the same does not apply to the grace that saves us. Christ makes direct and immediate contact with us by His personal action. To the extent that nature can be saved, it is through the intermediary of the person who is saved. How far do the effects of the grace of salvation go? Must the Christian be an eternal pessimist when he looks at the world around him, without any illusions about its possible progress, and await its destruction by fire on the last day? Or should he be an optimist, trusting not only in saving grace but also in the natures to be saved and in their capacity for improvement through the efforts of the men who have been saved?

On the above problem, which engrosses so many minds today, the following reading is suggested: D. Dubarle, "Optimisme devant ce monde," in the Collection *Foi Vivante* (Paris, Ed. de la Rev. des jeunes, 1949); the debate between L. Bouyer and Th.-G. Chifflot, in *La Vie Intellectuelle,* October, 1948 (L. Bouyer, "Christianisme et eschatologie," pp. 6-38; Th.-G. Chifflot, "De l'eschatologie considérée comme un des beaux-arts," p. 39-52). Also the luminous pages of Father Féret, "Sur la terre comme au ciel, le vrai drame de Hochwalder," in the Collection *Contestations* (Paris, Ed. du Cerf, 1953), pp. 75-88, from which we are quoting the second and third "certitudes":

If (man) realizes that one or another of his fellows, and a fortiori that whole segments of humanity are in a condition inferior to his own, unworthy of their common greatness, it is his inalienable duty to improve the condition of his less favored brothers to the extent that it lies in his power. Thus, justice and the exigencies that it creates have no limits except the limits of humanity.

But there is a still greater "certitude":

Charity, which is fraternal love extending to the whole human race and at the same time filial love communing through the Holy Spirit in the mystery of God, is the only Law whose practice gains admittance into the kingdom of God . . . "This is my commandment, that you love one another as I have loved you" (Jn. 15-12).

It is useless to multiply citations. Let us merely call to mind the great scene of the last judgment, in which the good and the wicked, the saved and the damned, will be ultimately differentiated according to whether they have or have not given food, drink, hospitality, clothing, care to the sick, and made fraternal visits to prisoners, for 'as long as you did it for one of these, the least of my brethren, you did it for me' (Mt. 25:40). For the Judge will say that He identified Himself with the mystery of each of those in need.

By this third and supreme light of revelation, we again see even more irrefutably that the only means of entering the kingdom of God to which the believer aspires is to work here and now to make this world a fraternal world, under the fatherhood of God. Henceforth we know that human labor (first certitude) does not suffice to establish the kingdom of God, regardless of how much it is aided by the most advanced technology. Nor does an acute sense of justice (second certitude) that refuses to acquiesce in any human servitude. The force of charity (third certitude) is needed, a force that assumes the order of justice in its entirety and all the demands of human labor, but that surpasses them in its communion, even in this life, with the infinity of the kingdom of God (pp. 80-82).

We shall not insist further on these questions, which apply quite as well to a theology of the cosmos. We shall merely invite the reader to see how they apply to that theology (cf. *Theology Library,* Vol. II, pp. 274-312) by studying the extent to which the powers of Christ and of the Church actually have a bearing on temporal matters. Does the temporal realm depend upon the kingship of Christ, upon the power and judgment of the Church? And if so, how? Some solutions to this grave problem are to be found in the chapter by Father Bouyer of Volume II of the *Theology Library* (pp. 465-496). Also in the book by Father Féret cited above. Another work by Father Féret that we recommend is: *L'apocalypse de saint Jean, Vision chrétienne de l'histoire* (Paris, Corréa); as well as the essay by G. Thils, *Théologie des réalités terrestres* (Paris, Desclée, 1947).

The universal efficacy of salvation. Two questions arise in this connection:

1. Theologians ask themselves whether Christ came principally to destroy original sin, which is the root of all our troubles, or to destroy actual sins (cf. Lexicon). Now, it was Christ's purpose first of all to destroy the greater sin. From this point of view, original sin is the greater, because it is the more extensive. It has corrupted the whole human race, and Christ even had to preserve the Blessed Virgin from it. And He even wipes it out in little children who have never committed any actual sin. Thus we can say that Christ came chiefly to wipe out original sin. He did this, not for the whole human race before any individual birth, but by removing this universal cause of spiritual corruption from each person.

2. How many men will be saved? This question is unanswerable. The most contradictory answers have been given, but none has a sound basis. The logion (see Lexicon) of the Lord: "Many are called, but few are chosen" (Mt. 20:16) has recently been the object of a careful study by Father E. Boissard (*Revue thomiste,* 1952, pp. 569-585). Father Boissard's conclusion is that these words of our Lord's signify: "Those who are called are the greater

number, and those who are chosen are the smaller number." In other words, it does not suffice to be called in order to be chosen. It is misleading to seek an indication concerning the number of the elect from this Gospel proposition. Actually, our Lord's words were solely an invitation to vigilance. And we can well believe that God's mercy is great enough to save many men.

Sin and salvation. Salvation consists at once in liberation from sin (its negative aspect) and in divinisation (its positive aspect). Both of these actions require the intervention of God, and man's cooperation.

God must intervene to liberate man from sin, for sin is an infinite offense that God alone can wipe out. But let us understand what we are saying when we speak of an infinite offense. Modern minds have little inclination to admit the "infinite magnitude" of sin, and they rebel against the consequences that are drawn from this magnitude. It is certain that man, a finite being, is incapable of performing an act that is infinite in its nature. Man, like all other creatures, performs only finite acts. Subjectively, sin is a limited act. But sin is an offense against God. Man in his smallness turns against God in His infinity. That gives sin an objective gravity that only God can remove.

Man must cooperate in his own salvation, even though this salvation comes entirely from the grace of God and consequently through His initiative. But man is a free being. He will not be "saved" unless his freedom, which has been wholly orientated toward evil, turns back to goodness. God's grace touches man in his very freedom, causing him to turn actively and freely and come back to God.

Suffering and salvation. Salvation is given to us through the Cross. That is to say, the meaning of suffering has changed since it was given to man as a punishment for sin. Or at least, it has been enriched with a new significance. Saints accept suffering in order to be more closely united to their Savior. And some, who are specially inspired by the Spirit of God, actually yearn for suffering. A fruitful study of the meaning of suffering might begin with the third chapter of Genesis and the Book of Job, and follow on through the Apocalypse.

BIBLIOGRAPHY

The fundamental work is:

Rivière, Jean. *The Doctrine of the Atonement,* 2 vols. London: Kegan Paul, Trench and Trübner, 1909.

Also, by the same author:

Le dogme de la Rédemption après saint Augustin. Paris: 1930.
Le dogme de la Rédemption chez saint Augustin. Paris: Gabalda, 1933.
Le dogme de la Rédemption au début du Moyen-Age. Paris: Vrin, 1934.
Le dogme de la Rédemption, Études critiques et documents. Louvain: 1931.

In addition to articles in reviews and dictionaries, the following should be noted:

Hamman, A. *La Rédemption et l'histoire du monde.* Paris: Alsatia.
Hugon, E. *Le mystère de la rédemption.* Paris: Téqui, 1910.
Laminne, J. *La Rédemption. Étude dogmatique.* Brussels: 1911.
Masure, Eugene. *The Christian Sacrifice.* New York: Kenedy, 1943.
―――. *The Sacrifice of the Mystical Body.* Chicago: Regnery, 1957.
Richard, L. *Le dogme de la rédemption.* Paris: Bloud and Gay, 1932.
Salet, G. *Richesses du dogme chrétien.* Le Puy: Ed. X. Mappus, 1946.
Thomas Aquinas, St. "The Life of Jesus," in *Summa Theol.,* III, 27-59.

For a comparison between the doctrine of expiation in the Old and New Testaments:

Medebielle, A. *L'expiation dans l'ancien et le nouveau Testament.* Rouen: 1924.
Also see the bibliography for Chapter IV.

Chapter IV

THE GLORIOUS EPIC OF JESUS CHRIST

by A.-M. Henry, O.P.

Chapter IV

THE GLORIOUS EPIC OF JESUS CHRIST

"The hour has come for the Son of Man to be glorified" (Jn. 12:23). These words which Jesus spoke at His triumphal entry into Jerusalem announced His Passion and death—"unless the grain of wheat falls into the ground and dies, it remains alone" (Jn. 12:24)—as well as His Resurrection, His Ascension, and His sitting at the right hand of the Father. It is a single mystery in its two aspects, the sorrowful and the glorious. It is Jesus' "hour."

I. THE DEATH OF CHRIST

It was fitting that Christ should accept death for our salvation. In inquiring into the motives behind the free acts of God, theology discovers a few "reasons" behind this mystery. However these reasons, as far as we can discern them, are the reasons of a gratuitous act of God, that is, they are simply reasons of fitness.

It was fitting that Christ, who came to make satisfaction for the whole human race, should Himself suffer the punishment inflicted on all men in the persons of Adam and Eve. And so He made total satisfaction for us in justice by dying, even though He was perfect and without sin: "Christ . . . died once for sins, the Just for the unjust, that he might bring us to God. Put to death indeed in the flesh, he was brought to life in the spirit" (I Pet. 3:18). Thus, our death was defeated and vanquished by the death of Christ, just as when one man suffers punishment for another the punishment of the latter is remitted by the punishment of the former.

Secondly, the death of Christ proved the truth of the Incarnation to us. If He had ascended to heaven without dying, many men would not have believed in the reality of His human nature and would have considered it a sort of collective mirage or hallucination. And yet, to prove that He did not die through any weakness of His nature, He did not die of sickness. He died from external violence to which He voluntarily submitted.

In the third place, by His death Christ delivered us from the fear of death, and from the fear of the devil who is the emperor of death: "that through death he might destroy him who had the empire of death, that is, the devil; and might deliver them, who throughout their life were kept in servitude by the fear of death" (Heb. 2:14-15).

Fourthly, by dying corporeally to this mortal body that bears the resemblance of sin, Christ invited us to die spiritually to sin: "For the death that he died, he died to sin once for all, but the life that he lives, he lives unto God. Thus do you consider yourselves also as dead to sin, but alive to God in Christ Jesus" (Rom. 6:10-11).

Finally, it was necessary that Christ die to prove His dominion over death by His Resurrection, and thus give us hope for our own resurrection: "Now if Christ is preached as risen from the dead, how do some among you say that there is no resurrection of the dead?" (I Cor. 15:12).

In death Christ did not cease to be our source of life; for He continued to possess this source of salvation inasmuch as He was God, and He died inasmuch as He was man. Even after His soul and body were separated, they remained individually united to the Word of God. By virtue of this fact, even though Christ ceased to be truly a man while in this state of separation of body and soul, and although He can no longer merit, His body and His soul can still serve as instruments of our salvation. The death of Christ destroyed the death of our soul: "Jesus . . . was delivered up for our sins" (Rom. 4:25). It also destroyed the death of our body: "Death is swallowed up in victory!" (I Cor. 15:54).

II. THE BURIAL OF CHRIST

No one is buried unless he is dead. Burial is a tangible proof of death, and Christ wanted to give us such a proof by His own interment. That is why Pilate took care to inquire whether Christ were dead (Mk. 15:44) before allowing Joseph of Arimathea to take His body and bury it.

Other reasons can be given for this burial. By undergoing burial Christ mysteriously gave hope to those who were already dead and buried. He had foretold it with the words: ". . . the hour is coming in which all who are in the tombs shall hear the voice of the Son of God" (Jn. 5:28). His burial also honored the devotion of those who had concerned themselves with this task: Nicodemus, Joseph of Arimathea, and the women who had acted in view of His burial (Mk. 14:8; 16:1, etc.).

Lastly, in His burial Christ gave Himself as an example to all Christians, who must die spiritually to sin and be as it were "buried" to the world, fleeing its attractions and its wicked enticements. For when Baptism immerses the Christian in water, it is sacramentally immersing him in the death of Christ. For the ancients, water was the figure of the kingdom of death, the empire of the dragon, of Leviathan or Satan, the domain of Sheol, the Styx of the pagans. Immersion into water symbolized plunging into death, and since it was done in imitation of the death of Christ, it symbolized in a very special way an immersion into the death of Christ. It was as if the Christian had gone down into Christ's tomb. That is why St. Paul says: "For we were buried with (Christ) by means of Baptism into death, in order that, just as Christ has arisen from the dead through the glory of the Father, so we also may walk in newness of life" (Rom. 6:4). And elsewhere he exhorts the baptized, saying: "For you have died and your life is hidden with Christ in God" (Col. 3:3). Thus the burial of Christ is the source of our life. God makes use of it to bury us in Him and to raise us up to a new life.

Indeed, the reasons for the burial of the Lord do not exhaust our meditation upon this subject. We see that Christ died the death of a criminal and a pauper, but He was buried in an honorable sepulcher through the care of a rich person, wrapped in fine cloths with aromatics, according to Jewish custom. Was it not fitting that His death should prove His patience to us, and that in His burial we should honor His condition as God-man? Moreover, Christ was buried in a stranger's tomb as if nothing belonged to Him, and to manifest that He died for the salvation of all men. The "garden" in which Jesus was buried (cf. Jn. 19:41) calls to mind the "garden" in which Adam had sinned. The stone that sealed His tomb was destined to make the truth of His Resurrection even more irrefutable. By causing this stone to roll away, Christ proved that even in death He was free, and that consequently He had died of His own free will.

III. CHRIST'S DESCENT INTO HELL

Christ's descent into hell has been a dogma of faith ever since it was inserted into the Creed in the fourth century.

Let us understand what this descent signifies. Christ did not descend into the hell of the damned, but into the abode of the dead, which the ancients imagined to be underneath—*infernus*—the earth. Christ came to visit the dead and bring them light. It was as if He forced the portals of the kingdom of death, where Satan was the prince not only of sinners but of all who, as sons of Adam, had to suffer the punishment of death. Thus Osee cried out prophetically: "O death, I will be thy death; O hell, I will be thy bite" (Osee 13:14). By forcing the doors of hell, Christ triumphantly wrested from the devil the souls of those whom he was detaining unjustly.

To sum up, the death that Christ suffered for the salvation of all had to be manifested in the land of the living as well as in the kingdom of the dead so that all might acknowledge His victory and that "every knee should bend of those in heaven, on earth and under the earth" (Phil. 2:10). The Passion of Jesus, which is the universal cause of our salvation, had to be applied to the living through the sacraments that configure them to His death, and to the dead by the Lord's visitation. "Thou also by the blood of thy testament hast sent forth thy prisoners out of the pit" (Zach. 9:11).

Even though Christ did not descend into the hell of the damned, His "visit" nevertheless had effects on all souls. It confounded the unbelief and the malice of the damned, it gave hope to those who were destined to suffer only a limited time in purgatory, it delivered the saints who were prisoners only by virtue of original sin and it gave them eternal light.

Finally, let us specify that since Christ's body was in the sepulcher, it did not descend into hell. It was His soul that in some way "touched" the souls of the fathers. This does not make it any less true that "Christ descended into hell," for in Christ the subject is always the Word to whom His soul is hypostatically united.

IV. THE RESURRECTION OF CHRIST

With regard to the Resurrection of Christ, we shall consider its fitness, and even its necessity, the qualities of the risen Christ, His manifestations, and the effects of His Resurrection.

Christ's Resurrection inaugurated the glorious epic of His exaltation upon earth and in heaven. After He had humbled Himself "taking the nature of a slave" (Phil. 2:7), after He had been obedient to death, even to death on the Cross, after He had descended into hell, God "exalted him and . . . bestowed upon him the name that is above every name" (Phil. 2:9).

It was fitting that Christ should rise from the dead, and it was even necessary for several reasons. He Himself declared this to the disciples of Emmaus: "O foolish ones and slow of heart to believe in all that the prophets have spoken! Did not the Christ have to suffer these things before entering into his glory?" (Lk. 24:25-26).

The Resurrection of Christ was an effect of God's justice who "has put down the mighty from their thrones, and has exalted the lowly" (Lk. 1:52). Since Christ had humbled Himself out of charity and obedience, even to the Cross, it was incumbent upon God to glorify Him.

Christ's Resurrection was also given to us to confirm our faith in His divinity. For it is clear that it was solely through the power of His Godhead that He rose from the dead: "For though he was crucified through weakness, yet he lives through the power of God" (II Cor. 13:4). And St. Paul also says that "if Christ has not risen, vain then is our preaching, vain too is your faith" (I Cor. 15:14).

By manifesting His Resurrection to us, Christ likewise gives us hope that we too shall rise again: "Now if Christ is preached as risen from the dead, how do some among you say that there is no resurrection of the dead?" (I Cor. 15:12).

Finally, by rising from the dead Christ offered us the model and the symbol of our new life: ". . . just as Christ has risen from the dead through the glory of the Father, so we also may walk in newness of life. For if we have been united with him in the likeness of his death, we shall be so in the likeness of his resurrection also. For we know that our old self has been crucified with him, in order that the body of sin may be destroyed, that we may no longer be slaves to sin; for he who is dead is acquitted of sin. But if we have died with Christ, we believe that we shall also live together with Christ; for we know that Christ, having risen from the dead, dies now no more, death shall no longer have dominion over him. For the death that he died, he died to sin once for all, but the life that he lives, he lives unto God. Thus do you consider yourselves also as dead to sin, but alive to God in Christ Jesus" (Rom. 6:4-11).

It should be noted that when we speak of Christ's exaltation, we do not mean His personal exaltation. For since His Person is the Word, it remained unchanged whether united to the soul and body separately or united to the whole human nature. Contrariwise, the human nature was exalted by the Resurrection. It is in the same sense that we say Christ rose from the dead by His own power. It was not His body alone that rose again, or His soul that restored His body to life; it was the Word of God who resurrected the body and the soul, each of which had not ceased to be individually united to the Word.

Finally, Christ willed to rise again on the third day to prove conclusively that He had died, and so that no one would have grounds for believing He was an impostor. We know that among the Jews, days were counted from sundown to sundown, and not from midnight to midnight. Accordingly He died on Friday evening, the evening of the Sabbath that would begin a few hours later, and rose again at dawn on the day after the Sabbath. Thus, He rose "on the third day," as He had prophesied.

The qualities of the risen Christ have been made known to us by the Gospel. First of all, Christ regained His real body, and He manifested it to His disciples in Jerusalem. As they were "startled and panic-stricken, and thought that they saw a spirit" (Lk. 24:37), Jesus said to them: "See my hands and feet, that it is I myself. Feel me and see; for a spirit does not have flesh and bones, as you see I have" (Lk. 24:39). Similarly, the episode with Thomas confirms our faith in the reality of Christ's risen body. The disciples also saw and worshipped Him (Mt. 28:17).

The body of Jesus is glorious and immortal, and He has complete power over His body. Thus, He could pass through closed doors (Jn. 20:19), and suddenly disappear from the sight of the disciples of Emmaus (Lk. 24:31). Jesus had worked a similar miracle at His birth when the Blessed Virgin brought Him forth while preserving her virginal integrity. Jesus' glorious body has no need of food, but it can nevertheless eat, as He proved by eating with His disciples (Lk. 24:41; Jn. 21:12,13). St. Bede said in this connection: "The parched earth absorbs water in one way, and the sun absorbs it in another; the earth absorbs water because of its indigence, whereas the sun does so through its power" (*In Luc,* cap. 97).

Christ's risen body has kept its scars. All the Fathers have held that these glorious wounds are not a deformity or a mark of ugliness, but on the contrary add to His body's beauty and perfection. They contribute to the greater glory of Christ: *majorem cumulum gloriae.* Indeed, these scars are the marks of His victory. They also served to confirm the faith of the disciples in Christ, and our faith through them. For all eternity they will be a reminder to the Father of the death of His Son, and they incline Him to listen to His Son's supplication. They are a help to all redeemed men, to whom they constantly reveal the signs of His Passion; for the virtue of His Passion remains in Him as it remains in the Eucharistic sacrament that contains His glorious body. Finally, they are an eternal testimony to condemn the incredulity of those who will not believe in Him.

The manifestations of the risen Christ were providentially ordered in such a way that His Resurrection might be made known to all believers through qualified and authorized witnesses. St. Peter says: "God . . . caused him to be plainly seen, not by all the people, but by witnesses designated beforehand by God, that is, by us, who ate and drank with him after he had risen from the dead" (Acts 10:41).

While women did not receive the function to preach, we know that He first manifested Himself privately to a woman: "He appeared first to Mary Magdalene" (Mk. 16:9). That reminds us that it was a woman, Eve, who first brought the word of death to man. Therefore it was fitting that the Apostles should receive from a woman the announcement of Christ's life after His death.

Jesus did not manifest Himself every day or continuously. But He did manifest Himself several times in a discontinuous way. He wanted to show that the time was past when He was obliged to share the life common to all mortals, for now He had become immortal. We also see that He appeared under different forms (cf. Mk. 16:12). The significance of this is that He allowed Himself to be seen by each one according to his dispositions, so that he might be brought to believe.

Finally, Jesus confirmed His Resurrection by all sorts of proofs or arguments: "To (the Apostles) also he showed himself alive after his passion by many proofs, during forty days appearing to them and speaking of the kingdom of God" (Acts 1:3). In fact, He showed them how the Scriptures had been fulfilled in Him (Lk. 24:44). Above all, He showed Himself, He pointed to His scars, and repeated the gestures that made Him easily recognizable, such as the breaking of the bread. Thus, we have all the proofs we could want of Christ's Resurrection.

God makes use of Christ's Resurrection instrumentally, as He uses all of Christ's acts, in order to work our salvation, and in this instance very specifically to accomplish our resurrection: "Jesus Christ . . . will refashion the body of our lowliness, conforming it to the body of his glory by exerting the power by which he is able also to subject all things to himself" (Phil. 3:21). The Resurrection of Christ constitutes the first-fruits and the cause of our resurrection: "Christ has risen from the dead, the first-fruits of those who have fallen asleep. For since by a man came death, by a man also comes resurrection of the dead. For as in Adam all die, so in Christ all will be made to live" (I Cor. 15:20-22).

But Christ's Resurrection is not only the cause and the model of our corporeal resurrection. First of all, it is the cause and model of our spiritual resurrection through Baptism, in which we are configured to His death and to His Resurrection, and receive the seed of glory. St. Paul tells us: "Jesus our Lord . . . rose again for our justification" (Rom. 4:25). And again: "For we were buried with him by means of Baptism into death, in order that, just as Christ has arisen from the dead through the glory of the Father, so we also may walk in newness of life. For if we have been united with him in the likeness of his death, we shall be so in the likeness of his Resurrection also" (Rom. 6:4-5).

V. THE ASCENSION

The fact that our Lord ascended to heaven forty days after His Resurrection does not mean that He remained forty days "upon earth." In truth, all the accounts of the Gospels and the Acts suggest, and the Pauline interpretation confirms, that Christ entered the glory of the Father at the moment of His Resurrection. According to St. John Chrysostom, our Savior's warning to Mary Magdalene, "Do not touch me" (Jn. 20:17), was meant to make her understand that He did not intend to resume His visible contacts with men. (*In Jo.,* Hom. 81.) Henceforth Christ would remain with His Father, and would come to earth several times only to manifest His Resurrection to men. His last public appearance and His last disappearance took place on the day of the Ascension—exception being made of His apparition to St. Paul on the road to Damascus (cf. Acts 9:5). After the Ascension, the angels announced to the disciples that the Lord would not return until judgment day: "Men of Galilee, why do you stand looking up to heaven? This Jesus who has been taken up from you into heaven, shall come in the same way as you have seen him going up to heaven" (Acts 1:11).

Where did Christ ascend to? The answer offered no difficulties to the ancients, because their cosmology was simple. They imagined that the earth was flat, that it rested upon "the waters below," and that its highest mountains, its columns of Hercules, supported the firmament and the waters above. As they saw it, Christ simply went up to heaven, that is, above the highest waters to the dwelling that the Greeks assigned to the Olympic gods. Even as late as the thirteenth century Giotto painted an Ascension in which Christ, after His upward journey, emerged above the heavenly waters.

But now that we have a better if still imperfect understanding of the universe, such a representation has become unacceptable to us. The earth is round, and what we call the physical sky or the heavens lies above, beneath, to the right, and to the left. We are resigned not to know just where Christ ascended to. It suffices that we believe in the reality of His Resurrection: Christ is alive right now. It matters little exactly where He is, for we know that according to His divinity He is always present among us: "Behold, I am with you all days, even unto the consummation of the world" (Mt. 28:20). We also know that according to His humanity Christ knows each of us by name, and sees our most secret thoughts. Distance has no effect upon this interior knowledge that Jesus has of us, or upon His love for us. It is as if a person were constantly to keep track of someone upon another continent through thought-transmission. Christ penetrates the depths of our minds and hearts at every instant, and He intercedes for each one of us before the Father. It is precisely this "contact" that He has with our souls through His intelligence and His love that permits Him to be the Father's "instrument" for our sanctification.

As to His corporeal absence from our midst, Christ has told us that it would be good for us: "It is expedient for you that I depart" (Jn. 16:7). Actually, it benefits our faith. Faith cleaves not to the visible but to the invisible. Moreover, Christ has left us a sacramental sign of His presence among us: the Eucharist. This sign does not hinder our faith, since we "see" Him in the Eucharist only with the eyes of faith; and it is a sensible sign, in the faith, of His companionship.

Christ's absence is equally beneficial to our hope. "And if I go and prepare a place for you, I am coming again, and I will take you to myself; that where I am, there you also may be. And where I go you know, and the way you know" (Jn. 14:3-4). Every just man who dies knows that he is going to join Christ, and this thought brings consolation. Where the head is, the members must be gathered together.

Finally, Christ's absence is good for our charity here below. Since we are risen with Christ, St. Paul counsels: "seek the things that are above, where Christ is seated at the right hand of God. Mind the things that are above, not the things that are on earth. For you have died and your life is hidden with Christ in God" (Col. 3:1-3). Besides, Christ has not left us orphans since He has left us His Spirit, the Spirit whom we receive in Baptism and who makes of us a single body, a single life, a single aspiration toward the Father, in union with Christ.

The Ascension of Christ is the cause of our salvation, not in the sense that it merited our salvation—for that was the privilege of His Passion—but in the sense that it opened heaven to us: "I go to prepare a place for you" (Jn. 14:2); in the sense that it liberated the souls of the saints that had until then remained outside of heaven: "Ascending on high, he led away captives" (Eph. 4:8); in the sense that our new high priest has penetrated into the Holy of Holies and never ceases interceding for us (Heb. 7:25); and finally in the sense that He accomplished all the things for which God created the world: "He . . . ascended also above all the heavens, that he might fill all things" (Eph. 4:10).

VI. THE SITTING AT THE RIGHT HAND OF THE FATHER

"So then the Lord . . . was taken up into heaven, and sits at the right hand of God" (Mk. 16:19). The "right hand" is the Hebraic symbol of honor and power. To "sit" or "be seated" immediately evokes the function of judging. To say that Christ sits at the right hand of the Father signifies that the Father shares with Him His honor, His power, and that He entrusts to Him His power to judge the living and the dead.

It is fitting that Christ according to His divine nature should "sit at the right hand of God," inasmuch as He is absolutely equal to the Father. But it is also fitting that Christ in His human nature—which possesses only a divine and eternal "I"—should share the honor and the power of the Father and the worship of the faithful. "Worthy is the Lamb who was slain to receive power and divinity and wisdom and strength and honor and glory and blessing" (Apoc. 5:12).

However if we consider in Jesus only the sanctifying grace that God communicated to Him, "to sit at the right hand of the Father" signifies that He received God's heritage in a greater degree than any other creature. And this is Christ's privilege: "Now to which of the angels has (God) ever said, 'Sit at my right hand . . .'?" (Heb. 1:13). The saints, who are Christ's members, will receive from Him glory and honor and the power to judge. In this sense, we can say that they too sit at the right hand of God, even though it is Christ's glory in which they share: "You who have followed me, in the regeneration when the Son of Man shall sit on the throne of his glory, shall also sit on twelve thrones, judging the twelve tribes of Israel" (Mt. 19:28). In the same sense, we can say that they sit at the right hand of Christ: "As for sitting at my right hand and at my left, that is not mine to give you, but it belongs to those for whom it has been prepared by my Father" (Mt. 20:23).

VII. CHRIST THE JUDGE

Christ received the power to judge the living and the dead. This power is fitting to Him by virtue of His primacy over all creatures and by virtue of His justice and His wisdom. "He it is who has been appointed by God to be judge of the living and of the dead" (Acts 10:42).

The power to judge belongs to Christ—as we have said with regard to His sitting at the right hand of the Father—both according to His divine nature and according to His human nature, but to each in its own way. It was fitting for several reasons that Christ as man should receive the power to judge.

In the first place, He is a man and we are men. Thus, God is preparing for us a judgment that is at once divine and very "human": "For we have not a high priest who cannot have compassion on our infirmities, but one tried as we are in all things except sin. Let us therefore draw near with confidence to the throne of grace" (Heb. 4:15-16). Besides, the judgment will coincide with the resurrection of the dead that God will bring about through the risen Christ. Finally, as St. Augustine remarks (*De verbis Domini,* ult. serm., cap. 7), since Christ will judge the good and the wicked, it is fitting that He should appear before the latter only in His human form. But to say that He will judge the just according to His manhood does not mean that He will give them eternal beatitude by virtue of what He possesses according to His human nature. It belongs only to God to grant eternal life. But when Christ judges the good, He will send them or lead them to eternal life. "This day thou shalt be with me in paradise" (Lk. 23:43).

The power to judge that Christ possesses extends to all men, to all human things, to all earthly realities, and even to the angels: "At the name of Jesus every knee should bend of those in heaven, on earth and under the earth" (Phil. 2:11). St. Paul tells us that we shall judge the angels (I Cor. 6:3). A fortiori, Christ, from whom we shall receive this power, will also judge them.

The judgment of Christ will take place twice: once at the death of each man, and once again universally on the last day. We shall try to explain this twofold judgment in the chapter on "The Return of Christ" at the end of this volume.

REFLECTIONS AND PERSPECTIVES

The Reign of the Spirit. We have just studied the various stages in the work of salvation accomplished by Jesus Christ. In so doing, we have merely followed the articles of the Creed that correspond to this glorious epic: "died, was buried, descended into hell . . ." Now, it is a remarkable thing that the Apostles' Creed does not stop with the Ascension, with the sitting at the right hand of the Father, or even with the judiciary power of the Savior. It closes with several articles of faith concerning the *Holy Spirit and His work.* The formula is as follows: "I believe in the Holy Spirit, the Holy Catholic Church, the Communion of saints, the forgiveness of sins, the resurrection of the body, and life everlasting. Amen."

The work of salvation did not terminate with the sending of Jesus Christ, but with the mission of the Holy Spirit, that is, with the institution of the Church whose members are united to Jesus Christ and among themselves by the Holy Spirit who has been given to us. Although our treatises on Christ and on the Church are separate, we should at once note the real unity of the work of salvation in which each divine Person has His part.

The Father, in whom the Son and the Holy Spirit have their origin, takes the initiative in the work of salvation. The Son assumes our humanity, fights the battle against Satan, sin, and death, and obtains our salvation by making reparation for our offenses, by meriting divine life for us, and by opening the door of reconciliation with the Father. The Holy Spirit, the Deifier, gives us divine life inwardly and joins us to Christ, so that the mysterious marriage between God and humanity may be accomplished between Christ and ourselves. It is thanks to the Holy Spirit that we can truly call God *Abba,* that is "Father." For we have truly received the Spirit of the Son, and together with the Son we are close to the Father "in the unity of the Holy Spirit."

To the three parts of the Creed correspond three states of Revelation. First, the Father revealed Himself "by the creation of heaven and earth" and by gathering Israel together. Then He prepared us to know the Son, who was revealed by His coming among us. Finally, we have known the Holy Spirit by His work of deification and unity. Although the Three Persons of the Holy Trinity are always at work, there is an economy in God's revelation just as there is in the fulfillment of salvation.

Thus, the Old Covenant appears to us as the reign of the Father, the coming of the Son as the reign of the Son, and the Church since Pentecost as the reign of the Spirit. The Christian believes in the Father by whom all things were made, in the Son who saved us by His death and Resurrection, and in the Holy Spirit who deifies us and gathers us together with Christ in the bosom of the Father. That is why catechumens were formerly immersed in water three times when they were baptized, at the same time as they made this threefold profession of faith according to the baptismal formula of the Apostles' Creed.

The different works appropriated to the divine Persons must be distinguished, as Revelation teaches us. It would have served no purpose for the Father, the Son, and the Holy Spirit to have made themselves known to us distinctly and personally, if we continued to speak without distinction of the works that are attributed to one or to the other of them. And we need have no fear of dividing God, inasmuch as God is One: the Father is in the Son, the Son is in the Father, and the Holy Spirit is the Spirit of the Father and of the Son.

Let us rather rejoice that when Christ ascended into heaven and deprived us of His visible presence, He did not leave us orphans but left us the Holy Spirit. For it is through the Holy Spirit that we are deified, and that we are one with Christ in the bosom of the Father. The Holy Spirit is the life of our souls, He is the soul of the one and holy Church. It is in Him that all the "saints" participate in the Son through the holy mysteries that Christ has left us. It is the Holy Spirit who inwardly works "the remission of sins," it is through Him that the Father resurrected Jesus from the dead, and through Him that the Father will resurrect us on the last day (cf. Rom. 8:11). It is the Holy Spirit who communicates "eternal life" to us. Hence the gift of the Holy Spirit constitutes the pledge of our heavenly inheritance (Eph. 1:14; II Cor. 1:22).

And while we must distinguish what is appropriated to the Son and what is appropriated to the Holy Spirit in the work of our salvation, we cannot separate the two. There is only one mystery—hidden in God until the coming of Christ, and now revealed by the Son and by the Holy Spirit. The Holy Spirit is the manifestation of Christ's work. It is He who reveals that we are children of God. The men whom the Apostles chose to help them with the various tasks of the Church were men "full of the Spirit" (Acts 6:3). Easter and Pentecost are the beginning and the end of the fifty-day celebration of a single mystery, accomplished in Jesus Christ, manifested and, in some way, applied on Pentecost. By His death and Resurrection, Christ merited the deifying Holy Spirit for us, and this Spirit has been given to us.

The Paschal Mystery as the center of our lives. When the Paschal Mystery is understood in its fullness, it is easy to see that it lies at the heart of our Christian life, that is, of our faith, of our worship, and of our morality.

It lies at the center of our faith. In the Paschal Mystery the history of salvation finds its consummation, God's plan is fulfilled, and the streams of living water that the Holy Spirit henceforth pours out upon all flesh are made to flow. It is in the Paschal Mystery that we gain access to the Father together with the Son and the Holy Spirit, and that we know the three Persons of the Blessed Trinity.

Easter lies at the center of our worship. Of all the feasts of the year, it is the greatest. Christmas exists for the sake of Easter. The Word came among us to conquer death and sin, and to reopen the lost paradise by bringing us back to the Father. The hierarchy of feasts corresponds to a hierarchy of the truths of our Faith and of the mysteries of our Religion. It would be heresy to give Christmas primacy over Easter. Christmas has meaning only insofar as it is ordered to the hour of salvation, and only through the Paschal act that already sanctified those who surrounded the Infant Jesus and that had efficaciously preserved the Virgin Mary from all stain of sin.

True, since the thirteenth and fourteenth centuries the West has given great importance to the feast of Christmas, no doubt through the influence of St. Francis of Assisi and his sons. This should not make us forget the fact of the *redemptive* Incarnation and of the Resurrection. Christ came that "His Hour" might be accomplished. The Paschal Mystery soars above the Mystery of the Nativity. Christmas is a feast of joyous intimacy, of silent recollection on the threshold of a great mystery. Easter is a triumphal feast, a glorious and solemn feast of deliverance and pure joy. As for Pentecost, coming at the end of the Paschal Season, it is really the extension of Easter to the whole Church and to the whole of human history, its manifestation in the Apostles, and its historical and dynamic reality until the end of the world.

What is true of the feasts of the liturgical year is equally true of all acts of worship and especially of the sacraments, for all the sacraments are Paschal Mysteries. Baptism, which the Easter liturgy invites us to celebrate during the Paschal vigil, is essentially a Paschal Mystery of death and resurrection. The Eucharist is the Paschal Mystery par excellence. That is why the Church celebrates it with great solemnity every Sunday, the day of the week dedicated to the Resurrection. As for Confirmation, it can be called "the confirmation of Baptism." Its relation to Baptism is comparable to the relation of Pentecost to Easter. Penance and Extreme Unction are likewise Paschal Mysteries, by reason of the deliverance that they bring. As for Holy Orders and Matrimony, they make it possible for the society of the Church, and not merely for the individual Christian, to represent the same Paschal Mystery.

Finally, the Paschal Mystery lies at the center of our moral life. For the whole of Christian morality consists in dying in order to live; in losing one's life in order to gain it; in dying to one's conceit and sins in order to live by the grace of God which is self-sufficient: in renouncing the glory that comes from men in order to receive the glory that comes from God. In the words of St. Paul: "Therefore, if you have risen with Christ, seek the things that are above, where Christ is seated at the right hand of God. Mind the things that are above, not the things that are on earth. For you have died and your life is hidden with Christ in God. When Christ, your life, shall appear, then you too will appear with him in glory" (Col. 3:1-4).

It would be interesting to pause here and study the psychological and pedagogical stages in the awareness of the mystery of life and of the mystery of renunciation among children, among adolescents —for whom renunciation is hard—and among adults for whom death has become a reality that must some day be faced. The important thing is not to discourage them, and to teach them to count as loss for the sake of Christ the things that were gain (Phil. 3:7). At the same time, care should be taken not to encourage an exclusive "dolorism" or pessimism that would not be truly Christian.

Media vita in morte sumus. While it is true that in the midst of life we are already engaged in death, it is true that each time we Christians are "in the midst of death" we are also already in the midst of life. The Eucharist is the sacrament of the Passion and death of Christ, and it contains the risen Christ. We receive the strength of the risen Christ to carry our cross with Him so that we may rise again and live with Him. In the Paschal Mystery that we celebrate here on earth, it is always erroneous to exclude life from death, or death from life.

Thus, from Easter to Easter, the Holy Spirit leads us in our faith, in our worship, and in our moral life, toward the perfect love of God with Jesus Christ in the bosom of the Father.

BIBLIOGRAPHY

The fundamental work is:

Durrwell, F. X. *Le résurrection de Jésus, mystère de salut.* Le Puy: Éd. X. Mappus, 1954.

Also:

Bouyer, Louis. *The Pascal Mystery.* Chicago: Regnery, 1950. (A theological commentary on the last three days of Holy Week.)
Thomas Aquinas, St. "The Life of Jesus," in *Summa Theol.,* III, 27-59.

See the bibliographies for the preceding chapters and the one for Chapter VII, "The Return of Christ."
On the doctrines of "the image of God" and the "recapitulatio," read the Fathers of the Church, particularly in such collections as "Sources chrétiennes" (Paris: Cerf), "The Fathers of the Church" (New York: Fathers of the Church, Inc.), and "Ancient Christian Writers" (Westminster, Md.: Newman). Also, see *Les deux Adams,* by P. Galtier, Paris: Beauchesne, 1947.
The meditations on the Passion are innumerable. There are the Gospel commentaries, the commentaries of the Fathers of the Church, of saints and theologians, of orators and Christian men of letters (Bossuet, Pascal, Bourdaloue, Lacordaire, etc.), of writers on spirituality. A classic work—of theology as well as "spirituality"—from this last group is *La Croix de Jésus* by L. Chardon. (Paris: Cerf.)

MARY AND THE CHURCH

THE MYSTERY OF THE NEW EVE

It is in the light of divine goodness that the theologian discovers a certain fitness in the Incarnation from God's point of view. God is good, and it belongs to goodness to communicate itself to others. Is it not fitting, therefore, that supreme Goodness should communicate itself in a supreme way through the Incarnation?

But the communication of divine goodness does not stop there. It wants to pour itself out upon all men, upon the whole universe. God became man so that men might become gods. God saves us not only by giving us a Savior, but also by making all those whom He unites to Himself cooperate in the work of salvation. The gift of God extends to the point of obtaining the free cooperation of those to whom He gives His favors.

This is the mystery of the spiritual creature, the daughter of God, and the "meaning"—at once mystical and mysterious—of woman.

From the beginning, God gave man a companion and a helper like to himself; and man named her, saying: "This now is bone of my bones, and flesh of my flesh" (Gen. 2:23). St. Paul explains this by declaring: "This is a great mystery—I mean in reference to Christ and to the Church" (Eph. 5:32). When the Lord created Eve, He had in mind the companion that He willed to associate with the future Adam, and He prophetically announced her coming.

For when Jesus Christ saved us, He did not intend us to be totally passive and not to cooperate in the work of our own salvation. There is within Him such a wellspring and superabundance of salvation that He grants to others the power of saving in union with Himself. The companion of the new Adam, whom Eve prefigured, is His associate in His gigantic combat against the Dragon. And this associate is at once and indivisibly the Blessed Virgin Mary and the Church.

God chose to assume human flesh within the womb of the Virgin Mary. After His union with Christ, God could not unite Himself to any creature more closely than through the mystery of mother-

227

hood. After the "grace of union," God could not grant a greater grace than that which corresponds perfectly to the Divine Maternity to which He had predestined Mary, the Mother of Jesus.

The open side of Christ on the Cross gave life to a companion that He would henceforth associate fully to His redemptive work. This companion is the Church, in which we all receive the life that comes from Christ. It is the Church that saves us, that is the fountain of salvation, the ark of the covenant, even though she receives everything she is and everything she has to give from her Lord and Spouse, from her Head, Jesus Christ.

Christ is our only Savior in the sense that all salvation comes from Him. But Christ does not save us by Himself without our cooperation. He has given to Mary and to the Church—and to all who, within the Church and in varying degrees, participate in her saving function—the power of saving through Him and in union with Him.

The mystery of Mary and of the Church is the mystery of this close cooperation, in which Mary, the figure and the perfect type of the Church, is personally what the Church is collectively: the Spouse of Christ.

Chapter V

THE BLESSED VIRGIN MARY

by R. Laurentin, S.T.D., Dr. ès-Lettres,

Professor at the Catholic University of Angers

Chapter V

THE BLESSED VIRGIN MARY

The definition of the dogma of the Assumption has brought the Marian question to the fore. The entire press, from theological reviews of all faiths to the evening papers, teemed with commentaries ranging from the most pertinent to the most absurd.

Amid all this excitement, Christians reacted in different ways. Some were delighted, for this decision simply enlarged the scope of their meditations and put an official seal on their certitudes. Others seemed disturbed. They had never given much thought to the Marian problem, and now that it was suddenly set before them a thousand questions crowded into their minds. Since faith has God as its object and since no saint has ever been the object of a definition, why give such a place in dogma to a mere creature? Granted "the silence of Scripture" with regard to Mary, how could she have assumed such a prominent role? In what measure does the extraordinary development of Marian doctrine have its source in Revelation or in the cavernous depths that psychoanalysis brings to light? In the upsurge that leads the soul toward Mary, what are the relative roles of sentiment and faith? If pious inventions and other dross so common in certain devout writings are eliminated, what is left of the mystery of Mary?

Those who somewhat confusedly asked themselves these and many other questions, sensed that the solution lay not in giving an improvised answer to each question, but in attaining to an over-all view which would be the starting point for the solution of all questions, just as the map of a city makes it possible for everyone to make out and follow his own itinerary. It is the purpose of the present Marian synthesis to give a brief and objective statement that will provide such an over-all view.

Now, if the word "synthesis" as used here meant an abstract construction expressed in rigid formulas, it would be most inappropriate. It would strike a dissonant note when used with the word "Marian." The deepest or at least the most characteristic aspect of Marian doctrine and of the personality of the Blessed Virgin Mary seems to be the important place that *time* plays in it: the law of duration and of progress. A "synthesis" that telescoped this basic element would overlook something essential.

Duration, progress: It is according to this law that Mary gradually became known to the Church. While she was almost absent from the primitive message, and totally absent from catechesis as long as she remained on earth in the midst of the Church, she was "discovered"—in the strongest sense of the word—even at the time of her initial presence.

Duration, progress: It was also according to this law, or rather primarily according to this law, that Mary lived. Her life progressed from the gratuity of her original gift to the superabundance of merits with which she left this earth; from her initial receptivity to the ultimate unfolding of her maternal mission, from the plenitude of the personal and secret grace of the first instant to the social and manifest plenitude that she radiates today from the heights of heaven.

In following this twofold progression, we shall first see how the Church gradually became conscious of the mystery of Mary. Then, taking our stand within the mystery itself, we shall contemplate the development of her destiny from the Immaculate Conception to the Assumption.

I. The Discovery of Mary in Time

Marian doctrine has developed in the Church according to a characteristic curve. It has been not a continuous but a rhythmic growth that reminds us of the ebb and flow of the tides. On the seashore each successive wave wells up, comes to a head, sweeps up on the beach, and then slides back while the succeeding wave wells up to invade the beach still further. So did each era of the Church sense a new aspect of the Blessed Virgin, discovering it with enthusiasm and often amid conflict, then relapsing into calm and silence. This rhythm was manifested in three ways: by the quantity of writings produced, by the quality of these writings, and by the swiftness of progress realized. Using these criteria, we can discern six great stages in the development of Marian doctrine: Scripture, the Patristic age until Ephesus, from Ephesus to the Gregorian Reform, from the end of the eleventh century to the end of the Council of Trent, the seventeenth and eighteenth centuries, and finally the nineteenth and twentieth centuries.

The preliminary phase: Presence and Silence

The development we are about to follow extends from the silent presence of the Blessed Virgin to the explicit recognition of this presence in the Christian mystery. And before we approach the earliest Marian teaching of the Church, it is important to stress this initial silence, this phase during which Mary lived in the Church without ever being mentioned in sermons.

In its primitive state, Christian catechesis did not begin with the account of the Annunciation. The Apostles' testimony was exclusively concerned with the public life of Christ: *from the Baptism of John to the Ascension* (Acts 1:22). Peter set these limits even before Pentecost and remained faithful to them throughout his preaching. The Acts give us another characteristic glimpse into his preaching (10:36-43), and we find the ultimate expression of Peter's preaching in the Gospel of St. Mark. Even in this final elaboration of Peter's doctrine, Mary was not named.

Thus, during a period of time whose precise duration we do not know, the Mother of Jesus, having reached the height of her perfection, lived in the Church although there was no explicit mention of her. She prayed and interceded for the Church, but in a hidden way. It would seem that she herself did not know the extent of her influence, and those around her did not realize it either. She was a living organ of the Body of Christ, but Christians were not taught about her. Like certain of the sacraments, she was a reality in the life of the Church before becoming the object of a dogma. Gradually this reality, which was dimly realized in the Communion of Saints, found expression in an explicit formula.

1. THE FIRST PERIOD: SCRIPTURE (CIRCA 50-90). PAUL AND MARK; MATTHEW, LUKE AND JOHN

The earliest explication of Mary's role is to be found in the New Testament, which was composed over a period of half a century. Here Mary was given a place that was materially unimportant but deeply significant. We must pay very special attention to these basic sources which are God's own words.

At first the Blessed Virgin appears in Scriptural writings in a wholly episodic way. The first testimony we encounter is characteristic in this respect. It is to be found in the Epistle to the Galatians, which may have been written before 50 A.D.:

But when the fullness of time came, God sent his Son, born of a woman, born under the Law, that he might redeem those who were under the Law, that we might receive the adoption of sons (Gal. 4:4-5).

Let us beware of glossing over this text. We can glimpse in it the divine maternity and also find in it a prelude to the spiritual maternity, inasmuch as Christ's human sonship is juxtaposed to our adoptive sonship. We may even go so far as to discover in it an echo of the mysterious prophecy of the Proto-Gospel (Gen. 3:15). But did Paul think of all these things? We should remember his laconic style. He spoke of Christ's Mother as an anonymous "woman," mentioning her in passing and in a parallel with the Law, which is not a title of glory. None of her privileges were emphasized. Paul bore witness to her fundamental reason for existing: *to make sure the Savior would be a member of the human race* "when the fullness of time came." And that is all he said.

The only two texts by Mark on "the Mother" of Jesus (3:31-35; 6:1-6) have the same mark of anonymity and casualness. Even more, can they be said to have a negative character. In the former, when Jesus hears someone interject His family into His ministry, He states that His true family consists of His disciples:

Now a crowd was sitting about him, and they said to him, "Behold, thy mother and thy brethren are outside, seeking thee." And he answered and said to them, "Who are my mother and my brethren?" And looking round on those who were sitting about him, he said, "Behold my mother and my brethren. For whoever does the will of God, he is my brother and sister and mother" (Mk. 3:31-35).

In the other passage, His fellow countrymen refuse to believe in Him precisely because He is only "the carpenter, the son of Mary" (Mk. 6:1-6). Their acquaintance with Jesus through their senses closes them off from any knowledge of Him according to the Spirit.

These three texts shut off one approach: the one that would have granted Mary greatness according to the flesh, as the mother of the sons of Zebedee conceived it (Mk. 10:37). They forbid us to exalt the Maternity of Mary without taking into account the gifts of grace that are bound up with it and that the remainder of the New Testament reveal to us.

The other three Evangelists open the following vistas. Between A.D. 50 and 70, Matthew, and after him Luke, tell us of Mary's role in the mystery of the Incarnation. Around the year 90, John, in completing his meditations, opens the way to an understanding of her role in the mystery of the Redemption. This first explanation seems to be closely related to the living presence of Mary in the primitive Church. It seems quite certain that Luke learned directly from her whatever he knew of the Gospel of the Childhood. Twice he referred to the memories she kept in her heart (Lk. 2:19 and 51). As for John, the Lord had entrusted His Mother to him as He was dying (Jn. 19:27). Thus, whatever John has revealed to us of the mystery of Mary, he learned from his own filial experience.

The texts we are about to glance over are brief. However, when we consider the ties between them and also to the Old Testament, their importance becomes manifest. Not only do they confirm one another, but some of them are repeated by the others. In their relation to the mysterious announcements of the Old Testament, notably Genesis 3:15, Isaias 7:14, and Micheas 5:2, they are, as it were, the last words that complete and give meaning to an unfinished sentence. In short, if we looked at each of them independently, their significance would escape us, just as anyone looking only at the dots on a pointillist drawing would fail to see the face it represents.

Matthew gives us the key to the prophecy of Isaias: "Behold a young girl (ha 'almah) shall conceive, and bear a son, and his name shall be called Emmanuel" (Is. 7:14). In this mysterious text, the "young girl" so unmistakably in question can not be identified with any person of the prophet's time. And here is a significant detail: she was to exercise a right that normally belonged to the father; it was she who received the mission to name her son. Can we deduce from this that there was no father in question, and that the reference was to a virgin? The context of Isaias would not suffice to assure this conclusion, but it suggests it. In fact, three centuries before Christ the translation of the Septuagint specifies without ambiguity: "Behold the Virgin (ἡ παρθένος) shall conceive." Matthew, who made use of this translation, recognized Mary as the mysterious "virgin." He clearly affirms the virginal character of her conception, the cause of which is the Holy Spirit (Mt. 1:20-21; cf. Is. 11:2), and insisted upon the Messianic character of her motherhood:

Now the origin of Christ was in this wise. When Mary his mother had been betrothed to Joseph, before they came together, she was found to be with child by the Holy Spirit. But Joseph her husband, being a just man, and not wishing to expose her to reproach, was minded to put her away privately. But while he thought on these things, behold, an angel of the Lord appeared to him in a dream, saying, "Do not be afraid, Joseph, son of David, to take to thee Mary thy wife, for that which is begotten in her is of the Holy Spirit. And she shall bring forth a son, and thou shalt call his name Jesus; for he shall save his people from their sins." Now all this came to pass that what was spoken by the Lord through the prophet might be fulfilled, "Behold, the virgin shall be with child, and shall bring forth a son; and they shall call his name Emmanuel"; which is, interpreted, "God with us" (Mt. 1:18-23).

"God with us": these words, which had a rather indeterminate meaning in Isaias and could be understood to refer to divine assistance, begin to take on in the Gospel of St. Matthew the meaning that the Church recognizes in them today: the divinity of the Messias. In the fullness of this meaning we find the joining of the two great groups of texts that extend throughout the Old Testament: those that apply divine attributes to the human Messias, and those that describe the descent of a hypostasis of God (the Word, Wisdom) among men.

In St. Luke we find all these elements, but on many points they are more completely developed. Like St. Matthew (1:1-17), he proved that the Messias is truly a member of the human race by giving us His genealogy (Lk. 3:23-38), but he took a more comprehensive view in this than Matthew. Going beyond Abraham, he went all the way back to Adam, by way of the patriarchs, and to God, Adam's creator. In Luke, the mystery of the virginal conception thus attains to its universal significance and appears as a renewal of the original creation. Like Matthew, Luke stressed the Davidic descent of the Messias, but he went further and explicitly referred to the prophecy that Nathan made to David.

Like Matthew, Luke affirmed that Jesus was conceived by the Holy Spirit, and that Joseph had no part in it (1:34-55), but he brought in new aspects of the mystery. First of all, he intimated that Mary had made a vow of virginity before the Annunciation. When the angel announced her glorious motherhood, she answered: "How shall this happen, since I do not know man?" (1:34). This was a surprising answer for a betrothed person, especially as betrothals at that time made the exercise of all the rights of marriage permissible. If we are not to strain the meaning of the text, this is what we must take it to mean: Mary, under the inspiration of the Holy Spirit, had decided not "to know man" in the Biblical sense of these words (cf. Gen. 4:1,17,25; 38:26, etc.).

The account of the birth according to St. Luke gives us a much vaguer indication of the mystery of the virginity *in partu:* the miraculous preservation of Mary's virginal integrity in the birth of the God-man. It was after a fatiguing journey, after vain attempts to find lodging (Lk. 2:7), in the discomfort of a stable that Mary brought forth her Son. And yet she took care of her newborn son herself: "She . . . wrapped him in swaddling clothes, and laid him in a manger" (2:7).

And we shall also see how Luke confirmed and clarified the two major doctrinal points of the operation of the Holy Spirit and the divine Messiahship of Mary's Son.

Not only did Luke develop St. Matthew's doctrinal points, but he added others. To Luke we owe the account of the Visitation; the Circumcision, by which the Savior submitted to a sacrificial rite; and of Jesus' two visits to the Temple: one at the time of the Presentation, and the other when He was twelve years old, at the time of the annual trip to Jerusalem. We can see how Luke delighted in bringing to the fore the bonds that united Jesus to the Temple, to sacrifice and to the priesthood.

But even more unique is the way Luke's Gospel makes us enter into the life of the Blessed Virgin. It places Mary (or rather it shows how she placed herself) at the end of the line of "poor and humble" folk who, according to Scripture, are the chosen portion of Israel. Mary spoke of her "lowliness" which the Lord had regarded (1:48); she offered herself as the prototype of the lowly that the Lord had exalted (1:52). These notions conjure up a whole spirituality that would deserve more extended study. Luke also revealed to us the secret of the Blessed Virgin's meditations (2:19 and 2:51), her reactions (1:29), her undertakings (1:39; 2:24,39,41, 44), her words—"Behold the handmaid of the Lord" (1:38), "My soul magnifies the Lord . . ." (1:46-55)—thereby unveiling her attitude toward God: her faith, humility, obedience, and thanksgiving. We should also stress that her faith, like our own in its obscurity (2:50; 1:29), inwardly burned bright (2:19,51) and was most pure and spontaneous in its expression (1:38,48).

One day when Jesus was speaking, "a certain woman from the crowd lifted up her voice and said to him, 'Blessed is the womb that bore thee, and the breasts that nursed thee.' But he said, 'Rather, blessed are they who hear the word of God and keep it' " (Lk. 11:27-28).

According to certain commentators, Jesus' words contradicted those of the woman and meant: "Blessed are those who have faith and *not* she who brought forth." That is not what St. Luke intended to say, for he had borne witness that Mary was blessed (1:45) and forever blessed (1:48) precisely because of her faith. Elizabeth said: "Blessed is she who has believed" (1:45); and Mary answered: "All generations shall call me blessed" (1:48). Besides, Luke had presented Mary as the first to listen to God's words (1:29) and to keep them in her heart (2:19,51). The conclusion, therefore, is inescapable: Jesus did not detract from His Mother's glory. In Luke 11:28, as well as in Mark 3:31-35, Jesus was merely dispelling a materialistic conception of this glory, and bringing to the fore its religious basis, which is faith.

Finally, Luke invites us to go still higher: to God who was well pleased with Mary (1:28) and who "has done great things" (1:49) for her.

There are many things we could say about Luke's Marian message. Let us pause only at the Gospel of the Annunciation (1:26-38). Since the treasures of this short passage exceed anything we could say about them, let us limit ourselves to giving its Scriptural context. It is a striking fact that this text is a veritable tissue of Scriptural allusions. Thus for example, the angel's words concerning the miraculous conception of Elizabeth: "For nothing shall be impossible with God" (1:37), are a literal repetition of the Lord's words to Sara in Genesis 18:14, concerning her equally miraculous conception. Why this Scriptural texture? A study of the *Magnificat* reveals the answer. Each clause of this Canticle echoes some passage of the Bible. It shows that Mary was so thoroughly imbued with God's words that she borrowed her own formulas from them. And it is not at all surprising that God should answer her in like manner. Speaking to a Virgin sustained by Scripture, the divine messenger spoke the language of Scripture. And for anyone who does not know this language, his message remains a closed book. Let us try to grasp the principal clues to its meaning.

The Gospel of the Annunciation is composed of three parts. First, the breaking of the good news (1:28-29), then two groups of explanations—one concerning the human origin of the Messias (30-33), and the other, more hidden, concerning His divine origin (34-36).

The first part is the announcement of the Messianic joy, and this joy is expressed by the word "χαῖρε" which ought to be translated

"Rejoice" rather than "Hail." It is couched in the formulas which several prophets (Zach. 9:9, Joel 2:21-27) and especially Sophonias (3:14,17) had used to announce the same joy and its same profound reason: the presence of Yahweh "in the midst" of Israel or (if we prefer to translate in its etymological sense the word *beqirbék* used here) "in the womb" of Israel. The Angel Gabriel took this announcement that the prophets had made to "the Daughter of Sion," the symbolic personalization of Israel, and addressed it to Mary personally. In Mary, the Daughter of Sion ceased being a symbol and became a personal reality; and the presence of Yahweh in the bosom of Israel took on a new meaning, the meaning of a divine maternity. Therefore, when we read the Gospel of the Annunciation let us not forget the text of Sophonias that reveals the Gospel's profound significance. To make this comparison easier, we shall present the texts side by side:

Sophonias' Announcement to Israel Soph. 3:14-17	The Angel's Announcement to Mary Luke 1:28-32
Rejoice (χαῖρε)	*Rejoice* (χαῖρε)
Daughter of Sion . . .	full of grace
The king of Israel, Yahweh	*The Lord*
is in thee (beqirbék)	*is with thee.*
Fear not: to Sion:	*Do not be afraid,* Mary.
Yahweh, thy God	Behold,
is *in thee* (literally, *in thy womb:*	thou shalt conceive *in thy womb*
beqirbék).	and shalt bring forth a son;
as a valiant *Savior* (yoshisa).	and thou shalt call his name
	Jesus. . . . he shall be king. . . .

We can understand that Mary was troubled by this announcement. And her anxiety came not from incomprehension or from cowardly fear as some would imply. It came from the shock of one of those encounters with God, from one of those immense joys that shake even natures of the highest caliber. In the light of Scripture which the angel took up again and applied to her personally, Mary understood that she was the new Israel in whose midst God was coming to dwell, and she caught a glimpse of how this promise would be fulfilled: through a maternity whose unprecedented object would be Yahweh Himself.

The angel clarified the human ancestry of the Messias, borrowing the terms of the fundamental Messianic prophecy: Nathan's oracle to David.

II Kings 7:12-16	Luke 1:32-33
Nathan's prediction to David (We are modifying the order to compare the parallel ideas.)	*Gabriel's Announcement to Mary*
Verse 12: *I will raise up* thy seed after thee, which shall proceed out of thy bowels, and I will establish his kingdom.	He shall be *great,*
Verse 14: I will be to him a father, and he shall be to me a *son:* Verse 16 b: and thy *throne* shall be firm for ever.	and shall be called the *Son of the Most High;* and the Lord God will give him the *throne* of David his father,
Verse 16 a: And thy house shall be faithful, and thy *kingdom for ever* before thy face, Verse 13: I will establish the throne of his *kingdom for ever.*	and he *shall be king* over the house of Jacob *forever;* and of his *kingdom* there shall be *no end.*

This passage (the angel's answer to Mary) clarified the divine origin of the Messias, just as the following clarified His human origin:

The Holy Spirit shall come upon thee and the power of the Most High shall overshadow thee; and therefore the Holy One to be born shall be called the Son of God (Lk. 1:34).

The significance of the title "Son of God" can be seen by comparing this passage with others where the title is solemnly conferred on Jesus: The manifestations of the Father at Jesus' Baptism (Lk. 3:22) and at the Transfiguration (9:35); the confession at Caesarea (Mt. 16:16); and the decisive testimony that cost Jesus His life (Mk. 14:62). As for the overshadowing of Mary, it clearly calls to mind the cloud that covered the tabernacle (Ex. 40:36) and was the sign of the divine presence. At the Transfiguration, this cloud rested above Jesus to attest to His divinity while the voice of the Father declared Him to be the *Son of God.* Likewise, at the Annunciation, it rested on Mary to attest to the divinity of her Son whom the angel had proclaimed to be the Son of God.

Thus the end of the message takes up again in new terms one of the most typical ideas of the beginning. Our parallelisms between Sophonias and Luke made of Mary "the Daughter of Sion," the personal epitome of Israel, and more precisely of Israel as the site of the divine presence. The evocation of the *Shekinah* (indwelling) makes us point to her now as the new ark of the covenant where this presence was realized. Mary is the Daughter of Sion in the sense that she is the holiest part of Israel, the consecrated place where God came to dwell.

Before leaving the Gospel of St. Luke, let us call to mind one last point, the prophecy of Simeon: "And thy own soul a sword shall pierce" (Lk. 2:35). According to the context, this sword was to consist in the repercussions in Mary's soul of her Son's sufferings. Simeon's prophecy was really the veiled announcement of Mary's sorrowful compassion. And Luke did not speak of this compassion again, nor did he mention Mary's presence on Calvary in any greater detail than the other Synoptics. But this should not surprise us. It was one of his habits to group all the facts about a particular person in a single passage, and to include in this report anticipations of coming events. That is what he did, for example, for John the Baptist (3:19-20). And he did the same for Mary. Thus Simeon's prophecy furnished him the opportunity of harmoniously suggesting, by anticipation, Mary's participation in the sorrowful Passion of the "Savior."

This association of Mary to the Redemptive Passion is more noticeable in the Gospel of St. John. St. John's interest in "the Mother of Jesus" is one of the marks, among others, that links it with the Gospel of St. Luke. The kinship between the two Gospels seems explicable in terms of a reciprocal influence: of John's influence on Luke through oral tradition, and of Luke's influence on John by way of the written word. As far as the Blessed Virgin is concerned, this affinity would be apparent even in St. John's Prologue, if with Father Braun, and according to the impressive testimonies of several of the Fathers, we use the following version:

> But to as many as received him, he (= the Word) gave the power of becoming sons of God; to those who believe *in the name of Him who was not born of blood, nor of the will of the flesh, nor of the will of man, but of God.* And the Word was made flesh, and dwelt in his tabernacle (ἐσκήνωσεν) among us (Jn. 1:12-14; cf. Apoc. 21:3).

This would be the virginal generation of Christ, and the last phrase concerning the Word who *dwelt in his tabernacle* (ἐσκήνωσεν) "among us" would coincide with the allusion by which Luke showed Mary to us as the new tabernacle in which God established His dwelling.

All this suggests the following bond between the Marian Gospel of Luke and John's Gospel. The Fourth Evangelist, having set out to complete the substance of the Synoptics rather than go over the same material they contained, merely alluded to what Luke taught concerning the role of the Blessed Virgin in the Incarnation (somewhat the way he made veiled allusions to the institution of the Eucharist at the Last Supper). On the other hand, John chose to elaborate the point that Luke had briefly indicated: the role of Mary in the Redemption.

Whatever John's actual intention was, let us consider the two major texts that indicate the nature of Mary's redemptive role. The first records the presence of Mary at the marriage feast of Cana (2:1-5); and the other speaks of her presence on Calvary (19:25-27). While both texts are very brief, they are replete with intentions that are made known to us by two facts.

First of all, there is a close *resemblance* between these two texts. Both of them concern the role of Mary at Jesus' *hour,* the "hour" that designates the Redemptive Sacrifice wherever it is used in the Gospels. In both passages, the Evangelist insistently called her the *Mother* of Jesus, and Jesus addressed her as *Woman.* Now these similarities are not insignificant. For it was not customary in Semitic usage for a son to call his mother "Woman." This trail, marked off by other parallelisms which we cannot discuss here, leads to Genesis 3:15, God's promise to Eve after the fall:

I will put enmities between thee and *the woman,* and thy seed and her seed: she shall crush thy head, and thou shalt lie in wait for her heel.

By a combination of converging strokes, John invites us to see Mary as the homologue of Eve in the new creation that the coming of the Word constitutes. She is *the woman* par excellence, the associate of the new Adam, and "the mother of all the living" (Gen. 3:20; cf. Jn. 19:27).

No less remarkable is the *place* John gives these two Marian texts. They encompass the entire ministry of Jesus. The first is placed at the time of Jesus' first miracle, the one that inaugurated His public life and rooted the faith of His disciples in Him (2:11). The other passage occurs at the "hour" when all was "consummated" (19:28-30). This is the Semitic procedure of inclusion. Its use by John leaves no doubt as to the importance he attributed to the Mother of Jesus.

We can now perceive the architecture of these texts: two master columns (Jn. 2 and 19:26-27) resting on a single Biblical substratum: Genesis 3:15. How are we to discover their mysterious meaning? The episode at Cana might well prove disconcerting:

> And the wine having run short, the mother of Jesus said to him, "They have no wine." And Jesus said to her, "What wouldst thou have me do, woman? My hour has not yet come" (Jn. 2:3-4).

These words of Jesus furnish us another analogy between John and Luke, in that they correspond to the words He addressed to His Mother when she found Him after His brief anticipation of His ministry at the age of twelve: "How is it that you sought me? Did you not know that I must be about my Father's business?" (Lk. 2:49). They signify the separation of the Son from His Mother during the days of His ministry. It was to be a temporary separation: Mary was with Jesus during the mysteries of His childhood and was to be reunited with Him in the mystery of His suffering, when His *hour* had come. And it was a fruitful separation: Jesus gave His Mother a pledge and an anticipation of its fruitfulness. At her request, He worked the inaugural miracle of His Messianic career.

We should pay attention to the context in which this inauguration took place. John saw in the feast and the marriage of Cana a symbol not only of the Eucharistic feast but also of the eschatological marriage between God and humanity that the Eucharist signifies and prepares. Let us call to mind the importance that the Fourth Evangelist gave to this eternal marriage at the end of the Apocalypse (19:7-8; 21:2,9). The earthly marriage of Cana in which Jesus inaugurated His ministry was presented as the figure and the pledge of the heavenly wedding feast that is to be the consummation of this ministry. Already at Cana, the intercession of the Mother of Jesus was an efficacious reality.

Mary was to be present again on Calvary, and there the dying Jesus entrusted her mission to her in more explicit terms:

> Now there were standing by the cross of Jesus his mother and his mother's sister, Mary of Cleophas, and Mary Magdalene. When Jesus, therefore, saw his mother and the disciple standing by, whom he loved, he said to his mother, "Woman, behold, thy son." Then he said to the disciple, "Behold, thy mother." And from that hour the disciple took her into his home" (Jn. 19:25-27).

Let us not minimize the significance of a text to which John has given such a prominent place. Many have seen in this only a private act. Jesus, as they saw it, simply entrusted His Mother to John so that he might take care of her in her abandonment. Such is not the meaning of this text. It was John who was entrusted to Mary *in the first place* (not Mary to John). And Christ's words are all the more amazing in that John's own mother was also present at the foot of the Cross. It was not John's intention, in this passage pregnant with meaning, to tell us about his private affairs. Here as elsewhere, the fact he reports raises our minds to the level of the mystery.

In this account, whose every portion relates to a prophecy, we are led to Genesis 3:15 and 19: Mary, present at Christ's side, inaugurating the new creation (that is, the order of grace), became, like Eve, "the mother of all the living," of all the Savior's disciples in the person of the beloved disciple.

The Marian teaching of John's Gospel throws retrospective light on the mysterious text of Chapter 12 of the Apocalypse, which is as it were the crossroads of all the Biblical avenues that lead to the Blessed Virgin Mary. Father Braun, to whose exegesis we refer the reader, has established that this text is primarily concerned with Mary. And yet—and this is still another similarity with Luke— John described Mary essentially in terms of Israel and of the Church of which she is the personal symbol.

Here is the text in question:

1. And a great sign appeared in heaven: a woman clothed with the sun, and the moon was under her feet, and upon her head a crown of twelve stars. 2. And being with child, she cried out in her travail and was in the anguish of delivery. 3. And another sign was seen in heaven, and behold, a great red dragon having seven heads and ten horns, . . . 4. And the dragon stood before the woman who was about to bring forth, that when she had brought forth he might devour her son. 5. And she brought forth a male child, who is *to rule all nations with a rod of iron* (Ps. 2:9). 6. And her child was caught up to God and to his throne. And the woman fled into the wilderness, where she has *a place prepared* by God, that they may nourish her a thousand two hundred and sixty days. . . . (Apoc. 12:1-6).

Then, Michael and his angels cast out of heaven "the ancient serpent, he who is called the devil and Satan" (12:9), who after he was cast down to the earth with his angels, continued to wage his battle:

13. And when the dragon saw that he was cast down to earth, he pursued the woman who had brought forth the male child. 14. And there were given to the woman the two wings of the great eagle (Deut. 32:11), that she might fly into the wilderness unto her place, where she is nourished *for a time and times and a half time* (Dan. 7:25). . . . 15. And the serpent cast out of his mouth after the woman water like a river, that he might cause her to be carried away by the river. 16. And the earth helped the woman, and the earth opened her mouth and swallowed up the river that the dragon had cast out of his mouth. 17. And the dragon was angered at the woman, and went away to wage war with the rest of *her offspring,* who keep the commandments of God, and hold fast the testimony of Jesus (Apoc. 12:13-17).

Let us admit from the start that this is an obscure text, in which the prophetic style intertwines events and perspectives. The order of the account is based not on chronology but on typology. Let us also admit that the Marian interpretation is the subject of controversy. On the other hand, Father Braun's recent exegesis seems convincing on the whole. Here are its principal Marian conclusions:

Chapter 12 of the Apocalypse applies *primarily* to Mary, but it *also* applies to the Church. John has chosen to describe the latter in terms befitting the former. This is a customary procedure, and indicates a typological relationship between two realities. (Such for example is the case of the discourse on the *bread of heaven,* which is at once the manna, the faith, and the sacrament of the Eucharist.) Here again John's Gospel coincides with Luke's: he designates the Blessed Virgin as a personal realization of the Church.

The beginning of the passage echoes the great prophecy of Isaias (7:14), which Micheas took up again (5:2). Like the *Almah* of Isaias, the woman of the Apocalypse is a *sign* (σημεῖον). But here she appears in triumph. The moon under her feet seems to indicate that she has risen above the course of history, above this world which is subject to the change and corruption which this satellite symbolizes. As in St. John's Gospel (with which this text offers many similarities), Mary is insistently called *the woman* (verses 1,4,13-17). She appears at once as the Mother of Christ and as the Mother of Christ's disciples, the latter being called her *offspring* (Apoc. 12:17). Here we find an echo of Genesis 3:14-15. In both texts, *the serpent* (Apoc. 12:9, 14) is at war against *the woman* and *her offspring:*

Genesis 3:14-15	Apocalypse 12:9, 13, 14, 17 the
God said to *the serpent:* . . .	ancient *serpent,* he who is called the devil and Satan, . . . pursued
I will put enmities between thee and *the woman,*	*the woman.* . . . And there were given to the woman the two wings of the great eagle, that she might fly into the wilderness . . . away from the serpent.
and thy seed	And the dragon was angered at the woman, and went away to wage war
and her *seed:*	with the rest of her *offspring,* who keep the commandments of God and hold fast the testimony. . . .

To the above-mentioned similarities between Genesis 3 and Apocalypse 12, we can add still another: *the anguish of delivery* (Gen. 3:16; Apoc. 12:2). This point is brought up as the major objection against the Marian interpretation of the passage, for it does not befit Mary's virgin birth. But this difficulty vanishes when we compare this passage to two other Johannine texts. In Apocalypse 5:6, Christ appears in the sky under the aspect of an immolated Lamb (cf. Jn. 19:36). The *anguish* of the woman who likewise appears in the heavens in Apoc. 12:2 is the counterpart of the *immolation* of the heavenly Lamb. Thus, we are not referred to the birth in Bethlehem (which John never even mentioned), but to the words of Christ from the Cross: "Behold, thy mother." The anguish refers to Mary's spiritual maternity, and to the compassion through which she shared the sufferings of the immolated Lamb. Clearly, John 19 and Apocalypse 12 are closely related.

In the Gospel text, the scene is laid on earth: Christ triumphs (Jn. 12:32, etc.) by His immolation, and Mary, through her suffering, becomes the mother of all men. In the Apocalypse, the scene is continued in heaven. The Savior keeps the stigmata of His sacrifice, and Mary retains the marks of her sufferings on Calvary. And meanwhile the effects of this sacrifice are perpetuated on earth, and the anguish of delivery will continue in Holy Mother Church until the end of time.

Among the riches of this obscure text, there *may be* an allusion to the Assumption, the only one that a literal reading of Scripture allows us to point to. It is not so much the flight of the woman into the desert with "the two wings of the great eagle" (Apoc. 12:13; cf. Ex. 19:4) that inspired the iconography of the Assumption as the mention of the place prepared (τόπος ἡτοιμασμένος) where the Mother of the Messias has gone according to Apocalypse 12:6. For St. John, this expression has an eschatological significance.

I go *to prepare a place* for you (πορεύομαι ἑτοιμασαι τόπον ὑμῖν). . . . *I am coming again, and I will take you to myself;* that where I am, there you also may be (Jn. 14:3).

Such were Jesus' words to His Apostles. The verb ἑτοιμάζω (to prepare), which is so often given an eschatological meaning in Scripture, is a term that occurs only once in the Fourth Gospel. If we hold to the term's true meaning, the *place prepared* where the woman of Apocalypse 12:6 goes, is heaven.

During the sixteenth century, Protestants and Catholics spoke too easily about "the silence of Scripture" concerning the Blessed Virgin. This was used as a pretext for Protestants to renounce all Mariology, and for Catholics to develop a para-Scriptural Mariology. It is urgent that we do away with this tenacious and harmful slogan. Already it is losing ground, for the Protestants have recently begun to find Mary again *through* Scripture, whereas the Catholics are finding Mary again *in* Scripture. It cannot be denied, of course, that the Blessed Virgin has a modest place *in* the Bible. She is presented entirely in relation to Christ and not for herself. But her importance consists precisely in the closeness of her bonds with Christ, described by so many converging texts.

In order to draw up the balance sheet of the Scriptural deposit concerning Mary, we must distinguish two areas: First, a few precise facts, and in the second place, a halo of suggestions that envelop these facts.

1. Mary is holy, a virgin, the Mother of the Savior; she was present not only at the beginning of Christ's life, at the Incarnation (Matthew and Luke), but also at the inauguration and consummation of His ministry (John), and finally at the birth of the Church on Pentecost (Acts 1:14); in other words, at all the fundamental moments of Christian history.

2. This presence was both one of faith and prayer, of love of the Lord and maternal love for men. And it takes on its full significance and scope when we consider not only the inter-relationships of all these texts among themselves and with the Old Testament,

but also when we see them within the context of the great movements of Biblical theology.

On the one hand Mary appears at the end of the history of the Chosen People, as the counterpart of Abraham. She is the summit and the completion of Israel, the personal realization of Israel, the supreme point at which it comes into possession of the promises and becomes the Church. On the other hand, in the cosmic perspective suggested by Luke and that dominates the Gospel of John, a perspective in which Christ inaugurates a new creation which is a restoration of the first creation, the Blessed Virgin appears by the side of Christ as the new Eve, the associate of His most secret intentions, of the hidden mysteries of the Incarnation and the Redemption, and as the mother of all the living.

This rich but vague outline was gradually to be clarified and amplified.

2. THE SECOND PERIOD: FROM THE GOSPEL OF ST. JOHN TO THE COUNCIL OF EPHESUS (90–431)

The Scriptural era was followed by a complex period which can be said to have ended in 431, the year of the Council of Ephesus in the East, the year after the death of St. Augustine in the West. During this period, light was progressively shed on the divine maternity, the integral virginity, and the holiness of Mary. We can discern three stages in this era: a time of calm and silence (90–190), a time of laborious hesitation (190–373), and a time of harmonious solutions (373–431).

A. The silent maturation. The discovery of the antithesis between Eve and Mary.

After the Scriptural era, there was first of all a period of regression. In the Christian literature of the second century (to the extent that we are acquainted with it), the Blessed Virgin occupied a very small place. Few texts have come down to us, and they generally were limited to drab repetitions of what Matthew and Luke had already said so zestfully: Mary is the Mother of Jesus; she conceived Him virginally. Scriptural sources were reduced as it were to their simplest expression, and a portion of their riches remained hidden. The countenance of the Blessed Virgin became blurred and partially obliterated.

However, there was one new development during this century of

The first image of the Blessed Virgin (second century). She is shown with the features of a beautiful Roman woman, holding her Child in her robust arms.

By her side we see a man draped in the mantle of the philosophers, holding his rolled manuscript in one hand and pointing to a star with the other hand. This "philosopher" is the prophet Isaias announcing the sign of salvation: "A virgin shall conceive, and bear a son" (Is. 7:14).

Rome. The Catacomb of Priscilla.

N.° 41958 Roma - Catacombe di Priscilla. Madonna (fine del II Sec.) F.lli Alinari 1932

discretion. The parallel between Mary and Eve, suggested by St. John, was made explicit by two authors: St. Justin, † 163, who initiated it, and St. Irenaeus, † c. 202. But the latter developed this major theme right from the start to a degree that was never to be surpassed, at least on certain points. He went so far as to call Mary (whose obedience had restored to the world the life lost through Eve's disobedience) "the cause of salvation for the whole human race."

We must stress the importance of this parallel, which was taken up again by a host of authors. It was not to be the object of controversy (as were other parallels we shall study later), but rather the object of eminently positive meditations. It proved to be a factor making for decisive progress. The thought of the Fathers was intuitive rather than deductive, symbolic rather than logical. They progressed not by way of syllogisms but by the confrontation of symbols that were bearers of truth.

Little by little, this truth became manifest through the use of the comparative method. Between Eve and Mary a parallel was discovered to exist in terms of situation, and an opposition in terms of loyalties. The parallel of situation consisted in the fact that in both cases a virgin called to a universal motherhood engaged in an act upon which the salvation of the whole human race depended. The opposition of loyalties consisted in the fact that Eve distrusted God and disobeyed Him, whereas Mary believed and obeyed. And the result in the first case was sin and death, and in the other, salvation and life for all. Concomitantly with this contrast between Eve and Mary—between Eve, the universal mother of death, and Mary, the universal mother of life—another contrast appeared: the contrast between Eve the wife of Adam, and the Church the Spouse of Christ.

And this twofold contrast led, appropriately to a comparison between Mary and the Church, as shown in the following diagram:

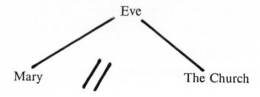

This three-sided relationship was to suggest a number of fruitful discoveries. According to Scriptural symbolism, womanhood is a sign and a mystery: woman represents redeemed creatures before almighty God. From these three Scriptural figures—these three feminine figures—a general idea emerges of the transfiguration of the human race saved by God, and of its cooperation in its own salvation. Mary thus appeared as the typical and eminent realization of this cooperation and transfiguration. This was to prove a focal point around which a great part of the progress in Marian doctrine took place, an axis to which other questions were referred. But for the present let us not anticipate further, but return to the chronological account.

B. The Divine Maternity, the virginity, and the holiness of Mary: The period of hesitations

After the phase of quasi-silence at the end of which the great and lone voice of Irenaeus was heard, there was a series of painful and frustrated efforts. This early theological reflection focussed on four points: the title of "Mother of God" (θεοτόκος), the virginity of Mary after the birth and also during the birth of Jesus (*virginitas post partum* and *virginitas in partu*), and finally, Mary's holiness.

1. The first notion unfolded gradually and without conflict. The title of "Mother of God" seems to have been attested to as early as the fourth century in the prayer *Sub tuum praesidium*. It was not seriously challenged until it was already universally accepted. Nestorius, who brought it into question, seems to have used it previously in his preaching. However, much controversy surrounded the clarification of the other three points.

2. The perpetual virginity of Mary (*virginitas post partum*) was denied by Tertullian and by several authors after him, the best known of the latter being Bonosus, who was condemned around 392.

3. The thesis of Mary's virginal integrity during childbirth (*virginitas in partu*) also stirred up difficulties, and left St. Jerome hesitant even though he was an intrepid defender of the perpetual virginity.

4. Mary's holiness came into its own still more laboriously. We could make a long list of those who did not hesitate to discover in Mary some doubt or other sin, especially among the Greek Fathers:

Origen, Basil, Gregory Nazianzen, John Chrysostom (who was particularly insistent on this point), and even Cyril.

Ambrose and Augustine laid the foundations of the acceptance of the third and fourth points by the West. More slowly and without any great controversy, the East soon was ready to accept them too. After Ephesus, the last shreds of error and indecision rapidly disappeared.

These difficulties and differences of opinion may shock some of our readers. And yet it would be unfitting to conceal them. For the truth cannot feed upon pretense, and its integrity demands the honest acceptance of all the facts. But we still have to explain what these facts mean. Why these gropings and errors?

First of all, God wants to leave to the efforts of human intelligence the discovery of certain aspects of the truth, whose principles He has adequately made known. Such an intellectual mission is not without greatness. It is one of the many aspects of God's plan to associate man actively in his own salvation. But here as elsewhere, the possibility of defeat is the reverse side of created freedom.

The way these failures came about might be illustrated by the following comparison. When a fresco is discovered hidden under the facing of some ancient monument, the first blows of the chisel sometimes mar the underlying picture. Absorbed in his scraping operations, the workman may have failed to notice at once the destruction he was causing. Something of the sort occurred in the third and fourth centuries, and was to be repeated every time a new feature of the Blessed Virgin's countenance was brought to light. Preachers in search of striking examples, and disputants carried away by the ardor of their refutations have at times unexpectedly come upon the Mother of the Lord, and, in their concern over something else, ignored one of her privileges which had not yet been clarified. Fortunately these momentary errors, these material errors, were reparable (by contrast with the damage done to the fresco in our example). For we are dealing here with an order of vital and spiritual realities: revealed truth bears within itself a principle of regeneration.

Let us inquire into the mechanism of these hesitations. They can be explained for the most part by the difficulty in reconciling two complementary aspects of the Christian mystery, a mystery whose truth cannot be reduced to geometric simplicity. At the out-

set, the Blessed Virgin was the object of a vague idea, of an indistinct spiritual experience. A new question would arise in connection with some conceptual comparison or under the pressure of
a powerful trend of ideas. Often the author, who was caught un-
prepared, offered some hasty formula, based on his preoccupations
of the moment and to the detriment of some other aspect of the
dogma to which he had not given thought. The conscience of
Christianity reacted, and a controversy broke loose. There was
hesitation, reflection, passion. Partial and contradictory answers
were followed in due time by the total answer, the true answer.
And thus the legitimate demands of the two opposing sides were
satisfied and became harmoniously integrated into the totality of
Christian doctrine.

This gives us an idea of the complexity of dogma and of how it
develops, and also puts us on guard against certain attempts at oversimplification in this area. A scrupulous examination of the facts
prohibits the hasty classification as "errors" or "truths" of the
opinions expressed before the problem was fully grasped. And it
would even more emphatically prohibit the division of the sup-
porters of these opinions, into "friends" and "enemies" of the
Blessed Virgin. The truth to which each phase of dogmatic development has led was less the refutation of an error than the golden
mean between two errors. To be more exact and to eliminate the
idea of compromise that the "golden mean" suggests, it might be
better to say that the truth defined was, as it were, the summit
where two slopes of the truth met, that is, the uniting of two partial
and complementary aspects which together constituted its integrity.

C. The progressive solution

What we have just said will throw light on the meaning of the
conflicts that arose in the Church from the end of the third century
until 431 over the four great Marian questions listed above. Let us
examine each of these questions individually.

1. Mary's perpetual virginity (*virginitas post partum*) was to be
defined as a mean between two deviations. It was a grave error
to propose it as a corollary of the Manichaean theses on the intrinsic perversity of marriage. Helvidius was an adversary of the
Manichaeans and suspected that their ideas had infiltrated into the
minds of promoters of asceticism. Carried away by his zeal, he tried
to take even this pretext away from his adversaries. In the heat of

controversy, he hastily seized upon the Gospel texts that refer to the brothers of the Lord (actually, according to Palestinian language, His cousins), and offered Mary as the integral model for mothers of large families. Who was right? Neither the Manichaeans nor their intemperate opponents. The fact of Mary's virginity had to be disassociated from any erroneous motive. The mind of Christianity quickly perceived this with Jerome, Ambrose, and Augustine.

2. The question of Mary's virginity during the birth of Christ (*virginitas in partu*) was still more delicate. Those most inclined to propose this doctrine were the Docetists, who looked upon Christ's body as simply an apparition. When proposed in this spirit, the thesis of virginity *in partu* was tainted with error. It was to remain suspect for a long time. It was not easy to reconcile the two exigencies of faith: an integral, physical and corporeal maternity on the one hand, and an integral, physical, and corporeal virginity on the other. Here again it was necessary to extricate the facts from the false principles with which certain minds had compromised them. St. Ambrose was the man who did this, in a way that we shall discuss below.

3. With regard to Mary's holiness, the opposition was more complex, less decisive, and was solved without any great controversy. The situation might be outlined as follows: On the one hand, there was a progressive discovery of the Blessed Virgin's holiness (closely related to the discovery of her virginity); on the other hand, there was a tendency to counteract the pharasaical conceit of certain ascetics by stressing that Christ alone is holy, and that all men are sinners. What a temptation for homilists to see in the Mother of the Lord the example of this universal frailty whose reality they wanted to impress upon their listeners! Many succumbed, and using Scripture with the alacrity that preachers sometimes display, they thought they discovered in Mary vainglory, doubt, or presumption. The use of such examples was startling only because it offended the delicacy and the very faith of the listeners.

These homilists had good intentions, and their principles were excellent. Christ alone is holy in His own right, He alone is metaphysically impeccable. He alone had no need of the Redemption. But they went astray in confusing Mary with the rest of humanity. Little by little the light of truth dispelled these errors.

4. It was with regard to the title of *Theotokos* that the most marked theological opposition arose. After this formula had already

been in the Church's peaceful possession for over a century, those who began to think about it discovered they had to find the right interpretation between two contrary errors. One error, the one that worried Nestorius, would have made of Mary the Mother of Christ in His divinity. Such an interpretation was all the more dangerous because mythology had left memories of a "mother of the gods." The other error, that of Nestorius reacting against the first one, would have proscribed the title of Mother of God, and disregarded the truth it contained. But to deny that Christ's Mother was the Mother of God was to deny that Christ is God. The golden mean consisted in realizing that the Blessed Virgin is the Mother of God inasmuch as she brought forth, according to His humanity, a Son who is personally God.

While we may have oversimplified the complex unfolding of these debates, there can be no doubt of their bitterness. For one thing, the healthy reaction against pagan cults created a climate of opinion unfavorable to the promoting of Mary's great privileges. Besides, those who were most eager to stress certain of these privileges were the very ones who were least conscious of their dogmatic aspects. The Manichaeans were more disposed to defend Mary's virginity after childbirth, the Docetists, to defend her virginity *in partu,* the Pelagians to extol her perfect holiness, and certain minds still under the influence of pagan cults to esteem the title of *Theotokos.*

Let no one conclude that heretics were the promoters of Mary's privileges. Rather they were the scarecrows that frightened others away from them. For their principles (or their explicit affirmations) bathed Mary's attributes in a false light. It was no easy matter to discern these caricatures from the original authentic affirmations concerning Mary's privileges. Those who eagerly fought error in all its forms were tempted to lump them all together and to consider them as branches of the one evil tree they wanted to uproot.

To the extent that we can recapture something of the climate of these outdated controversies, we realize the obsessions and suspicions that hampered the explanation of Marian doctrine. The Church's true servants were not so much those who attributed new titles of glory to the Blessed Virgin and added "new jewels to her crown," as those who set them forth in their true light. It was the great minds, not the narrow ones, that knew how to stand back, accept all aspects of the truth, and reconcile each new Marian privilege with its counterpart without which the privilege would have become a gnosis foreign to the body of Christian doctrine.

D. The position of the problem of the Immaculate Conception

We find a striking illustration of the situation we have just described at the very end of the period we are studying: This is in the twofold conflict between St. Augustine and the Pelagians over Mary's holiness. We shall not repeat what we have already said about the characteristics of Pelagian doctrine, which was a reaction against Manichaean pessimism by way of an excessive optimism as to the capacities of human nature, to the detriment of the necessary role of grace.

During the first phase of his controversy, Pelagius opposed St. Augustine by stressing the case of the Blessed Virgin "whom we must necessarily recognize to be without sin." No one had as yet put forth such a clear-cut formula of Mary's holiness. In this passionate controversy, there was danger of being tempted to reject the heretic's thesis. St. Augustine solved the difficulty most ingeniously. He accepted his opponent's affirmation, but with an entirely different meaning: Mary's holiness is an *exception,* and *its principle lies in the grace of God* and not in mere free will.

Julian of Eclanum focussed the conflict on a more delicate point: not the absence of actual sins, but the absence of original sin. This Pelagian was thus the first to make explicit the idea of the Immaculate Conception of the Mother of God. His objection was this: "By attributing original sin to her, you deliver up Mary in person to the devil!" In this case the Bishop of Hippo did not have the same mastery as in the preceding conflict. He offered only an equivocal text in answer. Looking back, we can see in Augustine's thought the progress of the two exigencies of Tradition. However, for centuries the authors who succeeded him saw in his answer the negation of the privilege of the Immaculate Conception.

In short, here as in many other cases the apparent defender of the Blessed Virgin (Julian) was a heretic. He proposed a genuine attribute under a false light. As he saw it, the Immaculate Conception was not a unique privilege, nor even a particular effect of divine grace, but the common lot of all Christians. Augustine was right in confronting him with the universality of original sin and the necessity of grace to conquer sin. Inasmuch as Augustine affirmed the *unique* character of the Marian privilege and the *preservation* through *grace* which is its very essence, he was infinitely closer to the dogmatic definition of the Immaculate Conception than his opponent.

Nevertheless, because the idea of Mary's conception without sin had first been presented prematurely and as a caricature by heretics, it remained suspect in the West for centuries. Thus, the Latins, who until then had been in the vanguard of Marian progress, remained for several centuries behind the Greeks among whom harmonious progress in this direction was to continue until the eighth and ninth centuries.

3. THE THIRD PERIOD: FROM THE COUNCIL OF EPHESUS TO THE GREGORIAN REFORM (431–1050)

The fundamental innovation that appeared at the start of this third period was the development of Marian feasts. The first feasts in honor of Mary made their appearance in the East shortly before the Council of Ephesus.

From that time on, Marian feasts continued to grow in number and in solemnity. The importance of this new fact cannot be over-emphasized: The Blessed Virgin Mary was assuming her liturgical stature. Every year, in each of the churches celebrating the feast, *homilies* were pronounced on Mary's mysteries, and *hymns* were sung whose beauty continually increased. These homilies and liturgical pieces constitute practically all the Marian writings of this epoch. The enthusiasm that filled men's souls during these feasts created a climate favorable to the disappearance of the last shreds of error, to the dispelling of remaining doubts, and to the discovery of Mary's last privileges. In the Byzantine homilies, especially of the seventh and eighth centuries, we see the emergence of three points of considerable importance: the original holiness of Mary, her mediation, and her Assumption.

Among the Latins, Marian feasts developed more slowly and with less enthusiasm, and, as it were, in the wake of the East. The three dogmas that were developing among the Byzantines remained stationary in the West. The doctrine of the Immaculate Conception was held back because of the authority of St. Augustine; the Assumption, through the authority of Pseudo-Jerome and as a reaction against the apocryphal writings that proposed this mystery in fabulous trappings. As for Mary's mediation, there seems to have been a movement in this direction during the Carolingian era with Radbertus and Autpert, but these fleeting beginnings did not develop. The tenth century, as far as we can evaluate it, seems to have been a stagnant period. In the East, homiletics went around in circles; in the West, the short-lived Carolingian ferment died down without fulfilling its promise. Everything was at lowest ebb. Once again we can see the alternate rhythm of progress and retrogression, of fervor and silence, that has been quite evident from the start.

4. THE FOURTH PERIOD: FROM THE GREGORIAN REFORM TO THE END OF THE COUNCIL OF TRENT (1050–1563)

From St. Ambrose to the end of the eleventh century, the Latins had remained stationary while the Greeks progressed. Now this relationship was reversed. From then on, only the West would contribute anything significant to the development of Marian dogma, and the East would have nothing more to offer. But before we close our discussion of the East we must do it justice: The Latin authors of the beginning of this era seem to have found their decisive inspiration in the Byzantines.

The first indications of this renaissance appeared shortly before the Gregorian Reform. The feast of the "Conception of the Virgin" (whose theological object was to remain undetermined for a long time afterward) began to be celebrated in England about 1060. After disappearing under William the Conqueror (1066–1087), it was revived around 1127–1128 on sounder theological foundations and was extended to Normandy, then to France, not without serious controversies in which St. Bernard was its opponent.

The rebirth of Marian theology, after a period of slow maturation, gradually increased in momentum at the juncture of the eleventh and twelfth centuries with St. Anselm († 1109), and suddenly took considerable proportions during the first half of the twelfth century when St. Bernard († 1153) flourished. The title of Mediatrix, until then exceptional in the West, began to gain favor everywhere. The Assumption began to make headway, the Immaculate Conception, too, although more timidly. A document of great theological value appeared at the start of the twelfth century, the *de Assumptione* by Pseudo-Augustine, which played a large role in the development of both of these doctrines. It counterbalanced the authority of Pseudo-Jerome, who opposed the corporeal glorification of the Mother of God.

Our brief summary will deal less with the details of the new ideas that abounded at this time than with the underlying intuition that gave rise to them. From this point of view we discover a new and prodigiously rich perspective, one whose possibilities have not been exhausted after eight centuries of reflection about them.

Until the end of the eleventh century, Mary's role had been restricted to the beginning of salvation, the Incarnation. Henceforth, her role was envisaged as relating to the fulfillment of the Redemption as a whole. She had been considered as the Mother of Christ, and not as His permanent associate (for this function was reserved for the Church). True, she was already looked upon as the new Eve, but only because she had introduced salvation, just as the first woman had introduced sin. The permanent role of spouse by the side of the Bridegroom had been the portion of the Church.

From then on Mary was given the role of associate. She was to be *by the side* of Christ what Eve had been through her divine vocation by the side of Adam, "a help like unto himself," *adjutorium simile sibi* (Gen. 2:18), according to the formula that soon became immensely popular. It was discovered that Mary's domain covered the same territory as that of the Church: thus there was not merely a resemblance between them but a subordination. The Blessed Virgin was no longer merely the type and exemplar of the Church; now she became the Church's queen, mother, and mediatrix: *collum ecclesiae,* according to the expression that made its appearance with Hermann of Tournai († after 1137).

In short, during this period (end of the eleventh century through the twelfth century), when the mystery of the personal presence of Christ came to the fore in the objective mystery of the Eucharist, the personal mystery of Mary was given first place in the objective mystery of the Church. And all this was only one aspect of the intellectual revolution then under way, which consisted in taking the point of view of the subject or of the person instead of the point of view of the object. Such a change in perspective called for many explorations and discoveries, and for many adjustments as well.

It was the thirteenth century, armed with the most lucid and powerful philosophical instruments, that accomplished an ordering in many fields of the effervescent discoveries of the twelfth century. The domain of Mariology was among the least favored in this respect. The most significant synthesis of the time, the one that exerted the greatest influence, was the great *Mariale super missus est,* which was attributed to Albert the Great until quite recently. It leaves much to be desired. Its basic principle—fullness of grace conceived as the universal inclusion of all graces—is narrow, and its application was carried on with a disconcerting fluency and spirit of systematization. It even went so far as to seek in Mary the grace of the seven sacraments (including penance), and the universality of human knowledge. The incontestable riches of the work were buried under this medley.

After making this harsh evaluation of a work that many have praised lavishly, we are relieved to be able to add at this late hour that St. Albert was not its author, as was hitherto unanimously believed.

St. Thomas Aquinas could have developed more satisfactorily the principles of a synthesis because of his profound insight into the doctrine of the divine maternity. But he did not make such a synthesis. And it would have been difficult for him to do so, for his thought was hampered by the difficulties concerning the Immaculate Conception that he had inherited and never overcame. Scotus († 1308), who led a decisive offensive against these difficulties, started a movement that was to go far, but he did not offer us a synthesis either. After him came Engelbert of Admont († 1331), who could be considered important if he were the source of the pseudo-Albert the Great; and then came the *Arbor vitae crucifixae* by Ubertino of Casale, written in 1305. Afterward there was a gradual regression into mediocrity.

However a few ideas continued to make headway, notably that of the Immaculate Conception. A few first-rate theologians appeared sporadically, such as Gerson († 1429), but in general there was a tendency to repeat what had already been said rather than to think things through anew. The philosophical apparatus became stiff and complicated. Nominalism raged. Theology was reduced to dust. In their efforts to escape a dessicated intellectualism, men sought life on the level of the imagination and sentiment. During this decadence, popular enthusiasm for the Blessed Virgin did not weaken. However it tended more and more to feed upon adulterated food, shoddy miracles, equivocal slogans and meaningless gossip.

Artistic trends manifested this transition from mystery to naturalism, and from naturalism to artifice. In the thirteenth century the majestic Romanesque Virgin, the immaculate throne of Wisdom incarnate, gave way to a new type of Virgin, graceful and smiling.

These thirteenth century Virgins showed their smiles rather than their Son, who was now moved from His central position to one on the side. The sober and hieratic costume of the earlier Virgins was replaced by more feminine attire, with increasingly complicated drapery. Gradually, artistic expression sank to affectation and melodrama. In the fifteenth century, the Virgin of the Presentation, who had always been presented standing, appeared kneeling; the Virgin on Calvary collapsed in a swoon. Sermons spoke of her tears, her moans, and her fainting spells, but they forgot to speak of her strength and her cooperation in the work of salvation.

The bottom of this decline had just about been reached when the Protestant crisis began. The popular Marian author of the time was Bernardine di Busti, whose *Mariale,* first published in 1496, went through many editions. We can infer the decadence of a period that established the reputation of this author. His compilation compromised excellent ideas by burying them in a meaningless mass of opinions, many of them outrageous.

A general house-cleaning was in order. Here, as in many other fields, after the indispensable clearing-away had been completed there was nothing but a vacuum left, for the theology of the time had done away with the indispensable bases of doctrine. Protestantism had returned to the situation of Ephesus, limiting Mariology to three points: Mary's holiness, her virginity, and her role as the Mother of God. And it sometimes even eliminated these fundamental points. Difficulties that had long since been resolved, which Tertullian and St. John Chrysostom had stumbled against, were returned to a place of honor by the reformers. When the Council of Trent terminated in 1563, it had not dealt with the Marian question, which remained in a particularly deficient state.

5. THE FIFTH PERIOD: FROM THE END OF THE 16TH CENTURY TO THE END OF THE 18TH CENTURY

At the very end of the sixteenth century, there was a rebirth of enthusiasm. This Marian renaissance began in the countries that had not been touched by the Reformation: Italy, and especially Spain, which was still at the height of its glory and set the tone in all domains, from mysticism to theology, from literature to fashions. The protagonists of this revival were the first great theologians of the Society of Jesus: in Spain, Salmeron († 1585) and Suarez, the founder of systematic Mariology (1590), and also Salazar, who in

1618 issued the first great work on the Immaculate Conception and the first exposition *ex professo* on the role of Mary in the Redemption. In the Germanic area there was St. Peter Canisius, in 1572, and in Italy, St. Robert Bellarmine.

It was the beginning of a great era. The Mariological movement spread rapidly, especially from 1619 to 1630, reached a peak between 1630 and 1650, and then slowly declined, as if exhausted from a too rapid growth. Several controversies seemed to bring about a short-lived revival. Among these sources of contention were: the *Avis salutaires,* from 1673 to 1678; Maria of Agreda, at the end of the seventeenth century and the beginning of the eighteenth; the "bloody vow" between 1714 and 1764. Several great Marian authors also appeared during this period: St. John Eudes († 1680), St. Louis-Mary Grignion de Montfort († 1716), and St. Alphonsus di Liguori, who published his *Glories of Mary* in 1750. Then the movement sank into deep silence for over half a century (1780–1830).

The beginning of the period we have thus delimited was characterized by a change in orientation, a renewal of inspiration, and an explosion of enthusiasm. There is a striking contrast between the first three-quarters of the sixteenth century and the start of the seventeenth. On the one hand, there were a few short and anemic works, preoccupied with polemic concerns; on the other, there was a superabundant literature, so thoroughly engrossed with constructive matters that it seemed to forget the existence of the Protestants.

The sixteenth century had limited itself to the negative task of preserving and defending a heritage that was reduced to a minimum. The seventeenth century was guided at times by an excess concern over promoting Mary's new glories and instilling new forms of devotion. In short, the end of the sixteenth century and the beginning of the seventeenth were in the Marian domain what springtime is in nature. Things that seemed dead showed signs of life; an abundant and overflowing vitality found innumerable ways of manifesting itself.

If we want to point to the central theological object of all these activities, we can do so without hesitation. It was the Immaculate Conception. This belief had been held back by weighty theological difficulties and by the opposition of such illustrious authorities as St. Bernard and St. Thomas Aquinas, and it was suspect in influential Roman circles. It was to be the central preoccupation of hundreds of Mariological works during the seventeenth century. Some of these works were catalogues of testimonies in favor of this doctrine; others argued; still others polemized. It was a vast and uneven labor, in which many would soon lose their way. And yet this effort was not in vain.

At the end of the seventeenth century, the last-remaining powerful opposition yielded. In Rome, the sanctions that prohibited the activities of the "Immaculists" were stopped. And the Thomists, who had waged war against the partisans of the Immaculate Conception in the name of St. Thomas, now deployed their efforts to find an affirmation of this doctrine in his writings. In 1854, the definition was promulgated amid general acceptance. And yet two centuries earlier it would have caused a revolution. A century of tranquil sifting was necessary. Just as a scientist may sometimes discover in his sleep the solution to some problem on which he has spent days of fruitless research, so at the end of a sterile period the Church definitively brought forth a solution in which many conflicts and complications were settled.

6. THE SIXTH PERIOD: THE 19TH AND 20TH CENTURIES

From the Marian point of view, the nineteenth century is quite remarkable. It began in the most extreme destitution. During the first thirty years of the century the rarity and mediocrity of Marian literature sank to a level never before reached, even in the sixteenth century.

The Marian renaissance that followed took the most surprising forms. It began in 1830 with an apparition, the first of a long series that characterized the century. The Blessed Virgin entrusted to Catherine Labouré the project of the Miraculous Medal, which was to be, as it were, the signal for a great movement of devotion and conversions. The image on the medal seemed to announce the entire program of the century: The Immaculate Conception and Mary's Mediation.

Inaugurated by an apparition, the era continued in 1854 with a dogmatic definition. Pius IX declared the Immaculate Conception to be a dogma of faith. And this infallible pronouncement came about without any great theological preparation, inasmuch as the efforts of the seventeenth and eighteenth centuries seemed to be forgotten for the moment and the work of the nineteenth amounted to very little. Pius IX carefully consulted the living tradition of the

Church. But the theological spadework was not very extensive. At best we can point to one general theological work that represents, if not a rigorous method, at least conscientious labors. And its author, L. Passaglia (who initiated Scheeben to Mariology) was to end his career in opposition to the Holy See—regarding an entirely different matter.

In short, during this disconcerting period a charismatic spurt preceded the theological and literary renaissance. The beginning of the century was marked by an absence of Marian works. Then, around 1840, there was a sudden transition to an even more distressing proliferation. Veuillot described this literature, whose abundance was the least of its defects, as follows:

Among the vast quantity of volumes produced each year, only a few are not utterly without merit: there are awkward and cold declamations, badly organized texts, lessons devoid of doctrine, of love, and too often devoid of grammar as well. It is amazing that the zeal that inspires the reading of these sorry productions fails to inspire those who write them.

These words reveal the drama of the whole nineteenth century. It was an epoch when ardent and authentic devotion was obliged to seek its nourishment in an inferior literature and a deplorable art.

However, the situation gradually improved. After the work of the Belgian Bishop, Malou, on the Immaculate Conception in 1857, Newman, in 1866, proposed a Mariology brought back to its sources and stripped of all dross. In 1882 Scheeben put forth a longer work which, after being buried for a half-century, was to achieve a considerable influence. Like Newman, he returned to Patristic sources, but he allowed himself to be more powerfully influenced by dogmatic developments. His work was motivated by a twofold concern: the concern to grasp the aspects of the Marian mystery in their order and unity and, what was newer, the concern to give Mariology its proper place in theology as a whole, between the treatise on Christ and the one on the Church, and thus to integrate organically Mariology into theology. With Scheeben, Mariology ceased being a gratuitous undertaking, and regained its authentic significance.

It was in Scheeben's footsteps that the movement of "scientific Mariology" began to take shape, especially after 1925. We are indebted to Scheeben both for the word "Mariology" and for the example he has left us. The great emphasis of this new trend has been

Marian mediation considered in its two phases: Mary's participation in the fundamental work of the Redemption; and Mary's participation in dispensing the fruits of the Redemption.

It was Cardinal Mercier who initiated the movement to study this question. The foundations of the movement were laid before 1913, and it was resumed after World War I. Since then, especially since 1926, it has continued to grow.

However, between 1940 and 1950, while this primary center of interest did not diminish, it was eclipsed by another: the Assumption. There is a striking difference between the quantity and the quality of the works that preceded Pius IX's Bull on the Immaculate Conception in 1854, and the Constitution of Pius XII on the Assumption in 1950. A successive reading of these two documents will reveal to us some measure of the progress that has been made in the past century in historical and theological precision.

In what direction is Marian theology now heading? The abundance of works and tendencies of the present day make us hesitate. We could mention first of all that the problem of the co-Redemption is regaining importance in the measure that the definition of the Assumption is no longer a current question. But something has changed in the position of the problem. Efforts are being made to relate it to some more fundamental doctrine that would manifest its significance.

What is the principle of this synthesis? Some say it is the Divine Maternity. The Spaniards say it is the "spiritual maternity," and they have given this notion an original turn. Certain Belgian authors stress Mary's association with Christ, insisting that even the Divine Maternity is only one aspect of this association. The German group would tend to stress Mary's mission as the representative of the human race. And so on. Through all of this debate, a single question is actually being asked: What is Mary's role in the plan of salvation? And this is the question that dominates theological thought at the present time. The twentieth century's concern about "demonstrating" Mary's mediation does not have the importance that the concern about "demonstrating" the Immaculate Conception had for the seventeenth. Less effort is being made to prove a thesis than to establish the role of the Blessed Virgin in the total Christian mystery, an effort that has led to the elimination of many factitious elements.

We can now see why first place is being given to an entirely new question: Mary and the Church. Scheeben, who was the first to present it with any breadth of perspective, long remained without anyone to echo his views. Beginning in 1926, and partially through his influence, two complementary trends took form: the ecclesiological movement has tended to present the Marian problem in a new light, and Mariologists have tended to consider Mary in an ecclesiological perspective. The documents produced by followers of both trends have increased overwhelmingly in the past few years. But there is no reason to complain about it. This effort is a return to the spirit of Patristic Mariology, while not renouncing legitimate acquisitions whose full meaning it helps to discover. It is restoring to Mariology a factor of equilibrium that it had gradually lost during the last few centuries.

II. The Course of Mary's Destiny

Now that we have glanced over the phases through which the Church passed in becoming aware of the mystery of Mary, it might seem that we ought to renounce the chronological order and adopt a logical order which would present the rational interrelationships of Mary's privileges. Such a method would start out from the central privilege that explains Mary, and deduce the other privileges as from a first principle. In short, we would abandon the temporal order and rise to the eternal order of predestination. We would strive to enter into God's mind, to grasp how He conceives of the mystery of Mary in a single idea.

Attractive as such a method may be, it unfortunately presents many disadvantages. First of all, it is too ambitious. It starts out from God's own intentions. But are we capable of defining these intentions with sufficient accuracy, especially at the present incomplete stage of doctrinal development? What was God's fundamental intention with regard to Mary? Was it to choose Himself a mother and shower her with perfections; to associate a creature to His whole work of salvation; to exalt, by the side of God made man, all the resources of grace that womanhood can offer; to give the Church a perfect exemplar in the new Eve? These are questions still under discussion. When God's thought is refracted in the diversity of human minds, it takes on various forms.

Let us not disregard God's thought, since it effectively governs all things, but let us consider it as a goal to be reached and not as a point of departure. We shall progress from the complex data of revelation to the divine intention that they manifest, and not from these intentions, which are beyond our grasp, to the known data.

Indeed if there is a logic in God's intentions, it is outside the bounds of our own logic. In certain domains, God's logic may be manifested so rigorously as to allow us to apply our deductive methods to it. But the case of Mary is more delicate and complex. We can have access to her mystery only by the comparison of several perspectives and not by a process of linear reasoning.

Besides, too logical a synthesis of Marian doctrine might be prejudicial to truth from two points of view. First, it would conceal the gratuitousness of God's intention, which is supremely free not only as a whole but even, in a certain respect, in its details. Moreover, such a synthesis would veil the role of Mary's freedom and her extraordinary cooperation with God's plans at every instant of her life. In short, it would dissolve the personal perspective which is so important wherever Mary is concerned. Mary's person would be absorbed into an abstract personification: maternity in itself, the *"consortium Christi Redemptoris,"* "the essence of the mystery of the Church" (*das Wesengeheimnis der Kirche*), transcendent womanhood, "the eternal feminine" in the noble sense of the word. Such a synthesis would reduce the most concrete of existences to a logically-deduced essence.

We should note the wonderful interrelationships of this destiny, whose center is the Divine Maternity. This Maternity is the culmination of all that preceded from the moment of the Immaculate Conception, and the point of departure for everything that followed, up to and including the Assumption and the heavenly exercise of the spiritual maternity. And yet, while we can *relate* everything to this central privilege, we can *deduct* practically nothing from it.

God granted Mary all that befitted the Mother of the Word Incarnate. We shall examine these fitting qualities, but we shall avoid presenting them as necessities. Even though the ordering of Mary's life and greatness may at times give the impression of a necessity, it is not a logical necessity but the type of necessity that occurs in the order of art and of love. In the creation of an artistic masterpiece as in the fateful meeting of two destinies, everything seems to be necessary; and yet everything is supremely free and gratuitous. The necessities that this masterpiece and this love impose cannot be reduced to a logical presentation. So is it with Mary's destiny.

Now that we have stressed the negative aspect, the danger of a deductive plan, we must stress how essential *time*—which is the ordering principle of this study—is to Mary's destiny. The importance of time will be made clear by two comparisons: one with the destiny of Christ, and another with the destiny of the saints.

1. St. Luke said of the child Jesus that He "advanced in wisdom and age" (2:52). Thus, Christ grew not only physically but also spiritually. But this latter growth was entirely accidental. Essentially, Christ was God from the very first moment, and in this order no growth was possible, contrary to the contentions of certain heretics of the Adoptionist kind.

In addition to His *substantial* possession of God through the hypostatic union, Christ also possessed God through His intellect (the beatific vision) from the first moment. Not only was He God, but He knew Himself as God. It follows that He was not a wayfarer in obscure faith as we are, on the way to the light of eternity: He possessed the completion of His personal destiny. In this sense He was not a *viator* but a *comprehensor,* to use theological language. Christ entered time, but His *personality* and His *knowledge* never ceased to transcend time. It was possible for Him to grow only superficially, according to the secondary and accidental aspects of His life.

Mary, on the other hand, lived the wayfarer's life common to all other mortals. The law of growth is therefore essential to her being and to her knowledge: she became the Mother of God; she lived in faith before attaining to the beatific vision at the end of her earthly destiny. Christ's career was the descent of an eternal Person into time. Mary's career was like our own, a progressive ascent from time toward eternity: it proceeded from gratuitous gift to merits, and from merits to new gifts.

2. And this brings us to our second comparison: time has greater importance in Mary's destiny than in that of the other saints. First of all, she knew how to "make the most of her time" (as St. Paul says, Eph. 5:16; Col. 4:5) better than all the other saints. Not only did she make greater use of her time subjectively, but objectively she was capable of greater progress. St. Thomas observes that growth in grace follows a law of acceleration that is comparable in the spiritual order to the falling of bodies in a vacuum. The closer a soul comes to God the faster He draws it to Himself; the higher a soul is in grace, the more rapid is its ascent.

Thus, Mary's growth, which began with a holiness that surpassed that of all the saints even at the start, rose to the greatest heights ever reached by man. She never experienced the negative progress which consists in the elimination of sin (a progress out of harmony with time because it implies sudden halts and regressions). Hers was the highest form of progress—that which consists in closer union with God and in the deepening of love. Finally, whereas the destiny of every other man wavers between nostalgia for the past and impatience for the future, Mary knew how to live on the level of time. She knew how to stay with the present, and to enlist her whole past in the service of the future with unfaltering hope.

Moreover, Mary had the privilege of belonging to all three phases of the era of grace: the era before Christ, the era of Christ's life on earth, and the era after Christ. She was born and grew up in the Old Testament. Then her life spanned the duration of her Son's, and continued during the beginnings of the Church. Not only did she participate in these three phases, but she seems to have received the mission to be the *transition* from one to the other (which is in harmony with the very essence of time). It was through her that Israel brought forth Christ on the day of the Incarnation. Later she was to play an analogous connecting role between the death of Christ and the birth of the Church. Finally, by her Assumption she anticipated the Second Coming: she is the bond between the present earthly condition of the Church and the future, heavenly, and resurrected condition toward which it is advancing.

Let us therefore follow the course of Mary's destiny, during which her life, her mission, and her being acquired their definitive stature under the motion of grace. In this development we can distinguish the following phases, in accordance with what we have just said:

1. Before the Annunciation: Mary, the completion of Israel.
2. Mary at the beginning of Christ's life: her cooperation in the Incarnation.
3. Mary at the end of Christ's life: her cooperation in the Redemption.
4. From the death of Christ to the Dormition: Mary, the bond between the era of Christ and the era of the Church.
5. The Assumption: Mary, "the eschatological icon of the Church."

1. BEFORE THE ANNUNCIATION: MARY, THE COMPLETION OF ISRAEL

We must begin by determining Mary's place in the history of salvation. The history anterior to Christ was the battlefield of two contrary movements. On the one hand, the human race was swept along by a dialectic of sin; on the other hand, gratuitous interventions by God were leading the human race toward the victory which would be the coming of Christ. Until the time of Abraham degradation held sway. Then God's interventions became increasingly efficacious, but in a more *restricted* sphere, and in an increasingly *spiritual* order. God chose Abraham's family; then He chose Jacob in preference to Esau. Then during a time when Israel's dreams of political grandeur and prosperity fell to the ground, grace became progressively centered in a elite, hidden according to the flesh: the "poor" and the "humble" who were the spiritual remnant of the chosen people, and finally in the flower of Israel, the Virgin Mary.

Reparation, preparation: these two words sum up the two aspects of humanity's ascent toward its Savior, two aspects that are closely related—the one negative and the other positive. God gradually purified a chosen lineage so that Christ might be born in a blameless environment. He inspired in this family an increasingly perfect and explicit faith, so that His divine coming might be the answer to a desire, an expectation, a hope on the part of man; so that it might not be a surprising intrusion or violence, but the work of freedom and love.

Thus from Abraham to Mary, a twofold progress took place: progress in the order of *moral purity,* and progress in the order of *faith:*

1. From the point of view of moral purity, there is a vast distance between Abraham and Mary. The behavior of the Father of believers was uncouth and often shocking. The Blessed Virgin's life began in the most perfect purity. With Abraham, whom Scripture compares to a "rock" from which God "hewed" the figure of His people (Is. 51:1-2), the stone age of salvation began. It was a time of vigor and ruggedness. With Mary, the golden age of perfection arrived.

2. From the point of view of faith, there is close resemblance, not a contrast, between Abraham and Mary: Everything began and ended with faith. In the beginning, there was the unconditional

faith of the Chosen People in the Promise; at the end, there was the unconditional faith of the Mother of God in the fulfillment of the Promise. And yet even here there was a considerable evolution. At the start there was a wholehearted but rather vague and material faith, in terms of its object; at the end, a faith spiritualized and enriched by the long unfolding of Revelation that the message of the Annunciation fulfilled. Let us look more deeply into this twofold mystery, the mystery of the Immaculate Conception, the transcendent completion of the long moral reparation realized by God in Israel; and the mystery of Mary's faith, the completion of the long preparation for the coming of the Messias.

Mary's destiny began by a totally gratuitous action on the part of God, by a unique action which, without any merit whatever on Mary's part, preserved her from all sin, and from even the slightest trace of sin:

> At the first instant of her Conception, through the grace and privilege of God Almighty and in consideration of the merits of Jesus Christ the Savior of the human race, the Virgin Mary was preserved and exempted from all stain of original sin (Bull *Ineffabilis* of December 8, 1854, Denz. 1641).

The gratuitousness of the divine intervention should not make us ignore the bond between this mystery and the anterior preparation. First of all, God did not alter the biological continuity essential to the unity of the human race, or even the ordinary process of human generation. To this perfect continuity in the order of the flesh corresponds an imperfect continuity in the order of grace. The Church has established two solemn and universal feasts in honor of the parents of the Blessed Virgin, the only two personages of the Old Testament she so honors. The purpose of this honor is to indicate that in them the long process of moral purification of the Old Testament attained a point of perfection which lacked nothing but actual deliverance from the bonds of original sin. And God accomplished this final step in Mary.

We must learn to look beneath the dry exterior of the dogmatic definition, whose every word must be weighed to prevent the danger of inadmissible interpretations, and discover the heart of the mystery. It is a mystery of love. God, yearning for the salvation of men, God who compared the chosen people to a beloved wife (see Osee 2; Jer. 31:17-22; Is. 54:4-8; 61:10-11; Cant.), gave free reign to His love. In Mary the adulterous people became a betrothed without spot (Osee 2:20; Cant. 2:8-12; Is. 61:10), not merely free from all sin and from all trace of sin, but also endowed with the fullness of grace. Divine love, which unlike our own does not depend upon its object but actually creates it, manifested itself untrammeled. It made Mary the most lovable object, the most attractive person among all mere creatures, the one in whom God could establish His dwelling without compromise with sin.

The force of grace unhampered by any interior reticence on Mary's part drew her toward God with her whole being in a rapture of faith and love. In accordance with the law that the creatures most favored by God are also the ones that thirst most for Him, Mary's ardent receptiveness, her violent desire for the Most High exceeded that of any other creature. Her burning faith, nourished by Scripture (as we have seen) was the living completion of the faith of Israel, and of its yearning for the Messias. In Mary, Israel's cry was to be answered.

But before considering this answer, we must point out another aspect of the mystery of the Immaculate One. So far we have approached this mystery in its relation to God. We must also consider the position it conferred upon Mary as a member of the human race. By her total holiness which restored the bond with the royal holiness of our first parents, Mary was raised above all men. She alone was perfectly agreeable to God in her whole being, as well as by all her acts. Thus, she was not only the first among creatures and the queen of creation, but also the representative, the advocate of the human race. She was the mediatrix of the human race in the sense that in her the mediation Israel had exercised since Abraham in favor of the sinful world (Gen. 18:17-33) attained to its highest efficacy. (This initial mediation was later to be modified by subordination to the transcendent mediation of the God-man and by Mary's participation in His mediation.) By reason of the love that impelled her to appeal to God in favor of all men, Mary was already, obscurely and in spirit, the universal mother. And the meaning of this motherhood was to be prodigiously enriched as her destiny unfolded.

The Church has chosen to point to various moments of the Blessed Virgin's life before the Annunciation: her Nativity, the first visible apparition of the one in whom salvation would be given; her Presentation, the first visible expression of her yearning for God. But all these moments are simply manifestations of a single mystery in which we can distinguish three aspects: the divine gift, Mary's answer to God, and her intercession for the world. This mystery made of her, in a certain sense, the peak of the human race. And yet this expression calls for two important limitations. First, Mary was only the *provisory* peak of the human race. Its true peak and its only head is Christ, whom she was destined to receive within her. Besides, she was the peak of Israel only *in the spiritual and interior order*. She had no place in the priestly hierarchy, in teaching, and in public worship: these functions were reserved for men. It was not Mary but John the Baptist who would officially prepare the coming of the Messias. Her mission, in keeping with her condition as a woman, was completely hidden, and consisted wholly of interior riches: the acceptance, the fructification, and the giving forth of divine grace.

2. MARY AT THE TIME OF THE INCARNATION: THE DIVINE MATERNITY

The crucial moment of Mary's destiny, the one to which all that preceded led and upon which all the rest was based, was the moment of the Annunciation. At that time the Blessed Virgin acquired a new greatness. She became the Mother of God. This mystery defies any linear exposition. Its riches cannot be encompassed in a single glance. Its logic is that of a masterpiece and not of a deduction. To describe it, we must juxtapose several perspectives and thus catch a glimpse of this logic and of these riches that are beyond anything we can conceive. We shall therefore approach in succession the fundamental reason for this privilege, the holiness with which God surrounds it, its essence, and its principal harmonics.

Mary's Maternity, the means of the Incarnation. To understand the significance of the Divine Maternity, we must go beyond the person of Mary. Indeed, the reason God became incarnate was not first of all to favor the most beloved of His creatures. It was *propter nos homines et propter nostram salutem*—for us men, and for our salvation. The Divine Maternity is first of all the means by which this mystery of salvation was realized.

Why did God will such a means? Why did the Word choose to descend from heaven, not with a body formed by God's hands like that of the first Adam (Gen. 2:7), but to be born upon earth with a body "born of a woman" (Gal. 4:4)? Because He wanted to be a member of the race He was to save; and He wanted to save it from within, not as with an alms thrown down from on high, but through salvation drawn from itself; not as a stranger but as a brother, as perfectly a man and of the race of the men to be redeemed as He was perfectly God, of the race of the offended God. In short, He wanted to be a perfect mediator, who perfectly united within Himself the two parties to be reconciled.

Mary's mission was therefore essentially to incorporate the Savior into the human race. This consideration dispels illusions to which Mariologists are sometimes too readily inclined, illusions that disfigure the plan of salvation. He who did not "come to call the just, but sinners" (Mk. 2:17) and who leaves the faithful sheep and goes "in search of the one that has strayed" (Mt. 18:12) did not come first of all for the joy of His Immaculate Mother, but for the salvation of the world.

Is this to say that Mary is a means without importance, a pure means, like the bread used at Mass to be changed into the Body of Christ? Such is the thought of many Protestants, and even Catholic theologians sometimes say that God *could have* made it so.

Let us note at once that this hypothesis has the disadvantage of abstracting from God's wisdom and love, and considers only His divine power. It would be very hazardous to imagine that this God who has such great respect for human liberty could have become incarnate without the consent of His Mother, that this God who has such great love for human persons could have treated the one who was closest to Him as a simple means, that this God whose presence transforms could have lived so close to His Mother without transforming her, and finally that He who gave the command "Honor thy father and thy mother" could have left without honor the one who brought Him forth. The hypothesis in which the Mother of the God-man would have no relation to the work of grace seems to conform less to another possible plan than to the idea of another God who would not be the One we know.

A Holy Maternity. Even apart from this hypothesis, we need only consider the facts to see that Mary's Maternity was penetrated with grace in a truly unique way. She was blessed not only because God had done great things for her (Lk. 1:49), but because "she had believed" (cf. Lk. 1:44). *From the point of view of God* who miraculously proposed and intervened, and *from the point of view of the Blessed Virgin* who was receptive to His message and to His action, the event was integrally pure, integrally religious. Let us examine both aspects of the holiness of the Annunciation, its human and divine aspects, its ascending and descending aspects.

1. *The one to whom* God addressed His message was holy: she was the κεχαριτωμένω (Lk. 1:28), the object of God's favors, and we know that God went so far as to bestow upon her the favor of preservation from original sin and of conferring upon her the fullness of grace. *Her state* was a holy one: she was a virgin (Mt. 1:18, 23; Lk. 1:27). And voluntary and vowed virginity (Lk. 1:34) very precisely fulfills the concept of holiness, inasmuch as it is a *separation* with regard to creatures with a view to a *total belonging,* in body and in soul, to God. Finally, the *act* by which Mary offered herself to the divine action was holy. It was an act of faith, obedience, and humility (Lk. 1:38; cf. 1:45).

When we consider the event of the Annunciation from this point of view, we may be tempted to see in Mary's Maternity the normal fruit of her perfect holiness. We can perceive a kind of continuity between Mary's perfection before that day and the perfection she acquired on that day. The Fathers have sought to express this fact by disconcerting formulas such as these: "Mary conceived in her spirit before conceiving in her body" or "she conceived the flesh of Christ through faith." What do such words mean? First of all, that the Divine Maternity was prepared by Mary's faith, proposed to her faith, and that it was accomplished by virtue of a consent that was an act of faith. Besides, this act of faith, of perfect faith completed by charity, was meritorious: Mary merited her Maternity, certainly not through merit in justice (*de condigno*), based on equality between the work accomplished and the reward, but through a merit of fitness (*de congruo*), based on delicacy and friendship. We can recognize God's plan in this, who chooses to make men not only desire but also merit the most gratuitous of His gifts.

There is still more to consider. Not only is Mary's Maternity a consequence and, as it were, a reward of her faith, but it seems to be its reflection or fruit. Indeed, there are close similarities and correlations between the spiritual act by which the Blessed Virgin accepted the Incarnation and the physical act by which she conceived the Savior. Both of these acts had the same object: the Word Incarnate. Both of them deserve the name of "conception," since "to conceive" can refer to an act of the intellect quite as much as to the act of generation. And there is more than a play on words involved. There is something here that pertains to the nature of faith. Like the conception of a child, faith is the active and fruitful receptivity of a seed of life. To quote the Fathers, every Christian, when he accepts the word of God, "conceives God in his heart." From this point of view, faith implies a kind of divine spiritual maternity; and the divine physical Maternity of Mary appears as the supreme realization of this gift—as the incarnation of the very essence of faith.

But let us beware of becoming absorbed by this point of view. It would lead us to an error contrary to the one we have just set aside. We would be refuting the false idea of an Incarnation realized without warning, without the cooperation of human liberty transformed by grace, only to fall into another error: the error of attributing to Mary a holiness by reason of which her Maternity would be due her in justice.

Is there, then, a continuity or a discontinuity between Mary's holiness and her Maternity? In this case as in that of modern physics, we cannot solve the alternative by the elimination of one of the terms. These terms are correlative: the remarks of the Fathers emphasize the existence of a relative continuity between Mary's faith in the Incarnation and the realization of this mystery within her. And yet, from another point of view there is discontinuity. What happened at the moment of the Annunciation had been harmoniously prepared by the whole of the Old Testament, by the Immaculate Conception and the spiritual progress that followed it. But all these things were completely gratuitous, in fact doubly gratuitous: God's *proposal* and the *action* that He exercised exceeded anything that knowledge of Mary's perfection could have led even the most intelligent angels to expect.

2. Let us therefore examine the divine and transcendent aspect of the holiness of the Annunciation. Not only did God govern the long preparation of grace that culminated in the Incarnation, but what He then proposed exceeded every hope He had ever aroused in man's heart. And suddenly He descended from on high, He intervened in an unprecedented way, and thus manifested the matchless holiness that He willed to confer upon the religious event that then took place.

It was the *Holy Spirit* who intervened (Lk. 1:35; Mt. 1:20). And we know from the Bible that the object of the Holy Spirit's intervention is sanctification. Here the intervention was unique, miraculous: The Holy Spirit made up in a transcendent way for the biological activity that belongs to man according to the order of nature. And this miracle brought about the integral reality of this holiness of which the Mosaic tabernacle—the holy of holies—had been the figure. By His supernatural action, the Most High granted a single answer to the two yearnings that were deepest in Mary's heart: her woman's yearning for motherhood, and her saint's yearning to belong totally to God. But He fulfilled them far beyond her fondest dreams.

A Divine Maternity. Our last consideration leads us toward a new phase. We at first visualized Mary's Maternity as the means of the Incarnation. We have just seen how holy this Maternity had to be, both from Mary's and from God's point of view. Now we discover that this Maternity is divine, and we must explore this fundamental dimension of the mystery.

Divine Maternity: This epithet can be understood in three ways —according to exemplary, efficient, and final causality. This Maternity had God as its model, as its principle, and as its term. Let us examine each of these points in succession.

1. Mary's Maternity might be called divine first of all because it was conformed to the model of the Fatherhood of God. God made of the human sonship of the Word an image of His divine sonship, and this is the ultimate explanation of the unique privileges belonging to the Maternity. He gave Mary perfect holiness, so that she might resemble the Father. He willed that the temporal generation of the Word be virginal, in the image of the eternal generation.

Let us also remember what the Fathers tell us about the role of Mary's faith in the Incarnation: her Maternity resembles the heavenly Fatherhood in that it is the fruit of faith, that is, of a spiritual act, a holy act. This harmony has far-reaching implications. We learn about the first Trinitarian procession through two concepts: *the conception of a Word* (by analogy with the act of the human intellect) and *the generation of a Son*. Similarly, Mary's action in the Incarnation was a *spiritual conception* through faith before it was a *physical generation* through the body.

However, we should not press this comparison to the point of identification; this is only a limited analogy. Whereas the conceptual duality (the intellectual act and the generative act) is entirely relative to our way of conceiving as far as the Trinity is concerned, this duality is real with respect to Mary. The Father accomplishes a single act that we grasp through two complementary modalities; Mary accomplished two distinct acts, even though they were very closely related—one in her mind and the other in her flesh.

Finally,—and this is the most profound analogy—the eternal generation and the temporal generation have the same term. The Son of the Father and Mary's Son are not two sons, but one and the same Son: the second *Person* of the Blessed Trinity. And it is this fundamental likeness that governs all the others. It draws the Divine Maternity into the orbit of the divine Fatherhood like a mysterious satellite.

2. Not only is Mary's Maternity divine through its resemblance to the Trinitarian archetype, it is also divine in its cause: Mary conceived by the Holy Spirit. Mary was a Virgin who had renounced "knowing" man (Lk. 1:34) in order to belong to God alone; and God Himself assumed, in a wholly spiritual and transcendent way, the role that belongs to man in human generation. It is this spiritual and transcendent character that the Fathers stress in their significant formula: Mary conceived the Word through faith. Just as the newly baptized Christian is reborn not of the flesh, nor of the will of man, but by faith and the Holy Spirit, so Christ, the exemplar of our adoption, was born in Mary.

3. Divine in its principle, Mary's Maternity is also divine in its term. Not only did she become a Mother through the power of God; she is the *Mother of God. And this is the fundamental reason why we speak of the Divine Maternity.* All the other reasons are ordered to this one. God conformed Mary to the model of the divine Fatherhood *in order to* make her worthy of His Son and to proportion her to her mission. The Fathers had a profound insight into this relationship, and in various ways said: A virginal generation, a generation whose principle was the intervention of God Himself, could have only God as its object, and the Divine Maternity could not be anything but virginal. Here again we have one of those deep fitnesses whose necessity is gratuitous in the sense we have used it above.

Thus, Mary is the Mother of God in the sense brought out by St. Cyril: She is not the Mother of the Godhead, but through human generation she is truly the Mother of a Son who is God. She is not the Mother of a man who was united to God, but of a man who, from the moment of His conception, was personally God. The fact that Mary did not give her Son His divine nature and personality takes nothing away from the authenticity of her title. For that matter other mothers do not confer upon their sons soul and personality, and yet they are truly mothers: mothers not only of the flesh that they form, but really mothers of the human person, created by God, that subsists in that flesh. In like manner, Mary is not simply the Mother of the flesh of Jesus: she is the Mother of *the Person* who subsists in that flesh; she is not the Mother of Jesus' body, but the Mother of Jesus who is God.

A Unique Relationship. It is this relationship to God that is the essence of the Divine Maternity and that places Mary above all other simple creatures. In many respects this is the most profound relationship that can exist between a human *person* and God. True, it is infinitely removed from the Trinitarian relations that are substantially divine. Again, it is less profound than the relationship of Christ's humanity to the Word who assumed it, and even, in certain respects, than the relationship of the Eucharistic species to the Body of Christ. These relationships presuppose the total absence of person, of created supposit. But the Divine Maternity is the noblest relationship compatible with a created personality, the closest bond uniting a divine Person to a human person: and that is why Mary is the noblest and the most favored of all simple creatures.

In order to bring out the various aspects of this superiority, let us compare the Divine Maternity, which is the basic gift Mary received, with the baptismal character, which is the basic gift the Christian receives. There are close analogies between the two terms of the comparison: like the Divine Maternity, the baptismal character is an ineffaceable gift, it incorporates us into Christ, makes us members of God's family, and wins for us His good will and His grace—providing we place no obstacle in the way. But that is as far as the resemblances go. Beyond this, there are only differences—all to Mary's advantage.

a) These two relations are ordered in opposite directions. One imitates the relation of *The Father to the Son,* for Mary was made a *mother*. The other imitates the relation of *the Son to the Father,* for the baptized Christian is made the *son* of God. True, in the order of divinity, fatherhood is not superior to sonship. But in the created order parents are superior to their children, and Jesus gave witness to this law in a disconcerting way by His submission during His childhood (Lk. 2:51), and even toward the end of His life when He declared in this connection: "The Father is greater than I" (Jn. 14:28).

Let us not conclude from this that the Second Person of the Blessed Trinity is inferior to the First, nor that the Blessed Virgin has no real superiority over her child! But we can confidently affirm that it is nobler for Mary to be the Mother of God than for baptized Christians to be the sons of God. This superiority is all the more evident in that the maternal relationship contracted by Mary on the day of the Incarnation *was added to the filial relationship* conferred upon her at the dawn of her existence. Before Mary became the Mother of the Word Incarnate, she was the daughter of the Father. For the Immaculate Conception implies the existence of a relationship to God that is analogous and superior in its effects to the relationship conferred by Baptism.

b) The Divine Maternity is founded on a true generation (even though it is temporal and concerns the flesh); and baptismal character is founded upon an adoption. In the case of Mary, there is a generation in the order of substance, and in the case of Baptism, a regeneration that is purely and simply accidental.

c) Following this line of thought we notice an important difference between maternity and baptismal character (a difference that will lead us to qualify the somewhat ponderous affirmation made above). The act of generation by which Mary brought forth a human being whose personality was divine was sufficient to win for her the title of Mother of God, abstracting from the effusion of grace which she personally received by reason of this mystery. The infusion of baptismal character, on the other hand, does not suffice, independently of the grace that normally follows from it, to make us sons of God, participants of the divine nature (II Pet. 1:4). Character implies a configuration to Christ the Son of God, but it is a radical, tendential, inchoate configuration in the order of the sign (*res et sacramentum*). Character is a *title* to divine sonship, a means of realizing it. But this sonship is formally realized only through grace (*res*). In short, whereas we are not truly and properly the sons of God by the *sole fact* of possessing the character of Christ, Mary is truly and properly the Mother of God by the sole fact of having conceived Christ. The following similarity nevertheless remains: Just as the consecration of the baptismal character orientates and specifies our vocation and our grace as the vocation and grace of sons of God, so the generation of the God-man orientated and specified Mary's vocation and grace to be the grace and the vocation of the Mother of God.

d) Baptized Christians become sons of God in dependence upon the mystery of the Incarnation. The Divine Maternity is a cooperation in the very fulfillment of this mystery. In other words, baptized Christians are conformed to the Son of God made man, and it is Mary who conformed the Son of God to our humanity.

e) Finally, Divine Maternity, like the baptismal character, brings with it God's favors, but in an incomparably greater measure. Here the theologian can prepare the way for the reader's contemplation, but he cannot offer a substitute for it. Each one must actually enter into the depths of this mystery by reason of which almighty and eternal God can forever and in all truth call a simple woman: "Mother," and she in turn can call her Creator: "Son."

A Transforming Relationship. However, Mary's Maternity effects no intrinsic change in the Trinity nor does it diminish God's transcendence. Metaphysics teaches us that God is immutable. Every new relation to Him is new from the point of view of the creature and not from His point of view. Thus, even the very real relation of the human nature to the Word who assumed it has its real foundation in this humanity and not in the Person of the Word.

This consideration brings us to the following question: Since every real relation between God and His creatures implies a real foundation in the latter and only in the latter, what ontological modification occurred within Mary when, on the day of the Annunciation, she contracted this real relation as Mother of God? Since every impression that God makes upon a created being leaves a mark on this being, what mark corresponds to the Divine Maternity?

This is a most difficult question to answer, because it plunges us into the very depths of the mystery, into the most hidden aspects of the relations between God and man. And yet we may not in all fairness avoid answering it.

First of all, the mystery of the Annunciation brought about a new relationship between Mary and God (the relationship by virtue of which Mary, full of grace—κεχαριτωμένω—became Mary, the Mother of God—θεοτόκος). It also resulted in new created grace for Mary. This is what the angel's words seem to indicate: "The Holy Spirit shall come upon thee and the power of the Most High shall overshadow thee" (Lk. 1:35). These words, in themselves, show that the Holy Spirit, the principle of sanctification, made Mary

Pictures of the Blessed Virgin reveal the faith and devotion of Christians through the course of Tradition. In this mosaic the artist's thought was still impregnated with the definition of the Council of Ephesus that declared Mary to be the *Theotokos,* the Mother of God. This glorious attribute of Mary's, in which Christian faith discovers itself, was to inspire the creation of an iconographic model of the Blessed Virgin holding her Child and presenting Him to the adoration of the angels, of the elect, or of the people.

Majestically poised between heaven and earth, she is the house of gold, the royal throne of the incarnate God. The hieraticism of the composition is intended to give more perfect expression to the dignity of her role: the Blessed Virgin's only reason for existing is that she may receive the Son of God. And already the hand of the Father in heaven is shown holding forth her reward.

French Romanesque Virgins, at the start of the Middle Ages, reproduced this Byzantine Theotokos, who is more a "definition" than a mother filled with maternal sentiments for her Son. And yet she was presented solely as a mother: faith discovers so much grandeur in her because it recognizes that her Son is God. In this lofty epoch, artists did not yet imagine a representation of the Virgin without her Son, human and smiling, as was to be done later.

Virgin in Majesty. Parenzo, in Istria (sixth century).

the object of His outpouring of virtue. In causing her to conceive, He conferred upon her a new privilege that was a complement to the relationship established at the time of the Annunciation.

But in what did the Spirit's gift consist? An analogy with what happens to a soul in Baptism will help us to understand this gift. Baptism makes man a son of God; this relation of sonship exists on two levels: 1) The baptized Christian receives the baptismal *character* that configures him to the Son. 2) This radical configuration that confers a basic connaturality with God is normally implanted in a living organism of supernatural virtues, thanks to which the baptized person can know and love God as a Father.

As we said earlier, Mary received all this equivalently and in an eminent manner in her Immaculate Conception. We can perceive what she received in addition at the Incarnation by means of the same analogy with Baptism. Just as Baptism makes man *a* son of God, the grace of the Annunciation made Mary *the* Mother of God. And this new relationship of Mary's can also be viewed from two levels. First, Mary received a mark that configured her to the Father, and made her worthy of addressing as "Son" the One who until then had been the Son of the Father only.

We have seen certain effects of this conformation in the spiritual and miraculous mode of the virginal generation. From this we can infer that the divine impress that thus penetrated Mary's activity at the Annunciation had more secretly penetrated her whole person. This radical configuration unfolded in Mary's living spiritual organism. It did not *confer* upon her the supernatural virtues that she already possessed, but it gave these virtues new scope. Until then, Mary's grace, like that of baptized persons, had the effect of making her repeat within the depths of her soul: *"Abba, Father"* (Rom. 8:16; Gal. 4:6), that is to say, "My God is my Father." Henceforth a new grace made her say of the One she was bearing, bringing forth, and bringing up: "My God is my Son."

In other words, the grace that Mary received at the Annunciation made her equal to her new condition as Mother of God. Without a grace of this sort, her Maternity would have been somewhat lacking in proportion, one might even say monstrous. Just as a mother devoid of human sentiments toward her human son would be a sad anomaly, so a Mother of God lacking divine sentiments would in a certain way be similarly heartless.

That is why Mary received in her person and in her supernatural organism a new connaturality with God, by virtue of which her Son was not a stranger to her but truly a Son: her adoration as a creature and her mother's love were fused by this grace into a single movement of the soul. In her tenderness and in her respect, in her authority and in her subordination, she had maternal sentiments for this God who was her Son.

In relation to her anterior grace, this new grace that Mary received was a deepening and a transfiguration. Not only was there question of a new orientation of her fullness of grace (which became a maternal fullness and not merely the fullness of grace proper to a daughter), there was a new expansion of this fullness to the measure of her new stature. We might be tempted to speak here of a sort of re-creation of Mary's being in the sense in which Scripture speaks of Baptism as a new creation (Gal. 6:15; cf. II Cor. 5:17). This is not to say that Baptism destroys our nature, nor that it takes anything positive away from it, but that it restores it in its very depths by giving it a deeper actuality and finality. Thus the re-creation by which Mary benefited altered neither her nature nor her anterior grace, but corresponded to a new mark made upon her by God and to the new finality to which she was destined as Mother of God.

Without claiming to have made an exhaustive analysis of the mystery nor even to have said all that can be said about it in human terms, we should like to add to this summary three particularly important points: the Divine Maternity is integrally virginal; it has a social significance; it implies a soteriological relationship.

A Virginal Maternity. It is necessary to elucidate a point that must already have caused the reader some anxiety. In reading the historical portion of this study, the question may have arisen why the point was made several times not only that there was a virginal conception (*virginitas ante partum*), not only that Mary remained a virgin after the birth of Jesus (*virginitas post partum*), but also that she conserved her virginity in the very birth of Jesus (*in partu*). And yet this is not one of those pious exaggerations that we find among so many Mariologists. It has been an undisputed notion for the past fifteen centuries and has been attested to by documents that place us under a strict obligation to believe.[1] It is the most

---

[1] Leo's *Tome to Flavian,* 4, Denz. 144. The Lateran Council of 649, Canon 3 (*incorruptibiliter genuisse*), Denz. 256. The 11th Council of Toledo, *Symbolum,* Denz. 282; cf. 314a, note 3; 782; 993. No discordant voice arose in

misunderstood of all points of Marian doctrine. The author of the present synthesis knows from experience how difficult it is to assimilate this point, but he also knows how much light it throws upon Mariological problems.

Why this difficulty? And what is the significance of this truth? We may not allow ourselves to elude these two questions, delicate as the subject may be.

The first obstacle arises from our cultural heritage, which is to a greater or lesser degree influenced by Plato and Descartes. Because of this idealistic influence, it is hard for us to believe concretely in the resurrection of the body, and we find little attraction in morals although we are entranced by mysticism.

The root of these defects lies in a more or less deep misunderstanding of the substantial unity of the soul with the body. According to certain current interpretations which have found their way even into some catechisms, the soul is presented as a replica of the body, as something apart from the body, whereas in reality it is the substantial form of the body. The body is conceived of as a garment, even as a "rag" or a prison for the soul, whereas it is the soul's living and transparent organ. Is it surprising, therefore, that the body should appear to be devoid of religious significance and that we should tend to be baffled by mysteries like the Transfiguration of Christ or the integral virginity of Mary, which imply a corporeal reflection of spiritual realities?

Another obstacle, one which is a stumbling block to our religious sensibility rather than our intelligence, is the extreme tedium and even indelicacy with which many manuals of theology deal with this question. These manuals inherited the gynecological inventions of the apocrypha which sought to give a midwife's certification of

---

Tradition after St. Ambrose (in addition to the article cited by Jouassard in *Maria*, Vol. I, cf. for example, J.-B. Terrien, *La Mère de Dieu*, Vol. II, p. 174, No. 2; G. Roschini, *Mariologia*, 1947, Vol. III, pp. 255-259; D. Bertetto, *Maria nel dogma*, Turin, S. E. I., 1949, pp. 160-166).

There are numerous testimonies in the liturgy: *Tu quae genuisti, natura mirante* (Antiphon Alma Redemptoris); *Communicantes et diem sacratissimum celebrantes quo beatae Virginis intemerata virginitas huic mundo edidit Salvatorem* (Communicantes for Christmas); *Peperit sine dolore* (Response to the 8th Lesson for the feast of the Circumcision, Roman Breviary); *Paries . . . Filium et virginitatis non patieris detrimentum; efficieris gravida et eris mater semper intacta* (Response of the 2nd Lesson for the feast of the Annunciation).

Mary's virginity. The result was the presentation of details that were as embarrassing as they were sterile. The Blessed Virgin's corporeal virginity, and her corporeal Assumption, are not historical events that have been transmitted to us by way of Scripture or oral tradition. They are mysteries whose existence the intuition of faith finds implicit in the revealed deposit. Just as the mode of the Assumption escapes us, so does the mode of the Virgin Birth. And it is an error in method to go beyond the essence of the revealed mystery and enter into descriptive details that God has not willed to give us.

What can we say about this mystery? Nothing more than has been said earlier: Mary's childbirth did not impair the integrity of her corporeal virginity; and this presupposes a miraculous intervention by God at the birth of the Savior no less than at His conception. However, the religious significance of this statement remains to be given. One meaning refers to the eternal generation of the Word to which, as we have seen, the temporal generation was conformed. It takes on a second meaning with relation to Christ, who attaches a high value to virginity and willed that no part of this privilege be destroyed in His Mother. A third meaning relates to Mary: her Immaculate Conception preserved her not only from sin but also from its personal consequences both with regard to the soul and to the body. The Blessed Virgin never knew the pains of childbirth or the corruption of the grave, the two punishments announced in Genesis 3:16 and 3:19. The mystery of the integral virginity of Mary, like that of the Assumption, which is a mystery of corporeal integrity—or as the ancients called it, of "incorruptibility"—reminds us of the bond between soul and body which is essential to the Christian mystery.

A Social Maternity. After discussing these personal aspects, let us pass on to the social aspect of the Divine Maternity. It is sometimes summed up in this inspired formula of St. Augustine's: "Being the Mother of the Head of the Mystical Body, Mary is also the mother of its members." At the moment of the Annunciation, this formula did not yet have its full meaning. True, as the God-man, Jesus was already by right and power the Head of all men; but He was to become fully their Head only by meriting their salvation through His Passion. And the incorporation of men would not be accomplished until Pentecost, with the Baptism of the 3,000 first Christians, the first-fruits of so many others. Likewise, Mary became progressively the mother of all men, first through the sufferings and merits of her compassion, then by effectively exercising her maternal role in the Mystical Body. But already at the Incarnation she possessed the fundamental title that pledged her to her vocation as the mother of all men.

Already, her Maternity was the first and hidden realization of the Church. Mary and Jesus did not constitute simply the society of a Son and His Mother. Together they formed the society of God and man, of the Savior and the first of the redeemed. All men are called to be incorporated into this society.

A Soteriological Maternity. This society into which Mary entered with Christ is a society of salvation. And Mary pledged herself to it with full knowledge and consent. She consented to become the Mother of the Messias who was destined to "save his people from their sins" as the name Jesus, declared by the angel, signifies (Lk. 1:31; Mt. 1:21). And the total and unconditional consent of "the handmaid of the Lord" (Lk. 1:38) virtually encompassed the whole work of the Redemption, to which the Annunciation was the prelude. From that moment on, Mary may well have thought of the prophecy by which Isaias clearly announced the painful "sacrifice" of the Messias (53:1-5;7,10) and its redemptive significance (53:5,6,10,12). In any case, Simeon specified the contradictions that her Son would suffer "for the fall and for the rise of many" (Lk. 2:34), and her own participation in her Son's sufferings: "And thy own soul a sword shall pierce" (Lk. 2:35). All this was preparation for the following phase.

3. MARY AT THE TIME OF THE REDEMPTIVE SACRIFICE

Between the Annunciation and the death of Jesus two periods unfolded which were in marked contrast to one another: the hidden life and the public life. In the first period Mary lived in intimate contact with her Son. In the second, she was separated from Him. And Jesus' words give us to understand that this separation was intentional: whenever there was question of His ministry, He kept His Mother at a distance. He did it the first time when, at the age of twelve—which is as it were the peak of childhood, its point of equilibrium and the prefiguration of adulthood—He anticipated the exercise of His teaching role (Lk. 2:49). A second time was at Cana at the start of His public life (Jn. 2:4; cf. 7:3-10). He did it again during His life of preaching (Mk. 3:31-35; cf. Lk. 11:27-

28): when His Mother and brothers were mentioned to Him, He turned His eyes toward His disciples (Mk. 3:34) and pointed to them as His new adopted family.

In short, Jesus lived each phase of His life with those whom He called to share it. He associated a woman, Mary His Mother, to His interior and hidden mission of prayer and holiness. He associated His Apostles to His official mission, and Mary was kept at a distance. But this was not a definitive separation. On the day of the sacrifice—that hidden sacrifice whose liturgical significance was veiled under the appearances of a condemnation and whose voluntary essence was concealed under a violent death—things changed. The disciples fled. And Mary, who had accepted the sacrifice of separation, was reunited to Jesus to commune in the sacrifice of the Passion. At the foot of the Cross, she resumed a role analogous to the one she had had in the hidden mystery of the Incarnation. However, it should be understood that her participation in the mystery of the Redemption was of a very different sort.

In both of these mysteries, her *activity* was a consent, enlisting her faith and her charity: consent to the life of her Son, consent to His redemptive death. These two consents were really only one, since the first, unconditioned and unrevoked, virtually had a bearing on the whole work of salvation which began at the Annunciation. But while Mary's activity remained the same, her situation and the scope of her acts changed. Before the Incarnation, Mary had been the provisory summit of the human race. As St. Thomas explains, it was in the name of the human race that she gave the Word her consent and her flesh. From that moment, her Son who was perfect man as well as perfect God, was the perfect representative of humanity. The role of representative that Mary played at the Annunciation was thus exceeded. And yet this role, in its dependence, still had some purpose.

It was God's intention to save man through man, as integrally as possible. This integrality, in which God's delicacy was pleased, found its completion in Mary. On Calvary she represented, in complete subordination, *the accidental aspects of humanity that her Son had not assumed:* the condition of a *created* and *redeemed* person living by *faith,* and *womanhood* (which symbolically summed up the others). From all these points of view her oblation was integrated to the sacrifice of the Cross, just as the oblation of the faithful is integrated to the sacrifice of the Mass. Mary's consent and her flesh had been incorporated into the mystery of the Incarnation. Now her consent and her suffering were incorporated into the mystery of the Redemption.

In addition to the perfection of these acts, which were the only human acts capable of being integrated to the Passion of Christ, because they alone were perfectly pure; in addition to what remained of her function as representative of men in union with the Savior, Mary had a third right to participate in the work of the Redemption: her Divine Maternity. Her Son belonged to her not by a strict right (*jus utendi et abutendi*) but according to the bonds of love and communion, according to the community of persons and goods that prolongs the initial community of flesh and blood between mother and son.

By calling Mary to Calvary, Christ extended this community to the sufferings and merits of the Redemption. In short, at the Cross, Mary was still able to say what every mother can say of her son: "He is my flesh and my blood." And she could also say what every mother united to her son can say: "What is yours is mine, and what is mine is yours." And by the grace of God, this affirmation assumed its supreme significance: "Your sufferings are my sufferings, Your work is my work, You have willed to communicate to me this treasure of sanctification that You are meriting."

This is the summit of Christ's work and the summit of Mary's association with her Son. By cooperating with Him in the salvation of the world, she acquired a new claim for being the mother of men. While Christ became effectively their head by meriting the graces of the Redemption, she became effectively their mother by participating in this universal merit. This was the hour when Jesus proclaimed her maternity: "Mother, behold your son."

4. FROM THE DEATH OF CHRIST TO THE DORMITION

In such a brief exposition, we cannot deal at length with the rather complex period following Christ's death.

Through Scripture we know only that Mary was there: after her presence on Calvary, she was present at Pentecost (Acts 1:14). And all that came before allows us to guess the significance of this presence, which took on different aspects at various moments: during the *triduum mortis,* during the period from the Resurrection to the Ascension, from the Ascension to Pentecost, and finally, during the first days of the Church. Just as Mary had been the bond between Israel and Christ at the Annunciation, she was now, in a lesser sense, the bond between Christ and the Church.

This period began with a tragic moment. During three days Christ was dead, and His prayer was no longer of this earth. It was an hour when humanity had put the capstone to its sins by the most odious of crimes, an hour when the best men sank to cowardice, when the sun was darkened, the earth shook, and the dead rose from their graves like terrible forewarnings of judgment. At that moment Mary alone was pleasing to God upon earth. She prolonged Christ's intercession and the living oblation of the redemptive sacrifice. Just as she had been the dawn before the Annunciation, she was now the sunset.

When Christ rose again, the living sun of justice that would never set, Mary's role took on a new significance: It was no longer to prolong Christ, but to prepare and maternally accompany the first days of the Church. She was the Church in a hidden but perfect way, insofar as the Church is defined by communion with Christ and by holiness.

On Pentecost, a scene unfolded very similar to the Annunciation: the Spirit who had secretly manifested Himself to form the physical body of Christ, manifested Himself with great magnificence to form Christ's Mystical Body. Mary was there, she who had been the first living member of the Savior. She had no part in the new hierarchical and visible dimension that the Church then acquired, but her prayer, which had prepared the birth of the Church, remained the highest point of the Church's prayer. Her prayer and her merit seem to have contributed greatly to the wonderful efficacy of the first evangelizations.

5. MARY'S ASSUMPTION. THE BLESSED VIRGIN AS THE "ESCHATOLOGICAL ICON OF THE CHURCH"

We shall not linger on Mary's "death." It was such a unique death that it seems equally true to say with one group of authors that "Mary died," and, with a much smaller group, that "Mary did not die." Her passing was full of mystery, as the ancient Epiphanius once remarked. And the Greeks had found a very apt formula to express this mystery. They called the state through which the Mother of God passed from her earthly to her heavenly life the "dormition."

For in the measure that death is the consequence of original sin and of corruption, it could not apply to the Immaculate Virgin, whose "incorruptibility" was so strongly attested to by the Greeks. And yet tradition seems clearly to favor a separation between Mary's soul and body at the end of her earthly life. To reconcile all points of view, we might speak of a brief separation between soul and body, exempt from any taint of corruption. In philosophical parlance, such a combination of notions scarcely seems viable. Is this the way we are to explain the mystery of the Dormition?

In any event, the Assumption marked a final transition in the destiny of the Blessed Virgin, and the significance of this transition should be understood.

First of all, we note an apparently negative aspect. When Mary's earthly and wayfaring life came to an end, she *ceased to merit*. Her merits had reached their maximum, and after that she acquired no new merits. All other aspects of the Assumption are positive.

First, Mary was reunited with her Son after a twofold separation: the separation of His public life and the separation that followed His death on the Cross. Henceforth they were permanently reunited, and nothing would come between them. Mary now knows her Son not through faith, not through earthly, obscure, and limited signs, but in the face-to-face vision of God.

In this beatific vision, Mary's spiritual maternity reaches its ultimate fulfillment. Even before the Annunciation, Mary had a maternal soul with regard to men, but her maternal grace had its foundations in the Incarnation and on Calvary, concomitantly with the capital grace of Christ. While Christ became radically the leader of all men, Mary became radically their mother. While He became formally their head by meriting their redemption, Mary became formally their mother by meriting with Him. That is why Christ proclaimed her maternal mission at that time. Mary's maternity became effective on Pentecost. In heaven her maternity became conscious. During her earthly life, she was plunged in the obscurity of faith just as we are, and could not know the power and the effect of her intercession. She did not know each of the sheep in the flock, the way Christ did (Jn. 10:14). Now she knows each of her children. She formerly loved them in her Son with a universal but indistinct love. In the beatific vision, she knows them individually and personally, with a warm and precise knowledge, with a more intimate maternal knowledge than that of the other blessed. A final aspect completes the warmth and intimacy of this knowledge: Inasmuch as Mary's body is risen like that of Christ, she preserves the physical connaturality and the affective capacity of which the other saints are for the present deprived.

Mary's heavenly maternity therefore implies a very perfect understanding of her children, perfect in its principle because it proceeds from the divine vision, and perfect in its integrity because her knowledge makes full use of the senses which are indispensable to all truly human knowing.

But to be a mother involves more than knowledge, it also involves action. In what does Mary's action with regard to her children consist? This is a difficult and controversial question. One point is certain: Mary exercises a universal intercession, a living intercession that stems from love. A mother does not know her children after the manner of a scientist who coldly records phenomena. Her knowledge is full of intentions and desires, like an artist's knowledge of his works. The difference here of course is that Mary's works are persons. Mary's desires for her children are God's own desires. And it is anthropomorphic mockery to contrast the justice of God with Mary's maternal mercy. The Blessed Virgin's merciful prayer is efficacious because it expresses the love of the God of mercy.

It may seem surprising that no mention has yet been made of Marian "mediation." Actually, there would be no need of discussing it explicitly if this question had not taken on so much importance. The word "mediation" embraces in a sometimes equivocal way many aspects of Mary's mission about which we have already spoken, using other terms.

In the first place Mary's mediation consisted in her very pure intercessory prayer before the Annunciation, an intercession that was already maternal. For even more than Deborra, Mary deserved to be called "a mother in Israel" (Judges 5:7). Then came her role as a link in the Incarnation: her holiness was a bridge between the God of holiness and sinful humanity. Through her, the Word was able to enter a sullied race without being sullied Himself. At that moment Mary was a mediatrix in the most powerful sense of the word, a mediatrix between sinful men and the thrice holy God. But from that moment on, the Word in becoming incarnate became the "one Mediator" (I Tim. 2:5); and Marian mediation took on an entirely different meaning.

Mary's mediation is not added to the mediation of the one Mediator, but participates in it. Even when her mediation seems to take on a sort of consistency of its own, when Mary plays the role of link between Christ and the Church, or between the Church of earth and the Church of heaven, she remains totally subordinate. Actually our Blessed Lady is less a mediatrix before the mediator than a mediatrix in Him and through Him.

In the last analysis, Mary's mediation is simply another name for her maternity. When we say that she is the universal mother we express in the fullest and most precise way the positive aspect of her mission, the element that differentiates her mission from Christ's and raises her above all the saints. When we say that she is the universal mediatrix we express only one aspect of this maternity: her subordinate participation in the mediation of the Son. And we must take care to add to the title of mediatrix the distinctions and reservations that it does not suggest by itself. In short, Mary's activity is specifically maternal. Just as Christ her Son is the universal head, she is the universal mother, in Him and through Him.

Over and above this universal and maternal action that Mary exercises daily in the Church, we must point out one last aspect of her role that is totally concerned with the future and that derives from her very being. It is a function in the order of exemplary and final causality that she exercises with reference to the Church as a whole. The Church, in her progress toward the Second Coming, even now realizes the completion of her mystery in the person of the Blessed Virgin risen with Christ. In Mary, her first member who has never ceased to go on before her, the Church attains to her term, her rest, and her plenitude: her corporeal presence, without veil and without end, beside the resurrected Christ. In defining the dogma of the Assumption, Pope Pius XII wanted to give the Church, shaken by adversity and threatened by storms, a solemn pledge of hope.

CONCLUSION

Christ, Mary, and the Church

We have seen how the law of time and progress has affected the Church's knowledge of Mary, and even Mary's very destiny. We must now try to see the relationship between these two movements. By one of these movements Mary goes on ahead of the Church, and by the other movement the Church learns to distinguish herself from Mary. Let us clarify these two points.

Throughout her destiny, the Blessed Virgin has realized in advance what the Church was to realize later on. Before the Church made her appearance, Mary was holy and immaculate. Before the Church, Mary united herself to Christ, formed a single body with Him, a single life, a single love. Before the Church, Mary communed in His sufferings and cooperated in His work of Redemption. Finally before the Church, Mary rose again with Him.

And yet all of these anticipations were not foreign to the life of the Church. For in Mary, the Church began her own hidden life. We could likewise say that in Mary the Church began being holy and immaculate, incorporated to Christ, began communing in His mysteries and rising again with Him. From this point of view, Mary appears as the first member of the Church, the member in whom the Church realized, in the most perfect way, and by anticipation, her deepest, most inalienable essence, which is communion in Christ.

Thus identified with Mary in her beginnings, the Church had to learn little by little to distinguish herself from Mary, somewhat the way a child learns to distinguish his body from his mother's, his smile from hers. At the outset and in certain respects until the twelfth century, Mary's face and the Church's remained indistinct. There are many texts and many pictures which we hesitate to classify as applying specifically to one or the other.

Gradually the Church learned to know herself and to know Mary more distinctly. And Mary appeared as the Church's supreme perfection, as her initial and her final golden age. The Church's initial golden age was the time when Mary alone was the Church, welcoming Christ upon earth through faith and living with Him in charity. The Church's final golden age is the Resurrection, the consummation toward which the Church militant is striving and which the Blessed Virgin has already personally attained. The further the Church gets from her initial golden age, the closer she gets to her final golden age, which will be the Second Coming of Christ, the more she discovers in her origins the perfection of holiness which is the mystery of Mary, and sees ahead of her the perfection of glory which is the other aspect of Mary's mystery. The more the Church becomes aware of her limitations, her imperfections, and her present toilsome state, the more she recognizes Mary as her ideal and her model, the more she honors Mary as the image and the program of her completion, and finally the more she understands the value of Mary's daily assistance.

These considerations lead us to clarify the link that unites the treatise on the Blessed Virgin on the one hand with the treatise on Christ which precedes it, and on the other hand with the treatise on the Church which follows it.

The link between the treatise on Mary and the treatise on Christ can be summed up in a single word that is the essence of Marian theology, a word whose overflowing riches we have already tried to understand: *Theotokos,* Mother of God. This title lays the foundation for all the ways in which Mary goes ahead of the Church, and the privilege by which she surpasses the Church. For it was Mary the Mother of God who alone brought forth the flesh of the Word Incarnate, and who thereby was more intimately associated than anyone else with His life and with His action.

The link between the treatise on Mary and the treatise on the Church could likewise be summed up in two words:

Maria = Ecclesia

These are two words whose mysterious identification involves a paradox and calls for some explanation. The problem lies in this alternative: Is Mary in the Church or is the Church in Mary? Is Mary greater than the Church or is the Church greater than Mary? Whence the methodological consequence: Should the treatise *de Maria* be considered as a part of the treatise *de Ecclesia,* or inversely is the treatise on the Church included in the treatise on Mary?

Actually, it is not a matter of choosing between two alternatives, but of accepting the co-existence of both. There exists between the Virgin Mary and the Virgin Church a reciprocal inclusion and interpenetration in which Scheeben liked to see an image of the Trinitarian circumincession. At the Annunciation, on Calvary, the Church was rough-hewn and hidden in Mary. Beginning with Pentecost, Mary was hidden in the Church and humbly obedient to the authority of the Apostles. On the one hand there was an inclusion of perfection, and on the other there was an inclusion of structure. There was an inclusion of perfection because Mary's faith and her union with Christ already contained all the perfection that would ultimately permeate the Church. There was an inclusion of structure, because the Blessed Virgin was contained in the Church visible where nothing distinguished her externally from the other members. She was not the head who epitomized the Church: on Pentecost it was Peter who spoke, and the Apostles who baptized. Mary was lost in the crowd and prayed in silence.

If the treatise on the Church were simply a treatise on the life of faith and charity, on the spiritual regeneration of humanity through grace, on the interior rooting and pouring forth of the gifts of the Holy Spirit, if it considered the Church only in her mystical communion with Christ, that is to say as distinct from Him, receiving everything from Him, and living in Him the life that will not pass away—then this treatise could be integrated into Mariology. But if we consider the Church in terms of her official mission to distribute the means of grace—to transmit the words and commands of Christ authoritatively, to administer the sacraments, to visibly represent Christ hidden until the day of His Second Coming—then the Blessed Virgin has no special function in the Church. The treatise on the Church is thus constructed parallel to and outside of Mariology.

In short, the Church, inasmuch as she is essentially Jesus Christ poured out and communicated, implies a twofold participation in Christ. She distributes divine gifts from above, and she also receives gifts from below. She exteriorizes the action of God by the sacraments, and she interiorizes them through faith. She administers the means of grace, and she makes them bear fruit. The first aspect is the official representation of Christ: it is epitomized in Peter and in his successors. The second is mystical communion with Christ: it is epitomized in Mary. If therefore we read the treatise on the Church in its relation to the treatise on Mary, we shall be led to make the following distinction: in the measure that the Church is an exterior, earthly, hierarchical society, whose function is visibly to take the place of Jesus Christ between His first and His second comings, the notion of the Church develops outside of Mariology. In the measure that the Church is an interior, heavenly, spiritual society, whose function is to communicate invisibly with Christ, we shall recognize the Blessed Virgin Mary in the Church.

REFLECTIONS AND PERSPECTIVES

The Mother of God. The foregoing theology of the Blessed Virgin has followed the course of her life from the Annunciation to the

Assumption. The advantage of such a method consists in the fact that it follows the evangelical deposit very closely, and simply comments theologically upon this deposit as it pursues the reading of Scripture.

There is another method, however, one that is bolder and more hazardous, but also—if it is successful—more explanatory. The theologian, in his hunger for a deeper understanding, seeks among all the elements of the "deposit" for a final principle of explanation that can take all factors into account. Instead of successively study-ing the various historical periods of Mary's life, the theologian takes each of her titles—Mother of God, Virgin Mother, Spouse of God, Queen of angels and of men, Mother of divine grace, Im-maculate Conception, etc.—and weighs them, so to speak, in rela-tion to one another. He hopes thereby to discover which title is most explanatory of the mystery of Mary and can in its own way explain all the others.

Certain theologians believe they have discovered the explanatory principle of the mystery of Mary in her maternity of grace, or in her Immaculate Conception, or perhaps in her spiritual marriage with Christ or with the Holy Spirit. However most theologians—and we unhesitatingly agree with them—give first place to her title as Mother of God. It is because Mary is the Mother of God that all her privileges were given her. In the present introduction to theology we shall not develop a Marian theology that can be deduced from this principle that explains the entire deposit. Actually, this theo-logical work has already been done by M.-M. Philipon, O.P. (cf. his article "Maternité spirituelle de Marie et de l'Église" in *Bulletin de la Soc. française d'études mariales,* Paris, Lethielleux, 1952, pp. 63-83). We are merely suggesting the broad outlines of a possible theology.

Let us first of all make it clear that when we speak of an "ex-planatory principle" of the mystery, we do not mean a rational ex-planation of the mystery. We are merely seeking an organizing principle for all the elements of faith relative to this mystery, so that we may not have a series of juxtaposed, unrelated notions, but truly a single mystery: "the" Marian mystery.

And we declare that the principle or explanatory title of the Marian mystery is the title of the Divine Maternity. Likewise, the principle that gives a theological explanation of the mystery of

Christ is the hypostatic union, that is to say, the union of two natures in *a single divine Person*.

Indeed, let us reflect on what the Divine Maternity means. Apart from the hypostatic union there can be no closer proximity between a creature and God than the union implicit in the Divine Maternity. We are often tempted to think of the hypostatic union as the mystery of a child who *became God*. But that is heresy. And we likewise tend to think of Mary's Maternity as the bringing forth of a man who became God. But that, too, is heresy. There is only one person in Christ. The "I" of Christ, even in His human nature, is a divine "I." It is the "I" of the Word of God. The relation of maternity which terminates in a person, terminates in Mary's case in the divine Person of the Word.

Mary is not the Mother of the Godhead, she is the Mother of the Word, the Mother of God. We must not conceive of Christ's humanity as *becoming* united to God by an intrinsic elevation, but rather of the Word of God assuming human nature and appropriating it in the unity of His being and person. In like manner we must not think of Mary as giving birth by her own power to a man who was to rise until he became God. Rather we must think of the Word of God as having taken the initiative and assumed flesh in Mary's womb.

The Son of Mary existed before Mary did, and His relationship with her was that of a man to his betrothed rather than of a son to his mother. He chose her among all women; He determined the place and the time; He asked her consent, and Mary answered with her Fiat. We see that there was perfect harmony in Mary's union to the Son of God, between her spirit and the being that was taking form in her flesh. While the Son of God took all the initiative in His human conception, Mary was not merely a "thing" of which He made use, not merely the instrument of His birth. On the contrary, she was spiritually aware of what was occurring within her. She was personally associated to the union that the Word was realizing in her body: she wholeheartedly wanted what the Son of God wanted. Thus, she became a mother not only corporeally, but spiritually, totally. While she played no active part corporeally, she cooperated spiritually to the full—even though this was done through grace.

God did not ask a sinful woman to be His mother. On the contrary, He prepared Mary for a total union, both spiritual and corporeal, a fully human union. It was the mystery of this union that was accomplished at the moment of the Incarnation. The proximity to God that the Divine Maternity gives Mary contains in an eminent way, and surpasses, the proximity of any nuptial union with God.

It can be said that the humanity of Jesus undergoes a kind of divinisation because His humanity has no personality but that of the Word. Likewise, Mary's Maternity manifested the concept of maternity in its divine absoluteness. For while Mary is not divine as a woman, she is divine as a mother. The Word of God assumed flesh in her flesh, and she gave birth to God Himself. The relationship of motherhood, which is one of person to person, is the relationship of the person of Mary to the divine Person of the Word made flesh. This ecstasy of maternity did not do away with Mary's human maternity, for she conceived a man. However it gave her human maternity its being, just as the Word gave the humanity of Christ its personal being.

This, then, is the "principle" of the Divine Maternity. We have seen that it contains in an eminent way the principle of the nuptial union between Mary and the Word. In addition, it has the advantage of accounting for all the facts without implying that this is a bizarre, artificial choice. For there is nothing about Mary that is of greater moment in the Gospel than her Divine Maternity. This principle presents itself as the most important one around which to "organize" the entire deposit of faith concerning Mary. We leave to our readers the task of carrying on this organization.

Mary's relationship with the Three Divine Persons. We have just spoken of Mary's nuptial alliance with the Word of God and we have pointed out in what sense we are to understand this union as included in the relationship of Divine Maternity that unites Mary to the Son of God.

Does not Mary also have a very special relationship with the Father and with the Holy Spirit? Can she not be said just as well to be the spouse of the Father, since she is the Mother of His Son? Can she not be termed the spouse of the Holy Spirit, inasmuch as she conceived by the Holy Spirit? Such was the thought of certain theologians who made of Mary the spouse of the Three Persons of the Blessed Trinity, by different rights. Thus Adam of St. Victor, a theologian and, even more, a poet of the twelfth century, in this famous stanza:

Mother of fair love, we name thee!
Famed triclinium we proclaim thee,
Which the Trinity all share;
Though thou dost a special dwelling
For the majesty excelling
Of the Incarnate Word prepare! [1]

We must remember, however, that Mary, like every other spiritual creature, was saved by Christ, and like every other member of Christ, she was a daughter of the Father. Besides, it cannot be said that the Holy Spirit is the "father of Jesus" or that "Jesus is the Son of the Holy Spirit," for that would be heresy. Obviously, we cannot affirm anything we please about the relationship that binds Mary to the three Persons. We must follow a rule, and Revelation alone points this rule out to us.

Thus we shall not say that "Mary is the spouse of the Father," even though Mary is privileged to be more closely united to the Father than any other creature. We shall not call this relationship one of *wife* to husband, because Scripture, as it has been transmitted to us, never says that any other creature has become the "spouse" of the Father, and it does not say it of Mary either. Mary is the daughter of the Father, from whom all graces come. If we want to express the special and unique love of the Father for Mary, we must find another word. Of course, exception might be made if we speak poetically, in which case we may allow ourselves some license—but not without risk—in using words that go beyond the common measure.

For the same reason we shall not say that Mary is the spouse of the Holy Spirit. Scripture does not declare this of any spiritual creature. The Holy Spirit is not the spouse but rather the bond of the nuptial alliance, the One who inspires the Love of each of the spouses.

In the light of what we have said, we may say only that Mary is the spouse of the Word. She is His spouse just as the Church is, since she is the figure and the type of the Church. She is His spouse like every creature in the Church is, together with the Church. The marriage between Christ and the Church is clearly affirmed and presented in Scripture, and there is no reason for not attributing to Mary what is attributed to every soul united to Christ through

[1] English translation by Digby S. Wrangham, *The Liturgical Poetry of Adam of St. Victor* (London: Kegan Paul, Trench, & Co., 1931), Vol. II, pp. 223-224.

Baptism, inasmuch as her Divine Maternity has already united her in an eminent and altogether unique way to the Son of God.

Mary's life. Although much has been written about the Blessed Virgin, the meagerness of the texts concerning her leaves indefinite room for research and study. The rule for such studies must be on the one hand to conform to the deposit of faith, and on the other hand to come as close as possible to what we know of the life of devout young Jewish girls at the time of Herod the Great. We can point out a few particularly important leads to follow which will complete the beautiful synthesis of this chapter.

The birth of Mary; the life of Anna and Joachim; the childhood of Mary. The psychology of young Jewish girls in the Messianic era; the psychology of a girl child who commits no sins, who has been preserved from all imperfection, who has never had within her the *fomes peccati,* that interior wellspring of pride and concupiscence which is such a powerful temptation to every human being. Can we picture to ourselves what this signified in her and for her?

The presentation in the Temple. Study the origin of this feast. The role of apocryphal writings in the establishment of this feast, and in a general way in certain descriptions of Mary's life. The reason for the importance of this feast in the Sulpician tradition, which seems to have taken a special interest in Mary's "interior" rather than in the objective mysteries of her life.

Mary's virginity. How was Mary induced to form the resolution to remain a virgin? What this signified in Jewish tradition and in Mary's conscience.

Mary's marriage. Was it a true marriage? Is Mary also the model of married women? Can we describe her sentiments as the wife of Joseph, her very pure affection for her husband, and reciprocally, Joseph's love for Mary? Can we base a theology of marriage on this case? (See on this subject, the chapter on marriage, *Theology Library* Vol. VI, and the Reflections and Perspectives at the end of the chapter.)

The Annunciation. How can we picture the scene? How can we picture the angel? Did he have a sort of artificial body that was visible and sensible, or was he merely a subjective vision whose immediate author was God? What was the value and significance of Mary's doubt or hesitation? Can we say that Mary's consent to the Incarnation preceded Christ's? On this question, read H.

Barré, C.S.Sp., "Le consentement à l'Incarnation rédemptrice, la Vierge seule ou le Christ d'abord?" in *Marianum,* 1952, pp. 233-266. In what sense can we say that the generation of Christ was natural or supernatural? The importance of this question.

The other facts of Mary's life have been sufficiently well presented to show possible developments. We shall simply suggest, with regard to the Assumption, a study to show how here again the Divine Maternity can be an adequate explanatory principle.

Finally, while Mary's apparitions were not part of her earthly life strictly speaking, they have been numerous and important enough in the life of the Church to be the object of a special study by theologians. Determine the deposit of faith, the significance of the apparitions as a whole and of each of them in particular. Determine what the believer's attitude should be on the one hand with regard to Revelation, and on the other hand with regard to private revelations. (See J.-H. Nicolas, "La foi et les signes," in *Suppl. de La Vie Spirituelle,* May, 1953, pp. 121-164.) The special meaning and value of pilgrimages to Mary's shrines.

The Marian liturgy. The liturgy of Mary's feasts in the West as well as in the East makes use of all sorts of Scriptural texts, some of which refer to the people of Israel, to Sion, or Jerusalem, and others to divine Wisdom, etc. The liturgy also makes use of poems by Christian authors such as the famous Introit by the poet Sedulius, *Salve, Sancta Parens.* Comment theologically on all these texts and show the reasons why the Blessed Virgin is like Sion, Israel, Wisdom, the Bride of the Canticles, the Dove, etc.

The poems of the liturgy bring up the whole problem of Marian art: iconography and sculpture. The history of the portrayals of the Blessed Virgin—from the royal and sovereign *Théotokos* of the Byzantines to the sorrowful Virgins of the Spaniards and the Flemish—is instructive for the theologian. A study of this history would bring out the series of major themes that the Church has successively recognized in the mystery of the Blessed Virgin. It would also help us to evaluate the "modern" portrayals of Mary.

Mary and the Church. Analogies are not lacking between Mary and the Church. Few are the qualities of the one that cannot be attributed to the other. The Litany of the Blessed Virgin contains several invocations that were attributes of the Church before being Mary's: ark of the covenant, tower of David, gate of heaven, refuge of sinners, etc. But these titles also suit Mary perfectly. Conversely, the images of the spouse, the tabernacle of God, etc. used in the liturgy of the Dedication suit Mary as well if not better than they do the Church.

In this chapter we have simply touched upon a liturgy of the relationships between the Church and Mary, which still remains to be fully developed. Such a study should begin by determining from what point of view Mary must be considered when she is compared or in a certain way identified with the Church. Then would come a study of the major Scriptural texts that provide the basis for these relationships (on this subject read the stimulating article by A.-G. Hébert, "La Vierge Marie, fille de Sion, in *La Vie Spirituelle,* August-September, 1951, pp. 127-139, which shows that a number of terms used by St. Luke are Old Testament terms referring directly to Jerusalem or Israel; also read Father Braun's study, *La Mère des fideles. Essai de Théologie johannique,* Tournai, Casterman, 1952). A study should also be made of the great figures of Mary and of the Church in the Old Testament: Eve, Sara, Ruth, etc.; the respective roles of Mary and the Church in the Redemption (or the Co-Redemption), in the mediation of graces; the respective ways in which the Church and Mary may be said to be Mother, Spouse, and Virgin; and finally, the way our prayer and our attachment to either the Church or Mary must also include our attachment to the other. (On all these points, read the reports of the French Society for Marian Studies, published in the *Bulletin de la Soc. fr. d'études mariales,* Paris, Lethielleux, 1951, 1952, and 1953.)

Mary and Womanhood. Mary is the perfect model of womanhood, as God conceived it in His plan of creation and salvation. Hence, a theology of womanhood can be constructed upon this model. Mary, the Virgin, Spouse, and Mother is the model of virgins vowed to Christ, the model of married women, the model of mothers, the model of every Christian woman who is always, spiritually speaking, virgin, spouse, and mother. The contemplation of Mary should also help to discover the profound sense of woman's perenniality in the Church and of her particular and irreplaceable mission. On this subject, see A.-M. Henry, "Le mystère de l'homme et de la femme," in *La Vie Spirituelle,* July, 1949; "Le mystère de la virginité," in *Chasteté,* included in the series *La religieuse d'aujourd'hui,* Editions du Cerf, 1953, and "Virginité de l'Église, virginité de Marie," in the *Bulletin de la Soc. fr. d'études mariales,* 1954.

BIBLIOGRAPHY

A complete Marian bibliography would include about 100,000 titles. Those listed here have been carefully selected on the basis of quality, documentary value and readability.

Bibliographical sources

Besutti, G. "Note di Bibliografia mariana," in *Marianum* (Rome), 9 (1947), pp. 115-137. Gives the sources and methods of Marian bibliography.
———. "Bibliografia mariana," in *Marianum*, 1950. Nine hundred and eighty-two books and articles published from 1948 to 1950 are carefully arranged here in a systematic order. Material on a given subject or author can be located by means of a name-and-subject index.

Later volumes of *Marianum* continue this bibliography. These fundamental works enable the bibliographical sketch that follows to be filled out in detail.

General works

1. *Manuals*

Roschini, G. *Mariologia*. 4 vols. Rome: Belardetti, 1947. Contains the most abundant documentation, which even though often of a secondary nature is indispensable. Furnishes many suggestions but always needs verification.

Also to be noted:

Carol, J. B., O.F.M. *Mariology*. 3 vols. Milwaukee: Bruce, 1954–1957. The first large-scale American Mariology, done with the collaboration of many scholars.
Keuppens, J. *Mariologiae compendium*. Louvain, 1947. A convenient size, 224 pp. and has an excellent collection of Mariological texts (pp. 158-222).
Merkelbach, B., O.P. *Mariologia*. Paris: Desclée, 1939.

2. *Comprehensive studies*

Bernard, R. *Le Mystère de Marie*. Paris: Desclée, 1933.
Burke, Anselm E., O.Carm. *Mary in History, in Faith and in Devotion*. New York: Kenedy, 1956.
Carol, J. B., O.F.M. *Fundamentals of Mariology*. Textbook ed. New York: Benziger, 1956.
Dublanchy, E. "Marie," in the D.T.C., 9, 2339-2474.
Dwyer, G., and Holland, T. *Mary Doctrine for Everyman*. London: Paternoster Publications, 1956.
Guitton, Jean. *The Virgin Mary*. New York: Kenedy, 1952.
Laurentin, R. *Queen of Heaven*. New York: Macmillan, 1957.
Most, W. G. *Mary in Our Life*. New York: Kenedy, 1954.
Neubert, E., S.M. *Mary in Doctrine*. Milwaukee: Bruce, 1954.
Nicolas, J. "Synthèse mariale," in *Maria*, vol. 1, pp. 707-744. Paris: Beauchesne, 1949.

Terrien, J. B. *La Mère de Dieu.* 4 vols. Paris: Lethielleux. A clear, reliable work, re-edited many times since 1902.
Vassall-Phillips, O. R., C.SS.R. "Mary, Mother of God," in *The Teaching of the Catholic Church,* ed. by Canon G. Smith, vol. 1, pp. 513-548. New York: Macmillan, 1951.

3. *Encyclopedias*

Maria. 5 vols., ed. by H. Du Manoir. Paris: Beauchesne, 1949. A rich source for documentation.
Katholische Marienkunde. 3 vols., ed. by P. Strater. Paderborn: Shöningh, 1947–1951.

4. *Periodicals (national bulletins of societies for Marian studies)*

Bulletins de la Société française d'Études mariales. Since 1935 (France).
Journées sacerdotales mariales. Since 1952.
Estudios Marianos. Since 1942 (Spain).
Estudos Marianos. Since 1944 (Portugal).
Mariale Dagen. Since 1931 (Belgium).
Marian reprints. Appears eight times a year (University of Dayton, U.S.).
Marian Studies. Since 1950 (U.S.).

5. *Reviews*

Theological reviews: *Ephemerides mariologicae.* Madrid. Founded in 1951.
Marianum. Rome. Founded in 1938.
Popular review: *Marie.* Quebec, Canada. Founded in 1947.

6. *Dictionaries*

Attwater, Donald. *A Dictionary of Mary.* New York: Kenedy, 1956.
Lexicon der Marienkunde. Regensburg: Pustet.

7. *Compilations*

Burke, T., S.J., ed. *Mary and Modern Man.* New York: America Press, 1954.
Fenton, J., and Beard, E., eds. *Studies in Praise of Our Blessed Mother.* Washington, D.C.: Catholic University Press, 1952.
O'Connor, E., C.S.C. *The Mystery of the Woman.* Notre Dame: University of Notre Dame Press, 1956.
Our Blessed Lady. Lectures on the Cambridge Summer School. London: Burns, Oates and Washbourne, 1933.

History of Mariology

1. *General works*

Until the histories of Mariology being prepared by G. Söll, and by Msgr. Jouassard, P. H. Barré, and R. Laurentin, are available, an outline of this history can be obtained from *Marie, l'Église et le Sacerdoce,* by R. Laurentin. Paris: Nouvelles éditions latines, 1953. This gives a view of the whole evolution of Mariology through the ages.

2. *Scripture*

Messenger, E. "Our Lady in the Scriptures," in *A Catholic Commentary on Holy Scripture*. New York: Nelson, 1953.

Robert, A. "La Sainte Vierge dans l'ancien Testament," in *Maria*, vol. 1, pp. 21-39.

William, F. M. *Mary, the Mother of Jesus*. St. Louis: Herder, 1954.

On Matthew and Luke—The classical commentaries are: *International Critical Commentary* (Edinburgh: Clark), *Études Bibliques* (Paris: Gabalda), Strack and Billerbeck (Munich: Beck).

On Luke—Féret, H. M., O.P. "Messianisme de l'Annonciation," in *Prêtre et Apôtre*, 29 (1948), pp. 37-38, 55-56, 71-73, 85-89.

Gallus, T. "De sensu verborum Luc 2, 35," in *Biblica*, 29 (1948), pp. 220-239.

Hebert, A. G. "La Vierge Marie, Fille de Sion," in *La Vie Spirituelle*, 85 (1951), pp. 127-140.

Lyonnet, S. χαῖρεκεχαριτωμέμη, in *Biblica*, 20 (1939), pp. 131-141.

On John—Braun, F. M., O.P. *Le Mère des fidèles*. Paris-Tournai: Casterman, 1953. This fully documented work eliminates the necessity of naming any others. Note that the Protestant, F. Quiévreux, "La Maternité spirituelle de la Mère de Jésus dans l'Évangile de saint Jean," (in *Supplément de la Vie Spirituelle*, 5 [1952], no. 20, pp. 101-134) arrives by different ways (and very original ones—the symbolism of numbers, for one) at the main conclusions of Father Braun.

3. *The Patristic Age*

Jouassard, G. "Marie à travers la patristique: Maternité, divine, virginité, sainteté," in *Maria*, I, pp. 69-157 (bibliography, pp. 15-157). A thorough, documented work, which can be supplemented on the Eve-Mary-Church theme by A. Muller's *Ecclesia-Maria* (Fribourg: Paulusverlag, 1951). Also see the articles by this author and H. Holstein in the *Bulletin de la Société française d'Études mariales*, 9 (1951), pp. 27-38.

4. *The Middle Ages*

Barré, H. "Marie et l'Église de vénérable Bède à saint Albert," in the *Bulletin de la Société française d'Études mariales*, 8 (1951), pp. 59-143. Contains an excellent survey of this period. There is no general work covering the following centuries (1270-1600). A series of monographs on the time from the origins of Benedictine monasticism to St. Francis de Sales can be found *Maria*, 2 (1951), pp. 540-1007.

5. *1600-1800*

Flachaire, C. *La Dévotion à la Vierge dans la Littérature catholique au commencement du XVII* siècle. Paris: Leroux, 1916.

Hoffer, P. *La dévotion mariale au déclin du XVII* siècle. Autour . . . des "Avis Salutaires."* Paris: Cerf, 1938.

For the eighteenth century: Dillenschneider, C. *Mariologie de saint Alphonse de Liguori*. Fribourg, 1931. The first volume of this work studies the relationship of St. Alphonsus to his times.

Finally, the numerous monographs arranged in chronological order in *Maria*, II and III, should be mentioned.

6. *1800 to the present*

Laurentin, R. *Marie, l'Église et le Sacerdoce,* pp. 346-628 and 649-770. This describes the gains and losses of this period.

7. *Mary in Protestant thought*

Crivelli, C. "Marie et les protestants," in *Maria,* I, pp. 675-695.

Hamer, J. "Les protestants devant la mariologie," in *Journées mariales sacerdotales,* I, pp. 125-149.

Schimmelpfennig, R. *Die Geschichte der Marienverehrung in deutschen Protestantismus.* Paderborn: Schöningh, 1952.

The bibliographies in the above works are completed by those in Roschini's *Mariologia,* I, pp. 306-316, and Besutti's *Bibliografia,* 1951, nos. 921-926, and 1952, nos. 1417-1454.

Carroll, E. R., O.Carm. "A Waldensian View of the Virgin Mary," in the *American Ecclesiastical Review,* Dec. 1956, pp. 380-397.

Hamer, J., O.P. "Mariology and Protestant Theology," in *Theology Digest,* Spring 1954, pp. 67-70.

————. "Protestants and the Marian Doctrine," in *The Thomist,* Oct. 1955, pp. 480-502.

Palmer, P., S.J. "Mary in Protestant Theology and Worship," Marian Library Study No. 3. Dayton, Ohio: University of Dayton.

Theology

1. *The Immaculate Conception*

Jugie, M., and Le Bachelet, X. "L'Immaculée Conception," in D.T.C., 7, 848-1218. This article is especially noteworthy.

Jugie, M. *L'Immaculée Conception dans l'Écriture et dans la tradition orientale.* Rome: Academia Mariana, 1952. Also the other volumes of the *Bibliotheca Immaculatae Conceptionis,* edited at Rome by Father Balié, Antonianum: Via Merulana.

Mathews, Br., S.M. *The Promised Woman: An Anthology of the Immaculate Conception.* St. Meinrad, Indiana: 1954.

Sericoli, C., O.F.M. "Immaculata B.M. Virginis conceptio iuxta Xysti IV constitutiones." Fasc. 5 of the *Bibliotheca mariana medii aevi.* Rome: Academia mariana, 1945.

2. *The Divine Maternity*

The two fundamental studies are: Manteau-Bonamy, H. M. *Maternité divine et Incarnation.* Paris: Vrin, 1949. Nicolas, J. *Le concept intégral de maternité divine.* St. Maximin: Revue Thomiste, 1937. On the difference between these views see the *Revue Thomiste,* 51 (1951), pp. 214-222.

Useful, but of unequal value, are the studies in *Estudios Marianos,* 8 (1949).

Also see:

Feckes, C. *The Mystery of the Divine Motherhood.* New York: Spiritual Books Associates, 1941.

Vonier, A., O.S.B. "The Divine Motherhood," in *Collected Works,* vol. 1, pp. 327-375. Westminster, Md.: Newman, 1952.

3. The Spiritual Maternity

Barré, H. "Marie et l'Église," in the *Bulletin de la Soc. fr. d'Études mariales,* 9 (1951), pp. 77-81 (documentation and bibliography on the historical aspect of the question).

Bartolomei, T. M., O.S.M. "La maternità spirituale di Maria," in *Divus Thomas,* 55 (1952), pp. 289-357.

Baumann, A. *Maria mater nostra spiritualis.* Brixen: Weger, 1948.

Geenen, G., O.P. "Mother of the Mystical Body," in *Cross and Crown,* 2 (1950), pp. 385-402.

Koehler, T. "La Maternité spirituelle de Marie," in *Maria,* I (1949), pp. 573-601.

Marvulli, L. *Maria, madre del Cristo mistico. La maternità de Maria nel suo concetto integrale.* Rome: Pontificia Facoltà teologica, 1948.

Stanley, T., S.M. *Mary and the Mystical Body.* Marian Library Study, No. 1: Dayton, 1953.

Terrien, J. B. *La Mère des hommes,* vol. 1. Paris: Lethielleux, 1902.

Estudios Marianos, 7 (1948).

Marian Studies, 3 (1952).

4. Coredemption

Dillenschneider, C. *Marie au service de la Rédemption.* Hagenau: Bureaux du Perpétuel Secours, 1947.

———. *Pour une corédemption mariale bien comprise.* Rome: Marianum, 1949.

———. *Le mystère de la corédemption mariale.* Paris: Vrin, 1951.

Laurentin, R. *Le titre de corédemptrice.* Paris: Lethielleux, 1951.

The largest study is that by J. B. Carol: *De Corredemptione.* Rome: Vaticana, 1950.

5. Mary's mediation

Bittremieux, J. *De mediatione universali.* Bruges: Beyaert, 1926.

Sebastian, W., O.F.M. *De beata Virgine Maria mediatrice.* Rome: Academia Mariana, 1952.

On the iconography of the subject: Perdrizet, P. *La Vierge de miséricorde.* Paris: Fontemoing, 1908; Vloberg, M. *Le Vierge notre médiatrice.* Grenoble: Arthaud, 1938.

6. Mary and the Church

Bulletins de la Soc. fr. d'Études mariales, 9-11 (1951–1953). A critical bibliography by R. Laurentin will be found here.

Congar, Yves, O.P. *Christ, Our Lady, and the Church.* Westminster, Md.: Newman, 1957.

Lubac, H. de, S.J. "The Church and Our Lady," in *The Splendour of the Church.* New York: Sheed and Ward, 1956.

Vollert, C., S.J. "A Bibliography on Mary and the Church," in *Theology Digest,* 4 (1956), pp. 34-36.

Cult, Devotion, Spirituality

1. Cult and Liturgy

Maria, I, pp. 215-416.

Mary in the Liturgy, 15th National Liturgical Week. Elsberry, Mo.: The Liturgical Conference, 1955.

2. *Lives of Mary*

Neubert, E. *Vie de Marie.* Salvator, Mulhouse, 1936.
Roschini, G. *Vita di Maria.* Rome: Belardetti, 1945.
Vloberg, M. *Vie de Marie.* Paris: Bloud and Gay, 1945.
William, F. M. *La vie de Marie.* Salvator, Mulhouse, 1947.

3. *Devotion*

The classic work, many times republished, is Louis-Mary Grignion de Montfort's *True Devotion to Mary,* Bay Shore, New York: Montfort Publications.

In modern times there is M. V. Bernadot's *Notre-Dame dans ma vie.* Paris: Cerf, numerous editions.

4. *The "presence" of Mary*

Gregorio de Jesús Crucificado. "La acción de Maria en las almas," in *Estudios marianos,* 11 (1951), pp. 255-278.

5. *Collections of texts*

Regamey, P. *Les plus beaux textes sur la Vierge Marie.* Paris: La Colombe, 1941.

Before the last war, the collection *Les Cahiers de la Vierge* (Paris: Cerf), in an edition that is now out of print, brought together some of the most beautiful of the ancient and modern texts.

6. *Apparitions*

There are two reasons why theologians tend to underestimate the value of apparitions: 1) They know that Revelation is closed and that they must base their work, not on heavenly manifestations, but on Scripture, Tradition and the directives of the Magisterium. 2) They are repelled by the mediocrity and the sometimes almost delirious tone of certain publications on these subjects.

This does not mean, however, that we should ignore the appeal of these manifestations, which, in the case of the two principal ones—Lourdes and Fatima—have received the highest approval of the Church. Even though we do not have a strict obligation to believe in apparitions, we would still have a poor sense of God and of the Church if we rejected, in theory and in actuality, everything that concerned them. A work which is both recent and objective and which contains all that is essential to know about the principal apparitions is: *Les Apparitions de la sainte Vierge,* by J. Goubert and L. Cristiani, Paris: La Colombe, 1952.

7. *Pedagogy*

"La doctrine mariale dans l'exposé de la foi," special number of *Évangéliser,* 7 (1953), pp. 315-317.
"La Vierge Marie et la formation religieuse," special number of *Lumen vitae,* 8 (1953), pp. 169-312.

Chapter VI

THE MYSTERY OF THE CHURCH

by P.-A. Liégé, O.P.

I. THE ETERNAL CHURCH OF GOD AND OF CHRIST

1. The Biblical expressions of the Mystery of the eternal Church
   (a) In the Old Testament
   (b) In the New Testament
   (c) The Church, the Body of Christ, according to St. Paul
2. The theological doctrine of the Mystical Body of Christ
   (a) The Church that has the glory of God
   (b) One Mediator, Himself man, Christ-Jesus
   (c) The capital grace of Christ the man
   (d) The capital grace of Christ, the cause of the Church
   (e) The dimensions of the Mystical Body of Christ

II. THE APOSTOLIC CHURCH

1. The wayfaring Church
   (a) The eternal Church and the historical Church
   (b) The Body of Christ in His earthly condition
   (c) The vocabulary relating to the Church
   (d) The theandric reality of the earthly Church
   (e) The Church, an incarnate community
2. The ecclesiastical ministry

   A. The depositaries of the hierarchical ministry
      (a) Christ, the Head of His visible Body
      (b) Apostolicity
      (c) The primacy of Peter
      (d) The apostolic succession
      (e) The Roman succession

B. The work of the ministry
- (a) The Church of faith and of the sacraments
- (b) The prophetic function of the Church
- (c) The priestly function of the Church
- (d) The pastoral function of the Church
- (e) The hierarchical ministry and the ministries
- (f) Christian life in the Church

C. The stages of the historical Church's growth
- (a) The Church, a Eucharistic community
- (b) The Church, a baptismal and evangelical community
- (c) A single ecclesial community
- (d) The truth of the Church and the perfection of the Church
- (e) The ecclesial community and other communities

D. Freedom and authority in the Church
- (a) Obedience to Christ and obedience to the Church
- (b) Initiatives and reforms in the Church
- (c) The danger of clericalism

3. The attributes and marks of the Church

A. The attributes of the Church

B. The marks of the Church and the apologetics of the Church
- (a) The theology and apologetics of the Church
- (b) Apologetics through the marks of the Church
- (c) The other "ways" of the Church's apologetics

4. The Members of the Church

A. The definition of the Church
- (a) The canonical definition
- (b) The theological definition

B. The rights to membership in the Church
- (a) Membership through baptismal character
- (b) Membership through grace
- (c) The degrees of membership

Chapter VI

THE MYSTERY OF THE CHURCH

I. The Eternal Church of God and of Christ

A Christian, according to St. Paul, is a man who has stripped his being of sin and put on the justice of God in Christ by participating in His mystery of Death-and-Resurrection. He is the man who walks in a newness of life according to the Spirit, the slave of the Lord, emancipated from sin and death: *the new man.* "If then any man is in Christ, he is a new creature" (II Cor. 5:17). But this individual Christian is a member of a whole people of saints. True, the mercy and eternal predestination of the living God touch him personally, but as caught up in a great successive people that is called in its entirety to God's heritage. The new man is this entire holy people, chosen even before God's blessed creation (see Eph. 2:15).

And this people was predestined only in the One who was willed and loved before all other creatures, the man Christ Jesus in whom the definitive union between God and men was accomplished. It is in Him that from all eternity God willed, for His glory, to gather together as in one large family heavenly spirits and earthly creatures, all adopted sons of the same Father. Such is the Mystery of the eternal Church of God and of Christ, the supreme Mystery, long hidden in God and finally manifested and realized in time. "The Church was created first, before all things . . . it is for her that the world was made." [1]

1. THE BIBLICAL EXPRESSIONS OF THE MYSTERY OF THE ETERNAL CHURCH

(a) *In the Old Testament*

How can we express the mystery of this union between the whole human race and the living God? In what does the completion of earthly creation consist? When the metaphors of Scripture are used to complement and correct one another, they present to our

[1] Hermas, *The Shepherd,* vision 2, chapter 4, no. 1.

faith a realistic concept of this marvelous new creation of God's free choice. We would have to be God Himself or at least possess the beatific vision to understand how deep the loving presence and the divine action of God are in His Church and also how, in spite of this gift of Himself to creatures, God remains God, the totally different One.

Even in the Old Testament God had called Israel His Chosen People, a holy people, the heritage of Yahweh. The covenant of Sinai, which was the fulfillment of the partial covenants that had preceded it and also the figure of the awaited Messianic covenant, dominates the whole history of the chosen people. The theocratic kingdom was simply the result of the Mosaic covenant, and a new kingdom was foreseen for the time of the Messianic covenant (Dan. 7). The Greek version of the Bible frequently speaks of the "Church of God," translating the Hebraic formula *Qahal Yahvé*. These words were meant to designate the religious convocation of the Chosen People, which had its origin in the convocation in the desert around Moses. The words "people," "kingdom," and "Church" were used interchangeably.

No doubt the reality expressed by these various images was, in the mind of Israel, filled with many racial and temporal hopes. The distinction between the carnal and the spiritual was not yet clearly defined, despite the prophets' efforts to call to mind the religious significance of the Covenant and of God's promises. The religious purity and the universalism of God's plan would be more clearly formulated later, when men were prepared to understand. But even then God's eternal intention to bring back to Himself the whole race of Abraham was being realized. Israel was the Church before the Church; it was the earthly prophecy of the eternal Church.

(b) *In the New Testament*

The New Testament's metaphors relating to the Church also show the continuity between the two covenants.

First, there are the sociological metaphors of the Church, the people, and the kingdom. The words *Church of God* (Acts 20:28; I Cor. 1:2; 15:9; Gal. 1:13; I Thess. 2:14; II Thess. 1:4) are used sometimes to designate a local community, and again the universal community of the elect of God in Christ: the etymology of the word "church" indicates God's initiative in the choice and in the gathering together of those called to His kingdom. Christians constitute the Israel of God (Gal. 6:16), the chosen race, the holy nation, the people purchased by God (cf. I Pet. 2:9-10) in a new and eternal covenant (I Cor. 11:25; II Cor. 3:6).

As for the *Kingdom,* it has become the wholly spiritual kingdom of Christ and of God (Eph. 5:5) in which, according to Daniel's prophecy, the holy people of the Most High participate in the kingship. It is a kingdom of holiness, already begun on earth and yet still to come, a kingdom whose founder is Christ (Apoc. 1:6).

The Old Testament had used images of construction in reporting Yahweh's words to His people: God is the architect and builder of Israel (Jer. 31:4; 33:7). Later, St. Paul said to the Corinthians: "You are God's tillage, God's building" (I Cor. 3:9). God's people are His building because He builds them and establishes His dwelling in them; because they are living stones built into a temple (I Pet. 2:5); because they are temples of the Holy Spirit (I Cor. 6:19) whose cornerstone and foundation is Christ: "In him the whole structure is closely fitted together and grows into a temple holy to the Lord; in him you too are being built together into a dwelling place for God in the Spirit" (Eph. 2:21-22; cf. also I Cor. 3:11).

The metaphor of the *Spouse,* as applied to the Church, indicates better than the preceding ones that the adoption of the people is a free work of love, that glory is simply the brightness of divine love's creative fruitfulness shining upon her. This metaphor manifests the close bond that unites God and Christ to their people.

The Old Testament had already sung of Israel's union with Yahweh as a marital union: God said to His people: "I will espouse thee to me forever" (Os. 2:19). And the prophets did not hesitate to chide Israel for its infidelity and its adulteries (Os. 1; Ezech. 16; Jer. 3). In St. Paul (Eph. 5:23-33) the Church is spoken of as the Spouse of Christ and not of God. Christ loved her and sanctified her as a husband loves his wife and takes care of her. He is also the Head of the Church as a husband is of his wife. Likewise, in Apocalypse 21:9-10, the Church is referred to as the Spouse of the Lamb.

St. John presents the Church under the image of the *Vine* (Jn. 15:1-17; cf. also I Cor. 3:6-9). Isaias had done so before him: "For the vineyard of the Lord of hosts is the house of Israel" (Is. 5:7); a vine that was loved, cultivated with care and made fruitful (Is. 5:1-2). St. John adds the allegory of the vine-stock and the branches. The same sap flows through them all. So is it of the oneness of life that must exist between Christ and His faithful. It is from within that the community of God's people is formed, a community of life. The metaphor of the vine lays great stress on this spiritual inwardness, as does the analogy of the human body, which plays such an important part in the theology of St. Paul.

(c) The Church, the Body of Christ, according to St. Paul

The image of the human body used by St. Paul has no counterpart in the Old Testament. True, it does seek first of all to manifest the union of the holy people with Christ, and not their union with God as God.

To the mind of St. Paul, humanity was predestined in Christ, and Christ was predestined jointly with the whole human race. The mystery of salvation and sanctification accomplished in the man Christ-Jesus concerns all men. In this sense, redeemed humanity cannot be separated from Christ the Savior. Actually, redeemed humanity is Christ: "For as the body is one and has many members, and all the members of the body, many as they are, form one body, so also is it with Christ" (I Cor. 12:12). In short, there is the one mystical person constituted by the Savior and His redeemed people, the one New Man (Eph. 2:15), the total Christ, as St. Augustine puts it.

But we must clarify the structure of this mystical Christ, which is comparable to a human body. While the Church is united to Christ, it is not identified with Him. He remains the Head who presides over the rest of the body. The physical Christ is the head of the mystical Christ: "And all things (God) made subject under his feet, and him he gave as head over all the Church, which indeed is his body, the completion of him who fills all with all" (Eph. 1:22-23).

True, Christ already possesses this sovereignty by nature, as the Word begotten by the Father before all creatures, through whom and for whom all things were created (Col. 1:15-17). But He also possesses it through predestination and acquisition, as man. And it is precisely as man that He can be the Head of the Church, inasmuch as through His mediation it has pleased God to reconcile all creatures to Himself, "making peace through the blood of his cross" (Col. 1:18-20).

The biological image of the head and the body should be taken literally: An influx of divine life is poured out into the whole Church from Christ the Head, by reason of His function as the one

Under the influence of St. Bernard, who vowed to the Blessed Virgin a cult full of tenderness, the Byzantine iconography of the Virgin *Théotokos* was gradually humanized. There was a decrease in the rigid hieraticism and an increase in maternal sentiment, and the attitude of the images became more relaxed and animated. But the Blessed Virgin continued to be represented as part of a group, ordinarily in the midst of the angels and saints. It was already a general law of compositions in primitive times (first to fourth centuries) never to represent an isolated detail but always to represent a group, or a progressive cycle in which the whole economy of salvation found expression. The details were added complements, but they were never separated from the over-all vision that the artists usually received from the liturgy.

The first isolated Virgin, standing and carrying the Child in her arms, dates from the end of the twelfth century (a Burgundian portal that is no longer extant). But the idea, or rather the devotion kept progressing, and soon the Virgin was to be seen everywhere. She is to be found along the piers in all the cathedrals of the Middle Ages. In the Cathedral of Notre Dame of Paris, four out of six doorways are dedicated to her.

We see her here in the north transept of this cathedral, the only great statue that the Revolution spared (in part, for the Child was broken).

Her beauty is wholesome, majestic, and simple. In a tender and proud movement she holds up her Child to the admiration of all, and this movement impresses a gentle motion to her hips, caused by the weight of her precious burden. The drapery accompanies the movement of the body, and the flexible and harmonious play of the folds forms upward lines that converge at the Child and draw the eye to Him despite His absence. This is one of the purest compositions of the thirteenth century. It was executed at the period when so-called Gothic art in France reached its peak, during the reign of St. Louis.

The Virgin of the cloister portal (north transept) of the Cathedral of Paris, executed between 1258 and 1260.

Mediator. All men are united to Adam in sin, as members of his family. All redeemed men are likewise united to Christ, the new Adam, in grace, as being included in His saving act. "For if by the offense of the one the many died, much more has the grace of God, and the gift of the grace of the one man Jesus Christ, abounded unto the many" (Rom. 5:15).

It is only by receiving of the fullness of Christ the man that the members of His body can have the life that He Himself receives from the uncreated fullness of God. This life consists essentially in the love of God, the charity with which God loves Himself. Writing to the Ephesians, St. Paul said: "Rather are we to practice the truth in love, and so grow up in all things in him who is the head, Christ. For from him the whole body . . . derives its increase to the building up of itself in love" (Eph. 4:15-16).

And when we consider the reality of the Body, we must say that the life of the members is none other than the life of the Head, poured forth and communicated. The members of Christ live in dependence upon their Head. The life of the trunk cannot be isolated from the life of the head. So is it with Christ. What union could be closer than that between the members and the head? St. Paul understood the mystery of the Lord's answer to him on the road to Damascus: "I am Jesus, whom thou art persecuting" (Acts 9:5). That is why he was able to write in all truth to the Galatians: "For you are all one in Christ Jesus" (Gal. 3:28). Even though the angels were not redeemed by Christ and do not have the same oneness with Him in the order of salvation as men do, they also recognize Him as their Head and cleave to this one Body for the sake of which all things were created: "to re-establish all things in Christ" (Eph. 1:10; ἀνακεφα λαιώσασθαι—to gather together under a single head).

The analogy of the body has so far manifested only the mysterious union of life which joins the Body to the Head in the mystical Christ. But Christ the man is simply a Mediator, and the unity of the Church in Christ cannot conceal the unity of the Church in God which the metaphors of the Old Testament expressed. Christ Himself comes from God and exists for God: that is, the total Christ predestined in the Person of Christ. In order to preserve the coherence and the biological sense of the Pauline image, we must say that the Triune God is the soul of the Body of Christ. And that is what St. Paul did equivalently by attributing this function to the

Person of the Holy Spirit. After having likened the unity of all Christians in Christ to the unity of the members of a single body, he justified his affirmation: "For in one Spirit we were all baptized into one body, . . . and we were all given to drink of one Spirit" (I Cor. 12:13).

The Holy Spirit dwells in the Body of Christ as a whole, just as He dwells in each of its members, and as He dwells in the Head in a unique way. This divine presence and this common participation in the Spirit assure the unity of the whole body, for there is "one body and one Spirit" (Eph. 4:4). It is a life-giving presence. The Spirit fashions the people of God (II Cor. 3:7 ff.). All progress in holiness by the members of Christ is His work (Eph. 3:16). He constantly works within them to guide the body to its completion and to make of it a holy temple in the Lord (Eph. 2:21-22). Just as He was active in Christ the man according to the fullness of God, from the Incarnation to the Resurrection, He now continues to make His Body conformable to Him, from justification to the glory of the resurrection (Rom. 8:11).

Through the gift of the Holy Spirit, Christians receive the spirit of the adoption of sons that makes them—in the image of Christ and dependent upon Him—co-heirs to the inheritance of God (Gal. 4:6-7). "If anyone does not have the Spirit of Christ (i.e., the Spirit who proceeds from Him as the Word and the Spirit that He received in plenitude as man) he does not belong to Christ" (Rom. 8:9). What the soul is to the human body, the Holy Spirit is in a totally unique and analogical way to the Body of Christ which is the Church: a life-giving omnipresence, the personal source of vital energy and the principle of unity in the way that the head is this principle for the other members.

2. THE THEOLOGICAL DOCTRINE OF THE MYSTICAL BODY OF CHRIST

The metaphor of the human body aptly expresses the mysterious reality of the spiritual community which came forth from God in Jesus Christ. This is not to say that the image never needs to be adapted to the reality and to the idea, nor that its expressive richness supersedes all other Biblical metaphors. But it has an over-all coherence and an intelligibility that make it particularly suited to theological use. St. Paul has given us quite a well-developed theology of the Mystical Body of Christ. It should be noted, however, that the expression "Mystical Body" did not originate with him. It dates from the Middle Ages and was long used to designate the Eucharist, in order to distinguish the sacramental Body of Christ from the Body of Christ which is the Church.

All that theologians need to do is to develop the Apostolic thought, which is often dense and synthetic, in order to manifest its full significance in terms of their theology of the Trinity and of Christ and in terms of their Christian anthropology. For theology takes on ecclesiological value the moment we consider God's new creation as a community, as the new Jerusalem that St. John saw in the Apocalypse, "coming down out of heaven from God" (Apoc. 21:10).

(a) *The Church that has the glory of God*

When the Biblical expression "the glory of God" is applied to creatures, it designates any gratuitous participation in the glorious life of God, any spiritual transformation that introduces souls, made for the infinite, into the vital realm of the Triune God, and renews them in His splendor. It is a spiritual life that makes an organism of God's people. It is not just an ordinary life of the spirit but the life of the Spirit of God, a life of knowledge and love whose object is the very object of the eternal contemplation and ineffable love of the Trinity. And this organism is not just an ordinary human super-organism, but the body of those who have been called by God unto His kingdom and His glory (I Thess. 2:12).

The glory of God consists in God's giving Himself and making spirits divine through His uncreated gift and His life-giving presence. The creative immanence of the Trinity in the new man works a transformation in the very structure of his soul and in his whole psychology that qualifies him to live as a member of the Triune family, and to adopt divine habits. The mysterious life of the three divine Persons in their eternal processions henceforth extends under the form of invisible missions to every regenerated spirit. We can in very truth speak of the Church as a divine organism. In the words of Tertullian: "Wherever the Three are, namely, the Father, and the Son, and the Holy Spirit, there is the Church: for the Church is the body of the Three" (*De Bapt.,* 6; P.L. I, col. 1206).

We usually speak of the Holy Spirit as the principle of the mystical life of the Church. This appropriation rests on the visible mission of Pentecost, which proclaimed the mysterious affinity between the procession of Personal Love and the work of fruitfulness and sanctification outside the Trinity that consists in the communication of divine life to men. But on the basis of this appropriation we must say that it is the whole Trinity that quickens the Church. To quote St. Augustine: "God therefore dwells in His temple; not only the Holy Spirit, but also the Father and the Son. . . . And this temple of God, I mean to say of the inaccessible Trinity in its entirety, is the Holy Church, the one Church that peoples heaven and earth" (*Enchir.*, 56, 15; P.L. 40, col. 259).

For, "now we are the children of God, and it has not yet appeared what we shall be. We know that, when he appears, we shall be like to him, for we shall see him just as he is" (I Jn. 3:2). The Church of heaven possesses the gift of God in its perfect state, with a consciousness that is totally imbued with the glory of the Trinity. God is all things in all men. The Church of this earth already possesses the gift of God, and the glory of God already illumines the whole city (Apoc. 21:23). However men's eyes cannot yet endure the brilliance of it, they cannot yet stand face-to-face contact with the Eternal One. This is the reign of faith. And yet it is through faith that God begins to communicate His glory to man in his earthly state. We have received the Holy Spirit, and with Him the pledge of our inheritance (I Cor. 1:22; Eph. 1:13 ff.). Through the love of charity and the Spirit's many ways of drawing us, we are introduced into the life of divine friendship which engrafts the community of souls onto God. For "God is love, and he who abides in love abides in God, and God in him" (I Jn. 4:16). Even now the eternal Church has begun to dwell in time.

(b) *"One Mediator . . . , Himself man, Christ Jesus"* (I Tim. 2:5)

Since Adam, the glory of God has rested in no man without first passing through a new Adam. Only the exigencies of theological analysis can justify the abstract and piecemeal approach we have so far taken. The Church of men is accepted by God only because her Head, Christ, was first of all acceptable to God.

Within the oneness of a single metaphysical personality, i.e., the personality of the Word, Christ is at once God and man: this is the hypostatic union. Obviously, it is as man that Christ can save men and be constituted as their Head. But Jesus the man could not have this privilege if He were not, even in His humanity, already in the sphere of the Godhead by reason of the Incarnation of the Word in His human nature. In short, He would not have this privilege if His were only an ordinary and individual human nature. Indeed, Christ was not constituted Mediator by any juridical decree of God. From the moment of His Incarnation, He was *by nature* constituted before God the envoy of destiny for the whole human race. And His redemptive epic was by this very fact accomplished and accepted by God in the name of all men.

(c) *The capital grace of Christ the man*

Theologians rightly distinguish in Christ's eminent holiness two kinds of grace. First of all, there is the grace of union which we have just discussed, by reason of which the man Jesus subsists in the Person of the Word. Secondly, there is the sanctifying grace of the man Jesus, by which His soul communes with the uncreated fullness personally united to it. Let no one be misled by this distinction. The sanctifying grace of Christ follows directly from His grace of union, as its necessary consequence. How could a human life thus possessed by God in the most radical center of its existence fail to be transformed and intimately united to God? How could it fail to receive the supreme fullness of sanctifying grace that a creature can receive? And it is precisely in virtue of the holiness of His human soul—which, it is true, follows from the grace of union— that Christ is the firstborn of a multitude of brothers (Rom. 8:29), that He is the Head of a Body whose life depends upon the divine life which dwells in Him in fullness.

This sanctifying grace that makes of Him the Holy One above all others is also a grace of headship, inasmuch as the supernatural destiny of the whole human race is included in Christ: whence the name capital grace. The total reality of the Mystical Body, which cannot be reduced to the reality of a juridical or moral body but which consists in a community of life according to the Spirit, is concentrated in the fullness of life that dwells in the Head, namely, in the capital grace of Christ. The life of the members, a gift of the riches of Christ's grace, is only a participation in the plenitude of this holiness. Did not God choose us in Christ "before the foundation of the world, that we should be holy and without blemish in His sight in love" (Eph. 1:4)?

(d) *The capital grace of Christ, the cause of the Church*

Let us try to clarify how the capital grace of Christ flows into His members, how it is the cause of the grace of the Church. First of all, we must set aside any fanciful notion of a quantitative over-flowing or effusion. Christ's personal holiness is His alone; the holiness of His Body could neither add to nor subtract from His fullness, for His Body's holiness depends necessarily upon His personal holiness. Of course, this dependence is not of the same degree as that of the creature upon its Creator, for Christ as man is not the first cause of holiness and His fullness is not uncreated. The glory of God illumines the city of the saints, and the Lamb is only His lamp (cf. Apoc. 21:23). The fact that the entire glory of the Church stems from the glory of her Head is a great mystery that we can try to explain as follows:

1. Christ's capital grace is the measure of the grace of His whole Body.
2. His capital grace is the human instrument for the acquisition of grace by the Body as a whole.
3. Capital grace is likewise the divine instrument for endowing the whole Body with grace. This multiform influence has its source in the personal union of Christ and the Word, which magnifies Christ's humanity and in which the Greek Fathers loved to contemplate the glory of the whole human race in God. For why should God have become man except so that man might become God?

Capital grace is the measure of the grace of the whole Body in the sense that the Church has been graced only in Christ. For Christ is complete only when united with His Body, and the Body's law of life is to conform to the life of the Head. This is true also in the sense that the grace of Christ possesses a plenitude that can never be granted to any other creature. All the gifts of God refer back to the fullness of the gift dispensed to Christ; all holiness, therefore, even that of the angelic world, finds in Him its model of participated glory.

Secondly, it was by reason of His capital grace that Christ was able to merit the salvation of all men by accomplishing the work that the Father had ordained for Him as "a propitiation for our sins, not for ours only but also for those of the whole world" (I Jn. 2:2). And let us understand this universal value of Christ's merit not only as a juridical substitution accepted by God, but more profoundly as an organic solidarity between the Head and all the members based on the personal union of the Savior to the Word.

Finally, the capital grace of Christ makes of His humanity, in the order of descending mediation, an animate instrument of the power of the Word who possesses it, and of the whole Trinity, for giving forth the divine life that He won for His redeemed members. Our Lord's humanity is life-giving to every spirit and to all mortal flesh. We must go that far in order to express the realism of Revelation and of all Tradition concerning the transforming immanence of the glorious Christ in His Church. The river of living water that flows through the city of God, according to Apocalypse 22:1, has its source in the throne of God and of the Lamb.

(e) *The dimensions of the Mystical Body of Christ*

Did God await the historical appearance of the one, necessary Mediator to form His adopted people? Were the people of the Old Covenant called only to the ephemeral role of a precursor, living in hope without participating in the reality of the promises? The Fathers certainly did not think so when they spoke of the Church of the redeemed as a long-lived people beginning in the days of Abel the just and reaching into eternity. The eternal Church embraces in her bosom the multitude of human beings who have found the paths to divine friendship, whether they lived before or after the coming of the Word to earth. Nor did God bind His eternal mercy that touches the depths of men's hearts to membership in the race of Abraham, nor in an absolute way to an exterior membership in the Church instituted by Christ.

Nevertheless, it is certain that no man has received the justice of God without a certain objective reference to the mystery of Christ; and that no son of Adam belongs to God and to His Church without also belonging in equal measure to Christ and to His Body. St. Thomas Aquinas echoes this certitude of faith when he affirms: "At no time, not even before the coming of Christ, could men be saved unless they became members of Christ" (IIIa, q. 68, art. 1, ad 1). "That they may be one, even as we are one: I in them and thou in me; that they may be perfected in unity" (Jn. 17:22-23). "That God may be all in all" (I Cor. 15:28). "Christ is all things and in all" (Col. 3:11). Therein lies the whole mystery of the eternal Church, the Church that God has loved and chosen in Christ before the creation of the world.

This reference to the Mediator applies to the men who lived before the Incarnation on the level of eternal divine predestination. And even for these saints, incorporation into Christ attained its full effect only after the historical fulfillment of the redemptive mystery. The Fathers and theologians see in the spirits that the sacred soul of our Savior visited (see I Pet. 3:19) all the just who had died before Him and who were waiting to enter into full possession of God's heritage in the wake of Christ, their Head.

With regard to this mystery of salvation, we should keep two perspectives simultaneously in mind, subordinating the second to the first: 1) the historical and progressive realization of the Christian economy through the stages of the Kingdom of God, as revealed to us by the Bible from Genesis to the Apocalypse; 2) the mystery of salvation considered at a meta-historical level, the level of divine predestination. On this latter level, regardless of the epoch of the Kingdom in which he lives and even though he may be ignorant of all exterior revelation, every man who deeply and sincerely awaits divine salvation encounters, outside of all history, the mystery of Christ which was accomplished in time for all men; and he thereby becomes a participant of the one Christian salvation.

Before the coming of our Lord Jesus Christ, there were many men who believed in the Christ to come, just as we believe in the Christ who has already come. *Times have changed, but the faith is the same.* Even words change with the times and with their diverse grammatical forms. The expression: "He is to come" does not have the same meaning as this one: "He has come." And yet the same faith unites both those who believed that He was to come and those who in their turn believed that He had come.

We see them all enter at different epochs by the same portal of faith, that is, through Jesus Christ. . . . The signs are different, but the faith is the same. . . . All who believed in the time of Abraham or Isaias, of Jacob or Moses, or of the other patriarchs and prophets who foretold the coming of Christ, were sheep and they listened to Jesus Christ. They did not listen to a stranger's voice, but to His voice. (St. Augustine, *In Joan* 45:9 P.L. 35, 1722–1723).

The fact remains that in the Church founded on Pentecost God's plan finds definitive expression and is perfectly realized in history. That is why those to whom she has given Christ and His Spirit in the fullness of Messianic times obviously have a more explicit awareness of the mystery of salvation accomplished in them than "the Christians of the periphery." Hence it follows that this mystery has made a deeper and more transforming mark on the former than on the latter: "As for us, we adore what we know. . . ."

Thus the whole of human history becomes the history of the Kingdom of God by reason of the fact that the Church reaches her fullest development within history. Henceforth history awaits the return of Christ, to inaugurate the last stage in God's eternal plan for humanity in time. This is the orientation of Christian hope, in its collective and cosmic terms. These are the dimensions of the Body of Christ.

II. The Apostolic Church

1. THE WAYFARING CHURCH

(a) *The eternal Church and the historical Church*

St. Thomas declares: "The true Church, our Mother, is in heaven. It is toward her that we are striving. It is by resembling her that our Church militant attains to her full stature" (*In Epist. ad Eph.,* Chapter 3, Lesson 3).

What we have so far said of the mystery of the Church applies fully only to the Church in her completed and glorified state, to the Church at the mature stature of the total Christ, "in all her glory, not having spot or wrinkle or any such thing, but . . . holy and without blemish" (Eph. 5:27). In this state, the Church's life will be totally inward, invariably dependent upon God and Christ in the immanence of divine glory: "The throne of God and of the Lamb shall be in (the city), and his servants shall serve him. And they shall see his face and his name shall be on their foreheads. And night shall be no more, and they shall have no need of light of lamp, or light of sun, for the Lord God will shed light upon them; and they shall reign forever and ever" (Apoc. 22:3-5).

The Mother of God in all her glory of soul and body—she who is the Church in her state of perfection—and the saints in the glory of their souls already constitute the eternal Church. But the earthly Church is part of it too, inasmuch as the substance of eternity, the invisible glory of charity, already shines forth in her. The present Church has begun to be what she will be beyond history. However she is to some extent provisory and incomplete. She is under the regime of faith, and subject to the law of growth in each of her members, as is every organic body. And so, insofar as her members are men in the wayfaring state, the earthly Church shows us a new face, one that is less essential since it is ephemeral and destined to be superseded by her eternal face. Her temporal face is less purely spiritual, but it is necessary and it has been fashioned by God and Christ. This is the Church as a visible society, instituted by Jesus to replace the Synagogue and charged by Him with the task of making His Redemption bear fruit in each successive human generation.

If a saintly Christian is questioned about the secret of his personality, he will answer: "It is the presence of the Spirit of Christ that dwells in me and fills me with a new vitality." But he will immediately add: "This Spirit has taken possession of me only in the vital center of a Christian community, and without any individualism in religious experience. In this community of persons communing in the same Spirit, I found structures and means that have placed me in contact with Christ." The experience of the Church under these two aspects—community of life and means of communion—cannot be dissociated from authentic Christian existence. That is what Bergson did not see in the admirable pages of his *Two Sources* concerning the saintly Christian.

(b) *The Body of Christ in His earthly condition, according to St. Paul*

When St. Paul speaks of the Church of this earth, he forcefully points out the unity of her two aspects: the Mystical Body considered in its invisible reality, and the visible society.

1. The visible society is the repository of the eternal Church, insofar as the latter already exists in time. Let us read the headings of Paul's letters. He addressed a very specific local community: "the church of God at Corinth" (I Cor. 1:2), for example. Equivalently, he addressed the Corinthians as "you who have been sanctified in Christ Jesus" (I Cor. 1:2); and he called the Philippians "all the saints in Christ Jesus that are in Philippi" (Phil. 1:1). The Body of Christ subsists in time and space. The metaphor of the Body can just as well express this aspect of visibility as the inwardness and unity of life which we pointed to earlier.

2. The human body possesses exterior organs that serve the life and growth of the organism. So it is with the Church. "And (Christ) himself gave some men as apostles, and some as prophets, others again as evangelists, and others as pastors and teachers, in order

to perfect the saints for a work of ministry, for *building up the body of Christ,* until we attain to . . . perfect manhood, to the mature measure of the fullness of Christ. . . . For from him the whole body (being closely joined and knit together through every joint of the system according to the functioning in due measure of each single part) derives its increase to the building up of itself in love" (Eph. 4:11-16). Whence we see that it is the same Body that lives inwardly by the divine life and that is the visible instrument of its own growth in the life of Christ. For St. Paul, the Church-as-Society is the Mystical Body insofar as it is externalized and given the adequate means for building itself, in accordance with the condition of its earthly subsistence. (Cf. Rom. 12:4-8; I Cor. 12:28-31.)

(c) *The vocabulary relating to the Church*

When we studied the Scriptural metaphors relating to the Church earlier in this treatise, we stressed their spiritual and eschatological significance. A clarification of vocabulary appears necessary, now that we have realized the complexity of the Church in her earthly phase.

The word "Church" can signify either the community of those sanctified in Jesus Christ, or the Institution of salvation founded by Jesus Christ in order to communicate holiness; or it may signify both aspects of the Church joined together. Scripture very rarely proposes analytical definitions. It uses the word "Church" in various contexts chiefly to suggest one or another of these designations. In the Old Testament, the spiritual, inward reality of the Church was one with her institutional structure, the latter being at once a concrete expression and a means of actualizing this interior reality. In the New Testament, we catch a glimpse of the final state of a purely spiritual community that is called the Church (Eph. 5:27). And yet we find that this same word retains the complexity it had in the Old Testament inasmuch as it refers to the same Church in her earthly state (Matt. 16:18, for example).

The term "people of God" calls for the same remarks. In the Revelation of the Old and the New Testaments this expression designates a sociological reality (and far more so in the Old than in the New), embracing a more essential reality of vital communion in God. The text of Leviticus (26:12): "I . . . will be your God, and you shall be my people" is paralleled by the one from the Apocalypse (21:3-4): "Behold the dwelling of God with men, and he will dwell with them. And they will be his people, and God himself will be with them as their God. And God will wipe away every tear from their eyes. And death shall be no more; neither shall there be mourning, nor crying, nor pain any more, for the former things have passed away."

The expression "Kingdom of God" might at first glance seem to designate solely the interior and personal aspect of the reality of the Church. (Cf. the parables of the Kingdom in the Synoptics.) True, the accent is on the spiritual and interior kingdom, the ultimate realization of God's plan inasmuch as it has already been accomplished and is as yet unfulfilled. And yet we must not forget that there is question here of a notion which is inseparable in Biblical tradition from a sociological realization. Just because Jesus reacted against an overly exterior Messianism is no reason for us to oppose the Kingdom of the Church. St. Matthew (16:18-19) actually identifies the Church with the Kingdom, including in the latter the present Institution of salvation. In the final state of things, the Kingdom will be the perfect Church (Apoc. 1:6). And if we want to talk about the aspect of the present Church that is already the communication of eternal life we use the term Kingdom.

When St. Paul speaks of the "Body of Christ," he explicitly adds the reality of the Church in Christ to the preceding expressions. And yet this image has the same expressive dimensions as the terms "Church" and "People of God." It designates the interior unity of those sanctified in Jesus Christ; and likewise the exterior unity of the various ministeries ordered to interior growth; finally, it designates both the interior and exterior unity simultaneously perceived.

In St. Paul, then, "Body of Christ" designates at once and according to the needs of pastoral teaching, the invisible and the visible aspects of the Church. In St. Augustine, however, and in many theologians dependent upon his ecclesiology (including St. Thomas, Bossuet, Scheeben, Franzelin, among the greatest), these words have come to designate first of all and principally the invisible aspect of the Church. In time, the term "Body of Christ" has become the "Mystical Body of Christ." When the latter expression is used from this point of view without further clarification, it does not give a sufficiently explicit definition of the Church upon earth. For the earthly Church possesses a visible organism of growth which must be clearly indicated by the term that defines the Church.

In general we are using this somewhat limited interpretation of the term "Mystical Body" in the present study, without hesitating to give the term a broader meaning when the context calls for it. Applying the term "Mystical Body" to the invisible aspect of the Church has the advantage of helping to formulate theologically the ordered duality of the wayfaring Church. Only if this term were used unilaterally to refer to the invisible aspect of the Church would there be reason to fear that it might orientate doctrine toward an invisible Church of the Lutheran type.

If we were to seek equivalents in Scripture for the expression "Mystical Body," we would have to use the word "Kingdom," already mentioned, and also the images of the Vine and the Spouse, noting that these last two terms abstract from the institutional aspect of the Church of Christ.

(d) *The theandric reality of the earthly Church*

In the wayfaring Church there is a coincidence of rights between the visible society and the mystical community of the justified. There are not two Churches, but a duality of aspects in the one Church. The visible aspect is only the shell of the eternal reality already present under the other aspect, and it is as indispensable to the invisible life of the Church as bark to a living tree; for the visible Church manifests the invisible Church at the level of phenomena, just as bark does the tree. However, it is truly "the same city that continues on this earth and that is already established in heaven" (St. Augustine, *Serm.,* 105, No. 9, P.L. 28, 622).

We could develop at great length, according to all the values and conditions of Christian life upon earth, this complex and contradictory picture of the Church.

It cannot be affirmed of the Kingdom of God that it is here or there. For it dwells in the secret of men's hearts. And the Church visibly recognizes her children. She is actualized in local communities. She claims that there is no Kingdom of God upon earth outside her societal communion: The *mystical* and *visible Body* in one.

To be a part of the Kingdom one must live in spiritual communion with God by faith and charity. God alone is the author of this supernatural life, which is His supreme gift to men in Christ. And the Church lays claim to the ministry of God's message of salvation, which she has preserved and transmitted visibly and socially: she possesses a *Magisterium*.

God is spirit, and those who adore Him must adore Him in

spirit and in truth. The new Israel is no longer dependent upon Jerusalem or on some other place of worship. And the Church continues to offer God an exterior cult of worship. The sacraments through which she communicates grace to men constitute the essential element of this cult. The spiritual Church is also the *sacramental* Church.

The citizen of the Kingdom is a free citizen. He carries within himself the law of his conduct. The grace that renewed him in the image of God performs the function of a new moral consciousness. His inspirations come to him from the Spirit, and the law no longer has dominion over him. He needs only to yield to the spontaneity of his faith and of his charity. Now, the Code of Canon Law contains over two thousand articles the contents of several of which stem back to our Lord Himself and to His Apostles; and the Church complements the inspiration of the Spirit with hierarchical guidance. The pope visibly represents Christ upon earth in the government of the Kingdom that He won at the price of His blood. The Church of freedom is also the Church of apostolic authority and hierarchy.

Before God, there can be no hierarchy except that set up in men's hearts through the love poured out on them by His Spirit, through spiritual proximity with Him. Now the visible hierarchy of the Church is only a missionary, ministerial hierarchy, that has no necessary link with the invisible hierarchy, known with certitude to God alone. For only God knows those who truly belong to Him. He discerns in His eternal prescience all those who will ultimately make up the elect of His holy and immaculate Church. But so long as the Church subsists in human form, she shelters indifferent and sinful men, her effective forces remain unstable and precarious, subject to evil and at war with Satan and his powers of darkness. There is a battle for the purity of the spirit of Christ even within the bosom of Holy Mother Church.

The Kingdom of God is an eternal kingdom that participates in the eternity of God and of the risen Christ. But the Church of Christ is also the wayfaring Church, the Church of labors and expectation, a body in process of formation, the tributary of time and progress. She will abandon her historical and mortal covering on the day of the Kingdom's triumph and of the end of the sacred history of the world (see I Cor. 15:24). On that day, she will cast aside that whole aspect of herself by which she is now the sanctifying Church, the instrument of her own growth and bound up with the earthly condition of her members.[1] We can see that what is given to the Church from the outside takes on an interior consistency within her, and that society gives rise to community within the Church. From this fact arises an eschatological tendency to become a pure community which will never be realized in the Church on earth.

While on the level of a clear, immediate, and descriptive view, visibility and invisibility seem to characterize respectively the society and community of the Church, it would seem that the terms "inwardness" and "outwardness" are more exact. In fact, all visibility is not excluded from the community. The wholly inward community of the heavenly Jerusalem will be accompanied by a glorious visibility that will spring from God's immanence in the new creation. And even now the community of believers manifests itself visibly by the fruits of the Spirit that dwell inwardly in it, and also by its missionary expansion. The question is one of the community's visibility as such, not of outwardness, even though the outwardness of the sanctifying society has previously presided over the inward movement of grace. To the extent that the Christian sacraments symbolically express the faith of believers and the mystery of Christ, they stem from the community. In the measure that they are instruments of divine life, they stem from the society.

(e) *The Church, an incarnate community*

Society in the present Church is therefore her institutional aspect in the order of means, whose whole task is to make the community ripen to maturity. Community is the already eternal and final reality of the Church: when God will be in all, and all in all. In the Church's completed state, the community will absorb all strictly societal and institutional outwardness. We can ask ourselves if something of the present structures of ecclesial society will subsist. Will the entire societal aspect of the Church be cast in the fire, leaving only charity? It would seem that in conformity with the indications of Revelation, the becoming of the Church and the structures that have edified her eternal reality will be assumed, to-

[1] It is from this view of the wayfaring Church that we can get some light concerning the theology of history. Now that Christ has come, history has reached the term of its hope. The Second Coming will make this hope a definitive reality. Profane history has no final sense except within sacred history; the former either leads men from a great distance toward the Kingdom or it raises obstacles to the Kingdom by setting itself up as self-sufficient. This point will be developed more fully below.

gether with the personal historicity of the saints, in the glorious community under a new and wholly interior form which will have no trace left of active mediation.

The term "community" used in the preceding lines, has been elaborated by contemporary thought to the point that it now presents itself as one of the most apt designations of the mystery of the Church. It evokes all the concrete riches of a people, it holds greater meaning for present-day minds, and it lends itself more easily to theological analysis.

A human community gathers together persons in the precise sense of the word, and makes them commune in the very principle of their personality. In the community of the Church Christ Himself is the "I," at once transcendent and immanent, of each of His elect. And each one is supremely himself under this impress of the living God and in communion with the others. Nothing could be less like a mass or a crowd, in which unconsciousness, anonymity, and the fatalities of instinct hold sway.

Reflecting on the condition of the incarnate person and of the human community, certain contemporary thinkers have insisted on a network of carnal and historical relations that condition their essentially spiritual reality, either on the basis of mediation or of expression. The saying is that man lives in a historical context, and every human reality is dependent upon history even if it is basically outside of history. The same is true of the Church. An idealistic trend of thought formerly made it difficult for many to accept the historical condition of the Church. Now that the pendulum has swung back toward realistic thought concerning the person, we have reason to hope for fruitful analogies that will help us to understand in faith the will of Christ for the Church on earth.

This Church is not purely a community: she is a community, and she is still becoming one; she is a community and she is the means of becoming one. And even the aspect by which she is already a community finds expression in a symbolism that stems from the world of flesh. The whole institutional and sacramental reality of the present-day Church finds its justification as the necessary accompaniment of a community still in search of its perfect personalization. And the risen Lord makes use of the mediations of His incarnate community, just as in the days of His mortal life He made use of the mediations of His historical humanity, to transmit eternal life. This function of mediation does not exhaust the institutional necessity of the Church, which is also in part brilliantly visible, and the symbolic expression of the eschatological community. For example, the liturgy and Catholic unity will have their equivalent in the eternal community from which mediations will be excluded. The Institution is justified as much by the indigence of the historical Church as by her perfection.

2. THE ECCLESIASTICAL MINISTRY

A. The depositaries of the hierarchical ministry

(a) *Christ, the Head of His visible Body*

Christ is essentially the Head of His Body inasmuch as *the life* of this Body depends upon His capital grace. But insofar as this Body takes the form of a society, Christ is also, in the primacy of His capital grace, the master of this *organ of growth* of His Mystical Body. He is Prophet, Priest, King and Pastor. In the glorified Church of eternity where everything will be spiritual, these functions will be reabsorbed into the function of the immanent communication of glory. The Church will be wholly prophetic, priestly, and royal, in vital dependence upon her Lord.

But the Church of earth needs a Prophet to give her the object of her divine faith. She needs a Priest who will place in her hands the life-giving sacrifice of the Savior and who will unite her to His acceptable worship of God. She needs a Pastor who will orientate her progress toward the city of the saints. Christ is the Way, the Life, and the Truth. He is the Head of the Church-as-Institution, as well as of the mystical Church, just as the Holy Spirit is the soul of the one Church in her dual aspects. Christ, in His glorified humanity, remains the one Minister of universal holiness in history.

When Jesus visibly departed from this world, He left His Spirit and His apostolic ministry to His Church: His Spirit as her inward reality, His ministry as her external reality. It is thanks to the Spirit and to the ministry that the Pasch of Christ becomes the Pasch of the Church. Pentecost, from which the earthly Church came forth, actualizes in time the life-giving power of the risen Lord. "All power in heaven and on earth has been given to Me. Go, therefore, and make disciples of all nations, baptizing them in the name of the Father, and of the Son, and of the Holy Spirit, teaching them to observe all that I have commanded you; and behold, I am with you all days, even unto the consummation of the world" (Matt. 28:18-20).

Evangelizing the nations is the *prophetic* office; baptizing them is the *priestly* office (and Baptism must be understood as the type of Christian worship); making them keep the Commandments is the *pastoral office*. And all three offices are exercised in the name of Christ who continues to act in His Church. This is the whole charter of the ecclesiastical ministry.

(b) *Apostolicity*

We cannot read the Synoptic Gospels without being impressed by the place that Jesus willed His Apostles to have in His Church. They were not simply the first believers destined to become witnesses of the life, death, and resurrection of their Lord. They were, in the words of St. Paul, the foundation on which the Church was built (Eph. 2:20-22). And yet is not Christ, by Himself alone, the foundation and the cornerstone of the Temple of God (see Eph. 2:20; I Cor. 3:11; I Pet. 2:4-8)? Most certainly. But the Apostles are by the will of Christ what He is by His own power as the Lord. Christ has said: "I am the light of the world" (Jn. 8:12); and He said to His Apostles: "You are the light of the world" (Mt. 5:14). Again: "I am the door" (Jn. 10:9); and in the Apocalypse the Apostles of the Lamb are the twelve gates of the holy city (Apoc. 21:13-14). Christ is the Shepherd (Jn. 10:11; 21:15-17; I Pet. 2:25); and the Apostles are shepherds (I Pet. 5:2-5). Christ alone holds the key to the Messianic Kingdom (Apoc. 1:18; 3:7); and He gave the keys of the Kingdom to the Apostles (Mt. 16:19; 18:18).

These Biblical images, as well as the powers with which Christ invested the Twelve, clearly show that the Church willed by Christ can be nothing if not the diffusion of apostolicity. We know the powers summed up in the text from Matthew cited above: to preach the Gospel (Lk. 16:15-16); to remit sins in the name of Christ (Mt. 18:18; Jn. 20:23); and to celebrate the Supper of the New Covenant (Lk. 22:19-20).

It is indeed Christ who retains full control of His Kingdom. His apostles do not take His place, but simply represent Him as permanent envoys, until He comes again.

(c) *The primacy of Peter*

Within the Apostolic College, Peter ranked first in apostolicity. The Gospel texts transmit our Lord's most explicit words concerning the primacy that He willed to confer upon him: "I say to thee, thou art Peter, and upon this rock I will build my Church, and the gates of hell shall not prevail against it. And I will give thee the keys of the kingdom of heaven; and whatever thou shalt bind on earth shall be bound in heaven; and whatever thou shalt loose on earth shall be loosed in heaven" (Mt. 16:18-19. Cf. Lk. 22:31-32; Jn. 21:15-17).

The record of the Apostles' words and deeds in the Gospels, the Acts, and the Pauline Epistles provides the most reliable proof that Peter translated the meaning of these words into action, and that the other Apostles acknowledged him to have effective superiority in the work of the ministry. When St. Luke speaks of the Apostolic College he often says: "Peter (with the) Eleven" (Acts 2:14); "Peter and the rest of the Apostles" (Acts 2:37); "Peter and the Apostles" (Acts 5:29). In the Acts of the Apostles, Peter takes the initiative in the election of Matthias (Acts 1:15-26). He speaks in the name of all the Apostles to bear witness to Christ (Acts 2:12-36; 4:5-22; 5:27-32). At the Council of Jerusalem, Peter sets forth his views with authority and all acquiesce (Acts 15:1-29).

In the Pauline Epistles, Paul goes up to Jerusalem to question Cephas (Gal. 1:18-19); in Paul's account of the Council of Jerusalem, Peter is presented as the leader of the apostolate of circumcision (Gal. 2:1-10). Moreover, a close study of the conflict of Antioch will reveal it to be an incontestable proof of Peter's supremacy (Gal. 2:11-14).

Since it is impossible for us to give a detailed exegesis of the Petrine texts in this study, we shall limit ourselves to making a few general reflections on the sixteenth chapter of St. Matthew:

1. The similarity in literary style will be noted between this passage and the promises made to the patriarchs in the Book of Genesis: After God had revealed His identity, He changed the name of the person to whom He was speaking, conferred upon him a newly created authority over the people, and promised him a numerous and royal posterity together with a territory to be governed. Through Peter's confession of faith, Christ made men acknowledge His divinity; by changing Simon's name to Peter (Rock),

He invested Peter with a vocation to be the permanent foundation of His Church. And Christ's promise was: the victory and eternal destiny of this Church, in which heaven and earth would be brought together.

2. It was not by virtue of his personal holiness but through his divine vocation and mission that Peter became the Rock of the Church. In fact, his weakness was pointed out on the occasion of each investiture (Mt. 16:22-23; Lk. 22:34). Christ's fidelity is the sole foundation of Peter's.

3. Peter's role was no different from that of the other Apostles. He simply epitomized their roles. Christ gave to Peter individually all the power that He gave to the Twelve undividedly (cf., e.g., Mt. 16:19 and Mt. 18:18). Peter was the head of the Apostolic College.

Protestant theology has contested the literary and historical authenticity as well as the meaning of the Petrine texts. But it is now tending more and more to approach the Catholic positions. At the heart of the primitive catechesis on the Church instituted by Jesus Christ there is a "Simon-Peter mystery," an apostolic primacy of Peter.

(d) *The apostolic succession*

The Catholic Church holds that the Episcopal College, inasmuch as its head is the Pope of Rome, succeeds the Apostolic College whose center was Simon-Peter, and that this is an historical succession. Two preliminary remarks will prevent errors concerning the Church's dogmatic position: 1) It is understood that the Twelve have an exceptional place in the Church and that their role as the first Apostles remains historically unique. 2) The Episcopal College succeeds the Apostles and not Christ Himself. In affirming these things, we have no intention of diminishing the role of the Holy Spirit, under the pretext of historical succession. For it is in the Spirit who is ever-active in the Church that the historical succession takes on the value of a mystery.

Now that we have made these things clear, we must establish the position of the Catholic Church. Scripture makes no explicit affirmation of this sort. It appears that the words of apostolic investiture cited above apply directly only to Peter and to the Eleven. Our Lord did not command them to choose their own successors in the apostolic ministry. The fact remains that Christ's promise to be with them until the end of the world seems clearly to be addressed beyond the Apostolic College to successors, inasmuch as the Twelve were to die before the Second Coming. And it goes without saying that when Christ founded a Church that was to be visibly prolonged upon earth, He intended to assure her an apostolic succession until His Second Coming.

We find this intention of Christ's particularly implicit in the command to celebrate the Lord's Supper. If Christ's sacramental Body was to remain the living treasure of the life of the Church, Christ's command called for a transmission of the apostolic powers; for He gave this power only to His Apostles. Jesus bequeathed to His Spirit quickening the Church the task of reminding the Church of what He had said, of keeping her faithful. Now, apostolicity was so clearly affirmed by Jesus that it could not help being a permanent element of His Church among men, a structure that the Spirit, far from supplanting, protects during the earthly life of the Church.

So it is that at the end of the apostolic generation a stable hierarchy was already organized in dependence upon the Apostles, as recorded notably in St. Paul's pastoral Epistles. Before the middle of the second century, we have proofs of the existence of a single bishop at the head of the local, established churches, a bishop who was surrounded by a college of presbyters and deacons (see St. Ignatius of Antioch [circa 110]: *Epistle to the Magnesians* 6:1; *Epistles to the Trallians* 3:1). Writing to the Smyrnians (8:2), the same St. Ignatius says: "Wherever the Bishop is, let the community be, just as wherever Christ is, there is the Catholic Church." His *Letter to the Romans* also contains a precious testimony in favor of the Roman primacy (3:1). The Episcopal College effectively succeeded the Apostolic College, and continued to multiply with the proliferation of local churches.

At the end of the second century, St. Irenaeus sought to establish the purity of faith of the local churches by affirming the uninterrupted succession of bishops in these churches since the Apostles. And as it would have taken too long to give the apostolic succession of all the churches, he felt it sufficient to give the apostolic succession of the Church of Rome, "the greatest, the most ancient, the best known by all and founded by the glorious Apostles Peter and Paul. Indeed, it is with this Church, because of its more powerful origin, that all the churches must be in harmony everywhere, for it is in the Church of Rome that all the faithful of the world have preserved the apostolic tradition" (*Adv. Haer.* 3:3). Even today, the Apostolic Church instituted by Christ is constituted by the Episcopal College in its entirety in communion with its head, the Bishop of Rome, Peter's successor. So will it be until the Second Coming.

(e) *The Roman succession*

The general problem posed by the apostolic succession is best seen with regard to the relation between Peter and the Bishop of Rome.

It is evident from the very nature of the promises Jesus made to Peter that He entrusted Peter with a mission that went beyond his historical person. These promises hold good for the entire duration of the Church. It is therefore for the temporal life of the Church that the power that corresponds to these promises must be exercised. The mission was to continue, according to the incarnational logic that governed the foundation of the Church-as-sacrament.

In actual fact, the Church of the first centuries recognized that the primacy of Peter was perpetuated in the Bishop of Rome. This general conviction held by the primitive Church implies Peter's coming to Rome and his episcopacy in that city. There is an historical fact involved here whose scientific proofs have become increasingly reliable, based on early testimony as well as on archaeological discoveries, even though the details of Peter's coming to Rome and of his death are still obscure.

The modalities of the primacy of Peter's successor were to become clearer amid many difficulties, as the Church took on geographical universality and developed through the centuries. It was not all clear and precise from the start, but the trend was toward the development of an effective Roman primacy in the matter of teaching and jurisdiction. Was it a human development? Yes, in the sense that it occurred in history and through historical circumstances. No, in the sense that the Holy Spirit has guaranteed the unbroken continuity between the very first tradition to which the New Testament texts bear witness and the present life of the Church. There is nothing in the Apostolic Church of today that contradicts the affirmations of Scripture. Rather the Church today constitutes a living commentary on them.

The *Apostolic* Church is, historically speaking, also the *Roman* Church, by which we do not mean the *Latin* Church.

B. The work of the ministry

(a) The Church of faith and of the sacraments

The whole work of the ecclesiastical ministry consists in putting men in contact with the life-giving Mystery of Christ, so that under its continuing influence they may be renewed in the likeness of Christ and receive the Holy Spirit. Now, according to Scripture, we become sons of God and members of Christ through faith in Jesus as the Son of God and as our Savior, and through the sacrament of faith, namely, Baptism. For this faith and the sacrament of faith constitute as it were two moments in a single process of entering into the mystery of salvation. And it is through the Eucharist, the sacrament of the same faith, that the grace of Baptism is made full.

Now the Church, ruled by the Apostles and their successors as vicars of Christ, was constituted and built by faith and the sacraments of faith. It is through these mediations of the Church that the power of Christ makes contact with us. The whole raison d'être of the pope and the bishops—and of all those to whom they have entrusted a subordinate part in their ministry, such as priests, deacons, etc.—is to preach the faith that saves, to administer the sacraments, and to raise up communities of holiness.

The Acts of the Apostles tell us that the faithful "continued steadfastly in the teaching of the apostles and in the communion of the breaking of the bread and in the prayers" (Acts 2:42). Could there be a better way of expressing the diverse functions of the ministry of holiness that the Church exercises?

(b) The prophetic function of the Church

Just as Christ the Prophet came to bear witness to the Truth (Jn. 18:37), so His Apostles and their successors received the mission of being His witnesses and of preaching the Gospel to every creature (Mk. 16:15; Acts 1:8). With the end of the Apostolic Age, Revelation came to a close. Thenceforth the prophetic function of the Church, "the pillar and mainstay of the truth" (I Tim. 3:15), was to guard the deposit (I Tim. 6:20), to transmit written or oral Apostolic Tradition (II Thess. 2:15), to understand and proclaim the meaning of these truths with the assistance of the Spirit of Christ. The saving truth of the Mystery of Christ has lived on in the divine memory and consciousness of the Church. Even the Bible—that privileged expression of God's Revelation—belongs to the Church. Scripture was born in the Church and is God's word only in the Church's act of faith. It is therefore only by living in the Church's communion of faith and love that Scripture can be understood, just as we understand the writings of someone whose thoughts are already familiar to us.

Only the whole Episcopal College united to Peter's successor enjoys infallibility in matters of faith, whether it expresses itself in many scattered localities (the ordinary and universal Magisterium) or whether it is assembled in an ecumenical Council (the extraordinary Magisterium). The same privilege is attached to the solemnly promulgated doctrinal definitions of the pope, according to the common faith of the Church formulated by the Vatican Council. According to the terms of this Council, the primacy of the Bishop of Rome, Peter's successor, has the infallibility in matters of faith which Christ promised to Peter (cf. Lk. 22:32):

> When the Roman Pontiff speaks *ex cathedra,* when in the exercise of his function as Pastor and Doctor of all Christians, and by virtue of his supreme apostolic authority, he defines that a doctrine of faith or morals must be held by the Universal Church, then thanks to the divine assistance that has been promised him in the person of Blessed Peter, he enjoys the infallibility with which the divine Redeemer willed to endow His Church when she defines a doctrine of faith or morals. It follows that such definitions by the Roman Pontiff are irrevocable in themselves and not by the fact of the Church's consent to them. (Session 4, Const. *Pastor aeternus,* Chapter 4, Denz. 1839.)

It should be noted that all the conditions specified in this definition must be conjointly present to assure the charism of infallibility. Rather than speak of the infallibility of the person of the Sovereign Pontiff, it would be more exact to speak of the infallibility of certain acts of his Magisterium (those that belong to the extraordinary Magisterium). Such is the position taken by the Vatican Council in its pronouncement after the discussion.

It is also very important to stress that the Council assigns this infallibility to certain of the Sovereign Pontiff's acts in their relation to the infallibility of the Church's Magisterium, that is, in their relation to the infallibility of the Episcopal College. The pope may never be held up in opposition to the Council, nor the Council in opposition to the pope. There is a *collegial infallibility* in which *all* the bishops, in communion with the Roman Pontiff, are judges of the faith. There is likewise a *personal infallibility* of the pope in which Peter's successor, *by virtue of the charism that belongs spe-*

cifically to him, epitomizes the infallibility of the whole Church as her principal member.

In earlier volumes of this *The Theology Library,* a detailed study has been made of the nature and functioning of the Church's various Magisteriums (Volume I, pp. 16-31; Volume III, pp. 26-28 and 43-46).

Indeed, the prophetic function of the Church should not be reduced to her dogmatic Magisterium, under the pretext that, sociologically speaking, this is its most exceptional and objective aspect. The principal axis of the Church's prophetic mission consists in evangelical preaching, and in all the forms of catechesis that actualize the word of God in the Church. By divine institution, every bishop has the responsibility of evangelizing his diocese. And the Roman See, using many forms through the centuries, strives to make the word of the living God heard throughout the world, for through His Church God's Revelation must ever govern the acts of the whole human race.

To this end, the hierarchy uses the help of priests, theologians, and even of the ordinary faithful, on the basis of their faith and of the character conferred upon them by the sacraments of Baptism and Confirmation. The customary distinction between the *teaching Church* and the *Church taught* should not be misinterpreted to mean that the community of believers is purely a passive one. On the contrary, there exists among believers a true *infallibility of the community,* a gift of the Spirit. The Holy Spirit can also give charisms of testimony to the faithful, obviously under the control of the teaching hierarchy; for Apostolic Revelation transmitted to the hierarchy remains the rule of faith. Through the bishops, it is the Apostles who teach; through the Apostles, it is the personal Christ who teaches the mystical Christ. Blessed be the Church, that majestic mother on whose knees we have learned everything we know!

The preaching of the Church is the same everywhere and remains equal, based on the testimony of the Prophets, of the Apostles, and of all the disciples, . . . acting through the action of God who effects the salvation of man and abides within our faith. This is the faith we preserve, having received it from the Church; this faith which under the action of the Spirit of God, like a precious liquor kept in an excellent vessel, restores youth and even renews the vessel that contains it. . . . For where the Church is, there also is the Spirit of God; and where the Spirit of God is, there also is the

Church and all her grace. And the Spirit is truth (St. Irenaeus, *Adversus Haereses*, Book III, Chapter 24).

(c) *The priestly function of the Church*

The priest is the one who offers up sacrifice. Christ offered up the sacrifice of all creatures once and for all. God accepted the glorification and love that this sacrifice expressed, and His acceptance inaugurated a New Covenant between God and men. The whole sanctifying cult of the Church flows from Christ's sacrifice (which began at the moment of His Incarnation and was consummated on the Cross). "For by one offering he has perfected forever those who are sanctified" (Heb. 10:14). And the entire cult of Israel prefigured it. The Church's priestly function consists in offering to God in the name of the total Christ the one, permanent sacrifice of Christ the Head, and in communicating to the Body the life-giving effects stemming from the divine acceptance, effects which are the glory of the Head.

All the Christian sacraments derive their unity from the great sacrifice that consists in the sacred and sacrificed humanity of Christ. Because of their symbolic aspect and because of the lively faith in the mystery of Christ demanded of those who participate in them, the sacraments constitute the supreme acts of Christian worship. Through the life-giving aspect of their symbolism they place the faithful in immediate contact with the universal source of all justification and of all communicated holiness, namely, "He who lives, . . . was dead, and (lives) forevermore" (Apoc. 1:18).

The Eucharist is the supreme fulfillment of this twofold reality of the Christian sacrament, and that is why it constitutes the central act of the Church's priestly ministry. The Eucharist contains the Victim of the one sacrifice of the New Covenant who was offered once and for all historically, and yet continues to offer Himself sacramentally in and for His Church. The other sacraments apply the influx of grace flowing from the Passion of Christ only partially and only in relation to the plenary sacrament of the Eucharist. In the Eucharistic celebration, however, the Church makes contact with life-giving Plenitude in itself. Even Baptism, that bath of regeneration in the mystery of Christ and of renewal in the Spirit which, according to St. Paul, is so vital to the constitution of the Body of Christ, calls for greater perfection: it is orientated to the Eucharist and prepares the way for it. We can understand why theological tradition is unanimous in looking upon the unity of the Mystical Body as the ultimate reality of the sacrament of the Body of Christ: "Because the bread is one, we though many, are one body, all of us who partake of the one bread" (I Cor. 10:17).

Thus the priestly function of the Church centers around the Christian sacraments, which for their part are polarized by the Holy Eucharist. But the sacramental act itself is only the summit of the sacral celebration of the Church. Actually, it is the whole liturgy with its commemoration of the mysteries of Christ, with its constellation of sacramentals, that establishes the life-giving contact between the people and God in the mystical mediation of Christ. The only thing to do is to enter with a lively faith into this mystagogy, and allow oneself to be transformed by the Church's sacral life, so as to progressively make one's own the salvation and the glory of God that are in Christ. The Church brings forth the Church; it is Christ who continues to beget Christ, perpetuating His Pasch.

The bishops, as the Apostles' successors, have the responsibility of exercising the priestly function. They are the leaders of the sacrificial and sanctifying liturgy in the wayfaring Church. Simple priests and sacred ministers are associated to this function by virtue of the priestly character in which they participate through the sacrament of Holy Orders. Now St. Thomas declares that every sacramental character constitutes a participation in the priesthood of Christ (IIIa, q. 63, a. 3). If we agree with him we must grant that all baptized Christians are in some lesser degree ministers of the Church's priestly function not only with regard to interior worship but also with regard to exterior and sacramental worship in its few non-hierarchical acts (such as the sacrament of marriage).

Scripture bears witness to the priestly function of the faithful: "You . . . are a royal priesthood" (I Pet. 2:9). These words of St. Peter's echo the text of Exodus 19:5-6. In the Apocalypse (1:6) we also read: "To him who has . . . made us to be a kingdom, and priests to God his Father—to him belong glory and dominion forever and ever." It is in virtue of their belonging to Christ-the-Priest that laymen have been allowed in certain cases to preside over assemblies of non-sacrificial worship and to celebrate the Eucharistic worship together with the hierarchical ministers. Prayer, offering, communion: these are the acts of worship exercised by laymen in the Church. The effect of excommunication is to deprive them of

these functions. Failure to exercise these functions is to behave like
an excommunicated person.

(d) *The pastoral function of the Church*

Christ is the one and only pastor of souls, He is the Good Shepherd of the Gospel parable (Jn. 10:7-16). But "the Prince of the
shepherds," as St. Peter says (I Pet. 5:4), has entrusted God's flock
to His Apostles and to their successors. The Epistles of St. Paul
are full of commands and counsels directed to the reign of charity
in the communities under his care. Indeed, how could the prophetic
and priestly functions be exercised in the Church-as-society, without a minimum of government? The one and only law of the New
Covenant is the law of the Holy Spirit living in men's hearts. And
yet in the present state of the Church, this law needs to be translated and its exercise aided by an exterior government. On the other
hand, to be content with the authoritarian aspect of the Church-as-
society without relating it to a concrete life, amounts to betraying
the Christian message as seriously as if one were content with the
Church of charity without passing through the hierarchy. It would
be preferring the letter to the spirit, and we know that "the Lord is
the spirit; and where the Spirit of the Lord is, there is freedom"
(II Cor. 3:17).

It is the pastoral function of the Church to assure the reign of
Christian morality in the Body of Christ; to see first of all that the
divine Commandments are obeyed through love, but also to specify
through her authority all that will nurture the spirit of Christ among
the faithful. In her pastoral function the Church has a broader
initiative, her power is less purely instrumental, and the object of
her power is less strictly determined than in her prophetic and
priestly functions. The Church exercises the power to legislate, to
judge, and to punish, like every other society, but she does all these
things in the Lord. She scrupulously guards all that pertains to
divine right, but she does not hesitate to adapt to diverse circumstances all which in her government constitutes the human wrapping
of the divine and apostolic deposit.

It is in her pastoral function that the Church reveals her human
countenance. The government of a society implies institutional and
administrative structures, customs that run the risk of being too
much bound up with temporal structures and of giving the Church
the appearance of a purely human society. And yet these institu-

tions and customs can serve the ends of Christian living to advantage in various times and places. The Christian can and must know how to judge those aspects of the Church's ministry that are of divine or apostolic institution and those that are of ecclesiastical institution or born of sociological contingencies. Thus, there are many things that could be otherwise, and it might even be better if they were.

Divine assistance has never been lacking to the Roman Pontiffs, but that does not signify that the government centralized through the organ of the Congregations, according to the type inherited from the sixteenth century and reinforced by the ultramontanism of the nineteenth century, has always existed. Opinions that are unfavorable to the temporal power of the popes are not a challenge to the Roman primacy. But while it is normal for the opinions of the faithful to be colored by the attitudes of their time, it is never permissible for them to be insubordinate or to deny the Church's authority. For their faith in the Church would be involved. A fundamentally anticlerical attitude would be proof of a deep infidelity to the spirit of Christ.

Government and jurisdiction are essentially episcopal privileges in the Church, in which simple priests are granted only a meager share. The pope holds effective pre-eminence in the entire Church through the Episcopal College, just as Peter did through the Apostolic College (see Jn. 21:15-17). The pope's jurisdiction has no territorial limits and its exercise is subject to no intermediary. To quote one of the canons of the Vatican Council:

> "If anyone says that the Roman Pontiff possesses only a function of inspection or direction, but no full and supreme power of jurisdiction over the entire Church, not only in matters of faith and morals, but in all that concerns the discipline and the government of the Church over the whole world; or if he says that the Sovereign Pontiff has only the principal part but not the fullness of this supreme power, or if he claims that this power is not ordinary and immediate with regard to each and every church as well as to each and every pastor and member of the faithful, let him be anathema" (Session 4, Const. *Pastor aeternus,* Chapter 3, Denz. 1831).

Let us note in passing that papal infallibility, like conciliar infallibility—under the conditions set forth above—extends to moral questions as well.

The bishop possesses the same governing powers in his own church as the pope exercises over the universal Church. St. Cyprian wrote to a schismatic deacon: "You must know that in the Church there is one bishop, and that the Church is in the bishop. If anyone is not united to the bishop, he is not in the Church. The members of the Church are those who form a people united to their priest, a flock cleaving to its shepherd" (Epist. 79, P.L. 4, 406). The fact that episcopal jurisdiction must be exercised in communion with the jurisdiction of Peter's successor in order to preserve its fully apostolic quality does not mean it is simply a power delegated by the pope. The Code of Canon Law affirms: "The bishops are the successors of the Apostles. They are appointed by divine right over the particular churches that they govern with an ordinary power under the authority of the Roman Pontiff" (C.J.C. 329).

The primacy of the pope does not correspond to the primacy of a head that creates its own body. Rather is it like a body that finds its unity in a head in which the body is epitomized without losing its identity. The constitution of the Church is unique and original. It is based on faith in the will of Christ, and this fact must not be forgotten when attempts are made to designate the Church's constitution by such political expressions as monarchy, oligarchy, etc., or by military comparisons.

It has sometimes happened, especially since the pontificate of Pius IX, that a legitimate but unenlightened devotion to the Sovereign Pontiff has led some persons to speak of the Roman primacy in inexact terms that eliminate the direct apostolic succession of the bishops. Such is certainly not the teaching of the Vatican Council, despite certain interpretations that are more Roman than Rome itself.

The Council took care to affirm: "The power of the Sovereign Pontiff does not impinge upon the ordinary and immediate power of jurisdiction of the bishops who, placed by the Holy Spirit, have succeeded the Apostles, and feed and govern like true shepherds the flocks that have been assigned to them respectively. On the contrary, the episcopal power is strengthened, affirmed, and defended by the supreme and universal shepherd" (Session 4, C. 3, Denz. 1828). As this text did not silence all discussion, Pope Pius IX, in January, 1875, approved the following declaration by the German Episcopate as authoritatively interpreting the thought of the Vatican Council:

. . . According to these doctrines of the Catholic Church, the Pope is the Bishop of Rome, but not the bishop of any other diocese or city. He is neither the bishop of Breslau, nor the bishop of Cologne, etc. . . . But in his quality as Bishop of Rome he is also Pope, that is, the pastor and supreme head of the Universal Church, the head of all the bishops and of all the faithful. . . . In this position the Pope must see that every bishop fulfills his duty over the whole area of his responsibilities. If a bishop is prevented from doing his duty, the Pope has the right and the duty, not as bishop of this particular diocese but as Pope, to order all that is necessary for the administration of the diocese.

The decisions of the Vatican Council do not offer the shadow of a pretext for claiming that the Pope has become an absolute sovereign because of these decisions. . . . The term "absolute monarch" may not be applied to the Pope in ecclesiastical matters, because he himself is subject to divine law, and he is bound by the intentions Jesus Christ has set forth for His Church. . . .

It is in virtue of this same divine institution, on which the papacy rests, that the episcopate is founded. The episcopate also has its rights and its duties in virtue of this institution given by God Himself, and the Pope has neither the right nor the power to change them. It is therefore completely erroneous to believe that by reason of the Vatican Council's decisions papal jurisdiction absorbs episcopal jurisdiction; that the Pope has replaced each individual bishop in principle; that the bishops are now simply instruments of the Pope and his functionaries without any responsibility of their own. . . . For the bishops were instituted by the Holy Spirit and put in the Apostles' places; and as true shepherds they feed and rule the flocks entrusted to their care. . . .

With reference to the affirmation that the bishops have become pontifical functionaries without any personal responsibility of their own, the Catholic Church does not accept the immoral and despotic principle that the command of a superior releases his subordinates without restriction from personal responsibility.

Finally, . . . infallibility extends exclusively to the Sovereign Pontiff's supreme teaching power, and this power extends over exactly the same area as the infallible teaching of the Church: it is bound to the contents of Sacred Scripture and to Tradition, as well as to the doctrinal decisions previously made by the teaching of the Church.

(e) *The hierarchical ministry and the ministries*

Christ associates the Church to the expansion of His Paschal mystery, not only as His beneficiary but also as His mediatrix. This mediation is the work of the hierarchical ministry. But the *whole* Church, and not just the hierarchy, is active in Christ for her self-edification. We have mentioned in passing the participation of the laity in the hierarchy's ministry, but that is not the whole story. There are two other sources of ministries in the Church: 1) The *spiritual ministries* that the "saints" of the Church triumphant as well as the Church militant exercise through their intercession and their merits in favor of the Body of Christ which is the Church (see Col. 1:24; I Pet. 3:12); 2) the *charismatic ministries,* which were very well developed in the early days of the Church, and which God continues to raise up in certain Christians to enable them to answer a specific need in the life of the Church.

Thus each of the Church's mediatory functions is accomplished in an organic manner on the threefold level of the institutional ministry, the spiritual ministry, and the charismatic ministry.

(a) As to the *prophetic function,* we have seen that the institutional ministry has the mission of teaching and preaching; the laity share in this function as public witnesses. The spiritual ministry consists in prayer (Col. 4:3) and in a fervent faith that corrects any tendency to formalism. The charismatic ministry establishes certain Christians in an exceptional vocation as evangelists capable of making Christ's message comprehensible to the mentality of their own time.

(b) As to the *priestly function,* all the faithful, by reason of their baptismal character, take an active part in praying, offering up, and communing in the sacramental worship over which the hierarchic priesthood presides. The corresponding spiritual ministry consists in the interior sacrifice (redemptive suffering) of the whole life of all Christians. The charismatic ministry may take on the form, for example, of a gift for public thanksgiving.

(c) As to the *pastoral function,* the authority that belongs specifically to the hierarchy is brought into play. This does not prevent the faithful from participating in this institutional ministry chiefly under the aspect of the institution of the family and in the charitable organizations of communities. Here the spiritual ministry consists in the support and edification that a life of evangelical integrity brings to the community. As for the charismatic ministry, it would consist in efforts to keep the Church young and to adapt it to each generation through such means as religious orders, forms of devotion, and various works.

So it is that "God has set the members, each of them, in the body as he willed. Now if they were all one member, where would the body be? . . . Now there are varieties of gifts, but the same Spirit; and there are varieties of ministries, but the same Lord; and there are varieties of workings, but the same God, who works all things in all" (I Cor. 12:18-19; 4-6). It follows that we must not set up the diverse ministries that build up the Church in opposition

If it is true that the faith of believers finds expression in images of their own creation, it is equally exact to say that the same faith seizes upon all the representations that spontaneously suit it or are capable in one way or another of becoming suitable to it, even if they are foreign to this faith in the beginning. Was it not by virtue of an analogous principle that the first Christian artists presented Christ with the features of Hermes or Orpheus?

"Whenever there reappears on the statue of a woman the mysterious reflection by which one recognizes the presence of the Blessed Virgin, the Church bows and prays in her turn." Could not this thought of André Malraux in his *Musée imaginaire de la sculpture mondiale* well serve as the key to this astonishing and devout work of art.

But do we even need to ask this question? Many examples could reassure us. We have only to think of the Chinese image of the famous Kouan-Yin, the Buddhist divinity of mercy and of the gift of life which, during the centuries when Christianity was severely prohibited and persecuted in Japan, was spontaneously used by Christians as an image of the Blessed Virgin (see P. Humbertclaude, S. M., *"Maria-Kwannon,* Marian iconography in Japan during the persecution," in *L'Apôtre de Marie,* August-November, 1953, pp. 97-104). Might it not amount to impiety on the part of Christians to pass by what is beautiful, or true, or good, outside their churches, without "recognizing" it?

Maternity, by Pablo Picasso (1901).

to one another. This is why the strictly apostolic ministry in its institutional form keeps its priority. We do not mean that everything stems from this ministry, but that all the other ministries must be carried on in communion with it and in the end be judged by it, in the name of the Spirit of Christ.

(f) Christian life in the Church

It is only by living integrally in the Church that the member of Christ is assured of meeting his Head and his God. It is only on board this ship that he will safely travel toward the shores of the city of the saints. The Church brought him forth in Baptism. Within the framework of the diocese and the parish she continues to nourish him with the words of life and with the Eucharist. Through her public prayer and her sacramental cult, she kindles devotion and eagerness for union with God and with Christ. At the same time she obtains for the Christian the divine assistance he needs to live his new life faithfully in accordance with the demands of his human life or with respect to the function that has been assigned to him in the Mystical Body.

By her pastoral government, the Church authoritatively inspires the charity of the faithful, orientating its interior dynamism in a spirit of Catholic unity toward works that are certainly pleasing to God. She protects the faithful from whatever could endanger their charity, and places it within a juridical and prudential order in which, without lessening the spontaneity of nature and grace, everything is conceived so as to favor the fruitful participation in the sources of divine life and the activation of the dynamism of grace in every aspect of life. Finally, in the Church the baptized Christian finds the efficacious fraternal support of charity and the mysterious solidarity of the communion of saints that make it easier for him to resist the Evil One and safeguard his Christian vitality.

St. Augustine used to say to his flock: "Keep close to this mother; for she brought you forth. No one can have God as his Father if he scorns Mother Church. Finally, it is this holy and wholly spiritual mother who prepares each day the food for your souls."

In the wayfaring state of the Church, society and community coexist, for God gives Himself to man externally under a social form, but He really gives Himself. A few laws of this coexistence can now be set forth.

To begin with, *there is a subordination of society to community* in the Church. The essence of the Church, the eternal Church, is the community. This is true even now, in spite of the Church's present incomplete condition in time. The common good of ecclesial society is the communion of all in God and of all in all: it is the fulfillment of God's words, whose purpose is to gather up all men in God and in Christ; it is glory and grace; it is a people of individual persons perfected in God. And even now the community constitutes this ultimate common good, in the measure to which God has already been given and partially assimilated in the Church of Pentecost.

Two important conclusions can be drawn from the fact of this subordination of society to community.

1. *Society has no autonomous value.* That is true of even the most perfect temporal society, which reaches its ultimate expression in the community of persons, the immanent common good of the human race—one that is at the service of human values and is measured entirely in terms of these values. And yet the human community is never actualized except in a close symbiosis with society. It has been reserved for the Church alone to tend toward a wholly spiritual and inward state. In the Church the distinction between society and community reaches its maximum expression because of the Church's human-divine nature. Human society, on the other hand, never gets beyond the time of education and outwardness.

Consequently, ecclesial society must take even greater care not to look upon itself as its own end. For the whole ministry of the Church is a ministry of mediation, and the absolute value that she mediates—namely, Christ—is absolutely transcendent to her. The ministries—the hierarchy and the sacraments—fashion the community as an instrument of God: in the words of the liturgy, *opus redemptionis exercetur.* To the extent that the ministries symbolize the community, they do so as a symbol of society rather than as a symbol of community, i.e., as the symbol of a common good to come rather than the externalization of a common good already possessed and assimilated.

The Church, as an institution, constitutes an all-embracing sacrament of the Reality of life that gives it its purpose. Christ, like an artist who models a work of art with the help of a mold, assimilates His Church to Himself by means of the institution. In other words, the features of the exterior Church are the same as those of the interior Church, just as the concavity of the mold is identical to the convexity of the work of art. There is an interrelationship between the sacramental unity and the interior unity, between sacramental holiness and moral holiness.

Everything about the Church-as-society must be justified by the end that constitutes the advent of the community. The power of society for its own sake would signify nothing but a patterning upon a profane society with a temporal goal. The grandeur of the Church-as-society consists in serving and in being totally defined in terms of her being ordered to the community. In this regard, the principal quality of ecclesiastical society must be purity in its steadfastness to its mission. Those in positions of authority in the Church will never have done meditating the example and the words of Christ when He washed His Apostles' feet at the Last Supper (Jn. 13:1-18; Lk. 22:24-28).

We could analyze in this light certain words such as "the power of the Church" or "the triumph of the Church." It must be clearly understood that in this approach the power of the Church consists first of all in holiness. The Church-as-institution will be powerful in times when she has favored the growth of holiness, and not necessarily in times when she has organized many conferences or signed many concordats with states, rallied many Christian parties, or been honored in political life. All these things must in the last analysis be judged by the interior growth of holiness.

The Church must never allow her societal aspect to take on autonomy, nor may she perform acts that are not strictly legitimized by her inward reality. Under no condition may the Church pattern herself upon a purely human society, with all that a human society involves in the way of distinctions, titles, and rewards, inasmuch as such a society is established wholly on a visible level of reality. On the contrary, the Church must always tend toward the perfection of her inward reality.

2. The Church-as-society must be concerned not only with referring her activity to her transcendent common good: God and Christ, manifested by divine Revelation. She must also refer her acts to her immanent and already assimilated common good: the community. The Church-as-society must be subject to the spirit of Christ living in the community.

This second conclusion is of great importance for teaching and discipline in the Church. When the hierarchic Church teaches God's

Revelation, it is in virtue of her own particular charism (*ex se, non autem ex consensu Ecclesiae*), and yet also in accordance with the truth of Christ assimilated by the *agape* of the community. We cannot conceive that the hierarchy should ever promulgate laws or definitions against the community. The hierarchic charism and the *agape* are correlatives, born of the same spirit which is the soul of the whole Church. There is a reciprocal causality of outwardness and inwardness. It would be as incorrect to construct an ecclesiology solely upon the external society of the Church as to postulate an ideal and abstract Church without any societal mediation. The almost constant tradition of the Church, in matters of faith or of essential practice, has been to secure explicit agreement between hierarchic initiative and the sentiment born of universal and inwardly assimilated faith, before making solemn promulgations.

A more practical example of how the testimony of hierarchic preaching must be articulated with the testimony of the life of the community can be found in the propagation of the faith.

C. The stages of the historical Church's growth

As we have already seen, the historical Church is in the process of becoming the eternal Church. To this end, she has been endowed with an institution that can be objectively described as follows: it is the totality of the sacramental mediations, of the prophetic, priestly, and pastoral ministries, by means of which Christ builds up His community in time. But this historical Church "in herself" subsists among historical men who live by Christ's life and who have become part of the institution of salvation. When the Church has completed her process of becoming within these men, the fullness of their participation in the institution should normally correspond to an adult state in the life of Christ. But until this process of becoming is completed, the historical Church will continue to *become* in her members, just as the man of adult vitality and member of society *has become* by passing through the stages of childhood and adolescence. In this connection, let us recall the parable of the grain of mustard seed and the parable of the leaven in the dough (Mt. 13:31-33).

This aspect of the growth of the historical Church will now hold our attention. Dependent upon the polarity between the historical Church and the eternal Church, we find another polarity developing: one between the reality of each of the partial realizations of the

Church as institution and the perfection (in the sense of totality) of the Church as institution. The solution of this institutional tension is one that gives rise to the most important pastoral problems.

The final state of every living reality explains all the stages of its growth. Just as we discovered the historical form of God's people first of all in the eternal Church, so we shall understand the stages in the growth of the historical Church by starting out with the final state of this Church.

(a) *The Church, a Eucharistic community*

What is the completed state of the historical Church? It is a community that truly lives the Pasch of Christ by actuating it sacramentally in the Eucharistic rite. Beyond that, there is only the eschatological Church toward which the Christian people are advancing from Easter to Easter. For this is an authentic celebration of the Eucharist, lived communally in faith in Christ's Pasch, lived in effective fraternal charity, in a thanksgiving that embraces the whole world in expectation of Christ's glorious return. In the Eucharistic celebration we rediscover the community as a reality in act, and we also find the sacrament in its twofold aspect as the expression and mediation of this reality.

If we consider each of the marks of the Church, we shall have more ample proof of the coincidence between the historical Church in her perfection and the Eucharistic community:

Is the Church ever more *one* than when, as a local Eucharistic community, she manifests herself as the people of the *agape* through the unanimity of her members and through her communion with all the Christians of the universe, all of whom are nourished by the same sacramental Body and by the same Spirit?

Is the Church ever more *Catholic* than when the members of the Eucharistic community gather together from all classes to give thanks to God in the name of the whole world?

The Church's *holiness* shines out in the celebration of a sacrament where Salvation Himself is present, communicating His own life, which is holiness, in the maximum degree.

As for the *Apostolicity* of the Eucharistic community, it is made manifest in that the only genuine Eucharist is the one that is celebrated in communion with the Bishop, the personified sacrament of apostolicity.

(b) *The Church, a baptismal and evangelical community*

We must sadly admit that the fulfillment of the Eucharistic communities does not always coincide—by a long way—with the exigencies of this perfect stage of the Church in her historical manifestation. Neither communion with the Pasch of Christ and with the brethren, nor the sacrament of this communion are lived in some communities with the realism of faith. How is it that some of our Eucharistic communities are so formal, if not false? It is because they were not preceded by genuine baptismal communities:

The baptismal community:

The Church receives her immediate capacity for being a Eucharistic community from the fact that she is an assembly centered around the baptismal font. She is the assembly of a people who, after a long catechesis, have inwardly assimilated the Christian mystery, the Christian faith, and Christian morals. In fact, they have assimilated these truths so thoroughly that they have come to "return" to the Eucharistic community the *Credo* that they received from it, and have publicly declared themselves members of God's people through Baptism. Here we find the two aspects of the earthly Church, the inward and the outward: communion in an eternal life bound to the death and resurrection of Jesus Christ; and a sacrament of faith pledged publicly that is the gateway to a more profound communion.

As the inscription on the baptismal font of the Lateran says so well: "Here a people of noble lineage is born for heaven. . . . Nothing any longer divides those who have been reborn. They are one: for Baptism is one, the Spirit is one, and faith is one. In the waters, Mother Church brings forth with virginal fruitfulness those whom she has conceived through the power of the Spirit."

The evangelical community:

Thus the Church is born as a baptismal community, under the direct control of the Eucharistic community. But she was begotten by God's Revelation before coming forth from the fruitful waters. And the reason our baptismal communities are sometimes so uncertain of their allegiance, so hesitant in choosing between the world and the kingdom, is because they did not start out as evangelical communities. And by evangelical community we mean a convocation around the announcement of the Good News. God's Revelation is seed. There will be no enduring fruitfulness unless God's words have first been planted in the depths of men's hearts and unless these words have inaugurated a secretly germinating life.

Now, baptismal catechesis represents a well-developed stage of God's Revelation. The Church began with the first announcement of Jesus Christ, the kerygma of Salvation, as St. Paul has said. It would serve no purpose to be instructed by catechesis concerning the Mystery, unless one had previously been converted to the Gospel. In her initial stages, the Church was a community of converts to Jesus Christ, called "unto his kingdom and glory" (I Thess. 2:12). She was a community whose primordial sacrament and the object of whose worship consisted in God's Apostolic Revelation; a community whose spiritual being and life were constituted by God's interior revelation. Here already were the *Res* and the *Sacramentum*. The Church was embryonic, and her unity was scarcely visible because the kerygma adapted itself to natural groups before transcending them, as in the case of the baptismal-Eucharistic community. And yet on this embryonic Church depended the authenticity of the whole ecclesial structure of the future.

The pre-evangelical community:

The historical kingdom of Christ, the anticipation of His eternal Kingdom, began with God's words. However, God's Apostolic Revelation is not His first gift. Certain dispositions of the heart are necessary to recognize His Revelation, and these dispositions are already a divine grace. During the period of waiting for God's words, or in the absence of His words, these dispositions constitute a link with the world of salvation. God knows His friends beyond the actual boundaries of the historical Church. They are outside her limits, and yet dynamically orientated toward her even if they are destined to know her only when she is gloriously unveiled.

This is not the proper place to enumerate in detail the qualifications of diverse sorts that can entitle men of good will to belong to this pre-evangelical cell of the Church. Here are assembled in a somewhat indiscriminable but real community those who live in a climate of human truth and moral aspiration. This community has its quasi-sacraments in the form of public acts and circumstances in which the gift of self affirms itself. In the words of St. Paul, "this will take place on the day when, according to my gospel, God will judge the hidden secrets of men through Jesus Christ" (Rom. 2:16). For those whom it summons, God's Apostolic Revelation is a judgment of Christ even during historical times. As for the others, the eschatological judgment will throw definitive light on their position with regard to God's Church.

The evangelical community created a preliminary gathering of men on the public place where God's Apostolic Revelation had been announced to them, before they were introduced into the Church. The pre-evangelical community leaves them to their ordinary lives, merely bound by the mysterious transcendence of their consciences obedient to the unknown God.

(c) *A single ecclesial community*

This analysis will not lead us astray. There is a single community consisting of communion in Jesus Christ and of the mediations of this communion. But this community, according to its two joint aspects as communion and sacrament, becomes more and more a communion of becoming that constitutes the Reality of the sacrament to come. The child is implicit in the adult, and none of the stages of an individual man's growth can be eliminated. So do successive Church communities overlap one another until they finally constitute the adult community of the Eucharist. From the world to the sanctuary, by way of the Gospel and the baptismal font.

There can be no true evangelical community that does not yearn for Baptism; nor any true baptismal community that does not reach fulfillment in the Eucharistic celebration. And conversely, there is no Eucharistic community that does not welcome the baptismal community; and no baptismal community that does not joyfully receive into its bosom those who have been evangelized. This dynamic vision of the Church and of her mission is exemplified by the Eucharistic community's recapitulation of its earlier stages during Lent, when its evangelization and baptismal catechesis are assumed as stepping stones to its Easter.

Need we add that the Eucharistic community must constantly sink the roots of its being deeper, become what it is, and thus get farther away from sin from Easter to Easter? The growth of the Church continues in the Eucharistic community in the measure that the Christian Reality is intensified within it thanks to the Sacrament, and the perfect Sacrament is also celebrated with greater truth. It is the whole historical Church that grows: both the communion and the means of communion.

There is a text in the Mozarabic liturgy—*oratio propter albas tollendas*—that gives magnificent expression to the unity in the Church's becoming:

> "Lord Jesus Christ, Savior of the world, true Man, born of our race, whom God the Father has recognized as His Son, strengthen in Your family these gifts that have marked it with Your image (*tua familia tuo nomine signata:* the catechumenate); purified by the holy water (*sacro liquore inundata:* Baptism); filled with the Holy Spirit (*tuo spiritu plena:* Confirmation); filled for its joy and its salvation with Your Body and Your Blood (*tuo corpore et sanguine satiata:* the Eucharist). Grant that these sacraments that have inaugurated a new life in (the members of Your Family) may be a perpetual pledge of their salvation (*ad usum salutis indesinenter obtineant:* the whole sacramental life of the initiate), so that they may safely attain to their blessed reward."

(d) *The truth of the Church and the perfection of the Church*

There might seem to be a conflict between a conception of the Church concerned with the truth of each of the communitarian stages enumerated above and a conception concerned with asserting the plenitude of sacramental forms. Actually, there is no need to choose between the two: God wants both the truth and the perfection of His Church at one and the same time. In Jesus Christ, the Head of the Church, the fullness of paschal life and the fullness of mediation coincide. It would be disloyalty to Jesus Christ to scorn even one sacramental element born of His mediation. And it would be still graver disloyalty to deliver up the sacraments of this mediation to formalism and indifference, for only the Spirit quickens.

And yet we must rediscover a fundamental category of the Church's pastoral function: *duration,* which is inseparable from human destiny. Sacramental mediations deal with moral situations, and concern subjects whose freedom affirms itself in the process of becoming. Evidently we can give objective definitions of the Church as an institution, the Christian Creed, and Catholic morality. But these holy realities receive their perfection from Jesus Christ, in order to *progressively* increase the fullness of His members. There is a great lesson for us in the fact that Jesus was born a child like any other man, and that His physical and psychic life and His mission followed the stages of development common to men.

The Church *becomes* among Christians. Her progression takes place by way of partial communities that are none the less real in their degree of completeness, and that are wholly orientated toward the Eucharistic community. Let us not be in too great a hurry to make a sacramental affirmation that might not be supported by an equivalent affirmation of faith. Falsehood threatens us. Let us not seek refuge behind an *ex opere operato* which has never covered our abuses of the sacraments, according to the authentic theology of the Council of Trent.

We have telescoped the vitally important initial stage of evangelization, for in Christian society the maternal education of the faith spontaneously brought about conversions. Now, catechesis which is not preceded by kerygma begets men "who know their religion" but not authentic believers. The *Sacramentum Verbi* has priority over the *Sacramenta*. Recent historical research has proven that the Church of the Fathers was faithful to this hierarchy, whereas the pastoral theology of the post-Tridentine period often jeopardized it.

The missionary function and the sacramental function of the Church are distinct and complementary. Without evangelization, the way is paved for a formalistic Eucharist. Without the Eucharist, the Gospel will not attain to its fullness. But in wanting to exercise these two functions at once, is there not the danger of lowering the Eucharistic cult to the level of "missionary para-liturgy"? A mediocre evangelization means a poor appreciation of the Eucharist. There is a vast difference between pseudo-communities in which worship does not translate an antecedent faith in Christ and communities in which conversion has already begun.

(e) *The ecclesial community and other communities*

When we speak of the Church as a community, we may mean one of several things: at times we may mean the local community, at others the universal community. Obviously there is no opposition here, for it is through the local community that the believer is a member of the universal community. The Church of Paris is the sister of the Church of Berlin, of Carthage, of Rome, and of all the others.

But what is the local community? Is it the diocese, or the parish? Or is it a group to which one may happen to belong?

According to law, there can be no hesitation. The local community is the diocese. For only the bishop possesses all the elements that bring together the Apostolic Church. There is no Church without a bishop and a flock. The parochial Eucharist is simply a participation of the episcopal Eucharist. The same is true of all ecclesial mediations, for priests are merely the collaborators of the bishop. The bishop, on the other hand, is not the collaborator but the colleague of the pope.

In actual fact, dioceses are often too vast to constitute a concrete community of life. And that is why parishes constitute the true nuclei of the Church: Each parish is an assembly of believers, a family of brothers, a Eucharistic people, a missionary nucleus. This fact must not make anyone forget that the parish belongs to the episcopal community, and that the bond of unity between parish and diocese finds expression on special occasions.

Even the parish seems at times to be supplanted as a concrete community by smaller and less stable regroupings such as the educational communities of youth movements, professional and Catholic Action communities, pious and charitable organizations. The parish stands only to gain from these peripheral communities, and yet it remains for all their members the center of ecclesial plenitude by reason of the Eucharistic celebration. These subordinate communities must find their communitarian axis in the diocese and in the parish, if they are truly to be cells of the Catholic Church.

D. Freedom and authority in the Church

Whether it be in praise or in blame, the Church has the reputation of being a society in which authority, discipline, and obedience are very highly cultivated. Some even go so far as to say that the Church shows contempt for freedom.

(a) *Obedience to Christ and obedience to the Church*

It would be easy to produce immediately several texts of St. Paul on the freedom of the Christian, the slave of Christ. If we were tempted to refuse this slavery in order to attain to true liberty, we would have to reflect on the difference between obedience to men and obedience to God. In addition to the fact that obedience to God has a more certain motive, it sets its mark on the personality of the one who abandons himself to it, because obedience to God is consent to the all-embracing Being and to infinite Love.

As we have seen earlier, the ecclesiastical ministry in its essential task adds nothing to God's Revelation. Its essential mission is to serve this Revelation and to make men docile to the Spirit. Faith is the free adherence of the heart. The moral practice of the Church is free and responsible submission to values recognized through faith. The sacramental cult also demands maximum lucidity of faith. Everywhere in the Church's mediation we encounter an outwardness that springs from Christ with a view to inwardness. Very often it is through lack of a profoundly spiritual life that the Church suffers from a narrow obedience that does not see the sacrament in exterior mediation.

Submission to the Church in the pastoral domain is more delicate. For there the margin of interpretation of Christ's thought and of the dispositions whose purpose is to preserve it is more completely controlled by the hierarchical ministers. The decision of those in authority on matters of secondary discipline may seem inopportune to me. I am then called to a religious submission of my will, but not to the conviction of my mind. A different decision might be better. I am free to think so and to wish for it.

In doctrinal matters that have only an indirect bearing on faith, an interior adherence based on trust in the Church's prudence is generally called for. And here again there would be many distinctions to make depending on the insistence of authority, one's own competence, and the concrete circumstances and necessities of the life of the Church. We should take pains to remember in such instances that every theologian is not the Church.

(b) *Initiatives and reforms in the Church*

Outside these domains that are subject to the immediate control of the hierarchy, initiative has a great role to play in the Church. And here we are speaking of an initiative that receives counsel and control from above, but which originates from below. Many of the problems of apostolic adaptation, piety, and theological thought, whose initiative has been fruitful for the Church, have sprung up in this spontaneous way. All that is required of initiators is concern for Catholic unity and Catholic communion. In concrete instances, serious problems can be raised in this domain of new or reformatory initiatives, in which the youth of the Church and the freedom of the Gospel are at stake.

We have an apostolic antecedent for this: Paul's behavior in his conflict with Peter must always serve as a guide in such circumstances. It is worth our while to recall the incident. In Jerusalem, where Peter and James governed the Church, the Gospel had not yet put an end to Jewish customs. Paul saw in this Judaeo-Christianity disloyalty to Christian freedom. What was he to do? Certain sentences in the Epistle to the Galatians seem to make light of the Apostolic Institution (Gal. 1:17; 2:6). The way Paul reproved Peter whom he deemed guilty of weakness in dealing with the Judaeo-Christians (Gal. 2:11-14) strengthens this impression. And yet Paul felt the need of being integrated in the apostolicity represented in Jerusalem: "I conferred with them on the gospel which I preach to the Gentiles, but separately with the men of authority; *lest perhaps I should be running, or had run in vain*" (Gal. 2:2). But this submissiveness did not lead him to agree that the Gospel be bound to the formalism of the Jews. "Now to these we did not yield in submission, no, not for an hour, *that the truth of the gospel might continue with you*" (Gal. 2:5).

Paul's attitude was a coherent one, but it has to be complemented by the attitude recorded for us in the Acts of the Apostles (21:17-26). St. Paul went up to Jerusalem for the fifth time and once more confronted Jewish formalism. But this time, condescending to the Apostles' opportunism, he agreed to submit to a ritual practice in order to preserve peace. And it was precisely for this that he had reprimanded St. Peter! Paul pushed his attitude of conciliation to the point of having his disciple Timothy circumcised, even though the latter was a Greek.

Paul's complex behavior must be recalled whenever reform takes on urgency in the Church. Let us draw a few conclusions from it: 1) In the Church there are no sects or autonomous bodies: unity must be preserved at all costs. 2) Apostolicity is the foundation of the Church: to separate from her is to separate from Christ. 3) Obedience is communion with the hierarchic authority, even though the initiative has not come from this authority. 4) The apostolicity of the Church being assured, it is normal to fight for the purity of the spirit of Christ in the Church. The greatest saints have used their fullest liberty in this connection. Witness St. Columban, St. Bernard, St. Catherine of Siena, St. Bridget, St. Thomas More, St. Clement Hofbauer, and many others. And there is no ground for seeing insubordination in their attitude. 5) A careful distinction must be made between the elements of the ecclesial Institution that constitute her fundamental structures willed by Jesus, and the contingent elements in which these structures find expression. Any *reformation* could affect only these contingent elements. Otherwise, there would be question of a *revolution,* and this is an impossibility within the Church of Christ. 6) When the occasion arises, fraternal correction will be exercised at every echelon of the hierarchy, as has in fact been done in the Church throughout her history.

(c) *The danger of clericalism*

As for those things that are obviously within the secular domain —techniques, culture, politics, etc.—it would be clericalism on the Church's part to legislate concerning them unless Christian faith or morals were in some way threatened. Anything that resembles personal power and the will to power in the Church has no right to force itself on Christian consciences. Christ emphatically founded His Church under the sign of service (Jn. 13:1-8); He has sufficiently stressed that the exercise of authority in the Church was to be entirely different from what it is in secular society (Lk. 22:24-27). He was stern enough in His condemnation of abuses by churchmen (Mt. 23) to invite those in charge of the Institution to the greatest purity (cf. also I Pet. 5:2-4).

And yet we must admit that history has unfortunately opened up a certain number of avenues for abuse of power in the Church. The fact that subordinates subjected to these abuses of power supported them in a holy manner does not lessen the serious guilt of the superiors. Christ did not leave us the Church to bully us; and the Church is powerless against a man's conscience, for conscience also comes from God. However, certain assents of the mind or certain acts of obedience may for the moment be hard to bear, and the Church's delays may try our patience. In such instances we must know how to wait, and not uselessly disturb our brothers; nor bring into question the pastoral prudence of a Church which, sometimes amid gropings, wants to safeguard the deposit of Christ *for all.* The only thing we can do is to refer the matter in question to those who have authority to deal with it. Perhaps what is needed most of all is an invincible trust in the truth that can never contradict the truth and that will certainly make itself known in the end.

Thanks to God who watches over His Church, the *Legend of the Grand Inquisitor* is scarcely more than a parody. In general the saints seem to have been more successful than others in finding true liberty in the Church, and yet they were always ready to demand their liberty when sin threatened it.

3. THE ATTRIBUTES AND MARKS OF THE CHURCH

A. The attributes of the Church

I believe in the One, Holy, Catholic, and Apostolic Church.

These four adjectives of the primitive profession of faith describe the whole mystery of the Church: the mystery of the eternal and wayfaring Church. The Creed simply took up again the expressions of the Fathers. St. Paul spoke of the *one* Church (Eph. 4:4), of the *holy* Church (Eph. 5:27). St. Ignatius (around 110) was the first to call the Church *Catholic*. The acts of the martyrdom of St. Polycarp (156) are addressed "to all the parishes of the *holy* and *Catholic* Church." The epithet *apostolic* dates from St. Irenaeus. But above and beyond all this, the reality which these words express was lived and preached from the time of the Apostles.

The Church is one through the unity of the Triune God and the unity of the divine plan that is epitomized in Christ-the-Head: one Spirit, one Head, and one Body. But there is also one Baptism, as St. Paul adds, signifying thereby the visible unity, the sacrament of the invisible unity; and there is a single Episcopal College having one Head, the symbol and guardian of the unity that comes from God. In the words of St. Ignatius (to the Magnesians 13:2), it is "a unity at once bodily and spiritual" that is not to be identified with external uniformity and does not necessarily tend toward centralization.

Let us conclude with Bossuet: "It is of the essence of the Church until the general resurrection to have an ecclesiastical ministry that makes her visible, but . . . the effect of this ministry is to bring the children of God to the perfect stature of Jesus Christ, that is, to the perfection which will first make them holy and then make them glorious in body and soul" (*Réflexions sur un écrit de Monsieur Claude,* Paris, 1727, p. 260).

The Church is holy with the invisible holiness of the Spirit who lives in her, and with the holiness of Christ whose Body she is. She is also holy in her visible institution; for the Spirit likewise quickens this institution in order to make it bring forth holiness.

The Church is Catholic because the predestination of God embraces the whole spiritual universe (Eph. 1:10), because Christ has made satisfaction for the sins of the whole world (I Jn. 2:2), and because the Gospel concerns all creatures (Mk. 16:15). The visible realization of this universality takes place through the geographical extension of the hierarchical Church. But we must take care not to restrict the Catholicity of the Church to this geographical aspect. It should be understood that the Church's Catholicity is part of her nature. The Church of Jerusalem was already the Catholic Church. Besides, the Church's Catholicity is qualitative as well as quantitative. "The Catholicity of the Church is the dynamic universality of her unity: the capacity her principles of unity have for assimilating, satisfying, exalting, winning over to God, and for bringing together within Him every man and all men, every human value" (M.-J. Congar, *Chrétiens désunis,* Paris, 1937, p. 117). And this is true for the duration of human culture as well as for its spatial extension.

The Church is apostolic not only with an historical apostolicity, but also with an apostolicity of the present moment. What has been said in our earlier chapters obviates the need for further stress on this point.

B. The marks of the Church and the apologetics of the Church

(a) *The theology and apologetics of the Church*

The four traditional attributes of the mystery of the Church are often called the *marks* of the Church in theological or catechetical teaching. We believe it is important to clarify what this comparison includes. Actually, there is question here of two different points of view: one theological, and the other apologetic.

The apologetic point of view has taken on great importance, one might even say the place of greatest importance, in modern treatises on the Church (exception being made of the theology of the last few decades). Ecclesiology was restricted to the question of the powers and the marks of the Roman Church as against Gallicanism or against the reformed Churches, until the time came to defend the Church against the eighteenth century atheists. Certainly this ecclesiology was useful, but secondary to the theological contemplation of the mystery of the Church in herself; and yet it sought to take the place of such contemplation.

(b) *Apologetics through the marks of the Church*

The Reformers reproached the Catholic Church for no longer being the Church of the Gospel and of the Fathers. The proof was to be given them that the Church of Christ has lived on in this Catholic Church, and nowhere else. On the basis of a common faith in Scripture and in the divinity of the Church of the Fathers, the essential properties of the Church willed by Christ and lived by the Fathers were established. As for the marks, at first there were a multitude of them, but they were reduced to four major ones in the nineteenth century. These marks, by the verification of their identical presence in the primitive Church and in the Catholic Church of the present day, have made it possible to prove the authentic succession of the latter. The demonstration established against the Protestants was quickly extended to the proof of the truth of the Catholic Church to unbelievers. This proof followed from the proof of Christ's divine mission, and was therefore purely historical and rational.

These proofs have incontestable value. However it must be admitted that their exact import, which is so hard to establish, has sometimes been contested and that it is too often overemphasized. Indeed, if *the way of the marks* is used in dogmatic fashion against dissident Christians, it can certainly be shown that the Roman Catholic Church possesses these marks in all perfection. But it is harder to demonstrate that this perfect realization excludes every other Church.

As for the purely rational proof following the same "way," the historians who establish so successfully the historical value of Christian origins do not hide the fact that it is very difficult—using only historical documents and excluding all other sources of light— to demonstrate scientifically from a purely historical point of view that the Church of Christ must possess these marks.

(c) *The other "ways" of the Church's apologetics*

To our mind, an analogous difficulty faces the "historical way" which appeared in the seventeenth century and which consists in establishing the same demonstration on the basis of the powers of the Church willed by Jesus. Beneath the homogeneous development that separates the primitive Church from the Church of Pius XII, the believer sees an identity that satisfies him. But this identity, so easily perceived with the eyes of faith, is more difficult to present simply with the resources of history.

Struck by this difficulty, Cardinal Dechamps, a nineteenth century prelate, proposed a new apologetics for the Church—new and traditional, for St. Augustine had already made splendid use of it. This method consists in starting out by proving the transcendent origin of the Catholic Church today by means of the contemporary fact of the Church's existence, which constitutes a multiform miracle for any mind that is the least disposed to see it. Once the Church has been recognized as divine, it is easy to go back to Christ, reversing the process of the previous "ways."

This is the *empirical way* that the Vatican Council was to recognize authoritatively, and that is increasingly permeating present-day apologetics. As the Council teaches:

Indeed, only the Catholic Church possesses all these facts that concur with admirable profusion in divinely establishing the evident credibility of the Christian faith. Far more important, when the Church's astonishing propagation, her eminent holiness, and her inexhaustible fruitfulness in all sorts of good works, and her unity in the universality of her invincible stability are considered, the Church in herself constitutes a great and perpetual motive of credibility as well as an irrecusable proof of her divine origin (Sess. 3, Const. *Dei filius*, chap. 3, Denz., 1794).

The apologetics of the miracle of the Church clearly proves her divine origin. And yet we cannot fail to remember certain extraordinary lives, such as the life of Seraphinus of Sarov, that we encounter in non-Catholic denominations. These other religious faiths might well lay claim to their less numerous and less brilliant experiences as proofs of their own miraculousness in the moral order. It will therefore be necessary for us to clarify a point in which the Catholic Church's loyalty to Christ shines forth like an ever-renewed miracle through the course of history: namely, the Church's apostolicity. The Church that manifests the greatest holiness (a recapitulation of the empirical miracle of the Church) and the most faithful apostolicity throughout its duration thereby proves that it is the integral Church of Christ.

4. THE MEMBERS OF THE CHURCH

Who belongs to the Church? The answer to this question calls for the most precise definition of the mystery of the Church. Such a definition emerges from the earlier chapters. The application we shall now make of it will give us a new insight into the great mystery that we are trying to understand through faith.

A. The definition of the Church

(a) *The canonical definition*

Our concern here is with the wayfaring Church. The difficulty in giving a truly balanced definition lies in establishing the proper relationships between the visible and invisible aspects of the Church. According to St. Robert Bellarmine, the great disputant of the Counter-Reformation, the Church is "the assembly of men associated by their profession of the same faith and their communion in the same sacraments under the governance of legitimate pastors, notably the Roman Pontiff, the one vicar of Christ on earth." This definition, with its anti-Protestant savor, has become almost universally *the* accepted definition in the theology and the pastoral function of the Church. We may well regret that this definition is so widely accepted, not because it is incorrect but because it holds too much to a juridical point of view of visible society and threatens to subordinate to society the mystery of the eschatological community.

(b) *The theological definition*

St. Bellarmine's definition is certainly valid from the canonical approach. If we begin, on the contrary, from the mystery of the Church whose essential and final values are spiritual (societal values, although indissolubly bound to the former in the present state of the Church, are secondary, ministerial values), we come to a rather different definition of the Church, one that might be called a theological definition. To quote Bossuet:

> Clearly, far from being a Church whose communion is purely external in nature and whose inwardness is merely accidental, the essence of the Church is the inward communion whose mark is its exterior communion, and the effect of which is to show that the children of God are preserved and enclosed in this seal. It is clear, too, that the elect are the last end for whom everything is done in the Church; it is principally for them that her ministry exists. Thus they are the most essential part and so to speak the very foundation of the Church" (*Conférence avec M. Claude*, Paris, 1727, pp.261-262).

B. The rights to membership in the Church

Depending on whether we choose one or the other definition of the Church and on whether we take the canonical or the theological point of view, we shall have a different conception of the basis for membership in the Church.

(a) *Membership in the Church through baptismal character*

In the light of the Bellarminian definition, the temptation is to consider only the visible aspect of the Church and to enumerate her members as one would citizens of a nation, as being those who are subject to her powers. The baptismal character is the infallible and indelible effect of the valid reception of the visible sacrament by which the Christian is admitted into the Eucharistic society. From the canonical point of view, this character is the fundamental right on which the membership of each individual in the Church is to be judged, and this judgment will be unappealable.

It should be noted, however, that baptismal character is not a claim to inward holiness, and this is so true that even the sinner retains his character. Baptismal character is an objective consecration by which the baptized person is made a participant of Christ in His function as sanctifier, in His social person. *In itself,* character does not assure participation in His inward holiness as Head of the Mystical Body. Thus character essentially constitutes a right to membership in the Church-as-society. Only indirectly, insofar as character invites grace and insofar as subjective holiness normally implies a belonging to the ecclesiastical organism, does character incorporate a person into the specifically spiritual reality of the Mystical Body.

(b) *Membership in the Church through grace*

Possession of the baptismal character, participation in the worship of the Christian religion—these are the normal conditions for belonging to God and to Christ. And anyone who would dare boast about belonging to Christ without fulfilling those requirements would be disregarding the whole positive economy of the distribution of Christian salvation: the visible Church, the priesthood, and the sacraments, expressly established by the Savior. But these external and even sacramental claims to membership in the Church do not lay bare the whole secret of souls.

From the theological point of view, membership in the Church is based on the inward possession of some element of the divine life communicated in Christ, and subordinately on exterior marks of incorporation in the visible community. Thus, belonging to the Church means—in the order of values (which does not signify in the order of causality)—first of all belonging to her spiritual and

vital reality. It also means belonging to her organism of sanctification. That is why, in the absence of absolute certitude on the presence of the Holy Spirit in the souls of baptized persons, we must
recognize the mysterious character of the true fold of Christ, leaving
to God, beyond empirical discernments and probable inductions,
the final judgment of the Shepherd who knows His sheep.

(c) *The degrees of membership*

Nevertheless, there is still room for a universal application of
principles somewhere between the theoretical and abstract a priori
judgment, as above presented, and the concrete judgment as to a
given person's membership in the Church. In short, wherever there
is at least divine faith, we can speak of a partial and imperfect but
real membership in the Church. And this membership will become
perfect with charity, even if in certain cases it is not a "normal" membership. Normally, the presence of this faith and charity presupposes the presence of baptismal character and life in the visible
community. In this connection, we have merely to refer to the picture of the member of the Church as given above.

And even though the link with the visible community is very
limited or baptismal character is absent, we may still be dealing
with authentic, even if imperfect or "abnormal," members of the
Church. We shall discuss the case of non-baptized persons later.
It is a well-known adage of the scholastics that grace is not always
bound, at least on God's part, with the sacraments. Conversely,
baptized persons, who are externally practicing members but lack
faith and charity, may be nothing more than paralyzed members
of Christ and of His Church.

St. Augustine wrote with regard to the perfect members of Christ:
"All who do not love God are strangers to Him. Though they enter
the basilicas, they cannot be counted among the sons of God. . . .
Even the wicked man can possess baptism; he may likewise have
the gift of prophecy and all the sacraments. . . . But no one can
have charity and remain wicked" (Epist. 70, P. L. 35, 2032).

C. Invisible membership in the Church

(a) *The Church outside the Church*

"Outside the Church there is no salvation": this formula of an
ambiguous truth has had great success in the Church's catechesis.

Its author was St. Cyprian, Bishop of Carthage in the middle of the third century. And we must admit that in the mind of St. Cyprian it was a question of the empirical Church in the strict sense, visibly assembled around the successor of the Apostles (Letter 73, 1:11,21).

Two centuries later, St. Augustine rectified St. Cyprian's narrowness of outlook, even while claiming to follow in his footsteps: "No one," says Augustine, "can attain to salvation and to eternal life unless he has Christ as his Head. And no one can have Christ as his Head unless he is in His Body which is the Church" (*De Unit. Eccl.*, P. L. 43, 429). The Church was to retain Augustine's affirmation under Cyprian's ambiguous formula. But does not Augustine's affirmation also raise many questions? How can we reconcile this exigency of means (being in the Body of Christ) with the divine intention of universal salvation (I Tim. 2:3-4)?

Actually, the faith necessary for salvation, and by means of which one becomes a member of the Body of Christ, can be interpreted more or less explicitly. And the less explicit interpretation seems quite far objectively from the content of the Catholic dogma concerning the Body of Christ which is the Church. We can first of all affirm with the whole of ecclesiastical tradition that the salvation of God has dwelt and certainly now dwells in certain men who, by reason of the historical circumstances of their existence, have not been able to find their salvation in the normal state of the Christian economy, within the life of the Church, and yet have had an implicit faith. God's mercy exceeds what theology can say about it. And although men are obliged to use means divinely instituted for salvation, God, for His part, has not bound Himself by these means. "For God did not send his Son into the world in order to judge the world, but that the world might be saved through him" (Jn. 3:17).

(b) *Invisible membership*

It is none the less true that the visible Church remains the one and only inn where Christ wants the future citizens of the heavenly Jerusalem to asemble here on earth. Now we must in fact grant a certain distinction in the earthly Church between the institution in its social, external, and visible aspect, and the Mystical Body in its spiritual and invisible aspect. However we cannot say purely and simply that these men have become members of the Mystical Body without any reference to the ecclesiastical institution.

In an earlier volume (Volume III, *Theology Library,* pp. 40-43), we have given an explanation of the conditions of a salutary faith in the absence of evangelization. These dispositions of soul by means of which non-evangelized persons can be justified imply the general will to obey God and to submit to everything recognized in conscience as flowing from this divine economy of salvation that finds its concrete realization in the Church: it is an implicit desire for the Church and for her sacraments. And this implicit reference to the visible Church is sufficient for certain persons only because it calls for a more complete actuation in terms of which the Church is defined and that exists among baptized persons who practice the life of the Church. The underlying truth of the adage: "Outside the Church there is no salvation" is this: *Salvation is attained only in the Church or through the Church's influence.*

A decree of the Holy See, dated August 8, 1949, and based on the texts of Pius IX (*Singulari quadam,* 1854, cf. Denz., 1647) and of Pius XII (*Mystici Corporis Christi,* 1943), has expressed the Catholic mind on this delicate question of the membership in the Church of non-baptized and non-evangelized persons:

For a person to obtain his eternal salvation, it is not always required that he be incorporated into the Church *de facto* as a member, but he must be united to the Church at least in *desire* or *wish.* However it is not always necessary that this wish be explicit as in the case of the catechumens. When someone is invincibly ignorant, God accepts an *implicit desire,* so called because it is included in the good dispositions of soul by which one desires to conform one's will to the will of God" (Cf. *Docum. Cath.,* November 2, 1952, 1396–1397).

These secret members of Christ belong to the Church in her two aspects, but imperfectly. To express with exactitude their status of membership, we must look not at the reality of the Church but at subjective incorporation into it. That is why we are using these expressions: visible membership and invisible membership in the one spiritual and visible Church. Ideally, the two factors—visible and invisible membership—should coincide. Normally, a visible member of the Church will be more closely bound to the Church, by the twofold right of the life of charity and life in the visible organism, than a secret member who participates only partially in the riches of grace deposited in the ecclesiastical organism. But God's grace has sublime whims, which can upset this objective order at least in part. More often than not, it is the infidelities of professed

Catholics that upset the objective order of things. For many who appear to be in the Church are perhaps outside her bounds, and many who seem outside are really at least partially inside.

(c) *The soul or the body of the Church?*

Since St. Bellarmine (*De Controv.,* Book 3, Chapter 2), efforts have been made to express the ecclesial status of the secret members of Christ by using the distinction between the body and the soul of the Church. This distinction was created in answer to the needs of the situation, even though it has been falsely attributed to St. Augustine. According to this view, the soul is held to be the whole spiritual reality of the Church, and the body her entire visible institution. At the present time many theologians are giving up this overly-neat mode of expression that threatens to betray the reality in question and to give currency to a dualistic conception of the Church that does not accord with Tradition.

The distinction between the body and the soul of the Church, understood in the modern sense, does not seem to us to have any further usefulness. No doubt it can be defended from the theological point of view, but it presents less analogical coherence than does traditional terminology.

Actually, it is the Holy Spirit, according to Tradition and to strict theological reasoning, who can rightly be called the soul of the wayfaring Church. It is the Holy Spirit who dwells in, quickens, sanctifies, and unites the whole ecclesiastical organism (see I Cor. 12:4 ff; Tit. 3:5; Acts 8:17; 13:2; 15:28; 19:6; 20:28). He is the soul of the Church in her societal and visible, as well as her spiritual aspect. (We have already shown that He is the soul of the eternal Church.) "Only the Catholic Church is the Body of Christ, of Christ who is the Head and Savior of His Body. Outside this Body, no one is quickened by the Holy Spirit." [1]

III. The Problems of the Church

1. CATHOLIC ACTION

(a) *The Laity and the Hierarchy*

In connection with the mission and the powers of the Church, we mentioned the place of the laity by the side of the hierarchy.

---

[1] St. Augustine, Letter 185, P. L. 23, 815.

Laymen, by reason of their Baptism and Confirmation, are incorporated in the Church in accordance with ministries that associate them intimately to the work of the hierarchy with a view to the growth of the Body of Christ. They are not to resemble, as someone once humorously remarked, "the Candlemas sheep in Rome, that were simply blessed and sheared." The laity has an active part to play in the tasks of the Church. To quote Pope Pius XII: "The faithful, and especially laymen, are on the front lines of the life of the Church. Through them the Church is the vital principle of human society. Consequently they above all others must have an ever clearer awareness not only of their membership in the Church, but of their being the Church" (Discourse to new Cardinals, November 20, 1946).

Every Christian is a witness to Christ in the world, from the moment he takes God seriously. His prayer for the coming of the Kingdom is incorporated in the prayer of the total Christ for the benefit of the whole human race. His life of faith and charity has the power to disturb the world, always inclined to get along without God and to exist only for itself. His brotherly love has the same power: it is by this sign that the true disciples of Christ are infallibly recognized. The vivifying flow of Christ's life into His members assures the apostolic value of the lives of contemplative religious in the Church. It also assures the testimonary value of the whole human life of those Christians who want to exist integrally in Christ while remaining in the world. Thus is the Gospel message extended to the very heart of natural communities, through the work that belongs specifically to the laity.

Moreover, every Christian who lives in the world may be faced one day or another with the duty of very explicitly proclaiming the disturbing message of his faith, of bearing witness to Christ, of exhorting to conversion, whether in private conversation or in public address. And he would do so as a delegated member of the Church.

(b) *Catholic Action*

It is sometimes thought that Catholic Action is an innovation in the Church. And yet we must consider the Christian testimony described in the preceding paragraph as Catholic Action, even when it is not part of an organization. In this sense, Catholic Action has always existed in the Church and has always been essential to her.

And yet it must be granted that the pontificate of Pius XI saw the blossoming and clarification of this function of the laity in the Church, as a reaction against the rebirth of paganism in Christian lands. In the words of Pope Pius XII:

> It would be an error to look upon Catholic Action, as certain persons have recently affirmed, as something essentially new. . . . There has always been in the Church a collaboration of the laity in the hierarchic apostolate, subordinate to the bishop and to those to whom the bishop has entrusted the responsibility for souls under his authority. Catholic Action has simply wanted to give this collaboration a new form, a new accidental organization, so that it might be exercised better and more efficaciously" (A.A.S. 43, p. 376).

According to the meaning of Catholic Action henceforth to be accepted, those who bear witness in an isolated manner are not doing Catholic Action. It is necessary to incorporate one's personal testimony and action in groups that have been specially organized and called for by the hierarchy to give public and collective testimony in the various human communities and environments. Baptism and Confirmation remain the ecclesial basis of Catholic Action. The hierarchy outwardly confirms this function of testimony and inwardly mandates it within movements organized by the hierarchy. Catholic Action has thus become a more explicit organ of the ecclesial Body, making precise the specific collaboration of the laity in the mission of the hierarchy, especially in the hierarchy's prophetic mission. One might say that Catholic Action has passed from the purview of private law to that of public law.

(c) Temporal Action and Evangelization

As a specific task of the Church, it would seem that Catholic Action has no obligation to work in the realm of temporal structures. St. Paul was not so much concerned, as an apostle, with abolishing slavery; nor did the first Christians, as such, seek to modify the political society of their time. The Christian awaits eternal life while living in time. His apostolic function consists first of all in reminding the world by his words and by his life of the question that God asks of the world; in making the world receptive to the presence of the Eternal; and in proclaiming the Good News. He is a witness to the living God and to Christ, and he communicates to the whole world, and first of all to those in his immediate environment, the fire that the Savior has come to bring to this earth. He knows very well that temporal structures will always be imperfect and he is content that they adequately serve man's spiritual vocation. To quote the words of Pope Pius XI:

"Inasmuch as Catholic Action does not differ from the divine mission entrusted to the Church and to her hierarchy, it is not of the temporal order but of the spiritual order; nor is it of the political order, but of the religious order" (Letter *Quae Nobis,* November 13, 1928).

But in the epoch in which we live, perhaps more than in other epochs, human structures often betray man instead of serving him, and threaten to make him deaf to God's Revelation. Can the Church, at this juncture, fail to interest herself in these structures which jeopardize the coming of the Kingdom of God? Is not the undertaking of this temporal work an eloquent testimony of charity? We are not trying to limit the Christian's obligations in the world, but to establish objectively just what Catholic Action is. The Christian owes it to himself to be present in a Christian way in the social and political structures of society so that they may not debase man, created in the image of God, below his normal stature. It is a Christian presence that presupposes a competent human activity in union with the other members of the human community. The same task is called for in the moral and intellectual structures, so that they may not traffic with paganism.

While this temporal activity of the Christian may be penetrated and motivated by a concern for Catholic Action, in itself it does not stem from Catholic Action in the strict sense of the word. Concretely speaking, it is difficult to establish the distinction between the tasks of the Church and the Christian tasks that are related to them. In the majority of cases institutional action and evangelizing action will have to be carried on side by side. Christian action must prepare the way for a visible expression of the specific Christian virtue of charity. The Christian's active presence in the human community will thus condition the apostolic testimony. Here are the two functions of Catholic Action: to exert influence by its presence and by its testimony.[1]

[1] Let us make ourselves clear: there is no question here of limiting the obligations to the world that a given Christian may take on, but to specify objectively the domain proper to Catholic Action, considered as an activity of the Church, by freeing it from all temptation to clericalism. Now that the

(d) The task of the Church and the political order

Politics consist in efficaciously ordering all techniques toward the realization of a human community in which persons blossom forth in a communion of like values: it is a work of justice and of unity. The Church, with divine efficacy and a transcendent end, carries on a task toward which the task of politics converges. Whence the temptation to deduce laws for the political order starting from the Church as final cause. But in the political judgments that inform his action, the Christian will find in his faith only an inspiration to be combined with the concrete and variable facts of the individual situation; whence the possibility of a plurality of political attitudes among Christians. In consequence, we would think that there is no politics of the Church, no Catholic politics, but only a Catholic inspiration.

What is the ideal human order, in its relation to the Church's mediation? True, we can imagine an inwardly Christian human community that would arrive at a uniformity of political judgment born of faith concerning particular matters: marriage, education, sexual morality. And yet we would be dealing only with elements, and not with a complete political order. The existence of a Christian party, outside this theological justification, can be explained only temporarily, to meet a danger threatening Christianity and demanding the maximum efficacy of the forces of Christian resistance.

(e) History, civilization, and the mediation of the Church

By history we understand the whole universe to the extent that it centers in man and his destiny, and to the extent that it is directed by man along the paths of a development and progress that underlies the ascent of conscience and the world of morality. This is the history to which God has bound Himself, to the point of identifying Himself with it. We shall not give up any of the terms: Jesus Christ is *God,* and that is absolute, unique, and definitive in its superhuman consequences. But He has intimately united Himself to history. History has neither been annihilated thereby nor halted in its course. And yet Jesus Christ is the Master, the supreme

---

sacral Christianity which succeeded so well in the Middle Ages has been dissolved, Christians are obviously invited to be the artisans of a new Christianity in a reborn world, but a Christianity of a secular sort. (See for the scope of these distinctions, J. Maritain, *True Humanism* (New York, Scribners, 1938).

Director of history. Everything must be subject to Him, and at the end of history all things will be revealed to us as having their source in Him. We may not decide in favor of human history devoid of the action of God in Jesus Christ; nor may we look to Jesus Christ independently of human history. This is a Christian certitude.

Human history has its reality, its development, its own laws. What relationship does faith allow us to proclaim between history and the Kingdom whose Author is Christ by reason of His first coming, and whose Perfecter He is by His second coming which we await? It would seem that this relationship is twofold:

1. *Human history prepares the content of the Kingdom.* For this Kingdom is not a kingdom of souls, but a kingdom of human lives that Christ has inaugurated by His Resurrection. And when Revelation speaks to us of "new heavens and a new earth" (Is. 65:17), it allows us to affirm that it is the totality of the first Creation together with the entire historical development that man has worked in it that, in accordance with God's plan, is to be gloriously recapitulated by Jesus Christ.

Such are the dimensions of the Church's Catholicity, into which all human values have been converted to Christ so that God may be glorified by them and so that the glory of God may transfigure them. For in the end, the reality of the second creation will consist of everything that has been offered up to God. Needless to say, however, it is man and his heart, before inanimate things and technical conquests, that are the first candidates for the Kingdom. Then comes the whole world of historical things, dependent upon the community of persons. History makes up, day after day, everything that will be saved—the stones of the heavenly city.

2. *Human history prepares the coming of the Kingdom.* In other words, it is under given historical conditions that the events of sacred history take place and that the Kingdom grows. These conditions may be favorable or unfavorable, occasions for the grace of the Kingdom or occasions for the shutting out of the Kingdom from the historical infra-structures of the human collectivity. Because this function is more external than the preceding one, the referring of history to the Kingdom is here of vital importance and encourages the Christian to act within history.

How will Jesus Christ reign effectively over human history? We can answer with this certitude: by the mediations that He has left to His Church and that assure the presence and the power of the

Risen One within us, the believers. We have no need of inventing anything: Jesus Christ Himself has provided for the way He would continue His Incarnation among us, and through us. For under the impulsion of the personality of Christ we must become as it were His channels through whom all the elements of history may come under His life-giving influence in the "Christophere." It is through us, through our faith, by our perpetual thanksgiving united to Christ's Eucharist, by our efficacious prayer and our contemplative action, that human history becomes in all truth sacred history.

Within the Church and through faith in Christ, history flows toward its eternal consecration. But, it may be asked: What are we to say of so many elements of history—and among them very large and rich elements—that are unaware that they are revealed in Jesus Christ? Will the history that has not found its mediations of salvation in Jesus Christ be condemned? In this connection let us be modest and not make glib affirmations that will contradict the universal plan of God's love for our world, a love that goes so far as to absorb even sin itself.

Without Jesus Christ, history does not possess the inward resources for reaching beyond itself. There is no salvation in the elements of the world and of history taken in themselves. We cannot leave Jesus Christ out of consideration when there is question of salvation. Let us not draw back before the tragedy whose only purpose is to intensify our faith: i.e., the fact that the human history that deliberately refuses to give itself to Christ and that proclaims its idolatry, and likewise the human values that have proclaimed their self-sufficiency, their greed, and their pride, are outside the history of salvation.

We have spoken of the refusal to accept Christ. But is there not a personal and collective way of being united to Christ, of accepting something of His sovereignty, outside the explicit knowledge of Revelation? With the grace of God, cannot man attain to supernatural existence through a certain love, a certain tendency of the heart to oblation? In this sense, could not genuine love be the salvation of large areas of human history? Might it not be the mediation that subjects human lives to Christ without their knowing it, and likewise brings into subjection all the historical realities bound up with their lives? Love would then give its meaning to all partial values, to all techniques, to all material and cultural progress. Indeed, how could love come from Satan, if it has cast aside selfishness and if it is the opposite of complacency and pride? While this is God's secret, it would appear that such love is, as it were, a gift of Christ and that it attains to God.

It must be quite clear that according to this hypothesis the power of Christ would reach far beyond the limits of the "explicit" faith of Christians. We can even ask ourselves in this connection if the "world" is not sometimes included in the society of Christians, and if the Kingdom does not sometimes quicken—in an incomplete way—persons and movements visibly outside the Church.

In any event, Jesus Christ remains the leaven of history, her eternal youth through her periods of growing old as well as in her upward flights and her creative activities. A certain conversion of human values is needed to make of them realities of sacred history in Jesus Christ. In the world of today many of the efforts toward love and peace doubtless constitute pre-Christian values in the process of conversion to the unknown or misunderstood Christ.

Christian clearheadedness must be as wary of notions of false transcendence as of a false incarnation. That is, it must beware of an incarnation which would consist solely in making history sacred or divine; or of a transcendence which would not be alarmed to see almost the whole of history go down to defeat.

This limited world, this passing history, this same world and this same history are the foundation of Christian hope, because Christ took them up into His glory when He rose from the dead; and because *we* are in the world and *we* exist in history.

Even though we are bound to Christ and touched by His glory in our mortal beings, we must remain in history. And we must remain in history not out of delusory resignation but in order to exert a serious influence on it. For henceforth we are in history as an element of Christ. The mystery of Christ reveals to us at each instant the true meaning of human history; it gives its meaning to all human matters.

Therefore, there is no time for sloth. Many incentives press the Christian to action: the missionary motive, with all its social and cultural implications; the motive of brotherhood, for Christian faith without active fraternal charity is a lie; the motive of thanksgiving, for the Christian people are delegated to the consecration of all human values in Jesus Christ. It is through their action within the course of history that all these motives achieve efficacy.

We must be competent, too, as if we were not even awaiting the

Kingdom. Faith does not dispense us from this. Christians too often give the impression that only the pious intention and utilization of temporal realities matter for them, instead of respecting creation and man in order to reveal them in Jesus Christ.

In the measure that we are present in the midst of the world in action, with all the lucidity and effective power of our faith, Jesus Christ will also be present in it. Then the idolatry and paganism of the sorcerers' apprentices will retreat. Then love will manifest itself, giving meaning to all material developments. Then, too, the divine direction of man's progress will be manifest, giving its own direction even to love.

Thus, the reign of Christ over history and civilizations can come only from within. A sociological annexation, an exterior utilization, the putting on of a Christian label too often tend to be nothing but the deceptions of a shallow clericalism. When seen in this light, the whole problem of what has been called "Christian civilization" finds its true solution. The baptism of societies and civilizations, like that of persons, presupposes faith in Jesus Christ, or at least a certain inward conversion.

2. THE MISSION OF THE CHURCH AND THE MISSIONS

(a) *The missionary Church*

Only a limited number of Christians go to the missions, but the whole Church is missionary. She has been sent by Christ for the growth of His Body among all peoples. She is catholic. And to this end the Church strives to root herself as an institution of salvation among all peoples. The pope as the supreme Pastor has special solicitude for those countries which do not yet have affiliations with any particular church. And it is up to all the bishops of the local churches to help him in this work by supplying him with missionaries, both priests and laymen.

Addressing the bishops, Pope Pius XI said: "It was not only to Peter, whose Chair we occupy, but to all the Apostles, whose place you have taken, that Jesus gave the commandment to 'go into the whole world and preach the gospel to every creature' (Mk. 16:15). Whence it is evident that the duty of spreading the faith is incumbent upon you in such a way that you are held, beyond any possibility of doubt, to join with Us in sharing the work and in assisting Us as much as each of you is free to do so in his own par-

Pentecost, the birth of the Church.

Vézelay, daughter of the Cluny Abbey, has a learned composition sculptured on the tympanum of its narthex.

In the middle is the figure of Christ enveloped in a mandorla (see pp. 114-115 above). From his hands go forth rays, the symbols of the Holy Spirit, extending to the heads of each of the Apostles. The figures of the lintel and the compartments show the various peoples of the earth to be evangelized by the Apostles. These peoples are represented in the way the Middle Ages imagined the peoples of antiquity to have been: skiapods (lower right) with gigantic feet with which they shaded their heads from the sun; cynocephalics (above, to the left of Christ) or dog-headed men; pygmies, on the right of the lintel, using ladders to get up on their horses; Scythians, with big ears, etc.

The unfolding of the scene begins from the center of the lintel, going to the left. First there are the peoples who are waiting or carrying offerings: they have not yet received the Gospel or even the Old Law. Then come those who receive God's Revelation and at the same time experience the power of the Spirit who works prodigies through the preaching of the Apostles: two persons are showing each other their healed arms or legs; a third is gazing at his foot.

To the right, it seems that a blind woman is being led, while a little further a lame man is approaching. The reception of the Good News inspires all these figures. Finally, the right portion of the lintel shows those who have been evangelized going in a procession toward St. Peter, who is recognizable by his keys, and toward St. Paul, both of whom are welcoming all peoples. The mutilated statue leaning against the center support represents St. John the Baptist carrying the lamb on a medallion: this is the figure of Baptism through which men enter the Church.

The Church's mission is evoked not simply in space but also in time. Around the circumference of the tympanum we can see the signs of the zodiac, alternating with the labors of the months that determine the rhythms of man's life.

Portal of the narthex in Vézelay (first quarter of the twelfth century).

ticular post. . . . In such a serious matter, the reckoning that God will some day ask will not be inconsiderable" (Encycl. *Rerum Ecclesiae*). Moreover, it is up to all the faithful to take an interest in the Church's expansion by their self-sacrifice, their help, and their prayers. All the members are jointly responsible for the Church.

What we have just said is valid first of all from a geographical and ethnical point of view. But there is no reason why it cannot be interpreted sociologically as well. Viewed in this light, the mission would consist in making the Church present in certain classes of men who are ignorant of her, even within an established local church. As Cardinal Suhard has pointed out: "In the Middle Ages and even up to the nineteenth century, missionaries 'went forth' from Christendom to preach to the 'infidel nations'. Paganism was 'outside' Christian Society. Today, on the contrary, the two 'cities' are no longer mutually exclusive, but one within the other, and closely overlapping." [2]

The canonical definition of the word *mission* is very precise: "Those places where the hierarchy is not yet constituted." But this definition does not cover everything. A given country may not yet have its own hierarchy and yet possess sectors of Christianity in full exercise; whereas a country with an established hierarchy may have vast sectors of people to evangelize. In order to avoid ambiguity, we shall therefore speak of "missionary sectors" rather than of "missionary countries."

It should be added that while *planting the Church* constitutes the essential work of the mission, this is not its whole work. Each individual church endowed with its own hierarchy must remain missionary through one of its functions. For it is always the Church that brings forth the Church. Obviously, here we are speaking of the Church as a whole, but we are speaking as much and more of the local church that has the responsibility for making Christ present by signs and words in the midst of a world tempted to return to paganism.

The role of signs in this connection is vitally important. It is the role of Christian communities to astonish the world, to pose a question to it by their very life. If they do not, then preaching will remain abstract and a matter of words, just like a merely human

[2] *The Church Today,* "Growth or Decline of the Church?" (Chicago: Fides, 1953).

system. Thus the interior life of the Church continually conditions her exterior life; evangelization is a doomed work unless the Church is able to show that the Spirit of Christ dwells within her.

(b) *The Theological Justification of the Missions*

There has been much discussion recently about the purpose and necessity of the missions. In general, the consideration has been limited to the spiritual yield of the missions. There are some who believe that the majority of non-baptized persons do not in actual fact have much access to the resources of divine grace; and they consequently look to evangelization as the means for their salvation. Others, who have greater trust in the good dispositions of these men in response to divine grace, admit that missions can be the cause *sine qua non* for the salvation of a certain number of souls, but they prefer to look upon the missions as the means of bringing to the greater number the fullness of life that they lack. Both of these points of view are correct, and must be retained—the second especially, to our way of thinking. But neither of these approaches provides an absolute, theological basis for the necessity of the missions. Actually, it is in the very nature of the Church of Christ, as He Himself has willed it, that the need for the missionary function is rooted.

The principal work of the missions, on the level of the Church, is to put an end to the abnormality of invisible membership in the spiritual and visible Church, and—needless to say—to establish the Church where she does not exist at all. The Church is a living being seeking its completion. In order for her members to participate in her life, they must be engrafted on her visible organism and thus assure her plenitude: fullness of spiritual life, bound up with fullness of life in the visible communion.

In this theological justification of the missionary function of the Church, the spiritual yield for the benefit of individuals is not forgotten. In fact, it is assured by the same token. But the justification which this spiritual yield postulates has been assumed into a view of superior wisdom based on the very essence of the Christian economy of salvation.

3. THE REUNION OF THE CHURCHES

(a) *Disunited Christians*

It is a fact—and a scandal—that while all Christians are unanimous in claiming they belong to Christ, they do not agree on the way to belong to Him. In His apostolic prayer, Jesus said: "That all may be one, even as thou, Father, in me and I in thee; . . . that the world may know that thou hast sent me" (Jn. 17:21-23). And yet Christians lay bare to the world the spectacle of their division into a number of churches. A true disciple of Christ cannot resign himself to the existence of these divisions. Even if he is certain of being in the true fold of Christ, he suffers because he has separated brothers, and he labors for reunion, as the Catholic Church has always done in her prayers and in her action.

(b) *The modes of reunion*

The abettors of schism and heresy have prodded the defenders of orthodoxy to set up a rigorous apologetics of the Church whose purpose is to prove that the Catholic Church, in spite of the human insufficiencies of her ministers and with all her dogmatic exigencies, remains the only Church of Christ. This controversial apologetics has been the charter of almost all Catholic efforts for reunion against the two great dissidences of Orthodoxy and of the Protestant Reformation. From this point of view, the dissidents are considered as men entirely cut off from Christian truth, who will recover it only by abjuring their erroneous faith and by being converted to the faith of the Catholic Church.

In itself, this apologetic approach is valid, and its dogmatic rigor is basically correct. Many converts have tested it. However, this view presents only one aspect of the truth, and then in an oversimplified way. Actually, a great many dissidents are not themselves abettors of dissidence. In their secession, they have kept a part of the Christian capital, and this capital continues to bear fruit among them. Thus the Church of Christ invisibly embraces them within her frontiers. They are not totally outside.

It would therefore be more exact to consider the dissidents in good faith as imperfect members of the Catholic Church and to present the return to unity to them as the fulfillment of their charity in the visible community of the "catholica," as a fuller participation

in the life-giving influence of Christ. Newman affirmed, at the end
of his long journey toward the Catholic Church, that his conversion
had changed nothing substantially in his Anglican life: it merely
brought him more total light, and more certain possession.

(c) *Ecumenicism*

While the effort for the reunion of individuals to the Catholic
Church is very fruitful, especially if it is understood as a fulfillment,
it calls for reunion on the level of whole groups. We know the attempts Anglo-Saxon Protestantism has made to create an ecumenical movement, and the evolution of this movement from a rather
pragmatic basis to a frankly doctrinal one. The present Ecumenical
Council of Churches, that groups the majority of Protestant
Churches and a part of the Orthodox Church, is not a super-
Church, but a friendly community of Churches that accept Jesus
Christ as their God and Savior, regardless of their conception of
the Church and without any one of them seeking to make its own
particular point of view dominate the others.

A Catholic cannot fail to rejoice over such initiatives inspired
by the nostalgia for unity, even though he may have fears that they
will not in the end attain to the reunion that, he knows, is the only
authentic one. For, to the mind of the Catholic, the unity of the
Church is not purely eschatological, nor something to be accomplished here below. As he sees it, this unity has already been given
and it exists in the Catholic Church. It is a truth to be recognized
and lived. In other words, the Catholic's idea of ecumenicism cannot have the same meaning it has been given by Protestants. The
Catholic's ecumenicism leads him to an irenical and positive consideration of dissidences; his dogmatism is not a doctrine of authoritarian triumph, but consists in simple fidelity to the truth that has
come from God in Christ, and without which there is no true
charity.

God alone knows the hour and the means of the reunion of the
separated churches to the Church. This does not lessen the obligation of Catholics to work for it with all their strength in a great
spirit of truth and charity, by fighting for the triumph of the purity
of the spirit of Christ in His Church. And they will gladly recognize every element of positive Christianity in their separated
brethren, while pointing out that the Church possesses the plenitude
of the Christian values to which they legitimately hold fast. And

Catholics will do all this without liberalism, but also without the Pharisaism of those who think they have been constituted judges over their brothers, simply because God has deigned to allow His truth to dwell in them. It can happen that a dissident Christian may be truer than his Church, and that a Catholic may be less true than his Church.

CONCLUSION

The pedagogy of the mystery of the Church. Entrance through faith into the plenitude of the mystery of the Church is the achievement of an adult faith. The progressive awakening of believers to the meaning of the Church should be a major concern of every Christian educator. To succeed in this, it is necessary to have assimilated this total mystery over a long period of time and to sense the difficulties that its presentation can meet in the contemporary mind. While the following suggestions are far from telling the whole story, they seem to us to be fundamental:

1. The mystery of the Church is a lived mystery. Here more than in other aspects of the Christian mystery, an *initiation* is needed. It is more important to give Christians an authentic experience of the Church than to give them treatises on the Church. Now, an experience is based on concrete and immediate conditions. In other words, initiation into the Church will begin as an experience in living in a local community: a local community of faith, fraternal love, the Eucharist, missionary expansion, a community in which the priesthood guarantees the apostolic bond. This community is a true cell of the Church, from which the Christian will come to know the universal Church. Catechesis will unfold the significance of this experience of the Church in the measure that it is lived.

2. This catechesis will constantly subordinate the institutional aspect to the aspect of spiritual mystery in the infrangible unity of the historical Church. Images will be useful in helping faith grasp this point.

First image: The Temple, during its construction, needs scaffolding (*The Shepherd of Hermas,* Vision 9). The Church will one day be the completed Temple of God and of the Lamb. At the present time she is inseparable from her scaffolding, for until the end of time she will be in progress of construction; however, the scaffolding has meaning only for the building of the Temple.

Second image: A broken limb needs the support of bandages until it recovers its free movement. Thus will the Church some day enjoy her total and free vitality for all eternity. Now she must receive her vigor through the means of humble but necessary human mediations. St. Augustine, who makes use of this image, says: "Everything that is accomplished in the Church of time resembles these medical bandages." (*Enarr. in psal.* 146,8; P.L. 37, 1904.)

Third image: The ear of grain is carried on its stalk, and it is the ripe ear that counts. On the feast day of the harvest, the straw will be burned and the wheat will be housed. But the ear will not reach maturity unless it is carried on its stalk, through which it receives its vitality. So is it with the Church as she prepares for the feast of the eternal harvest by attaining to her maturity in history, through institutional mediations that are temporary and yet indispensable.

Fourth image: The mold used by the modeler to fashion a work of art. The Church is a work of art, God's masterpiece. Christ is the ever-active artisan of God's plan. To this end He makes use of the institution that He founded and to which He has given the marks of His eternal Church. When the work of art is completed, the mold is no longer of any use. So will it be with the Church after history.

3. When the Church is presented as a *community,* it will be stressed that her collective aspect in no way diminishes the reality and the demands of personal vocations. To the same extent that the Church contradicts individualism, she must also be distinguished from a mass or an instinctive collectivity. It is normal that the total discovery of the Church as a community should come about only after initiation into the personal faith that marks the beginning of adulthood.

4. As to the *institutional aspect* of the Church, stress should be laid on the wisdom of Christ who founded an institution of holiness perfectly adapted to human nature, in accordance with the intentions of the Incarnation. Christ did not found the Apostolic Church to humiliate us, to subject us to arbitrary rule and to force us to obey. He founded it to serve us. The fact remains that in the historical Christ, the Incarnation made God present to men under the features of the Holy One, whereas in the Church God gives Himself to us through a humanity that is less pure and that is not exempt from sin. But it is the same faith that makes us recognize

the coming of God through the historical person of Christ and through the historical face of the Church as mediatrix. Consequently greater emphasis will be placed on the personal character of the Church's mediations, as being "acts of Christ" and not merely "things."

5. Finally, the relativism of historical forms in which the Institution of Christ finds expression should be pointed out. To attribute to purely ecclesiastical dispositions a value of divine stability is no homage to Christ, but a weakness of faith. First of all, there is the eternal reality of the Church, as imperishable as the life of God Himself; and then there is the historical reality of the Church instituted by Christ, as lasting as Christ's will concerning the duration of His Church. There are historical expressions of both of these realities, which vary with the historical conditions of humanity in its progress toward the Kingdom. The source of true freedom of faith in the Church lies in the distinctions between these two points of view. The faithful of the present day are legitimately conscious of these distinctions.

*   *   *

Let us allow the liturgy to have the last word, by quoting from the splendid Preface of the Mass of the Dedication of a church inscribed in the Proper of certain French dioceses:

"It is truly meet and just, right and availing to salvation, that we should give thanks unto Thee, O Lord, eternal God, the dispenser of all good things, who hast chosen this house of prayer as your dwelling, which we have raised up with our hands, and who dost sanctify by Thy unceasing action the Church that Thou hast founded. For it is this Church, the true house of prayer, that our visible edifices seek to represent, the temple of Thy glory, the seat of incommutable truth, the sanctuary of eternal charity. She is the ark in which, having escaped from the flood of humanity, we are sailing toward the haven of salvation. She is the beloved and only Spouse that Christ won at the price of His blood, and that He quickens by His spirit.

"In her bosom we were born anew to life by the gift of Thy grace; There we were nourished with the milk of Thy words, strengthened by the Bread of life, comforted by the help of Thy mercy. It is this same Church that fights with faith and loyalty here on earth, with the help of her Spouse, and that, triumphant in heaven, receives from Him the crown of glory forever."

REFLECTIONS AND PERSPECTIVES

The present position of ecclesiology. We have chosen to present the present position of ecclesiology by quoting from a judicious commentary by Étienne Borne (*La Vie Intellectuelle,* December, 1953, pp. 21-38), on Father Yves Congar's work, *Lay people in the Church* (Westminster, Md., Newman, 1957). With a wisdom worthy of the book he is evaluating, the author of this commentary says that today, as indeed in all times, we are faced in ecclesiology with the temptation to make two "approximations," which he distinguishes in terms of the place they respectively give to the laity and to the clergy.

According to one approximation, the laity seem to be in the Church like sick men in a hospital or like pupils in a school. Indeed, the laity are sick spiritually, for the world in which they live is an unfailing occasion of sin. Therefore the laity need to be admitted into this hospital-school which is the Church, that they may be cared for and cured, instructed and enlightened. For in the Church are the clergy who have the authority, the competence, and the powers to do these things. They are the doctors, nurses, and teachers who have access to the efficacious means of grace which will change sickness into health, and ignorance into knowledge.

Our author goes on to say that such a theology of the laity can be reconciled in the conscience of the layman, with the most contradictory political philosophies.

At times the layman will lean to the right and admire, in this sacred Society in which the people are bound by an obedience that is also a devotion, an exemplary image of the universal human order that calls for the subjection of son to father, of woman to man, and of subject to sovereign. At other times, the layman will lean to the left, and show his concern for the freedom of his temporal involvement, and will stay in a state of insurrection against any kind of clerical interference; and yet he will declare himself blindly obedient to the hierarchical Church in the purely spiritual order of things.

This separatism is rather common: complete independence on the one hand, and radical dependence on the other. Thus, a right-wing layman and a left-wing layman can profess this same theology of a wholly passive and obedient laity, not without an inferiority complex and false humility—and these tendencies are sometimes encouraged either consciously or unconsciously by the many conflicts that tend to be identified with the active and guiding portion of the Church.

According to the second approximation, on the contrary, the Church is a growing body, a building under construction, and—

There is no other breath of life, no other architectural thought than the breath and the thought that come from the Holy Spirit through Christ. Differences in function between the clergy and the laity are evident, but they do not entail a religious inferiority of some in relation to the others. In the spiritual search, the sick man and the pupil before the physician and teacher can just as well be the cleric before the layman as the layman before the cleric. Thus are accomplished the vital exchanges of a developing organism. . . . The laity, fully integrated into the Church, would fruitfully remind her that her role is not to remove men from the world, one at a time, but to save both humanity and the world.

Here again theology can reconcile diverse philosophies:

One may become a Bergsonian to oppose ready-made and non-essential structures of the Church in favor of the creative "élan" of a living community which is the most pure, and the divine, essence of the Church. Throughout the history of biological evolution, life is the cause and structure is the effect. And yet sometimes the effect turns against its cause, and life at a standstill turns against life in motion. Then the clergy is motionless and the laity is on the move.

But since the Church is always inspired by the Holy Spirit, and this is the definition of an infallibility that holds for the total community, the falling back of the "élan" cannot prevail over the ever-renewed springing up of the fountain of life. Finally, in order to bring human anxiety and religious hope closer together, one may even at times dare to use a vocabulary of Marxist origin. Has not the laity long held in the Church the position of a nomadic rather than of an integrated proletariat, that could participate in religious culture and life only through the mediation of a priestly class? And has this not hardened the laity in an intolerable state of hostility?

These are the two ecclesiologies, or at least the two tendencies of the "approximations" that confront each other in contemporary Catholic consciousness.

The first was static, authoritarian, bearing the marks of Jansenism and pessimism as to the natural capacities of man both for the future and for his temporal adventure. It was clear and precise, perhaps because resentment and negation have more distinct outlines than do "élan" and generosity. In the other theology there is vehemence and impatience, the vocation of the Church, the identification and intermingling of the most clearly distinct orders, but there is also a vast intuitive wealth and the surge of creative energy.

The truth is that this dilemma must be overcome. In the words of Étienne Borne:

We must substitute the philosophy of the *and* for the philosophy of the *or*. We must not think of the Church as either structure or life, institution or community, hierarchy or brotherhood. On the contrary, the Church is structure and life, institution and community, hierarchy and brotherhood. A synthetic approach disposes of the dilemma from the start.

This is not to say that each of these two aspects represents a half-truth that might need to be balanced by the complement of another half-truth. Such a dialectic of insufficiency would be an insufficiency of thought. In reality, each aspect is *pars totalis,* partial when separated from the other, according to a psychological, historical, or sociological analysis, but total according to theological intuition—it is at one and the same time one aspect of the Church and the whole Church. Indeed, the whole Church existed before the faithful, from the time of the first Apostolic College; and she possessed the powers of consecration, forgiveness, and preaching that had been given her from above by Christ. It is the whole Church that is the community of the faithful, and constituted by them one living body which is the Body of Christ Himself. The Church as institution is the whole Church. The Church as community is the whole Church. The Church as community and the Church as institution are one and the same Church.

We shall therefore avoid any ecclesiology that might develop one of these aspects of the Church *to the detriment* of the other, that is to say, one against the other. The truth must assume everything without conflict. The Church is not only a hierarchical society endowed with certain "powers"; she is also a living body quickened in its entirety by the Spirit of God. An ecclesiology that was only a "hierarchology" would be quite as false as one that was exclusively a "pneumatology" (see Lexicon). Likewise, the Church is without sin, but she is made up of sinners. *Immaculata ex maculatis.* Finally, the Church is not made up principally or essentially of the authority of some and the obedience of others. She is composed of the love of charity that unites all the members of Christ to one another in the Holy Spirit.

And yet the unity of the Church is not the result of a "Sobornost" (see Lexicon), a sisterhood of Churches that are inwardly and outwardly equal. She is the effect of a hierarchical arrangement, which does not harm the sisterhood of the individual Churches and of the bishops among themselves. Even over against the hierarchy there is a "public opinion" to be defended, as Pope Pius XII called to mind on February 18, 1950, before the International Press Congress. Even over against the Bishop of Rome, who is the Pope, the other bishops are his "brothers" and not his "sons." He himself calls them "Venerable brothers."

The general trend of ecclesiology since the sixteenth century and especially since Cardinal Bellarmine, has been to insist upon the visible, exterior, and hierarchical aspect of the Church, to the detriment of her interior, organic, "pneumatic" aspect; to insist upon the powers of the Magisterium and of the priesthood rather than on the grace of the Holy Spirit that is poured out on all the members of the Church; in short, to identify the Church with the clergy and to hold the laity in low esteem. The contrary tendency that is now taking shape must guard against the contagion of an exclusivism that could be just as vicious even though it tends in the opposite direction.

The Church and the World. It is not as of today that the question of the relationship between the Church and the world has come up. Already in the second century, the nature of this relationship was clearly indicated in the famous *Letter to Diognetus.* Only recently Pope Pius XII cited what he called "a magnificent sentence" from this letter which seemed "a warning for the present time: 'Christians inhabit individual countries, but they do so as wayfarers; every foreign region is a homeland for them, and every homeland is foreign soil' " (Encyclical *Evangelii Praecones,* June 2, 1951). Actually the Greek word πάροικοι, which has been translated "tenants," should be "guests" or "strangers."

Nevertheless, the perpetual temptation of the Church, or at least of the Christians in the Church, is twofold. On the one hand there is the temptation to withdraw from the world and to oppose it: to be strangers in this world, no longer to speak the language of everyone, and because of that no longer to be listened to by men. At its limits, this would mean that the Church would cease being an institution of salvation for the men of this world. The second temptation is the contrary one of mingling too much in the world, of not being sufficiently on one's guard against it. The danger then is that the salt of the Gospel will lose its savor and that Christianity will be prostituted to false gods. A sound theology of the relationship of the Church to the world must in every era maintain these two terms of the dialectic: The Church is of this world and not of this world.

This problem has recently had a historical significance that we cannot fail to mention here, especially as it will help to see the question under a different light. In the general crumbling of institutions in Europe or at least in France during the years 1940–1945, even the best Christians were often tempted to give up all thought of restoring these institutions and these works that had seemed so necessary in eras of "glorious Catholicism," that is, when Catholicism was apparently and institutionally triumphant within nations. In 1937 the J.O.C. (Young Christian Workers) declared at its Congress: "We shall build the Cathedral." But by 1946, it was not far from saying: "We shall build the Catacomb," that is, a true brotherhood, unencumbered by any institution.

What is the golden mean in this matter? Must the Church renounce the thought of having her own works and institutions, distinct from those of the world? Or else must she simply renounce certain works and not others? Must she seek to be seen, to show herself, to express her spiritual power temporally, as in the days of the Inquisition—and even show her temporal power, as in the epoch of what has been called "Cesaropapism"? Or should she on the contrary withdraw into the background, renounce the pageantry and honor given to her ministers, and all her pomp?

Father Liégé's beautiful chapter on theology will, we hope, give the essential elements of the answer. We shall simply present here a few pointers that seem to indicate the direction that thought on these questions ought to take.

1. The Church is not of this world. There is no homogeneity between the people of God and the peoples of earth. God's people do not have the same origin, nor the same end, nor the same perfection as other peoples. Whereas the Church, instituted by Christ, finds her perfection at every moment and also eschatologically in something beyond this earth, the people of earth seek their perfection here below. God's people do not develop according to the same laws as do other peoples. The law of constant "progress" which is that of the development of the peoples of earth is not transposable to the people of God. For the latter, defeat, humiliation, loss in numbers and in prestige, and even death may be just as important, and sometimes more important than anything else. Finally, God's people and the peoples of earth do not use the same means of development. Earthly peoples need many complex materials. The people of God have only one means, apparently the lowliest of all: God's Revelation and the sacraments of His Revelation.

Thus, the Church, considered as the people of God, is fundamentally different from this world. However:

2. The people of God are men of this world. The best means by which Christians can make sure they are not of this world is to live the life of their time, to speak the language of their own world, and to live with their contemporaries not as strangers but as true fellow-citizens.

Merely to live in the twentieth century according to the ways of living, thinking, and speaking of the sixteenth century, or perhaps of the twelfth or sixth centuries, is not necessarily equivalent to "not being of this world." It is simply living in the twentieth century according to the mode of another era. And if these institutions are perpetuated in order to regain temporal power, to keep ancient riches, to develop earthly possessions, and to preserve the ancient human means of a society that no longer exists, then this life in an outworn style is a camouflage and a scandal for the true Christian.

Now, there is no denying that God's people are perpetually tempted to preserve their means of expression, especially those that succeeded in the beautiful epochs of faith because they were the work of believers who *sincerely* expressed their faith in their own language, which was the language of their epoch.

We might choose church architecture as an example, although the same remarks might be made concerning charitable institutions, schools, theological teaching, religious communities, good works, the religious or ecclesiastical habit, and so on. In the case of architecture, there is a temptation in epochs when faith is declining to take up again styles that flourished in ages of faith. Thus the twentieth century has revived the Baroque style that had its fullest meaning at the time of the Counter-Reformation in Italy or in Spain; even the so-called "Gothic" of the thirteenth and fourteenth century French cathedrals and the Romanesque style have come back into fashion.

To plunge back into the past in this way is *not* to be an authentic Christian who is outside the world because he is inwardly living in a spiritual realm that is beyond this world. Flirting with other epochs, other customs, other attitudes, does not make anyone less of this world. Often enough it is a rather powerful bond to this world, for estrangement from the present presupposes that a person is not sincere with his true self or with the present moment. And can anyone find God if he is not sincere with himself, or with this instant or this time that can communicate with Eternity? Besides, anyone who does not live in his own time is depriving his contemporaries of a testimony of faith by which neither the men of the past nor the men of the future can profit. Even though God's people are not of this world, they exist none the less here and now.

3. God's people have a radical need to express themselves. The people of God are proud of their faith and want to show it forth in broad daylight. They build cathedrals, compose "Summas" of the-

ology, organize great pilgrimages and ceremonies of all sorts, launch works of mercy and charity, publish magazines and pictures, etc. And as in all visible matters, a certain material show is necessary in all these works of "expression."

There is always the temptation to develop this material display either by multiplying Church ceremonies and increasing their pageantry, or by inventing new works: schools, hospitals, various administrations, bureaus, etc. But sometimes too great material wealth is detrimental to "expression." Signs which should be a help to lead the mind to the realities they signify can be screens and obstacles if they make the mind stop and become engrossed in the signs themselves.

A golden mean is therefore necessary quite as much in the pageantry of the Church's activities as in the multiplication of these works, which are helps to profane society, so that visible things may always be conformable to the Spirit who dwells in the Church. We know that Providence periodically sees to it that God's people, who are tempted to glorify themselves in their structures, are brought back to "poor means."

This "golden mean" will determine the amount of splendor that may be allowed or must be denied the Church's temples and ceremonies. There can be no doubt that the evangelical primacy of charity forbids Christians from gilding their temple when men are dying of hunger against its walls; it keeps them from closing their church at night if men would die of cold without this shelter. Our Savior's words: "The poor you have always with you, but you do not always have me" (Mt. 26:11) do not mean that the magnificence of churches need have no limit or that we can be vain about them under the pretext that they serve divine worship. We know today that the tower of Babel was essentially a religious structure, "God's stepladder." And yet might it not be the symbol of those monuments or ceremonies that are intended to honor God but call down His curse because of men's vanity about them?

The Church and the Dissidents. The Church is visible, and yet she contains more than appears to the eye. We know that there are "just men" outside her visible boundaries, that is to say, men who are invisibly attached to the visible Church.

In other words, the Church is not a private religion, as are certain present-day Negro and Indian religions, which are so well guarded that no white man has so far been able to see all their ceremonies

NAME	ORIGIN	NUMBER
THE CHURCHES		
I. The Roman Catholic Church.		422,000,000.
II. The Orthodox Church.		140,000,000.
Old National Churches separated from Rome and Byzantium in the 5th and 6th centuries.		
1. Nestorians.	Disciples of Nestorius, condemned by the Council of Ephesus in 431 and by the 2nd Council of Constantinople in 553.	about 100,000.
2. Armenians.	Separated at the beginning of the 6th century.	about 2,500,000, of whom 900,000 are in the U.S.S.R.
3. Syrian Jacobites.	Monophysites (schism born of refusal to accept the Council of Chalcedon, 451), organized by the monk James Baradas.	about 80,000.
4. Christians of St. Thomas.	Nestorians.	about 220,000.
5. Monophysite Coptic Church.	Egyptian Monophysite dissidents (6th cent.).	about 1,000,000.
6. Abyssinian Monophysite Church.	Ethiopian Monophysite dissidents (6th cent.).	about 3,000,000.
III. Protestantism:		
Lutherans.	Luther.	68,000,000.
Reformed (Calvinists and Zwinglians).		41,000,000.
Lutheran-Reformed.		
Anglican Church.	Schism of Henry VIII.	30,000,000.
THE SECTS		
A. *Sects separated from the Catholic Church.*		
The Gallican Catholic Church. The Anti-Concordat Church (1801).		
1. German Catholics.	Founded in 1844–1845 by two misguided priests, John Rong and Gerski.	barely 2,000.

DOCTRINAL AND HIERARCHICAL STATUS

There has been no break in continuity between the Apostolic College and the succession of bishops in these two Churches. They therefore both possess an authentic hierarchy, an authentic priesthood, and authentic sacraments. Concerning the word "Orthodox" and the differences between the two Churches, see *Introduction to Theology*, Vol. I, p. 112. Concerning the different rites of these Churches, which are the rites of "the Church," see Tables, Vol. I, pp. 114-117.

Patriarch at Kotschanès.

Catholicos at Etchmiadzin.

Patriarch at the convent of Dar-us-za (Iraq).

Valid episcopate and priesthood. Controversial points of doctrine have often been obscured through the centuries.

(Syria, Persia, India, China).

Patriarch at Cairo.

Autonomous hierarchy of recent date.

There has been a break in the continuity between the Apostolic College and the hierarchy, where the latter exists.
A hierarchy without hierarchical force, without a priesthood. In Sweden, Lutheranism has bishops, but they are only theoretically necessary.

The "hierarchy" is represented by a system of "presbyters" (that is, *elders*), who are elected in principle. Break in the continuity.

Possesses an episcopal hierarchy, but one that the Catholic Church cannot accept, since there has been a break in the continuity *de facto* between the Apostolic College and the hierarchy.

Note: These two Churches have no more priests.

This sect has no real importance today, although it had an ephemeral success in the United States in the 19th century. It has evolved toward a purely secular thought. Theoretically and practically, it no longer has any priesthood.

NAME	ORIGIN	NUMBER
2. National Czechoslovakian Church.	Schism of Dr. Ch. Farsky, of Aug. 1, 1920.	about 700,000.
3. National Church of the Philippines.	Schism of Gr. Aglipay y Aléban, Aug. 3, 1902.	now only 100,000 active members.
4. Old Catholics.	Schism of Catholics who opposed the Vatican Council. Founder: Dollinger, who was against schism but forced into it.	about 80,000 (In Germany, Austria, Switzerland).
Polish-Catholic Church.		
5. Church of Utrecht.	Jansenist origin.	about 12,000.
6. Liberal Catholic Church.	Founded by Wedgwood in England in 1916.	99,000,000.
Mariavites.	Originated in Poland, 1887.	10,000.

B. *Sects separated from the Russian Church.*

1. The Raskol.	Schism of the old-believers in 1667.	about 9,000,000.
2. Christians of the Spirit.		
3. Rationalist Sects.		about 6,000,000.
4. Protestant Sects.		

C. *Sects stemming from Protestantism or connected with it.*

Mennonites.	Founded in Switzerland in 1523.	about 500,000.
Unitarians or Anti-Trinitarians and Socinians.	Sect born of Renaissance humanism.	about 150,000.
Baptists.	Various origins (America and Germany).	40,000,000.
Quakers.	Founded by G. Fox in 1649.	about 200,000.
Methodists.	Founded by John Wesley in 1729.	about 30,000,000.
Mormons.	Founded by Joseph Smith in 1830.	about 700,000.
Adventists.	Founded by William Miller in the 19th century.	about 80,000.

DOCTRINAL AND HIERARCHICAL STATUS

This sect had valid priests. In January, 1946, it asked for and obtained allegiance with the patriarchate of Moscow. It is therefore now included in the Orthodox Church.

Gr. Aglipay, a priest, assumed the title of Archbishop. But the schism had the spirit of naturalistic and rationalist free inquiry. The old Catholics offered to regularize their orders, but this did not take place. Their priesthood is fictitious in the eyes of the Roman Catholic Church.

Valid episcopate and priesthood.
Note: It was Old Catholics who gave valid orders and a valid episcopate to the National Yugoslav Church.

The Polish-Catholic Church, which exists only in the United States, received priests and bishops from the Old Catholics.

Valid episcopate and priesthood.

Sets up an "Apostolic succession" but it must be considered as doubtful in view of the doctrinal positions held.

They received one Old Catholic bishop. Valid priesthood.

The Bezpopovtsi have no priests.
The Popovtsi have valid priests.

Without priests.

All these sects are without authentic priests. We shall name only the most important ones here, for they are innumerable. The reader is referred to the tables set up by Father Congar in *Chrétiens desunis* (Paris: Ed. du Cerf, 1937), p. 353 ff., and to the recent presentation by H.-Ch. Chéry, "Les sectes bibliques" in *Lumière et vie*, No. 6, October, 1952, pp. 67 and 108, with a short bibliography on p. 108. Father Chéry is also preparing a work on the sects.

Calvinist Anabaptist Sect.

Religious subjectivism.

"Evangelical Society."

Its basis has been set forth in "The Book of Mormon" written by the founder.

The founder prophesied the end of the world for 1843-1844.

or to discover their essential beliefs. (In this connection, read two exciting accounts: Pierre-Dominique Gaisseau, *La forêt sacrée, magie et rites secrets des Tomas,* Albin Michel, 1953, and A. Gheerbrant, *L'expedition Orénoque-Amazone 1948–1950,* Gallimard, 1952.) The Church is a universal religion, open "to every man who comes into the world." Therefore in relation to the Church we can evaluate the religions that men profess in terms of the measure of truth they possess, and of the economy of means of salvation that they offer. While all the so-called "pagan" religions are more or less equal in this regard, the same is not true of the purely Christian dissidents or of the Abrahamite dissidents (Israel and Islam). The theologian must be able to weigh the portion of truth and the authentic means of salvation that each of them contains.

So great is the confusion concerning this subject, that we have seen fit to give a brief summary in the following table of what should be known about each "Church." (We are using the word here in the broad sense in which it is used in certain documents of the Magisterium dealing with "the dissident Churches." See for example the rescript of June 12, 1907, of the Sacred Congregation of Indulgences.) The Churches that are listed as having "valid episcopates and priesthoods" also validly possess all the other sacraments.

After the Christian religions, what place is to be given to Judaism and Islam?

We cannot consider the Jews and Moslems in the same light as the pagans and idolaters. They believe in the true God. They are children of Abraham like ourselves, they share a part of Scripture with us. And as far as the Jews are concerned, their present-day life often bears witness providentially to the truth of the traditions of the Old Covenant. On the other hand, they differ from true Christians who are united in the ecumenical movement in that they do not believe in the divinity of Jesus or in His Resurrection. That is why the Chair of Unity Octave held from January 18 to January 25 each year gives them a special place in its prayers, between the Christians and the pagans. They are our brothers only in Abraham.

And yet even this is a vast heritage which these groups share with us, and it deserves to be honored. When Pope Gregory VII received a delegation from the Moslem King Setifienna of Mauretania in Rome in 1076, to discuss the problem of the Christian subjects the latter still had in North Africa, the Pope declared with the breadth of vision proper to the universal Pastor: "We pray God from the

bottom of Our heart to receive you after a long life into the bosom
of the beatitude of the most holy Patriarch Abraham" (cited by Pol
Roussel, "Le christianisme en Mauritanie" in *Maroc-Monde,* July
5, 1952).

As to the countless non-Abrahamite religions that the human race
has known, we cannot forget that we have inherited certain traditions from them, either through their interpretation by Judaism or
at the moment of their conversion to Christianity. We have already
had occasion to point out these traditions, and we shall do so again.
We must also remember that these religions sometimes prepare
men's minds in a providential way for the message of faith. The invasion of the West by Oriental cults was a providential "transition
that was ultimately to assure the expression of the new faith in a
large portion of humanity" (Franz Cumont, *Lux perpetua,* Paris,
P. Geuthner, 1949, p. XXV).

This eminent historian of the Magusians or Western magi, the
priests of the Mazdean diaspora, developed his assertion by saying
that "the preaching of the Asiatic priests prepared . . . the triumph
of the Church, in spite of them, and this triumph was the completion
of the work whose unconscious artisans they had been. . . . By affirming the divine essence of man they strengthened in man the
sentiment of his eminent dignity; by making interior purification the
principal object of earthly existence, they refined and exalted psychic life, and they gave it an almost supernatural intensity that the
ancient world had not known before" (*Les religions orientales dans
le paganisme romain,* Paris, 1906, p. XII, cited in *Lux perpetua,*
p. XXVI).

Indeed, it is permissible to agree with this same author that "the
obvious purpose of the episode of the Magi in the first Gospel was
to show the clergy of the most powerful and the wisest of the Eastern
religions bowing before the Child who was to found the religion of
the future" (*Lux perpetua,* p. XXII). Christ was willing to be recognized by these foreign priests just as Abraham had been by Melchisedech. And the Church devoutly remembers their adoration in
her celebration of Christmas and Epiphany. The religion of "the
children of light" and of Him who said "I am the truth," must honor
what is true and good in every religion, as she has actually done
through the centuries. It would be easy to condemn everything in-
discriminately, but that would not be in accordance with the truth
that the Church professes. For then the Church would be acting like

a private religion in imitation of and on the same level with all the other religions. That would be a far cry from her goal, which is to be "the gathering" of all the "nations" and of all religions, helping them to surpass their own limits and attain to the true God in Jesus Christ our Lord.

The Church and the Missions. In these "Reflections and Perspectives," we shall discuss only two of the questions brought up by the problem of the missions in the world of new exchanges and of unprecedented relationships that we know today:

1. *The Constantinian and Mediterranean inheritance.* The message of salvation in our Latin West has become profoundly bound up with a Christian heritage that was once Constantinian, then medieval, and included the whole Greco-Latin culture slowly formed and nurtured in the Mediterranean civilizations. In fact, so great has this commingling been that we cannot always discern what belongs to the pure message of the Gospel and what stems from this heritage of Mediterranean civilization and Christianity.

There is a tendency for this impasse to become aggravated at the present time because of the crushing predominance of the Latin element in the present-day Roman Church, to the detriment of the Greek and Arabic elements, which are equally Mediterranean. This tendency is visible not only among the faithful, but also among those who govern them and among theologians. The theologian will not deny the providential aspects of these deadlocks between faith and civilization. And yet he must strive to discern what is essential in the message of faith, which must of necessity be communicated to everyone, and what is accidental, the particular heritage of a geographical and social structure or of a specific historical juncture.

In order to bring the faith to the Negroes of Africa, to the Indians of America, or to the Japanese, the missionary does not need to bring them also our Latin grammar, our social customs, our peculiar ways of thinking and praying. On the contrary, there are many things that Christianity can receive from these peoples through which it can become for them the authentic fruit of God's grace *and also* of their own nature.

The mystery of the Church is a mystery of marriage. Wherever the Church appears upon earth, her presence is in some way the result of a marriage. It may prove useful to explain this proposition in a few words.

We know that the Fathers of the Church already conceived of the mystery of the Incarnation as a mystery of a marriage feast: the marriage of the Godhead to humanity in the person of Jesus. But that was only an allegory, for a marriage calls for two persons, and in Christ there never was more than one. It is more exact, as some have indeed done, to consider the "wedding of the Incarnation" not as within the one person of our Lord, but as between our Lord and the Church (see St. Gregory, Hom. on St. Matt., 22).

This mystery of marriage is to be found in the *faith* of every Christian. The word *faith,* to which the word *affiance* (betrothal) is etymologically related, evokes this mystery. Faith comes to us by hearing God's words; but it is likewise a quality of mind, the fruit of the soul in which the grace of God dwells. When we hear God's Revelation, it is as if someone awoke within us a sense that had been dormant since our creation. Faith is something that is within us, the fruit of our own heart, endowed with God's grace. A marriage has taken place between the Word of God and our soul, and our faith is the expression of this marriage.

Like missionary evangelization, the gift of faith is not a message that the missionary can impose from without. Preaching is not a dictatorial command. The latter is a violation of conscience, whereas missionary evangelization always seeks to bring about a marriage between God's Revelation and a given form of mentality, of mind, of civilization, or of humanity. God did not fear to be conceived by a woman, nor does He fear to be conceived spiritually by our various types of minds. He has no fear lest He no longer resemble His true Self when He comes into our minds. On the contrary, He must be understood in a thousand ways in order to be well understood.

God is ineffable. We do not even begin to understand Him unless we conceive Him in intimate union with all our Catholic brothers. Thus, there is a marriage between Christ and the Church, and at the same time there are a thousand marriages, as many marriages as there are minds and forms of humanity to receive Christ. Missionary evangelization must strive to honor these authentic human values everywhere, and to make a success of these "marriages" everywhere.

In recent years a number of good books have been published on the missionary question. We refer the reader to the following works, and to the bibliographies they contain: A. Rétif, S.J., *Foi au Christ et mission* (Paris, Ed. du Cerf, 1953); V. Seumois, O.M.I., *Introduction à la missiologie* (Beckenried, 1952); Guy de Bretagne, O.M.I., *Pastorale catéchétique* (Paris, Desclee de Brouwer, 1953).

2. *Episcopal and territorial jurisdiction.* The Church's jurisdictions in the ancient Christian lands as well as in the so-called mission lands, are solely territorial jurisdictions. The sectors entrusted to the bishops are territorial, as are those entrusted to the apostolic vicars or prefects, or to the "provincials" of religious orders.

As it happens, territorial delimitation no longer suffices for pastoral or missionary needs. France, for example, has long been a Christian land territorially, in which the hierarchy has been established and has never ceased being established. However there are "areas" and "social classes" in France—or to use Canon Boulard's term, "sociological territories"—that impinge upon "ecclesiastical territories" and sometimes almost completely escape the influence of territorial ecclesiastical jurisdictions.

While France is not territorially speaking a "mission country," the working class in France is *de facto* a missionary sector. Wherever the working class exists anywhere in France, it is evident that for the most part it escapes the influence of the Church (or perhaps that the Church escapes from the working class). In certain parishes composed principally of working class families, the majority of the practicing Catholics come from the middle or bourgeois class. The dioceses with the best statistics for church attendance are in fact dioceses where the working class is still small. And even in these "good" dioceses, the working class, in great part, does not come under the Church's influence. Thus, a problem of social groupings exists for the missionary, and the territorial structure of the Church seems poorly adapted to meet this problem.

Does that mean that it is better to create "bishoprics" or apostolic vicariates made up of social groupings or classes, with their own bishop or apostolic vicar, their own clergy and their own seminary? Would it be equally desirable for the apostolic religious orders to create autonomous nonterritorial missions, upon the model of the religious provinces, each of them having their provincial, their novitiate, their house of studies, and their own administration? Decisions of this sort obviously must be made exclusively by the hierarchy or by the superiors of religious orders. But it is the theologian's task to throw light on the question in regard to several points:

What is the origin of the territorial structure of the Church? This point calls for careful study. The primitive Church had two very different types of government: 1) a government according to which the Churches disseminated over very widespread areas were all under the "surveillance" of a single Apostle who governed them through the intermediary of colleges of "presbyters" or "episcopes" (Phil. 1:1; Acts 20:17, 28; 14:22), or through "presidents" (Rom. 12:4,8); 2) a government with a monarchical and fixed basis. A useful study could be made on the bond between territory and hierarchy in the Church. Actually, the primitive Church did not have many nomadic members. She addressed her message almost entirely to farmers and artisans. Are we to say that the territorial structure for government and pastoral guidance is simply bound to this historical conjuncture, or are we to attribute a more fundamental value to this structure?

The second point is this: From the viewpoint of law and not fact, those who are militantly in favor of the territorial structure of the hierarchy sometimes say that this structure is intangible because the "charity" of the Christians in each territory must not show favoritism for certain classes, social groupings, or persons. This is a powerful argument that should hold the theologian's attention. However, it is likewise necessary that charity not show favoritism for any country or language. In Christ, there are no longer Frenchmen or Germans, Americans or Russians. Although neither the parish nor the diocese can bear witness to this universal oneness, the Eucharistic community of "class" or "social grouping" could well do so. Thus authentic and total testimony to unity must come from Christians united in the same territory and in the same social grouping.

The third point to consider would be the evolution of ecclesiastical institutions in this direction. It would then be obvious that the "intangible" principle of territorial jurisdiction is often in default. In Occupied Germany there exists a French jurisdiction superposed *de facto* upon the German jurisdiction. In Paris as in other countries, there is a "bishop for foreigners" whose title indicates that his jurisdiction is not territorial. There is still a "Vietnamese parish" in Paris, and there are many other "national parishes" as well. There are many cities and even villages in the United States and Canada where the same territory includes an English parish, a German parish, a French parish, etc. There are many cities in the Near East where there are several patriarchs or bishops whose territorial jurisdiction is common and who are distinct only by reason of their rites. These examples could be multiplied. What lesson can we draw from these facts?

The fourth point to remember is that the great majority of the human race lives a settled life. Modern men are divided among several communities that do not coincide as they once did: there are city communities and neighborhoods, industrial and rural communities; communities of independent wealth and middle-class communities. How can the ecclesiastical structure adapt itself to this diversity?

It would seem that the Christian community based on locality (the parish), inasmuch as it is usually the community of homes, is destined to remain the basic Eucharistic community where Baptisms and marriages tend to be celebrated. But communities of social groupings can also legitimately aspire to their own Eucharistic celebrations, their own preaching, and their itinerant clergy.

However this presupposes that these groups have at least a fixed habitat. At the present time there are many exceptions to this hypothesis. Homes, and not merely working men, have become more and more mobile. The ancient rhythm of leading flocks to the mountains to pasture according to the seasons has now been replaced by the rhythm of work and leisure (Sundays and holidays and paid vacations). This rhythm is more capricious and yet it brings vast masses of people at regular intervals into parishes that are ordinarily almost deserted (parishes by the sea, in the mountains, or in the country). This poses a serious problem of pastoral guidance for the pastors of these "vacation" parishes, inasmuch as summer and winter visitors ask them to administer almost all the sacraments even though they are total strangers.

From another point of view, the vicissitudes of labor or of unemployment tend to make homes more mobile, and less bound to one particular locality. Even when the industrial worker's home is fixed, it is much less soil-bound or locality-bound than was the peasant home of former times. All the factories producing the same sort of products tend to resemble one another all over the world. And so is it with the working population. Thus, the relationship between an industrial population and the land it inhabits has become progressively weaker. The general indication is that the world is becoming "nomadic," less and less determined by geographical locality either sociologically, ethnologically, or psychologically. Should not these things have significance for pastoral guidance and for the missions? In this connection, the reader is referred to our "Reflections" on the ministries of the priest (see Chapter VI, Volume VI).

Toward a theology of pastoral guidance: The theology of the Church that we have read considers the Church in her being and in a certain manner in her essence. Such a study is necessary and fundamental, but it fails at least in part to consider the Church in her action, her progress, her life, and her becoming. The theology "of the Church" should be completed by a theology "of the mission of the Church," that is, of her life and her action, and especially of her action on men whether baptized or not, whether believers or unbelievers. This second side of the diptych would then be the theology of pastoral guidance. For lack of this theology, modern pastoral guidance has become a matter of slogans, fashionable procedures, "tricks" that have wild success but often last for a day. Because of lack of coherent thought, action is in a state of grave incoherence.

The Church has a threefold mission that corresponds to the threefold role of Christ as prophet, priest, and king. Starting from this threefold mission, here are the possible chapter-headings of a theology of pastoral guidance. (The inspiration for the following outline has come in great part from Father Liégé's article "Pour une théologie pastorale catéchétique" that appeared in *Bible et Mission,* No. 1, Éditions du Cerf).

I. *The Prophetic Mission.*
   The Pastoral function of evangelization and pre-evangelization.
   (a) The theology of God's Word.
      The human phenomenon of the word.
      The word of Scripture in religions.
      The Word in the historical economy of salvation.
      The saving Word.
   (b) The theology of catechesis and of preaching.
      1. The place of evangelization in the Church.
         The work of evangelization.
            The spoken word.
            The word as gesture.
            The word as sign.
         The contents of evangelization.
         The artisans of evangelization.
            The special role of the laity.
         Pre-evangelization.
            The adaptation of Christianity to different cultures.

2. The theology of preaching.
The different types of preaching.
The preaching of the Bible, perpetually renewed in its expression.
The different ages of faith.
Preaching in the different ages of faith.
Catechism: contents and methods.

II. *The Mission of Worship.*
The pastoral function of worship and of the liturgy.
The theology and pedagogy of sacred things.
The theology of the relationship between the secular life and the sacred life:
Sociology, ethnology, psychology, of social rites.
The history, evolution, and geography of these rites.
Social rites and religious rites.
The theology of signs.
The sign and human life.
The different sorts of signs. Efficacy.
The theology of the so-called sacred languages.
The theology of the symbolism of gestures, things, times, and places. The religious value of music, dance, etc.
The theology of sacred art.
The theology of the priesthood and of sacrifice.
The theology of the divine office, of praise, thanksgiving, prayer, and sacrifice.
The theology of sanctification through worship.
The para-liturgies.
(In this connection, cf. "Reflections and Perspectives," *Theology Library,* Vol. III, pp. 427-441)

III. *The Government of "Charity."*
The pastoral theology of Christian groups and of reunion in Charity.
The theology of the diocese.
The theology of the parish.
The theology of movements, groups (Catholic Action, associations, the family), and of social groupings.

In all these studies, the category of *time* and *duration* should be given an important place. In actuality, the Church lives and progresses in time. Pastoral guidance does not complete its work in an instant. Man does not acquire his full rights to citizenship in the Church without passing through laborious stages. And his sanctification is equally slow. Pastoral guidance must take into account this most important factor of duration. In this connection it is a protest against too frequent use of the sacraments in childhood, that is often followed by infrequent recourse to the same sacraments in maturity.

BIBLIOGRAPHY

General works

Until Msgr. Journet's monumental work is completed (*The Church of the Word Incarnate,* vol. I, New York: Sheed and Ward, 1955), any of the following will be helpful in gaining a comprehensive view of the subject:

Broutin, P. *Mysterium Ecclesiae.* Paris: Orante, 1947. A well-balanced, stimulating work, not too technical or detailed. In French, despite the title.

Hasseveldt, Roger. *The Church, A Divine Mystery.* Chicago: Fides, 1955. A readable general treatment.

Lubac, H. de, S.J. *The Splendour of the Church.* New York: Sheed and Ward, 1956. A rich personal synthesis which needs to be supplemented by a more technical study.

Montcheuil, Yves de, S.J. *Aspects of the Church.* Chicago: Fides, 1955. Good, brief treatment of specific problems; an excellent introduction.

Philips, G. *La sainte Église catholique.* Paris-Tournai: Casterman, 1947. A good handbook with full explanations.

The Church in Biblical Theology

Bardy, E. *Le Saint-Esprit en nous et dans l'Église d'après le nouveau Testament.* Albi, 1950.

Cerfaux, L. *La théologie de l'Église suivant saint Paul.* Paris: Cerf, 1947. A technical work to be read in conjunction with the texts in question.

Gelin, A. *La Révélation biblique de l'Église—L'Idée universaliste dans la Bible—Présentation de l'Église dans le nouveau Testament, in Équipes enseignantes,* 1949–1950. Paris, 18 rue Lacoste.

Goossens, W. *L'Église, Corps du Christ, d'après saint Paul, Étude de théologie biblique.* Paris: Gabalda, 1949. A popularization of Cerfaux's work.

Villain, M., and Baciocchi, J. de. *La vocation de l'Église. Étude biblique.* Plon, 1954.

Warnach, Dom. *Die Kirche in Epheserbrief.* Münster, 1949.

The Mystical Body

Guerry, Em. *Dans le Christ total.* Paris: Desclée, 1953.

Mersch, E., S.J. *The Theology of the Mystical Body.* St. Louis: Herder, 1951.

Mura, E. *Le Corps Mystique du Christ.* 2 vols. Paris: Blot, 1947. Scholastic treatment; clear and well-ordered.

Pius XII. *Mystici Corporis Christi,* Encyclical. Washington, D.C.: NCWC.

The Apostolic Church

Bossuet. *IVe lettre à une demoiselle de Metz.* 1659.

Clérissac, H. *Le mystère de l'Église.* Paris: Cerf, 1934. In the form of pensées; poetic and evocative.

Congar, Yves, O.P. *Esquisses du Mystère de l'Église.* Paris: Cerf, 1953. A careful study of the relationship between the various aspects of the Church.

Grosche, Msgr. R. *Pilgernde Kirche.* Fribourg, 1938.

Leclercq, J. *La vie du Christ dans son Église.* Paris: Cerf, 1944. Penetrating and well-grounded theological meditations.

Suhard, Emmanuel Cardinal. "Growth or Decline," in *The Church Today.* Chicago: Fides, 1953.

Vonier, Dom Anscar. "The People of God" and "The Spirit and the Bride," in the *Collected Works.* Westminster, Md.: Newman, 1953.

Apolloni-Ghetti, B. M., Ferrua, A., Kirschbaum, E., Josi, E. *Explorasioni sotto la Confessione di S. Pietro in Vaticano.* 2 vols. Vatican, 1951. The state of the archaeological question on the tomb of St. Peter in Rome.

Battifol, P. *L'Église naissante et la catholicisme.* Paris, 1913. An historical study which remains a classic work on the primitive organization of the hierarchical Church.

Beauduin, L. *Liturgy, the Life of the Church.* Collegeville: The Liturgical Press, 1929.

Carcopino, J. *Études d'histoire chrétienne: les fouilles de Saint-Pierre et la tradition.* Paris: Albin Michel, 1953.

Colson, J. *L'Évêque dans les communautés primitives.* Paris: Cerf, 1951.

Cullmann, O. *Peter: Disciple, Apostle, Martyr.* Philadelphia: Westminster, 1953. A technical exposition of the orthodox Protestant position. To be studied with the reports by Congar in *La Vie Intellectuelle,* Feb. 1953, pp. 17-43, and Daniélou in *Études,* Feb. 1953, pp. 206-219.

Cyprian, St. *The Lapsed. The Unity of the Catholic Church.* vol. 25 in *Ancient Christian Writers.* Westminster, Md.: Newman, 1957.

Guardini, Romano. *Vom Sinn der Kirche.* Mainz, 1934.

Ignatius of Antioch, St. *Epistles.* vol. 1 in *Ancient Christian Writers.* Westminster, Md.: Newman, 1946.

Irenaeus, St. *Against Heretics.* Library of Nicene and Post-Nicene Fathers. Edinburgh: Clark.

Journet, Charles. *The Church of the Word Incarnate.* vol. I, "The Apostolic Hierarchy." New York: Sheed and Ward, 1955.

————. *The Primacy of Peter as seen from the Catholic and from the Protestant Points of View.* Westminster, Md.: Newman.

Leuba, J. L. *L'Institution et l'Événement.* Delachaux, 1950. A Protestant work which contrasts the historical Church and the Church of the Spirit.

Martimort, A. G. *De l'évêque.* Paris, 1946.

Menoud, P. H. *L'Église et les ministères selon le nouveau Testament.* Delachaux, 1949. An objective study by a Protestant.

Pius XII. *Mediator Dei,* Encyclical. Washington, D.C.: NCWC.

Scheeben, M. J. *Mysteries of Christianity.* St. Louis: Herder, 1946.

Vatican Council. Const., *Pastor Aeternus.*

Adam, K. *The Spirit of Catholicism*. New York: Doubleday, 1954.

Braun, F. M. *Aspects nouveaux du problème de l'Église*. Fribourg: 1942. A non-Catholic critique of the origins of the Church. Re-worked and completed in *Neues Licht auf die Kirche*, Cologne: 1946.

Brière, Yves de la. *L'Église et son gouvernement*. Paris: Grasset, 1950.

Congar, Y., O.P. *Vraie et fausse Réforme dans l'Église*. Paris: Cerf, 1950.

Goerres, Ida F. *Die leibhaftige Kirche*. Frankfurt: Knecht Verlag, 1950.

Heris, C. V. *L'Église du Christ*. Juvisy, 1930.

Jugie, M. *Où se trouve le christianisme intégral?* Paris: Lethielleux, 1947.

Jung, N. *Le magistère de L'Église*. Paris: Bloud and Gay, 1935.

Lubac, H. de, S.J. *Catholicism*. New York: Sheed and Ward, 1958.

Poulpiquet, A. de. *L'Église catholique*. Paris, 1923. Apologetic study.

Sertillanges, A. D. *Le miracle de l'Église*. Paris: Spes, 1933.

Thils, G. *Les notes de l'Église dans l'apologétique catholique depuis la Réforme*. Gembloux, 1937. Historical and critical study; technical.

L'Église et la liberté. Semaine des Intellectuels catholiques. Éd. de Flore, 1952.

Études mariales. Marie et l'Église. 3 vols. Paris: Lethielleux, 1951–1953.

Problems of the Church

Caryl, J., and Portier, V. *La mission des laïcs dan l'Église*. Lyon-Paris: Éd. Chronique Social, 1940.

Congar, Y., O.P. *Lay People in the Church*. Westminster, Md.: Newman, 1957.

Congar-Varillon. *Sacerdoce et laïcat dans l'Église*. Paris: Vitrail, 1947.

Guerry, E. *L'action catholique; textes pontificaux classés et commentés*. Paris: Desclée, 1936.

———. "Action catholique," in the encyclopedia *Catholicisme*, vol. I, col. 98-101.

Lecler, J., S.J. *The Two Sovereignties*. London: Burns, Oates and Washbourne, 1952. A study in Church-State relations.

Tiberghien, P. *L'Action catholique*. Lille, 1945.

———. *L'Action catholique, précisions*. Paris: J.E.C.F., 1949.

Charles, P. *Missiologie*. Paris: 1939.

Daniélou, J. *The Salvation of the Nations*. New York: Sheed and Ward, 1949.

Lubac, H. de, S.J. *Le fondement théologique des missions*. Paris: 1946.

Masson, J. *Vers l'Église indigène; catholicisme ou nationalisme?* Brussels: 1944.

Olichon, A. *Les missions: histoire de l'expansion catholique dans le monde*. Paris: Bloud and Gay, 1936.

Perbal, A. *Premières leçons de théologie missionnaire*. Paris: 1937.

Pius XII. *Divini Praecones*, Encyclical. Washington, D.C.: NCWC.

Rétif, A. *Introduction à la doctrine pontificale des missions*. Seuil, 1953.

Seumois, A. *Introduction à la missiologie*. Beckenried, 1952.

Adam, K. *Vers l'Unité chrétienne*. Paris: Aubier, 1949.

Aubert, R. *Le Saint-Siège et l'Union des Églises*. Brussels: Éd. Universelle, 1947. Pontifical texts with an historical and theological commentary.

Beauduin, L., Chavasse, A., Michalon, P., Villain, M. *Église et Unité*. Lille: Éd. Catholicité, 1948.

Bouyer, L. *Newman, His Life and Spirituality*. Westminster, Md.: Newman, 1958.

Congar, Y., O.P. *Divided Christendom*. London: G. Bles, 1947. Principles of Catholic ecumenism. Fundamental, but difficult.

——.*Vraie et fausse Réforme dans l'Église*. Paris: Cerf, 1950.

Dumont, C. J. *Les voies de l'unité chrétienne*. Paris: Cerf, 1954. Doctrine and spirituality.

Villain, M. *Pour l'Unité chrétienne*. Arthaud, 1943–1945.

La Sainte Église Universelle, confrontation oecuménique. Paris: Delachaux, 1949.

Tolerance and the Catholic. New York: Sheed and Ward, 1955.

Irenikon. Quarterly review. Chevetogne, Belgium.

In studying the history of the Church, we gain a concrete knowledge of its progress, of its gradual completion in space and human existence; this is the work of the Holy Spirit, through the Church's ministry and the spread of sanctity, and it continues in spite of sin and human weaknesses. For the study of this process, the following works would be useful:

Daniélou, J. *Essai sur le mystère de l'histoire*, Seuil, 1953.

Fliche, A., and Martin, V., eds. *Histoire de l'Église, depuis les origines jusqu'à nos jours*, 26. vols. Paris: Bloud and Gay. A tool for scientific research. Volumes that have been translated into English are: *The History of the Primitive Church*, by Lebreton and Zeiller, 2 vols., New York: Macmillan, 1949, and *The Church in the Christian Roman Empire*, by Palanques, Bardy, and de Labriolle, 2 vols., New York: Macmillan, 1949–1952.

Huby, J., and Rousselot, P. *Christus, la religion chrétienne*. Paris, 1919.

Plinval, G. de, and Pittet, R. *Histoire illustrée de l'Église*. 2 vols. Paris: Cerf.

Senarclens, J. D. *Le Mystère de l'histoire*. Geneva, 1949. A Protestant work.

THE RETURN OF CHRIST

We have already dealt with the end of human life in our study of morals (Volume III of this series, pp. 26-67). Before analyzing the movement of our moral activity, it was necessary to know the end that sets it in motion and specifies it. However it sufficed to consider this end in its essential and even timeless aspect, namely: the vision of God that constitutes our beatitude.

In this chapter of our theology we are considering the "end" in an altogether different way. Starting with the Incarnation studied at the start of this "Economy" and continuing on to the Return of Christ, we are studying the facts in themselves and for themselves, in their historical context. We are no longer trying to discover the end toward which we are tending, but to know what has already been revealed to us of its execution, how concretely it will terminate the history of salvation, what circumstances will accompany it, how the Sovereign Judge will manifest Himself, and how the good will be rewarded and the wicked punished. This is the object of Chapter VII.

Chapter VII

THE RETURN OF CHRIST

by A.-M. Henry, O.P.

I. THE GLORIOUS MANIFESTATION OF CHRIST IN GOD'S PLAN

1. The day of Yahweh and the expectation of Israel
   - (a) "Who was, and who is, and who is coming"
   - (b) The manner of God's coming
2. The day of the Lord in the New Covenant
   - (a) Come, Lord Jesus
   - (b) Christ the Lord
   - (c) The revelation of Christ's return
   - (d) The time of patience, the time of the nations, the time of vigilance
   - (e) The day of the Lord: judgment and resurrection
   - (f) The first-fruits of eternal life

II. THE PILGRIMS TO THE NEW JERUSALEM

1. The ages of the world
2. The sacraments of the pilgrims
3. The judgment of the pilgrims
   - (a) The glory of the elect
   - (b) Reprobation
        The punishments of hell
        Who pronounces judgment?
   - (c) Purgatory
4. The expectation of the saints

REFLECTIONS AND PERSPECTIVES

BIBLIOGRAPHY

Chapter VII

THE RETURN OF CHRIST

God's plan, as meant to be revealed to us by the Bible, calls for an ultimate act on the part of the Father: God must in truth visibly manifest His Son's triumph, bring to an end the activity of the powers of evil, clothe His elect with the glory of Christ, and renew the whole of Creation. The economy of salvation which we have just studied theologically must close with the consideration of this last act of the mystery, that is, of "the revealed plan of God."

I. The Glorious Manifestation of Christ in God's Plan

Jesus has assured us that He will reappear visibly among us: "A little while and you shall see me no longer; and again a little while and you shall see me" (Jn. 16:16). St. Paul tells us that we look "for the blessed hope and glorious coming of our great God and Savior, Jesus Christ" (Tit. 2:13).

Let us not be disturbed by this "little while," of which our Lord speaks, and which we have seen continue century after century. Rather let us listen to St. Augustine's remark: "When everything is over, we shall realize how short the time has been." Let us remember that for the Lord, and for us during eternity, a day is as a thousand years and a thousand years are as a single day (II Pet. 3:8; Ps. 89).

It is a fact, therefore, that our Lord will come back. He Himself has said so. The first disciples believed in His return, the Apostles preached it, and St. John has written an Apocalypse about Christ's definitive triumph, as the concluding book of our inspired Scriptures.

Was the hope of such a triumph new? Was the promise of Christ's return, the announcement of a last judgment, of a renewal of all things, of the hope of a universal salvation—were all these things new, unheard-of, and strange for the men and women who heard the Gospel preached? How did the Jews understand this message? Do the eschatological discourses of Paul to the Thessalonians and the Corinthians, the discourses of Peter, and those of John in his

Apocalypse, teach something absolutely new? Or did they simply fulfill a doctrine of long standing, even if imperfect, obscure, and still vague? In a word, to what hope of Israel was the hope manifested in New Testament writings opposed, or did it superimpose itself on the former?

1. THE DAY OF YAHWEH AND THE EXPECTATION OF ISRAEL

(a) *"Who was, and who is, and who is coming"* (Ap. 4:8).

The whole history of Israel is underpinned by the personal initiatives of its God. It was God—the still unnamed God—who commanded Abraham to go forth from his land and who made him the father of a multitude. It was God Himself who saved Israel in Egypt, and during famine in Canaan. It was Yahweh who gave battle to the Amorrhites near Gabaon by casting so many great stones upon them (Jos. 10:11) that more of them died from the hail of stones than by the sword of the children of Israel (*ibid.*). It was Yahweh who delivered up to the children of Israel the kings assembled near the waters of Meron (Jos. 11). And it was Yahweh again who delivered the Philistines into the hands of David at Baal Pharisim (II Kgs. 5:20). All these battles haunt the memory of Isaias. Woe to those who trust in human covenants:

> For the Lord shall stand up as in the mountain of divisions:
> He shall be angry as in the valley which is in Gabaon (Is. 28:21).

The warlike initiatives and the victories of God are inscribed in the book of Yahweh's wars which has been made known to us in the Book of Numbers (21:14).

Among all these acts of Yahweh, there are two of exceptional importance. God intervened so miraculously in them that His name was henceforth bound up with these two events. We are referring to the epics of the Red Sea and of Mount Sinai. Yahweh is the God who delivered Israel from Egypt: this is an article of faith in the Israelite creed (see Deut. 26:5-9). And Yahweh is the God who manifested Himself on Sinai and who gave His commandments to Moses. Inversely, Israel is the people whose existence and reason for being are founded upon this twofold initiative by its God. Its national hymns perpetuate the memory of this twofold event. First, here are the Psalms that celebrate Yahweh's triumph over Egypt:

Come and see the works of God;
Who is terrible in his counsels over the sons of men.
Who turneth the sea into dry land,
In the river they shall pass on foot:
There shall we rejoice in him (Ps. 65:5-6).

He divided the sea and brought them through:
And he made the waters to stand as in a vessel.
And he conducted them with a cloud by day:
And all the night with a light of fire (Ps. 77:13-14).

The sea saw (Israel) and fled:
Jordan was turned back.
The mountains skipped like rams,
And the hills like the lambs of the flock.
What ailed thee, O thou sea, that thou didst flee:
And thou, O Jordan, that thou wast turned back?
Ye mountains, that ye skipped like rams,
And ye hills, like lambs of the flock?
At the presence of the Lord the earth was moved,
At the presence of the God of Jacob:
Who turned the rock into pools of water,
And the stony hill into fountains of waters (Ps. 113:3-8).

For Isaias, Yahweh was He

Who made a way in the sea,
And a path in the mighty waters.
Who brought forth the chariot and the horse, the army and the strong:
They lay down to sleep together, and they shall not rise again (Is. 43:16-17).

Conscious of this divine protection, the prophet no longer needed to fear nations. He denounced their deeds, and announced the ruin of their perverse projects. He restored Israel's courage. The entire Old Testament is a hymn to the glory of the heavenly Leader of Israel's army: Yahweh sabaoth, Yahweh the Lord of hosts. For example after the victory against Sisara, Debora sang a canticle of triumph to Yahweh:

I will sing to the Lord the God of Israel.
O Lord, when thou went out of Seir,
And passed by the regions of Edom,
The earth trembled, and the heavens dropped water.
The mountains melted before the face of the Lord,
And Sinai before the face of the Lord the God of Israel (Judges 5:3-5).

And when the Levites returned from exile, they made a solemn thanksgiving to celebrate the benefactions of Yahweh to their fathers, as reported by Esdras:

And thou didst divide the sea before them, and they passed through the midst of the sea on dry land: but their persecutors thou threwest into the depth, as a stone into mighty waters. And in a pillar of a cloud thou wast their leader by day, and in a pillar of fire by night, that they might see the way by which they went. Thou camest down also to Mount Sinai, and didst speak with them from heaven, and thou gavest them right judgments, and the law of truth, ceremonies, and good precepts (II Esd. 9:11-13).

Sometimes the themes of the Red Sea and of Sinai are fused into a single theme that is the leitmotif of remembrance that underlies the hope of Israel.

> The waters saw thee, O God,
> The waters saw thee: and they were afraid,
> And the depths were troubled.
> Great was the noise of the waters:
> The clouds sent out a sound.
> For thy arrows pass: the voice of thy thunder in a wheel (Ps. 76:17-18).

The waters that withdrew in fear refer to the passage over the Red Sea; the torrents of water and the thunder refer to the theophany of Sinai. All of this is summed up in the First Commandment of the Law, which is also the foundation of the Israelite Creed:

> I am the Lord thy God, who brought thee out of the land of Egypt, out of the house of bondage (Ex. 20:2).

Yahweh is not an unknown God, a God whose brilliant deeds and actions have never been seen. He has manifested Himself. He has made Himself visible to a certain extent, at least through His acts. He entered into the history of Israel, and Israel has preserved the memory of this astonishing God who saves it from mortal perils, who leads it miraculously in the desert, who gives it His Commandments. Israel is the people of a God, as are other peoples, but its God is Yahweh, and Yahweh is not like other gods. He is not a cold and remote God, or a cruel God who must be appeased by barbaric sacrifices and actions. Yahweh is a God who is close to men, a fatherly God and yet a powerful God before whom all the other gods are but dust and a puff of wind. Israel has always been conscious of being in the hand of a living, powerful, God, a God who is very close.

This trust in Yahweh is heavy with hope. Yahweh is a God "with a mighty hand and with a stretched out arm" (Ps. 135:12). He liberated Israel, He gave it its law; He led it in the desert, and He continues to lead it. *Therefore He will save Israel from all its enemies, from all its ills.* Yahweh has come, and therefore He will come again:

that is why He makes men hope for Him. The very name of Yahweh is a hope. It is the certitude of final victory, of a triumph whose outlines have been gradually delineated by the prophets and that rejoices the hearts of the people. The name of Yahweh is heavy with a glorious eschatology. It is like seed planted deep within the heart of His people that slowly develops eschatological faith and hope. He is both the God who has already come in a glorious manner and the God who is to come. The Power of God, whose favors the people have already received and continue to receive unceasingly, slowly broadens the people's perspectives of salvation and happiness.

Moreover, the people are reminded that in the beginning God had placed His servant in a paradise which alone could correspond to Yahweh's power and goodness. It was through his own fault that man lost this paradise and all its attendant privileges, and it is through Yahweh's power that he will return to it. The last things are the answer to the first things, the Apocalypse is the answer to Genesis. The picture of the last days brings us back to the primitive times, the nostalgia for a future paradise draws its inspiration from the paradise lost. We might even go so far as to say that the thought of the last days impresses in the mind of the sacred writer, imbued with eschatological trust, the picture of this lost paradise.

In a certain sense, the first two chapters of Genesis are eschatological. I am Yahweh, the God who has come, the God who comes each day, the God who is coming and who is coming in power far beyond all hope, just as He came prior to any possible recollection before man's sin. I am Yahweh, the living God upon whom the history of Israel depends in its every facet. The God who is to come is the same who manifested Himself in the storm and lightning of Sinai, in Israel's victorious wars, in the judgment of the nations, in the miraculous protection of the holy people. He is an avenging God, a judging God, and at the same time a redeeming God, a God who is a Father. The face of God that is gradually delineated thus corresponds to the partial glimpses of Him obtained in the past or in the present.

The God who is to come is first of all the Lord of storms: this is the first title of the avenging God.

> The Lord is a jealous God, and a revenger:
> The Lord is a revenger, and hath wrath: . . .
> The Lord's ways are in a tempest, and a whirlwind,
> And clouds are the dust of his feet (Nah. 1:2-3).

The prophets often express Yahweh's anger in terms of a storm:

> I beheld, and lo there was no man:
> And all the birds of the air were gone.
> I looked, and behold Carmel was a wilderness:
> And all its cities were destroyed at the presence of the Lord,
> And at the presence of the wrath of his indignation (Jer. 4:25-26).

Thus, according to at least one tradition, at the end of the world the earth will be plunged in darkness as before a great storm. According to another tradition, there will be a great light. But these two views are not contradictory.

The God who is coming is likewise a warlike leader:

> The Lord shall go forth as a mighty man,
> As a man of war shall he stir up zeal:
> He shall shout and cry:
> He shall prevail against his enemies (Is. 42:13).

Yahweh is like a general passing his troops in review before the final attack, or like a commander-in-chief:

> The noise of a multitude in the mountains,
> As it were of many people,
> The noise of the sound of kings,
> Of nations gathered together:
> The Lord of hosts hath given charge to the troops of war (Is. 13:4).

> And the Lord hath uttered his voice before the face of his army:
> For his armies are exceeding great,
> For they are strong and execute his word:
> For the day of the Lord is great and very terrible:
> And who can stand it? (Joel 2:11).

The eschatological armies which Yahweh will use are the troops of the nations, the enemies of His people, the instruments of His vengeance (Is. 10:5). Such for example were the Assyrian armies whom God summoned to chastise Israel:

> And he will lift up a sign to the nations afar off,
> And will whistle to them from the ends of the earth:
> And behold they shall come with speed swiftly.
> There is none that shall faint, nor labor among them:
> They shall not slumber nor sleep,
> Neither shall the girdle of their loins be loosed,
> Nor the latchet of their shoes be broken (Is. 5:26-27).

Yahweh, the God who is coming, is also a judge: "For the Lord will enter into judgment with his people, and he will plead against

Israel" (Mich. 6:2). Lastly, He is a king: an all-powerful king who will cast all His enemies under His feet. In the day of Yahweh there will be only one kingdom, and Yahweh will be its head: "The Lord shall reign for ever and ever" (Ex. 15:18). What an honor for the messenger who is to announce the inauguration of the eschatological kingdom:

> How beautiful upon the mountains
> are the feet of him that bringeth good tidings,
> and that preacheth peace: of him that sheweth forth good, . . .
> that saith to Sion: Thy God shall reign! (Is. 52:7).

Several Psalms, especially those concerning the "enthronement of Yahweh," sing in advance of the joys of the crowning:

> Sing praises to our God, sing ye:
> Sing praises to our king, sing ye.
> For God is the king of all the earth:
> Sing ye wisely.
> God shall reign over the nations:
> God sitteth on his holy throne (Ps. 46:7-9).

But side by side with these formidable titles, there are others that inspire trust and dispel all possibility of fear. Yahweh is a Father, nay, a Mother, a Bridegroom, a Redeemer, a good Shepherd:

> For thou art our father,
> And Abraham hath not known us,
> And Israel hath been ignorant of us:
> Thou, O Lord, art our father, our redeemer,
> From everlasting is thy name (Is. 63:16).

As one whom the mother caresseth, so will I comfort you (Is. 66:13).

> And it shall be in that day, saith the Lord,
> *That* she shall call me: My husband . . .
> And I will espouse thee to me for ever (Os. 2:16-19).
> In that day, saith the Lord, I will gather up her that halteth:
> And her that I had cast out, I will gather up:
> And her whom I had afflicted (Mich. 4:6).

These last-mentioned titles that Yahweh appropriates suggest that He is always something more than a terrible war chief, even when He is convoking the nations against Israel and inspires dread. Yahweh is a Father who loves His child. It is in this sense that the prophets "know" Him better and better, and reveal Him to Israel.

(b) *The manner of God's Coming*

The certitude that all evil will be abolished in the end, that the enemies of Yahweh will be punished, that God will recover His universal dominion and that men will live happily and at peace under His eschatological scepter, inspired the sacred writers with a rather definite vision of the last days. According to the exegesis of G. Pidoux,[1] we can distinguish two outlines of the eschatological drama, one simple, the other complex.

According to the simple outline, the day of Yahweh will include two phases: a phase of destruction and a phase of restoration of the "remnant." According to the composite outline, the drama becomes more complicated in the process of organization. First, the eschatological armies called by Yahweh will rise up against Sion. This will be followed by God's victory over these very armies for having attacked the holy people. Then will come the restoration of Jerusalem, the return of the captives. Yahweh will be king of Sion. Finally, the lordship of the God of Israel will extend over all nations, and even over the universe, the stars and the other gods. Jerusalem will be the royal high place where all peoples, now at peace with one another, will come and adore Yahweh. The pilgrims' hymn recorded for us by Isaias and Micheas, sings of the sweetness of these irenical times:

> And in the last days
> The mountain of the house of the Lord
> Shall be prepared on the top of mountains,
> And it shall be exalted above the hills,
> And all nations shall flow unto it.
> And many people shall go, and say:
> Come and let us go up to the mountain of the Lord,
> And to the house of the God of Jacob,
> And he will teach us his ways,
> And we will walk in his paths:
> For the law shall come forth from Sion,
> And the word of the Lord from Jerusalem.
> And he shall judge the Gentiles,
> And rebuke many people:
> And they shall turn their swords into ploughshares,
> And their spears into sickles:
> Nation shall not lift up sword against nation,
> Neither shall they be exercised any more to war (Is. 2:2-4).

[1] *Le Dieu qui vient* (Neuchâtel: Delachaux et Niestlé, 1947).

Let us take note of the idea of a "remnant," which is ancient and persistent in the eschatology of Israel. Since the drama that precedes the eschatological drama is universal, few will escape. It is this limited number, this "remnant," that is to form the nucleus of the new Israel (cf. Is. 26:20-21).

Let us also remark once more that the categories used for expressing eschatological conceptions are borrowed from past times: from the time of Moses, the time of the desert, the Davidic monarchy. The day of Yahweh is a reflection of the events that happened long before, it is a projection into the future and into the absolute of past joys. It is paradise regained, the land where milk and honey flow (Ex. 3:8,17; 13:5; 33:3), the land of waters and fertility (Ez. 47). It will be the time when even animals will be at peace with one another, as in the beautiful days of Eden:

> The wolf shall dwell with the lamb:
> And the leopard shall lie down with the kid:
> The calf and the lion, and the sheep shall abide together,
> And a little child shall lead them (Is. 11:6).

We have no way of knowing whether the ideas relating to past things have influenced eschatological themes, or whether the reverse is true. The Garden of Eden is a theme of the past and of the future. In the person of Yahweh, whose name contains the goodness of the first days and the sweetness of the future, it is also a certainty of the present moment.

2. THE DAY OF THE LORD IN THE NEW COVENANT

(a) *Come, Lord Jesus*

Thus, when John the Baptist arrived, Israel already possessed a very ancient and very solid eschatological doctrine. This doctrine was quite naturally cultivated in such Israelite liturgical feasts as the enthronement of Yahweh, the Pasch, or the Feast of the Tabernacles.

This has not been true of all religions. In Babylon, for example, religion did not culminate in the formation of an eschatology. And it is interesting to note once again that the hope of Israel was rooted in the very Name of Yahweh. Israel expected all things of its God. He was its Creator, its Rock, its Buckler, its Strength, its Head, its Commander-in-chief, its King, and its Father. The name of Yahweh, as we have already pointed out, has a strongly eschatological meaning.[2] Let us not fear to show these relationships and to make these deductions.

The fact that eschatology has in a certain respect been "deduced" from the Name of Yahweh does not prevent it from having been divinely revealed. God directs the course of history. It is He who revealed His holy Name. It is He who has given such power to His name, who has made it capable of inspiring such great trust in those who believe in Him. It is He who has lead Israel, who was the author of the passage over the Red Sea as well as of the revelation on Sinai. Even though eschatological doctrine developed from the starting point of inward trust in God, it is transcendent as well. It is God who planted this trust in the hearts of His people. He might well have chosen to inspire only His prophets and to reveal His plans explicitly to them alone. He chose to lead all His people in such a way that their epic would be a perpetual testimony to the doctrine that He wanted to teach them, and so that His doctrine would always be bound up with historical facts and with divine interventions that were in some degree palpable.

Christ came and did not destroy Israel's hope. He came to fulfill it. He was to purify it of all anthropomorphism, of all instinct of temporal possession and domination. He unveiled the true countenance of this hope, that had tended to be obscured by the bright raiment of certain prophecies and the tenacious instincts of a still primitive people. Christ took what Israel had anticipated on the carnal, temporal, and political level, and revealed it to us on a specifically spiritual level.

The words "Let us sing to the Lord, for he is gloriously magnified" (Ex. 15:21) are comparable to St. Peter's brilliant profession of faith: "This Jesus God has raised up, and we are all witnesses of it" (Acts 2:32, cf. also 3:15); or to St. Stephen's vision: "Behold, I see the heavens opened, and the Son of Man standing at the right hand of God" (Acts 7:56).

(b) *Christ the Lord*

The God who delivered Israel from the slavery of Egypt also delivered Jesus from the bonds of death. The God who is to inaugurate the messianic kingdom made this Jesus whom Israel crucified both Lord and Christ. The eschatological faith of Christians is entirely bound up with this new and definitive fact: Jesus is the

[2] Cf. Pidoux, *op. cit.*, pp. 51-52.

Lord. The very name of *Kyrios,* "Lord," which is the equivalent of "Yahweh" in the translation of the Septuagint and in the usage of the Hellenized Jews, is attributed to Christ in New Testament literature (see I Cor. 8:6; and compare with Tit. 2:13; Ap. 1:6).

The Resurrection of Jesus manifested that He is Christ and Lord. He is even now sitting at the right hand of God, sharing His power, and possessing the place and the powers of the Sovereign Judge of eschatological times. He is already reigning invisibly. Yahweh showed His power on Sinai: a cloud covered the summit and Moses was there listening to Him and speaking to Him face to face. God showed His power in the Resurrection of His Son. He had announced it on Mount Tabor when a cloud had enveloped Jesus and His disciples, Peter, James, and John, and when He spoke to His beloved Son in glory. And Moses and Elias, the great witnesses of God's power, were there. At the present time, we know that Jesus reigns, that He is the awaited Messias, the King, Judge, and Bridegroom. We are waiting for His glorious manifestation, prophetically announced by Scripture and confirmed by the Transfiguration, according to St. Peter (II Pet. 1:17-19).

Let us enter into this mystery of the Christian expectation, and consider successively: 1) The revelation of the return of Christ; 2) the significance of the expectation; 3) what the day of the Lord will be like; 4) what has already happened.

(c) *The Revelation of Christ's Return*

The eschatological prophecies of the Old Testament are not without relevance for the New. Jesus took them up again in His discourses on the end of the world. In the one recorded for us in the twenty-fourth chapter of St. Matthew, Daniel is cited three times, Isaias twice, and Zacharias once. And Jesus never tired of repeating: "Watch therefore, for you do not know the day nor the hour."

Jesus compared His terrible and glorious "coming" first to a fig tree whose leaves are a sign that summer is near, then to the days of Noah, the days of the Flood which, according to St. Peter (II Pet. 3:6-7) are the type of the flood of fire at the end of the world. He also compared His second coming to the servant who has won his master's confidence and who is constantly watching while he waits for him; and finally, He compared it to the ten virgins invited to the wedding of one of their friends and who await the arrival of the Bridegroom. "Then will the kingdom of heaven be like ten virgins who took their lamps and went forth to meet the bridegroom" (Mt. 25:1). All these comparisons, and especially the last-named, which is so sweet for those who watch and so terrible for those who allow their minds to go astray among worldly concerns, have their place in the New Testament perspective of the last days, the perspective which our Lord had brought out in the preceding discourse.

It is now clear that He is the Messias, the long-awaited King. He has already come. He has arrived. He has announced His return in clear terms in the consoling discourses after the Last Supper, recorded for us by St. John. He made Himself so clear that His disciples said to Him: "Behold, now thou speakest plainly, and utterest no parable" (Jn. 16:29).

The "manifestation" of Christ is at the very heart of our hope. It is our hope: "We . . . live . . . looking for the blessed hope and glorious coming of our great God and Savior, Jesus Christ" (Tit. 2:13). "You turned to God from idols, to serve the living and true God, and to await from heaven Jesus, his Son, whom he raised from the dead, who has delivered us from the wrath to come" (I Thess. 1:10). "But our citizenship is in heaven from which also we eagerly await a Savior, our Lord Jesus Christ, who will refashion the body of our lowliness, conforming it to the body of his glory" (Phil. 3:20-21). The Lord came the first time not to judge us but to save us (Jn. 12:47; cf. 3:17 and Lk. 19:10), not in glory but in humiliation (Phil. 2:6-8), not as a King but as a servant (Phil. 2:7; Mt. 20:28), even though He was the Son of God, in virtue of which He was already the King of men and of the universe. But God manifested His power over Him, and on the last day He will manifest Himself definitively in glory and His reign will have no end.

(d) *The Time of Patience, the Time of the Nations, the Time of Vigilance*

The time in which we live, between the first and second comings of Christ, is a time of expectation and trials. It is the time of the patience of God.

Indeed, God is patient. He did not judge the world as soon as He had given it the means of salvation. He gave it a respite; He allowed time for the whole world to hear the evangelical announce-

This is how Christians, even in the eleventh century, still pictured the risen Christ descending into hell.

The Savior carries in His right hand the instrument of His triumph: the Cross. The stigmata of His wounds appear on His left hand and on His feet. And penetrating into "hell," that is, the sojourn of the dead, He breaks down its "doors," whose locks seem to fly in all directions, and He walks on the body of Satan, the prince of darkness, the one who possesses the keys to the dwelling of the dead and who is henceforth enchained.

With His left hand He raises up Adam from his knees, whom Satan still holds by one foot. Behind them we can distinguish Kings David and Solomon. Finally, at the right, we see John the Baptist the Precursor and a few of the just.

The *Anastasis* of the church of Daphni, near Athens (eleventh century mosaic).

ment of salvation, to repent, and to enter into the "convocation," *Ecclesia,* the Church of God. The scoffers say: "Where is the promise of his coming? For since the fathers fell asleep, all things continue as they were from the beginning of creation" (II Pet. 3:4). They do not know that "the Lord . . . is long-suffering, not wishing that any should perish but that all should turn to repentance" (II Pet. 3:9), that is, to conversion.

Christ is thus a kind of second Noah. Before the deluge of fire is unleashed against the nations, judgment has been in a certain way suspended and a respite has been given men so that they may be converted. Yahweh had said to Noah: "After seven days, I will rain upon the earth forty days and forty nights" (Gen. 7:4). Between the announcement of God's sorrow—Yahweh repented of having made man on the earth and was inwardly saddened because of it (Gen. 6:6)—and the judgment by water, seven days elapsed, the time of God's mercy and patience, the time "when the patience of God waited . . . while the ark was building" (I Pet. 3:20).

The day of judgment by fire is also the eighth day following on the week of mercy in which we are now living. That is why the symbols of the week and of the number eight have such importance in ancient Tradition. St. Peter, calling to mind God's various judgments in the Old Covenant, calls Noah himself the eighth (cf. II Pet. 2:5). Actually, the seven others were his wife, his three sons and their wives. But the number of his entourage would have had little significance if it had not culminated in the figure eight, which designated Noah as a type of the Messias. The number eight which adds unity to the number seven, the perfect number, is the number of the highest perfection. The Fathers did not fail to note that Christ rose from the dead on the day after the Sabbath, that is, on the eighth day, and that He was the eighth to come after Adam, Noah, Abraham, Isaac, Jacob, Moses, and David.

This intermediary week that St. John simply called an "hour" (I Jn. 2:18), can last for centuries. We know that "one day with the Lord is as a thousand years, and a thousand years as one day" (II Pet. 3:8). God alone knows when it will end. "But of that day or hour no one knows, neither the angels in heaven, nor the Son, but the Father only" (Mk. 13:32). "It is not for you to know the times or dates which the Father has fixed by his own authority" (Acts 1:7). And yet the mystery, i.e., God's plan as revealed to St. Paul, consists in this: "A partial blindness only has befallen Israel, until the full number of the Gentiles should enter, and thus all Israel should be saved, as it is written, 'There will come out of Sion the deliverer and he will turn away impiety from Jacob; And this is my covenant with them, when I shall take away their sins' " (Rom. 11:25-27).

Thus the intermediary time is truly the time of the nations. The fulfillment of salvation follows a path inverse to that followed by judgment before the Messias. God had set one people apart and had made a covenant with them. He had led them into the Promised Land, although only a remnant entered. Nor had the political and religious life in Canaan been without successive purifications. Only a remnant had come back from exile. A small remnant of believers still remained at the time of our Lord's preaching. And we call those who believed in Him "believers," for if they had really believed in Abraham they would also have believed in Him. Finally, a single just man, Christ, was the last representative of Abraham's posterity, in whom all nations were to be blessed. Now the opposite course is being followed, the path of "integration." One after the other, all the peoples of the earth are to be incorporated into Christ and to fill the bosom of the Church. Thus Israel will also come back, and Christ will restore all things to His Father.

The time between the first and second comings is a time of God's mercy first of all for the nations, and then for Israel. From another point of view this is also the time of faith, hope, and of the testing of the faithful. St. Peter tells us that in the hope of the incorruptible heritage prepared for us, we rejoice, "though now for a little while, if need be, you are made sorrowful by various trials, that the temper of your faith—more precious by far than gold which is tried by fire—may be found unto praise and glory and honor at the revelation of Jesus Christ" (I Pet. 1:6-7). Our faith and our hope are put to the rack, but at the same time they fill us with joy, "for I reckon that the sufferings of the present time are not worthy to be compared with the glory to come that will be revealed in us" (Rom. 8:18). Trials strengthen our faith and spur us to hope: "For we know that all creation groans and travails in pain until now" (Rom. 8:22). It awaits with eager longing, with impatience, "the revelation of the sons of God" (Rom. 8:19) at the moment of Christ's return.

However there is a difference between the expectation and hope of Israel under the Old Covenant and the expectation of believers under the New. The Jews awaited the Messias; they were as captives awaiting their Liberator. But we know that our Deliverance has been won, that it is an accomplished fact, that our place has been prepared and reserved for us in heaven. Our Liberator has come. He is merely absent for a little while. "For it is like a man going abroad, who called his servants and handed over his goods to them" (Mt. 25:14). The Church awaits Christ as a wife awaits her husband. Apparently she is a widow, deprived of the visible presence of her Spouse, but she knows that He is alive and she waits for Him with steadfast hope. She is watching for Him.

She is watching, and Christians must join in watching with her: "Watch therefore" (Mt. 24:42; 25:12). "You also must be ready, because at an hour that you do not expect, the Son of Man is coming" (Lk. 12:40). "Let your loins be girt about and your lamps burning" (Lk. 12:35), that is to say, do not let yourselves be misled by thoughts of this world. Hold your hearts steadfast in the faith and hope of your Master and your Spouse. Do not allow yourselves to be delayed or caught by the invitations of this passing world: "Time is short; it remains that those who have wives be as if they had none; and those who weep, as though not weeping; and those who rejoice, as though not rejoicing; and those who buy, as though not possessing; and those who use this world, as though not using it" (I Cor. 7:29-31).

(e) *The Day of the Lord: Judgment and Resurrection*

The return of Christ will be what all the prophets from earliest times have announced concerning the day of Yahweh: a judgment, a destruction, and at the same time a completion, a fullness, a realization, a salvation and the inauguration of a Kingdom of peace.

First of all, it will be a judgment. The judgment of Yahweh will be accomplished by the judgment of Christ. It is He who is to judge the living and dead (II Tim. 4:1). It is He who is to separate the weeds from the good grain (cf. Mt. 13:39). "Before Him will be gathered all the nations, and He will separate them one from another, as the shepherd separates the sheep from the goats" (Mt. 25:32; cf. 19:28). The satanic powers that ruled over sin and death were disarmed at the Resurrection (cf. Col. 2:15), and on the day of Judgment Christ will have a definitive victory over them. No one will henceforth be able to harm His elect.

The return of Christ will also be a triumph, a fulfillment, a veritable re-creation. "All these things are to be dissolved" (II Pet. 3:11): the heavens will be violently destroyed and the elements will catch fire. "But we look for new heavens and a new earth, according to His promises, wherein dwells justice" (II Pet. 3:13). Just as Christ was the Mediator of the first creation (Jn. 1:1; Heb. 1:2; I Cor. 8:6 and Col. 1:16), He will likewise be the Mediator of the second. Already, at the time of His death, the whole earth manifested its submission and its terror by trembling. At the time of His glorious manifestation the entire universe will obey Him. Even the invisible powers will once more be subject to Him (Phil. 2:6-11; I Pet. 3:22) "that in all things He may have the first place" (Col. 1:18).

Above everything else, Christ's triumph will be manifested by His triumph over death, by the definitive and glorious resurrection of bodies. This is the great hope of Christians. For "if there is no resurrection of the dead, neither has Christ risen; and if Christ has not risen, vain then is our preaching, vain too is your faith" (I Cor. 15:13-14). But we know that "our Lord Jesus Christ . . . will refashion the body of our lowliness, conforming it to the body of his glory by exerting the power by which he is able also to subject all things to himself" (Phil. 3:21). For the Christian, therefore, death becomes the seed of glory and of a blessed eternity: "what is sown in corruption rises in incorruption; what is sown in dishonor rises in glory" (I Cor. 15:42-43).

How will this come about? St. Paul's explanations are a bit brief, and all the arguments of the theologians leave the intellect ill-equipped for serious investigation. Let us preserve the discretion of our faith and our hope on the secret of this mystery.

Is it possible to advance certain considerations as to the picture we may form in our minds of the place in heaven that Christ now occupies? We usually think that after His Resurrection our Lord lived forty days "upon earth," and that He afterward ascended to "heaven." In this connection, it would be interesting to give a history of the pictures of "heaven" that have been formulated through the centuries. The first Christians imagined the earth was flat, supported by the "waters from below," the dwelling of "Hades," "Sheol," the kingdom of the dead, and holding up the firmament and "the waters above" on its highest mountain peaks. It was thus quite natural for them to suppose that Christ had risen above the "third heaven" into the "paradise" (II Cor. 12:2) where St. Paul says he was caught up. Our present conception of the universe no longer allows such imaginings. If Christ is "in heaven," i.e., the physical heaven, He is just as much beneath us and around us as above our heads.

In truth, the question of Christ's "place" seems badly put. A more careful reading of the Synoptics, St. John, and the Acts, confirms the idea that the Resurrection, the "Ascension," the sitting at the right hand of the Father are concomitant acts both for Christ and in the economy of salvation. The risen Christ passed immediately into a better world, where He is "preparing a place" for us. The Evangelists themselves call His encounters with Mary Magdalen, the disciples, Thomas and others, "apparitions" or manifestations. The last of these was the "apparition" of the Ascension, or at least it was the next-to-the-last, since we are awaiting His last and definitive coming. Christ did not live "upon earth" in a continuous manner during those forty days, or at least if He did we know nothing about it. We know only His intermittent "manifestations," outside a tomb whose stone He Himself rolled away, in rooms whose doors were shut, on the shores of Lake Tiberias. It may be that He has remained in our midst through the centuries, and that He whose body is naturally capable of going through walls has not allowed Himself to be seen. That is how the saints have pictured Him, for example St. Catherine of Siena who somehow sensed His presence by her side while she prayed.

Such a mental picture of Christ is not forbidden. It is at least as fitting as one which would locate the Body of Christ on a star or a planet, sorely tempting the imagination. In fact, it seems more in harmony with the Scriptural accounts of Christ's apparitions, even if the last of these apparitions has been foretold in a setting and with a ritual that are more terrifying.

However, let us not linger over these imaginative representations. The flesh profiteth nothing, for it is the Spirit that quickens. These words which Christ spoke to His disciples with regard to the sacrament of His Body is well suited to this purpose also. The essential is that we really possess His Spirit within us, and that we have the sacrament of His Body and His Blood in our midst to unite us to Him inwardly and to make us live increasingly by His Spirit. The truth is that Christ knows and loves us, and penetrates in to the very depths of our hearts. Not even infinite distance or space can prevent this contact between Christ's soul and ours.

(f) *The First-fruits of Eternal Life*

Salvation has been brought to us by Christ, and it consists in this: Through His Passion, Death, and Resurrection, He has merited the Holy Spirit, the deifying Spirit, the Power of life, for us. And after He ascended to His Father, He sent this Spirit to us. Christ's mission came to an end with the sending of His Spirit. That is why He said to His disciples: "It is expedient for you that I depart" (Jn. 16:7). Before Christ left His Apostles, "The Spirit had not yet been given, since Jesus had not yet been glorified" (Jn. 7:39).

Who is this Spirit? In what manner do we possess Him at the present time? The Spirit is He whom the prophets had said would be poured out at the time of the Messias:

> For I will pour out waters upon the thirsty ground,
> and streams upon the dry land:
> I will pour out my spirit upon thy seed,
> and my blessing upon thy stock (Is. 44:3).

The Holy Spirit is He who gives life, He is the Spirit of fruitfulness. He was over the waters in the beginning, fecundating them. He overshadowed Mary and made her to conceive Christ in her flesh. For these reasons He is compared to water in the desert that restores life and vigor. We find this comparison frequently in Scripture:

> And the Lord will . . . deliver thy bones,
> and thou shalt be like a watered garden,
> and like a fountain of water
> whose waters shall not fail (Is. 58:11).

In Ezechiel's vision of the heavenly Jerusalem, waters, the symbols of God's benedictions, spring up from beneath the threshold of the sanctuary where God resides, as a sort of emanation of His life:

> And behold waters issued out from under the threshold
> of the house toward the east (Ez. 47:1).

The description ties in with that of the first paradise. These two descriptions are related, as we have already seen. Even more explicit is the following oracle by the same prophet:

> And I will pour upon you clean water,
> and you shall be cleansed from all your filthiness,
> And I will cleanse you from all your idols.

> And I will give you a new heart,
> and put a new spirit within you:
> And I will take away the stony heart out of your flesh,
> and will give you a heart of flesh.
> And I will put my spirit in the midst of you (Ez. 36:25-27).

And Zacharias says:

> In that day there shall be a fountain open to the
> house of David, and to the inhabitants of Jerusalem:
> for the washing of the sinner, and of the unclean
> woman (Zach. 13:1).

> And it shall come to pass in that day, that living
> waters shall go out from Jerusalem: half of them
> to the eastern sea, and half of them to the western sea:
> they shall be in summer and in winter. And the Lord
> shall be king over all the earth: in that day there shall
> be one Lord, and his name shall be one (Zach. 14:8-9).

One day, our Lord revealed to His listeners the meaning of these Scriptural passages, when He was in Jerusalem during the solemn Feast of the Tabernacles:

> "If anyone thirst, let him come to me and drink. He who believes in me, as the Scripture says, 'From within him there shall flow rivers of living water.'" He said this, however, of the Spirit whom they who believed in him were to receive (Jn. 7:38-39).

The Holy Spirit, the power of life, is the pledge of eternal life: "And in this we know that (God) abides in us, by the Spirit whom he has given us" (I Jn. 3:24). He is even an anticipation of and a participation in it, since "He who believes in the Son has everlasting life" (Jn. 3:36), and no one can say Jesus is the Lord except in the Holy Spirit. The Spirit is the first-fruits, the pledge of eternal life: "God . . . has . . . stamped us with his seal and has given us the Spirit as a pledge in our hearts" (II Cor. 1:22; cf. II Cor. 5:5). "The Holy Spirit . . . is the pledge of our inheritance, for a redemption of possession, for the praise of his glory" (Eph. 1:14).

Through the Spirit whom we have received we are even now united to Christ in heaven, we are raised up with Him to the right hand of the Father, as we say in the Communicantes of the Feast of the Assumption. We have already been emancipated from all servitude and even from corruption. We no longer live according to the flesh but according to the Spirit who is the power of life for all eternity: "You, however, are not carnal but spiritual, if indeed the Spirit of God dwells in you. But if anyone does not have the Spirit of Christ, he does not belong to Christ" (Rom. 8:9).

The Christian, living entirely hidden with Christ in the Holy Spirit, a stranger to this world and ignored by it, will appear in all his glory when Christ returns: "For you have died and your life is hidden with Christ in God. When Christ, your life, shall appear, then you too will appear with him in glory" (Col. 3:3-4). Then the Holy Spirit will also manifest from Whom He proceeds. The Holy Spirit is Christ's steward until His return. By making us participate even now in the life of the Trinity, His role is to purify us of all sin, to unite us to one another, to consummate us in unity, and to make us hear all that Christ has said to us. His final action will be to restore life to our mortal bodies and to make them resemble Christ totally: "But if the Spirit of him who raised Jesus Christ from the dead dwells in you, then he who raised Jesus Christ from the dead will also bring to life your mortal bodies because of his Spirit who dwells in you" (Rom. 8:11). "And the last enemy to be destroyed will be death" (I Cor. 15:26).

Is this to say that in this life our participation in the Resurrection of Christ concerns only our souls and not our bodies? Such a distinction between body and soul is foreign to the thought of Scripture and in particular to that of St. Paul. It even stems from a philosophy that does not entirely agree with that of St. Thomas. If we are to hold to St. Paul's view, the Spirit within us is a pledge of eternal life and resurrection. Inasmuch as we have been grafted in Christ, we have received a seed of resurrection that affects our whole being even though its present effects are chiefly spiritual.

The spirit that quickens the Church of true believers is the Spirit of the glorious Christ who is absent at the present moment. Everything concurs, in union with the Spirit and under His vital influence, to complete Christ's work, to consummate men in Unity. "And the Spirit and the bride say, 'Come!' And let him who hears say, 'Come!'" (Ap. 22:17).

The Spirit, the sign of the last days announced by the prophets, the inauguration of the Kingdom to come in this present world, makes us ardently desire the end. "May glory come and the world pass away! Hosanna to the God of David! Come, Lord!" (Didache 10:6).

II. The Pilgrims to the New Jerusalem

Now that we have established the theological bases of our faith, that is, the totality of realities in which we believe and hope, we must consider these same realities from another point of view: the point of view of the man who has yet to win eternal life. In short, we shall approach these realities not as the object of the Church's faith, but as the personal drama of the believing Christian. We shall approach them no longer by analyzing the elements of our heavenly heritage, but by trying to understand the manner in which we take part and possess it, the way in which we reach the Father's House, by whom we shall be glorified with Christ in the Holy Spirit. We shall approach them not from the point of view of the mystery, that is, of God's plan definitively revealed which we have tried to understand, but from the point of view of the one who is plodding onward in the desert of this world to reach the heavenly Jerusalem, and in whom the mystery will be accomplished; and also from the point of view of the one who is lagging behind and perhaps will never reach the goal.

1. THE AGES OF THE WORLD

The fundamental fact for a Christian to hold on to is that history has a direction. There is no such thing as a wheel of destiny. Man is not subjected to a 'Aνάγκη or a *fatum,* to a cycle of causes, influences, and effects that are perpetually being renewed and yet are perpetually the same. The vision of the world that corresponds with our faith is not circular, but linear. The world had a beginning, and it will come to an end some day. And this last day has even been given a name in Scripture and Tradition. It is called the day of Yahweh, or simply "that day." The formula "in that day," by which several prophetic oracles begin, recurs more than fifty times in the Bible.

However, there is a certain ambiguity in this linear formula of the vision of the world because we see a certain pattern of recurrence in the Bible as well as in the liturgy. And there is also an ambiguity as to the eschatological day, since many of the prophecies concerning "that day," the day of Yahweh, have already been partially realized by the coming of the Messias. Let us try to clear up this twofold ambiguity.

We have already seen that the prophets announced events to

come with expressions and images borrowed from the events and things of the past such as the crossing of the Red Sea, the theophany of Sinai, the trek across the desert, episodes from the reign of David, and finally the descriptions of paradise contained in the first books of the Law. The Church considers these events as being still in progress, and therefore returns to them each year in her liturgy. They are the paradigms of spiritual realities and of the life of the Christian. The Church strives to make her children relive all these epochs and the spiritual trials which they signify. They are not simply memories, or mere reminders of the past. They are typical states. The Fathers of the Church even called them sacraments: the sacrament of the Red Sea, the sacrament of the desert, the sacrament of the Promised Land.

Thus on the one hand, there has been an incessant progress, a linear advance of history, a forward march. St. Augustine liked to distinguish six ages of the world: Adam, Noah, Abraham, Moses, David, and Christ who inaugurated the reign of the Spirit, that is, the last days, the last hour. Elsewhere he applies the parable of the laborers in the vineyard to this same history of the world, comparing the first hour to Adam, the third hour to Abraham, the sixth hour to Moses, and the ninth hour to David. We are the laborers of the eleventh hour. The thought is the same, and we find it in the writings of all the Fathers of the Church (see de Lubac, *Catholicism*). Everything flows toward this gathering up, this recapitulation of all things in Christ and toward the consummation of all things in unity.

But there is also an incessant return to David, whose kingdom has once again been promised to the Messias; to Moses, the legislator, to whom the scribes, the wise men of Israel, and the Pharisees refer, and who was to bear witness to the truth of our Lord's teaching at the moment of the Transfiguration; to Abraham, the father of all believers, whose faith serves as a model and example to all the faithful (see Heb. 11:8-19), and to whom St. Paul refers to establish his doctrine of justification (Rom. 3:31-4:8); and finally to Noah, the type of the savior and judge, and to Adam, who is the figure of the one who was to come (Rom. 5:14).

Thus God's pedagogy of history consists in impelling us forward, always forward, and in continually broadening our horizons. The Christian is not a man who sifts through the past. He is a pilgrim to the Promised Land which is the life of the Trinity. In the measure that his faith, his hope, and his charity develop in the Holy Spirit, the more drawn he is to the spiritual realities toward which he is running. But on the other hand, divine pedagogy presents typical states of the spiritual life. And just as Providence led the Hebrews step by step from Abraham to Christ, passing by the dark paths of the father of all believers, who started out "not knowing where he was going" (Heb. 11:8), by way of the Law of Moses, the Kingdom of David, the teaching of the prophets and the wise men, so must the Christian slowly follow this road if he wants to know the plenitude of Christ some day.

But what the history of Israel sketched on the political and temporal level in a religious atmosphere that was still primitive and uncouth, Christ has accomplished in His own life on the spiritual level by His victory over the powers of evil and His glorious entrance into the Jerusalem on high on the day of His Ascension. Now the Church, and every Christian with her, lives these things each year in the Holy Spirit, by following the whole pilgrimage of Israel in union with Christ, by rediscovering the course of divine teaching from the revelation of Yahweh's name to Moses to the omnipotence and universality of God revealed to the prophets, and thence to the revelation of the Blessed Trinity. And in following this path she passes through the same salutary trials, and enjoys the same spiritual fruit contained in the events of this sacred pilgrimage. This path follows the linear course of history which is really a spiral ascension, like a path which winds its way upward around a mountain.

The typical states to which the Church and Christians continually come back are rediscovered each time at a deeper spiritual level. The Event has never stopped giving all the spiritual fruits with which it is pregnant. It is the joy of the pilgrim, beginning with the springs of earthly water in the desert, or the temporal Kingdom of David, gradually to enjoy the living waters of the Spirit and the patrimonial possessions of the promised Kingdom. Like the sap which provides the tree with its shoots, buds, leaves, flowers, and fruit, the Spirit quickens the march of history and slowly opens up humanity to the many dimensions of divine life within the bosom of the Father.

We have now also cleared up the second ambiguity that we had encountered. The Day of Yahweh has in part arrived, and is still in part expected. When our Lord inaugurated the age of the Spirit, He also inaugurated the eschatological age. But for all that, everything has not yet been accomplished. "Now we are the children of God, and it has not yet appeared what we shall be. We know that, when he appears, we shall be like to him, for we shall see him just as he is" (I Jn. 3:2).

The "interim" Church, in her societal, juridical, hierarchical, and sacramental aspect, is a prolongation of the Synagogue. Although the Scriptures of the Christians fulfill those of Moses and the prophets, although the sacraments of the New Law contain the grace of the Holy Spirit, although the visible hierarchy of orders is the minister of grace and of all truth, it is through Scriptures, the sacraments, and the hierarchy, that the Synagogue has been continued at a superior level in the Church. The Scriptures, the sacraments, and the hierarchy are provisory and destined to disappear. On the contrary, the Church of the Holy Spirit, in her "pneumatic" aspect, has inaugurated the kingdom of God. Christians have one foot in the Synagogue and the other foot in heaven. Whatever they can perceive or enjoy of the sacraments of faith comes close to heavenly joys in the measure that they live by the Spirit that is in them.

2. THE SACRAMENTS OF THE PILGRIMS

The pilgrims who are plodding toward the Promised Land are not without guideposts and provisions for the journey. The Scriptures, the hierarchy, in a word all that can be called the sacramentality of the Church, is at their service. We include in the word "sacramentality" not only the sacraments proper but everything in the Church that has a spiritual meaning, bearing, and efficacy. It is in this sense that we say that the Church is sacramental in her every aspect.

We have seen the sacramental bearing of Biblical events and of their liturgical renewal. We could also analyze, within each liturgical cycle, the eschatological significance of feasts. This eschatological meaning is particularly notable for Advent, which is the time of expectation and hope. The reason the Church at this season goes over the prophecies of Isaias and Israel's history and anxious waiting, is not purely and simply to return to the past. Such a return would be meaningless. For Christians are also waiting. They are awaiting and hoping for the glorious end of the Kingdom inaugurated with the Incarnation. Thus Israel's hope is a lesson for Christians, although it must be understood and fulfilled at a superior level. Christians would not know what to do with the past unless it assured them of a reality already attained and gave them the hope of a reality still to be fulfilled. Using the prophetic words of the Old Dispensation, the Church makes us relive this hope during Advent, in the Holy Spirit.

Likewise, in the liturgy Sunday is the sacrament of the last day. It was on Sunday that the Lord rose from the dead. That is the day that the Lord made. *Haec dies quam fecit Dominus.* Throughout the Paschal season, the Church never tires of singing this anthem borrowed from the prophets, thus clearly indicating that the day awaited by the ancients, the eschatological day, is already defined as the day when Christ despoiled Satan of his princely power and took definitive possession of His Kingdom.

It was also on Sunday that Christ appeared several times to His disciples, giving rise to their conviction, after the Ascension, that Christ would return on a Sunday. They may well have expected Him on Pentecost, which was also a "day after the Sabbath." In any event, they expected Him every Sunday, and that is why at sundown after each Sabbath (we know that days began and ended in the evening for the ancient Jews), they would gather together for prayer and to read the Scriptures.

In their concern to allow no breach in the unity of the community awaiting its Lord, and so that no foolish virgin should lead astray the assembly of those who were awaiting the Bridegroom, all the Christians were there together. And when dawn came, the hour of the Resurrection, and Christ had not come back despite their liturgical supplication—*Maranatha*—the breaking of the bread and the renewal of the Last Supper took place. They did not go away until they had received the viaticum of the glorious Christ, absent but always fervently awaited. The Eucharist, the manna of our earthly pilgrimage, was for them, as it must be for us, the eschatological sacrament, the first-fruits of the meal in which we shall once more eat and drink with Christ, in the Kingdom of heaven.

Like the Eucharist, all the sacraments have an eschatological significance and bearing. But this is especially true of Baptism, the Paschal sacrament par excellence, that we must quickly glance at now.

Theology has often made of Baptism a simple sacrament of purification, thus confusing certain ideas about Baptism and Penance. That is not the way Baptism is primarily presented to us in Scripture and Tradition. The water of Baptism is not there simply to purify us. It is there to make us die and to raise us up again, that is, to bring us forth anew.

The reason for this is that water, for the ancients, was a mysterious and dangerous cosmic reality. Water is the kingdom of death. Ancient and Jewish cosmology was in fact defined by the triple division of heaven, earth, and hell. And hell, signifying that which is below, was localized in the *waters* underneath the earth. The ancients imagined that the earth was situated upon the waters: "Who established the earth above the waters" (Ps. 135:6). "For he hath founded (the earth) upon the seas" (Ps. 23:2). He established the earthly element upon the seas, upon the waters. The trilogy of heaven, earth, and hell corresponds to the trilogy of sky, earth, and waters. There is this difference, however, that the waters of hell are "the waters from underneath," the waters that we see spring up from the earth almost everywhere in springs, rivers, lakes, and seas; they are not "the waters from above," i.e., from the sky. They are the deep waters referred to by the author of the Book of Job in the words: "He hath set bounds about the waters, till light and darkness come to an end" (Job 26:10).

This trilogy of "waters, earth, and heaven" reappears several times in Scripture: "Thou shalt not make to thyself a graven thing, nor the likeness of any thing that is in heaven above, or in the earth beneath, nor of those things that are in the waters under the earth" (Ex. 20:4). "And every creature that is in heaven and on the earth and under the earth" (Ap. 5:13). "Him . . . who created heaven and the things that are therein, and the earth, and the things that are therein, and the sea and the things that are therein" (Ap. 10:6). Yahweh rules over this tri-form universe with a limitless power. Sometimes the Psalms strive to manifest His power by saying that even the sea, that is, the foundation of the world, trembled before Him:

> Then the fountains of waters appeared,
> and the foundations of the world were discovered:
> At thy rebuke, O Lord,
> at the blast of the spirit of thy wrath (Ps. 17:16).

In pagan religions, for example in the religion of Babylon, the primitive sea, chaos, the *Téhom,* is the enemy of God, an enemy that God has subjugated from the moment of creation. While Israel considers that even the *Téhom* belongs to God, it holds that the sea has become the residence and property of the Evil One, of the powers of evil. That is why God manifested His sovereignty by imposing a limit upon the waters:

> Thou hast set a bound which they shall not pass over;
> neither shall they return to cover the earth (Ps. 103:9).
> *Terminum posuisti quem non transgredientur neque convertentur operire terram.*

The conquest, the measurement, the limitation, and the ordering of the primitive *Téhom* represent a victory and an outpost of the sovereign God against the powers of evil:

> Hitherto thou shalt come, and shalt go no further,
> And here thou shalt break thy swelling waves (Job 38:11).

Every victory over the waters such as the end of the Flood, the crossing of the Red Sea, etc., is a manifestation of Yahweh's supreme domination:

> Thou rulest the power of the sea: and appeasest the
> motion of the waves thereof (Ps. 88:10).
> Thou by thy strength didst make the sea firm:
> Thou didst crush the heads of the dragons in the waters (Ps. 73:13).

The spirit of evil personified by the monster, the "Leviathan," the "Dragon," lives in the sea. He is the enemy of God, the power of evil, the leader of Satan and of all the evil spirits, the author of all man's servitudes. And hence in the day of God's triumph over His enemies, Yahweh will kill the Leviathan:

> In that day the Lord with his hard, and great,
> and strong sword
> Shall visit leviathan the bar serpent,
> and leviathan the crooked serpent,
> And shall slay the whale that is in the sea (Is. 27:1).

The theme of the combat between God and the marine dragon, the paradigm of all the powers of evil, is common in Scripture. Psalm 73, so often used in baptismal liturgies, is another proof of it:

> *Tu confregisti capita draconis super aquas* . . .
> Thou didst crush the heads of the dragons in the waters.
> Thou hast broken the heads of the dragon (Ps. 73:13-14).

The reason the waters of the Red Sea or of the Jordan drew back to let the Hebrews pass was that "they saw God" and trembled: "The waters saw thee, O God, the waters saw thee: and they were afraid, and the depths were troubled" (Ps. 76:17). These are the waters of the kingdom of death, the abysses of demons. After the Sanctus in its Easter Mass, the Gothic missal includes the following acclamation, which is a paraphrase of Psalm 76: *"Viderunt te inferi, Deus, viderunt et timuerunt a voce tonitrui tui dicentes: absorpta est mors in victoria tua. Ubi est mors aculeus tuus?*—Hell saw Thee, O God, it saw Thee and trembled at the voice of Thy thunder, crying out: Death has been engulfed in Thy victory. Where, then, is thy sting, O Death?" (P.L., 72, 279). St. John tells us in his Apocalypse that after the Judgment the sea will be no more (Ap. 21:1).

The eschatological theme of the crushing of the Dragon is to be found in the descent of Jesus into the Jordan at the time of His Baptism. The Syrian liturgy for the feast of Epiphany sings: "Thou, Lord, hast sanctified the waters of the Jordan when Thy Holy Spirit left heaven and descended upon them, and when Thou didst crush the head of the Dragon who writhed, powerless to resist." In the Ethiopian book, *The Miracles of Jesus,* Jesus said before His Baptism: "Today I shall crush the Evil one, I shall abolish his power, I shall drown him in the waters" (P. G., 17, 844).

Every catechumen does at the time of his Baptism the same thing that Jesus once did. He descends into the waters, that is, into the kingdom of death. He imitates the Savior in His Baptism and in His burial in the tomb. As St. Paul says, he is *consepultus cum Christo,* buried together with Christ. Then he raises himself up, he comes forth from the kingdom of death, and he rises again with Christ.

For the water on which the Spirit rests possesses a new quality. It becomes fruitful, it begets life, it gives life. It calls to mind the primordial waters on which the Spirit of God moved before the creation of life (cf. Gen. 1:2). It is because the Christian is born of water that the ancient frescoes portrayed him in the form of a fish, and that Christ, his Model, was the great Fish, *Ikhtus.*

Thus Baptism recalls and sacramentally reproduces Israel's descent into the Red Sea where God already manifested His power over the Abyss, the descent of Jesus into the Jordan, the descent into hell, the descent into the tomb, and at the same time the Resurrection, the Re-creation. Baptism is not only a sacrament of purification, but also a sacrament of death and resurrection. The themes of all the crossings and all the liberations of the Old Testament are the figure of this sacrament.

Baptism is a Paschal and an eschatological sacrament in the same measure that Easter itself is eschatological. It is a salvation, a deliverance, a re-creation, a rebirth, each of which calls for fulfillment. The baptized Christian is a man reborn, and yet he awaits the new Birth (Mt. 19:28), that is, the manifestation of Christ. The Christian is a man who has already triumphed over death, Satan, sin, and the powers of evil. He is a fellow citizen of heaven, risen with Christ. And yet he must still die and fight against Satan and against sin. The power of the resurrection does not deprive him of the merit and dignity of fighting and triumphing in his own right. It gives him the power to conquer, and the hope of victory.

This is true not only of Baptism, but of the other sacraments as well. Each of them in its own way represents future glory and prepares for it. They signify the Passion of Christ, the grace presently communicated by the sacrament, and the glory to which it leads. As for the Eucharist in particular, St. Thomas has expressed its threefold significance in the memorable prayer, *O sacrum convivium:* "O sacred banquet, in which Christ is received, the memory of His passion renewed, the mind filled with grace, and a pledge of future glory given to us." The same prayer could be said in reference to every sacrament.

We have just seen how Baptism, because it is a liberation, opens up the Kingdom of heaven to us. All these considerations also apply to Confirmation, which is the "seal of Baptism"; to Penance, which is a second Baptism, as it were, a second sheet-anchor after Baptism; and to Extreme Unction, which frees us from all the consequences of sin—punishments, infirmities and weaknesses of soul.

Holy Orders and Matrimony deserve special mention.

The hierarchic priesthood of the Church Militant is not entirely an earthly priesthood. The priesthood of the Christian "priest" is never more than the sacrament of the priesthood of Christ who is our only Priest and who acts in all our "priests." The priests of the Old Covenant "were numerous, because they were prevented by death from continuing in office; but he (Christ), because he continues for ever, has an everlasting priesthood. Therefore he is able at all times to save those who come to God through him, since he lives always to make intercession for them" (Heb. 7:23-25).

The hierarchic priesthood is sacramental. It is part of the provisory economy of signs. Inasmuch as it is only the shadow and the sign of the eternal and authentic priesthood of Christ, it constantly turns the mind to this heavenly priesthood and this divine liturgy in which the elect celebrate with Christ, and at His side, divine praise, thanksgiving, and jubilation. *Beatus populus qui scit jubilationem.* Blessed are the people who know jubilation! The Christian people are preparing for this rejoicing under the efficacious direction of their hierarchic and sacramental priesthood.

Again, this priesthood is like a scaffolding that masons set up to build a house. When the house is built, the scaffolding is taken down. When the construction of the Church has been completed, the hierarchic priesthood will no longer have any reason for being. True, there exists another hierarchy in heaven, but it is not founded on the sacramental powers of sanctification. It is a hierarchy of interior values wholly founded upon charity and upon the conformity of each individual soul with Christ. Inasmuch as the sacramental priesthood builds the Church here on earth, it invisibly organizes this interior hierarchy of souls according to the way they understand the Word and receive grace. In heaven, the invisible will become visible, and the things that were visible before will be relegated to second place. When at last the temple of the eternal Church has been built, it will appear in all its luminous splendor. The scaffolding of the ministerial priesthood that was only the sign and the instrument of Christ the Priest, of "the Lamb (who) is the lamp (of the city) (Ap. 21:23), will lose its provisory function. When the One who had been signified appears, the sign will lose its function and will subsist only as a memory, as a mark of glory. The hierarchic rank of holy priests will not depend so much on their ministerial power as on their holiness. The eschatological meaning of the ministerial priesthood is the construction of this invisible Church that celebrates the eternal liturgy of heaven in union with the Lamb.

As for Matrimony, its eschatological significance is clear. Christ's marriage with the Church, which this sacrament signifies, was not celebrated until the Passion. The Church Militant is a Bride whose marriage contract was signed in the blood of Christ, but who is still waiting to participate in the nuptial banquet in a more direct way than through a sacrament, and to enter the chamber where she is to live a life of union with her Bridegroom for all eternity. Matrimony is the eschatological sacrament of the day when Christ will say without ever having to repeat it: "This now is bone of my bones, and flesh of my flesh" (Gen. 2:23).

3. THE JUDGMENT OF THE PILGRIMS

At the end of the pilgrimage "when the Son of Man shall come in his majesty, and all the angels with him, then he will sit on the throne of his glory; and before him will be gathered all the nations, and he will separate them one from another, as the shepherd separates the sheep from the goats" (Mt. 25:31-32).

How does God judge? God is just and He judges according to justice, that is, according to each one's merits. But are not merits the fruits of divine gifts? Does not God reward His own gifts? Yes, that is true, and that is why God's justice is founded on His mercy. God rewards our merits only because He first came to rescue us in our misery and has favored us with His gifts. Thus God's mercy is at the beginning of His judgments: God rewards things that do not come exclusively from us, and He punishes us less than we deserve.

The good that is in us and that we have received from God is measured by our faith. It is faith that justifies us, and it is on faith that we shall be judged. But let us take care to understand this word in its full Pauline or Johannine significance, that is, not as a simple intellectual assent but as an act of our whole being, a movement of wholehearted adherence, of trust and love; in a word, a movement of lively faith:

If anyone hears my words, and does not keep them, it is not I who judge him; for I have not come to judge the world, but to save the world. He who rejects me, and does not accept my words, has one to condemn him. The word that I have spoken will condemn him on the last day (Jn. 12:47-48).

And again:

Now this is the judgment: the light has come into the world, yet men have loved the darkness rather than the light, for their works were evil. For everyone who does evil hates the light, and does not come to the light, that his deeds may not be exposed. But he who does the truth comes to the light that his deeds may be made manifest, for they have been performed in God (Jn. 3:19-21).

(a) *The Glory of the Elect*

The most firmly established point in the doctrine of faith is first of all the fact of the final resurrection. St. Paul tells us: "If there is no resurrection of the dead, neither has Christ risen; and if Christ has not risen, vain then is our preaching, vain too is your faith" (I Cor. 15:13-14). The resurrection of the flesh has been an article of faith since the beginning of the Church. It was written into the baptismal creed of the Roman Church (the Apostles' Creed) as early as the second century. To deny it, one must be as far removed from the Church as the Docetists and the Gnostics.

Christ conquered death. While a respite has been given to "the prince of death," "the father of lies," it is only provisory. On the day of judgment and of ultimate triumph, the dead will rise again and the elect will join with Christ in forming not merely an eternal society of friends, but the family of God Himself. All who have received the Holy Spirit, the Spirit of sons, will form within the bosom of the Father and for the praise of His glory, the completed Christ, the total Christ, Head and members.

Together with the elect, the whole world will reach its consummation. The elect will live on a new earth and in a new heaven. Everything will be transformed for the better, so as to be in harmony with the state of the blessed.

"How do the dead rise?" (I Cor. 15:35). St. Paul's explanation borrows its figures and comparisons from the physics of his own time. But the language is of no concern to us. His conclusion is clear: "What is sown in corruption rises in incorruption; what is sown in dishonor rises in glory; what is sown in weakness rises in power; what is sown in the natural body rises a spiritual body" (I Cor. 15:42-44). What does the expression "spiritual body" mean? First of all, it is certain that it is a real body. Spiritual does not mean unreal. It means: entirely subject to the Holy Spirit. The Church has condemned those who held that the dead will rise again with an ethereal and spherical body (Canon 5 of Pope Virgilius against Origen, and the Council of Toledo, 675).

We shall rise again like Christ in "the same flesh in which we live, we stand, and we move" (Creed of the Council of Toledo). But our flesh will be spiritual like Christ's. The body we have inherited from Adam and from sin is an earthly, animal, and corruptible body. It is not completely "in the hand" of the Spirit. The soul is ashamed of what it is incapable of governing. The body that we shall inherit and that we have already inherited from Christ in the seed of Baptism, will reflect the glory of the Holy Spirit who dwells in it. It will be young, immortal, exempt from infirmities and defects. To quote St. Isidore, the resurrection "does not change nature or sex, but simply does away with corporeal frailty and defects." That is to say that on the day of Resurrection men will recognize one another, friends will find each other again, husbands and wives will love each other with a very pure love of eternal friendship because they will love each other in God.

And yet will the glory be the same for all? It seems not, since our Lord Himself has declared: "In my Father's house there are many mansions" (Jn. 14:2). However the elect will not be jealous of one another. On the contrary, the diversity of the gifts of glory will bring supplementary joy to each one. Inasmuch as the elect are members of one another, St. Augustine says, the glory of one will be the glory of the other; and one will rejoice to see in another what he himself does not possess. Likewise, the proclamation of sins on the day of judgment will not bring shame or dishonor to the blessed who will be known to have been great sinners. For, St Augustine also tells us, the fervor of their conversion and of their repentance will be admired all the more when the gravity of their follies is more widely known.

Certain of the elect, as Christ had promised His Apostles, will sit with Him on the seat of judgment: "You who have followed me, . . . shall also sit on twelve thrones, judging the twelve tribes of Israel" (Mt. 19:28). The Tradition of the Latin Fathers usually divided men into four categories, with regard to judgment. For example, St. Gregory says in his *Moralia* (Bk. 26) that some will reign and be judged, i.e., the ordinary Christians who have sinned and done penance; others will reign and not be judged, i.e., the perfect who have lived according to the Evangelical counsels. Among the condemned, some will perish, i.e., the godless and the idolaters who have not known God; the others will perish and be judged, i.e., the wicked Christians.

Finally, the peaceful, complete, and definitive possession of the Holy Spirit together with the Son in the bosom of the Father will give the elect a perfect and definitive beatitude. What will be the nature of this intimacy with the Three? St. John simply tells us: "We know that, when (God) appears, we shall be like to him, for we shall see him just as he is" (I Jn. 3:2). Does this similitude signify the vision of the divine essence in itself? And yet St. John says elsewhere that "No one has at any time seen God. The only-begotten Son, who is in the bosom of the Father, he has revealed him"

(Jn. 1:18). And St. Paul says that God "dwells in light inaccessible, whom no man has seen or can see" (I Tim. 6:16).

We can understand that the Greek Fathers, and especially the School of Antioch, hesitated before this mystery. St. John Chrysostom admits that the elect see God within the limits of their capacity, but he denies that they really see the divine essence. According to him, neither the prophets, nor the angels, nor the archangels have seen or now see God as He is in Himself "for how could the whole of created nature see the Uncreated?" (Hom. 15 on St. John).

The doctrine of the Latin Fathers is more definite. In the fourteenth century Pope Benedict XII, in his Constitution *"Benedictus Deus,"* defined that the elect see God "with an intuitive vision and even face to face, without any intermediary created objective, inasmuch as the divine essence reveals itself to them in an immediate, naked, clear and open manner." The dogma of the immediate vision, as St. Thomas has shown, is inseparable from the dogma of immediate creation by God and of the dogma of the immortality of the soul. The end corresponds with the beginning. To have refused to admit the possibility of an immediate vision—without any objective intermediary—would simultaneously have ruined the dogma of the immediate creation of the soul by God and its natural immortality. It would have abolished the traditional conception of immaterial spirit, capable of the infinite, "capable of God." It is in the Light of God that we shall see the Light. *In lumine tuo videbimus lumen.*

(b) *Reprobation*

The existence of eternal reprobation was clearly announced by our Lord in Chapter 25 of St. Matthew: "Before him will be gathered all the nations, and he will separate them one from another, as the shepherd separates the sheep from the goats" (Mt. 25:32). "Then he will say to those on his left hand, 'Depart from me, accursed ones, into the everlasting fire which was prepared for the devil and his angels'" (*ibid.,* 41). St. John also says in his Apocalypse that he saw Satan and his satellites thrown into a pool of fire and brimstone "where are also the beast and the false prophet; and they will be tormented day and night forever and ever" (Ap. 20:9-10).

St. Paul goes still further. He does not even allude to the "resurrection" of sinners. To his mind, the resurrection is the last work of the Holy Spirit in those in whom He dwells. Thus there can be no resurrection in the strict sense of the word for sinners (cf. Rom. 8, and I Cor. 15). And indeed the wages of sin is death—death for all eternity. Death develops all its fruits and its consequences only beyond this life, where it establishes its Kingdom and where sinners, far from ultimately escaping it, belong to it forever. Hell is like an eternal death, a death of the soul, and a death of the whole man in a body that has not stopped suffering the agonies of death and that therefore cannot be said to be "risen." This is true although St. John implies an after-life for the damned when he speaks of a "resurrection of judgment" as opposed to a "resurrection of life" (Jn. 5:29).

Hell is like a gigantic and unlimited amplification of the death of man. It is a shutting out from the true life which is in God and which is lived by the blessed. St. Fulgentius says that "on the day of retribution the reprobate will not be immortal; they will become corrupt but they will not be consumed; they will be as dying but they will not die . . . the death of the soul and of the body will never terminate because the torment of the body and soul is never to end" (*De remiss. pecc.* 2:13). We can say in all truth that the wages of sin is death in this world and in the next. And so reprobation is clearly affirmed in Scripture, whether through the figure of the separation of the good and the wicked, of a pool of brimstone and tortures, or of a kingdom of death. And to this may be added the fact that the Church has never prayed for the damned.

On the other hand, there are other Scriptural texts which have troubled all the doctors of the Church, such as for example: "If his work burns he will lose his reward, but himself will be saved, yet so as through fire" (I Cor. 3:15); "every kind of sin and blasphemy shall be forgiven to men; but the blasphemy against the Spirit will not be forgiven" (Mt. 12:31). What is this fire through which we must pass before being saved? What sins and blasphemies are not sins against the Spirit? The Church was very slow to take cognizance of the fundamental demands of revealed truth. It was not until the fifth and sixth centuries that the dogma of eternal punishment became firmly established in Christian belief.

Meanwhile, it is true that Origen had set forth his famous theory of "Apocatasis." Relying on obscure texts of the Bible, the Alexandrian doctor had taught—or allegedly taught—that after successive trials all intelligent creatures, including demons and sinful men, would finally be restored to God's friendship. Hell would be no more. Origen hoped in this way to "save" the universality of salvation and the infinite mercy of God. This doctrine, which was to be condemned by Pope Anastasius in the year 400 and later by Pope Vigilius in the year 543 (Denz. 211), influenced the Doctors and pastors of the Church. We find a somewhat mitigated version of it in the "Ambrosiaster" and in St. Jerome. The latter was a fiery partisan of Origen before 394, but later rejected these opinions. In the end he admitted a progressive mitigation of the punishments of hell and continued to think that the torments of Christians, even of the sinners among them, would not be eternal. Then only unbelievers would experience the pains of hell. In his own words:

"He who has entrusted himself to Christ with his whole soul, even if death finds him in sin like a man who has fallen, will live eternally because of his faith. A common death touches believers and unbelievers alike, and all will likewise rise again. But the latter will rise again to their shame, while the others, because they have believed, will rise again for eternal life" (Letter 119).

St. Ambrose likewise admitted that faith would succor sinners and will win forgiveness for them although there be injustice in their works. St. Augustine, who was acquainted with the doctrine of the progressive mitigation of the pains of hell, abstained either from supporting or opposing it: *"Quod quidem non ideo confirmo quoniam non resisto"* (Enchiridion 112).

Regardless of damnable sins and damned sinners, the faith of the Church is that eternal punishment is a fact. And yet the Church has never pointed to any man as having been damned. She does not canonize the reprobate. She knows that the slightest movement of faith and charity suffices to win of God's mercy the reduction of eternal punishment to a trial by temporary fire.

The Punishments of Hell

Whatever kind of hell we may be speaking of, we must distinguish two sorts of punishment within it: the punishment of damnation that St. Augustine calls *"alienatio a vita Dei,"* exclusion from divine life, and the punishment consisting of sensible, afflictive sufferings.

The sufferings of damnation are common to all the damned and even to those who are deprived of eternal life only for a time. Before the coming of our Redeemer, the souls of the just suffered the common punishment, the damnation inflicted upon the human race since Adam and Eve; and they awaited the Messias in the hell that is sometimes called the "limbo of the patriarchs." That is where our Lord descended after His death, to deliver them and to reintegrate them into the second paradise. The benefits of the Redemption were then extended to the souls of the just. Since the Resurrection, this hell, or the limbo of the patriarchs, no longer exists.

Damnation is also visited upon those who have not committed personal sins but have none the less been immersed at their birth in the sin of human nature: original sin. They share with the damned the privation of glory and of the beatific vision, even though they have not committed any actual sin. St. Augustine says that they suffer the least stringent of the punishments of hell: *"Mitissima omnium poena."* That means that for them damnation is not accompanied by sensible sufferings. It is merely a privation. We now call this part of hell "the limbo of children." "Gentle" as this punishment may be, we cannot fail to see that it is extremely serious since it consists in the privation of God's life and exclusion from His beatitude. What holy soul would not prefer (at least in its loving zeal) to suffer a thousand torments if only it could be with Him?

The existence of limbo (or hell, according to ancient terminology) for children obliges us in strict justice to consider the gravity of original sin and the nature of the bond that unites us as members of the human race. Because of Adam's sin we are all of us by nature—and hence by birth—deprived of divine help and of God's beneficent friendship. This is not to say that each of us is personally responsible for this "original sin," any more than the eye or the hand are responsible when we commit a sin of the eyes or of the hand. Adam is responsible for the sin of the whole race, for he is not only the father and head of the race, but also the one who constituted it in the state of original sin; just as the soul is responsible for an impure look or for the hand's theft.

Man incurs original sin at birth, as a defect which affects the whole race and which is transmitted by generation. At birth, man is related to Adam as one of his members. Since every sin involves responsibility on the part of the sinner, the responsibility for original sin rests with Adam and not with each child at birth; just as the responsibility for the sin of the eye or of the hand must be attributed to the soul and not to the eye or to the hand. And since all responsibility means merit or condemnation, we must conceive the just retribution for original sin in the same way. But as long as a child is not bound to Christ, who alone gives life, he remains a member of this human race that has deprived itself of divine friendship. Moreover he is passible, and if he dies he must go to the "limbo of children."

In declaring that the child suffers no afflictive punishment, the doctrine of limbo manifests the child's non-responsibility. In declaring that he does not see God, it stresses the depth of our solidarity and the absolute gratuity of divine help. But what does this "privation" of divine life, even though free of any painful punishment, mean for the soul of the child, and later for his body? It is hard to imagine or describe it.

It should be noted that this punishment is reserved for children who have not attained the use of their reason and who have not received the grace of Baptism. As soon as the child becomes capable of a free act, that is, of an act of reason or a human act in the strict sense, he expresses his fundamental being in this act, or, to put it another way, his basic orientation. This orientation is either good or bad. If it is good, this indicates that God's mercy has come to the aid of the child and given him the help of His grace. If it is bad, this indicates the child has refused to give himself to God. In any event, original sin does not remain the only sin after the age of reason has been attained. If the child chooses the good, God's grace which helped him has necessarily remitted this sin. If on the contrary he makes his choice in favor of evil, his first act is a personal sin for which he himself accepts the responsibility and which cannot be punished merely in limbo. His punishment then is not a simple privation, but must include suffering.

On the other hand, it should be noted that when we speak of the "grace of Baptism" we do not mean that all children who have not effectively received the Baptism of water are shut out from heaven. For one thing, God's mercy is infinite, and the grace He gives to whomever He pleases is not bound up with the sacraments as far as He is concerned. Why, for example, should He not grant His mercy to anyone who asks Him? Besides, the doctrine of the Baptism of desire could, it seems, be applied to the children of Christian parents. In this sense, parents who efficaciously believe, who have the firm intention of having their children baptized, receive Baptism of desire in the name and place of their children. Actually, the parents are the Church's representatives with their children; and children who are baptized before the age of reason are always baptized in the faith of the Church. We are not forbidden to believe that if such a child should die before being baptized, he would be saved in the faith of his parents.[3]

But apart from the children of Christian parents—and even in cases where hope takes the place of certitude—we have no assurance concerning the fate of children born without Baptism. Only the sacred sign of Baptism can give certitude to our faith. Just as we cannot condemn with certitude those whom God's mercy may exempt from eternal death, out of consideration, for example, for certain prayers, so too we must not underestimate the "human" possibilities of very small children to whom God sometimes grants, in spite of their tender years, the power to make free and meritorious acts.

Whereas damnation is a privation that does not allow of degrees and that is common to all who do not share divine life, there are all sorts of degrees in the punishment of the senses, corresponding to the personal and actual culpability of each individual. The fate of children who have committed no actual sin and who are not subject to any afflictive, sensible punishment, is one thing; the lot of great sinners and demons is quite another.

Exactly what is meant by the fire, the gnawing worms, and the rust, referred to in the Gospels? The holy Doctors have given various interpretations, but nothing has been defined by the Magisterium. This is a matter about which we should avoid indiscreet flights of imagination that have no solid foundation. The men of the Middle Ages, haunted by the fire of hell and the deviltries of the demons, have represented or transcribed all sorts of infernal scenes, but their representations are more often than not direct descendants of paganism,[4] and do not stem from the Bible, which offers very little to feed the imagination.

Who Pronounces the Judgment?

We know this much: those who have sinned mortally, that is, those who have voluntarily turned away from God, go to hell.

[3] Cf. Ch.-V. Héris, "Le salut des enfants morts sans baptême," in *La Maison-Dieu*, No. 10, pp. 86-105.

[4] Michel Carrouges has brought out this fact in his admirable study, "Images de l'enfer," in the collection entitled *L'enfer*, Coll. Foi vivante, Ed. de la Revue des j., 1950.

However the infernal punishment inflicted upon the sinner must not be understood after the manner of the sanctions or punishments inflicted by human judges in our courts. Regardless of the fairness of the court before which a condemned man stands, his crime is never so clear-cut that his conviction involves no deliberation or choice on the part of the judges. Man sees appearances. Only God sounds the reins and the heart. It can also happen that the same crime may be punished in one way by one court and in another way by a different one, or even differently by the same court at a different time or in different circumstances. Unless a criminal knows his judges very well and exactly what they know of his crime, he is rarely sure in advance of what his verdict will be. And this gives him reason to hope.

The same does not hold true of the sinner who has completely turned against God. He is not permitted to hope. Even if God wanted him, he would not want God. Hell is in the heart of man before being in the judgment that outwardly pronounces judgment. The candidate for hell never finds hell a surprise or a punishment he didn't expect. It is the place where he has long since placed himself inwardly, before being thrown into it outwardly.

As Jouhandeau says very precisely, "the reason man does not understand hell is that he has not understood his own heart." [5] And elsewhere he also writes: "Wherever I am, there is my free will; and where my free will is, absolute and eternal Hell is in power." Man is free to love God, but he is also really free to flee from Him completely. "Hell is only the horrible guarantee of human freedom. Men are truly free before the Creator only if God has granted them the power to refuse their love to Him eternally. If the odyssey of angelic and human creatures *must necessarily* end by a final and total reconciliation between God and themselves, then the freedom of creatures is nothing but flight. Hell must at least be open as a *possibility*." [6]

Jouhandeau is therefore justified in hurling this terrible apostrophe, worthy of a Luciferian Prometheus: "I can, by myself alone, set up in opposition to God an empire over which God is powerless: that is Hell" [7]—in other words, his proud ego petrified in refusal. Jouhandeau seems to have trembled before the consequences of his

[5] *Algèbre des valeurs morales*, p. 229.
[6] M. Carrouges, *op. cit.*, p. 70.
[7] *Algèbre*, p. 214.

own inflexibility and hesitated before certain conclusions, since he also wrote: "Hell is God's greatest suffering before being mine." And yet he has merely [8] "transcribed into extravagant language, with psychological lucidity that is at times extraordinary, the situation of Christians who profess the faith but spend their lives *preferring themselves to God,* without understanding that they are weaving their own damnation. Jouhandeau bears witness to the presence in man of the seeds of hell. And at the same time he has proven, by breaking away from the horrible fascination that these seeds released for him, that the game isn't up, and that here on earth, close as a man may be to the abyss, he isn't there yet and can hear the call of love with great suddenness." [9]

We ought, however, to complete Jouhandeau's lucid but partial analyses. Hell is not only "the supreme pedestal of the ego." [10] It is also the "collectivity of the reprobate, the terrible reverse of the communion of saints in the heavenly Jerusalem. It is the unleashing of the hatred of all against all." [11] If even on this earth "man is often a wolf to other men, what will it be in the world deprived of all grace and hope?" [12] We have merely to think of certain scenes from Sartre's *Mouches* and *Huis-Clos,* or of certain words spoken by the Staretz Zossima, Dostoievsky's saint in *The Brothers Karamazov.*

All these pictures are not delirious nightmares from some deranged psychologies. They belong to every century and to every type of man. They stem from the very depths of the person conscious of the tragic possibility within him of being in contradiction with everything he truly wants. Hell is as it were "the immanent fruit of sin," [13] the deep-seated suffering "of no longer being able to love" to use the words of the Staretz Zossima. Hell is the suffering that the damned has freely chosen here below and that inexorably controls his future life.

There is something a bit primitive, even pagan, in certain descriptions of a purely exterior hell, which have no corresponding interior state within the candidate for hell. There are even scenes

[8] *Ibid.,* p. 228.
[9] M. Carrouges, *op. cit.,* p. 74-75.
[10] *Ibid.,* p. 78.
[11] *Ibid.,* p. 78.
[12] *Ibid.,* p. 78.
[13] *Ibid.,* p. 83.

from Dante's *Divine Comedy* that are not exempt from this criticism. The judgment of the damned is not a human judgment that man might pronounce simply on the grounds of external acts and without taking into account the heart's interior intentions. On the contrary it is a judgment that reveals these intentions. If God punished someone for his exterior acts and not for his intentions that were better than his acts, He would be unjust and He would no longer be God.

And if God rewarded the sinner against his will, He would be like a straw man who is insulted and neither moves nor reacts. He would not be Love, who is pleased to find an answering love or saddened by a refusal of love. He is alive, and He cannot look with the same countenance upon those who love Him and those who hate and insult Him.

But even though hell, no less than heaven, is a sort of immanent sanction, an interior judgment of the heart, that does not mean that there is to be no last judgment, that is, no external proclamation. Neither the conception of an exterior judgment or the conception of an interior and immanent judgment should be chosen to the detriment of the other. One does not preclude the other, any more than God's transcendence prevents Him from also being immanent. We must consider the two together.

Moreover we know that while the sanction is immanent, it is also exterior and afflictive. The Gospel speaks to us of the "gehenna of fire," which is a reality distinct from and outside the inwardly tortured soul or mind. It may happen that the torture of a gnawing remorse, even though devoid of real regret, may be the essence of the punishment. Indeed, what would physical sufferings amount to if they allowed the soul to escape its interior hell? He who has refused love and now knows that although he was made for God he will never be able to give Him his measure of love, experiences a kind of suffocation for which there can never be any counterirritant. But this interior suffocation does not mean that all of hell is within. There is also the exterior sanction, the "sufferings of the senses" to which we have already referred. Inasmuch as the latter cannot be separated from the immanent suffering, they must be considered as a sort of material correlative to the interior fire that burns and consumes the spirit.

Need we add once again that we must not conceive this "punishment of the senses" the way Dante conceived it in his imagination,

A commentary on the Apocalypse was composed by Beatus, the abbot of Liébane, in Spain, in 734. The book was a great success and was recopied in various monasteries in Spain and elsewhere. The manuscript of Saint-Sever, a double page of which is represented in the adjoining illustration, was illuminated in Gascony in the abbey by the same name, after a Spanish model, and under Abbot Gregory, that is, between 1028 and 1072.

The scene here reproduced illustrates Chapters 4 and 5 of the Apocalypse. On the central throne is the figure of Christ who does not hold a book (Ap. 5:1), but a sort of medallion with the figure of a lamb (Ap. 5:6). In His left hand He holds a long staff (scepter?) terminating in a ring in which there is a figure of a bird.

Around Him are the four Evangelical animals with the heads of a man, a lion, a bull, and an eagle. Each one has six wings, and—except the man—they are covered with eyes (Ap. 4:8). They each hold a book, with the exception of the eagle who is clasping a rolled scroll.

All around are the twenty-four elders, sitting on thrones, holding their harps in one hand and with the other holding up to the Lord "the golden bowls full of incense, which are the prayers of the saints" (Ap. 5:8). And finally on the outer edge is the multitude of angels (Ap. 5:11) praising the Lamb.

We may well admire the originality of this composition and the artist's concern to avoid monotony by the diversity of attitudes, costumes, and thrones, all of which are made still more lifelike by the brilliant colors. This "Apocalypse" served as the model for several others, both paintings and sculptures, and can be considered as an iconographical type.

Manuscript of Saint-Sever (Bibliothèque nationale).

fed on the heritage of paganism far more than on the Gospel itself. The Gospel tells us that he who believes "shall live." He alone will live, at least in the sense that to exist for all eternity without being united to God, without seeing Him, is not really living. From this point of view, the punishment of the damned seems above all to be a kind of "sleep" of the real life, to which his existence is reduced. And what is more excruciating for a being created for life and who knows that he was created for life, than not to live? Regardless of the corresponding suffering in the senses of which we were just speaking, it seems that the essence of the punishment of hell lies in this unsatisfied appetite: the suffering of one who wants to love but cannot love.

(c) *Purgatory*

Belief in purgatory gradually developed in the living consciousness of the Church from two principles: on the one hand from everything in Scripture and Tradition that exalts the demands of divine justice and mentions a purifying fire; and on the other hand from the liturgical custom of prayers and suffrages for the dead. However it was not until 1439 that the Council of Florence officially defined its existence on the occasion of controversies with the Greeks.

Moreover it seems that the conception of purgatory current at that time corresponded to specifically Latin ideas of the Redemption, in which the juridical notions of debt, satisfaction, and reparation invaded the field of theology to the detriment at times of notions of purification, improvement, sanctification, to which the Greeks ordinarily limited themselves. In other words, while the faith of the Church is now fixed with regard to the existence of purgatory, it is vague as to the nature of this fire, its duration, and its specific efficacy. And yet the Fathers of the Church did not want the faithful to take refuge in the notion: "The duration of purgatory doesn't matter to me, since I know I shall ultimately attain eternal life." In consequence, they usually laid great stress on the extreme gravity of the punishment meted out in purgatory. This punishment will be more severe, St. Cesarius says, than anything that can be thought of or experienced in this world in the way of suffering . . . (Serm. 104).

However there is one aspect of the Church's practice that has remained constant, namely, the suffrages for the deceased. This obviously means that the souls in purgatory can be helped. It is an application to them of the dogma of the communion of saints, by virtue of which we are all members of one another and can make satisfaction for one another. It is also a pressing appeal to God's mercy. That is why the faithful apply prayers, good works, alms, and above all the Holy Sacrifice of the Mass to the needs of their beloved dead. The Church also opens up the treasury of her indulgences to the dead, that is, the treasure of merits accumulated by her saints and entrusted to her care, so that all may benefit from them.

Can the souls in purgatory pray for the living and help them? Certain Fathers have timidly advanced this proposition. However it is not a commonly accepted doctrine. The souls in purgatory are in a state in which they need first of all to be helped so as to arrive as soon as possible to eternal happiness. The common doctrine is that we can and must help them, but that they are not yet in a position to help others.

4. THE EXPECTATION OF THE SAINTS

All that we have said so far applies in a general way to the Last Judgment at the end of the world. What of the interval between the death of each man and the day of judgment? Do the elect have only the first-fruits of their beatitude then, and are the reprobate granted a respite before entering into eternal torments?

The answer to this question is scarcely touched upon in Scripture. The first Christians had little interest in it either, because they believed the end of the world was at hand. A little later, a commonly accepted view was that certain provisory dwellings awaited the souls of the dead. Such in particular was the thought of St. Ambrose in the fourth century. However the dwellings were not the same for everyone. Some were already suffering, and others were already in glory. This indicates that a "particular judgment" had already been made. Finally in 1336, Pope Benedict XII condemned the opinion that held that the souls of the elect had to wait until the final resurrection to enjoy the beatific vision. This was not merely an opinion held by a certain number of theologians. Benedict XII's own predecessor in the Chair of Peter, John XXII, had vehemently preached it in a series of sermons to the people of Avignon in 1331 and 1332, and he had even upheld it during the last years of his life, notably at the Consistory of January 3, 1334.

The fact is that this opinion, already passionately discussed, had in its favor a long succession of witnesses, and among them some of the great names of both Latin and Greek Tradition. The future blessed whose trials had come to an end were often represented as "held in a sort of pleasant sleep" or in a state of quiet and hopeful joy, waiting at the "door of heaven" in an "atrium," in a "place of rest." All these figurative expressions indicated, with various nuances, the delay imposed upon all souls until the end of the world, in accordance with current belief (cf. de Lubac, *Catholicism,* New York, 1958, Sheed and Ward). John XXII had defended this thesis, but by declaring that he was speaking only in his capacity as a private theologian he had taken care not to commit the papacy. At his death, he retracted this opinion in the presence of his cardinals.

Thus the elect possess the essentials of beatitude as soon as they die: they enjoy the beatific vision. While this doctrine does not have the same foundations, defined in Scripture and in primitive Tradition, as the doctrine of the resurrection of bodies, it is none the less of faith. Benedict XII defined it in the Constitution *Benedictus Deus* of January 29, 1336, and the Church professes it every time she celebrates a canonization and addresses prayers to the saints.

We must therefore distinguish two judgments: the particular and individual judgment that takes place when the soul leaves the body, and the general judgment on the day of the resurrection of the dead. Indeed, justice demands a second judgment. True, God knows the soul perfectly, since He searches the reins and the heart, and He can judge the soul immediately. And yet justice demands that the soul's cause be completely pleaded or manifested, and this is possible only at the end of time when the soul's works will have produced their last effects. On that day we shall see that a small act of charity, small at least to the superficial eye, may have produced a fruit which in turn produced another, and then another, and so on until the end of the world. We shall continue to witness the fruitfulness of the charity possessed by the saints even to the last day. And on the other hand, we shall see the successive accumulation of ruins that has followed the lives of sinners. It is therefore necessary that at the end of the world when the concatenation of effects has been terminated, that a general judgment make outwardly manifest to the eyes of all the justice of the first judgment of the just and even more of the damned, and proclaim the promises of this judgment.

With regard to the first judgment we have already said that we must not think of it after the manner of a wholly external affirmation that might take the soul by surprise either in sin or righteousness, as if a saintly soul could expect anything except to enter into the joy of its master and as if the damned soul could expect anything except to be separated from the Life that it has refused. If it is true that God judges, it is also the soul that seals its own judgment. And this judgment consists in the soul itself, as it is, with its burden of love or hate.

The second judgment will be more complete and decisive because the blessed who have already been judged must yet recover their bodies for final happiness. Everything is not over for them inasmuch as everything is not over for the Church. How could they remain strangers to the painful road of pilgrims, to the fate of sinners who have not yet done penance? Like Christ and with Christ who intercedes with His Father until judgment, they participate in the Church's expectation, they pray, intercede, hope, and wait without anxiety, with the assurance but also the strong desire of finally seeing Christ's definitive triumph and the decisive defeat of all the powers of evil.

In a word, the blessed in heaven are also members of the Church. They, too, can say to us: we are members of one another. They are our brothers in heaven and continue the combat although in a different mode, peacefully and trustingly. This doctrine is the foundation of the Church's prayers to the saints and of the worship we render them. It also implies that the non-purified elect pass through purgatory immediately after their death, and that the damned enter their punishment the moment their souls are no longer able to repent.

Glory, peace, vision, and the tranquil possession of God, which are the divine and essential elements of beatitude, are possessed even now by the elect. But their beatitude still lacks a complement without which their happiness would not be perfectly human: the recovery of their bodies and the visible company of their friends. When these things come to pass, the Church will be definitely victorious and glorious, and all the elect will be filled with the luminous joy of Christ.

REFLECTIONS AND PERSPECTIVES

"I am the resurrection and the life; he who believes in me, even if he die, shall live; and whoever lives and believes in me, shall never die" (Jn. 11:25-26). "This is the will of my Father, . . . that whoever beholds the Son, and believes in him, shall have everlasting life, and I will raise him up on the last day" (Jn. 6:40; cf. 6:44).

The Church's belief in the Resurrection, in eternal Life, in the immortality of the soul, is not the conclusion of laborious studies on the immateriality of the human soul, or the fruit of certain anthropological and cosmological theses. Our faith is founded on God's revealed words.

It is true that representations of death and the imagined "dwellings" of the dead may change, and have in fact changed considerably through the centuries, in response to philosophical and cosmological conceptions. However there has been no change in Christ's words to Martha cited above, which the Roman liturgy repeats at every funeral Mass. He who believes does not die, and Christ will raise him up again on the last day. This does not mean that the godless man will not rise again. But his "resurrection of judgment" (Jn. 5:29) cannot be called a "resurrection of Life." Being sure of Christ's Words, and also of St. Paul's teaching (see especially I Cor. 15), we can approach the philosophical study of the soul with greater serenity, criticize the various historical "representations" of the other world, and seek rational relationships between them and established dogma.

"First things" and Eschatology. Let us first pose the question of vocabulary. We speak of "heaven" to designate the abode of the blessed, and we also speak of "heaven" to designate the air above our heads: the clouds, moon, sun, and stars. Why is the same word used to designate the physical and the spiritual heaven? Is it legitimate to say that the heaven of the elect is "Above," and to juxtapose the present life to it as life "here below"? What do we mean when we say that our God is the "Most High," the God of Heaven above?

On the other hand, we speak of "hell" to designate several distinct realities. For example, Christ's descent into "hell" does not signify that Christ visited the damned in "hell." The very word signifies etymologically what is underneath, what is in an *inferior* situation. Whence this localization and the corresponding imagery?

These two very simple examples remind us that our eschatological pictures are bound up with a certain conception of the world— with a specific cosmology. Should this cosmology cease to be valid, then our religious words, because of their identification with a given cosmological vocabulary and also because of the heritage of outdated religious ideas that they carry along with them, may easily lead us into error.

Franz Cumont writes in *Lux perpetua* (Paris, Paul Geuthner, 1949, pp. 3-12): "The speculations of the ancients on the fate of souls were closely bound up with a specific conception of the world that we no longer hold. The Greeks debated the question of whether this world is eternal or not, and certain ones thought the life of the world was made up of long periods, 'great years,' that were repeated ad infinitum. They imagined a perpetual linkage of causes which would have governed the totality of the cosmos from all eternity and would continue guiding it forever. But they had not even a vague notion of man's antiquity upon earth. Their imagination never dreamed of the millions of years that have elapsed since the beginning of life on our planet. They thought our species was merely a few thousand years old. For them, it was only recently that the gods still mingled in the society of mortals. If the ancients had a false idea of our human condition because of their chronological evaluation, they were led still further astray by the narrow limits of their cosmology, for their eschatology was modeled on their cosmology and adopted its outlines.

"At the dawn of modern times, the discoveries of Copernicus and Galileo, by transforming our conception of the structure of the universe, destroyed the notions that 'earthbound' men had of the grandeur of their destiny. Of all the scientific conquests that have broadened the intellectual horizons of humanity, none, not even the theory of universal gravity, have been more disturbing to traditional beliefs than those of Copernicus and Galileo. This new concept of the universe would no doubt have provoked a great moral crisis even in the sixteenth century if all its consequences had been immediately perceived. This moment marked the definitive rupture with a past over a thousand years old. The reversal of the roles of the sun and the earth destroyed the postulates on which rested all the notions extant up to that time concerning the 'place' of life after death.

"Neither religion, nor even the philosophy of the ancients before Plotinus, regarded the posthumous condition of the soul as purely spiritual: it was a diaphanous breath analogous to the wind, an impalpable shadow visible to the eyes, or a mixture of air and fire.

Even the Platonists, who proclaimed this essence to be immaterial, taught that it took on a form as soon as it descended from the heavenly heights to enter our world. And they thought it was wrapped in ethereal or aerial envelopes before it came to shut itself up in a body. Thus it did not remain a pure spirit that escaped the limitation of space. We cannot say of it, as we do of the universal soul, that it is nowhere and everywhere. It travels in the sensible world and successively inhabits its various parts. After death, it moves into a specific region of the universe.

"Let us see how this universe was constituted. It was composed of four elements. The heaviest of these, earth, by virtue of its very density, had fallen toward the center and been agglomerated into a compact sphere that remained suspended in equilibrium without moving. Water had spilled over its surface, giving birth to rivers which flowed into the seas, or into the Ocean that surrounded this island or *oïkoumenè,* the continent inhabited by man. Or else this liquid principle rose in vapors into the inferior zone of the atmosphere which was thickened by humid fogs or clouds.

"The two other and lighter elements had their place above the first two. The air enveloped the earthly globe with a mobile layer, continually agitated by the winds: of its nature it was dark, when the light of the stars and sun did not light it up. Muddied in its proximity to the earth by the exhalations of waters, it is purified in the measure that it escapes from them in its higher spheres. And it extends to the zone of the moon, where it touches the ether. This fourth element, both volatile and light, has a natural tendency to rise, and its subtle fire, which occupies the upper portion of the cosmos, shines forth in the brilliance of the stars. The sphere of the moon is the limit between the world of the gods and of eternity, a world subject neither to becoming nor corruption, and our earthly world, subject to birth, change, and death.

"Above the moon, rose six other spheres of transparent crystal, that imprinted their sinuous movements upon the planets: first, those of Mercury and Venus, the brilliant star of the morning and evening, then that of the sun. The latter ranked fourth, that is, in the middle of the seven superimposed circles, from which, according to a well-authorized opinion, it directed the complicated course of the 'erring stars' and, by regulating the revolutions of the heavens, governed all of nature. Beneath this 'heart of the world,' moved Mars, Jupiter, and Saturn. Finally, embracing the seven others in its immense orbit, the sphere of the fixed stars was, according to certain thinkers, the motor that put all the wheels of the celestial machinery into motion, and it deserved to be adored as the supreme god: this sphere marked the limits of the world. Beyond that, the physicists saw nothing but ether or emptiness. But the theologians saw in this astronomical Olympus the dwelling of the Immortals, or else, if they were followers of Plato, they imagined this empyrean was peopled with transcendent and purely intelligible powers.

"It was in a universe, thus constituted, that were located the dwellings of souls that had left their fleshly wrapping. The earth, which was the center of this universe, was, according to very ancient myths, scooped out of an immense cavity in which the internal gods reigned over the people of darkness. Beyond the Ocean that surrounded the *oïkoumenè,* the Fortunate Islands, so it was believed, welcomed the blessed heroes. Hades, the domain of death, was sometimes located in the then inaccessible southern hemisphere. Moreover, the air that surrounds the earth was filled with disembodied souls transformed into beneficent or harmful demons. The most virtuous of them rose as high as the moon, to the limits of the dwelling of the gods. Or else, according to certain theologians, man's reason, purified of all alloy, returned as an "intelligent fire" to the sun from which it had come forth. According to another doctrine, the souls that came down to earth to shut themselves up in flesh acquired their qualities and their passions successively from the stratified spheres of the planets, according to the nature proper to each, and inversely were stripped of these qualities in seven stages when they ascended to the highest heaven where, as sublime essences, they were to enjoy unending felicity in the company of the gods. We can see that all this is closely bound up with the cosmic system taught by the astronomers of antiquity.

"Thus, the great *All,* where dwells the society of the living and the innumerable souls of past generations, is conceived as a closed vase, whose outer wall is the sphere of the fixed stars, within which the spheres of the seven planets are fixed one within the other. And below, under the zone of air and vapors in perpetual movement, the immobile earthly globe is the stable point around which the whole heavenly machinery revolves.

"Ancient physics had established a strong contrast between the sublunary world, a closed field in which the elements were at war, and the heavenly spheres which moved regularly around it in the luminous ether. Thus creation was divided into two parts ruled by opposing principles. Modern astronomy has integrated the earth into the general economy of the cosmos and has looked upon it as a cell of this great body, subject to the same laws as the infinite multitude of its fellows in a whole restored from duality to unity.

"The ancient universe, when compared to the one we see through our giant telescopes, is very tiny indeed. Although since Posidonius the smallness of our earth as compared with the universe as a whole has been commonly accepted by philosophy, the Greeks always thought the firmament was very close to us. They knew neither the infinitely large nor the infinitely small, but created a world in proportion to man, without even realizing that in reality the universe is doubly incommensurable with man, both because of its immensity and its infinitesimal size. While they did have a momentary intuition of the solar system, they did not penetrate or even surmise the mysteries of the stellar world, whose depths Herschel began to fathom during the eighteenth century.

". . . Recently Sir James Jeans was moved by the 'terrifying' impression made upon us by the immensity of the universe, its glacial solitudes, the prodigious duration of cosmic phenomena, the indifference or even apparent hostility of nature with regard to our sentiments, our ambitions, and our ideal of perfection with its spiritual values.

"It was not fear but admiration that the spectacle of the cosmos inspired in the Greeks and in their Roman disciples. They never tired of celebrating the magnificence of nature, giving lavishly of its riches, the infallible laws that govern the course of the stars and the constant return of the seasons. This order and beauty were already pointed to by them, as they have often been by others since, to prove the existence of a Creator. But they were especially impressed by the splendor of the skies illumined for an eternal feast and by the unchanging harmony of their revolutions that made it possible to mathematically calculate its coordinated movements in centuries to come. To their mind, this harmony was not only mechanical but also musical.

"The rotation of the spheres produced such sweet harmonies that the instruments that called them to mind here on earth awakened in the soul the nostalgia for this inebriating concert and filled it with raptures that raised it up toward the heavens. Similarly, the contemplation of the gleaming stars aroused deep emotion, accompanied by a vast desire to soar up toward these luminous gods. Filled with mystical ecstasy, the fervent observer thought himself to be transported into the center of the sacred choir of the stars and participated in their eternal existence. But this double exaltation, only temporary here below, is no more than a foretaste of the joys that will be given after death to reason emancipated from the bonds of matter, when the former goes to live among the constellations. By taking part in their harmonious evolutions it will understand their divine causes and will at the same time be delighted by the sublime concert produced by their perpetual movements. Such was the beatitude that a religion of the stars held out for its elect.

"Thus everything seemed to exist for the service and the delight of man in this life, and for his reward after death. As the king of this earth, he could think he was the center of a world created for him and subordinated to his ends. It was for him that the plants grew and animals were born, that nature multiplied her gifts. It was for him that the heavens revolved and the sun warmed and illumined the atmosphere. . . .

"The limited knowledge of the ancients still allowed them to imagine that their philosophy knew all the essentials of what happened in heaven and on earth. They prided themselves for understanding the system of the world and for having discovered the mechanism of the heavens. In this spherical world, limited by the animated orbits of circular movements, in which all the sublunary phenomena resulted from the mingling of the four elements and were commanded by the principles of heat, cold, dryness, and humidity, nothing seemed an impenetrable mystery. Never has reason felt it was so close to having guessed all the secrets of nature and attained to an understanding of the very essence of things in this vast domain in which man was both the observer and the usufructuary. . . .

"All the reasons that, through the centuries, have nourished faith in an existence after death led the ancients to constantly modify their doctrine of immortality to adapt it to the ever-illusory science of their epoch, and to replace by new forms of after-life those that seemed inacceptable and obsolete.

"Extenuated phantoms vegetating in the night of the tomb, imperceptible shadows hidden in the deep caverns of the earth, souls plunged in the dark abyss of the invisible hemisphere, igneous vapors carried by the winds through the atmosphere, lunar demons nourished by vapors rising up from the earth, rational essences returning to the sun that created them, or reascending through the starry sky toward the empyrean from which they had descended—all these conceptions that were born of the naïve faith of an archaic epoch and ended as the loftiest religious speculations, are proof of the unceasing efforts of thinkers to make man's future life harmonize with the psychology and cosmology that they professed. . . .

"Antiquity bequeathed a singularly complex composite of beliefs and speculations from various epochs to the Middle Ages, whose theology and superstitions they nourished up to the moment when the crumbling of the geocentric system upset all notions of the cosmos and stripped medieval eschatology of a mainstay on which it was absolutely dependent. When the earth ceased being the center of the universe, the only fixed point surrounded by the moving circles of the heavens, and became a paltry planet turning around a star which in turn moved in a fathomless immensity among an infinity of others, the ancients' naïve idea of the soul's journey in a narrowly-bounded world became inacceptable. Hence the progress of science, by discrediting the erroneous solution that antiquity had bequeathed us, brought us face-to-face with a mystery undreamt-of by the pagan mysteries."

Indeed, Christian scientific inquiry during the first centuries adopted ancient conceptions of the universe as formulated by Ptolemy. It assumed that souls rose toward heaven by crossing the "planetary spheres" of the Iranian astronomer-astrologers, and thus attained to the "supra-earthly" light of beatitude, which St. Basil called Ἐν τῷ ὑπερκοσμίῳ φωτί (Hexam. 2:5; cf. also Cumont, *op. cit.*, p. 188). In the fourteenth century, Dante still pictured heaven in this way. "To destroy this tradition, Copernicus and Galileo had to ruin Ptolemy's system, and stellar astronomy had to open up to the imagination the infinite spaces of a limitless universe" (*ibid.*).

St. Paul pictured the universe after the manner of the ancients and everyone understood him when he said he had been "caught up to the third heaven" (II Cor. 12:2). Likewise, St. John pictured the woman of the Apocalypse, the sign of Mary and of the glorious Church, with "the moon under her feet, and upon her head a crown of twelve stars" (Ap. 12:1). St. John did not invent this image, but used it spontaneously. It belonged to the "lunar and stellar" eschatology, according to which the moon and the stars in a lesser degree were the glorious and triumphant seat of blessed souls. "A

Roman bas-relief in the Copenhagen Museum shows us the attached busts of a brother and sister, and the little girl is seen to rest on a large crescent and is surrounded by seven stars, representing the planets" (Cumont, *op. cit.,* p. 178). The ancient representations of the Iranian astronomer-priests and of the Pythagorians were still valid for Christian imaginations, or at least offered themselves as symbols of the beyond.

Thus, until the seventeenth century, eschatological representations and conceptions were closely bound up with the cosmological conceptions of the time. (On this subject, reread Father Dubarle's important chapter in Volume II of the present series.) The discovery by Copernicus, which is certainly one of those that have caused the greatest upheaval of all time in the human race, revolutionized cosmology, and by the same token revolutionized eschatological "beliefs" or *representations*. We have kept the same word—heaven—to designate both the physical area that surrounds the earth and also the dwelling of the blessed. And yet the two realities are now distinct in our minds, if not always in our imagination. The discovery that caused so much trouble for Galileo purified Christian thought of what it still retained of the scientific-religious heritage of the Iranians and the Pythagorians. St. Thomas Aquinas taught that the first paradise was on earth because it was not yet an immutable state of beatitude, but that "in the state of final beatitude it will be transferred to the empyrean heaven" (Ia, a. 102, a. 2, ad 1). We have a better understanding today of what Christ teaches us. We realize that our souls will not "rise" into the physical heaven but will simply live eternally with Him, and that we shall rise again on the last day.

However there is a certain relationship between the order of our end willed by God and the order of our origins, between eschatology and the "first things." This relationship is made known to us by Revelation. In the first part of this chapter, we have shown that Israel's hope and its notion of what its future was to be were continually nourished by the memory of past favors. The hope of a future paradise is nourished by the memory of the first paradise, to the point that the sacred writer's description of the Garden of Eden is actually an eschatological picture. The beginning of Genesis and of the Apocalypse are closely interrelated: Man, Woman, and the serpent are the characters in both of these books. St. Thomas also teaches that the description of the location of paradise given in

Genesis is not without importance, for "although the place of the earthly paradise avails not man for his use, it avails him for a lesson; because he knows himself deprived of that place on account of sin, and because by the things that have a bodily existence in that paradise, he is (symbolically) instructed in things pertaining to the heavenly paradise, the way to which is prepared for man by Christ" (IIa IIae, q. 164, a. 2, ad 4). Moreover the theme of the "return" to paradise has always been honored by Christianity. Christ is the second Adam who reopens paradise to the one who decides to "follow" Him to the end (see A. Stolz, *L'ascèse chrétienne,* Chevetogne, 1948, especially Chapter II, "Adam et la mystique").

Will this return to paradise come about by a violent re-establishment that excludes all real progress from the earthly city toward the heavenly city, inasmuch as judgment will create an absolute break in continuity between the history "before" and the history "after" the judgment? Or will this return come about by a progressive re-establishment? On this point theologians may be divided into those who are "pessimists" and those who are "optimists" (see D. Dubarle, *Optimisme devant ce monde,* Paris, Ed. de la Revue des jeunes). Actually, we know that the judgment will involve a radical transformation of the universe and that all we need to know is what can and must happen through and beyond this transformation, and what cannot. Theology must respect the revelation on the flood of fire quite as much as the one in the Epistle to the Romans on the painful bringing forth of creation (Rom. 8:19-22).

Finally if the last things and the first things are related in this way, then it is also a thesis of theology which the thoughtful believer cannot help accepting, that the doctrine of the beatific vision corresponds to the immediate creation. It is because the human soul was immediately created by God that it is "capable" of seeing God face to face. It is because God destines the soul for this immediate vision that He creates it Himself without any intermediary. The end of a thing corresponds to its "nature," that is, to its "birth," and its beginning.

Philosophers who see man as a product of the species without any special intervention of God, without any break in continuity with the evolutionary causality of Nature, are obliged to lower the human soul to the level of animal and mortal "souls." The human soul, because it is spiritual, escapes in its noblest parts the causality of the species, and with regard to its end it is outside the species.

Inasmuch as it was destined for a divine life it can be immediately created only by God (cf. *Theology Library:* Vol. II, pp. 300-301).

The Day of the Lord. For the believer who lives *after* the time of Christ, "the day of the Lord" is an ambiguous expression. The day that the prophets of the Old Covenant announced has already arrived, and in this respect it is past. It is also present and to come.

For the prophets, "the day of the Lord" meant the day of the Messias' coming. From this point of view, the day of the Lord was the day of His Incarnation, or the day of His birth, or the day of His first Epiphany at the time of the adoration of the Magi, or the day of His first public manifestation at the time of His Baptism in the Jordan. The day of the Lord also designated the day of our Messianic salvation, or of our liberation by the Messias. From this point of view, "the day of the Lord" designates the time of Christ's Passion and Resurrection that consummated His work of salvation. That is the time that our Savior referred to when He spoke of "His hour" (Jn. 2:4; cf. Mk. 14:41; Jn. 5:28; 7:30; 12:23,27; 13:1; 16:2,4,21,25; 17:1; 19:27), or when He spoke to His enemies of "their hour" (Lk. 22:53). For the same "hour" that was His or the hour of His Father, was from the point of view of His enemies the hour of "the power of darkness" (Lk. 22:53). In a general way, the "day" or the "hour" of the Lord was every moment of Jesus' life. If the hour was still "to come," it had already "come" and "was" every time He spoke, from the fact that He was "there" and that in that way the hour of His Passion was already beginning (Jn. 4:23; 5:25; 16:32).

Thus the day of the Lord, in the sense that it designates the time of Christ's salvific work, is over. Salvation is a fact. Everything is consummated. And yet nothing is accomplished as long as the battle continues. As long as a soul can still be lost, how can it be said to be saved? Salvation is accomplished, therefore, in the sense that paradise has been reopened by Christ, that God's patrimony has again been offered to man and that man has been given the strength to escape the grasp of the Evil One and to obtain this patrimony. But salvation is still to come in the sense that nothing is decided in a definitive way for the one who has not ended his earthly career. In this last sense, for the Church Militant "the day of the Lord" is the day (or the hour) of the Resurrection and of Judgment (Mt. 24:36-50; 25:13; Mk. 13:32; Lk. 12:40; 17:31). And for each individual soul, the day of the Lord is the day of death. No one knows this terrible, happy, and glorious day, "not even the angels of heaven, but the Father only. And as it was in the days of Noe, even so will be the coming of the Son of Man" (Mt. 24:36-37).

Between the two events is the intermediary time that is, depending on one's point of view, the time of conversion and penance, the time of God's patience, the time of grace, the respite given by God to the Nations, the time of the dominion of the Holy Spirit, the "Advent" of the Church, the time of Anti-Christ, the time of the wayfaring Church, the time of the Church's widowhood. It is the time announced by Christ in the parables of the servant who awaits his master's return and of the wise and foolish virgins who await the arrival of the Bridegroom. It is the time that our Lord designates as the "eleventh hour" (Mt. 20:12) of the world, or at least the hour that the Fathers of the Church have spontaneously recognized as the eleventh hour in the parable of the laborers in the vineyard. This is the time when everything has already been accomplished definitively as far as we are concerned, also the time when everything begins to be accomplished within us and in the Church Militant. It is the time of the sacraments of the Church that bring us, under the veil of certain signs, the mystery of the Passion accomplished in the past, and the reality of its fruit today in our souls and in the Church. And through this reality, we enter even now into the Blessed Eternity that the Passion inaugurated and that the sacraments announce.

These sacraments that make us in some respect coexist with the time of the Passion of Christ and the time of His glorious Return, and with eternity in the present instant when we receive them, are the seven sacraments of the Church which are the seven sacraments of the Christian Pasch, but understood with all their prolongations and explanations throughout the symbolism and the occasions of the liturgy. Thus the sacrament of the Pasch which is the Eucharist, is most fittingly celebrated on Sunday, from the point of view of its sacramental significance in our own time, inasmuch as Sunday is the day of the week that commemorates "the day of the Lord." And the same is true of Easter, which is the annual anniversary of the day the Lord made.

And yet, even though "the day of the Lord" is sacramentally celebrated only on certain days, it is His day every day at every instant, and no less on somber days than on the (sacramentally) glorious days of Easter and the other feasts. And even though the hour of

the Lord corresponds sacramentally to certain celebrations, it really
exists at every instant of the Church and of each of our lives, by
day and by night. Behind the curtain of signs that are feasts and
celebrations, the Lord effectively holds out His helping hand to us
and periodically consoles us. But whether the Lord consoles us or
not, He is always there in our midst.

Judgment. Concerning the circumstances of judgment, what will
precede it, the signs that will accompany it, the glories of the
blessed, the various sufferings of the damned, there is abundant
Christian as well as non-Christian literature. We know very little
in this sphere, and the little we know has been handed down to us
through enigmatic signs. Theology must therefore maintain a certain sobriety in dealing with it. Its work must consist in regrouping
the various texts of Tradition that treat of eschatological realities, in
interpreting them in the light of exegesis and of all the disciplines
of textual analysis, and in comparing and organizing them insofar
as possible.

The fundamental eschatological sources are in the New Testament. On the signs that will precede Judgment, read: Matthew 24
and 25; Luke 21:5-26; I Corinthians 15:51-53; I Thessalonians
5:1-11; II Peter 3. We shall cite the Apocalypse once and for all
as the proper source of the theology of eschatological judgment.
Concerning the doctrine of millenarism in particular, consult the
authorized commentaries on the Apocalypse.

Concerning the Resurrection in the strict sense, read I Corinthians 15, and the references that we have given in the course of
this chapter. It should be noted that the authors of the New Testament do not explicitly teach the immortality of the soul. But this
immortality, which is of faith, is an immediate and inescapable
corollary of the dogma of the Resurrection. Nothing rises again
unless it already exists. If the resurrection has no subject, or no
longer has a subject, it is not a resurrection but a new creation.
This implies a break in the continuity of existence. Immortality
under such circumstances would amount to the creation of a new
person. Authentic immortality is implicitly contained in words
such as those our Lord spoke to the good thief: "This day thou
shalt be with me in paradise" (Lk. 23:43). Everyone understood
that the thief would be with Jesus not before but after his death.

There is perhaps another reason for our disturbing lack of texts
on immortality. Today we conceive of man as being composed of
a soul and a body after the manner of Plato, or Aristotle, or Des-

cartes. The anthropologies of all these philosophies differ noticeably from the anthropology of the authors of the New Testament. The latter do not divide "the soul" and "the body" in the same way, and on the contrary distinguish in man between the soul and the mind. When St. Paul tells us that we have been resurrected in our Baptism, he does not mean a resurrection that would touch only the "soul" in the Aristotelian sense, and would resurrect the body only in the next life. He means that we have received a seed of resurrection that affects our whole "substance" even if all its effects are not immediately felt and if we must provisorily divest ourselves of our bodies. We are members of Christ, and in His risen flesh we have the first-fruits of our resurrection. For St. Paul, the essential is to know and to announce that Christ is risen and always living, and that our life depends infallibly upon His, as the graft depends on the trunk on which it has been engrafted, as fruit depends upon the seed, as a limb depends upon the life of the whole body.

In what place will judgment be passed? There is a whole tradition based on Joel 3:2 that answers: In the valley of Josaphat. But the foundation of this doctrine is weak. It is more prudent to say that we know nothing as to the time and the place of judgment.

Concerning the authors of judgment, certain texts (e.g., Mt. 19:28 or 12:41) give us reason to think that the just will judge together with Christ. And yet we must reconcile these texts with John 5:22 according to which all judgment has been given to the Son. On the basis of these texts St. Thomas distinguishes the judgment of authority from the judgment that passes sentence, and the judgment of the one who pronounces it and of the one who transmits it. Thus the just will judge even the angels (I Cor. 6:3) in the measure that these have had a part in the actions of men.

Heaven. Questions concerning the resurrection of the blessed relate to: 1) the way they will rise again; 2) the qualities of their risen bodies; 3) the factors surrounding beatitude; 4) the place where they will live.

1. Inasmuch as resurrection presupposes a pre-existing "subject," does it suffice that the soul alone subsists at the moment of resurrection or will the resurrection start from the "remains" of the body disseminated in the universe? The view that the "remains" of the body will be reunited has been traditionally honored until now. It presupposes that there is a certain evolution of matter upon earth and that the principle that nothing is lost and nothing creates itself is not true. For according to this opinion, the corporeal sub-

stance that belongs to a man must not also belong, by way of exchange, to another man or to several others. Now in this regard, we know that there is an evolution, that the sun, for example, consumes its heat and always gives forth "new" heat, and that this will continue until its chemical transformation has been accomplished and it dies out. Science seems to show the possibility of this second opinion.

2. The qualities of the risen body have been developed at length by the ancients: integrity, the age when the blessed will rise again, impassibility, subtlety, agility, clarity. St. Thomas has even felt the need of refuting the opinion that all will rise again with masculine bodies (Suppl., q. 81, a. 3), a view that proves the low esteem in which the female sex was held by some, and a proof also of the dependence of certain "theological" theses upon certain current ideas. We have little knowledge as to the qualities of resurrected bodies, but it is certain that we shall rise again as men and women the way God made us and the way we have lived.

3. Essential beatitude consists in the immediate vision of God. This beatitude is lived in a certain context that is its garment, as it were (see the image of Is. 61:10, one used by certain theologians). The soul will be reunited with its body, and this restitution of the plenitude of human nature is no insignificant part of perfect beatitude. The blessed is surrounded by the friends that he had known on earth and especially his relatives, whom he finds again with all the more joy because he now loves them with a pure love free of any admixture of selfish or sensual emotions.

Moreover, theologians weigh the value of certain special glories possessed by certain saints by reason of their own individual victories and that are called "aureoles." These include the palms of the martyrs, the fidelity of virgins, the apostolic fruitfulness of preachers, etc. As for the "dowries," about which medieval theologians waxed enthusiastic, they are gifts received by the soul that has been definitively wedded by Christ, so that it may share the perfect life with Him. They include the "vision" that corresponds to the faith of the militant life; the "comprehension" or possession, that corresponds to hope; perfect joy or "delectation" that corresponds to charity.

4. Finally, we can say nothing concerning the place where the risen blessed will live, any more than we can of the place where Christ and the Virgin Mary now live. We can only criticize certain traditions of which Dante, for example, is the heir and the witness,

and that stem in great part from ancient pagan traditions, as we have already pointed out. Concerning the Resurrection, see "La resurrection de la chair," special number of *Lumière et vie,* No. 3, April, 1952.

Hell. The same or analogous questions arise concerning hell. 1) What are the various punishments of hell? 2) Where is hell located? 3) Are justice and mercy reconcilable? 4) Are there different hells?

1. We can consider punishment from the point of view of the one who inflicts it and from the point of view of the one who endures it, and also from the point of view of the intrinsic order of justice disturbed by sin, justice which it is the object of punishment to re-establish. This gives us the following picture of hell:

Punishment, depending on the point of view from which it is seen, is:

on the part of *the one who inflicts it*	on the part of *the one who endures it*	from the point of view of *the order of justice that it reestablishes*
total rejection (punishment inflicted upon an enemy; object of the virtue of vengeance).	*total* punishment, for it is contrary to the will of the recipient.	the punishment of *damnation:* infinite punishment that corresponds with the infinity of the One offended.
		punishment of the senses: finite, avenges sins committed
corrective punishment (chastisement inflicted upon a friend). This punishment may be:	*satisfactory punishment* that the friend inflicts on himself. It is less a "punishment" than the others, because it is accepted voluntarily. But from the point of view of the effect of the punishment, the restoration of order, it is the most excellent punishment (i.e., sacramental satisfaction).	punishment that is merely *satisfactory,* that repairs the order of justice established in the universe by God.
	purgative punishment that the offender suffers in justice.	*medicinal punishment,* that is a remedy, and repairs the interior harmony of the powers of the *subject.*

The punishment of hell is therefore essentially a rejection and an absolute punishment, both from the point of view of the one who inflicts it and from the point of view of the one (an enemy) who endures it. From the point of view of the punishment, strictly speaking, it is a punishment of damnation, that is, a total privation of happiness that corresponds to an infinite offense. That does not mean that the act that offended God is infinite. The sinner is incapable of an infinite act; but the *Person* offended is infinite and that suffices to make the offense infinite. Hell moreover involves, for those who have sinned personally, a punishment of the senses that positively and painfully afflicts the sinner.

2. The ancients have always situated hell in the "lower" regions beneath the earth. We know that in the primitive mind hell was simply the dwelling of the dead, whatever the condition of their posthumous life—whether sorrowful or happy, or simply different from life on earth. To "descend to hell" simply meant to die, or more precisely to pass from the present life to the invisible life of the dead. Under the influence of Persian Mazdeism (see Cumont, *op. cit.*, p. 217 ff.) and that other doctrine that located the dwelling of the dead in heaven, "hell was transformed" and became a place of judgment, punishment, and fire.

In the third century before Christ (see Cumont, *op. cit.*, p. 226), the representation of infernal fire was accepted and in some degree assumed by Judaism and spontaneously passed into the preaching of our Lord and into Christianity. And yet our Lord never spoke of "infernal" fire, but only of everlasting fire (Mt. 18:8; 25:41) or of unquenchable fire (Mk. 9:42) or of the gehenna of fire (Mt. 18:9; Mk. 9:44-46), the sign that He used to indicate the sanction of divine justice rather than the place of punishment. The word "hell" is used only in Matthew 16:18, but here the "gates of hell" are a personification of the powers of evil that are responsible for death.

Thus there is no revealed "localization" of the dwelling of the dead, or of the specific inhabitation of the damned. The notions of ancient representation were simply taken up again by the sacred authors to designate certain realities that everybody designated by these names. We continue to call "hell" the dwelling of the damned, and "heaven" the dwelling of the blessed. But the "low" and the "high" that these words originally signified have become merely symbols of spiritual realities since the discoveries of Copernicus.

However it is not surprising that the first Christian generations, that still clung to the cosmology of the ancient Greeks and Romans, pictured the dwelling of the elect in the stars and planets, beyond the heavenly "spheres" (see Fr. Dubarle, *Theology Library:* Vol. II, pp. 275-305). The imagination of peoples is hard-headed, if we may use the expression. And Christian generations have long held to traditions of after-life held by the pagans, starting with Homer (Ulysses' descent into hell) and Virgil (the descent of Aeneas into hell) and continuing on until Dante and even later. Moreover, there were different categories of dead to be localized: the patriarchs, children who died without Baptism, the damned. For each of these groups there were specific places such as the "limbo of the patriarchs," the "limbo of children," and the dwelling of the damned that we now call "hell." It was also asked whether "Abraham's bosom" to which our Lord referred (Lk. 16:22) was to be assimilated to the limbo of the patriarchs. We have lost the naïve boldness our ancestors had in locating these places.

Likewise the descriptions of the torments of hell, and especially the fires of hell, that we find in Dante's *Divine Comedy* deserve strong criticism in the light of what the Gospel and Christian tradition teach. In this sphere, the contamination of pagan notions was more serious, and neither theologians nor poets, including Dante, were always exempt from them (see M. Carrouges, "Images de l'enfer," in *L'Enfer, op. cit.*).

3. The "justice" suffered in hell leaves no place for friendship in the strict sense. We cannot speak of a "society of the damned" in the sense that we speak of a "society of the blessed." Charity unites, and hatred divides. There is no "Body" or society of Anti-Christ. And yet God is good. And because He is good, He allows the just man to receive more than his rightful measure of created goods through a gratuitous gift of grace. And also because He is good, He does not permit evil to reach its ultimate consequences. He tempers punishment *citra condignum* and makes it less severe than sinners deserve, so that even in His justice His mercy is always active without, however, destroying the order of justice that His mercy has created.

In this regard, a question arises concerning the reward of "dead works," that is, "good" works performed by sinners in the state of sin. Actually, the sinner does not do only evil works by reason of the fact that he is in the state of sin. Even though his heart may be devoid of charity, he may pay his debts, accomplish a certain justice, perform certain acts that objectively stem from temperance even though they are not inspired by perfect virtue. St. Thomas thinks that these relatively good works of the sinner are rewarded temporally by God during this life—and this should arouse our concern about certain temporal successes—or else in the next life by a mitigation of the condemnation. This is what he says about it:

"God remembers the good deeds a man does in a state of sin, not by rewarding them in eternal life, which is due only to living works, i.e., those done from charity, but by a temporal reward: thus Gregory declares (*Hom. de Divite et Lazaro 41 in Ev.*) that unless that rich man had done some good deed, and had received his reward in this world, Abraham would certainly not have said to him: 'Thou didst receive good things in thy lifetime.'" (IIIa, q. 89, a. 6, ad 3.) A fortiori, we must say the same thing of works performed in charity which are "mortified" by sin and do not "revive" through penance. Regardless of the way He goes about it, we know that God is just and that He takes everything into account; and that first and above all He is merciful.

4. We have distinguished two sorts of punishment: the punishment of the damned and the punishment of the senses. This opens up the possibility of several places of punishment—the place where both sorts of punishment are endured (hell), the place where only damnation is endured (the hell of children that we now call limbo), and the place where souls are not condemned to damnation forever and where they must suffer the punishment of the senses: that is purgatory, a temporary abode.

The punishment of damnation inflicted on children who die in the state of original sin is purely a privation. It is a privation of "eternal life" for those who have been deprived of grace, which is the seed of eternal life.

Purgatory. The doctrine of purgatory, "a point of disagreement between our separated brothers and ourselves" represents a maturing within the Church of the mystery of salvation and specifically of the Pascal mystery. We shall find the main outlines of this development in an excellent study by Y. Congar, "Le purgatoire," in *Le mystère de la mort et sa célébration* (Paris, Ed. du Cerf, 1951, pp. 279-336).

Burial Rites. It would be desirable to study not only funeral rites but all prayers for the dead, "suffrages," anniversary Masses, the

Masses for the seventh and thirtieth day, the "month's mind" Masses, and to try to attain to a theological understanding of these rites, customs, and prayers.

There would be much to say also on the ways in which Christians buried their dead in the past and the ways in which they now bury them. We know that formerly Christians buried their dead around their church, thus making of the front of their church a "paradise" or a "parvis." It would be equally interesting to study the way Christians care for the graves of their dead and remember them. Christianity has not abolished many ancient customs that were not incompatible with its beliefs. However, the weakening of faith and a fortiori the growth of unbelief have found rather spontaneous expression in an insistence on certain practices that can easily be given a superstitious interpretation. Pastors must zealously "watch" that at services for the dead the faith is kept at a high level, and that the tears of those who legitimately weep for their dead are tempered by the hope of eternal life and Resurrection.

On the celebration of services for the dead, read the excellent book cited above in the collection Lex Orandi: *Le mystère de la mort et sa célébration.* Concerning cemeteries, see also *L'Art Sacré,* Nov.-Dec., 1949, "Cimetières et tombeaux." Concerning superstition, see the excellent theological study by A. Léonard, "La métamorphose du sacré dans la superstition," in *Supplément de la Vie Spirituelle,* February, 1954, pp. 5-29.

BIBLIOGRAPHY

1. *The Last Things:* Revelation and theology

The sources for a theology of the last things are scattered in many places in Scripture; scriptural commentators usually list these in studying the Apocalypse, which is the major source of Revelation on the last things. A work of particular importance on this subject is that by P. Allo in the collection *Études Bibliques* (Paris: Gabalda); less technical but rich theologically is H. M. Féret's *L'Apocalypse de saint Jean, Vision chrétienne de l'histoire,* Paris: Correa.

Read also Oscar Cullman's *Le retour du Christ, espérance de l'Église selon le nouveau Testament,* in *Cahiers théol. de l'act. prot.,* Neuchatel: Delachaux and Niestlé, 1943. And from the same collection, G. Pidoux's *Le Dieu qui vient,* 1947.

Finally, see J. Cantinat's excellent work: *Comment prêcher les fins dernières,* in *Cahiers du Clergé rural,* 1953.

There are few works that give a comprehensive treatment of the theology of the last things, as it has been outlined in the preceding chapter. For this, reference must be made to monographs and dictionary articles on individual questions. The following works can be mentioned, however:

Guardini, Romano. *The Last Things*. New York: Pantheon, 1954.

Michel, A. *Les fins dernières*. Paris: Bloud and Gay, 1932.

Roguet, M., Féret, H. M., Daniélou, J., etc. *Le mystère de la mort et sa célébration*, in the collection *Lex orandi*. Paris: Cerf, 1951.

Thomas Aquinas, St. "The Last Things," in *Summa Theol.*, Suppl., 69-99. This first part of Thomistic eschatology treats of the soul's state after death, purgatory, prayers for the dead, prayers of the elect in heaven, the last judgment. Also, see "The Life of Jesus," in *Summa Theol.*, III, 27-59.

On secular history and the economy of salvation, see:

Daniélou, J. *Advent*. New York: Sheed and Ward, 1951.

——. *The Salvation of the Nations*. New York: Sheed and Ward, 1949.

——. *Essai sur le mystère de l'histoire*. Éd. du Seuil, 1953.

There is also valuable material in the following:

Cerfaux, L. *La théologie de l'Église suivant saint Paul*. Paris: Cerf.

Diétrich, Suz. de. *Le dessein de Dieu*. Paris: Delachaux and Niestlé.

Guardini, Romano. *The Lord*. Chicago: Regnery, 1955.

Lubac, H. de, S.J. *Catholicism*. New York: Sheed and Ward, 1958.

Sertillanges, A. D. *Le miracle de l'Église*. Paris: Spes, 1933.

Also see Chapter XII of Volume II of the *Theology Library*: "The two economies of divine government: Satan and Christ," by L. Bouyer.

2. *The Resurrection and the Life of Glory*

The life of heaven is a prolongation of the interior life of grace; thus many works on grace treat the life of glory and sometimes contain a bibliography on the subject. Useful works are the following:

P. Ant. de Jesus. *L'au-delà béatifique*. Tournai: Casterman, 1947.

Garrigou-Lagrange, R., O.P. *Life Everlasting*. St. Louis: Herder, 1952.

Lattey, Cuthbert, S.J. *Man and Eternity*. London: Burns, Oates and Washbourne: 1937.

Leroy, O. *La splendeur corporelle des saints*. Paris: Cerf.

Schneider, W., and Thurston, Herbert, S.J. *The Other Life*. New York: Wagner, 1920.

Thomas Aquinas, St. "The Resurrection," in *Summa Theol.*, Suppl., 69-99.

Vaughan, J. S. *Life after Death*. New York: Benziger, 1904.

3. *Hell*

Carrouges, M., Spicq, C., Bardy, G., Héris, C. V., etc. *L'Enfer*, in the collection "Fai vivante." Paris: Éd. de la Revue des j., 1949. An excellent work.

4. *Purgatory*

Congar, Yves, O.P. "Le purgatoire," in *Le mystère de la mort et sa célébration*, op. cit., pp. 279-336. An outstanding treatment, with a full bibliography.

Jugie, Martin. *Purgatory*. Westminster, Md.: Newman, 1950.

Also read the beautiful *Treatise on Purgatory,* by St. Catherine of Genoa, London: Sheed and Ward, 1950.

5. *The liturgy of the dead*

All the problems of the funeral liturgy, of preaching on the dead, of music, of types of burial, etc., are touched on or treated fully in *Le mystère de la mort et sa célébration.*

Useful information on all these questions can be found in the dictionaries and encyclopedias under such headings as "Death," "Damnation," "Judgment," "The Last Things," "Parousia," "Purgatory," "Resurrection," etc.

INDEX OF PROPER NAMES

ANALYTICAL INDEX